Practical Econometrics

The McGraw-Hill/Irwin Series in Economics

ESSENTIALS OF ECONOMICS

Brue, McConnell, and Flynn
Essentials of Economics
Third Edition

Mandel
Economics: The Basics
Second Edition

Schiller
Essentials of Economics
Ninth Edition

PRINCIPLES OF ECONOMICS

Colander
Economics, Microeconomics, and Macroeconomics
Ninth Edition

Frank and Bernanke
Principles of Economics, Principles of Microeconomics, and Principles of Macroeconomics
Fifth Edition

Frank and Bernanke
Brief Editions: Principles of Economics, Principles of Microeconomics, and Principles of Macroeconomics
Second Edition

McConnell, Brue, and Flynn
Economics, Microeconomics, and Macroeconomics
Nineteenth Edition

McConnell, Brue, and Flynn
Brief Editions: Economics, Microeconomics, and Macroeconomics
Second Edition

Miller
Principles of Microeconomics
First Edition

Samuelson and Nordhaus
Economics, Microeconomics, and Macroeconomics
Nineteenth Edition

Schiller
The Economy Today, The Micro Economy Today, and The Macro Economy Today
Thirteenth Edition

Slavin
Economics, Microeconomics, and Macroeconomics
Eleventh Edition

ECONOMICS OF SOCIAL ISSUES

Guell
Issues in Economics Today
Sixth Edition

Sharp, Register, and Grimes
Economics of Social Issues
Twentieth Edition

ECONOMETRICS

Gujarati and Porter
Basic Econometrics
Fifth Edition

Gujarati and Porter
Essentials of Econometrics
Fourth Edition

Hilmer and Hilmer
Practical Econometrics
First Edition

MANAGERIAL ECONOMICS

Baye and Prince
Managerial Economics and Business Strategy
Eighth Edition

Brickley, Smith, and Zimmerman
Managerial Economics and Organizational Architecture
Fifth Edition

Thomas and Maurice
Managerial Economics
Eleventh Edition

INTERMEDIATE ECONOMICS

Bernheim and Whinston
Microeconomics
Second Edition

Dornbusch, Fischer, and Startz
Macroeconomics
Twelfth Edition

Frank
Microeconomics and Behavior
Eighth Edition

ADVANCED ECONOMICS

Romer
Advanced Macroeconomics
Fourth Edition

MONEY AND BANKING

Cecchetti and Schoenholtz
Money, Banking, and Financial Markets
Fourth Edition

URBAN ECONOMICS

O'Sullivan
Urban Economics
Eighth Edition

LABOR ECONOMICS

Borjas
Labor Economics
Sixth Edition

McConnell, Brue, and Macpherson
Contemporary Labor Economics
Tenth Edition

PUBLIC FINANCE

Rosen and Gayer
Public Finance
Tenth Edition

Seidman
Public Finance
First Edition

ENVIRONMENTAL ECONOMICS

Field and Field
Environmental Economics: An Introduction
Sixth Edition

INTERNATIONAL ECONOMICS

Appleyard and Field
International Economics
Eighth Edition

King and King
International Economics, Globalization, and Policy: A Reader
Fifth Edition

Pugel
International Economics
Fifteenth Edition

Practical Econometrics

data collection, analysis, and application

Christiana E. Hilmer
San Diego State University

Michael J. Hilmer
San Diego State University

PRACTICAL ECONOMETRICS: DATA COLLECTION, ANALYSIS, AND APPLICATION
Published by McGraw-Hill Education, 2 Penn Plaza, New York, NY 10121.

Some ancillaries, including electronic and print components, may not be available to customers outside the United States.

This book is printed on acid-free paper.

1 2 3 4 5 6 7 8 9 0 DOW/DOW 1 0 9 8 7 6 5 4 3

ISBN 978-0-07-351141-2
MHID 0-07-3511412

Senior Vice President, Products & Markets: *Kurt L. Strand*
Vice President, Content Production & Technology Services: *Kimberly Meriwether David*
Managing Director: *Douglas Reiner*
Executive Brand Manager: *Michele Janicek*
Managing Developmental Editor: *Christina Kouvelis*
Marketing Manager: *Katie Hoenicke*
Marketing Coordinator: *Jennifer M. Jelinski*
Director, Content Production: *Terri Schiesl*
Lead Project Manager: *Jane Mohr*
Buyer: *Jennifer Pickel*
Cover Designer: *Studio Montage, St. Louis, MO*
Cover Image: *Stuart Dee/Getty Images*
Compositor: *Laserwords Private Limited*
Typeface: *10/12 Times New Roman PS*
Printer: *R.R. Donnelley*

Library of Congress Cataloging-in-Publication Data

Hilmer, Christiana E.
Practical econometrics / Christiana E. Hilmer, San Diego State University, Michael J. Hilmer, San Diego State University.—First edition.
pages cm
ISBN 978-0-07-351141-2 (alk. paper)
1. Econometrics. I. Hilmer, Michael J. II. Title.
HB139.H555 2014
330.01'5195—dc23

2013018530

www.mhhe.com

Dedication

For Kieran and Skylar

About the Authors

Christiana E. Hilmer is a Professor of Economics at San Diego State University. She received her PhD in economics with a co-major in statistics from North Carolina State University and her BA in economics–mathematics from the University of California, Santa Barbara. Dr. Hilmer previously held academic positions at Virginia Tech and Brigham Young University. She has published more than 20 articles in leading economics journals, such as the *American Journal of Agricultural Economics* and *Economic Inquiry.*

Michael J. Hilmer is a Professor of Economics at San Diego State University. He previously held positions at Virginia Tech, the University of Louisville, Brigham Young University, the University of North Carolina, Greensboro, and FMI Corporation. He holds a PhD in economics from the University of California, Santa Barbara, and a BA in economics from California State University, Northridge. Dr. Hilmer has published more than two dozen articles in internationally recognized journals. He has served as an associate editor for the *Economics of Education Review,* and a content expert for the U.S. Department of Education's "New ERIC" project.

The authors did, in fact, first meet in an econometrics class.

Preface

Econometrics is among the most valuable tools in an economist's toolkit. As any experienced craftsman knows, for a tool to be truly useful, one must have both the desire and the know-how to make use of it. One of our former professors liked to drive home this important point by saying that "the true power of a given test is the power of the test times the probability that someone actually uses it." This lesson stayed with us throughout our years studying econometrics, as we (not so fondly) recall the many times that we would anxiously sit down to apply a newly learned tool, stare at a blank computer screen, and think to ourselves "OK, what do we do now? Where do we get the data for which this econometric tool is appropriate? Once we have that data, how do we actually execute the commands required to perform the estimation?" Unfortunately, student feedback suggests that many of our first-time econometrics students find themselves in similar predicaments. Consequently, as each semester progresses, our office hours and e-mail inboxes become inundated with students seeking help with more practical questions, such as: Where do we get appropriate data? How do we understand which econometric tool to use in which situation? What information should we include in the write-up of our project?

Our goal with this text is to bridge the gap between theoretical and practical knowledge of introductory econometrics, thereby providing readers with not only the desire but also the practical know-how to correctly utilize the econometric tools introduced. In doing so, we hope to increase the true power of the introductory econometrics course.

In our view, one of the reasons that large numbers of first-time econometrics students are left feeling lost when moving from theory to practice is that existing texts generally proceed by (1) introducing data sets that are either made up or are taken from peer-reviewed journal articles without explaining to readers how they might locate such data on their own and (2) assuming that readers either already know or will be able to quickly learn how to ask their chosen statistical package to perform the necessary calculations for them. In doing so, the texts fail to provide students with the practical tools required to make maximum use of the econometric tools presented. This is unfortunate because for most individuals, particularly those who plan to directly enter the labor market rather than pursuing graduate degrees in economics, the true excitement associated with gaining econometric knowledge lies in the practical application of the acquired tools rather than the understanding of the econometric theories underlying the development of those tools.

This text bridges the gap between the theoretical and the practical knowledge of introductory econometrics in a number of ways. The text begins with a detailed discussion of how to identify a sufficiently interesting question and how to assemble a data set appropriate for empirically examining the answer. From that point forward, we continue to develop these important practical skills by only analyzing data sets that are publicly available and by detailing the steps taken to assemble each individual data set in either the given chapter or in Appendix A. When introducing new econometric tools, we strive to clearly explain the intuition underlying each individual tool, both verbally and visually whenever possible, before introducing the technical details required to actually implement the tool. Because correctly interpreting the resulting estimates is every bit as important as understanding how to implement a given econometric tool, we pay particular attention to developing correct interpretation skills. Likewise, because a tool lacks value unless it can actually be used, every time we introduce a new econometric tool, we provide the commands required to perform the analysis in a statistical package. Finally, because an empirical research project cannot be judged successful unless each of the individual steps is effectively communicated to the reader, we conclude the text with a detailed discussion of the how-to's associated with effectively communicating the quality of one's work, culminating in a capstone example of how to conduct and effectively write up an empirical research project.

The Use of Software

While many software packages are potentially available to readers, we focus on Microsoft Excel and Stata. We do so because Microsoft Excel (1) is relatively easy to use; (2) is available on almost every computer to which a student will have access, including those of their future employers; and (3) helps solidify the intuition underlying the econometric tools being introduced through the manner by which many calculations are performed. While true, because Microsoft Excel is limited in its ability to perform more advanced econometric analysis, in the concluding chapters of the text, we rely on calculations performed in Stata because it is not only the most user-friendly, more advanced statistical package, but because it also offers a reasonably priced version that is available to students. To steepen the learning curve associated with learning to work with what is likely a new statistical package, we provide a comprehensive description of Stata commands in Appendix B that includes the commands necessary to perform all of the calculations introduced in the text.

Organization of the Book

To maximize the practical value of the material covered, the text is organized as follows.

Chapter 1 introduces the general themes of the text by reviewing the five steps to conducting an empirical research project, providing a general overview of econometrics, discussing the relationship between populations and samples, and introducing the importance of sampling distributions.

Chapter 2 begins the development of practical tools by providing a detailed discussion of data collection and management techniques, including potential sources of appropriate data, the how-to's of transferring data into Excel, the effective management of data once they are collected, and the Excel commands most commonly used in the data collection and management process.

Chapter 3 reviews summary statistics used to develop a general of sense of the data collected in the previous chapter, including measures of central tendency, measures of dispersion, histograms, scatter diagrams, covariance, and correlation coefficients.

Chapters 4 through 8 provide a detailed introduction to one of the most important tools in an econometrician's toolkit—linear regression analysis. *Chapter 4* starts by introducing simple linear regression analysis, the how-to's of ordinary least squares (OLS) estimation, the correct interpretation of the estimated OLS coefficients, the different potential measures of the goodness-of-fit of the OLS estimates, and the appropriate way to read regression output in Excel. *Chapter 5* introduces the six assumptions required for OLS to be the best linear unbiased estimator (BLUE), the correct approach to performing hypothesis tests for the significance of individual coefficients and the overall significance of the estimated sample regression function, and the correct approach to constructing confidence intervals around predicted values. *Chapter 6* extends linear regression analysis to the case of multiple independent variables by discussing the multiple linear regression assumptions required for OLS to provide estimates that are BLUE, the correct interpretation of the estimated OLS coefficients, and the correct method for performing hypothesis tests of the individual significance of the estimated slope coefficients, and the overall significance of the estimates sample regression function. *Chapter 7* introduces methods for incorporating qualitative independent variables and other nonlinearities, including interaction terms, quadratic terms, and log terms into multiple linear regression analysis. Finally, *Chapter 8* discusses issues related to the assumption that the model being estimated is "correctly specified," including the potential importance of omitted independent variables; included irrelevant independent variables; missing values for independent variables; outliers associated with given independent variables; and the Reset, Davidson-MacKinnon, and "eye" tests for determining the correct model specification.

The next seven chapters of the text introduce more advanced econometric tools. *Chapter 9* discusses the implications associated with heteroskedastic data, the correct approach to testing for heteroskedasticity, and the correct approach to correcting for its presence. Chapters 10 and 11 introduce the issues presented by time-series data, with *Chapter 10* introducing tools for estimating time-series models, including static and distributed lag models, approaches to dealing with time-trends and seasonality, and approaches to testing for structural breaks, and *Chapter 11* discussing the implications associated with autocorrelation, the correct approach to testing for autocorrelation, and the correct approach to correcting for its presence.

Chapters 12 through 15 provide introductions to more advanced econometric tools. *Chapter 12* introduces tools for dealing with dependent variables that only take on two possible outcomes—linear probability, logit, and probit models—or that take on multiple discrete outcomes—multinomial logit, multinomial probit, and ordered probit models. *Chapter 13* introduces tools for dealing with panel data, including pooled cross-section, fixed effects, and random effects models. *Chapter 14* introduces instrumental-variable approaches to dealing with the empirical issues presented by simultaneous equations, endogenous independent variables, and measurement error in independent variables. *Chapter 15* provides an overview of more recently developed econometric tools, including quantile regression, Poisson and negative binomial models, and difference-in-differences models.

Chapter 16 provides a detailed demonstration of how the newly acquired skills can be put to practical use by choosing a specific application, working through the individual the steps required to conduct a successful empirical research project related to the chosen topic, and providing a specific example of the write-up that might accompany such a project.

Key Features

To aid the development of the intuition, technical, and practical skills required to successfully conduct an empirical research project, every chapter in the text begins with the same three features.

Chapter Objectives: Approximately four to seven chapter objectives are listed at the beginning of each chapter to serve as a quick introduction to the material and concepts to be mastered.

A Student's Perspective: Rather than simply listing a number of topics that we believe students might be interested in addressing, we begin each chapter with a topic that a former student actually chose to address in his or her empirical research project.

Big Picture Overview: This feature provides a roadmap to the tools introduced in each chapter. A primary focus of this feature is visual depiction of the goals of the chapter demonstrating how the material covered in the chapter expands on the material covered in previous chapters.

To review the importance of the tools introduced, we conclude every chapter with three corresponding features.

Empirical Research Tool Boxes: These boxes provide a quick reference to the econometric tools introduced. They include the goal, implementation, and correct interpretation of the tool as well as a discussion of why the tool works.

Excel Example Boxes: These boxes demonstrate the correct implementation of given econometric tools in Excel by implementing the commands for a specific empirical example and by discussing the correct interpretation of the results.

Excel Regression Output Boxes: These boxes contain the regression output for the example being discussed in the chapter. Immediately following these boxes, in select chapters, *Interpreting the Regression Output Boxes* provide further analysis.

Hypothesis Testing Boxes: In applicable chapters, these boxes work through testing hypotheses and provide both a numeric and visual explanation.

Empirical Results Boxes: Rather than estimate models step-by-step in Excel, for select examples throughout the text, Stata commands are given and the results are displayed in these boxes.

Additions to Our Empirical Research Toolkit: Each chapter concludes with a review of the econometric tools introduced in the chapter.

Our New Empirical Tools in Practice: Using What We Have Learned in This Chapter: This feature ties back to the topic introduced in "A Student's Perspective" to demonstrate the practical value of the tools introduced in the chapter by describing how actual students utilized the tools in their empirical research projects.

Looking Ahead to (the Next) Chapter: This feature provides an introduction to the material presented in the next chapter, with particular focus on how the new material builds on the reader's existing knowledge base.

In addition to these common beginning and ending features, we introduce a number of learning aids within the body of each chapter.

Problems and Exercises: The end-of-chapter Problems are crafted to help reinforce the core concepts, while the Exercises require students to use a host of different programs and require more data-driven analysis.

Supplements

To make this textbook user-friendly for both the instructor and the student, we provide PowerPoint slides, a test bank, and other supplementary material. The PowerPoint slides follow the information presented in each of the chapters, and the test bank includes multiple-choice, short-answer, and essay questions. All of the supplements for students and instructors are available at www.mhhe.com/hilmer1e.

For Instructors:

- The Solutions Manual provides detailed answers to the end of chapter problems and exercises.
- PowerPoint presentations outline the chapters for easy class preparation.
- The Digital Image Library provides electronic images of the figures and tables in the book.
- The Test Bank contains multiple-choice, short-answer, and essay questions.

For Students:

- Excel files with all of the data sets discussed in the text help students learn the material by allowing them to replicate all of the work on their own.
- Files with the commands required to perform all of the analysis in the text in other statistical packages, such as SAS, are provided.

CourseSmart is a way for faculty to find and review eTextbooks. It's also a great option for students who are interested in accessing their course materials digitally. CourseSmart offers thousands of the most commonly adopted textbooks across hundreds of courses from a wide variety of higher education publishers. It is the only place for faculty to review and compare the full text of a textbook online. At CourseSmart, students can save up to 50% off the cost of a print book, reduce their impact on the environment, and gain access to powerful web tools for learning including full text search, notes and highlighting, and email tools for sharing notes between classmates. Your eBook also includes tech support in case you ever need help.

Finding your eBook is easy. Visit www.CourseSmart.com and search by title, author, or ISBN.

Acknowledgments

We would like to thank all of the instructors and students who took the time to review the drafts of this project before it was published. We incorporated many of their suggestions and we are grateful for their insight.

Anton Bekkerman
Montana State University

John Bowblis
Miami University of Ohio

Juan Cabrera
Ramapo College of New Jersey

Gregory Coleman
Pace University

Steven Cuellar
Sonoma State University

Luciana Echazu
Clarkson University

Susan He
Washington State University

Paul Johnson
Vassar College

Elia Kacapyr
Ithaca College

Manfred Keil
Claremont McKenna College

Rehim Kilic
Georgia Institute of Technology

John Kreig
Western Washington University

Quan Le
Seattle University

Jim Man Lee
University of Illinois, Chicago

Patrick Mason
Florida State University

Vicki McCracken
Washington State University

Fabio Milani
University of California, Irvine

Douglas Miller
Missouri State University

Daniel Millimet
Southern Methodist University

Todd Nesbit
Pennsylvania State University, Erie

Heather O'Neill
Ursinus College

William Parke
University of North Carolina, Chapel Hill

Christina Peters
Metropolitan State University of Denver

Dick Startz
University of California, Santa Barbara

Joseph Sulock
University of North Carolina, Asheville

Jennifer Vangilder
Ursinus College

Chiung-Hsia Wang
Colorado State University

Christopher Warburton
John Jay College

William Wood
James Madison University

Yongsuhk Wui
University of Arkansas, Pine Bluff

We would also like to thank the team at McGraw-Hill, especially Douglas Reiner, Christina Kouvelis, and Michele Janicek for their hard work, dedication, and invaluable help in bringing this book to publication.

We would like to thank our parents, Keith and Sheri Hilmer, Jane Connelly, and Tim Ruefli, for their continuing support and for instilling in us a lifelong love of learning and a great respect for the value of education.

Christiana E. Hilmer

Michael J. Hilmer

Contents in Brief

Table of Contents

PART TWO
LINEAR REGRESSION ANALYSIS 70

Chapter 4
Simple Linear Regression 70

Chapter 5
Hypothesis Testing for Linear Regression Analysis 103

Chapter 6
Multiple Linear Regression Analysis 147

Chapter 10
Time-Series Analysis 284

Chapter 11
Autocorrelation 313

PART 4
ADVANCED TOPICS IN ECONOMETRICS 345

Chapter 12
Limited Dependent Variable Analysis 345

Chapter 13
Panel Data 371

Chapter One

An Introduction to Econometrics and Statistical Inference

CHAPTER OBJECTIVES

After reading this chapter, you will be able to:

1. Understand the steps involved in conducting an empirical research project.
2. Understand the meaning of the term *econometrics*.
3. Understand the relationship among populations, samples, and statistical inference.
4. Understand the important role that sampling distributions play in statistical inference.

A STUDENT'S PERSPECTIVE

empirical research project
A project that applies empirical analysis to observed data to provide insight into questions of theoretical interest.

Suppose that having enrolled in an introductory econometrics course you are wondering what you are going to learn and why doing so is going to be valuable to your future. What is the answer to this most important question?

This is exactly the situation encountered by all of our former students. The short answer is that you will learn to conduct an **empirical research project** from start to finish. The long answer is that you will acquire important skills that are highly valued in the modern labor market.

BIG PICTURE OVERVIEW

> *"Hal Varian likes to say that the sexy job in the next ten years will be statisticians. After all, who would have guessed that computer engineers would be the cool job of the 90s? When every business has free and ubiquitous data, the ability to understand it and extract value from it becomes the complimentary scarce factor. It leads to intelligence, and the intelligent business is the successful business, regardless of its size. Data is the sword of the 21st century, those who wield it well, the Samurai".*

—Jonathan Rosenberg, senior vice president of product management at Google, February 16, 2009, http://googleblog.blogspot.com/2009/02/from-height-of-this-place.html

As the quote implies, empirical research skills are extremely valuable. The market value of possessing such skills is evidenced by the fact that in 2011, college graduates with economics degrees (one of the most empirically focused majors) were among the highest-paid nonengineering majors in terms of their median mid-career earnings, as shown in Figure 1.1.

FIGURE 1.1
The 20 Best-Paying College Degrees by Mid-Career Median Salary in 2011 according to PayScale, www.payscale.com

College Degree Mid-Career Median Salary
Petroleum engineering $155,000
Chemical engineering $109,000
Electrical engineering $103,000
Material science & engineering $103,000
Aerospace engineering $102,000
Physics $101,000
Applied mathematics $98,600
Computer engineering $101,000
Nuclear engineering $97,800
Biomedical engineering $97,800
Economics $94,700
Mechanical engineering $94,500
Statistics $93,800
Industrial engineering $93,100
Civil engineering $90,200
Mathematics $89,900
Environmental engineering $88,600
Management information systems $88,200
Software engineering $87,800
Finance $87,300

To maximize your chances of becoming a samurai in the world of empirical research, this textbook focuses on helping you acquire four skills: (1) the creative-thinking skills required to identify sufficiently interesting questions of interest and appropriate economic theories, (2) the data collection and management skills required to assemble and work with appropriate data sets, (3) the empirical skills required to perform valid statistical inference, and (4) the communication skills required to successfully convey the quality and importance of the work to potential readers.

We depict the goals of this text in Figure 1.2. To get started, we need to introduce the individual steps involved in conducting an empirical research project in the following section.

FIGURE 1.2
A Visual Depiction of the Goals of This Textbook

Goal → Learn to Conduct an Empirical Research Project

We want to learn to do this

To do so, we need to acquire:

(1) Creative-thinking skills required to identify questions of interest and appropriate economic theories.
(2) Data collection and management skills required to assemble and work with appropriate data sets.
} Chapter 2

(3) Empirical skills required to perform valid statistical inference. } Chapters 3–15

(4) Communication skills required to successfully convey the quality and importance of the work to the potential reader. } Chapter 16

1.1 UNDERSTAND THE STEPS INVOLVED IN CONDUCTING AN EMPIRICAL RESEARCH PROJECT

In broad terms, there are five steps to conducting a successful empirical research project: (1) determining the question of interest; (2) developing the appropriate theory relating to that answer; (3) collecting data that are appropriate for empirically investigating the answer; (4) implementing appropriate empirical techniques, correctly interpreting results, and drawing appropriate conclusions based on the estimated results; and (5) effectively writing up a summary of the first four steps that conveys to readers the value of the work that was completed.

Step 1: Determining the Question of Interest

In many ways, this is the most important step in producing a quality empirical research project. Without an intriguing question, even the most technically proficient project is likely to fall on deaf ears because the reader is likely to have no investment whatsoever in the outcome. Conversely, a project addressing a question of great interest is likely to grab and hold a reader's attention regardless of the degree of technical rigor with which it is executed.

Determining a sufficiently interesting question is, of course, the million-dollar question for researchers. Unfortunately, there is no clear answer as to how to best determine those questions that will be of the greatest interest to the greatest number of readers. Some individuals are gifted with the innate ability to identify such questions, while others have great difficulty mastering the art. In general, given that we are all more passionate about subjects in which we are personally invested, we suggest starting by identifying topics that you find particularly interesting. For instance, a restaurant server might be interested in analyzing the factors associated with receiving higher tips; a macroeconomics student might be interested in analyzing the factors associated with lower unemployment in certain states and countries; a football fan might be interested in analyzing the factors associated with a team making the playoffs in a given season.

Once we have identified a general topic, we need to determine an appropriate question related to that topic. How can we be sure that our chosen question is likely of sufficient interest to potential readers? A useful tip is to write down the proposed question and read it aloud to see whether it passes the sound test (i.e. does it sound like a question that will interest potential readers?). If it passes this test, then we can proceed to the next step in the process. If it does not, then we will need to repeat the process until we identify a question that does pass the test.

Step 2: Developing the Appropriate Theory Relating to the Answer

This step bears the fruit of previous coursework that has been completed. For instance, drawing on their accumulated knowledge, the server mentioned earlier might hypothesize that the couples dining out on weekend nights are more likely to tip well than couples dining out on weekday nights; the macroeconomics student might hypothesize that states with more educated citizens are likely to have lower unemployment rates; and the football fan might hypothesize that the greater a team's payroll, the better the team is likely to perform on the field.

Step 3: Collecting Data That Is Appropriate for Empirically Investigating the Answer

Before even attempting to perform empirical analysis, we *must* collect data that are appropriate for investigating our chosen question of interest. In practice, this step is likely as important as any other in determining the ultimate success of our project because without appropriate data, we will be unable to complete the project regardless how clever or important our chosen question. For this reason, learning how to collect (and eventually manage) data is a vitally important skill that every budding empirical researcher needs to develop. Starting to acquire these skills is the focus of Chapter 2 in this textbook.

Step 4: Implementing Appropriate Empirical Techniques, Correctly Interpreting Results, and Drawing Appropriate Conclusions

Once a sufficiently interesting question has been identified, the correct underlying theory has been determined, and the appropriate data have been collected, we must be able to properly execute the empirical analysis required to perform the necessary statistical

An Important Caveat about the Relative Importance of Each Step

While the text focuses almost exclusively on introducing the tools required to perform appropriate empirical analysis (step 4 in conducting an empirical research project), once those tools are acquired (which itself is a difficult and time-consuming process), steps 1 through 3 and step 5 generally require at least as much, if not more, actual time than step 4. There are several reasons for this. For one, identifying questions of sufficient interest and identifying and collecting appropriate data are often both quite difficult and time-consuming, particularly for those who are new to the practice. For another, once the appropriate data have been collected, the appropriate econometric analysis performed, and the correct conclusions drawn, producing an effective write-up takes time because doing so is often an iterative process that requires several drafts before successful completion.

For this reason, we encourage students tasked with conducting empirical research projects to start their work sooner rather than later. We cannot count the number of times that just before the project deadline, we have been contacted by students who have been stuck on one of the early steps (most often finding appropriate data for analyzing their chosen question) and have therefore been having great difficulty completing their work. Almost invariably, these students have commented that they now wish they had taken our advice about the relative importance of the other steps more seriously.

inference to answer the question of interest. Developing the skills required to successfully perform this step is the focus of Chapters 3 through 15.

Step 5: Effectively Writing Up a Summary of the Empirical Work

This is our opportunity to sell the significance and the quality of our work to potential readers. While this might sound somewhat easier than several of the preceding steps, its importance should not be discounted: Regardless of how well-executed steps 1 through 4 are, if the quality of those steps is not communicated sufficiently well in the write-up, then the reader is unlikely to be left with a positive view of the work. Given the importance of this step, as a capstone, Chapter 16 provides a detailed example of how to tie steps 1 through 4 together in an effective write-up.

Before embarking on our journey, we need to introduce the term that is at the heart of the empirical tools that we discuss.

1.2 UNDERSTAND THE MEANING OF THE TERM *ECONOMETRICS*

econometrics
The application of statistical techniques to economic data.

In broad terms, **econometrics** is the intersection between the disciplines of economics and statistics. This should be evident from the term itself. Refer to Figure 1.3 below.

FIGURE 1.3
An Introduction to the Study of Econometrics

Econometrics

Economics Statistics

economics
The study of how people chose to use scarce resources.

statistics
The science of collection, organization, analysis, and interpretation of data.

How do these root words combine to create the field of econometrics? And how is the study of econometrics potentially of great value? To answer these questions, it is important to consider the words in more detail. **Economics** is a social science examining the human behavior of "how individuals respond to incentives." **Statistics** is "the mathematics of the collection, organization, and interpretation of numerical data, especially the analysis of population characteristics by inference from sampling."

This combination of words interacts as follows. To examine human behavior, economists develop scientific models known as *economic theory* that predict how individuals, firms, and so on, respond to incentives in different situations. While economic theories can certainly be developed to explain almost any human behavior, they are only valuable if they accurately explain how humans actually behave. This brings us to the intersection between economics and statistics. How might we determine whether a given economic theory is indeed consistent with actual human behavior? By collecting data that results from actual human behavior and applying appropriate empirical techniques to determine whether the observed behavior is consistent with the theoretical model.

Venn diagram
A tool for visually depicting the overlap between the total variation in two or more different factors of interest.

As an alternative way to think about the study of econometrics, we introduce the **Venn diagram** in Figure 1.4. Letting the lighter circle represent the entire discipline of economics and the slightly darker circle represent the entire discipline of statistics, the overlap between these two disciplines, which is demonstrated as the darkest area, is econometrics.

FIGURE 1.4
A Venn Diagram Explanation of Econometrics

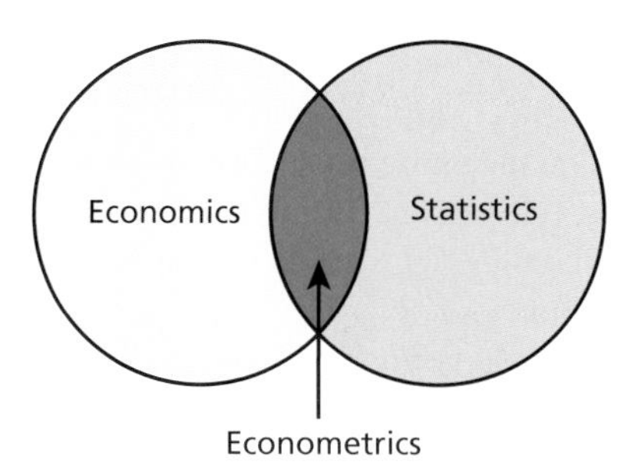

What does Figure 1.4 tell us about the study of econometrics? On the one hand, it tells us that not all of economics involves the application of statistics and that not all of statistics is applied to economics. Indeed, it is the case that much of the work in both disciplines is performed independent from the other. While true, there is most definitely an important overlap between the two fields, and as indicated in Figure 1.4, that overlap forms the field of econometrics.

Note that while we couch the preceding discussion in terms of economics, we could just as easily place other social science and business disciplines in the green area, suggesting that the tools introduced in this text can be applied to questions of interest in other many other disciplines. Indeed, many of the data sets that we analyze touch on questions of importance to disciplines other than economics.

With this discussion in mind, we turn to the fundamental issue that lies at the heart of statistics.

1.3 UNDERSTAND THE RELATIONSHIP AMONG POPULATIONS, SAMPLES, AND STATISTICAL INFERENCE

By definition, *statistics* is

> *"the mathematics of the collection, organization, and interpretation of numerical data, especially the analysis of population characteristics by inference from sampling."*
>
> www.thefreedictionary.com/statistics

This definition introduces three important terms that play a vital role in the study of econometrics—*population, sampling,* and *inference.* Given that these three terms form the very basis of statistical analysis, we need to consider their meanings in detail.

Populations and Samples

As discussed earlier, once we have developed a given economic theory, we can attempt to determine whether that theory is indeed consistent with actual human behavior by (1) collecting data resulting from actual human behavior and (2) using appropriate techniques to estimate the degree to which the observed behavior is consistent with the underlying theory. The question is, in order to adequately answer our chosen question, do we need to collect data on the observed behavior of all individuals subject to the given theory? This question becomes increasingly important when we consider that in many cases, a given economic theory affects potentially millions and millions of individuals. For instance, suppose that we wish to test the economic theory that reductions in marginal tax rates increase consumer spending in the United States. Given that there are more than 300 million citizens in the United States, it is important to ask whether determining if our theory is correct requires data on the level of spending at different marginal tax rates for every single one of those 300 million citizens. Fortunately for us, the answer is no. Understanding why not is where the three important terms, *population, sampling,* and *inference,* come into play.

population
The entire group of entities that we are interested in learning about.

sample
A subset or part of the population; what is used to perform statistical inference.

confidence
A statement about the chance that an event (or group of events) will occur.

Continuing with the marginal tax rate example, the 300 million plus U.S. citizens represent the **population** that we are interested in learning about. To answer the question of whether we need to collect data on the entire population to determine whether our economic theory is indeed consistent with observed human behavior, we need to consider the potential costs and benefits associated with collecting data for the entire population versus collecting data for only a given **sample** drawn from the population.

Returning to our question of the size of the sample that we must collect in order to learn about the population of interest, on the one hand, the greater the percentage of the population for which we collect data, the greater the **confidence** we have in our results. In fact, if we collect data on the entire population, we will have 100 percent confidence in our results, as we will be 100 percent certain that they accurately reflect the entire population. On the other hand, collecting data is expensive because every single observation collected requires expenditures of time and effort, which can potentially sum to a very, very significant expense for a larger population (i.e., there is a reason that the U.S. census is only conducted once every 10 years). Given these competing concerns, we would like to find a middle ground that balances the benefit of collecting data on a larger percentage of the population with the cost of assembling a very large sample. The question we must address is how large a sample we need to collect in order to have sufficient confidence that the conclusions we draw from the observed sample are likely to be accurate reflections of the population we are trying to learn about. As we will see, the answer is that for our conclusion to be considered valid, the number of observations in the sample drawn from the population need only be what many would consider a surprisingly small number.

statistical inference
The process of drawing conclusions from data that are subject to random variation.

It is important to note that the fact that we generally only observe a specific sample drawn from the population means that the population values we are interested in learning about are generally unobserved. Instead, the only information available to us is the statistics that are observed for the given sample drawn from the population. As a result, we generally need to use the statistics observed for the given sample drawn from the population as our best indication of the true (but unobserved) population parameters. The process of using statistics observed for a given sample as the best estimate of parameters that likely exist for the population of interest is referred to as **statistical inference.**

As a concrete example to help make the previous topics easy to visualize, we like to consider fishing for rainbow trout in a beautiful alpine lake, such as the one pictured in Figure 1.5.

FIGURE 1.5
A Beautiful Lake Containing Thousands of Rainbow Trout

Source: S. Greg Panosian/Getty Images

representative sample
A sample indicative of what would be found with access to the entire population.

independent random sampling
A technique in which each individual is chosen entirely by chance and each member of the population has a known, but possibly nonequal, chance of being included in the sample.

sampling with replacement
Takes place when a unit is drawn from a finite population, the value is recorded, and then returned to the sample.

To determine the typical size of rainbow trout in this lake, do we need to catch and measure all of the millions of rainbow trout that live there? No. We only need to catch a relatively small **representative sample** of rainbow trout to generate a valid estimate. This is true because as long as the sample of fish that we catch is truly representative of the population from which it is drawn, then we should be able to perform valid statistical inference on the basis of that sample (i.e., the typical size of the fish in the sample should provide an accurate indication of the typical size of the fish in the entire lake).

How do we know whether the specific sample drawn from the population is indeed representative of the population itself? One guarantee is that the chosen sample is collected through **independent random sampling,** which is ensured if we **sample with replacement** by returning each observation to the population once we have selected it and recorded its value. In the case of our rainbow trout example, we would do so by releasing all fish back into the lake once we catch and measure them. If we return each fish to the lake after catching it, then presumably there is an equal chance of catching a given fish every single time we cast our line and, as a result, the likelihood of catching a given fish with one cast should be independent of the likelihood of catching a given fish with a different cast. In practice, most sampling is conducted without replacement. This tends not to be an issue as long as the size of the population is much, much larger than the size of the sample because, in such cases, the probability of drawing two of the same observations is extremely small.

Visually, we depict the statistical inference process in Figure 1.6.

FIGURE 1.6
An Introduction to Independent Random Sampling

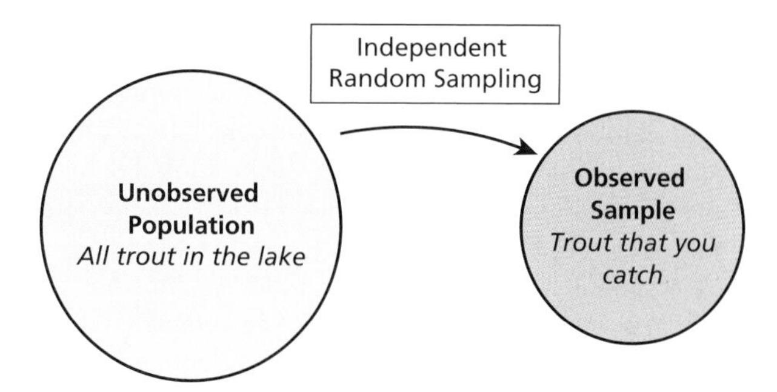

Once we have collected our specific independent random sample from the population, what do we do with it? We use the observed values for the sample as our best estimate of the values that are likely to exist within the entire population. As discussed earlier, we refer to this process as performing statistical inference, and we visually represent it in Figure 1.7.

FIGURE 1.7
A Visual Depiction Statistical Inference

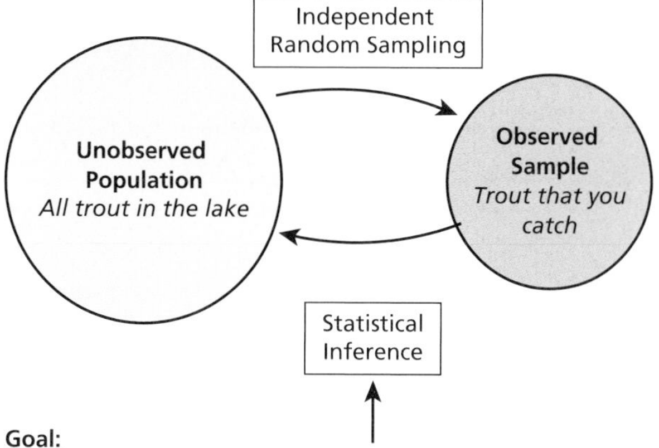

Before continuing our discussion, we need to define a few important terms related to populations and samples that will be used throughout the remainder of the textbook. The true (but unobserved) value for the variable of interest that exists within the population is

parameter
A function that exists within the population.

statistic
A function that is computed from the sample data.

point estimate
A single valued statistic that is the best guess of a population parameter.

referred to as a **parameter.** The value for the variable of interest that is observed for the specific random sample drawn from the unobserved population is referred to as a sample **statistic.** Finally, because the sample statistics serve as our best estimates of the true population parameters, we often refer to sample statistics as being our best **point estimates** of the unobserved population parameters.

What does this discussion mean in practice? A simple example that is likely familiar to most readers provides context.

A Real-World Example of Statistical Inference: The Nielsen Ratings

Suppose that we own a retail business and that we are interested in purchasing televison advertising time in hopes of increasing revenue and, ultimately, profit. What information would we need to make an informed decision as to the time of day and the program during which we should purchase advertising time? The answer to this question is complicated by the fact that the number of consumers predisposed to favor our product is likely to vary by time of day and type of program, meaning that there are likely certain times that are more profitable than others for our ad buys. How can we determine which times are more profitable and which times are less profitable to advertise? By collecting a specific sample of a given size from the population and using information observed for that sample to draw conclusions about the population from which the sample is drawn.

Do we need to perform this calculation ourselves? No. In America, the task of collecting information on household viewing habits is performed by Nielsen Media Research that, according to the website www.nielsen.com/us, "tracks the television and media-viewing habits of homes across the country" and produces a statistic commonly referred to as the Nielsen Ratings. According to its website, there are currently roughly 112.8 million television households in the United States. Is it possible to observe the viewing habits of all of these 112.8 million households? No! So what does Nielsen Media Research do? It surveys the viewing habits of a randomly selected sample of roughly 12,000 households and uses observations from that sample to draw conclusions about the population of roughly 113 million households. This means that the company is attempting to determine the viewing habits of nearly 113 million television households based on observations of only 12,000 households, or 0.01 percent of the population. Figure 1.8 visually depicts this process.

FIGURE 1.8
A Visual Depiction of the Real-World Nielsen Ratings Example

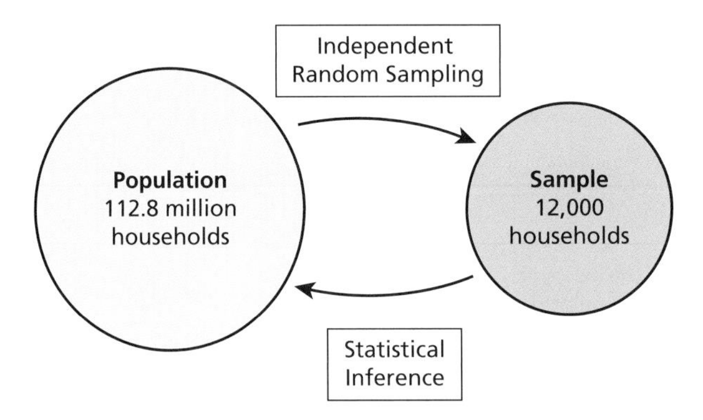

A question that may occur to you at this point is how can such a small sample (12,000 households) provide valid information as to such a large population (more than 112 million households)? This is where the statistical inference process becomes rather amazing to many individuals. Based on the laws of statistics, if our data are collected through independent random sampling, then we can draw accurate conclusions about the population of interest from even a relatively small-seeming sample drawn from the population. Indeed, on its website, Nielsen Media Research highlights the importance of its sampling approach by stating that the first crucial step is to "scientifically select a group of households that mirrors the population at large . . . Selecting a representative sample of homes is vital to collecting data that mirrors the population's viewing habits . . . Nielsen TV families are a cross-section of households from all over the United States . . . We carefully draw our samples in a way that offers every American household with a television an equal chance of being selected."

While this discussion might seem rather complicated, the issues discussed are summarized quite nicely by the following joke:

> *A statistics professor was describing sampling theory to his class, explaining how a sample can be studied and used to generalize to a population. One of the students in the back of the room kept shaking his head. "What's the matter?" asked the professor. "I don't believe it," said the student, "why not study the whole population in the first place?" The professor continued explaining the ideas of random and representative samples. The student still shook his head. The professor launched into the mechanics of proportional stratified samples, randomized cluster sampling, the standard error of the mean, and the central limit theorem. The student remained unconvinced saying, "Too much theory, too risky, I couldn't trust just a few numbers in place of ALL of them." Attempting a more practical example, the professor then explained the scientific rigor and meticulous sample selection of the Nielsen television ratings which are used to determine how multiple millions of advertising dollars are spent. The student remained unimpressed saying, "You mean that just a sample of a few thousand can tell us exactly what over 112 MILLION people are doing?" Finally, the professor, somewhat disgruntled with the skepticism, replied, "Well, the next time you go to the campus clinic and they want to take a sample to perform a blood test . . . tell them that's not good enough . . . tell them to TAKE IT ALL!!"*

sampling distribution The distribution of a sample statistic such as the sample mean.

Given the preceding discussion, an important question is how can we use the observed sample statistics to learn about the unobserved population parameters that we are attempting to estimate. The key to answering this question lies in our knowledge **sampling distributions.**

1.4 UNDERSTAND THE IMPORTANT ROLE THAT SAMPLING DISTRIBUTIONS PLAY IN STATISTICAL INFERENCE

Notation:

n number of observations in a sample

N number of observations in the population

As we will discuss in Chapter 5, a key to understanding the statistical inference process is the realization that the specific independent random sample of size n that is drawn from the *unobserved* population of size N is but one of many, many potential samples of size n that could have been drawn from the population. Given that each of the many, many potential independent random samples of size n are likely to provide different information, an important concern is the degree to which each individual sample is likely to provide a valid estimate of the unobserved population. As Chapter 3 will (hopefully) make clear, the root of statistical inference is knowledge of the distribution that would result if we (1) collected all possible samples of size n that could be drawn from the unobserved population of size N, (2) calculated the value of a given statistic (say, the sample mean) for each of those samples, and (3) placed those values in order on the number line to create a distribution known as a sampling distribution.

Visually, we depict the process of constructing a sampling distribution in Figure 1.9.

Notice that while we need to consider what a given sampling distribution would look like in theory, in practice, we will never put forth the extreme effort required to construct an entire sampling distribution. Instead, we will only collect a specific, independent random sample from the population—sample 1 as boxed in Figure 1.9—and combine information from that sample with our theoretical knowledge of what the sampling distribution would look like (were we to construct it) to learn about the population.

To aid understanding of this important concept, in Chapters 3 through 8 we specifically choose examples for which we can collect data for the entire population and, rather than analyzing those populations themselves, we select and analyze data for specific, independent random samples of given sizes drawn from those populations. We believe that this approach is advantageous for the following reason: Because we actually observe the entire population (which is extremely rare in practice), we have advanced knowledge

FIGURE 1.9 **A Visual Depiction of the Construction of a Sampling Distribution**

Specific Sample Drawn

Random Sampling

Sample 1 n observations *sample mean* $= \bar{x}_1$

Sample 2 n observations *sample mean* $= \bar{x}_2$

Sample 3 n observations *sample mean* $= \bar{x}_3$

Population N observations

True (unobserved) population mean

Sample 4 n observations *sample mean* $= \bar{x}_4$

All q possible samples of size n that can be drawn from the population of size N

Sample q n observations *sample mean* $= \bar{x}_q$

If we calculate the sample mean for each of the q possible samples of size n, and plot the values on a number line, we get the sampling distribution of the sample mean

Sampling Distribution of the Sample Mean

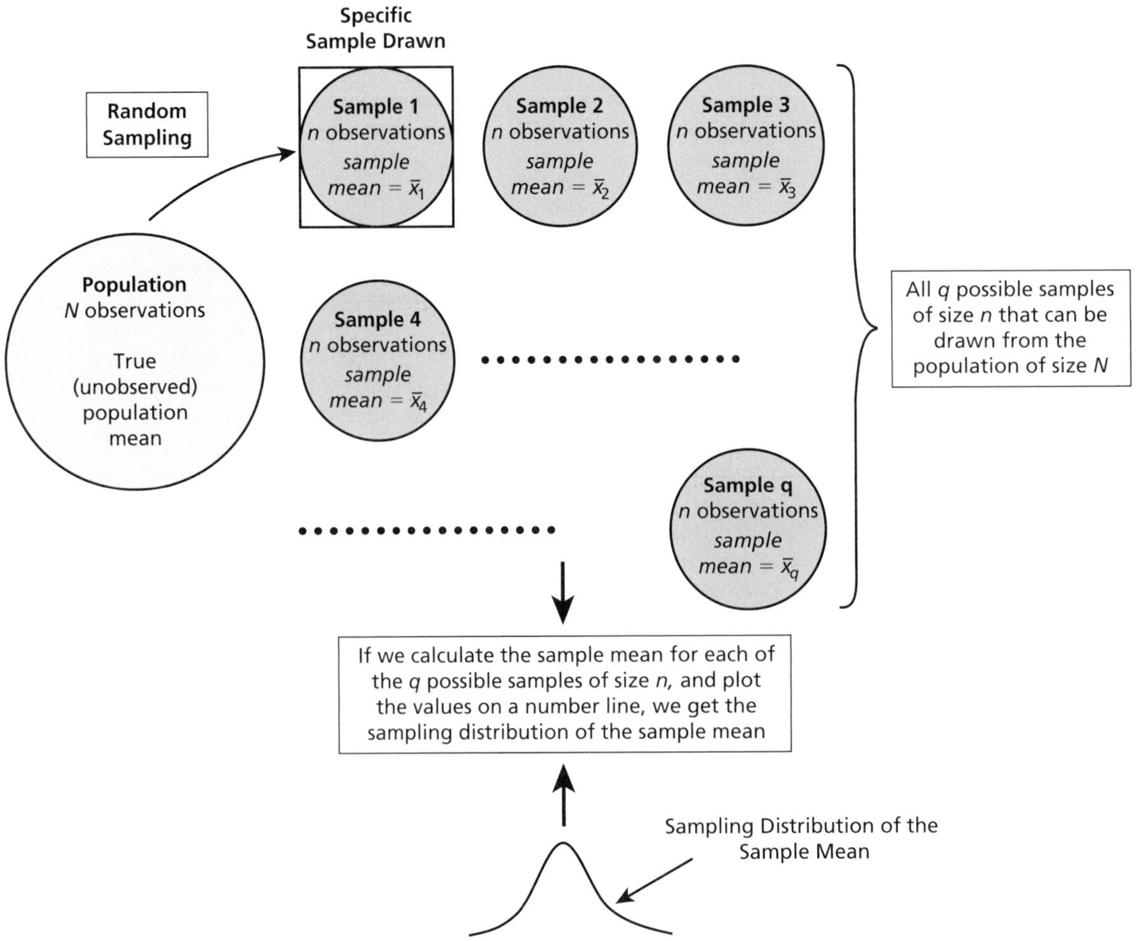

of the population parameters that we wish to estimate. We find this potentially valuable for two reasons: (1) In Chapter 3, we are able to start constructing a sampling distribution by drawing multiple, independent random samples from the population and placing calculated values for those different samples on the number line, and (2) In Chapters 3 through 8, whenever appropriate, we are able to compare sample statistics between the one independent random sample on which we focus and the known population parameters that they are intended to estimate—an approach that helps us consider the potential strengths and weaknesses of the statistical inference process.

It is important to note that we follow this approach for illustration purposes only. Beyond our desire to create a concrete example for introducing the concepts of sampling distributions and statistical inference, there is absolutely no reason to randomly select a sample from a known population (if we are lucky to have access to the entire population) or to randomly draw a smaller sample from a larger sample (if we are not lucky enough to have access to the entire population).

ADDITIONS TO OUR EMPIRICAL RESEARCH TOOLKIT

In this chapter, we have introduced a number of tools that will prove valuable when performing empirical research. They include:

- The individual steps to conducting an empirical research projects.
- The relationship between population, samples, and statistical inference.
- A general understanding of the importance of sampling distributions.

OUR NEW EMPIRICAL TOOLS IN PRACTICE: USING WHAT WE HAVE LEARNED IN THIS CHAPTER

On the basis of our introduction to the material to be covered in the course, most of our students find themselves anxious to get started learning this most valuable subject.

LOOKING AHEAD TO CHAPTER 2

As discussed earlier, there are generally five steps associated with conducting a successful empirical research project. While step 4—implementing appropriate empirical techniques, correctly interpreting results, and drawing appropriate conclusions based on the estimated results—is the focus of the majority of this textbook, before being able to perform such analysis, we must first identify a question of interest, develop appropriate theory, and identify and collect appropriate data. Chapter 2 discusses these three steps in more detail.

Problems

1.1 What is something you are interested in for which you could either directly collect data or survey individuals to obtain data? Explain how you would accomplish steps 1, 2, and 3 in conducting an empirical research project for this idea.

1.2 For each of the following, state if it is a population or a sample. Why?

a. U.S. census

b. Unemployment rate

c. Consumer confidence

d. Housing prices in New York City

1.3 Answer the following:

a. Flip a coin 10 times. Put a 1 each time the coin comes up heads and a 0 each time the coin comes up tails. Count the number of heads you obtained and divide by 10. What number did you get? This is your estimate of the probability of obtaining heads.

b. Is the number you obtained in part (a) a parameter or a statistic?

c. Now flip the coin 25 times. Put a 1 each time you obtain a heads and a 0 for tails. Count the number of heads you obtained and divide by 25. What number did you get?

d. What is the chance you obtain a heads in a fair coin flip? How do you believe this number is obtained using your results from parts (a) and (c)?

e. How does this process relate to the idea of a sampling distribution?

1.4 Answer the following:

a. Roll a die 10 times. Put a 1 each time the die is a one and a 0 each time the die comes up any other number. Count the number of ones you obtained and divide by 10. What number did you get? This is your estimate of the probability of obtaining a one.

b. Is the number you obtained in part (a) a parameter or a statistic?

c. Now roll the die 25 times. Put a 1 each time the die comes up as a one and a 0 for any other number. Count the number of ones you obtained and divide by 25. What number did you get?

d. What is the chance you obtain a one with a fair die? How do you believe this number is obtained using your results from parts (a) and (c)?

e. How does this process relate to the idea of a sampling distribution?

Chapter Two

Collection and Management of Data

CHAPTER OBJECTIVES

After reading this chapter, you will be able to:

1. Consider potential sources of data.
2. Work through an example of the first three steps in conducting an empirical research project.
3. Develop data management skills.
4. Understand some useful Excel commands.

A STUDENT'S PERSPECTIVE

Suppose that given your interest in public health, you know that you would like to conduct an empirical research project that is related in some way to obesity in America. Where should you begin?

This is exactly the situation encountered by one of our former students. As she quickly learned, a very important fact related to empirical research is that before performing any analysis, researchers must determine a sufficiently interesting question to be addressed and must identify and collect data that are appropriate for empirically investigating the answer. Because collecting and managing data is likely relatively new to many readers, Chapter 2 presents an overview of data collection and data management techniques that should prove useful when beginning to conduct your own empirical research.

BIG PICTURE OVERVIEW

The goal of this textbook is to help students acquire the tools required to complete empirical research projects. Given this goal, the vast majority of the textbook focuses on econometric tools for analyzing data once they are collected. While this is the necessary approach for an introductory econometrics textbook, it does potentially downplay a very important fact: A dirty, little secret about empirical research is that determining a question of sufficient interest/importance to potential readers and successfully identifying and collecting data appropriate for empirically investigating the answer are, in many ways, the most crucial (and time-consuming) parts of producing a successful empirical research project. As evidence of this fact, most seasoned empirical researchers can recite war stories concerning promising projects that were derailed by the inability to collect appropriate data—sometimes after their having devoted considerable time and other resources to the project.

One reason that econometric textbooks generally start from the point at which an interesting question has already been identified and an appropriate data set already assembled is that those skills are often more art than science, and therefore, the skills required to perform them are rather difficult to instill through written words. Indeed, our experience suggests that these skills are best acquired by rolling up your sleeves and practicing the skills on your own, making sure to use every available opportunity as a chance to better hone your skill set. On a positive note, through our own experience and that of our students, we find that the learning curve for acquiring these skills is rather steep once you start to get the hang of it. Nonetheless, in hopes of providing the best possible starting point from which to start developing your own skills, this chapter introduces a number of tips to help develop your ability in data collection and management.

We depict the goals of the chapter in Figure 2.1.

FIGURE 2.1
A Visual Depiction of the Empirical Tools Introduced in This Chapter

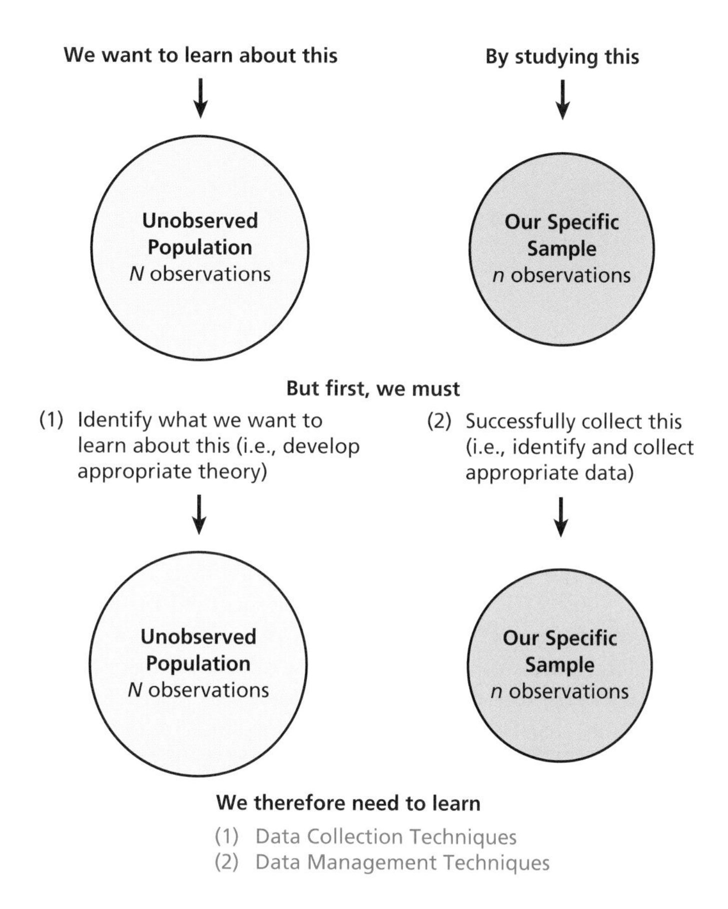

In the following sections, we attempt to achieve these goals by reviewing potential sources of data, introducing data collection and data management techniques, working through an example of constructing an actual data set, and reviewing some of the most valuable Excel commands for collecting and managing data.

2.1 CONSIDER POTENTIAL SOURCES OF DATA

cross-sectional data
Data collected for many different individuals, countries, firms, etc., in a given time period.

time-series data
Data collected for a given individual, country, firm, etc., over many different time periods.

In general, there are three distinct types of economic data that we are likely to encounter. **Cross-sectional data** are collected for many different individuals (or firms, nations, etc.) at one specific point in time. For instance, labor economists that are interested in determining the relationship between earnings and educational attainment might collect data for 10,000 different individuals in a given time period—say, 2011—and ask whether additional years of education are associated with higher earnings. **Time-series data** are collected for a given individual (or firm, nation, etc.) over multiple different time periods. For instance, macroeconomists interested in determining the relationship between various factors of production—such as labor productivity and a given country's GDP—might collect data on that country's GDP and labor productivity from the first quarter of 1990 to the fourth quarter of 2010 and ask whether changes in labor productivity are associated

Some Notable Data Sources on the Internet

www.rfe.org	Resources for Economists provides links to U.S. macro data, other U.S. data, world data, financial data, and data that were used in journal articles. This is a great place to begin your search for data and to get ideas of what kind of data are available.
www.icpsr.umich.edu/icpsrweb/ICPSR/	Inter-University Consortium for Political and Social Research has many public data available. You can either search for a specific topic or browse papers that have online data available.
http://nces.ed.gov/	National Center for Education Statistics has excellent data on education-related data.
www.census.org www.bls.org	U.S. Census Bureau and the Bureau of Labor Statistics, respectively, have a wealth of information on labor-related topics.
www.bts.gov	Bureau of Transportation Statistics has data on airlines, ferries, freight, bridges, and other transportation-related issues.
www.oecd.org	Organisation for Economic Co-operation and Development has country-level data on GDP, financial aid, education, health, and unemployment.
http://research.stlouisfed.org/fred2/	Website maintained by the St. Louis Federal Reserve that has a plethora of macroeconomic data, both current and historical.

panel data
Data collected for a number of individuals, countries, firms, etc., over many different time periods. Also known as *longitudinal data.*

with changes in GDP. **Panel data (or *longitudinal data*),** are collected for multiple individuals (or firms, nations, etc.) over multiple time periods. For instance, financial economists interested in determining the relationship between firm stock prices and firm profitability might collect data on a group of firms over a number of different time periods.

Regardless of the type of data being sought, there are generally three broad sources of data: (1) private-use data, such as the results of government surveys or internal, firm-level data that can be obtained through formal request and/or by having the appropriate connections; (2) publicly available data, which can usually be obtained through the Internet or through formal Freedom of Information Act (FOIA) requests from the appropriate agency; and (3) personal survey data, which can be attained by personally conducting a survey asking people for information and recording their responses. While academic researchers frequently rely on government survey and/or proprietary, firm-level data, undergraduates are far more likely to get their data from one of the final two sources.

As an example of how to identify publicly available data that one might be able to collect and analyze, suppose that we are interested in empirically analyzing the factors associated with a country's macroeconomic performance. In this case, we would definitely be in luck, as the Internet contains a veritable treasure trove of websites offering country-level macroeconomic data and/or aggregating other potential sources of such data. We list a few of the more prominent sources in the box at the top of this page.

Suppose we are interested in identifying publicly available data that are not included among the sources in the box but for which we expect data to exist. The best place to start locating such data is a simple Internet search. While there is certainly an art to performing successful Internet searches, with a little practice it is possible to quickly become quite adept at doing so. Our advice is to start by asking a search engine to perform a search on exactly the data desired. In fact, as we demonstrate in the following example, this is exactly how we identified most of the data that we analyze in this text.

On a related point, do not be too hasty to jettison ideas that might be of great personal interest simply because it might seem, at first blush, that the necessary data are unlikely to exist. We say this because we are continually surprised by the data that some of our students are able to identify and collect. A particularly memorable, recent example is the former student who had a particular interest in medical marijuana dispensaries in California. Much to our surprise, the student was able to locate a website, www.weedtracker.com, that contained data allowing him to estimate the relationship between medical marijuana prices and the number of dispensaries within a given radius, the number of strains sold at each dispensary, and user-submitted ratings of quality of the different of the product offered at different dispensaries. In summary, our advice is that no matter how outlandish-seeming the desired data, it is likely worth devoting at least a little time searching the Internet because it is often surprising what can be accomplished.

Suppose that we spend sufficient time on the Internet and are unable to locate publicly available data that are appropriate for addressing our chosen question. What can we do? One obvious answer is to start over by identifying a new question of interest for which we can collect appropriate data. Rather than crying defeat, however, another approach is to create our own data set by surveying individuals and collecting their responses to our questions.

Where might we find individuals willing and/or able to answer our questions? There are several possibilities: We could ask permission from a fellow professor to conduct a survey in his or her class (assuming we had first received appropriate legal permissions for working with individual subjects); we could stand in the middle of campus and ask students to provide responses; we could go door-to-door in our neighborhood, asking residents for their responses; or we could use one of the many available Internet programs designed to collect responses from anonymous users. To demonstrate how easily this final approach can be employed, in the following example, we create, administer, and collect responses to a survey using the SurveyMonkey website, www.surveymonkey.com (we note that there are many competing survey design websites that would be just as useful). The underlying question guiding our survey is the potential effect that social media use is having on American teenagers (which has received considerable recent media attention). The questions we developed appeared on the SurveyMonkey website as depicted in Figure 2.2:

FIGURE 2.2
An Example Survey on SurveyMonkey, www.surveymonkey.com

Factors affecting GPA

1.

1. What is your current GPA?

2. How many years have you spent in college?

3. What is your major?

4. During the fall semester, on average, how many hours a week do you play video games?

5. During the fall semester, on average, how many hours during the week do you work?

6. During the fall semester, on average, how many hours a week do you work out?

7. During the fall semester, how many text messages do you send a week?

8. During a typical week, how many hours do you spend studying?

9. What was your high school GPA?

10. Are you a male or a female?

- Male
- Female

Note that from start to finish, creating our survey required less than 30 minutes. To actually collect responses, we needed to alert potential respondents to the existence of our survey. We did so by sending an e-mail asking former students to voluntarily provide responses. Within a few days, we received 37 anonymous responses, for which the first five entries look like Figure 2.3:

FIGURE 2.3
Sample Responses from Our Example Survey on SurveyMonkey, www.surveymonkey.com

1	College	Video Games	Work	WorkOut	Text Messages	Studying	High School
2	GPA	Hours/Week	Hours/Week	Hours/Week	/Week	Hours/Week	GPA
3	2.57	3	6	12	1000	6	3.41
4	2.90	0	20	0	50	3	3.40
5	3.70	0	6	6	0	6	3.90
6	3.32	0	0	6	25	9	3.30
7	3.00	4.5	8	10	40+	10	3.60

If so desired, we could perform an empirical analysis of these data to produce our empirical research project. We note that a surprisingly large fraction of students in our classes have chosen this avenue for assembling the data sets that they analyze in their empirical research projects.

The upshot of this discussion is that a great deal of different data are available these days and, with a little practice, you should be able to quickly develop data collection skills that will prove valuable in many of your future endeavors. To aid the development of these skills, all of the examples contained in this text are collected from publicly available sources; the details of how we identified and assembled those data sets are included either in the relevant chapters or in Appendix A. It is our hope that reading through the details of how we assembled these data sets will help you quickly move up the learning curve related to data collection.

2.2 WORK THROUGH AN EXAMPLE OF THE FIRST THREE STEPS IN CONDUCTING AN EMPIRICAL RESEARCH PROJECT

Chapter 1 discussed the fact that of the five steps for conducting an empirical research project, the first three—identifying a question of interest, determining the appropriate theory for addressing that question, and collecting data appropriate for determining the answer—need to be performed before beginning the econometric analysis. As a comprehensive example of how we might perform these three steps, suppose that having followed with great interest the recent media focus on the potential impacts of the Great Recession, we are generally interested in researching how the recent economic downturn might have affected the lives of U.S. citizens. How should we proceed?

What might a question of sufficient interest be in this case? Among other things, an important concern for many citizens is the likelihood that they or their loved ones will be the victim of crime. Accordingly, we might wish to answer the question, Is there a relationship between the health of the economy and the prevailing crime rate? Does this question sound sufficiently interesting to many potential readers? We think that it does.

Now that we have identified a general question of interest, we need to determine the appropriate economic theory underlying our chosen question. In this case, we might recall from previous courses that economic theory predicts that general economic conditions should affect individual incentives to participate in crime. In particular, economic theory suggests that individuals who are out of work should have more incentive to participate in crime because they have fewer productive alternatives, and therefore, they should possess higher marginal benefits of participating in crime. Accordingly, when unemployment rates increase, economic theory would predict that we should see more individuals turning to crime and prevailing crime rates increasing. Conversely, when unemployment rates decrease, economic theory would predict that we should see fewer individuals turning to crime and unemployment rates decreasing. In other words, the underlying theory related to our chosen question would be this: All else constant, crime rates should be positively related to the unemployment rate (i.e., higher crime rates should be associated with higher unemployment rates, and lower crime rates should be associated with lower unemployment rates).

How might we collect the data necessary to test our theory that crime rates are positively associated with unemployment rates? We should start by recognizing that in order to test this theory, we need to collect data on a large number of observations containing different combinations of crime rates and unemployment rates. In reality, there are two potential sources of such data: We could attempt to collect data on crime rates and unemployment rates (1) for a given unit of observation (i.e., a given city, state, or country) over a long period of time or (2) for different units of observation (i.e., different cities, states, or countries) in the same period of time. While both approaches might seem plausible, in our experience, the more fruitful approach is to collect cross-sectional data on a large number of observations in the same time period.

When attempting to collect cross-sectional data, an important concern is the unit of observation that we should pursue. In this case, we might ask whether we should attempt to collect data at the city, state, or national level. As we discuss in future chapters, to generate the most precise estimates, we wish to collect samples with the largest possible number of observations. Accordingly, when determining the appropriate unit of observation, an important question is what level of data is likely to provide the largest possible sample size. For our crime rate example, we might choose to collect data at the city level because, for the individual, crime is a local rather than a state or national issue (i.e., I do not care whether the state crime rate is higher or lower if I am being mugged). This approach has the added advantages that (1) there are a large number of U.S. cities that report crime statistics, thereby greatly increasing our sample size relative to what we would have if we collected state-level data and (2) the other data that we wish to collect are also likely available at the city level, meaning that we will be able to seamlessly merge the individual pieces of data.

How might we do so? A natural starting point would be the Internet search shown in Figure 2.4:

FIGURE 2.4
The Internet Search for Identifying Our City Property Crime Data

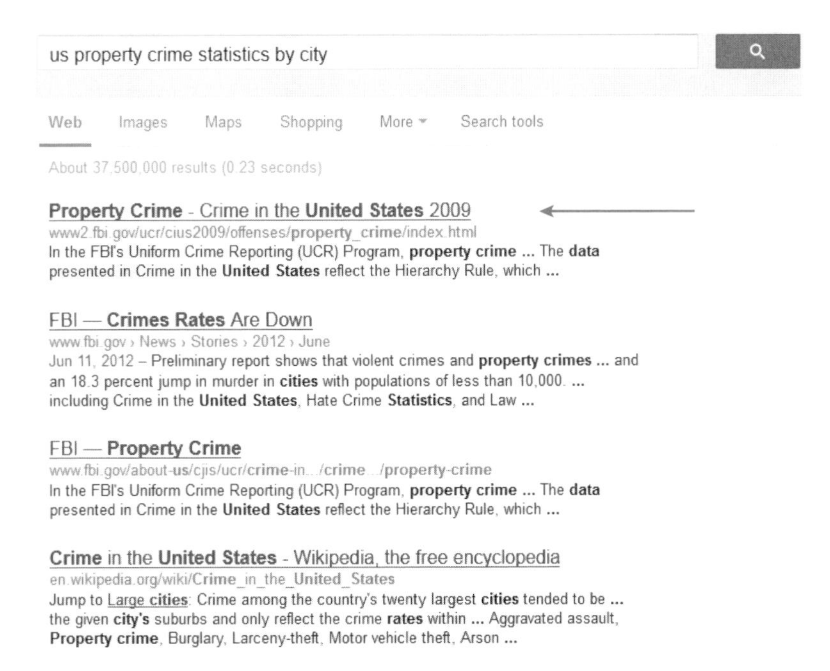

Just like that, we are well on our way to collecting the data that we desire. Clicking on the first link in the webpage above "Property Crime—Crime in the United States 2009" takes us to the website in Figure 2.5:

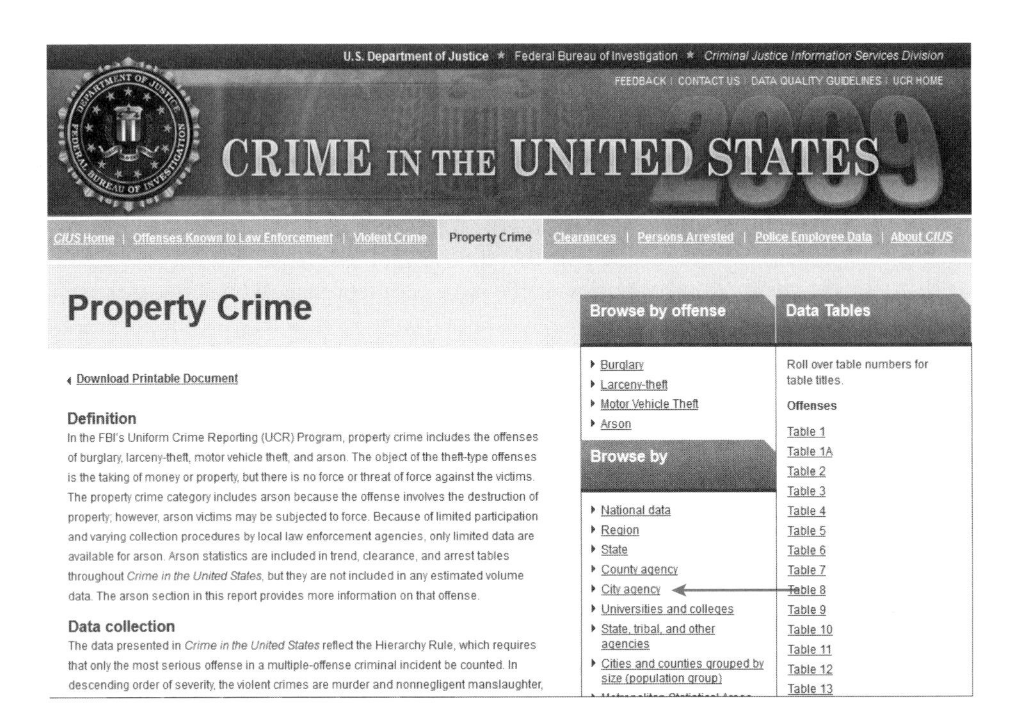

FIGURE 2.5
The Property Crime Webpage from Which We Get Our City Property Crime Data

Because we are interested in city-level data, in the "Browse by" window we click on the "City Agency" tab. Doing so takes us to the webpage in Figure 2.6:

FIGURE 2.6
Identifying the Table That Contains Our City Property Crime Data

This webpage reveals to us that we have already arrived at the home for our desired crime data. Clicking on the "Table 8, Offenses Known to Law Enforcement, by State by City, 2009" tab takes us to Figure 2.7:

FIGURE 2.7
Identifying the Webpage from Which We Download Our City Property Crime Data

As is sometimes the case, we luck out and find that the data we desire are already available in Excel format (if it is not, as we discuss in Section 2.4, it is fairly easy to import data into Excel that are not originally in Excel format). Clicking on the "Download Excel" tab pulls up the pop-up window in Figure 2.8:

FIGURE 2.8
The Dialog Box That Allows Us to Open Our City Property Crime Data in Excel Format

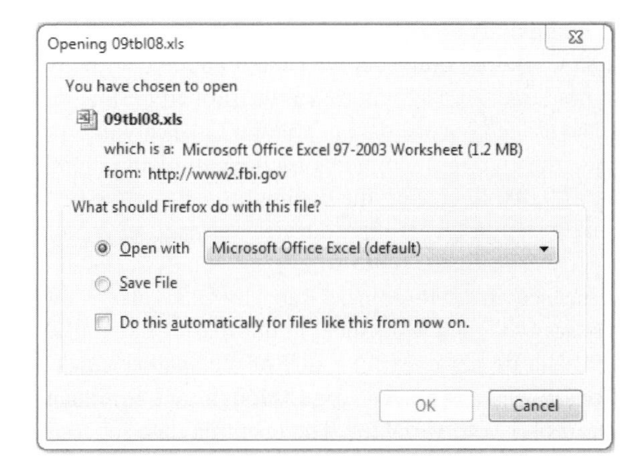

Clicking "Open with" and "OK" we get our desired data in Excel format, which looks like Figure 2.9:

FIGURE 2.9
Our City Property Crime Data in Excel Format

	B	C	D	E	F	G	H	I	J	K	L	M
1												
2	**Enforcement**											
3												
4	City	Population	**Violent crime**	Murder and nonnegligent manslaughter	Forcible rape	Robbery	Aggravated assault	**Property crime**	Burglary	Larceny-theft	Motor vehicle theft	Arson[1]
5	Abbeville	2,932	9	0	1	0	8	53	18	33	2	
6	Adamsville	4,704	25	0	1	17	7	342	33	291	18	
7	Addison	710	5	0	1	0	4	29	4	22	3	
8	Alabaster	30,002	41	0	2	12	27	635	82	522	31	
9	Albertville	20,078	82	0	11	12	59	928	233	659	36	
10	Alexander City	15,057	132	2	10	31	89	843	180	631	32	
11	Aliceville[2]	2,456	22	0	0	3	19		7		4	
12	Andalusia	8,994	54	1	5	7	41	484	61	408	15	
13	Anniston	23,598	584	5	27	113	439	2,379	966	1,258	155	
14	Ardmore	1,275	0	0	0	0	0	13	2	11	0	

The first thing we like to do once we reach this stage is to save the data with a descriptive name. At this point, we like to include the identifier "Master" so that we know these are the initial data that we downloaded. For instance, in this case, we would save the downloaded data to an Excel file titled "**City Property Crime Sample - Master.xlsx**." We then have some decisions to make. As we can see in Figure 2.9, the data set that we have downloaded actually contains data on 10 different types of crime. At this point, we must choose the type of crime on which we wish to focus. While we could conceivably choose any of the 10 crime types, because economic theory suggests that less violent crimes are likely more closely related to economic conditions, we might choose to focus on property crimes, meaning that we will only be interested in the property crime data in column I.

At this point, we have two different options for managing the downloaded data: (1) We can delete all crime columns other than column I, leaving us with only those crime data in which we are interested, or (2) we can create a new worksheet and copy the data columns in which we are interested into that new worksheet. Because it protects all of the data that we initially downloaded, we recommend the latter method, lest we decide to focus on a different type of crime at some later date, in which case we would rue the day that we decided to delete all of the other columns in Figure 2.9.

An important point to notice about the data in Figure 2.9 is that all of the different crime types in columns D–M are listed in terms of the number of crimes committed rather than the crime rates. To convert the data to crime rates (which we should do to scale for differences in community size), we need to divide the property crime data by the population data in column C. Before doing so, we should notice that the population data in column C are many times larger in magnitude than the property crime data in column I. Accordingly, to convert the property crime data in column I to easily interpretable property crime rates, we can divide the entries in column I by the entries in column C, and multiply the resulting value by 100,000 to convert the data to property crime rates per 100,000 citizens.

The next step in assembling our desired data set is to add unemployment rate data to our property crime data. To do so, we essentially repeat the preceding process for the initial Internet search "2009 Jobless Rates by U.S. City." Downloading these data (which we promptly save to a new worksheet in our master Excel file), we quickly notice that unemployment data do not exist for many of the smaller cities included in the property crime data. Consequently, we need to go through and eliminate the cities that do not provide observations for both variables. The resulting data set contains observations on 359 cities and is presented in Figure 2.10:

FIGURE 2.10
Our City Property Crime and Unemployment Data in Excel Format

	A	B	C	D	E
1	id	Metro Area	State	Property Crimes/100,000	April 2009 Jobless Rate
2	1	Anchorage	AK	3,641	0.073
3	2	Fairbanks	AK	3,904	0.073
4	3	Anniston-Oxford	AL	8,571	0.091
5	4	Birmingham-Hoover	AL	6,832	0.077
6	5	Decatur	AL	5,745	0.089

2.3 DEVELOP DATA MANAGEMENT SKILLS

While we have stressed the importance of collecting appropriate data, the data collection process is not the only concern we have when conducting an empirical research project. As discussed in later chapters, conducting the appropriate empirical analysis entails trial and error and potential changes to our initial variables that, if not managed correctly, can lead us to overwrite and lose the initial data that we are attempting to analyze. From personal experience, we can affirm that little is more frustrating than devoting hours upon hours to identifying, collecting, and starting to analyze a given data set before making a simple mistake and losing the initial data for good, thereby requiring us to spend hours upon hours reconstructing our previous work (if doing so is even possible). We are not afraid to admit that in our learning process, we made such mistakes more times than we care to remember. As a result of learning from these mistakes, we have developed a number of tips that we always try to follow when managing data that make it possible for us to relatively easily re-create our initial data set should the need arise. We like to think of these as tips for avoiding the "Agony of Delete:"

1. We always collect and assemble our data set in one "master" file (e.g., **City Property Crime Data - Master.xlsx**). We are then very careful to never perform any calculations and/or data transformations in that file. Instead, we create a new "working" file in which we perform all of our new work (**City Property Crime Data - Working.xlsx**). To highlight this fact, a screen capture of the folder in which we saved these files looks like Figure 2.11:

FIGURE 2.11
Our "Master" and "Working" City Property Crime Excel Files

Name	Type
City Property Crime Data - Master	Microsoft Office Excel Worksheet
City Property Crime Data - Working	Microsoft Office Excel Worksheet

The reason for this precaution is that if we were to make a mistake with the data and/or lose any of the initial values in the "working" file (**City Property Crime Data - Working.xlsx**), we would not have to go back through the previous data collection steps to entirely re-create our master data set. Instead, we could simply return to the "master" file (**City Property Crime Data - Master.xlsx**), copy the initial values into a new Excel file, and create a new "working" file in which we could start performing our new econometric analysis.

2. If the master data does not already contain a unique identifier for each individual observation, we always assign one. For instance, in our master data set **City Property Crime Data - Master.xlsx**, we created the variable "id." The reason for this precaution is that in managing and analyzing our data, we may frequently wish to sort the data in different ways; having the unique identifier for each observation will allow us to always be able to return the data to the initial order.
3. We always try to make our file and variable names as intuitive as possible. For instance, the variable name "Property Crimes / 100,000" conveys much more information than the variable name "Crimes." As such, the data in our "working" file **City Property Crime Data - Working.xlsx** look like Figure 2.12:

FIGURE 2.12
The Variable Names Included in Our City Property Crime File

id	Metro Area	State	Property Crimes/100,000	Unemployment Rate
1	Santa Barbara-Santa Maria-Goleta	CA	2,528	0.076
2	Honolulu	HI	3,679	0.057
3	Fort Smith	AR-OK	5,861	0.07
4	Hattiesburg	MS	4,568	0.063
5	Billings	MT	4,360	0.042

The reason for this precaution is that if we ever return to the project at a later date, we will have a much quicker learning curve for getting back up to speed on what we had already accomplished.

4. In our "master" file, we always include a worksheet titled "Data Sources" into which we copy the website addresses from which we collect data, references to other sources of data, and notes about what the different variables mean (i.e., a list of variable definitions). For instance, in our "master" file **City Property Crime Data - Master.xlsx**, we include the worksheet in Figure 2.13:

FIGURE 2.13
The "Data Sources" Worksheet in Our City Property Crime Excel File

Property Crime
http://www2.fbi.gov/ucr/cius2009/offenses/property_crime/index.html

Unemployment Rate
http://blogs.wsj.com/economics/2009/06/03/unemployment-rates-by-metro-area/

Data Sources | Master Data | Sample Data

The reason for this precaution is that it helps greatly if we ever need to re-create or construct new variables for use in our empirical analysis and it helps keep track of what we have already done when returning to the project.

5. When working in a given file, we are never afraid to create new worksheets. We can make data adjustments, report results, and so forth, on additional worksheets without worrying about overwriting the initial data. Again, it is best to give each worksheet a clear name. For instance, in our "working" file **City Property Crime Data - Working.xlsx**, we construct the worksheets in Figure 2.14 to complete the empirical analysis in Chapter 4.

FIGURE 2.14
The Different Worksheets Created in Our City Property Crime Excel File in Chapter 4

6. Before merging information from different files into one file, we always spot check common rows in the two different files to make sure that we are copying information for the same observation. The reason for this precaution is that if we do not, we run the risk of cross-pollinating the data, leading to incorrect entries for some variables.
7. Whenever we run regressions in a statistical package other than Excel, we create a new worksheet and save the results to that worksheet. We then paste the regression commands that we used to generate the results to the first row of the worksheet, so that we can easily re-run the models in the future without having to recreate the commands we used from scratch.
8. Finally, and perhaps most importantly, when working in a given file, we try to remember to save our work as often as possible. The reason for this precaution is that if the file were to crash, all of the work that we had performed since the last active save would be lost, and we would need to re-perform all of the same calculations once the file was reopened.

As you begin to work with data, you will likely develop your own techniques for helping to manage your data sets. We encourage you to identify such techniques and to uniformly apply them in your work (and to make note of them so that you can recall what you did previously should you return to the project in the future).

2.4 UNDERSTAND SOME USEFUL EXCEL COMMANDS

While the Excel commands required to estimate the econometric models introduced throughout the textbook are important, a number of Excel commands also prove quite useful when getting started with data collection and management.

Installing the Data Analysis ToolPak

Given that we cannot perform regression analysis without it, perhaps the most important Excel feature we use throughout the remainder of the text is the Data Analysis ToolPak. Because this feature does not come preloaded in Excel, we must take steps to make it available.

To load the Data Analysis ToolPak, start by opening an Excel workbook and clicking on the Windows symbol in the upper left corner of the screen (Figure 2.15):

FIGURE 2.15
The Windows Symbol That Provides Access to Downloading the Data Analysis ToolPak

Doing so pulls up a drop-down window listing "New," "Open," "Save," and so on, on the left side and "Recent Documents" on the right side. In the bottom right corner of that drop-down window, there is a tab titled "Excel Options." Clicking that tab brings up the pop-up window in Figure 2.16:

FIGURE 2.16
The Pop-Up Window for Adding Options in Excel

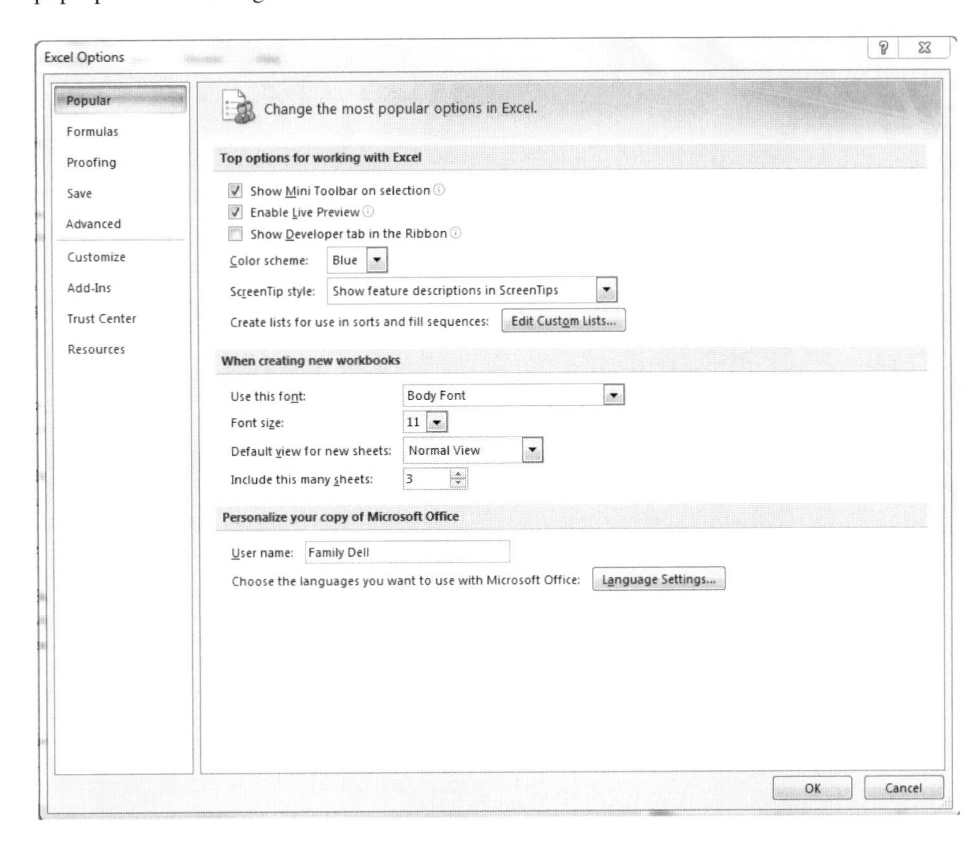

Clicking the "Add-Ins" tab in the left panel of this window takes us to the pop-up window in Figure 2.17:

FIGURE 2.17
Selecting the Add-Ins Option in Excel

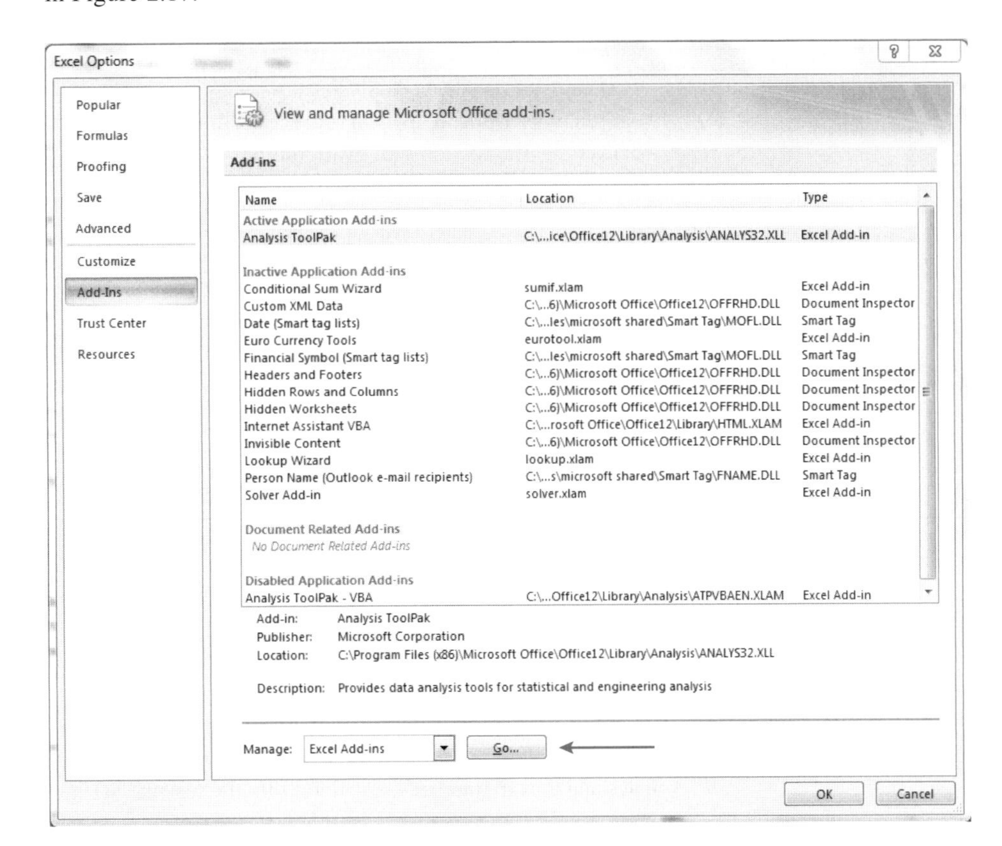

Because we want to access the Excel Add-Ins, we highlight the "Add-Ins" tab and click the "Go" tab near the bottom of the window. Doing so takes us to the pop-up window in Figure 2.18, which includes the Data Analysis ToolPaks we wish to install:

FIGURE 2.18
Selecting the Analysis ToolPaks from the Potential Add-Ins Available in Excel

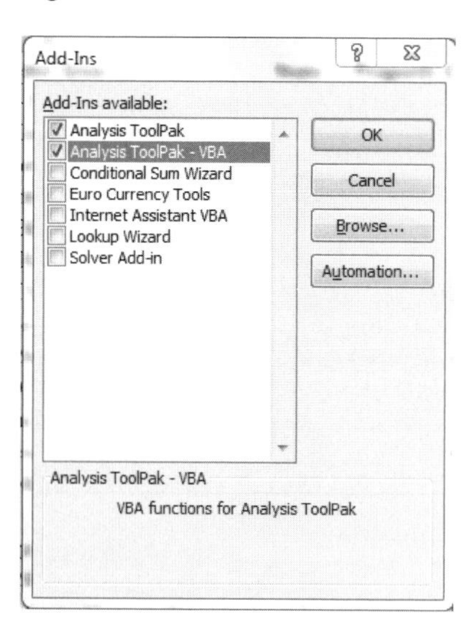

Checking the two "Analysis ToolPak" Add-Ins and clicking "OK" installs these feature into Excel.

From now on, when we open Excel and click on the "Data" tab, we will see the desired "Data Analysis" tab to the very right of the screen (Figure 2.19):

FIGURE 2.19
Selecting the Data Analysis Tool When Working in Excel

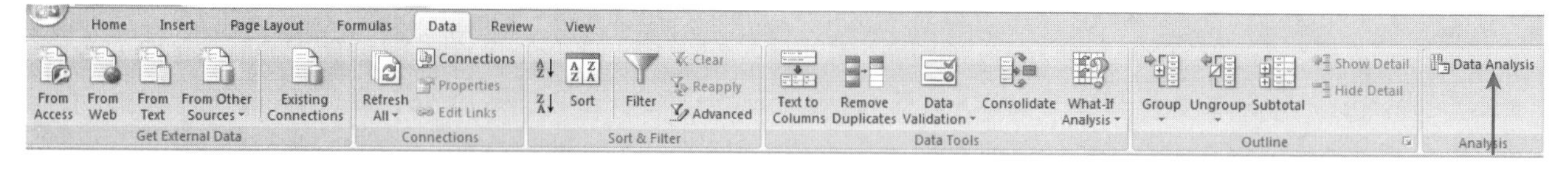

Clicking on the "Data Analysis" tab brings up a pop-up window containing all of the Data Analysis tools available to us in Excel. Scrolling down the list of possible Data Analysis tools, we reach the Regression tool by highlighting "Regression" and clicking "OK" (Figure 2.20):

FIGURE 2.20
Choosing a Given Tool from the Data Analysis ToolPak

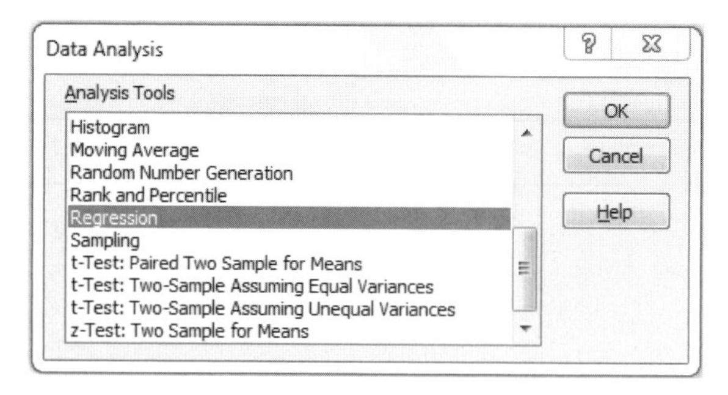

Note: In order to install the Analysis ToolPak to a Mac instead of a PC, we need to download a free program from the web.

Importing Data from the Web

Suppose that we would like to import Internet data that are not originally provided in Excel format. Fortunately, Excel contains a fairly simple command for doing so. The first thing we need to do is identify the source of the data that we wish to download. As an example, suppose that we are interested in comparing standardized student test scores across states in the United States and that an Internet search identifies the website in Figure 2.21 as a source of such data:

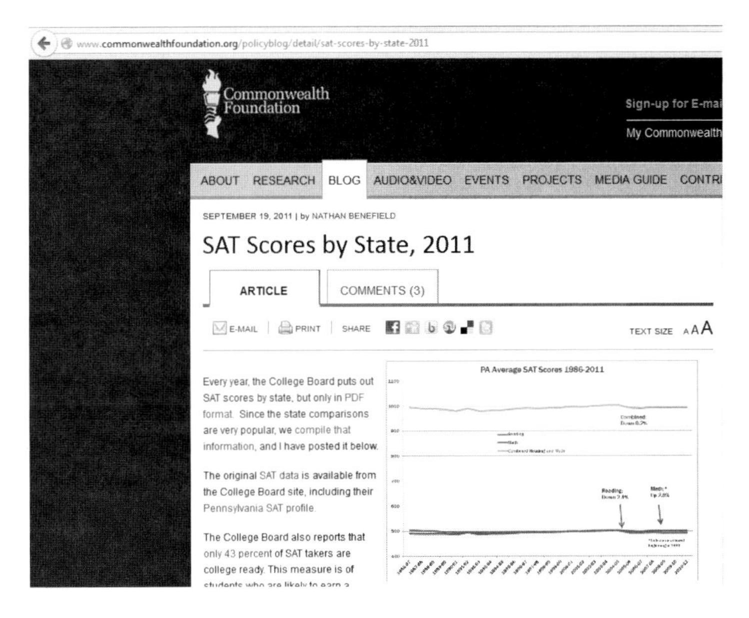

FIGURE 2.21
SAT Scores by State, Commonwealth Foundation Website, www.commonwealthfoundation.org/policyblog/detail/sat-scores-by-state-2011

Scrolling down this webpage, we find that the data in which we are interested are contained in the table shown in Figure 2.22:

FIGURE 2.22
Mean 2011 SAT Scores by State According to www.commonwealthfoundation.org/policyblog/detail/sat-scores-by-state-2011

SAT Scores 2011

Mean 2011 SAT Scores by State

States are listed by total 2011 SAT Scores

Rank	State	Critical Reading	Math	Writing	Combined	Participation Rate
1	Illinois	599	617	591	1807	5%
2	Minnesota	593	608	577	1778	7%
3	Iowa	596	606	575	1777	3%
4	Wisconsin	590	602	575	1767	5%
5	Missouri	592	593	579	1764	5%
6	Michigan	583	604	574	1761	5%
7	North Dakota	586	612	561	1759	3%
8	Kansas	590	595	567	1752	6%
9	Nebraska	585	591	569	1745	5%
10	South Dakota	584	591	562	1737	4%
11	Kentucky	576	572	563	1711	6%

Our goal now is to import these data into Excel without having to enter them by hand (which is both time-consuming and introduces the potential for data-entry error). To do so, we need to copy the web address for this webpage, which is www.commonwealthfoundation.org/policyblog/detail/sat-scores-by-state-2011.

Our next step is to open a new workbook in Excel and click on the "Data" tab. At this point, we can see that the very left tab is titled "Get External Data." Because we want to import data from the Internet, we click the "From Web" tab as shown in Figure 2.23:

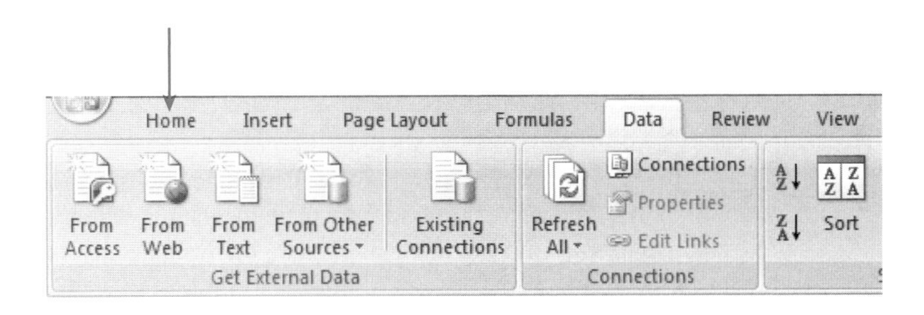

FIGURE 2.23
The Tab for Importing Data from the Web into Excel

Doing so brings up the "New Web Query" pop-up window. Once this window arises, we can paste our copied web address into the "Address" tab and click the "Go" tab, all of which produces Figure 2.24:

FIGURE 2.24
The New Web Query Window for Importing Data into Excel

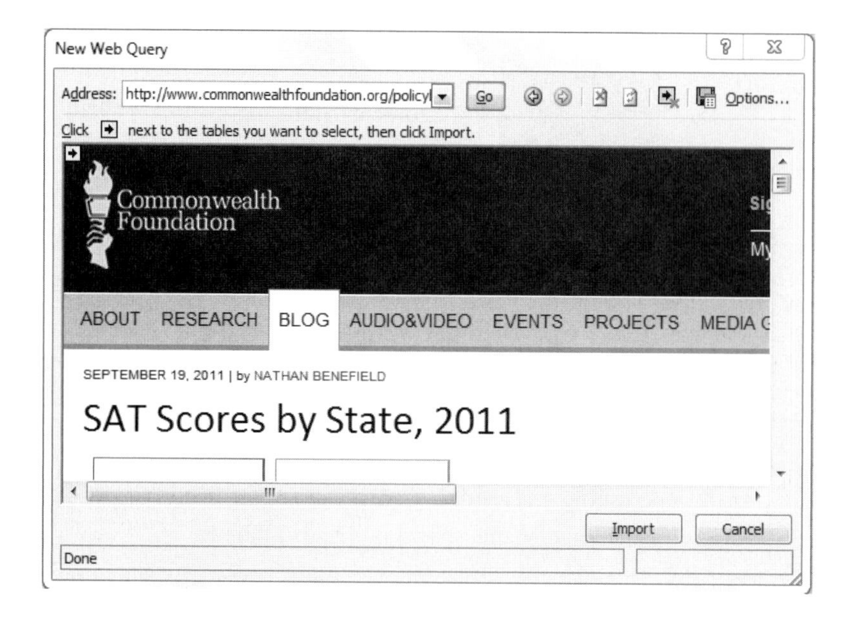

Note the yellow arrow tab in this pop-up window. This feature is very important because it allows us to limit the information that we import to contain only the data table in which we are interested. In this case, we should scroll down until we see the data shown in Figure 2.25:

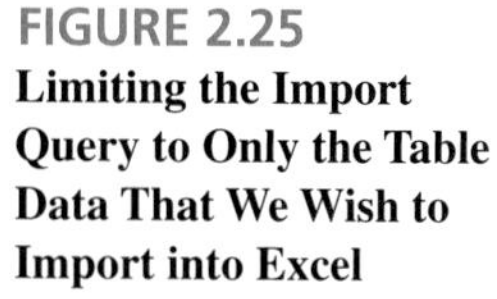
FIGURE 2.25
Limiting the Import Query to Only the Table Data That We Wish to Import into Excel

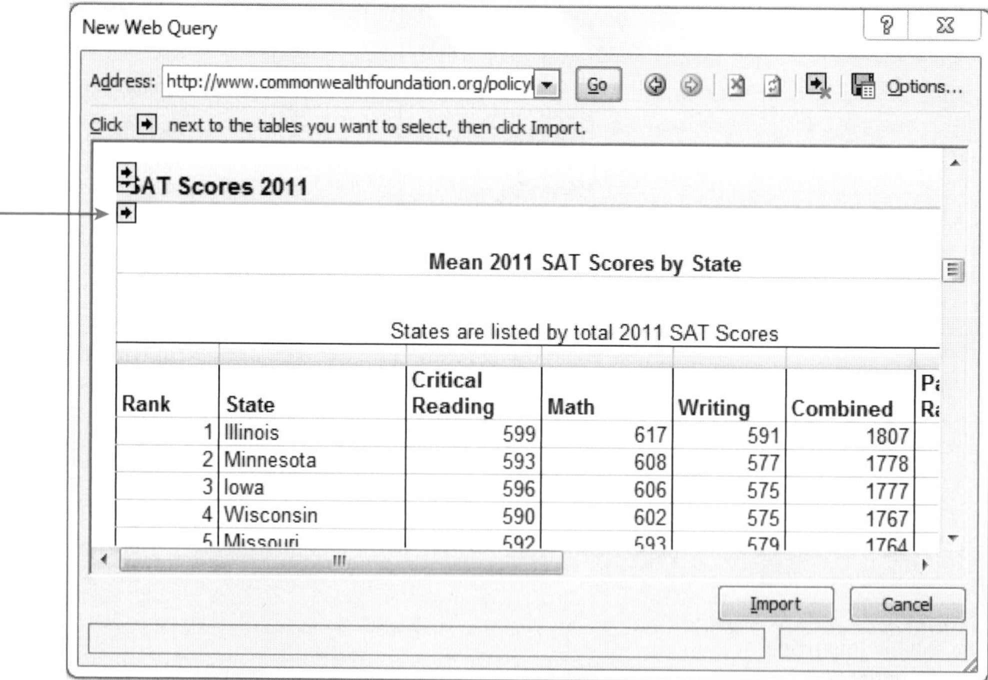

If we click on the yellow arrow tab immediately above our desired table, and click "Import," then we will import only the table data in which we are interested and not all of the extraneous information contained on the webpage. Doing so first produces the pop-up window in Figure 2.26:

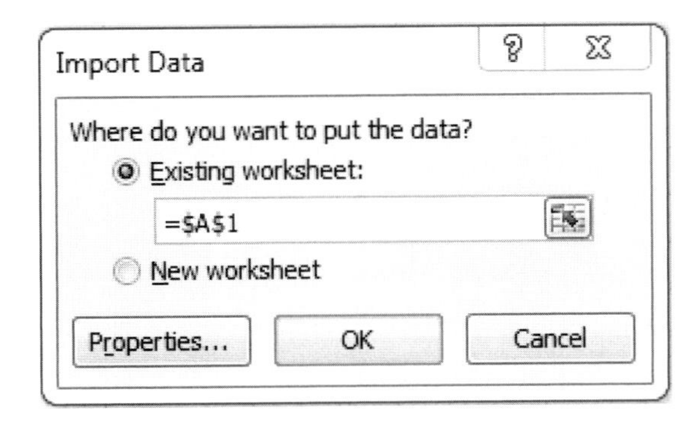

FIGURE 2.26
The Pop-Up Window That Allows Us to Select the Cell into Which the Data Are Imported into Excel

This window allows us to specify the exact worksheet and cell into which we want the data to be imported (this is actually important when we need to import multiple pages of tables and want to place each new page immediately below the last line of the previous page). In this case, because we are only importing the data from this one table, we are good with placing them in the upper-left corner (cell $A$1); click "OK." Doing so, we get Figure 2.27:

FIGURE 2.27
The Data That We Import into Excel from www.commonwealthfoundation.org/policyblog/detail/sat-scores-by-state-2011

	A	B	C	D	E	F	G
1	Rank	State	Critical	Math	Writing	Combined	Participation Rate
2	1	Illinois	599	617	591	1807	5%
3	2	Minnesota	593	608	577	1778	7%
4	3	Iowa	596	606	575	1777	3%
5	4	Wisconsin	590	602	575	1767	5%
6	5	Missouri	592	593	579	1764	5%

Creating New Worksheets

Once we have downloaded our data, one of the more valuable tools that we control is the ability to create new worksheets in our Excel workbook. The reason that this ability is so valuable is that creating new worksheets allows us to copy our data to a new place where we can work with it without fear of losing our master data, thereby having to start over with the initial data collection. Instead, if we make a mistake on the new worksheet, we simply delete the data and replace it with a copy of the master data that are contained in a different worksheet.

To create a new worksheet, we go to the bottom of the Excel file and click on the first tab to the right of the existing worksheets (Figure 2.28):

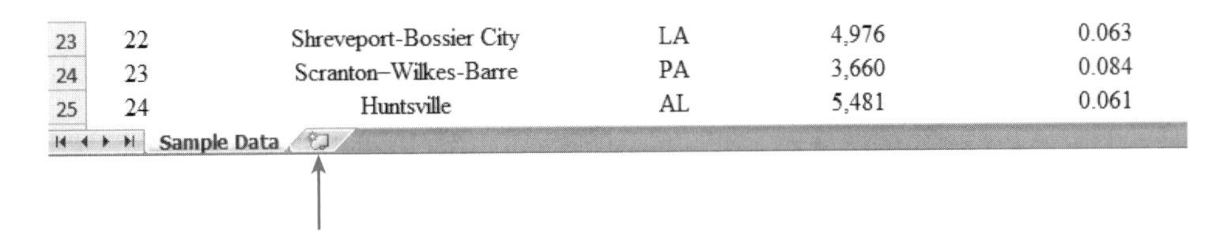

23	22	Shreveport-Bossier City	LA	4,976	0.063
24	23	Scranton–Wilkes-Barre	PA	3,660	0.084
25	24	Huntsville	AL	5,481	0.061

FIGURE 2.28
The Tab That We Click to Create a New Worksheet in Our Excel File

Doing so creates a new worksheet in which we can copy our master sample data and work without fear of permanently overwriting it (Figure 2.29):

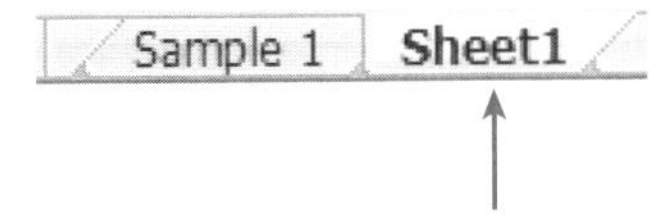

FIGURE 2.29
The New Worksheet Created in Our Excel File

Note: We can give the new worksheet a new title by double-clicking the "Sheet 1" tab and typing in our desired title, such as "Covariance" (Figure 2.30):

FIGURE 2.30
Renaming the New Worksheet Created in Our Excel File

Sorting Data from Lowest to Highest and Highest to Lowest

When working with data, it is often useful to sort the data from either lowest to highest or highest to lowest because doing so not only gives us a better sense of the data themselves, but also proves to be an easy way of checking for data-entry error (i.e., if the minimum or maximum values are far out of line with the remaining data, then we might conclude that we entered certain values incorrectly).

Suppose that we wish to sort our state test score data by the participation rate variables. We would start by moving to the "Data" tab before clicking on the "Sort" tab (Figure 2.31):

FIGURE 2.31
The Sort Tool in Excel

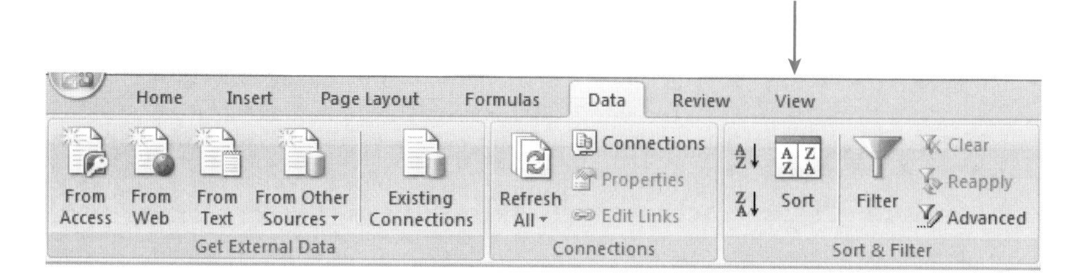

Doing so produces the pop-up window in Figure 2.32:

FIGURE 2.32
The Column Containing the Data to Be Sorted

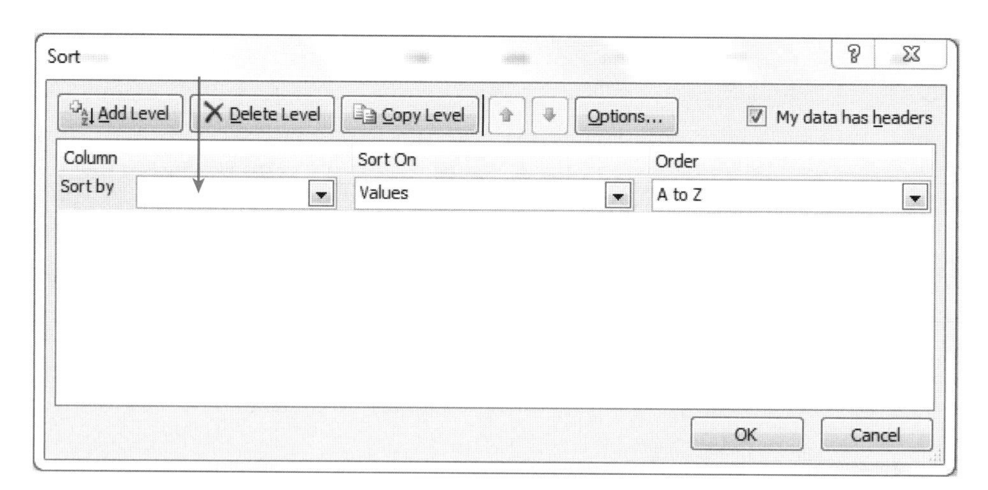

To sort our data by a given variable, we need to scroll down and select that variable by which we wish to sort in the "Sort by" window. For the current example, we select "Participation Rate," which looks like Figure 2.33:

FIGURE 2.33
The Order in Which "Participation Rate" Is to Be Sorted

Depending on the direction in which we want to sort our data, we can then either select "Smallest to Largest" or "Largest to Smallest" in the "Order" window. Selecting "Smallest to Largest," the results of sorting our data are as shown in Figure 2.34:

FIGURE 2.34
The Results of Sorting "Participation Rate" from Smallest to Largest

	A	B	C	D	E	F	G
1	Rank	State	Critical	Math	Writing	Combined	Participation Rate
2	3	Iowa	596	606	575	1777	3%
3	7	North Dakota	586	612	561	1759	3%
4	10	South Dakota	584	591	562	1737	4%
5	18	Mississippi	564	543	553	1660	4%
6	1	Illinois	599	617	591	1807	5%

Cut, Copy, and Paste Columns and Rows

When managing a data set, it is often useful to cut, copy, and paste entire rows and/or columns of data in order to move them to different rows and/or columns for data management purposes. As an example, suppose we decide that our student test score data would be more clearly presented if the "Combined" column were moved before the "Critical," "Math," and "Writing" columns. To do so, we would simply need to click on cell at the top of column F in order to highlight column F. We then need to simultaneously hold down the "Ctrl" and the "X" keys to cut that column from the table. Finally, we need to highlight the destination column—in this case, is column C (which we do by clicking on cell at the top of column C)—and simultaneously holding down the "Ctrl" and the "V" keys to paste the cut column into column C. Doing so, we get Figure 2.35:

FIGURE 2.35
The Results of Cutting and Pasting "Combined" to Move It from Column F to Column C

	A	B	C	D	E	F	G
1	Rank	State	Combined	Critical	Math	Writing	Participation Rate
2	1	Illinois	1807	599	617	591	5%
3	2	Minnesota	1778	593	608	577	7%
4	3	Iowa	1777	596	606	575	3%
5	4	Wisconsin	1767	590	602	575	5%
6	5	Missouri	1764	592	593	579	5%

Suppose that instead of moving a column of data, we wish to replicate a column of data. We could do so by highlighting the specific column that we wish to replicate, copying the column by simultaneously holding down the "Ctrl" and the "C" keys, and pasting the copied data into the target column by highlighting that column and pasting the copied cells into that column by simultaneously holding down the "Ctrl" and the "V" keys. Doing so for the column "Critical," we get Figure 2.36:

FIGURE 2.36
The Results of Copying "Critical" to Replicate It in Column G

	A	B	C	D	E	F	G	H
1	Rank	State	Combined	Critical	Math	Writing	Critical	Participation Rate
2	1	Illinois	1807	599	617	591	599	5%
3	2	Minnesota	1778	593	608	577	593	7%
4	3	Iowa	1777	596	606	575	596	3%
5	4	Wisconsin	1767	590	602	575	590	5%
6	5	Missouri	1764	592	593	579	592	5%

Note: We can do the exact same things for rows of data by following the preceding instructions but doing so for rows instead of columns of data.

Use the Function Tool in Excel

Suppose that we are interested in working with one of the canned functions in Excel but we do not know the exact command for doing so. We can find likely find the command we are looking for using the Function tool. To do so, we place the cursor in the cell in which we wish to make the calculation, and then we click on the "f_x" tab above the column headings (Figure 2.37):

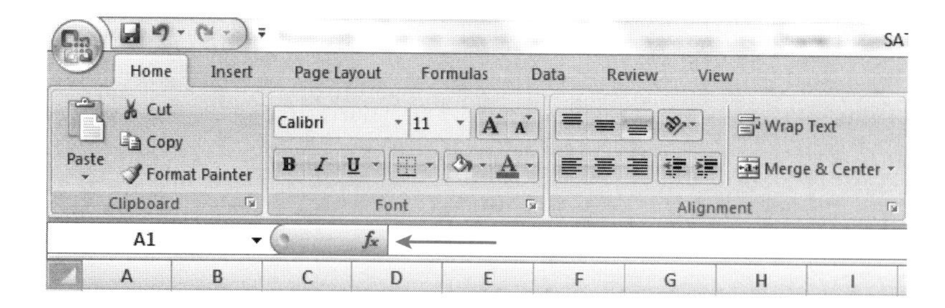

FIGURE 2.37
How to Access the Function Tool in Excel

Doing so pulls up the pop-up window in Figure 2.38, in which we can either search for our desired function in the "Search for a function" window, or we can locate it by scrolling through the "Select a function" window.

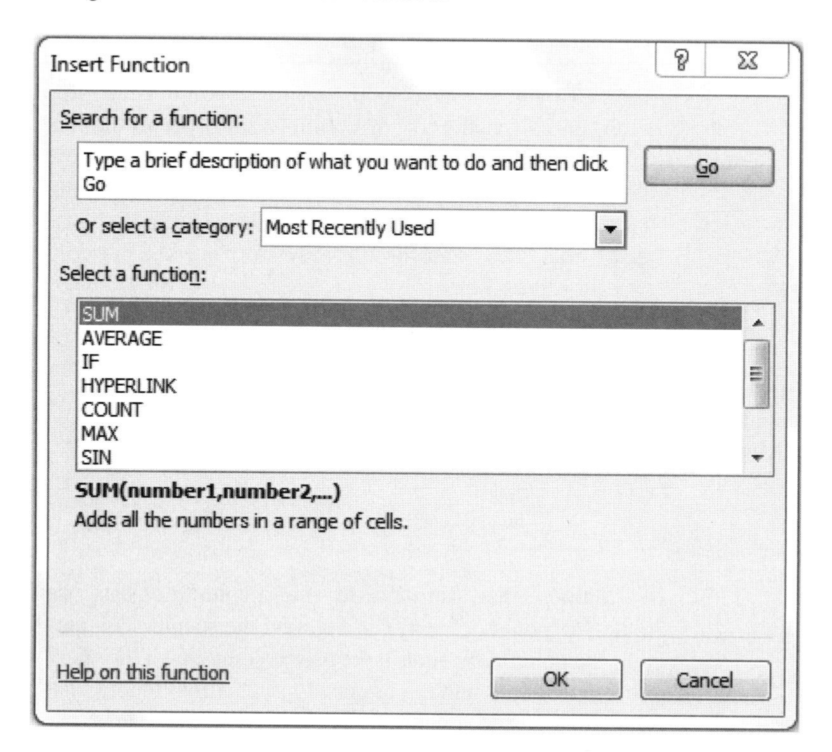

FIGURE 2.38
Functions That Are Accessed by Clicking on the Function Tool in Excel

Copy Cell Entries Down a Column

Suppose that we want to copy the contents of a given cell down the remaining cells in a column. While we could do so using the copy and paste functions, there is a quicker and easier way. Excel is programmed so that double-clicking on the bottom right corner of a cell copies the calculations in that cell to the remaining cells in the column.

As an example, suppose that we wish to calculate the "Average" test score for each state. To do so quickly and easily, we perform the desired calculation in the top cell in the column (cell F2). We then double-click on the bottom-right corner of that cell (Figure 2.39):

F2 fx =SUM(C2:E2)/3

	A	B	C	D	E	F
1	Rank	State	Critical	Math	Writing	Average
2	1	Illinois	599	617	591	602.3333
3	2	Minnesota	593	608	577	
4	3	Iowa	596	606	575	
5	4	Wisconsin	590	602	575	
6	5	Missouri	592	593	579	

FIGURE 2.39
The Spot to Click to Paste the Operation in Cell F2 Down the Remainder of Column F

Doing so copies the calculation in that first cell into all remaining cells in the column, giving us Figure 2.40:

FIGURE 2.40
The Results of Pasting the Operation in Cell F2 Down the Remainder of Column F

F2 fx =SUM(C2:E2)/3

	A	B	C	D	E	F
1	Rank	State	Critical	Math	Writing	Average
2	1	Illinois	599	617	591	602.3333
3	2	Minnesota	593	608	577	592.6667
4	3	Iowa	596	606	575	592.3333
5	4	Wisconsin	590	602	575	589
6	5	Missouri	592	593	579	588

This feature is extremely valuable when we wish to utilize the data management tip of assigning a unique id for each observation. To do so most easily, we would create the new column "id"; we would type "1" and "2," respectively, in the first two cells. (Note that if we only typed a "1" in the first cell in the column and we double-clicked the bottom right corner of that cell, Excel would copy a "1" into all remaining cells in the column.) We would then highlight those two cells and double-click on the bottom-right corner of the second cell (Figure 2.41):

FIGURE 2.41
The Spot to Click to Paste a Successive id Number Down the Remainder of Column A

	A	B	C	D	E
1	id	State	Critical	Math	Writing
2	1	Illinois	599	617	591
3	2	Minnesota	593	608	577
4		Iowa	596	606	575
5		Wisconsin	590	602	575
6		Missouri	592	593	579

Doing so copies the subsequent values in the pattern started in the first two cells to the remaining cells in the column, giving us unique "id" numbers for each observation (Figure 2.42):

FIGURE 2.42
The Results of Pasting Successive id Numbers Down the Remainder of Column A

	A	B	C	D	E
1	id	State	Critical	Math	Writing
2	1	Illinois	599	617	591
3	2	Minnesota	593	608	577
4	3	Iowa	596	606	575
5	4	Wisconsin	590	602	575
6	5	Missouri	592	593	579

Use the Paste Special Command to Copy Values

Suppose that we have performed specific calculations in a number of cells and that we wish to paste the resulting values into a different worksheet (cell, file, etc.) without carrying through the calculations used to determine the values. We can use the "Paste Special" command to do so by copying the initial cells which, in this example, are the "Average" calculations in column F (Figure 2.43):

FIGURE 2.43
The Formulas That We Do Not Wish to Paste into the Destination Cells

F2 fx =SUM(C2:E2)/3

	A	B	C	D	E	F
1	id	State	Critical	Math	Writing	Average
2	1	Illinois	599	617	591	602.3333
3	2	Minnesota	593	608	577	592.6667
4	3	Iowa	596	606	575	592.3333
5	4	Wisconsin	590	602	575	589
6	5	Missouri	592	593	579	588

We next click on the cell into which we wish to paste these data—say, column H—right-click the mouse, and highlight "Paste Special" in the drop-down menu. Doing so produces the pop-up window in Figure 2.44:

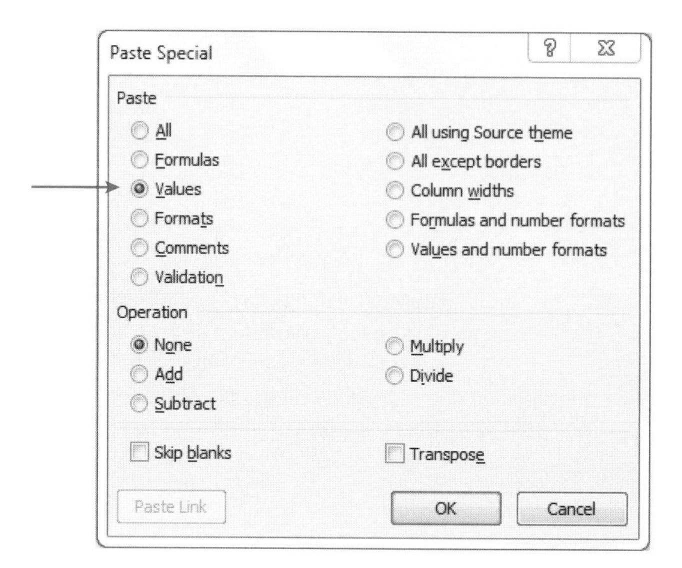

FIGURE 2.44
The Paste Special Command That Allows Us to Copy the Calculated Values Rather Than the Formulas into the Destination Cells

To paste the calculated value without carrying through the calculations themselves, we need to click the "Values" tab and "OK," resulting in Figure 2.45:

FIGURE 2.45
The Results of Pasting the Calculated Values Rather Than the Formulas into the Destination Cells

H2 | *fx* 602.333333333333

	A	B	C	D	E	F	G	H
1	id	State	Critical	Math	Writing	Average		Average
2	1	Illinois	599	617	591	602.3333		602.3333
3	2	Minnesota	593	608	577	592.6667		592.6667
4	3	Iowa	596	606	575	592.3333		592.3333
5	4	Wisconsin	590	602	575	589		589
6	5	Missouri	592	593	579	588		588

Note that the results of the calculations in column F have now been repeated in column H, but that the calculations themselves have not been carried forward (i.e., the entry in cell H2 is now 602.33 rather than = Sum(C2:E2)/3). This proves extremely useful when managing data because, if we simply copy and paste the original cells to a new location without taking this step, the calculations in the cell are automatically performed using columns E through G rather than columns C through E, which is obviously not what we want (Figure 2.46):

FIGURE 2.46
The Results of Pasting the Initial Formulas into the Destination Cells

H2 | *fx* =SUM(E2:G2)/3

	A	B	C	D	E	F	G	H
1	id	State	Critical	Math	Writing	Average		Average
2	1	Illinois	599	617	591	602.3333		397.7778
3	2	Minnesota	593	608	577	592.6667		389.8889
4	3	Iowa	596	606	575	592.3333		389.1111
5	4	Wisconsin	590	602	575	589		388
6	5	Missouri	592	593	579	588		389

Use the Paste Special Command to Transpose Columns

Another valuable option available in the "Paste Special" tool is the ability to transpose data from rows to columns and columns to rows. As an example, suppose that we wish to shift the first two columns in our state test score data—"State" and "Combined"—to rows. We would highlight those two columns as in Figure 2.47:

FIGURE 2.47
The Column Data That We Wish to Transpose to Row Data

State	Combined
Illinois	1807
Minnesota	1778
Iowa	1777
Wisconsin	1767
Missouri	1764

We would then transpose those columns into rows by clicking on the destination cell for the transposed data, right-clicking the mouse to produce "Paste Special," and clicking the "Transpose" tab, which looks like Figure 2.48:

FIGURE 2.48
The Paste Special Command That Allows Us to Transpose Column Data into Row Data (and Vice Versa)

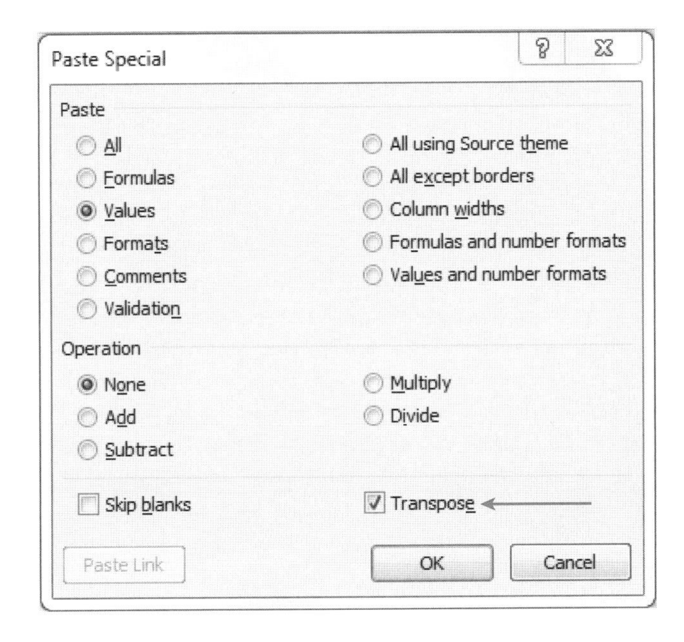

We would then click "OK" to transpose the initial data from columns to rows, with the results looking like Figure 2.49:

FIGURE 2.49
The Results of Transposing Our Column Data into Row Data

State	Illinois	Minnesota	Iowa	Wisconsin	Missouri
Combined	1807	1778	1777	1767	1764

ADDITIONS TO OUR EMPIRICAL RESEARCH TOOLKIT

In this chapter, we have introduced a number of tools that will prove valuable when performing empirical research. They include:

- Various methods for obtaining data, including Internet searches for publicly available data and self-administered surveys.
- Data collection and management skills for assembling and working with appropriate data sets.
- Excel commands that prove useful when managing data.

OUR NEW EMPIRICAL TOOLS IN PRACTICE: USING WHAT WE HAVE LEARNED IN THIS CHAPTER

Using the tools introduced in this chapter, our former student collected data for her empirical research project. She started by identifying a question of sufficient interest by recalling a reading from one of her classes suggesting that at least some portion of the rise in obesity rates in the United States could be tied to the reduction in smoking rates. Drawing on her economic training that excise tax rates should be tied to consumption of the taxed good, she theorized that if the underlying theory were true, then states with higher tax rates on cigarettes should have lower obesity rates than states with lower tax rates on cigarettes.

Based on this preliminary work (steps 1 and 2 of conducting an empirical research project), our former student realized that she needed to collect state-level data on cigarette taxes and obesity rates. To identify the former, she conducted an Internet search for "state cigarette tax rates" and was taken to the website www.ncsl.org/default.aspx?tabid=14349, which contained data on state cigarette excises taxes per 20-pack per state. To identify the latter, she conducted an Internet search for "state obesity rates" and was taken to the website www.usnews.com/opinion/articles/2010/08/10/us-obesity-rates-by-state, which contained data on 2010 state obesity rates.

Downloading these data and combining them into one Excel worksheet, our student constructed the master data set that formed the basis for her empirical research project (Figure 2.50):

FIGURE 2.50
Our Former Student's State Cigarette Tax and State Obesity Rate Data

	A	B	C
1	**State**	**2010 Tax Rate Per 20 Pack**	**2010 State Obesity Rates**
2	Alabama	0.425	0.28
3	Alaska	2	0.27
4	Arizona	2	0.25
5	Arkansas	1.15	0.32
6	California	0.87	0.23

LOOKING AHEAD TO CHAPTER 3

Before utilizing econometric techniques to analyze our data, we must first get a general sense of the data that we are dealing with. To provide such information, Chapter 3 presents a review of the summary statistics that form the basis of our understanding of the data.

Problems

2.1 What are the three different types of data? Give an example not contained in the chapter of each of these types.

2.2 Answer the following:

a. Give an example of where you may need to create a survey to obtain data.

b. Give two different examples of how you would distribute the survey.

c. How does the method of distributing the survey in part (b) affect the results you obtain? For example, how do you think that your results would change if you surveyed your friends by e-mail versus if you surveyed individuals exiting your local grocery store?

d. Why does it matter that the results may be different depending on your chosen method?

2.3 Why is it important to carefully manage the data you collect? Describe the steps you would follow once you located data on the web and read it into Excel.

Exercises

E2.1 Do the following:

a. Search the web to obtain GDP (gross domestic product) and population data for the last 20 years in the United States. Read these data into Excel.

b. Create a new variable called GDP/Capita by dividing the GDP by Population.

c. Use "Paste Special" on the GDP/Capita variable to remove the function you used in part (b) from these data.

d. Sort the data from low to high, and write down the years when GDP per capita was the largest and smallest.

e. Are the data you collected in this exercise cross-section, time-series, or panel data?

E2.2 Do the following:

a. What were the unemployment rates in 2012 for New York, Los Angeles, Chicago, Phoenix, Houston, and Philadelphia? Put these data into an Excel spreadsheet.

b. Find the population of each of these cities for 2012, and put these data into the Excel spreadsheet you created in part (a).

c. Create a new variable called Total Unemployed by multiplying the unemployment rate by population.

d. Use the Function key in Excel to obtain the total number of unemployed in the six cities combined. What is this number?

e. Use the "Paste Special" command to transpose all observations in these data.

E2.3 Do the following:

a. Go to the Bureau of Transportation Statistics website at www.bts.gov; find the urban utility report for the previous year, and obtain all the data in an Excel spreadsheet. Save your spreadsheet.

b. Create a new worksheet, and copy over the daily vehicle miles of travel and average state gasoline cost for all the cities listed by all years listed. Name the worksheet "Miles and Gas."

c. Create a new column in the worksheet from part (b) and label it "id" (short for identification number). Number the observations in your spreadsheet from 1 to the number of observations you obtained. This is the best way to keep track of how the data were initially ordered.

d. Sort the data to find the answer to the following two questions: (1) In what year and city did the residents travel the most and the least daily miles? (2) In what year and state was the average state gasoline cost the highest and lowest?

E2.4 Go to the OECD website at www.oecd.org and click on the statistics link at the top. Download the Excel file that contains the basic statistics for Africa for the most recent year.

a. Which country had the highest GDP growth, and which country had the lowest GDP growth?

b. Which country had the highest population density, and which country had the lowest population density?

c. How do you think that the last row for all of Africa was obtained for land area and population? Try various functions to verify your answer. Note that the functions will likely yield slightly different numbers.

Chapter Three

Summary Statistics

CHAPTER OBJECTIVES

After reading this chapter, you will be able to:

1. Construct relative frequency histograms for a given variable.
2. Calculate measures of central tendency.
3. Calculate measures of dispersion.
4. Use measures of central tendency and dispersion for a given variable.
5. Detect whether outliers are present for a given variable.
6. Construct scatter diagrams for the relationship between two given variables.
7. Calculate the covariance and the correlation coefficient between given two variables.

A STUDENT'S PERSPECTIVE

Suppose that you work for a large pizza delivery chain and that you are concerned as to whether it is financially sensible to take the risks necessary (speeding tickets, accidents, etc.) to make your deliveries in quicker times. How would you go about empirically determining whether faster deliveries result in bigger tips?

This is exactly the situation encountered by one of our former students. To make a more informed decision, the student collected data on the tip amount and the minutes from order to delivery for his 50 most recent calls, illustrated in Table 3.1.

How should the student start his empirical analysis of these data? This chapter discusses visual and numerical methods that are used to answer this question.

BIG PICTURE OVERVIEW

The goal of empirical analysis is to learn something about a population of interest (in the tip example, the population would be all of the deliveries that the individual could ever work). Achieving this goal is complicated by the fact that we rarely, if ever, observe the entire population that we are hoping to learn about. Instead, the best that we can typically do is to collect a random sample from the population and use information observed for that given sample as our best guess as to the unobserved values that exist for the population.

As an example, consider that in the 2008 presidential election, 131,257,328 Americans cast votes for president of the United States, with Barack Obama receiving 66,882,230 votes and John McCain receiving 58,343,671 votes. In the days leading up to the election, the American public was keenly interested in learning about who was more likely to win the election. To provide such information, several polling organizations contacted American citizens and asked who they were most likely to vote for. Was it necessary for the organizations to question all 131,257,328 citizens who eventually cast ballots in order to generate a reasonably accurate picture of the likely outcome of the election? No. Based on statistical principles, it was only necessary to poll rather small-seeming samples drawn from the voting population. For instance, by interviewing only 714 likely voters between October 30, 2008, and November 1, 2008, the CNN/Opinion Research poll was able to

TABLE 3.1
Tip Data Collected by Our Former Student

Delivery	Tip Amount ($)	Minutes to Delivery	Delivery	Tip Amount ($)	Minutes to Delivery
1	$10	19	26	$10	15
2	0	35	27	0	49
3	2	30	28	5	24
4	5	15	29	3	30
5	5	24	30	7	13
6	0	63	31	0	48
7	3	7	32	2	23
8	8	20	33	0	35
9	0	43	34	5	41
10	5	7	35	1	49
11	10	12	36	0	23
12	0	25	37	0	29
13	0	32	38	5	38
14	20	8	39	3	18
15	3	11	40	0	39
16	2	14	41	2	26
17	0	34	42	0	30
18	10	17	43	5	10
19	0	28	44	10	18
20	0	18	45	0	24
21	6	9	46	4	26
22	3	18	47	0	19
23	2	46	48	3	49
24	0	33	49	6	8
25	15	21	50	0	12

estimate that Barack Obama would win the general election by a 53–46 margin, which amazingly enough, is the exact margin by which he did win the popular votes.

This anecdote raises a very important question—how can such a small sample (roughly 0.0005% of the population in the preceding example) provide such accurate information about an entire unobserved population? The answer to this question lies at the heart of statistics and provides the starting point for our work in this text.

statistical inference
Uses statistics and random sampling to learn about the population.

We refer to the process of using a specific observed sample to draw conclusions about an unobserved population as **statistical inference.** To set the concept of statistical inference in our minds, we find it useful to think of the simple visual example represented in Figure 3.1.

FIGURE 3.1
A Visual Depiction of the Statistical Inference Process

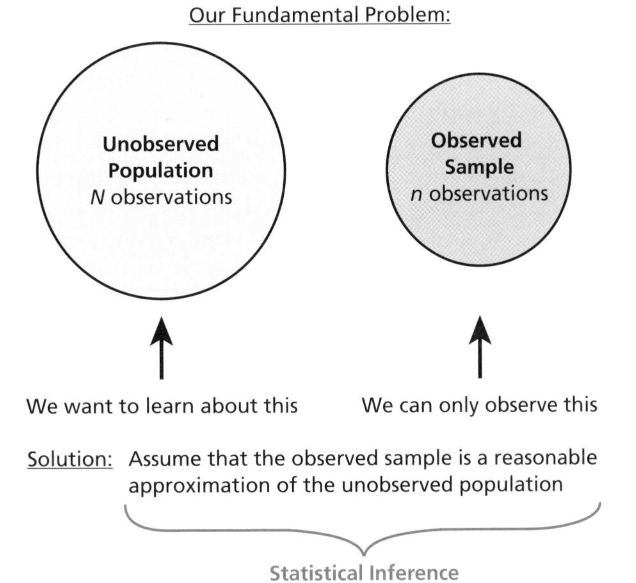

summary statistics
Numerical values that summarize the observed data.

In this chapter, we start our discussion of statistical inference by introducing visual and numerical values that summarize the observed data for the specific random sample that is drawn from the population of interest. We refer to such values as **summary statistics.** As we will see, while these are some of the most basic values that we can calculate, they are extremely important in providing a general sense of the empirical probability distribution of our given sample. Given their importance to understanding the nature of the data being analyzed, empirical research projects generally start with the presentation and discussion of summary statistics when introducing the data that is the focus of the project.

In broad terms, when thinking about the data points for an individual variable in our observed sample, there are two main things we wish to know: (1) Where do the observed data points tend to fall? (2) How widely spread do the observed data points tend to be from each other? Likewise, when thinking about the relationship between two variables in our observed sample there are two main things we wish to know: (1) the manner in which the variables are related to each other and (2) the strength of that relationship. In this chapter, we introduce numerical and visual tools for beginning to answer these questions. Visually, we summarize the goals of this chapter in Figure 3.2.

FIGURE 3.2
A Visual Depiction of the Empirical Research Tools Introduced in This Chapter

Q: What can we learn about the observed sample?

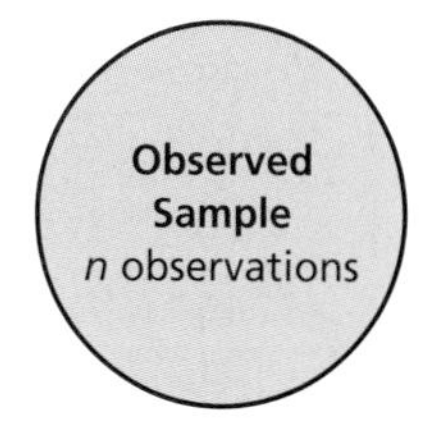

A: We can

(1) Visually summarize the observed data.

- For one variable } Histograms
- For two variables } Scatter Diagrams

(2) Numerically summarize the observed data.

- For one variable } Measures of Central Tendency, Measures of Dispersion
- For two variables } Covariance, Correlation Coefficient

As a final point, notice that we are careful to use the terminology "unobserved" whenever talking about populations for which we are performing statistical inference. We do so because we find it valuable to use terminology that reminds us why we are doing what we are doing—which, in this case, is trying to learn about population parameters that we cannot directly observe.

Before continuing with our discussion, we need to introduce the data sets that we analyze in this chapter. For the sake of continuity, throughout the text of the chapter, we focus on the 150-observation city property crime sample that we introduced in Chapter 2. In the Excel boxes, we focus on the 2011 CEO compensation and firm profit for a 200-observation sample that is randomly selected from the population of *Fortune* 500 companies. While these data sets both contain two variables of interest, we begin the chapter by focusing on only one given variable, city property crimes rates and CEO compensation, respectively, before moving on to the relationship between both variables in the data sets.

3.1 CONSTRUCT RELATIVE FREQUENCY HISTOGRAMS FOR A GIVEN VARIABLE

We strongly suggest beginning the analysis of a given data set by simply looking through the data in an effort to identify anything that might stand out. For instance, when looking at our former student's tip data in Table 3.1, we quickly notice that a disproportionate number of entries are 0, which suggests that a large number of customers in the student's area refused to tip the delivery driver. Another advantage of starting with this approach is that it can help identify observations that were recorded incorrectly. For instance, if the visual inspection revealed that our former student had recorded $200 instead of $20 for delivery 14, then he would have been able to correct the mistake before beginning his empirical analysis (or, if it were not a mistake, he would have known to offer excellent service to the address on future orders).

relative frequency histogram
A graph that displays a relative frequency distribution and provides a visual summary of an empirical probability distribution.

Beyond these simple, yet potentially important points, visual inspection of the data is unlikely to provide much knowledge about our observed sample. Accordingly, we need to consider more formal ways for gathering useful information. Given that a picture is worth a thousand words, we might wish to construct visual images of where the observed data points in our sample fall relative to each other. For our 150-observation property crime sample, a **relative frequency histogram** is shown in Figure 3.3.

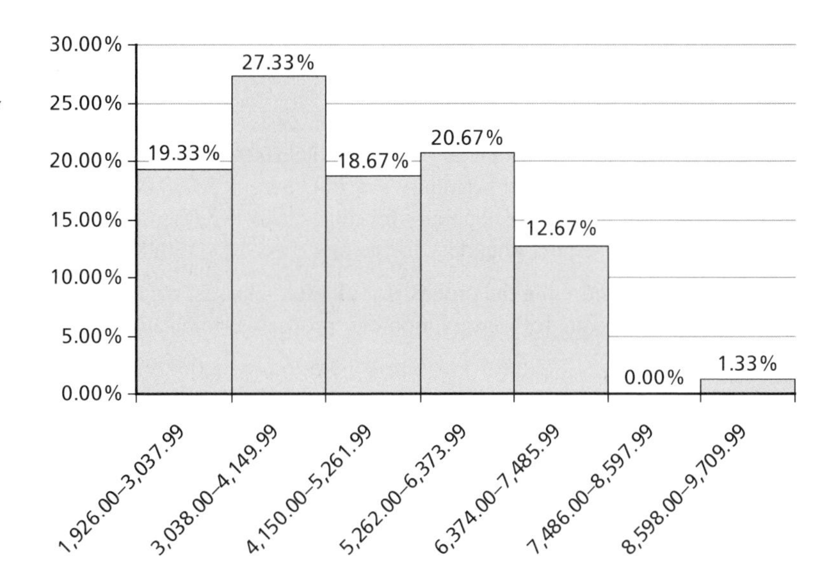

FIGURE 3.3
Relative Frequency Histogram of the Property Crimes/100,000 Citizens for Our 150-Observation City Property Crime Sample

relative frequency table
A tabular summary of a set of data that shows the percentage of items that fall in each of several distinct classes.

How did we construct the picture in Figure 3.3? The first step is to construct a **relative frequency table** based on the underlying relative frequency distribution of the observed sample data. A frequency distribution is created through a four-step process: (1) select the number of classes, (2) choose the class interval, (3) select the class boundaries, and (4) count the number of values in the sample that fall within the boundaries of each class.

Specific rules governing each of these steps are as follows.

Step 1: Select the number of classes

classes
The distinct categories that the data are divided into in a relative frequency table.

The rule-of-thumb for determining the approximate number of **classes** in a relative frequency table is

$$Approximate\ number\ of\ classes = [(2)(Number\ of\ observations)]^{(1/3)} \quad \textbf{3.1.1}$$

The actual number of classes is the integer value that just exceeds the calculated number value. For our 150-observation city property crime sample, the approximate number of classes is $[(2)(150)]^{0.3333} = 6.69$, which is rounded up to 7.

Step 2: Choose the class interval

class interval
The width of each class in a relative frequency table.

Once the number of classes has been determined, the appropriate **class interval** is

$$Approximate\ class\ interval = \frac{Largest\ data\ value - Smallest\ data\ value}{Number\ of\ classes} \quad \textbf{3.1.2}$$

Again, the actual class interval width is the integer value that just exceeds the number value. For our 150-observation city property crime sample, the approximate interval width is $(9{,}705 - 1{,}927)/7 = 1{,}111.28$, which we round up to 1,112.00.

Step 3: Choose the class boundaries

class boundaries
The starting and ending values for each class in a relative frequency table.

Once the number of classes and the class interval have been determined, the appropriate **class boundaries** are determined such that

- Each data item belongs to one and only one class.
- The lower boundary for the first class is set just below the lowest value in the data set.
- The lower boundary for the second class is found by adding the class width to the lower boundary for the first class.
- The upper boundary for the first class is found by subtracting .01 from the lower boundary for the second class.
- The remaining class boundaries are determined by repeating the process for the remaining classes.

For our 150-observation city property crime sample, the lowest value in the data set is 1,926.53, and the appropriate interval width is 1,112.00. To determine the lower boundary for the first class, we round down the lowest value to 1,926.00. Applying the previous rules, we then get

$$\begin{aligned} \text{Lower boundary for first class} &= 1{,}926.00 \\ \text{Lower boundary for second class} &= 1{,}926.00 + 1{,}112.00 = 3{,}038.00 \\ \text{Upper boundary for first class} &= 3{,}038.00 - 0.01 = 3{,}037.99 \\ \text{Lower boundary for third class} &= 3{,}038.00 + 1{,}112.00 = 4{,}150.00 \\ \text{Upper boundary for second class} &= 4{,}150.00 - 0.01 = 4{,}149.99 \end{aligned} \qquad \textbf{3.1.3}$$

Continuing the process for all eight classes, we find that the appropriate class boundaries for our 150-observation city property crime sample are

$$\begin{array}{c} 1{,}926.00 - 3{,}037.99 \\ 3{,}038.00 - 4{,}149.99 \\ 4{,}150.00 - 5{,}261.99 \\ 5{,}262.00 - 6{,}373.99 \\ 6{,}374.00 - 7{,}485.99 \\ 7{,}486.00 - 8{,}597.99 \\ 8{,}598.00 - 9{,}709.99 \end{array} \qquad \textbf{3.1.4}$$

Step 4: Calculate the relative frequency

relative frequency
The number of observations that fall into each class in a frequency table.

We calculate the **relative frequency** within each class by first determining the number of observations (or the frequency) in each class and then, determining the percentage of observations in each class. Combining these pieces of information, for our 150-observation city property crime sample, we get the relative frequency table in Table 3.2.

TABLE 3.2
Relative Frequency Table for Our 150-Observation City Property Crime Sample

Property Crime Class	Frequency	Relative Frequency
1,926.00 – 3,037.99	29	19.33%
3,038.00 – 4,149.99	41	27.33%
4,150.00 – 5,261.99	28	18.67%
5,262.00 – 6,373.99	31	20.67%
6,374.00 – 7,485.99	19	12.67%
7,486.00 – 8,597.99	0	0.00%
8,598.00 – 9,709.99	2	1.33%
Total	150	1.00

Constructing a Relative Frequency Histogram

A relative frequency histogram is simply a visual representation of the information contained in the relative frequency table. For the data in Table 3.2, the relative frequency histogram looks like Figure 3.3.

EXCEL EXAMPLE 3.1

Using the Histogram Wizard to construct relative frequency histograms for our CEO compensation sample

Once you have the Data Analysis Toolpak, which you can download following the instructions in Chapter 2, you can more easily create histograms using the Histogram Wizard.

Using the Histogram Wizard

1. Determine the appropriate bin ranges using the rules in the text.
   Place the lower bounds in empty cells (**F7:F14**).
   Place the upper bounds in empty cells (**G7:G14**).
2. Click on the "Data" tab.
3. Click the "Data Analysis" tab, which is the furthest tab on the right.
4. In the "Analysis Tools" menu, highlight "Histogram" and click "OK."

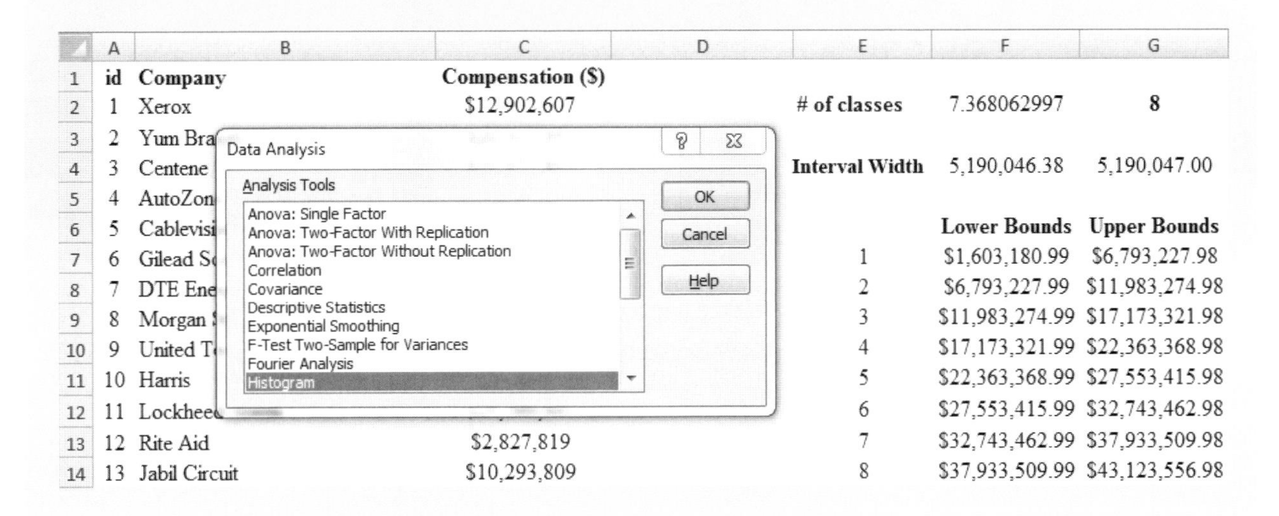

5. Click the "Input Range" tab, and highlight the CEO compensation data (**C2:C201**).
   Click the "Bin Range" tab and highlight the upper bounds (**G7:G14**).
   Click the "Output Range" tab and highlight an empty cell (**I3**).
   Check the "Chart Output" box.
6. Click "OK".

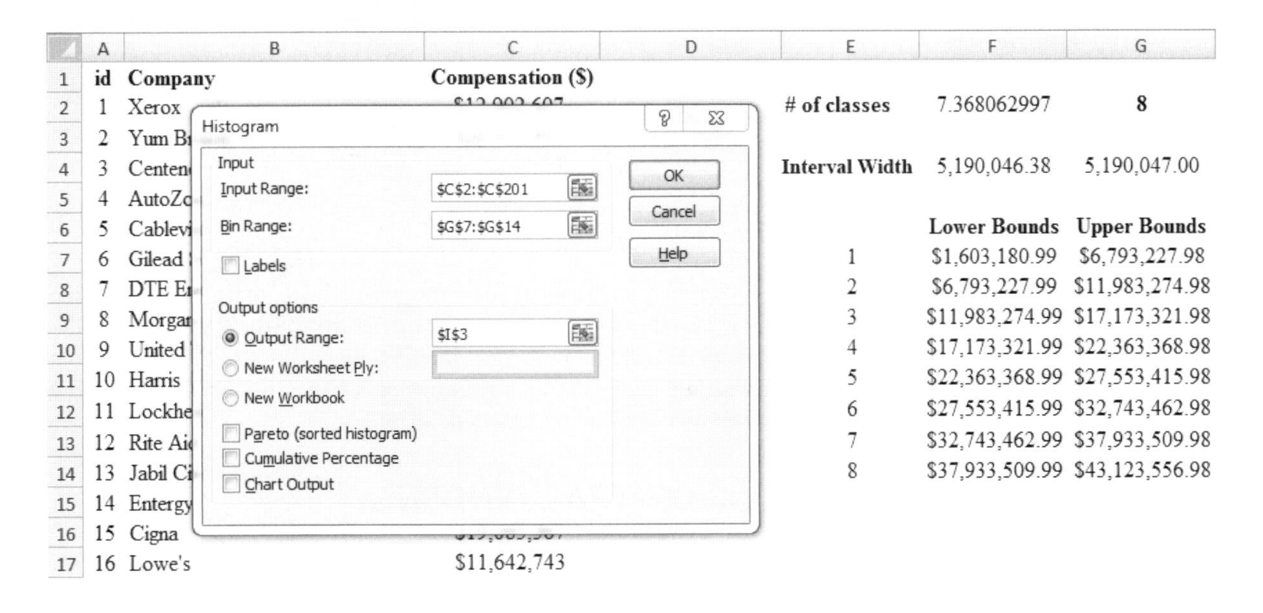

Bin	*Frequency*
$6,793,227.98	55
$11,983,274.98	66
$17,173,321.98	49
$22,363,368.98	17
$27,553,415.98	5
$32,743,462.98	5
$37,933,509.98	2
$43,123,556.98	1
Total	200

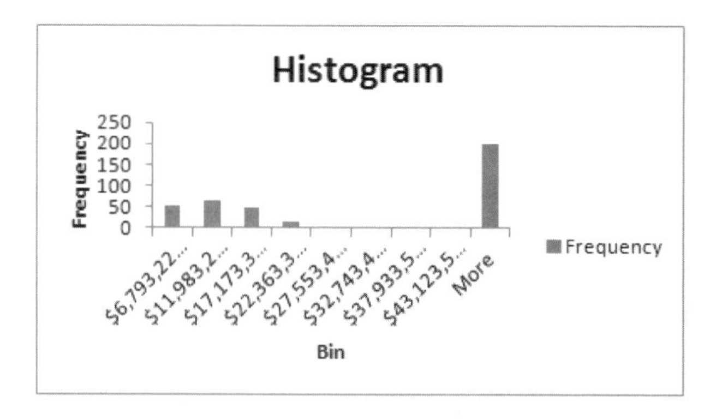

There are two important things to note about the above chart: (1) While the item initially created by Excel is a basic histogram, it is possible to make the histogram more visually appealing using "Design," "Layout," and "Format" features under the "Chart Tools" tab, as shown here.

(2) Once the preceding frequency table has been produced, a relative frequency table can easily be constructed by converting the data in the frequency column into relative frequencies and creating a bar chart of the bins and relative frequencies. For our example, doing so looks as follows:

Bin	*Relative Frequency*
$1,603,180.99 - $6,793,227.98	27.50%
$6,793,227.99 - $11,983,274.98	33.00%
$11,983,274.99 - $17,173,321.98	24.50%
$17,173,321.99 - $22,363,368.98	8.50%
$22,363,368.99 - $27,553,415.98	2.50%
$27,553,415.99 - $32,743,462.98	2.50%
$32,743,462.99 - $37,933,509.98	1.00%
$37,933,509.99 - $43,123,556.98	0.50%

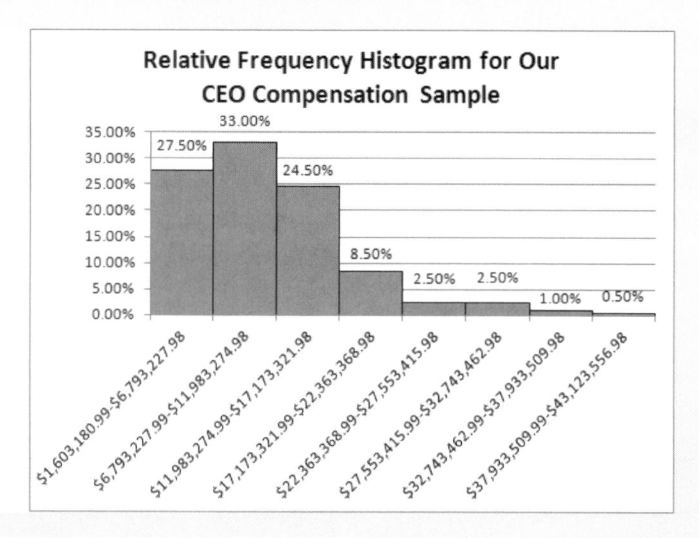

empirical probability distribution
A distribution that is created from the sample data.

While visual depictions, such as relative frequency histograms, provide valuable information as to the overall nature of the **empirical probability distribution** of our observed sample, they lack specific numerical interpretations. As a result, to complement our visual summary of the data we may wish to calculate specific numerical values that summarize the distribution in a quick and simple manner.

3.2 CALCULATE MEASURES OF CENTRAL TENDENCY FOR A GIVEN VARIABLE

If we were to rearrange property crime rates from smallest to largest, we would learn that the minimum value in our sample is 1,926.53 property crimes per 100,000 citizens while the maximum value is 9,705.45. We refer to the difference between these two values as the

EMPIRICAL RESEARCH TOOL 3.1: VISUAL SUMMARIES OF THE EMPIRICAL PROBABILITY DISTRIBUTION

Goal:
Constructing visual images of where the observed data points in our sample fall relative to each other.

Tools:
Histograms
A relative frequency histogram is a graph that displays a relative frequency distribution.

range
The difference between the maximum and the minimum values in the data set.

range of the data, meaning that for our 150-observation city property crime sample the range of the data is 9,705.45 − 1,926.53 = 7,778.93.

These simple summary statistics provide a general sense of the spread between the smallest and largest observations in our sample. They do not, however, provide any indication as to where the remaining values tend to fall between those extremes. Accordingly, they do not provide any information as to whether most of the observations fall closer to the minimum, closer to the maximum, or closer to the middle of the range.

EXCEL EXAMPLE 3.2

Commands for calculating the minimum, maximum, and range for our CEO compensation sample

Determining the Minimum, Maximum, and Range

1. In an empty cell (say, F3), type=**min(C2:C201)**
2. In an empty cell (say, F5), type=**max(C2:C201).**
3. In an empty cell (say, F7), type=**F5 - F3.**

	A	B	C	D	E	F
1	**id**	**Company**	**Compensation ($)**			
2	1	Xerox	$12,902,607.00			
3	2	Yum Brands	$20,411,852.00		Minimum	$1,603,181.00
4	3	Centene	$10,473,912.00			
5	4	AutoZone	$11,360,019.00		Maximum	$43,123,552.00
6	5	Cablevision Systems	$11,445,228.00			
7	6	Gilead Sciences	$15,615,645.00		Range	$41,520,371.00

These data indicate that the minimum compensation for a *Fortune* 500 CEO in our sample is $1,603,181, that the maximum compensation is $43,123,552, and that the difference between the largest and smallest compensation, or the range of the data, is $41,520,371.

measures of central tendency
The numerical values that summarize where the central mass of an empirical probability distribution tends to fall.

How can we generate a better sense of where the observed data points tend to fall within the sample range? **Measures of central tendency** are individual values that describe an empirical probability distribution by asking, "If you were forced to provide one number that best describes the observed sample data, what would it be?" There are three primary measures that answer this question by indicating where the central mass of the empirical probability distribution tends to be located.

The Sample Mean

sample mean
The arithmetic average of the observed sample data.

The **sample mean,** $\bar{x}$, is the arithmetic average of the observed sample data and is calculated as

$$\bar{x} = \frac{1}{n}\sum_{i=1}^{n} x_i = \frac{1}{n}(x_1 + x_2 + x_3 + \ldots + x_n) \qquad 3.2.1$$

In words, the sample mean is calculated by summing the observed values for each of the observations in the sample and dividing that sum by the number of observations in the sample. This statistic provides a sense of the "average" value in the sample by balancing all of the observations equally. Note that this does not imply that most (or even any) observations in the sample have values equal to the sample mean. Rather, it implies that if the data were on a seesaw, the sample mean would be the value that would perfectly balance the two sides.

For our 150-observation city property crime sample, the sample mean is

$$\bar{x} = \frac{1}{n}\sum_{i=1}^{n} x_i = \frac{1}{150}(2{,}527.56 + 3{,}679.21 + \ldots + 2{,}934.58)$$

$$= \frac{1}{150}(682{,}536.41) = 4{,}550.24 \qquad \textbf{3.2.2}$$

We interpret the value in formula 3.2.2 as indicating that the mean property crime rate in our 150-observation 2009 city property crime sample was 4,550.24 per 100,000 citizens.

The Sample Median

sample median
The numerical value of the middle observation when the observed data are arranged from smallest to largest.

The **sample median** is the numerical value of the middle observation in a data set that is ordered from smallest to largest (i.e., the observation dividing the data set so that the number of observations smaller than the median value equals the number of observations larger than the median value). Correctly determining this value depends on whether we have an odd or even number of observations in our random sample. If we have an odd number of observations, there will be exactly one observation that defines the middle of the sample. We can identify this observation by dividing the total number of observations by 2 and rounding up to the next highest integer. As an example, if our random sample has 53 observations, the middle observation will be the 27th in the ordered data set (because 53/2 = 26.5, which rounds up to 27), and the sample median value will be the numerical value associated with that observation. Note that this observation divides the ordered sample so that 26 observations are smaller than the 27th observation and 26 observations are larger.

If we have an even number of observations, there will be two observations that define the middle of the sample. We can identify these observations by dividing the total number of observations by 2 and selecting the resulting observation and the one directly above it as the middle observations [i.e., observations $n/2$ and $(n/2) + 1$]. As an example, if our one specific random sample has 84 observations, the middle observations will be the 42nd and 43rd, and the median value will be the arithmetic average of the numerical values associated with those observations. Note that the two median observations divide the ordered sample so that 42 observations are smaller than the median and 42 observations are larger than the median.

To calculate the median for our 150-observation city property crime sample, we start by reordering our data from smallest to largest. In this case, because we have an even number of observations, we have two uniquely identified middle observations, the 150/2 and the (150/2) + 1, or the 75th and 76th observations. Because these observations have numerical values of $10,040.90 million and $10,187.00 million, we calculate that the median 2010 city property crime rate in our sample is (4,303.64 + 4,339.22)/2 = 4,321.43). Noting that the "Order" column is added for illustration purposes, our calculations for correctly determining the sample median are provided in Table 3.3.

TABLE 3.3
Our 150-Observation City Property Crime Sample Ordered from Lowest to Highest Crime Rates with the Middle Two Values Highlighted

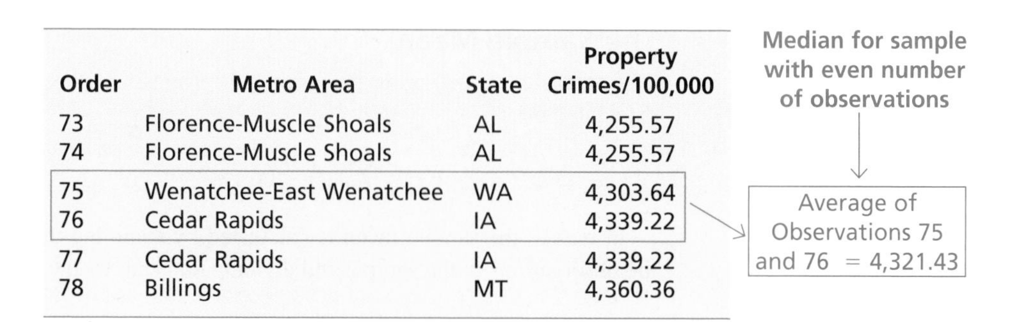

Order	Metro Area	State	Property Crimes/100,000
73	Florence-Muscle Shoals	AL	4,255.57
74	Florence-Muscle Shoals	AL	4,255.57
75	Wenatchee-East Wenatchee	WA	4,303.64
76	Cedar Rapids	IA	4,339.22
77	Cedar Rapids	IA	4,339.22
78	Billings	MT	4,360.36

EMPIRICAL RESEARCH TOOL 3.2: MEASURES OF CENTRAL TENDENCY

Goal:

Determine individual numerical values that describe the empirical probability distribution of the observed sample data by asking, "If you were forced to provide one number that best describes the observed sample data, what would it be?"

Tools:

Sample mean — The sample mean is the arithmetic average of the observed sample data.

Sample median — The sample median is the numerical value of the middle observation in a data set that is ordered from smallest to largest.

Notation:

$\bar{x}$ Sample mean

Estimator for:

μ Population mean

Formula:

$$\bar{x} = \frac{1}{n}\sum_{i=1}^{n} x_i = \frac{1}{n}(x_1 + x_2 + x_3 + \ldots + x_n)$$

To summarize, for our 150-observation city property crime sample, we now know that

Minimum = 1,926.53
Sample mean = 4,550.24
Sample median = 4,321.43
Maximum = 9,705.45

Adding these to the previously determined minimum and maximum values, we now have a better understanding of the empirical probability distribution for our specific sample. Figure 3.4 provides a visual representation of what we now know.

FIGURE 3.4
Measures of Central Tendency for Our 150-Observation City Property Crime Sample

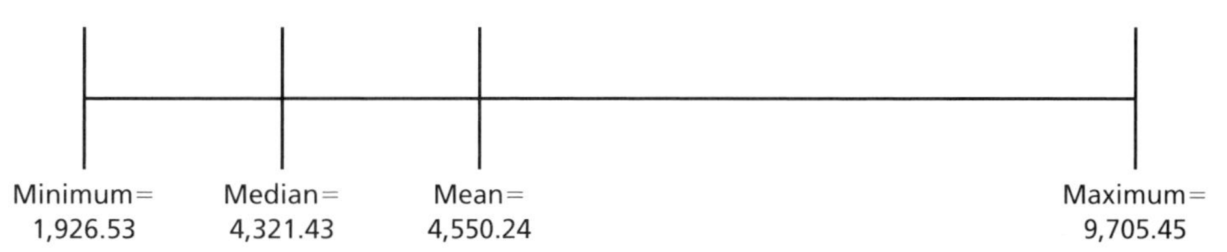

Statistics Joke

Q: Why are the mean, the median, and the mode like a valuable piece of real estate?
A: LOCATION! LOCATION! LOCATION!

EXCEL EXAMPLE 3.3

Commands for calculating measures of central tendency for our CEO compensation sample

Calculating the Mean and Median

1. Calculating the mean:
   In an empty cell (**F3**), type=**average(C2:C201)**
2. Calculating the median:
   In an empty cell (**F5**), type=**median(C2:C201)**

	A	B	C	D	E	F
1	**id**	**Company**	**Compensation ($)**			
2	1	Xerox	$12,902,607.00			
3	2	Yum Brands	$20,411,852.00		Mean	$11,612,180.62
4	3	Centene	$10,473,912.00			
5	4	AutoZone	$11,360,019.00		Median	$10,235,726.50
6	5	Cablevision Systems	$11,445,228.00			

This can be interpreted as indicating that the mean CEO compensation in our specific sample is $11,612,180.62 and that the median CEO compensation is $10,235,726.50.

As Figure 3.4 indicates, these statistics provide a general sense as to where important points in an empirical probability distribution lie. They do not, however, provide an indication of how close or how far away the remaining observations tend to fall from those specific values.

3.3 CALCULATE MEASURES OF DISPERSION FOR A GIVEN VARIABLE

measures of dispersion
The numerical values that express the degree of variability that is present in the data.

total deviation from the mean
The sum of each of the observations subtracted from the mean value.

sum of squared deviations
A method of measuring how far individual observations fall from the mean.

variance
A non-negative number that gives an idea of how widely spread the values of the random variable are likely to be; the larger the variance, the more scattered the observations are on average. The units on the variance are squared.

Notation:
s^2 Sample variance
s Sample standard deviation

degrees of freedom
The number of values in the final calculation that are free to vary.

How can we generate a better sense of how close the individual observations in the sample tend to fall to each other? **Measures of dispersion** are numerical values that express the degree of variability present in a specific sample by asking, "If you were forced to provide a number that best describes how close or how far the observed data points tend to fall from each other, what would it be?" We calculate such values as follows. Given that we already know the calculated sample mean, we start by asking how far each individual observation in the sample falls from the observed sample mean. As a first approximation for this calculation, we (1) determine the sample mean, (2) figure out how far away each observation in the sample lies from that mean, and (3) calculate an aggregate measure of the differences for all observations in the sample known as the **total deviation from the mean.** This measure cannot be our final calculation, however, because its sum always equals 0 due to the fact that the sample mean divides the sample so that the sum of deviations below the mean is always equal to the sum of deviations above the mean. As a result, if we sum the individual deviations from the mean, the positive and the negative values always cancel, and the resulting total deviation is always 0. We can solve this problem by turning the negative deviations into positive deviations by squaring each individual deviation from the mean before summing them up. The resulting value is known as the **sum of squared deviations** and is the basis for much of our work in econometrics, including our desired measures of dispersion.

Variance and Standard Deviation

The **variance** of an empirical probability distribution, s^2, is the sum of squared deviations from the sample mean for observations in the sample divided by the number of observations minus 1. We calculate this value as

$$s^2 = \frac{\sum_{i=1}^{n}(x_i - \bar{x})^2}{n - 1} \qquad \textbf{3.3.1}$$

In words, formula 3.3.1 states that the sample variance is calculated by determining how far each individual observation lies from the sample mean, squaring that calculated value, summing all of the individual squared values, and dividing the resulting sum by the number of observations minus 1. This statistic provides a general sense of the average distance that our values tend to lie from the sample mean. Accordingly, we would, in general, conclude that in samples with lower calculated variances, the observed values tend to lie closer to each other, while in samples with higher calculated variances, the observed values tend to lie farther from each other. Note that there is no definitive rule governing what specific values constitute "lower calculated variances" and "higher calculated variances" because the calculated values depend on the units of observation (e.g., property crimes versus property crimes/1,000 citizens versus property crimes/100,000 citizens.) and the scale of the data.

Special notice should be given to the denominator in formula 3.3.1. This term is referred to as the number of **degrees of freedom** of the calculated statistic. Degrees of freedom are the number of independent pieces of information that can be freely chosen when calculating the value of the statistic. The number of degrees of freedom in this case is $n - 1$ because, to calculate the sample variance, we first need to calculate the sample mean (instead of using the true population mean) and doing so costs us one degree of freedom. To see why, consider the following simple example. Suppose that the sample mean is 8 and that the first two values in a three-observation sample are 5 and 10. In such a case, we will not be "free" to choose any potential value for the third observation because with the values of the first two observations defined, there will only be one specific value that makes the sample mean equal to 8. In our simple example, that value is 9 (i.e., $5 + 10 + 9 = 24/3 = 8$). The fact that we are not "free" to choose any value for the last observation in the sample means that we are only "free" to choose values for $n - 1$ of the observations in our sample. Hence, the number of degrees of freedom in determining the sample variance is $n - 1$. An intuitive way to understand this value is to think that we are essentially paying for estimating the sample variance by subtracting off one from the number of observations in the sample because we estimated the population mean.

While the preceding calculation provides some sense of the average distance each observation tends to fall from the sample mean, because the results of the calculation are necessarily denominated in squared units, they are somewhat difficult to interpret. For this reason, we often prefer to convert the calculated sample variance into the sample **standard deviation,** s, by taking the square root of the variance,

standard deviation
A measure of the dispersion of a set of data that is calculated by taking the square root of the variance. The units on standard deviation are the same as the units of x.

$$s = \sqrt{s^2} \qquad \textbf{3.3.2}$$

For our city property crime sample, calculating the sample variance and the sample standard deviation requires us to first calculate the values $\bar{x}$, $\sum(x_i - \bar{x})$, $\sum(x_i - \bar{x})^2$, and $(n - 1)$. The resulting values are shown in Table 3.4.

TABLE 3.4 Calculated Values That Are Required to Calculate the Variance and the Standard Deviation of Our 150-Observation City Property Crime Sample

id	Metro Area	State	Property Crimes/100,000 (x_i)	$(\bar{x})$	$(x_i - \bar{x})$	$(x_i - \bar{x})^2$	
1	Santa Barbara-Santa Maria-Goleta	CA	2,527.56	4,550.24	−2,022.68	4,091,250.44	$\sum(x_i - \bar{x}) = 0.00$
2	Honolulu	HI	3,679.21		−871.03	758,697.46	
3	Fort Smith	AR-OK	5.860.87		1,310.63	1,717,756.02	
4	Hattiesburg	MS	4,567.87		17.63	310.83	$\sum(x_i - \bar{x})^2 = 335{,}294{,}649.93$
5	Billings	MT	4,360.36		−189.88	36,054.28	
6	Rome	GA	5,197.97		647.73	419,551.91	
7	Napa	CA	2,554.32		−1,995.92	3,983.689.45	$(n - 1) = 149$
8	Reno-Sparks	NV	3,813.64		−736.60	542,580.59	
9	Davenport-Moline-Rock Island	IA-IL	4,914.01		363.77	132,329.34	Variance = 2,250,299.66
10	Chico	CA	2,776.07		−1,774.17	3,147,678.68	
11	Sebastian-Vero Beach	FL	3,216.13		−1,334.11	1,779,846.86	Standard Deviation = 1,500.10
12	Texarkana	TX-AR	6,910.79		2,360.55	5,572,183.12	

Based on these calculations, we see that the sample variance is

$$s^2 = \frac{1}{n-1}\sum_{i=1}^{n}(x_i - \bar{x})^2 = \frac{1}{149}(335{,}294{,}649.93) = 2{,}250{,}299.66 \qquad \textbf{3.3.3}$$

and the sample standard deviation is

$$s = \sqrt{s^2} = \sqrt{2{,}250{,}299.66} = 1{,}500.10 \qquad \textbf{3.3.4}$$

These statistics provide a general sense of the average numerical distance that each individual observation falls from the sample mean. As mentioned earlier, due to the units of denomination, we generally focus on the standard deviation rather than the variance. In this particular case, the standard deviation indicates that, on average, the property crime rates in our 150-observation sample lie 1,500.10 away from the mean rate of 4,550.24. Unfortunately, there is no steadfast rule for determining whether this particular value is small or large.

Percentiles

percentile
A number such that the *p*th percentile is a value so that $p\%$ of the data are smaller than the value and $(100 - p)\%$ of the data are larger than the value.

A **percentile** is a number that divides an empirical probability distribution into two parts such that for a given value p^*, p^* percent of the sample lies below that value and $(1 - p^*)$ percent of the sample lies above that value. In other words, the 53rd percentile is a number such that 53 percent of the sample lies below that value and $(1 - 53) = 47$ percent of the sample lies above that number.

There are three steps for computing a given percentile p^*:

1. Sort the data from low to high.
2. Count the number of observations (n).
3. Select the $p^* (n + 1)$ observation.

Because we are unlikely to be so lucky as to have $p^* (n + 1)$ result in a whole number, we must consider the following contingencies:

1. If $p^* (n + 1)$ is not a whole number, then select the closest whole number.
2. If $p^* (n + 1) < 1$, then select the smallest observation.
3. If $p^* (n + 1) > 1$, then select the largest observation.

According to these rules, the 25th percentile for our 150-observation city property crime sample is the 38th observation in our ordered data set because $p^* (n + 1) = 0.25(151) = 37.75$, which rounds to 38. The numerical value associated with the 38th observation is the 3,363.06 of Greeley, Colorado. Given that this is the 25th percentile, we interpret this statistic as saying that 25 percent of the city property crime rates in our sample are less than 3,363.06, while 75 percent are greater than 3,363.06.

The 75th percentile for our sample is the 5,595.36 of El Centro, California, which is the 113th observation in the ordered data set $(0.75(151) = 113.25)$. We interpret this as saying that 75 percent of the cities in our sample observe property crime rates less than 113.25 per 100,000 citizens, while 25 percent observe property crime rates greater than 113.25 per 100,000 citizens.

quartiles
Those percentiles that divide a data set into four parts.

interquartile range (IQR)
The difference between the third and the first quartile.

Note that there are a number of percentiles that are so well known that they go by other names. The 50th percentile divides the data such that exactly 50 percent of all observations in the sample lie below that value while 50 percent of all observations lie above it. As such, another name for the 50th percentile is the *median*. Similarly, values that divide the sample into fourths (i.e., the 25th, 50th, and 75th percentiles) are known as **quartiles,** and the **interquartile range (IQR)** is the difference between the 1st (25th) and 3rd (75th) quartiles.

The Five-Number Summary

five-number summary
A measure of dispersion. It consists of the minimum, first-quartile, median, third-quartile, and the maximum.

We can combine the preceding measures of central tendency and dispersion into one comprehensive statistic known as the **five-number summary.** This measure consists of (1) the minimum, (2) the first quartile, (3) the median, (4) the third quartile, and (5) the maximum.

For our 150-observation city property crime sample, the five-number summary is

$$\text{Minimum} = 1{,}926.53$$
$$Q_1 \text{ or 25th percentile} = 3{,}363.06$$

EMPIRICAL RESEARCH TOOL 3.3: MEASURES OF DISPERSION

Goal:

Determine individual numerical values that describe the degree of variability present in the observed sample by asking, "If you were forced to provide one number that best describes how close or how far the observed data points tend to fall from each other, what would it be?"

Tools:

Sample variance	The sample variance is the average total squared deviation from the mean for all observations in the sample and is denominated in squared units.
Sample standard deviation	The sample standard deviation is the square root of the variance and is denominated in regular units.
Percentiles	Percentiles are numbers that divide an empirical probability distribution into two parts such that for a given value p^*, p^* percent of the sample lies below that value and $(1 - p^*)$ percent of the sample lies above that value.
Five-number summary	The five-number summary is a summary statistic that lists the minimum, the 25th percentile, the median, the 75th percentile, and the maximum for an empirical probability distribution.

Notation:	Estimator for:
s^2 Sample variance	σ^2 Population variance
s Sample standard deviation	σ Population standard deviation

Formulas:

$$s^2 = \frac{\sum_{i=1}^{n}(x_i - \bar{x})^2}{n-1} \quad \text{and} \quad s = \sqrt{s^2}$$

Median	= 4,321.43
Q_3 or 75th percentile	= 5,595.36
Maximum	= 9,705.45

To summarize, in addition to our measures of central tendency, we now know that the

Sample standard deviation	= 1,500.10
25th percentile	= 3,363.06
75th percentile	= 5,595.36

Adding these to the previously determined values, we now have a better understanding of the empirical probability distribution with which we are dealing. Figure 3.5 illustrates what we now know.

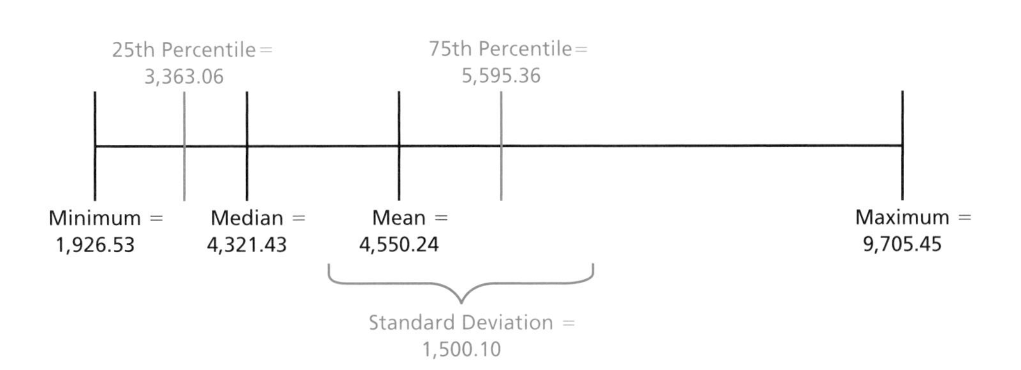

FIGURE 3.5
Measures of Central Tendency and Dispersion for Our 150-Observation City Property Crime Sample

EXCEL EXAMPLE 3.4

Commands for calculating measures of dispersion for our CEO compensation sample

Calculating the Variance, Standard Deviation, and Percentiles

1. Calculating the variance: In an empty cell (F3), type=**var(C2:C201).**
2. Calculating the standard deviation: In an empty cell (F5), type=**stdev(C2:C201).**
3. Calculating the *p*th percentile:
   In an empty cell, type=**percentile(C2:201,P),** where P is the exact percentile desired (i.e., 0.25 for the 25th percentile (F7), 0.75 for the 75th percentile (F9)).

	A	B	C	D	E	F
1	id	Company	Compensation ($)			
2	1	Xerox	$12,902,607.00			
3	2	Yum Brands	$20,411,852.00		Variance	$46,122,273,517,083.60
4	3	Centene	$10,473,912.00			
5	4	AutoZone	$11,360,019.00		Standard Deviation	$6,791,338.12
6	5	Cablevision Systems	$11,445,228.00			
7	6	Gilead Sciences	$15,615,645.00		25th Percentile	$6,565,110.75
8	7	DTE Energy	$7,389,279.00			
9	8	Morgan Stanley	$12,981,856.00		75th Percentile	$14,256,553.75
10	9	United Technologies	$27,671,331.00			

This can be interpreted as indicating that the variance of the CEO compensation in our sample is 46,122,273,517,083.60 squared dollars and that the standard deviation is $6,791,338.12. The 25th percentile is $6,565,110.75, meaning that the CEO compensation of 25 percent of the companies in our sample fall below $6,565,110.75 and that the CEO compensation of 75 percent of the companies in our sample fall above $6,565,110.75. Likewise, the 75th percentile is $14,256,553.75, meaning that the CEO compensation of 75 percent of the companies in our sample fall below $14,256,553.75 and that the CEO compensation of 25 percent of the companies in our sample fall above $14,256,553.75.

Note that Excel uses a different methodology for calculating percentiles than the one we suggest in this chapter, but the results are very similar.

EXCEL EXAMPLE 3.5

Commands for calculating the five-number summary for our CEO compensation sample

Calculating the Five-Number Summary

1. Minimum: In an empty cell (F3) type=**min(C2:C201).**
2. 25th percentile:
   In an empty cell (F5) type=**percentile(C2:C201,.25)** or =**quartile(C2:C201,1).**
3. Median: In an empty cell (F7), type=**median(C2:C201).**
4. 75th percentile:
   In an empty cell (F9), type=**percentile(C2:C201,.75)** or =**quartile(C2:C201,3).**
5. Maximum: In an empty cell (F11), type=**max(C2:C201).**

	A	B	C	D	E	F
1	id	Company	Compensation ($)			
2	1	Xerox	$12,902,607.00			
3	2	Yum Brands	$20,411,852.00		Minimum	$1,603,181.00
4	3	Centene	$10,473,912.00			
5	4	AutoZone	$11,360,019.00		25th Percentile	$6,565,110.75
6	5	Cablevision Systems	$11,445,228.00			
7	6	Gilead Sciences	$15,615,645.00		Median	$10,235,726.50
8	7	DTE Energy	$7,389,279.00			
9	8	Morgan Stanley	$12,981,856.00		75th Percentile	$14,256,553.75
10	9	United Technologies	$27,671,331.00			
11	10	Harris	$8,575,820.00		Maximum	$43,123,552.00

These values have all been summarized earlier, but are presented here in one convenient format.

If you have access to Excel's Data Analysis toolpak, the preceding values, except for percentiles, can easily be calculated using the "Descriptive Statistics" command as follows.

EXCEL EXAMPLE 3.6

Using Excel's Descriptive Statistics Wizard to summarize the data for our CEO compensation sample

1. Click on the "Data" tab.
2. Click the "Data Analysis" tab, which is the furthest tab on the right.
3. In the "Analysis Tools" menu, highlight "Descriptive Statistics" and click "OK".
4. Click the "Input Range" tab and highlight the GDP data (**C2:C201**).
   Click the "Output Range" tab and highlight an empty cell (**$E$1**).
   Check the "Summary Statistics" box.
   Click "OK".

	A	B	C	D	E	F
1	**id**	**Company**	**Compensation ($)**		*Compensation ($)*	
2	1	Xerox	$12,902,607.00			
3	2	Yum Brands	$20,411,852.00		Mean	$11,612,180.62
4	3	Centene	$10,473,912.00		Standard Error	$480,220.12
5	4	AutoZone	$11,360,019.00		Median	$10,235,726.50
6	5	Cablevision Systems	$11,445,228.00		Mode	$10,219,189.00
7	6	Gilead Sciences	$15,615,645.00		Standard Deviation	$6,791,338.12
8	7	DTE Energy	$7,389,279.00		Sample Variance	$46,122,273,517,083.60
9	8	Morgan Stanley	$12,981,856.00		Kurtosis	$3.45
10	9	United Technologies	$27,671,331.00		Skewness	$1.55
11	10	Harris	$8,575,820.00		Range	$41,520,371.00
12	11	Lockheed Martin	$25,369,641.00		Minimum	$1,603,181.00
13	12	Rite Aid	$2,827,819.00		Maximum	$43,123,552.00
14	13	Jabil Circuit	$10,293,809.00		Sum	$2,322,436,123.00
15	14	Entergy	$10,130,771.00		Count	200

We have discussed all of the values listed in the descriptive statistics wizard except for kurtosis and skewness. These are typically thought of as more advanced topics, but simple definitions are that *kurtosis* measures the thickness of the tails of the distribution, while *skewness* is a measure of the degree of asymmetry around the mean.

Now that we know how to calculate measures of central tendency and dispersion for a given variable, it is important to consider how to best use them. At this point, it is worth noting that simply because we possess the ability to use a given empirical tool does not mean that we must always use it. The choice of whether to include a specific tool in a given context should be governed by a reasonable analysis of how much information the tool adds to the understanding of the reader of your project.

3.4 USE MEASURES OF CENTRAL TENDENCY AND DISPERSION FOR A GIVEN VARIABLE

While all of the summary statistics introduced in this chapter provide valuable information about the empirical probability distribution of our observed sample data, they provide different types of information. What should we make of these differences? In general, each of the measures has potential upsides and downsides. The biggest potential upside of the sample mean is that it is likely the most well-known and understood measure of central tendency (think of your current GPA, which is the sample mean of all of the grades that you have received during your college studies). For this reason, when people refer to something as being an "average," they are normally referring to the sample mean for a given empirical probability distribution. The biggest potential downside of the sample mean is that it is subject to potential bias caused by the presence of one or more **outliers,** which pull the mean away from the center of the distribution and toward the outlying observations.

outlier
An observation in a data set that is far removed in value from the others in the data set. It is an unusually large or an unusually small value compared to the others.

To see this, consider the simple example in Table 3.5, which compares two different five-observation samples that could be drawn from our population of *Fortune* 500 firms.

TABLE 3.5
Comparing Measures of Central Tendency for Two Property Crime Distributions with (Almost) the Same Mean

Sample 1		Sample 2	
Metro Area	Property Crimes/100,000	Metro Area	Property Crimes/100,000
Vallejo-Fairfield	3,985.00	Madera-Chowchilla	2,160.15
Cedar Rapids	4,339.22	Barnstable Town	2,755.92
Nashville-Davidson-Murfreesboro-Franklin	4,517.88	Pittsburgh	3,771.23
Olympia	4,637.85	Billings	4,360.36
Cleveland	5,274.34	Florence	9,705.45
Sample Mean	4,550.86	Sample Mean	4,550.62
Sample Median	4,517.88	Sample Median	3,771.23

If we focus only on the sample mean, we might conclude that the two empirical probability distributions are (almost) exactly the same. If, however, we focus on the median, we might conclude that the two empirical probability distributions are quite different. We can highlight this difference by plotting the data points for the two property crime distributions on the number line as shown in Figure 3.6.

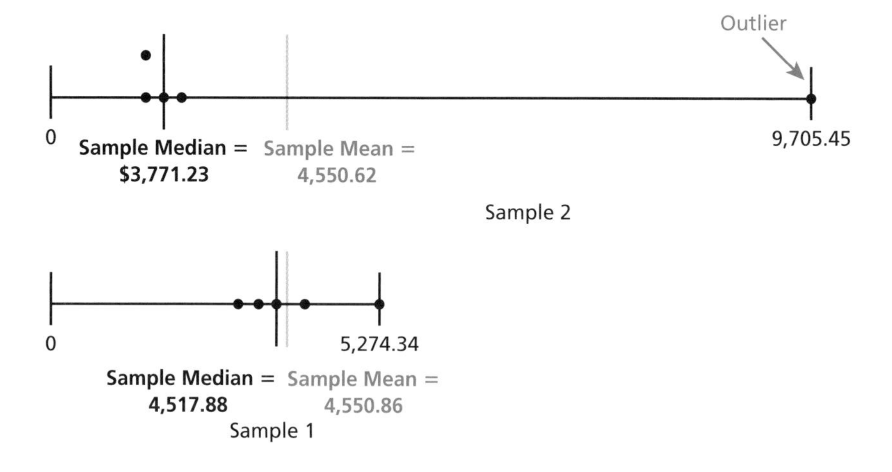

FIGURE 3.6
Visual Depiction of the Distribution for Our Two Five-Observation Samples

> **Statistics Joke**
>
> Q: Did you hear the one about the statistician who put his head in the freezer and his feet in the oven?
> A: On average, he felt fine.

This brings us to a primary advantage of the sample median. The calculation of the sample median limits the influence of potential outliers. To see this, consider again the two property crime distributions presented in Table 3.5. The sample median for Sample 1 is 4,517.88, while the sample median for Sample 2 is $3,771.23. Given these values, we should conclude that despite having (almost) equal sample means, the middle observation in the first property crime distribution was nearly 750 more than the middle observation in the second property crime distribution. Why? Because in Sample 2, one high-valued observation (9,705.45) has undue influence on the calculation of the sample mean, suggesting that the second distribution is subject to outlier bias while the first offers a much more equal distribution of salaries. Note that given the (almost) equal sample means, this insight only comes to light once we compare the sample medians.

skewed distribution
An empirical probability distribution for which the observed values are asymmetric so that values on one side of the distribution tend to be further from the "middle" than values on the other side.

By definition, when outliers cause empirical probability distributions to have sample medians that are much different than sample means, we refer to them as **skewed distributions.** Before discussing the types of skewed distributions, we note that a **symmetric distribution** is one for which the mean and the median are equal and for which the left side of a distribution looks exactly like the right side. Such a distribution is depicted in Figure 3.7.

FIGURE 3.7
Visual Depiction of a Symmetric Distribution

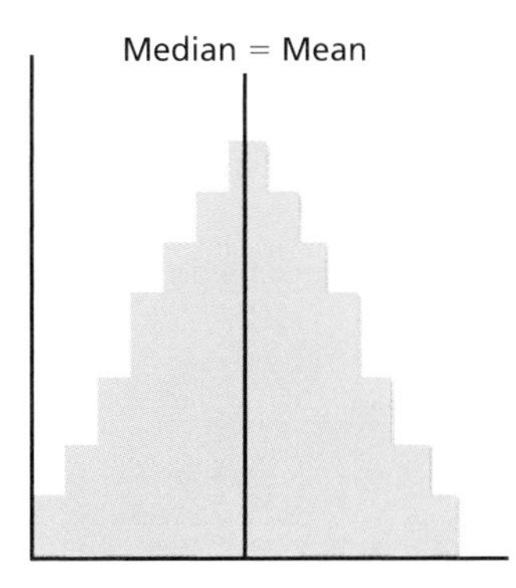

symmetric distribution
Empirical probability distribution for which the observed values on one side of the distribution tend to be equally spaced from the "middle" as the values on the other side.

right-skewed distribution
One that has most of the mass on the left and the outliers on the right.

There are two different types of skewed distributions that we can encounter. **Right-skewed** (or positively skewed) **distributions** are those for which the sample mean lies well to the right of the sample median, a situation that is depicted as shown in Figure 3.8:

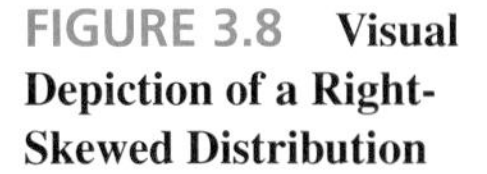
FIGURE 3.8 **Visual Depiction of a Right-Skewed Distribution**

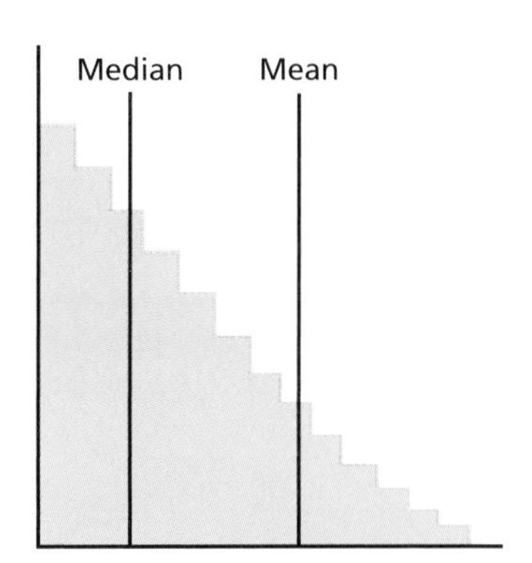

A well-known example of a right-skewed distribution is the distribution of household income in the United States, shown in Figure 3.9 for 2010.

left-skewed distribution
One that has most of the mass on the right-hand side and the outliers trailing off to the left.

Left-skewed (or negatively skewed) **distributions** are those for which the sample mean lies well to the left of the sample median, a situation that is depicted in Figure 3.10.

In reality, left-skewed distributions are observed much less frequently than right-skewed distributions. A previously determined example of a left-skewed distribution is student performance on traditional posttest exams (which are administered after the subject matter has been taught), such as that found by Amanda M. Klein in her 2005 thesis entitled, "The Effects of Computer-Assisted Instruction on College Algebra Students at Texas Tech University." The data from her study are depicted in Figure 3.11.

What about empirical probability distributions that are not perfectly symmetric but are also not obviously skewed to the same degree as Figures 3.9 and 3.11? As an example, suppose that the empirical probability distribution for our specific sample looks like Figure 3.12 on page 55.

Is the distribution in Figure 3.12 skewed? Some readers might reasonably say yes, while some might reasonably say no. To bring more rigor to our determination of which answer

FIGURE 3.9 Example of a Right-Skewed Distribution

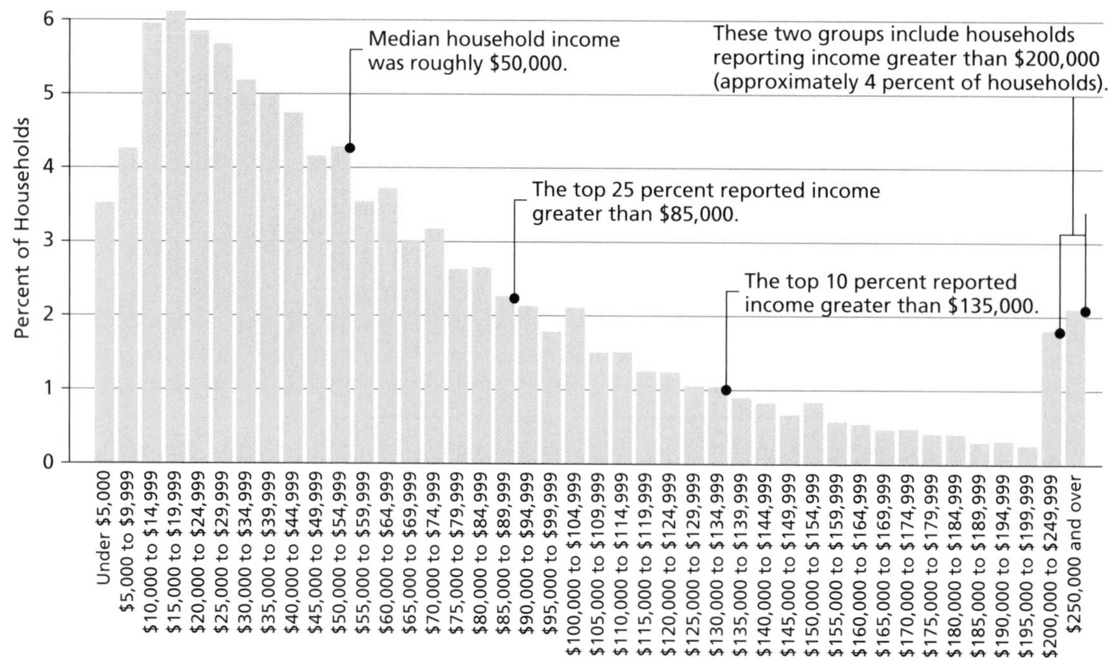

Source: U.S. Census Bureau, Current Population Survey, 2011 Annual Social and Economic Supplement.

FIGURE 3.10
Visual Depiction of a Left-Skewed Distribution

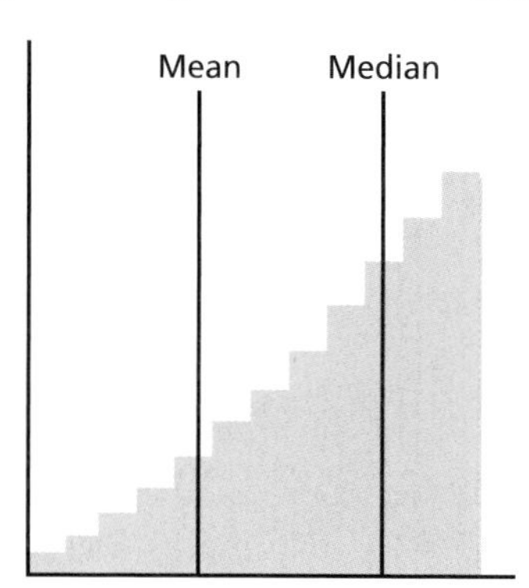

FIGURE 3.11
Example of a Left-Skewed Distribution

Source: http://thinktech.lib.ttu.edu/ttu-ir/bitstream/handle/2346/1419/Thesis.pdf?sequence=1.

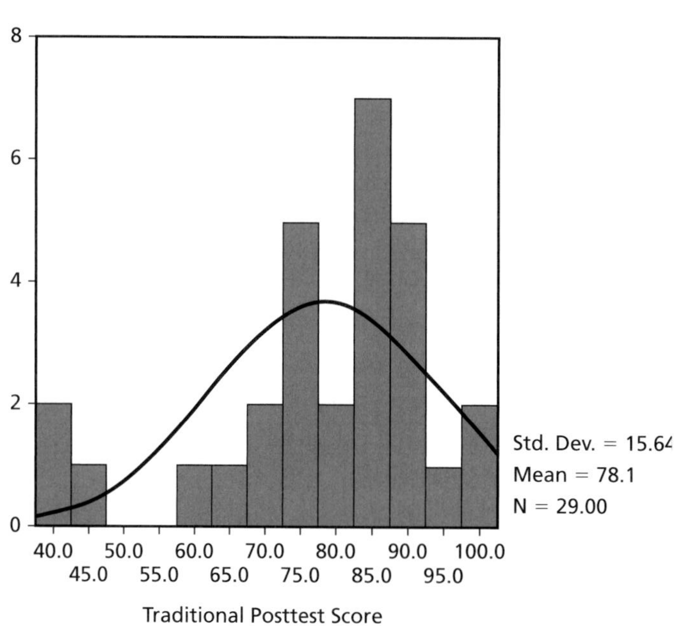

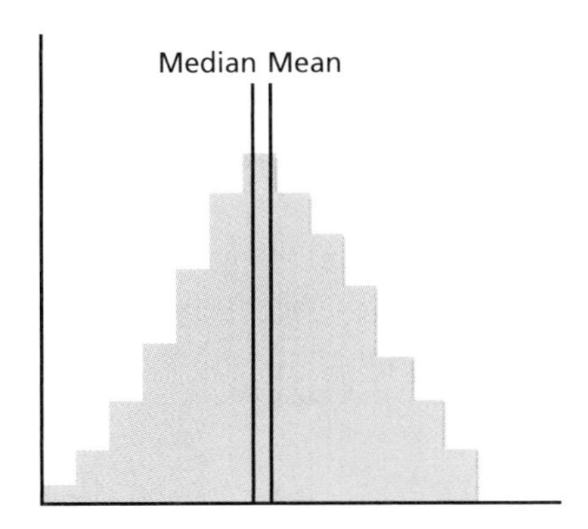

FIGURE 3.12
Visual Depiction of a More Symmetrically Skewed Distribution

is correct, we can calculate the degree to which an empirical probability distribution is skewed using a numerical measure known as **Pearson's coefficient of skewness.** This measure is calculated as:

Pearson's coefficient of skewness
A numerical measure of the skewness of a data set.

$$sk = \frac{3(Mean - Median)}{Standard\ deviation} \quad \textbf{3.4.1}$$

The general rule of thumb for interpreting the resulting statistic is that

If $sk < -0.5$ or $sk > 0.5$, then the distribution is skewed.
Otherwise, the distribution is symmetric.

Accordingly, the decision rule can be summarized as shown in Figure 3.13.

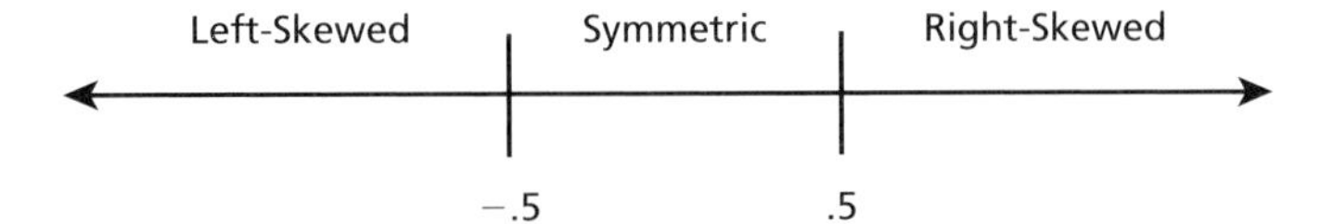

FIGURE 3.13
Interpretation of Pearson's Coefficient of Skewness

What should we do with this statistic once we have calculated it? If we conclude that the empirical probability distribution is symmetric, then we should report the mean as our measure of central tendency and the standard deviation as our measure of dispersion. If we conclude that the empirical probability distribution is skewed, then we should report the five-number summary as our combined measure of central tendency and dispersion.

For our 150-observation city property crime sample, we calculate Pearson's coefficient of skewness as:

$$sk = \frac{3(4{,}550.24 - 4{,}321.43)}{1{,}500.10} = 0.1525 \quad \textbf{3.4.2}$$

and we conclude that the empirical probability distribution is nearly symmetric. Accordingly, in this case we are probably safe summarizing the sample using the sample mean.

3.5 DETECT WHETHER OUTLIERS FOR A GIVEN VARIABLE ARE PRESENT IN OUR SAMPLE

Given the important effects that outliers potentially have on the skewness of our empirical probability distribution, we would like a more formal method for identifying their presence. Our preferred method for detecting whether outliers are present in our sample depends on whether our empirical probability distribution is symmetric or skewed.

EMPIRICAL RESEARCH TOOL 3.4: DETERMINING THE SKEWNESS OF AN EMPIRICAL PROBABILITY DISTRIBUTION

Goal:

Determine whether the empirical probability distribution is symmetric or skewed.

Tools:

Pearson's coefficient — A numerical measure that uses the distance the median lies from the mean to determine whether a distribution is symmetric or skewed.

Notation:

sk Pearson's coefficient of skewness

Formula:

$$sk = \frac{3(Mean - Median)}{Standard\ deviation}$$

Conclusion:

The distribution is left-skewed if $sk < -0.5$.

The distribution is right-skewed if $sk > 0.5$.

The distribution is neither left-skewed or right-skewed if $-0.5 < sk < 0.5$.

Detecting Outliers if the Data Set Is Symmetric

If our data are symmetric, then the method we use relies on the empirical rule which states that the percentages of the normal probability distribution that fall within one, two and then three standard deviations of the mean are represented in Table 3.6.

TABLE 3.6
The Empirical Rule

For a unimodal symmetric distribution:

68% of the observations should fall within 1 standard deviation of the mean.
95% of the observations should fall within 2 standard deviations of the mean.
99.7% of the observations should fall within 3 standard deviations of the mean.

Detecting Outliers if the Data Set Is Skewed

Because the empirical rule is based on a symmetric distribution, it cannot be used for skewed data. Instead, for skewed data sets, we rely on the interquartile range (IQR). Using this value, we define "moderate outliers" as observations that lie either between ($Q_1 - 1.5IQR$ and $Q_1 - 3IQR$) or ($Q_1 + 1.5IQR$ and $Q_1 + 3IQR$), and we define "extreme outliers" as values that lie beyond $Q_1 - 3IQR$ or beyond $Q_3 + 3IQR$, where Q_1 is the first quartile and Q_3 is the third quartile.

If we look back at the five-number summary for our city property crime sample, we see that $Q_1 = 3{,}376.71$, $Q_3 = 5{,}583.22$, and the $IQR = 5{,}583.22 - 3{,}376.71 = 2{,}206.51$. From this information, we can determine that the cutoffs for moderate and extreme outliers in our sample are as follows:

Negative Outliers:

$$Q_1 - 1.5IQR = 3{,}376.71 - 1.5(2{,}206.51) = 66.95$$
$$Q_1 - 3IQR = 3{,}376.71 - 3.0(2{,}206.51) = -3{,}242.82$$

Positive Outliers:

$$Q_3 + 1.5IQR = 5{,}583.22 + 1.5(2{,}206.51) = 8{,}892.98$$
$$Q_3 + 3IQR = 5{,}583.22 + 3.0(2{,}206.51) = 12{,}202.75$$

Because the minimum value in the data is 1,926.53, we clearly do not have any moderate or extreme negative outliers in our sample. We do, however, have one moderate positive outlier (a value between 8,892.98 and 12,202.75, which we can see looking back to Figure 3.3). These calculations suggest that city property crime rates are perhaps slightly skewed, with cities being more likely to have disproportionately high property crime rates than disproportionately low property crime rates.

While we have motivated this discussion with the need to identify potential outliers in order to determine the appropriate measures of central tendency to use when describing our sample data, we note that there is another potentially valuable reason to identify whether outliers are indeed present. Namely, once we have so identified their presence, we need to determine the likely reason that the outliers exist. Outliers typically exist within a data set for one of two reasons. The first is **data-entry error.** Because most data are collected by humans, it is certainly possible that human error leads to incorrectly entered data. In such cases, it is obvious desirable to catch and correct such mistakes. Rather than going back through entry-by-entry, identifying outliers in the data provides a much simpler method for correcting for such mistakes. As an example, suppose that we are entering student GPAs on a four-point scale and we noticed that there existed an outlier with a value of 36. Given that such a value is impossible, we would quickly catch the mistake and re-enter the observed value as the correct 3.6.

data-entry error
Occurs when data are mistakenly entered incorrectly in a data set.

The second potential source of outliers is true variation in the data. For instance, according to *Forbes*, the $54 billion estimated 2010 net worth of the richest person in the world, Carlos Slim Helu and family, vastly exceeds the median net worth of American families in 2007 (the most recent year for which the data were available from www.census.gov/compendia/statab/2010/tables/10s0705.pdf). Based on these facts, in the case of personal net worth, we would conclude that such outliers were due to true variation in the data rather than human data-entry error, and we would conclude that they are true facts. As such, while it might be tempting to do so, we strongly argue that such values should never be discarded because they have been determined to be a viable part of the data and should, therefore, be included in any empirical analysis regardless of any impact that they might have on the results (see Table 3.7).

TABLE 3.7
Rules Governing When to Use Which Descriptive Statistics

Type of Data Set:

Symmetric: ($-0.5 < sk < 0.5$)

Measure of central tendency: mean ($\bar{x}$)
Measure of dispersion: standard deviation (s)
How to detect outliers: values beyond $\bar{x} \pm 3s$

Skewed: ($sk < -0.5$ or $sk > 0.5$)

Measure of central tendency: median
Measure of dispersion: five-number summary, which consists of

- Minimum
- Q_1, 25th percentile
- Median
- Q_3, 75th percentile
- Maximum

How to detect outliers:
Moderate outliers are values between $Q_1 - 1.5IQR$ and $Q_1 - 3IQR$ or $Q_3 + 1.5IQR$ and $Q_3 + 3IQR$.
Extreme outliers are values beyond $Q_1 - 3IQR$ and $Q_1 + 3IQR$.

While we are certainly interested in examining the individual variables in our observed sample, in many cases, we are more interested in examining the relationship between different variables of interest. Just as we did earlier, we can begin our analysis of such relationships by constructing basic visual depictions of our observed sample data.

3.6 CONSTRUCT SCATTER DIAGRAMS FOR THE RELATIONSHIP BETWEEN TWO VARIABLES

scatter diagram (or scatterplot)
A way to visualize bivariate data by plotting pairs of measurements on a collection of individual data.

The primary visual tool that we use to describe the relationship between two random variables of interest is a **scatter diagram** (or scatterplot). Such a diagram is constructed by: (1) placing the dependent variable on the y-axis and the independent variable on the x-axis and (2) plotting each individual salary/experience observation in the resulting two-dimensional space. For our 150-observation city property crime sample we get the plot shown in Figure 3.14.

FIGURE 3.14
Scatter Plot of Property Crimes versus Unemployment Rate for Our 150-Observation City Property Crime Sample

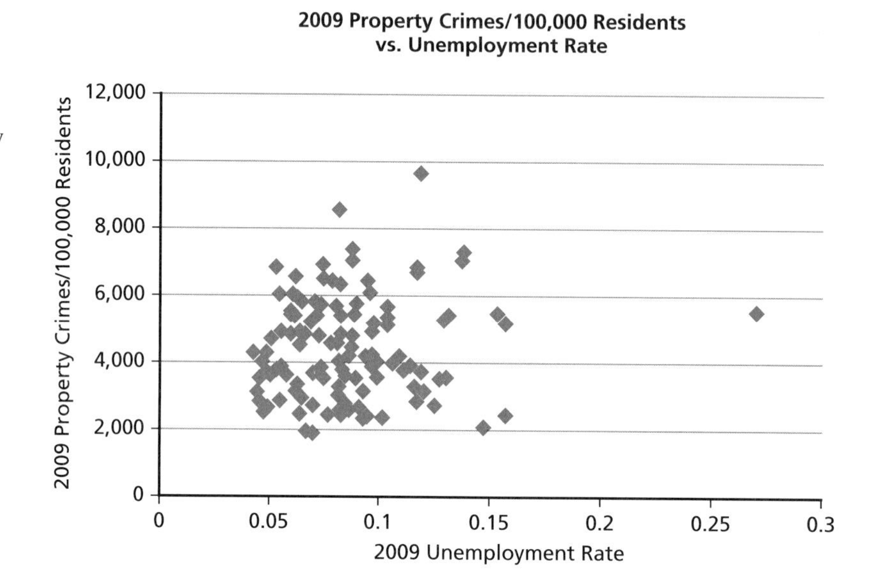

Such diagrams are valuable for two reasons. First, they provide a general indication of the direction of the relationship between the two random variables. If the data appear to be related in a general upward direction, then the diagrams would suggest that a positive relationship exists between the variables. If the data appear to be related in a general downward direction, then the diagrams would suggest that a negative relationship exists between the variables. If the data appear to as either a U-shape or an inverted U-shape, then the diagrams would suggest that a **quadratic relationship** exists between the variables. Second, by indicating whether the data points are more tightly or more loosely scattered, they provide a general indication of the **strength** of the relationship between the random variables. If the data points are more tightly scattered, then the diagrams would suggest that a stronger relationship exists between the two variables. If the data points are more loosely scattered, then the diagrams would suggest that a weaker relationship exists between the two variables. Visually, combining these points we have Figure 3.15.

quadratic relationship
When the variables have a relationship that looks like a *U* or an inverted *U*.

strength
In terms of the relationship between two random variables, a measure of how closely x and y move together in a linear fashion.

Returning to the scatter diagram for our city property crime sample in Figure 3.3, we might conclude that (1) there appears to be a general upward-sloping relationship between observed salary and observed years of experience and (2) the individual data points appear to be fairly widely spaced. Combined, these facts might suggest that a positive relationship is likely to exist between these two random variables but that the underlying nature of the relationship is likely to be weak. While this conclusion lacks specificity, it does suggest the need for further exploration of the potential relationship between property crime and unemployment rates for our 150-observation city property crime sample.

FIGURE 3.15
Types of Relationships That Can Exist between *x* and *y*

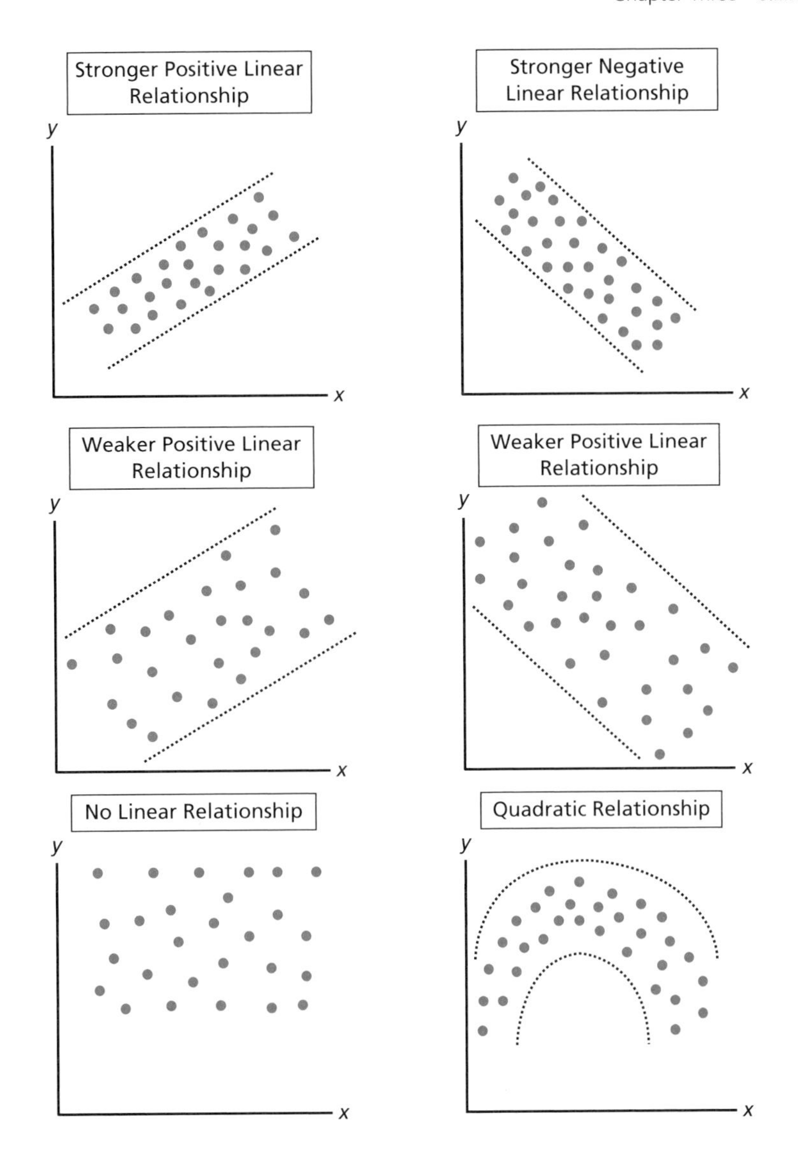

The visual tools that we have introduced so far provide a general indication of the likely linear relationship between our two random variables. At this point, we have learned that U.S. cities with higher unemployment rates tend to have higher rates of property crimes than those with lower unemployment rates. We might now wish to calculate summary statistics that provide specific numerical context to our understanding of the relationship between the variables.

3.7 CALCULATE THE COVARIANCE AND THE CORRELATION COEFFICIENT FOR THE LINEAR RELATIONSHIP BETWEEN *y* AND *x* FOR TWO VARIABLES OF INTEREST

covariance between *y* and *x*
A measure of how two variables move together in a linear fashion.

The first summary statistic that we consider is a measure of the simultaneous deviations of random variables y and x from their respective means. This value is referred to as the **covariance between *y* and *x*** and is calculated as

$$cov(x, y) = s_{xy} = \frac{\sum_{i=1}^{n}(x_i - \bar{x})(y_i - \bar{y})}{n - 1} \quad 3.7.1$$

EXCEL EXAMPLE 3.7

Commands for creating a scatter diagram for our CEO compensation sample

Creating a Scatter Diagram for Our CEO Compensation Sample

In Excel, a scatter plot can be constructed using the Chart Wizard.

1. Highlight the cells in the third and fourth columns [**Profit ($ millions)** and **Compensation ($ millions)**] while holding down the CTRL key. Make sure that the variable you want on the *y*-axis is the right-hand column.
2. Click on the "**Insert**" tab.
3. In the "**charts**" tab click on the "**Scatter**" feature.

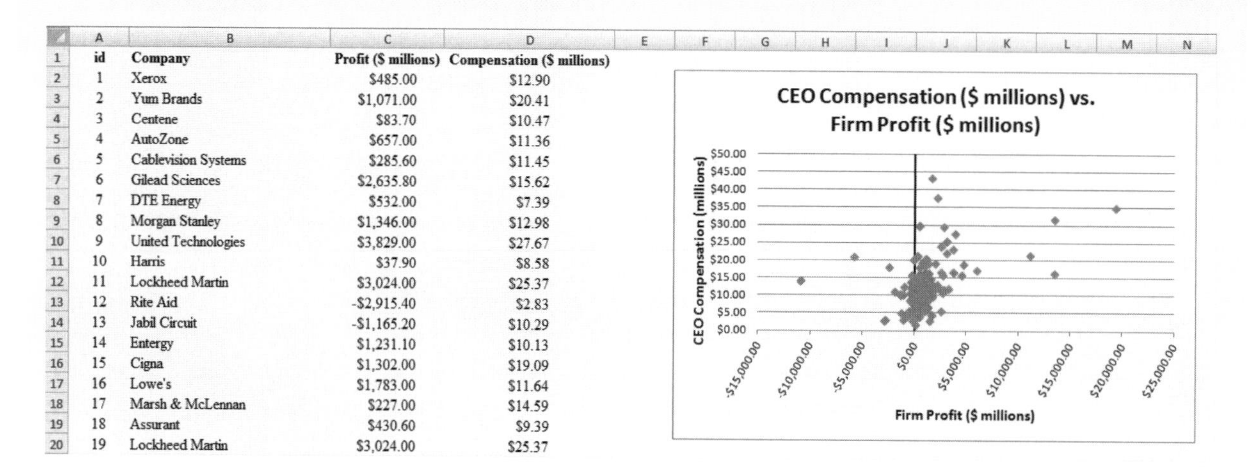

	A	B	C	D
1	id	Company	Profit ($ millions)	Compensation ($ millions)
2	1	Xerox	$485.00	$12.90
3	2	Yum Brands	$1,071.00	$20.41
4	3	Centene	$83.70	$10.47
5	4	AutoZone	$657.00	$11.36
6	5	Cablevision Systems	$285.60	$11.45
7	6	Gilead Sciences	$2,635.80	$15.62
8	7	DTE Energy	$532.00	$7.39
9	8	Morgan Stanley	$1,346.00	$12.98
10	9	United Technologies	$3,829.00	$27.67
11	10	Harris	$37.90	$8.58
12	11	Lockheed Martin	$3,024.00	$25.37
13	12	Rite Aid	-$2,915.40	$2.83
14	13	Jabil Circuit	-$1,165.20	$10.29
15	14	Entergy	$1,231.10	$10.13
16	15	Cigna	$1,302.00	$19.09
17	16	Lowe's	$1,783.00	$11.64
18	17	Marsh & McLennan	$227.00	$14.59
19	18	Assurant	$430.60	$9.39
20	19	Lockheed Martin	$3,024.00	$25.37

The data appear to be upward-sloping, which suggests that a positive relationship likely exists between CEO compensation and firm profit.

EMPIRICAL RESEARCH TOOL 3.5: SCATTER DIAGRAMS (SCATTERPLOTS)

Goal:

Provide a visual summary of the relationship between the dependent and independent variables by plotting where the data points in the observed sample lie in two-dimensional space.

Tools:

Scatter diagram   Plots the data with the dependent variable on the *y*-axis and the independent variable on the *x*-axis.

Usefulness:

Allows us to look at all of the data points in the sample to get a sense of the likely relationship between the two variables.

Notation:

s_{xy} Sample covariance between *x* and *y*

The information that we learn from this calculation depends on whether the value is positive or negative. A positive covariance results when above-average values of *x* are generally associated with above-average values of *y*, in which case a positive linear relationship likely exists between *y* and *x*. A negative covariance results when above-average values of *x* are generally associated with below-average values of *y*, in which case a negative linear relationship likely exists between *x* and *y*.

As formula 3.7.1 indicates, to determine the covariance for our sample of 150-observation city property crime sample, we need to first calculate the individual deviations from the mean for all observations for both random variables (i.e., we need to calculate $(x_i - \bar{x})$ and $(y_i - \bar{y})$). We then need to multiply those values together for all observations before summing the products to determine the estimated covariance. Performing these calculations, we get Table 3.8.

TABLE 3.8 Calculations Required to Determine the Covariance of Our 150-Observation City Property Crime Sample

id	Metro Area	Unemployment Rate (x_i)	Property Crimes/100,000 (y_i)	($\bar{x}$)	($\bar{y}$)	$(x_i - \bar{x})$	$(y_i - \bar{y})$	$(x_i - \bar{x}) \cdot (y_i - \bar{y})$
1	Santa Barbara-Santa Maria-Goleta	2,527.56	0.076	4,550.24	0.09	−2022.68	−0.01	19.61
2	Honolulu	3,679.21	0.057			−871.03	−0.03	24.99
3	Fort Smith	5,860.87	0.07			1310.63	−0.02	−20.57
4	Hattiesburg	4,567.87	0.063			17.63	−0.02	−0.40
5	Billings	4,360.36	0.042			−189.88	−0.04	8.30
6	Rome	5,197.97	0.103			647.73	0.02	11.21
7	Napa	2,554.32	0.085			−1995.92	0.00	1.38
8	Reno-Sparks	3,813.64	0.11			−736.60	0.02	−17.90
9	Davenport-Moline-Rock Island	4,914.01	0.065			363.77	−0.02	−7.53
10	Chico	2,776.07	0.124			−1774.17	0.04	−67.96
11	Sebastian-Vero Beach	3,216.13	0.119			−1334.11	0.03	−44.43
12	Texarkana	6,910.79	0.052			2360.55	−0.03	−79.53
13	Midland	3,636.52	0.045			−913.73	−0.04	37.18
14	St. George	2,042.68	0.066			−2507.56	−0.02	49.38
15	Appleton	2,680.17	0.086			−1870.07	0.00	−0.57

$\sum_{i=1}^{n}(x_i - \bar{x})(y_i - \bar{y}) = 1{,}100.08$

$(n - 1) = 149$

$Cov(x,y) = 7.3831$

$\sum_{i=1}^{n}(x_i - \bar{x}) = 0$

$\sum_{i=1}^{n}(y_i - \bar{y}) = 0$

As these calculations demonstrate, for our 150-observation city property crime sample, we calculate the covariance between x and y to be

$$cov(x, y) = s_{xy} = \frac{\sum_{i=1}^{n}(x_i - \bar{x})(y_i - \bar{y})}{(n - 1)} = \frac{1{,}100.08}{150 - 1} = 7.3831 \qquad 3.7.2$$

This value should be interpreted as follows. The positive value suggests that, on average, higher property crime rates are associated with higher unemployment rates, while the numerical value 7.33831 tells us something about the magnitude of the relationship. Unfortunately, no clear decision rule for determining whether the magnitude is large or small exists because the chosen units of measurement have undue influence over the calculated covariance between x and y. For instance, if we enter our independent variables as the total number of property crimes rather than the number of property crimes per 100,000 citizens, the calculated covariance changes from 7.3831 to 738,307.84. This is an issue, because while the calculated value became much smaller with this change in denomination, the underlying relationship between salary and experience did not change.

We can develop a more easily interpretable summary statistic that removes the undue influence of the chosen demonination by dividing the calculated covariance between y and x by the product of the standard deviations of y and x. The resulting value, referred to as the **correlation coefficient,** is calculated as

correlation coefficient
A number between −1 and 1 that measures how nearly a scatter diagram falls to a straight line.

Notation:
r_{xy} Correlation coefficient between x and y

$$r_{xy} = \frac{Cov(x, y)}{Stdev(x)Stdev(y)} = \frac{s_{xy}}{s_x s_y} \qquad 3.7.3$$

This calculation provides a measure of the degree of joint variation between y and x as a fraction of the individual variations in y and x. Scaling the calculation in such a manner produces a statistics that does not depend on the chosen unit of measurement because the covariance in the numerator is denominated in units of x times units of y, while the product of the standard deviations in the denominator is also denominated in units of x times units of y. In other words, the units of measurement in the quotient in formula 3.7.3 cancel, which removes the interpretation problem for the calculated covariance discussed above.

By way of interpretation, note that the calculated value of the correlation coefficient is constrained to fall between -1 and 1 because the covariance between y and x can equal—but never exceed—the product of the standard deviations of y and x. This fact allows us to develop a set of rules governing the interpretation of the calculated value. If $r_{xy} = 1$, then all of the data points in the sample fall on the same positively sloped line. If $r_{xy} = -1$, then all of the data points in the sample fall on the same negatively sloped line. If $r_{xy} = 0$, then there is no linear relationship between the variables.

Because it is unlikely for data that we actually encounter to all fall on the same line, we need to consider the more likely case in which the data are scattered around a line. In such cases, the calculated correlation coefficient falls between -1 and 1, with values falling closer to -1 lying closer to (but not on) the same negatively sloped line, indicating a stronger negative relationship between y and x, and values falling closer to 1 lying closer to (but not on) the same positively sloped line, indicating a stronger positive relationship between y and x. Finally, values falling closer to 0 than to either -1 or 1 tend to lie further from any potential line, indicating a weaker linear relationship between the two random variables.

To calculate the correlation coefficient, we first need to calculate the sample standard deviations for and x and (s_x and s_y). From simple calculations in Excel, we know that

$$s_x = \sqrt{s_x^2} = \sqrt{\frac{335{,}294649.93}{149}} = \sqrt{2{,}250{,}299.66} = 1{,}500.10 \qquad \textbf{3.7.4}$$

$$s_y = \sqrt{s_y^2} = \sqrt{\frac{0.1386939}{149}} = \sqrt{0{,}0009308} = 0.0305095 \qquad \textbf{3.7.5}$$

Plugging these values into formula 3.1.3, we get

$$r_{xy} = \frac{Cov(x, y)}{Stdev(x)Stdev(y)} = \frac{s_{xy}}{s_x s_y} = \frac{7.3831}{(1{,}500.10)(0.0305095)} = 0.1613 \qquad \textbf{3.7.6}$$

Because 0.1613 is positive and closer to 0 than it is to 1, we can conclude that for our 150-observation city property crime sample, the linear relationship between property crime rates and unemployment rates appears to be positive but weak.

EXCEL EXAMPLE 3.8

Commands for calculating the covariance and the correlation coefficient for our CEO compensation sample

The covariance command in Excel calculates a slightly different value than the one we discussed earlier. To convert the Excel value to our desired value, we need to multiply the Excel value by $n/(n - 1)$.

Calculating Our Covariance

In an empty cell (G2), type **=covar(C2:C201,D2:D201)*(201/200).**

Calculating a Correlation Coefficient

In an empty cell (G4), type **=correl(C2:C201,D2:D201).**

A screen capture of the worksheet with the preceding commands appears as follows:

	A	B	C	D	E	F	G
1	id	Company	Compensation ($ millions)	Profit ($ millions)			
2	1	Xerox	$12.90	$485.00		Covariance	$6,993.02
3	2	Yum Brands	$20.41	$1,071.00			
4	3	Centene	$10.47	$83.70		Correlation Coefficient	0.39238316

These results indicate that the relationship between CEO compensation and firm profit is positive because the covariance and the correlation coefficient are both greater than 0.

EMPIRICAL RESEARCH TOOL 3.6: SUMMARY STATISTICS FOR THE LINEAR RELATIONSHIP BETWEEN TWO RANDOM VARIABLES

Goal:

Determine individual numerical values that summarize the linear relationship between two random variables of interest.

Tools:

Covariance	Unit-based measure of the degree of linear relationship between y and x.
Correlation coefficient	Unitless measure of the degree of linear relationship between y and x.

Notation:

s_{xy} Sample covariance r_{xy} Sample correlation coefficient

Formulas:

$$s_{xy} = \frac{\sum_{i=1}^{n}(x_i - \bar{x})(y_i - \bar{y})}{n-1} \qquad r_{xy} = \frac{Cov(x, y)}{Stdev(x)Stdev(y)} = \frac{s_{xy}}{s_x s_y}$$

Conclusions:

If $s_{xy} > 0$ and/or $r_{xy} > 0$, then we conclude that the estimated linear relationship is positive.

If $s_{xy} < 0$ and/or $r_{xy} < 0$, then we conclude that the estimated linear relationship is negative.

While the calculated covariance and correlation coefficients provide numerical measures of the direction and strength of the linear relationship between y and x, they do not provide a sense of where the individual data points lie in relationship to each other. As we did when considering individual variables of interest, we can construct visual summaries of the data that expand our knowledge of the relationship beyond these simple numerical measures.

ADDITIONS TO OUR EMPIRICAL RESEARCH TOOLKIT

In this chapter, we have introduced a number of tools that will prove valuable when performing empirical research. They include:

- Methods for constructing visual summaries of the empirical probability distribution for a given variable.
- Numerical values that measure the central tendency of the empirical probability distribution for a given variable.
- Numerical values that measure the dispersion of an empirical probability distribution.
- Methods for determining the skewness of an empirical probability distribution.
- Methods for detecting whether outliers are present in an empirical probability distribution.
- Methods for constructing visual summaries of the relationship between two variables.
- Numerical values for the relationship between two variables.

OUR NEW EMPIRICAL TOOLS IN PRACTICE: USING WHAT WE HAVE LEARNED IN THIS CHAPTER

Using the tools introduced in this chapter, the student collecting data on the relationship between his observed tips and the number of minutes from order to delivery summarized his sample data as shown in Table 3.9.

TABLE 3.9
Summary Statistics for Our Former Student's Tip Data

	Tip Amount	Minutes to Delivery
Mean	$ 4.40	23.56
Standard Deviation	$ 5.39	13.70
Minimum	$ 0	7.00
25th Percentile	$ 0.00	14.00
Median	$ 3.00	20.00
75th Percentile	$ 6.00	32.00
Maximum	$21.00	63.00

Based on these summary statistics, he concluded that his average tips were actually quite low, in large part due to the fact that more than 25 percent of his clients offered no tip whatsoever. He also realized that there was a wide variance in delivery times, with nearly 75 percent of the sample receiving their pizza within the 30-minute goal time but with clients waiting as long as 1 hour and 3 minutes for their order. To further learn about the relative empirical probability distributions of these two variables, the student constructed the histograms shown in Figure 3.16.

FIGURE 3.16
Relative Frequency Histograms for Our Former Student's Tip Data

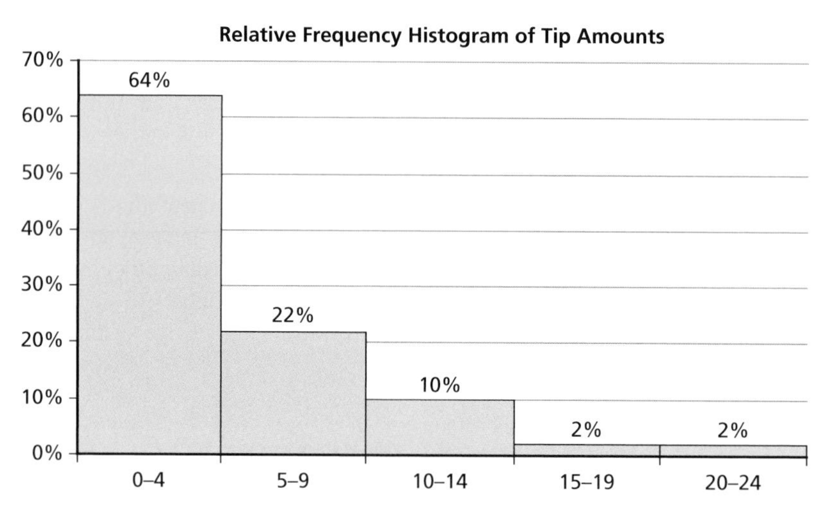

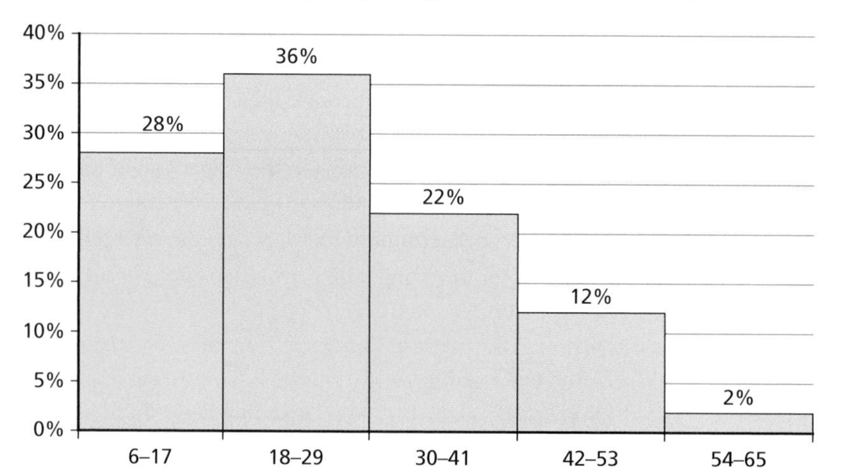

These histograms suggest that tips are heavily skewed to the low end, with nearly two-thirds of all tips being between $0 and $4 and with only 4 percent of tips being $15 or more. Conversely, the empirical probability distribution of minutes to delivery appears closer to symmetric, with the middle two bins, 18–29 and 30–41 minutes, respectively, comprising 58 percent of the sample.

While informative, these visual and numerical tools do not provide much indication of the likely relationship between the two variables. To get a better sense of the likely relationship, the student plotted the scatterplot in Figure 3.17.

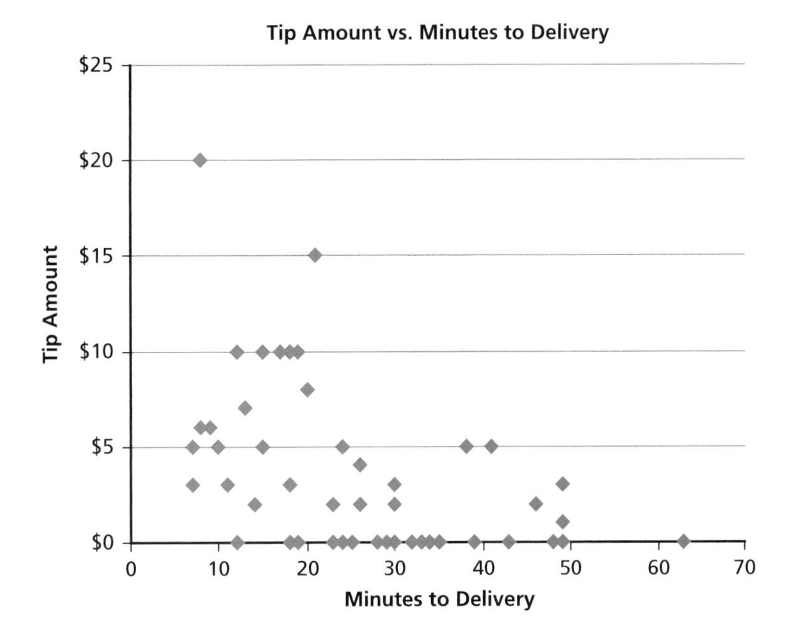

FIGURE 3.17
Scatterplot of Tip Amount versus Minutes to Delivery for Our Former Student's Tip Data

Visual inspection of this scatterplot suggested that there may well be a negative linear relationship between the observed tip amount and the number of minutes to delivery. To further confirm this potential, the student calculated that for his observed sample

$$\textit{Covariance} = -27.798$$
$$\textit{Correlation coefficient} = -0.479$$

The fact that the estimated correlation coefficient is negative and close to 0.5 in absolute value suggested that the linear relationship between the observed tip amount and the number of minutes to delivery was likely negative and somewhat strong. Based on this initial analysis, our former student was well on his way to producing a successful empirical research project.

LOOKING AHEAD TO CHAPTER 4

This chapter has introduced visual and empirical research tools for summarizing the empirical probability distribution for individual variables. While valuable, economists are often more interested in learning about the relationship between two or more variables (how salary is related to experience and productivity, how GDP is related to capital investment, education, tax rates, etc.). Chapter 4 introduces the most powerful tool in the economist's arsenal for learning about such relationships—linear regression analysis.

Problems

3.1 Why is the mean not a good measure of central tendency for data that are skewed to the right? Draw a picture to demonstrate your answer.

3.2 Explain why the standard deviation would likely not be a reliable measure of variability for a distribution of the data that includes at least one extreme outlier.

3.3 A histogram from diameter of rods manufactured from two machines is presented on the next page.

a. Based on this histogram, what would you conclude about these two machines?

b. If your manager wanted a measure of central tendency for these data, what would you tell her?

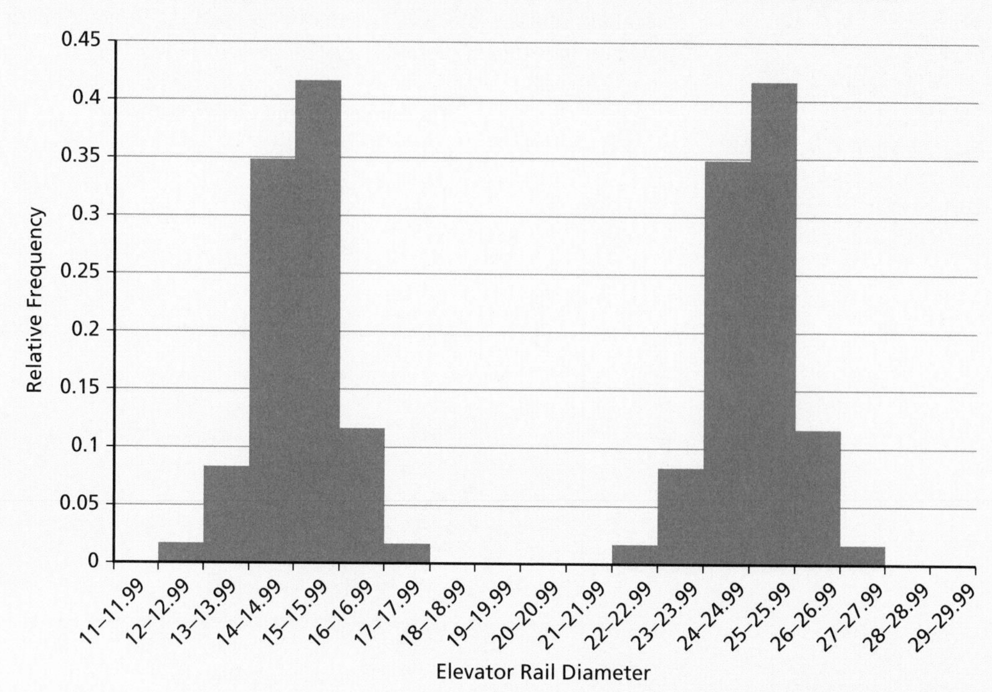

3.4 A human resource manager in concerned about employee job satisfaction. A sample of 26 employees was selected to complete a questionnaire designed to measure job satisfaction. The data are shown here. Higher scores indicate a greater degree of job satisfaction.

31	36	42	47	47	56	56	59	60	61	64	69	70
72	73	74	75	76	76	77	78	82	82	84	84	85

$$\sum_{i=1}^{26} x_i = 1{,}716, \sum_{i=1}^{26} x_i^2 = 119{,}234, \sum_{i=1}^{26} (x_i - \bar{x})^2 = 5{,}978$$

a. Compute Pearson's coefficient of skewness, and explain what it tells you about the histogram for these data.

b. Compute the summary statistic that best measures the central tendency or norm in these data.

c. Compute the summary statistic(s) that *best* measures the variation in these data.

3.5 Annual sales, in millions of dollars, for 21 pharmaceutical companies follow.

8,408	1,374	1,872	8,879	2,459	11,413
608	14,138	6,452	1,850	2,818	1,356
10,498	7,478	4,019	4,341	739	2,127
3,653	5,794	8,305			

a. Provide a five-number summary.

b. Do these data contain any outliers?

c. Johnson & Johnson's sales are the largest on the list at $14,138 million. Suppose a data-entry error (a transposition) had been made and the sales had been entered as $41,138 million. Would the method of detecting outliers in part (c) identify this problem and allow for a correction of the data-entry error?

3.6 The manager of a local fast-food restaurant is interested in improving the service provided to customers who use the restaurant's drive-up window. The manager asks his assistant to record the time (in minutes) it takes to serve 200 customers at the final window in the facility's drive-up system. The following 50 customer service times are observed for an hour in the day.

0.0774	0.0953	0.1338	0.1645	0.1788	0.1880	0.2041	0.2240	0.2303	0.2426
0.2641	0.2715	0.2798	0.2990	0.3019	0.3181	0.3374	0.3475	0.3534	0.3538
0.3734	0.3746	0.3798	0.3799	0.3845	0.3996	0.4029	0.4145	0.4152	0.4184
0.4233	0.4257	0.4259	0.4434	0.4573	0.4629	0.4629	0.4714	0.4841	0.5007
0.5071	0.5117	0.5162	0.5168	0.5177	0.5179	0.5219	0.5227	0.5343	0.5344

$$\sum_{i=1}^{50} x_i = 18.5668, \sum_{i=1}^{50} x_i^2 = 7.6657, \sum_{i=1}^{50} (x_i - \bar{x})^2 = 0.7712$$

a. Compute the summary statistic that *best* measures the central tendency or norm in these data.

b. Compute the summary statistic(s) that *best* measures the variation in these data.

c. Show whether there are any outliers in these data.

d. What is the 90th percentile of these data?

3.7 As a human resource manager for Comcel, you have been assigned the task of evaluating a new employee training program. You have the following production data (units during the month of January) for 25 employees who were participants in the program.

760	850	870	890	910	950	960	990	1,030	1,050	1,070	1,080	1,090
1,110	1,130	1,140	1,160	1,170	1,180	1,190	1,280	1,290	1,300	1,380	1,390	

$$\sum_{i=1}^{25} x_i = 27{,}220, \sum_{i=1}^{25} x_i^2 = 30{,}304{,}800, \sum_{i=1}^{25} (x_i - \bar{x})^2 = 667{,}664$$

a. Compute the summary statistic that best measures the central tendency or norm in these data.

b. Compute the summary statistic(s) that best measures the variation in these data.

c. Show whether there are any outliers in these data.

3.8 Identify whether the following variables are positively correlated, negatively correlated, or not correlated.

a. People who drink diet soda tend to weigh more, and people who drink less diet soda tend to weigh less.

b. Students who spend a lot of time on Facebook have a lower GPA, and students who spend less time on Facebook tend to have a higher GPA.

c. Sometimes the team who wears black wins the football game, and other times the team who does not wear black wins the football game.

3.9 For each of the following graphs, comment on the strength and direction of the relationship between the x and y variables.

a.

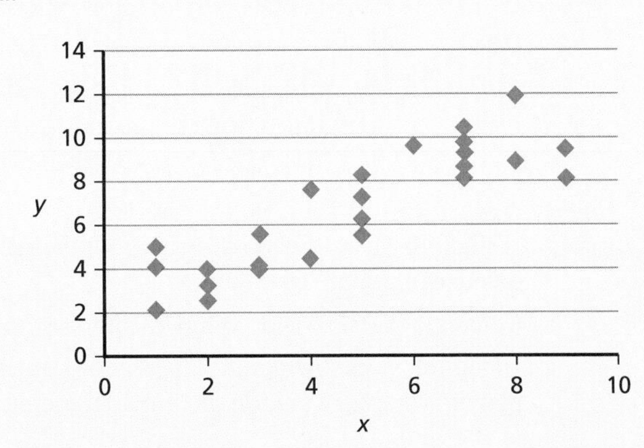

b.

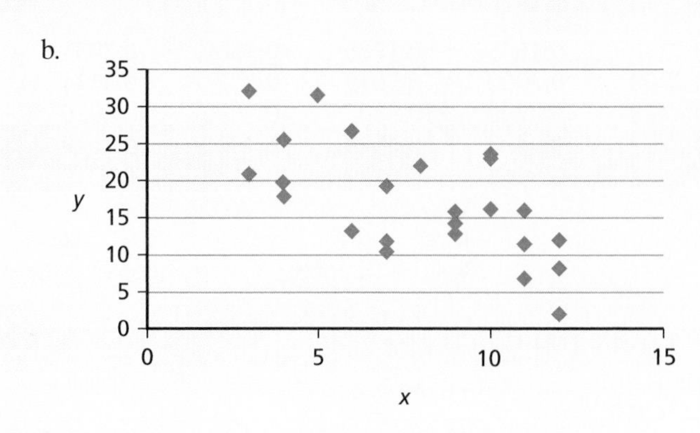

c.

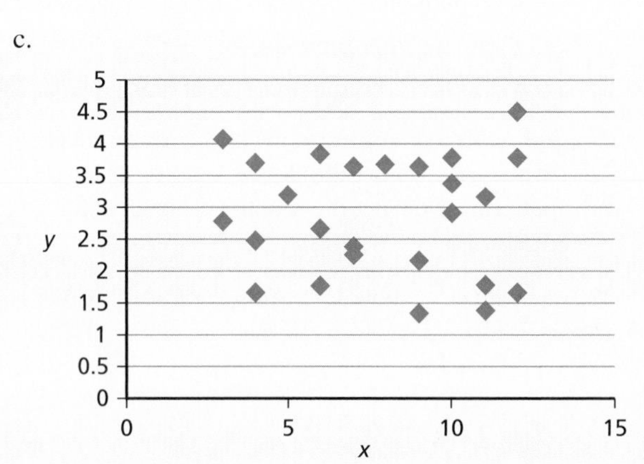

3.10 For each of the graphs in Exercise 3.9, pick out which of the three correlation coefficients are most likely.

a. $r_{xy} = 0.3346$, $r_{xy} = 0.8788$, or $r_{xy} = -0.0124$

b. $r_{xy} = -0.6242$, $r_{xy} = -0.2321$, or $r_{xy} = -0.1231$

c. $r_{xy} = -0.2249$, $r_{xy} = -0.0323$, or $r_{xy} = 0.1532$

3.11 For the following three sets of covariances and standard deviations, find the correlation coefficient.

a. $s_{xy} = 6.20$, $s_x = 2.58$, $s_y = 2.74$

b. $s_{xy} = -18.14$, $s_x = 2.97$, $s_y = 8.30$

c. $s_{xy} = -0.11$, $s_x = 2.97$, $s_y = 0.92$

d. How does the sign and magnitude of the covariance affect the correlation coefficient?

Exercises

E3.1 The Federal Deposit Insurance Corporation provides information on the top 50 banks and their total deposits. The information is contained in **Too Big to Fail.xls.**

a. What are the mean, standard deviation, and median for total deposits?

b. Create a histogram using the method described in Section 2.2.

E3.2 The **Base.xls** workbook contains annual revenue figures for Major League Baseball players (in terms of hundreds of thousands of dollars) for 2009.

a. Open the workbook and create a histogram of the players' salaries using the method discussed in class. Print both the frequency table (including relative frequencies) and the histogram.

b. Calculate the 10th and 90th percentiles of the salaries.

c. Using the value for the 90th percentile, filter the player data to show only those players who were paid in the upper 10 percent of the revenue range. Print the list of players.

d. What is the average player's revenue? If a player made the average revenue, at what percentile would he be ranked in the data?

e. Summarize your results.

E3.3 Create summary statistics and a histogram for the data found in **tax.xls.** Comment on your results in terms of the best statistics to summarize these data, as well as what the different values you found indicate.

E3.4 Open the file **scatter.xls.** For each of the four data sets listed, create and print a scatter plot. Then comment on the strength and direction of the linear relationship between the two variables.

E3.5 Calculate the covariance and the correlation coefficient for the following sets of numbers.

a.

x	y
1	5
2	3
3	4
5	7
6	10
7	9
8	12
8	9

b.

x	y
3	36
4	30
6	17
9	16
9	24
10	12
11	20
12	15

c.

x	y
3	3
4	2
6	2
7	2
9	1
10	3
11	3
12	2

E3.6 Consider the economic development data in the file **P02_06.xls.**

a. Create a scatterplot for each variable versus the size of the household's monthly home mortgage or rent payment. Print the graphs.

b. Which of the variables have a positive linear relationship with the size of the household's monthly home mortgage or rent payment?

c. Which of the variables have a negative linear relationship with the size of the household's monthly home mortgage or rent payment?

d. Which of the variables have essentially no linear relationship with the size of the household's monthly home mortgage or rent payment?

E3.7 Open the file **scatter.xls.** For each of the data sets listed, calculate the covariance and the correlation coefficient without using a canned command in Excel. Print your work. What do each of the correlation coefficients imply about the strength and direction of the linear relationship?

E3.8 One of your friends is interested in investigating if there is a relationship between how many baseball hats a person owns and their education level. They took a random sample of 60 individuals, and the result of their survey is listed in **hats.xls.** Create a scatter plot, find the covariance and correlation coefficient, and explain what this information tells your friend about the relationship between baseball hats and education level.

Chapter Four

Simple Linear Regression

CHAPTER OBJECTIVES

After reading this chapter, you will be able to:

1. Understand the goals of simple linear regression analysis.
2. Consider what the error term contains.
3. Define the population regression model and the sample regression function.
4. Estimate the sample regression function.
5. Interpret the estimated sample regression function.
6. Predict outcomes based on the estimated sample regression function.
7. Assess the goodness-of-fit of the estimated sample regression function.
8. Understand how to read regression output in Excel.
9. Understand the difference between correlation and causation.

A STUDENT'S PERSPECTIVE

Suppose that your roommate, who spends hours a day playing video games rather than attending class and studying, complains endlessly about receiving poor grades. As a responsible student who is tired of hearing such complaints, how would you handle the situation? Would you simply lend a sympathetic ear, or would you try to provide inspiration for change?

This is exactly the situation that one of our former students found himself in. As a budding econometrician, this student took the opportunity presented by the empirical research assignment to examine whether the roommate's devotion to video games was affecting his performance in the classroom. To collect appropriate data, the student used SurveyMonkey to create a survey that fellow classmates were asked to complete (after receiving permission from his instructor, of course). Suppose that summary statistics for the survey results are as shown in Table 4.1.

TABLE 4.1
Summary Statistics for Our Former Student's Hours of Video Game Play Sample

	GPA	Hours of Video Games
Mean	3.07	4.67
Standard Deviation	0.47	6.86
Minimum	1.96	0.00
25th Percentile	2.81	0.00
Median	3.01	3.00
75th Percentile	3.38	5.00
Maximum	3.98	40.00
Observations	66	66

Looking at these summary statistics, we see that the mean GPA for the 66 respondents was 3.07, while the mean number of hours spent playing video games was 4.67. Moreover, the distribution of reported video game hours appears to be quite skewed, with more than 25 percent of the class playing 0 hours, more than 75 percent playing fewer than 5 hours, and the biggest video game enthusiast playing 40 hours of video games per week. While informative as to the empirical distributions for the two variables, these summary statistics provide no indication as to the degree to which student's GPA and hours of weekly video game play are related. Given that learning this information is the entire reason for undertaking this particular project, we clearly need to develop additional empirical tools that provide the information we seek.

BIG PICTURE OVERVIEW

linear regression analysis
Empirical tool that fits the relationship between the dependent variable and independent variable(s) using a linear function.

As economists, we are often interested in learning about not only individual variables, but also about the relationship between different variables. In this chapter, we introduce **linear regression analysis,** which is a powerful empirical tool that determines the degree to which a linear relationship exists between a given dependent variable and one or more independent variables of interest.

Note that when performing linear regression analysis, we will again generally be unable to observe the entire population and will, instead, be forced to rely on analyzing a specific random sample drawn from the population to draw conclusions about the unobserved population. We visually summarize the empirical tools introduced in this chapter in Figure 4.1.

FIGURE 4.1
A Visual Depiction of the Empirical Research Tools Introduced in This Chapter

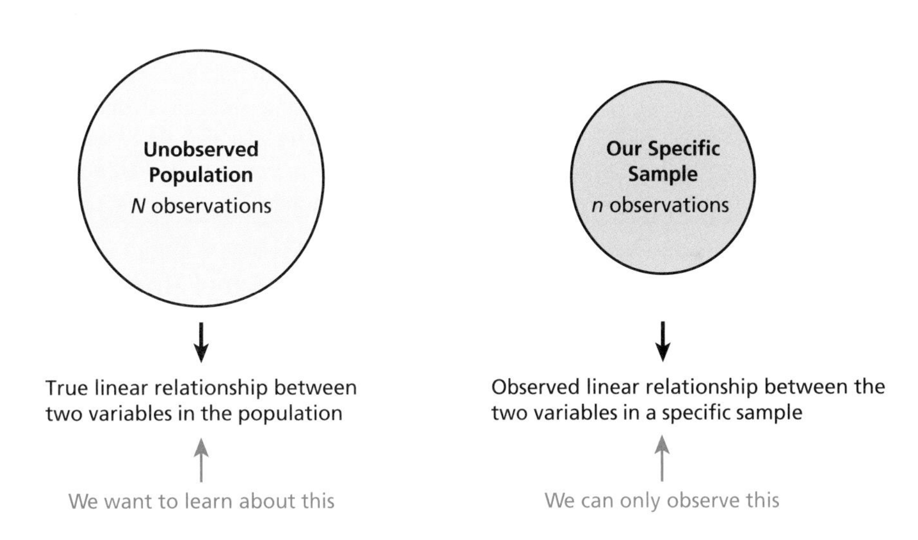

Question: How can we learn about a population that is never observed?

Answer: We can start by learning about the observed sample by

(1) Summarizing the linear relationship between the variables } Correlation, Scatterplots

(2) Estimating the linear relationship between the variables } Simple Linear Regression

(3) Determining how well the estimated linear relationship describes the observed sample data } Goodness-of-Fit

We discuss the calculation and use of these tools in the remainder of the chapter. Before doing so, we introduce the data sets that will be the focus of our discussion in the text and the basis for our examples in the Excel boxes.

DATA TO BE ANALYZED: OUR CITY PROPERTY CRIME AND CEO COMPENSATION SAMPLES

For consistency, we will continue to analyze the same data that we collected in Chapter 2 and started to analyze in Chapter 3.

Data Analyzed in the Text

Our goal in collecting these data is to investigate the theory that a city's property crime rate is a function of its unemployment rate. Using the tools introduced in Chapter 3, we know that simple summary statistics for our specific 150-observation city property crime sample are as shown in Table 4.2.

TABLE 4.2
Summary Statistics for Our 150-Observation City Property Crime Sample

	Property Crimes/100,000 Residents	Unemployment Rate
Mean	4,550.24	8.57%
Minimum	1,926.53	4.20%
25th Percentile	3,376.71	6.43%
Median	4,321.43	8.20%
75th Percentile	5,583.22	9.78%
Maximum	9,705.45	26.90%
Variance	2,250,299.66	0.09%
Standard Deviation	1,500.10	3.05%
Observations	150	150

As these data indicate, the mean number of property crimes per 100,000 residents was 4,550.24 in 2009, while the minimums and maximums were 1,926.53 and 9,705.45, respectively. At the same time, the mean unemployment rate was 8.57 percent, while the minimum was 4.20 percent and the maximum was 26.90 percent. The fact that the median number of property crimes per 100,000 residents and the median unemployment rate are fairly close to the mean suggests that these two empirical distributions are fairly symmetric.

Data Analyzed in the Excel Boxes

Our goal in collecting these data is to investigate the theory that the compensation of a *Fortune* 500 firm's CEO should be related to the firm profits. Simple summary statistics for our specific 200-observation CEO compensation sample are noted in Table 4.3.

TABLE 4.3
Summary Statistics for Our 200-Observation CEO Compensation Data

	Compensation ($)	Profits ($ millions)
Mean	11,612,180.62	807.40
Minimum	1,603,181.00	−10,949.00
25th Percentile	6,565,110.75	65.50
Median	10,235,726.50	427.95
75th Percentile	14,256,553.75	1,216.78
Maximum	43,123,552.00	19,280.00
Variance	46,122,273,517,083.60	6,886,834.84
Standard Deviation	6,791,338.12	2,624.28
Observations	200	200

As these data indicate, the mean compensation for *Fortune* 500 CEOs in our sample is $11,612,181, while the minimum and maximum compensations are $1,603,181 and

Correctly Identifying the Dependent and Independent Variables

In order to correctly perform linear regression analysis, we must first correctly identify the *dependent variable* (*y*) and the *independent variable* (*x*) in our analysis. By definition, the dependent variable is the variable that changes in response to changes in the independent variable. While identifying which variable is which might sound straightforward, we find that confusing them is one of the more common mistakes our students make when performing their own empirical research projects. As an example, one of our students was recently interested in determining how the elevation of a MLB stadium affects the number of home runs hit. For such an analysis, the dependent variable should be the number of home runs hit and the independent variable should be the elevation of the stadium. Unfortunately, the student switched these variables, thereby asking whether the number of home runs hit affected the elevation of a team's stadium rather than asking whether the elevation of the team's stadium affected the number of home runs hit. To see why this was problematic, consider that if the student had identified a positive relationship for his specification, he would have concluded that every additional home run hit by a team increased the elevation of the team's stadium. In other words, he would have concluded that if the San Diego Padres hit enough home runs they could raise the elevation of their stadium (20 feet) to equal that of the Colorado Rockies (5,280 feet).

To avoid making such mistakes, we encourage students to write down their question of interest, their suspected dependent and independent variables, and the way they would interpret their potential results before reading those values out loud to see whether they pass the ear test. As an example, for the stadium elevation example, we would write down that "We are interested in determining the relationship between the number of home runs hit and a stadium's elevation," "We think that the dependent variable is the number of home runs hit and the independent variable is the stadium's elevation," and "We would interpret the results as indicating the effect that variation in stadium elevation have on the number of home runs hit." Given that all three of these thoughts make sense, we would conclude that we have correctly identified the dependent and the independent variables for our linear regression analysis.

dependent variable
The variable that is being explained.

independent variable
The variable that does the explaining.

Notation:
- y The dependent variable in our linear regression analysis
- x The independent variable in our linear regression analysis

\$43,123,552, respectively. At the same time, the mean firm profit is \$807.4 million, while the minimum and maximums are −\$10,949 and \$19,280 billion, respectively. The fact that the median CEO compensation of \$10.24 million and the median firm profit of nearly \$430 million are so much closer to the minimum values than the maximum values might suggest that the distributions for both of these variables are skewed to the right.

As a final point relating to the data analyzed in this chapter, note that for the city property crime sample, the **dependent variable,** which we denote as *y*, is the city's property crime rate per 100,000 residents and the **independent variable,** which we denote as *x*, is the city's unemployment rate. Likewise, for the CEO compensation sample, note that the dependent variable is the CEO's compensation and the independent variable is the firm's profit.

4.1 UNDERSTAND THE GOALS OF SIMPLE LINEAR REGRESSION ANALYSIS

simple linear regression analysis
A statistical method that relates a dependent variable to an independent variable.

As an introduction to this powerful tool, we start by discussing **simple linear regression analysis.** Each of the words in this term has a specific meaning. The word *simple* refers to the fact that we are estimating the relationship between the dependent variable and a single independent variable; the word *linear* refers to the fact that we are estimating a linear relationship between the variables; and the word *regression* refers to the specific manner in which we estimate the relationship.

To understand simple linear regression analysis, we begin by focusing on the word *linear*. Recall that the slope-intercept formula for a line is

$$y = mx + b \qquad \textbf{4.1.1}$$

where

y = Dependent variable
x = Independent variable
b = Intercept (or the value that y takes on when $x = 0$)
m = Slope (or the effect that one-unit changes in x have on y)

This formulation is extremely valuable because it defines the relationship between y and x in a numerical form that provides the answer to two important questions:

marginal effect
The effect that a one-unit change in the independent variable has on the dependent variable, *holding all else constant.*

1. What is the **marginal effect** that a one-unit change in the independent variable is expected to have on the value of the dependent variable?
2. What is the predicted value of the dependent variable that is likely to be associated with a given value of the independent variable?

As an example of the value of this specification, suppose that you are spending the current semester studying abroad in Europe and that you awake in the morning to find the day's forecast to be as depicted in Figure 4.2.

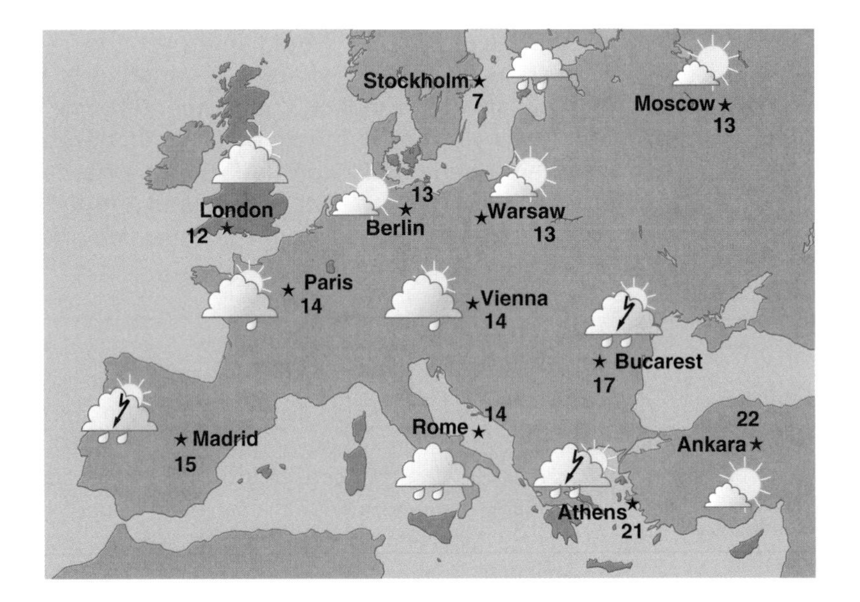

FIGURE 4.2
The Day's European Weather Forecast in Celsius

Based on this information, how would you dress for the day's activities? To answer this question, you would need to convert the forecast Celsius temperatures into the more familiar Fahrenheit temperatures. Celsius and Fahrenheit temperatures are related through the specific linear relationship $F = (9/5)C + 32$. This formula is valuable because it provides our two desired pieces: (1) from the formula, we see that each 1-degree change in the Celsius temperature corresponds to a 1.8-degree (9/5) change in the Fahrenheit temperature, and (2), if the current temperature is 21 degrees Celsius, then the corresponding temperature in Fahrenheit is $F = (9/5)(21) + 32 = 37.8 + 32 = 69.8$ degrees. Graphically, these facts are shown in Figure 4.3.

Before discussing how to determine the estimated linear relationship between two variables, we need to introduce terminology. Figure 4.3 depicts a specific type of relationship in which the variables exhibit an exact linear relationship to each other: each 1-degree increase in Celsius temperature corresponds to exactly a 9/5-degree increase in Fahrenheit

FIGURE 4.3
Graphing the Relationship between Celsius and Fahrenheit

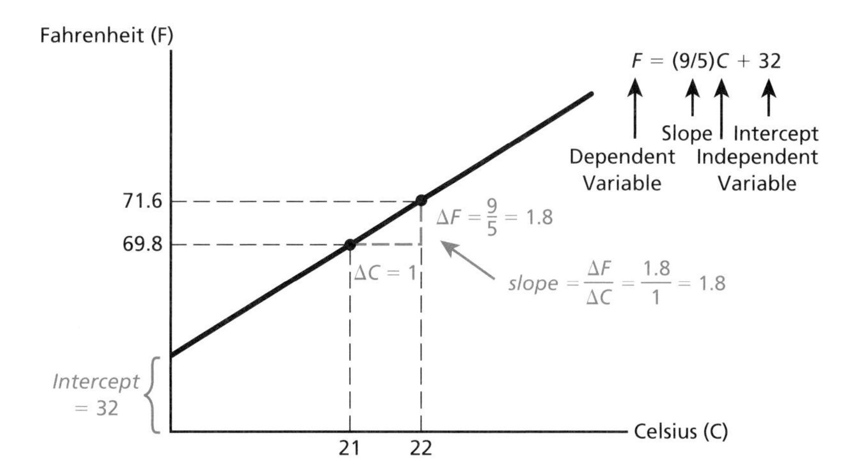

deterministic
A relationship in which an exact linear relationship exists between two variables.

temperature. Such exact linear relationships are referred to as being **deterministic** because the value of one variable perfectly "determines" the value of the other variable.

Deterministic relationships are not often encountered in real-world relationships because most outcomes encountered in the real world are the result of natural phenomena containing strong random components that make deterministic relationships unlikely. Instead, we normally observe relationships in which the observed values of y and x are linearly related to some degree but do not all fall on the same line. Such relationships are referred to as being **probabilistic** because the value of one variable does not perfectly determine the value of the other, meaning that, while related in a specific way, the observed data points do not all fall on a straight line (i.e., there is some "probability" that the observed value of y is located away from the predicted value of y).

probabilistic
A relationship in which an exact linear relationship does not exist between two variables.

The difference between deterministic and probabilistic relationships is summarized in Figure 4.4.

FIGURE 4.4
Scatter Diagrams of Deterministic and Probabilistic Relationships

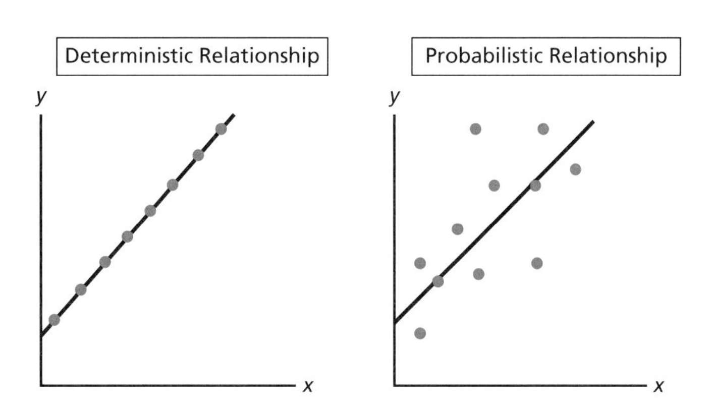

Given that every data point in the deterministic relationship falls on the same line, it is easy to see that the correct formula for the deterministic linear relationship is $y = mx + b$. But what is the correct formulation for the probabilistic relationship? We begin to answer this question by noting that the vertical distance that an observed data point falls away from a specified linear relationship is referred to as the **residual** and is denoted as e. Because each observed data point in a probabilistic relationship possesses a random error component, we can write the formula for the probabilistic relationship as

residual
The fluctuation away from the deterministic model in a regression model.

$$y = mx + b + \varepsilon \quad \textbf{4.1.2}$$

where

y = Dependent variable
x = Independent or explanatory variable
b = Intercept (the value that y takes on when $x = 0$)
m = Slope (the affect that one-unit change in x has on y)
ε = Residual

At this point, we must again introduce new terminology and notation. First, to allow for the fact the specific values of the dependent and independent variables differ for each individual observation in a sample, we add an i subscript to every variable (i.e. x, y, and ε become x_i, y_i, and e_i) and our equation for the line becomes

predicted value of y_i The value that is obtained by putting a value of x into the regression equation.

$$y_i = mx_i + b + e_i \qquad 4.1.3$$

Second, the **predicted value of y_i**, denoted as $\hat{y}_i$, is the value of y predicted by the linear relationship between y and x. As an example, if $x_i = 6$, then $\hat{y}_i = mx_i + b = m \cdot 6 + b$.

Finally, note that the residual e_i for each observation is the difference between the observed value of y_i and the predicted value $\hat{y}_i$, meaning that the residual is $e_i = y_i - \hat{y}_i$.

Proceeding with our discussion, suppose that our probabilistic linear relationship is given by $y_i = 4x_i + 7 + e_i$ and that Table 4.4 presents hypothetical observations for the values of y_i and x_i in a given sample.

Notation:

$\hat{y}_i$ Predicted value of y for a given value of x

ε_i Random error term for a given observation

TABLE 4.4 Data to Demonstrate a Probabilistic Linear Relationship

y_i	x_i
9	1
19	2
20	3
18	4
27	5
30	6

The predicted values of y and the associated random error components are then given in Table 4.5.

TABLE 4.5 Computing Predicted Values and Random Errors

Observed value of x (x_i)	Predicted value of y $\hat{y}_i = (E(y\|x))$	Observed value of y (y_i)	Random error component ($e_i = y_i - \hat{y}_i$)
1	$(4 \cdot 1) + 7 = 11$	9	$9 - 11 = -2$
2	$(4 \cdot 2) + 7 = 15$	19	$19 - 15 = 4$
3	$(4 \cdot 3) + 7 = 19$	20	$20 - 19 = 1$
4	$(4 \cdot 4) + 7 = 23$	18	$18 - 23 = -5$
5	$(4 \cdot 5) + 7 = 27$	27	$27 - 27 = 0$
6	$(4 \cdot 6) + 7 = 31$	30	$30 - 31 = -1$

These entries correspond to Figure 4.5.

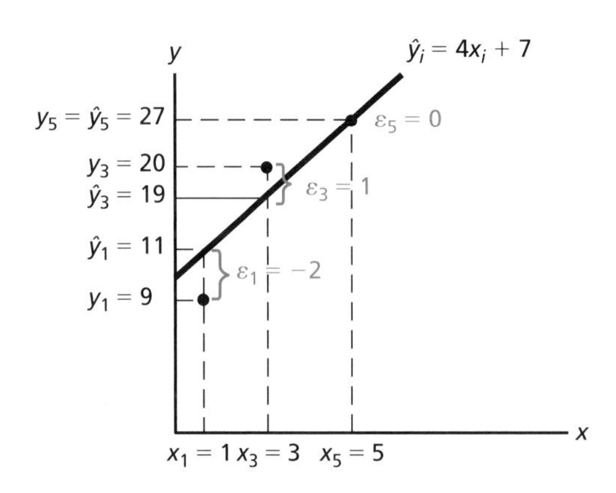

FIGURE 4.5 Finding Predicted Values and Errors on a Graph

As Figure 4.5 demonstrates, in a probabilistic relationship, the observed value of y can either be greater than the predicted value of y (in which case, $e_i > 0$), less than the predicted value of y (in which case, $e_i < 0$), or equal to the predicted value of y (in which case, $e_i = 0$). Because the calculated value of ε_i plays a pivotal role in performing linear regression analysis, it is important to consider the factors that theory suggests should be included in the term.

4.2 CONSIDER WHAT THE RANDOM ERROR COMPONENT CONTAINS

error term
Another name for the random error component.

The random error component (or the **error term**) measures the exact degree to which an observed value of y differs from the value of y that is predicted for a given value of x in the population. It is important to consider the factors that are likely contained in this term because they are the factors that cause the observed value of y to differ from the predicted value of y. While there are many, many potential factors that might cause this deviation, we discuss four that are of primary importance to econometricians.

The first potential factor is referred to as *omitted variables.* Omitted variables are independent variables that vary with the dependent variable, y, but are not explicitly included in the regression model. In the case of simple linear regression, the number of omitted variables is typically large because we would reasonably expect far more than one independent variable to be related to the dependent variable. For instance, at this point, our simple linear regression of property crime rates on unemployment rates likely omits many factors that play an important role in determining a city's property crime rate, such as population, income and education levels, police force size, concealed carry laws.

The second potential factor is referred to as *measurement error.* Measurement error, which is defined as the difference between the measured value of the observation and the actual value of the observation, occurs when the data collected are for some reason not equal to the true values of the observations. One potential source of measurement error is incorrect data entry. As an example, suppose that instead of entering the true property crime rate of 2,528 for Santa Barbara–Santa Maria-Goleta, the first city in our 200-observation sample, we accidentally add a 0 and enter a value of 25,280. In such case, the estimated relationship between x and the entered value of y will not reflect the true relationship between y and x. A second potential source of measurement error is indirect observation of the data being collected. As an example, consider an economic consultant working for a private firm. Because individual salaries for private firms are not a matter of public record, when collecting salary data, we have to rely on asking the individual to provide such information. Should the individual either incorrectly recall or choose to misrepresent this value, the data entered will be subject to measurement error.

The third potential factor is referred to as *incorrect functional form.* By definition, incorrect functional form occurs when we fit the wrong model to the data. As an example, suppose that our data look like those in Figure 4.6 and that we fit a line through the data as depicted in line A. In such a case, the estimated model is an incorrect representation of the true relationship between y and x, and the resulting mistakes are included in the error term of the linear regression. Note that in this case, the model that should be fit is not linear but is quadratic as depicted in line B. We return to this possibility in future chapters.

FIGURE 4.6
Fitting Lines through the Possible Scatter Diagram

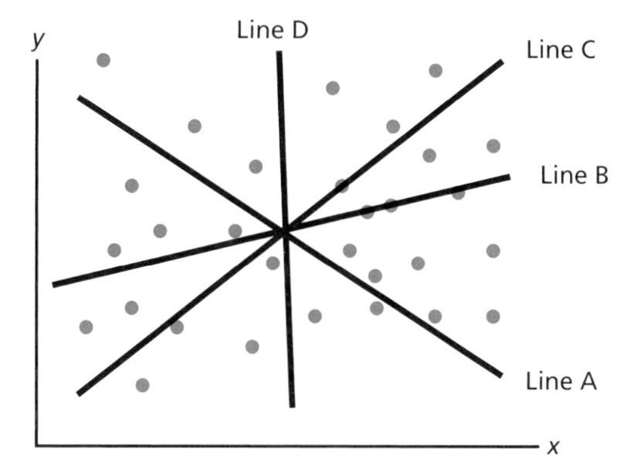

The final potential factor is referred to as a *random component*. The random component picks up the fact that the variable being studied is inherently random. As an example, consider an individual's daily choice of lunch. If the individual normally frequents a restaurant serving burgers and tacos for exactly the same price, would we expect him or her to purchase exactly the same meal each day? Likely not. Instead, we might expect him or her to purchase a burger some days and a taco others, depending on his or her preferences on each given day. Because the individual's daily preferences likely vary randomly, any estimated relationships based on his or her observed behavior will contain a random component, and this component and its accordant effects are included in the error term.

With this in mind, we can move on to the mechanics of performing linear regression analysis.

4.3 DEFINE THE POPULATION REGRESSION MODEL AND THE SAMPLE REGRESSION FUNCTION

population regression model
The underlying relationship that holds for the population.

By definition, there is a true underlying linear relationship between the two variables within the population (which is what we are trying to learn about). We refer to this true relationship as the **population regression model,** and we write it as $y_i = \beta_0 + \beta_1 x_i + \varepsilon_i$, where

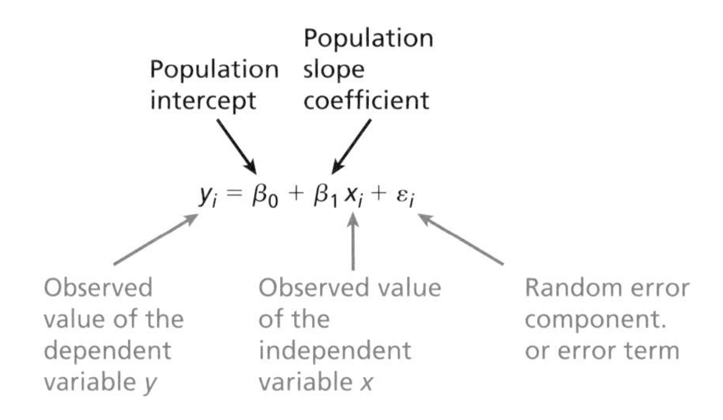

4.3.1

Notice that because the population regression model describes the relationship between y and x that actually exists in the population, the model includes an error term because the values of y that are actually observed in the population do randomly vary around the values of y that are predicted for given values of x.

Because the population is generally unobserved, we need to use our observed sample to generate our best possible estimate of the unobserved population regression model. We do so by calculating the best-fit linear relationship for our observed sample and using it as the estimate of the unobserved population regression model. The best-fit linear relationship that holds for our specific random sample is referred to as the **sample regression function** and is written as $\hat{y}_i = \hat{\beta}_0 + \hat{\beta}_1 x_i$, where

sample regression function
The regression function that is fit to the sample data.

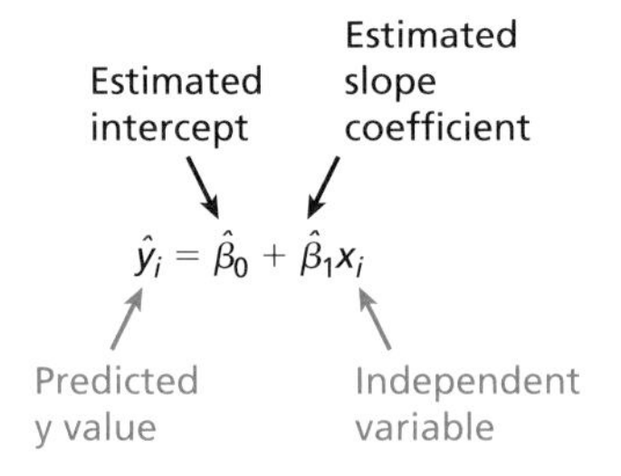

4.3.2

Notation:

$\hat{\beta}_0$ Estimated intercept
$\hat{\beta}_1$ Estimated slope coefficient

Note that in moving from the population regression model to the sample regression function, we change our notation for the slope and the intercept from β_0 and β_1 to $\hat{\beta}_0$ and $\hat{\beta}_1$ (pronounced "β_0 hat" and "β_1 hat"). We make this change to indicate that the values calculated for the specific random sample are merely estimates of the true (unobserved) population parameters and not the true population parameters themselves. In other words, the sample slope coefficient estimate, $\hat{\beta}_1$, is an estimate of the population slope, β_1, and the sample intercept estimate, $\hat{\beta}_0$, is an estimate of the population intercept, β_0.

Note further that within the sample regression function, the residual, e_i, is the difference between the observed value of y and the predicted value of y, or

$$Residual = e_i = y_i - \hat{y}_i \quad \textbf{4.3.3}$$

and is our best estimate of the population error term, ε_i.

In order to understand how we determine our best-fit line, it is useful to visually consider the relationship between the estimated sample regression function and one individual sample data point (see Figure 4.7).

FIGURE 4.7
A Graphical Representation of the Sample Regression Function

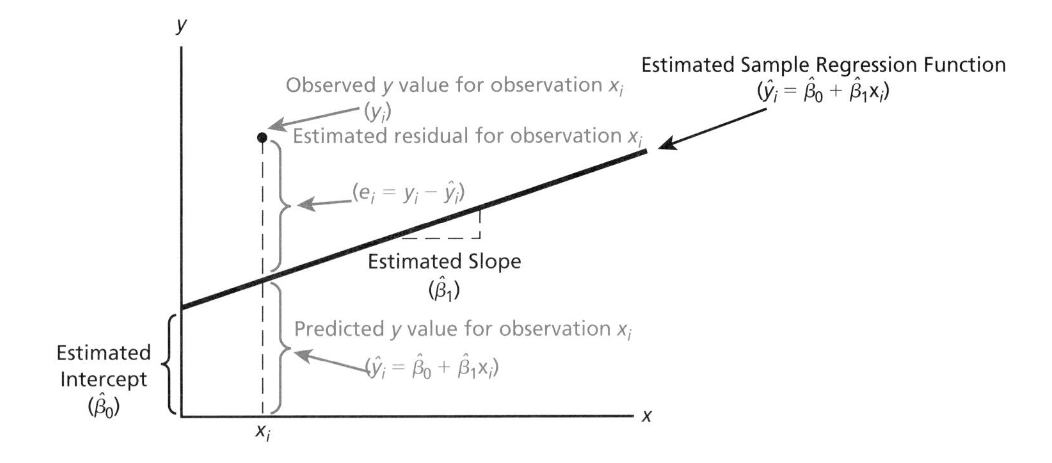

As Figure 4.7 demonstrates, the value of y that is actually observed for a given x is divided into two parts: (1) the portion that is explained by the estimated sample regression function, or $\hat{y}_i$, and (2) the portion that is not explained by the estimated sample regression function, or e_i.

For the calculations that we will perform later, it is important to recognize that instead of the individual data point in Figure 4.6, we will actually have many, many data points, each of which has its own predicted value of y and its own residual. In other words, the visual for the data with which we will be working will look more like Figure 4.8.

FIGURE 4.8
A Graphical Representation of the Residuals for a Sample with Multiple Observations

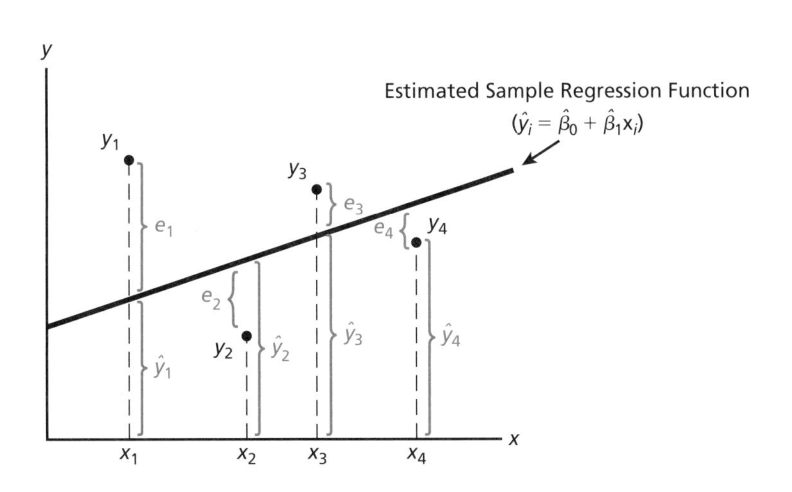

With these thoughts in mind, we can now consider how to determine the best-fit estimated sample regression function for our observed sample data.

4.4 ESTIMATE THE SAMPLE REGRESSION FUNCTION

Determining the linear relationship that "best describes" the underlying relationship between the two random variables in our specific sample is complicated by the fact that many, many different linear relationships describe any given data set. For example, we could argue that lines A, B, C, and D all define the observed linear relationship between y and x in Figure 4.6 to some extent.

The question is which of these lines "best describes" (or "best fits") the true underlying relationship between y and x. The answer, as you might expect, is the line that is "closest" on average to each of the observed data points.

Because we want our estimated best-fit line to be "closest" on average to the observed data points, we want to minimize some measure of the difference between the values of y that are actually observed and the values of y that are predicted by our estimated best-fit line. A first impulse for determining the total difference between the observed and predicted values of y might be to simply sum the individual deviations from $\hat{y}$ by calculating the value $\sum_{i=1}^{n}(y_i - \hat{y}_i)$. This will not work in practice, however, because the estimated linear relationship is averaged across all observed values of y, resulting in total positive deviations from $\hat{y}$ that exactly balance the total negative deviations from $\hat{y}$, resulting in the summation always being equal to 0. For this reason, we need to turn the negative deviations into positive deviations by squaring each individual deviation from the mean before performing the summation. We then can determine the specific line that "best fits" our sample data by minimizing the sum of the squared deviations from the predicted value of y.

minimizing the sum of squared residuals
The process by which the "best fit" line for sample data is determined.

least squares criterion
The linear relationship that best fits the observed sample data is the one that minimizes the sum of squared residuals.

Because individual deviations from the predicted value of y are also known as residuals, satisfying our objective function for determining the "best-fit" regression line is referred to as **minimizing the sum of squared residuals.** Formally, to determine the specific line that minimizes the sum of squared residuals (or that satisfies the **least squares criterion**), we start by writing the problem as

$$Minimize \sum_{i=1}^{n} e_i^2 = \sum_{i=1}^{n}(y_i - \hat{y}_i)^2 = \sum_{i=1}^{n}\left(y_i - (\hat{\beta}_0 + \hat{\beta}_1 x_i)\right)^2 \qquad \textbf{4.4.1}$$

We solve this minimization problem by taking the derivatives of formula 4.4.1 with respect to $\hat{\beta}_0$ and $\hat{\beta}_1$, setting them equal to 0, and solving for the values of the parameters that satisfy the optimality condition (in this case, $\hat{\beta}_0$ and $\hat{\beta}_1$). Doing so yields the following formulas:

$$\hat{\beta}_1 = \frac{\sum_{i=1}^{n}(x_i - \bar{x})(y_i - \bar{y})}{\sum_{i=1}^{n}(x_i - \bar{x})^2} = \frac{Cov(x, y)}{Var(x)} \qquad \textbf{4.4.2}$$

and

$$\hat{\beta}_0 = \bar{y} - \hat{\beta}_1 \bar{x} \qquad \textbf{4.4.3}$$

which are the values that define our estimated sample regression function $\hat{y} = \hat{\beta}_0 + \hat{\beta}_1 x$. Note that when estimating sample regression functions, statistical packages are simply programmed to calculate formulas 4.4.2 and 4.4.3.

To calculate these values for our 150-observation city property crime sample, we first need to determine the values $Cov(x,y)$, $Var(x)$, $\bar{x}$, and $\bar{y}$, which we do in Table 4.6).

TABLE 4.6 Using the Formulas to Calculate the Slope Coefficient for Our 150-Observation City Property Crime Sample

Metro Area	Property Crimes/ 100,000 (y_i)	Unemployment Rate (x_i)	$(y - \bar{y})$	$(x - \bar{x})$	$(y_i - y)(x_i - \bar{x})$	$(x - \bar{x})^2$
Santa Barbara-Santa Maria-Goleta	2,528	0.076	−2,022.68	−0.010	19.60654995	9.4E-05
Honolulu	3,679	0.057	−871.03	−0.029	24.99282337	0.000823
Fort Smith	5,861	0.070	1,310.63	−0.016	−20.56818355	0.000246
Hattiesburg	4,568	0.063	17.63	−0.023	−0.400092065	0.000515
Billings	4,360	0.042	−189.88	−0.044	8.29647518	0.001909
Rome	5,198	0.103	647.73	0.017	11.2100306	0.0003
Napa	2,554	0.085	−1,995.92	−0.001	1.383836616	4.81E-07
Reno-Sparks	3,814	0.110	−736.60	0.024	−17.90430769	0.000591
Davenport-Moline-Rock Island	4,914	0.065	363.77	−0.021	−7.527634429	0.000428
Chico	2,776	0.124	−1,774.17	0.038	−67.96253333	0.001467
Sebastian-Vero Beach	3,216	0.119	−1334.11	0.033	−44.43472417	0.001109
Texarkana	6,911	0.052	2,360.55	−0.034	−79.5347039	0.001135
Midland	3,637	0.045	−913.73	−0.041	37.18261802	0.001656
St. George	2,043	0.066	−2,507.56	−0.020	49.38218761	0.000388

$\sum(y_i - \bar{y})(x_i - \bar{x}) = 1{,}100.08$

$\sum(x_i - \bar{x})^2 = 0.138694$

$\hat{\beta}_1 = Cov(x, y)/Var(x) = 7{,}931.70$

$\bar{y} = 4{,}682.36$

$\bar{x} = 0.083$

$\hat{\beta}_0 = \bar{y} - \hat{\beta}_1\bar{x} = 3{,}870.55$

Based on these entries, we see that our estimated slope coefficient is

$$\hat{\beta}_1 = \frac{\sum_{i=1}^{n}(y_i - \bar{y})(x_i - \bar{x})}{\sum_{i=1}^{n}(x_i - \bar{x})^2} = \frac{1{,}100.08}{0.138694} = 7{,}931.71 \quad \textbf{4.4.4}$$

and our estimated intercept is

$$\hat{\beta}_0 = \bar{y} - \hat{\beta}_1\bar{x} = 4{,}550.24 - (7{,}931.71)(0.086) = 3{,}870.55 \quad \textbf{4.4.5}$$

Combining these values, our estimated sample regression function is

$$\hat{y} = \hat{\beta}_0 + \hat{\beta}_1 x = 3{,}870.55 + 7{,}931.71x \quad \textbf{4.4.6}$$

Superimposing this estimated sample regression function over the scatter diagram for our 150-observation city property crime sample (which we first constructed in Chapter 3), we have Figure 4.9.

FIGURE 4.9
The Estimated Sample Regression Function for Our 150-Observation City Property Crime Sample

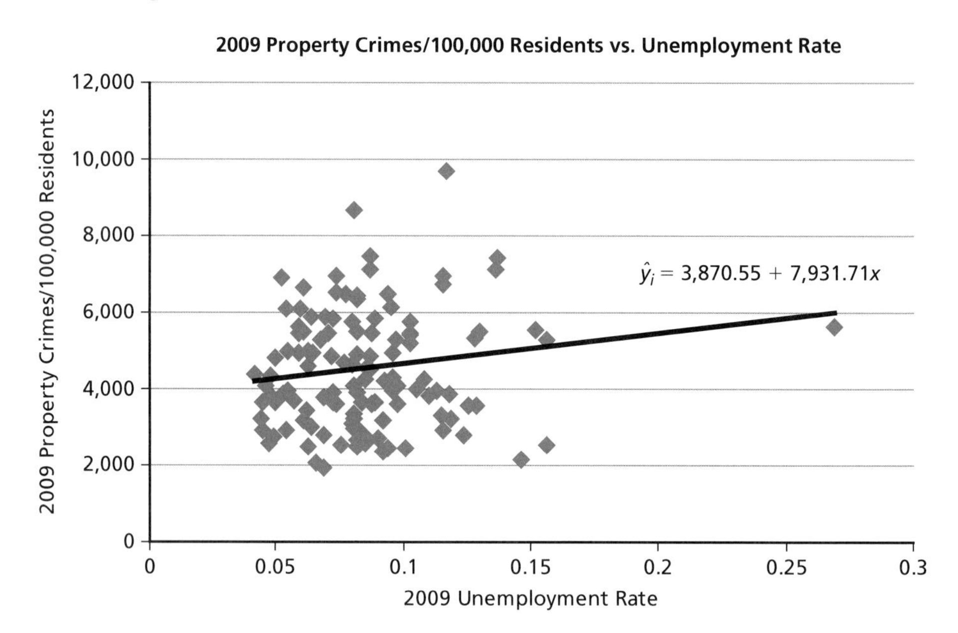

EMPIRICAL RESEARCH TOOL 4.1: THE ESTIMATED SAMPLE SIMPLE LINEAR REGRESSION FUNCTION

Goal:
Estimate the linear relationship between *y* and *x* that best fits the observed sample data.

Tools:
Minimizing the sum of squared residuals by solving the problem

$$\text{Minimize} = \sum_{i=1}^{n} e_i^2 = \sum_{i=1}^{n}(y_i - \hat{y}_i)^2 = \sum_{i=1}^{n}\left(y_i - (\hat{\beta}_0 + \hat{\beta}_1 x_i)\right)^2$$

Formulas:
The estimated sample simple linear regression function is

$$\hat{y}_i = \hat{\beta}_0 + \hat{\beta}_1 x_i$$

where

$$\hat{\beta}_1 = \frac{\sum_{i=1}^{n}(x_i - \bar{x})(y_i - \bar{y})}{\sum_{i=1}^{n}(x_i - \bar{x})^2} = \frac{Cov(x, y)}{Var(x)} \text{ and } \hat{\beta}_0 = \bar{y} - \hat{\beta}_1\bar{x}$$

As mentioned previously, linear regression analysis is one of the most powerful tools in our empirical research arsenal. To get the most benefit from this powerful tool, it is absolutely critical that we be able to interpret our estimates correctly. We cannot stress this enough. In fact, given the importance we place on correct interpretation, when grading our students' empirical research projects, one of first things we look at is their offered interpretation of the results.

4.5 INTERPRET THE ESTIMATED SAMPLE REGRESSION FUNCTION

The estimated sample regression function allows us to answer our two important questions of interest:

1. What is the marginal effect that a one-unit change in the independent variable is expected to have on the value of the dependent variable?
2. What is the predicted value of the dependent variable that is likely to be associated with a given value of the independent variable?

To answer these questions, we must be able to correctly interpret our estimated sample regression function.

EXCEL EXAMPLE 4.1

Plotting the estimated sample regression function for our CEO compensation sample

Plotting the Estimated Sample Regression Function

Return to the scatterplot of CEO compensation versus firm profit.

1. Right-click on one of the data points in the scatterplot.
2. Select the "Add Trendline . . ." option, and keep "linear" selected.
3. Select "Add Equation" to see the estimated equation on the graph.
4. Change the line color, etc., as desired from the menu provided.

A screen capture looks as follows:

id	Company	Compensation ($)	Profit ($ millions)
1	Xerox	$12,902,607	$485.00
2	Yum Brands	$20,411,852	$1,071.00
3	Centene	$10,473,912	$83.70
4	AutoZone	$11,360,019	$657.00
5	Cablevision Systems	$11,445,228	$285.60
6	Gilead Sciences	$15,615,645	$2,635.80
7	DTE Energy	$7,389,279	$532.00
8	Morgan Stanley	$12,981,856	$1,346.00
9	United Technologies	$27,671,331	$3,829.00
10	Harris	$8,575,820	$37.90
11	Lockheed Martin	$25,369,641	$3,024.00
12	Rite Aid	$2,827,819	-$2,915.40
13	Jabil Circuit	$10,293,809	-$1,165.20
14	Entergy	$10,130,771	$1,231.10
15	Cigna	$19,085,567	$1,302.00

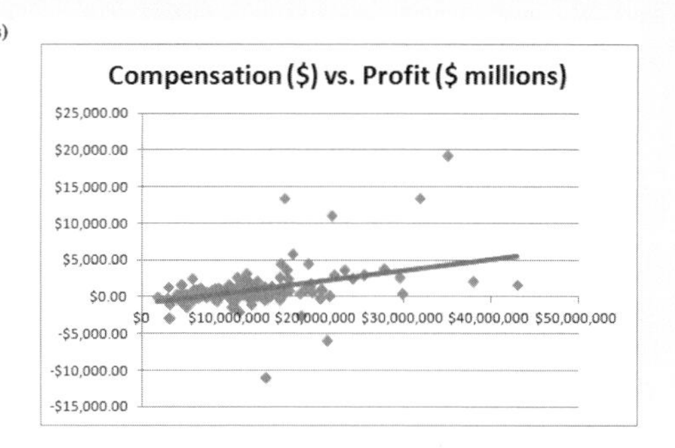

Interpreting the Estimated Sample Regression Function

$$\widehat{Compensation} = 10{,}792{,}308.27 + 1{,}015.44\ Profit$$

Based on these results, we would estimate that

1. For a firm with a profit of 0, CEO compensation would average $10,792,308.27.
2. On average, for each $1 million increase in profit, CEO compensation would increase by $1.015.44.

---

estimated intercept
Provides an estimate of the value that the dependent variable is expected to take on when the independent variable is equal to 0.

The **estimated intercept** ($\hat{\beta}_0$) provides an estimate (based on the observed sample data) of the average value that the dependent variable is expected to take for an observation with an observed value of 0 for the independent variable. For our 150-observation city property crime sample, we would expect a city with an unemployment rate of 0 to observe 3,401.39 property crimes per 100,000 residents.

We offer one word of caution here when it comes to interpreting the estimated intercept. In practice, because we do not often observe values of continuous independent variables that are close to 0 (the lowest property crime rate in our 150-observation sample is only 1,926.53), the intercept often fails to provide a reliable estimate of the value that y would take on if x were indeed equal to 0. Moreover, for reasons that we discuss later, the estimated value often turns out to be nonsensical. Fortunately, the estimated intercept rarely plays a central role in the types of economic analyses that we wish to perform.

estimated slope coefficient
Provides an estimate of the how much the dependent variable changes when the independent variable changes by one unit.

The **estimated slope coefficient** ($\hat{\beta}_1$) provides an estimate (based on the observed sample data) of the *average* effect that each one-unit change in the independent variable is likely to have on the dependent variable. For our 150-observation city property crime sample, we would expect each one-point increase in the unemployment rate to increase the number of property crimes per 100,000 residents by an average of 15,460.59.

Note that we highlight the word *average* in the preceding explanation for an important reason. The marginal effects that we estimate through linear regression analysis are averaged over all individuals in the sample. Accordingly, it would be incorrect to interpret an estimated coefficient as indicating that every observation in the sample observing a one-unit increase in the independent variable will observe exactly the same $\hat{\beta}_1$ increase in the dependent variable. Instead, all observations observing a one-unit increase in the independent variable will observe different changes in the dependent variable, with the average of those changes being $\hat{\beta}_1$.

EMPIRICAL RESEARCH TOOL 4.2: CORRECTLY INTERPETING THE ESTIMATED INTERCEPT AND ESTIMATED SLOPE COEFFICIENT

Goal:
Explain what the estimated slope and estimated intercept mean from the simple linear regression equation.

Tools:

The estimated intercept ($\hat{\beta}_0$) is the predicted value of the dependent variable, y, when the explanatory variable x is equal to 0.

The estimated slope coefficient ($\hat{\beta}_1$) is the average effect that each one-unit change in the independent variable has on the dependent variable.

4.6 PREDICT OUTCOMES BASED ON OUR ESTIMATED SAMPLE REGRESSION FUNCTION

prediction
The value of the dependent (y) variable that is obtained by putting in a value for the independent (x) variable into the sample regression function.

We can estimate the value of the dependent variable that is most likely to be associated with a given value of the independent variable by inserting a specific value for the independent variable into the estimated sample regression function and calculating a **prediction** for the likely value of the dependent variable. As examples, for cities with unemployment rates of 9 percent ($x = 0.09$) in our 150-observation city property crime sample, the predicted number of property crimes per 100,000 residents would be

$$\hat{y} = 3,870.55 + 7,931.71 \cdot 0.09 = 4,584.39 \qquad \textbf{4.6.1}$$

while for a cities with unemployment rates of 13 percent ($x = 0.13$), the predicted number of property crimes per 100,000 residents would be

$$\hat{y} = 3,870.55 + 7,931.71 \cdot 0.13 = 4,901.67 \qquad \textbf{4.6.2}$$

EMPIRICAL RESEARCH TOOL 4.3: CALCULATING PREDICTED VALUES BASED ON OUR ESTIMATED SAMPLE REGRESSION FUNCTION

Goal:

Predict the value of the dependent variable that is most likely to be associated with a given value of an independent variable.

Tools:

After determining the simple linear regression equation, $\hat{y} = \hat{\beta}_0 + \hat{\beta}_1 x$, plug the value of the independent variable, *x*, into the right hand side of the equation and solve for the predicted value of *y*.

4.7 ASSESS THE GOODNESS-OF-FIT OF THE ESTIMATED SAMPLE REGRESSION FUNCTION

Given the process by which we calculate it, we commonly refer to calculating an estimated sample regression function as determining the "best-fit" line through the observed sample data. This terminology raises an important question: Just how well does the best-fit line actually fit the observed data?

Using the term *best fit* in relation to the process of determining the estimated sample regression function can be somewhat misleading for the following reason. The OLS estimated sample regression function is only the "best fit" in the sense that it has a smaller sum of squared residuals than all other potential linear estimators, a fact that does not in any way guarantee that this "best-fit" line actually fits the sample data well. As an example, consider the scenarios in Figure 4.10 in which the same estimated sample regression function describes two different hypothetical samples.

FIGURE 4.10
Comparing the Goodness-of-Fit of Two Hypothetical Data Sets

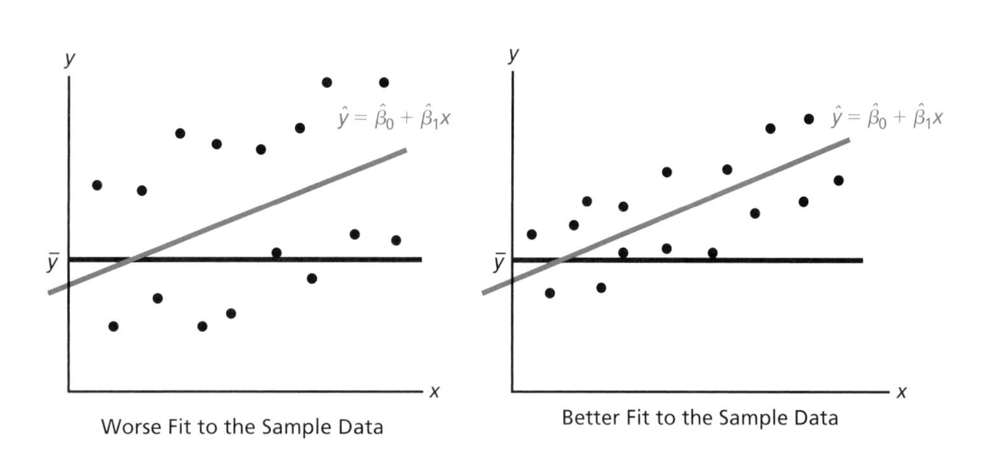

While the estimated sample regression function $\hat{y} = \hat{\beta}_0 + \hat{\beta}_1 x$ is the best-fit line in both cases, it clearly does not describe the underlying relationship between *y* and *x* equally well. Rather, because the observed data points on the right tend to fall closer to the estimated sample regression function than the observed data points on the left, we might conclude that the estimated sample regression function is a "better fit" to the data on the right than to the data on the left. The remainder of this section addresses the following question: Once we have calculated the estimated sample regression function for our observed sample data, how do we know whether our estimated sample regression function is a "better fit" or a "worse fit" to the observed sample data? We refer to this as a question of the **goodness-of-fit** of our estimated sample regression function.

goodness-of-fit
How well a model describes the observed data.

To assess the relative degree to which the total variation in *y* is explained by the joint variation between *y* and *x*, we need to calculate and compare the different types of

Venn diagram
Shows the relationship between different sets.

variation present within our observed sample data. A convenient tool for discussing the different types of variation inherent in our observed sample data is the **Venn diagram.** In the Venn diagram in Figure 4.11, the lighter circle represents the total observed variation in y while the darker circle represents the total observed variation in x.

FIGURE 4.11
Introduction to the Venn Diagram

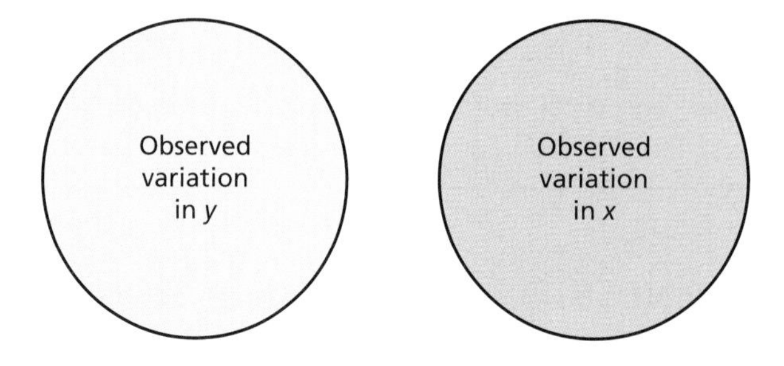

explained variation in *y*
The percentage of total variation in y that is explained by the joint variation between y and x.

unexplained variation in *y*
The percentage of total variation in y that is not explained by the joint variation between y and x.

In this case, because the circles do not overlap, we conclude that there is no observed joint variation between y and x. In Figure 4.12, the circles do overlap, meaning that there is observed joint variation between y and x. By definition, the **explained variation in *y*** is the percentage of the total variation in y that is explained by the observed joint variation between y and x, or the darkest area in Figure 4.12. Likewise, the **unexplained variation in *y*** is the percentage of the total variation in y that is not explained by the observed joint variation between y and x, or the lightest area in Figure 4.12.

FIGURE 4.12
A Venn Diagram Demonstrating Joint Variation between *y* and *x*

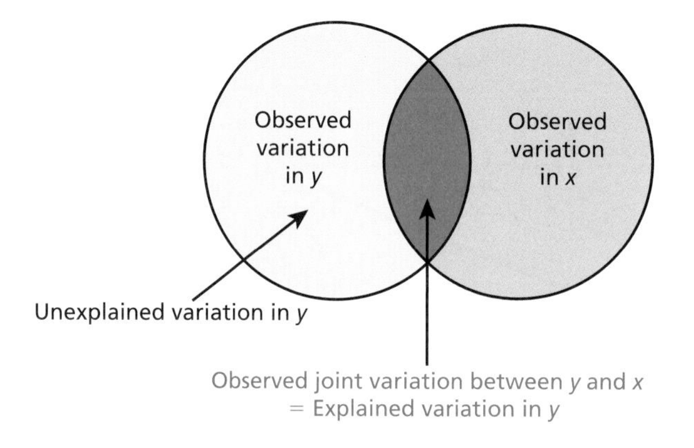

As we discuss in the remainder of this section, we can use these concepts to measure the relative goodness-of-fit of our estimated sample regression function.

Measure the Explained and Unexplained Variation in *y*

To start our discussion, consider that if no statistical relationship exists between y and x, then the estimated slope coefficient is 0 (i.e., $\hat{\beta}_1 = 0$). In such a case, because y and x are statistically unrelated, the value of x has no influence on the predicted value of y, and our best guess for each value of y is the average value of y, or $\bar{y}$ (i.e., if $\hat{\beta}_1 = 0$, then the predicted value of y is $\hat{y}_i = \hat{\beta}_0 + \hat{\beta}_1 x_i = \hat{\beta}_0 + 0x_i = \hat{\beta}_0$). In other words, if $\hat{\beta}_1 = 0$, we conclude that $\hat{y}_i = \hat{\beta}_0 = \bar{y}$. This fact relates to the concept of explained and unexplained variation in the following way. Because there is no joint variation between y and x, the total observed variation in y would equal the unexplained variation in y, a situation that would be represented as shown in Figure 4.13.

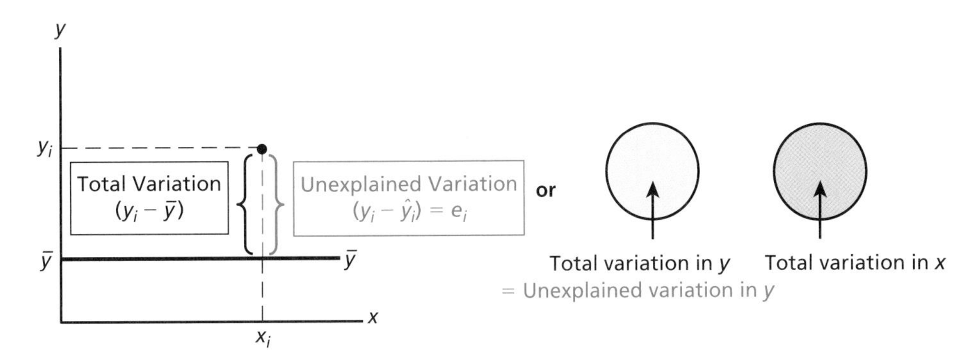

FIGURE 4.13 **A Scenario in Which the Estimated Sample Regression Function Explains None of the Variation in *y***

Suppose that a statistical relationship does exist between y and x and that, as a starting point, the estimated sample regression function perfectly explains the total observed variation in y. In such a case, each individual data point would fall exactly on the estimated sample regression function and the total observed variation in y would be perfectly explained by the joint variation between y and x, a situation that would be represented as shown in Figure 4.14.

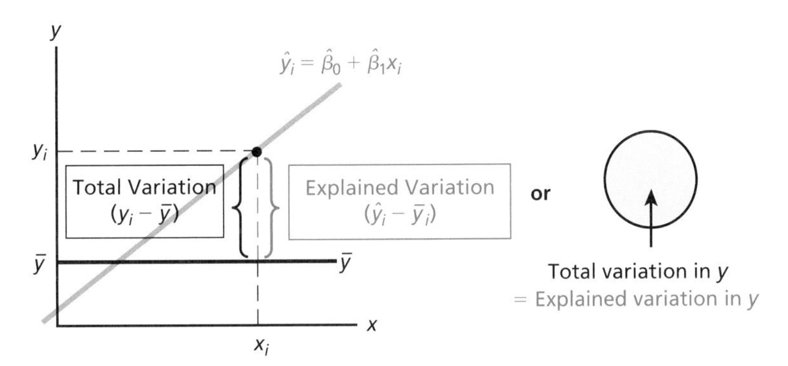

FIGURE 4.14 **A Scenario in Which the Estimated Sample Regression Function Explains All of the Variation in *y***

In more general terms, the difference between the estimated sample regression function and the no-relationship predicted value of y (i.e., the difference between the blue and black solid line in Figure 4.14) represents the percentage of the total variation in y that is explained by the observed joint variation between y and x. In other words, the explained variation in y is the difference between the predicted value of y and the mean value of y (or $\hat{y}_i - \bar{y}$).

With this in mind, we turn to the most realistic scenario that we are likely to encounter—the case in which the observed sample data points are distributed around the estimated sample regression function rather than on the estimated sample regression function. This scenario compares to the earlier examples in the following ways. First, because the observed joint variation between y and x will not explain all of the variation in y, we observe both explained and unexplained variation in y. To calculate these different types of variation, note that the observed total variation in $(y_i - \bar{y})$ is divided into two parts: the explained variation in y $(\hat{y}_i - \bar{y})$ and the unexplained variation in $(y_i - \hat{y}_i)$. We can represent this fact visually as shown in Figure 4.15.

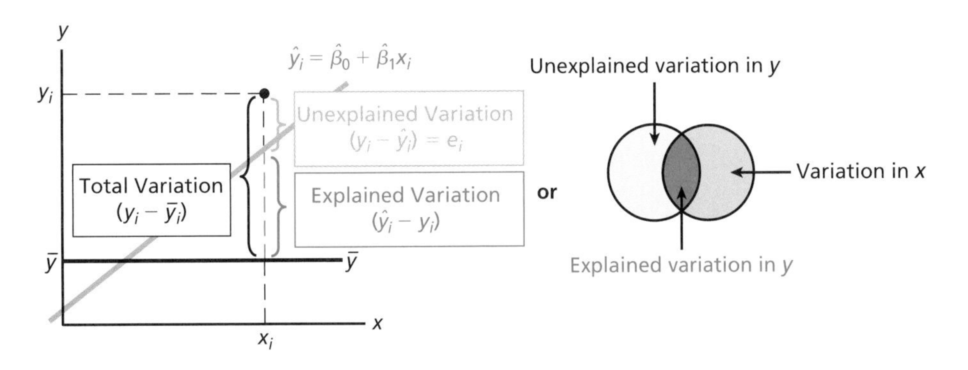

FIGURE 4.15 **A Scenario in Which the Estimated Sample Regression Function Explains Part of the Variation in *y***

While the preceding depictions include only one data point, the samples that we are likely to encounter in the real world will include multiple data points. As an example, as we will discuss in detail later, the estimated sample regression function for our 150-observation city property crime sample is depicted as shown in Figure 4.16.

FIGURE 4.16
The Estimated Sample Regression Function for Our 150-Observation City Property Crime Sample

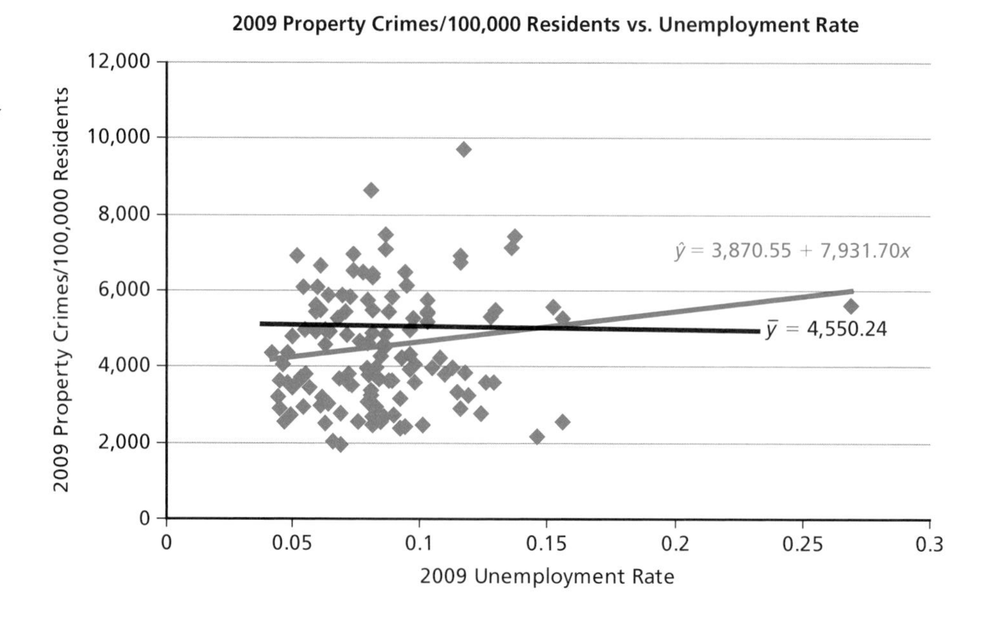

total sum of squares (TSS)
The total variation in y, which is measured by summing the squared deviations between the observed value of y and the mean value of y or $\sum_{i=1}^{n}(y_i - \bar{y})^2$

explained sum of squares (ESS)
The portion of the variation in y that is explained by the relationship between y and x, which is measured by summing the difference between the predicted value of y and the mean value of y, or $\sum_{i=1}^{n}(\hat{y}_i - \bar{y})^2$

unexplained sum of squares (USS)
The portion of the variation in y that is not explained by the relationship between y and x. It is measured by summing the squared residuals, or $\sum_{i=1}^{n}(y_i - \hat{y}_i)^2$

The scenario in Figure 4.16 differs from that in Figure 4.15 in the following way. Rather than having calculated total, explained, and unexplained variations for only one observation, we have them for all 150 observations. This makes it more difficult to interpret our calculated measures of variation. Fortunately, we can convert the 150 individual values into one sample value by aggregating from the individual level to the sample level. While a first impulse for this aggregation might be to sum the calculated values across all of the individual observations, such an approach will not work because the positive and negative deviations cancel so that the aggregated values always sum to 0. Again, we solve this problem by squaring the value for each individual observation before summing them up. In other words, we calculate our aggregate measures of the total, explained, and unexplained variation present in our sample by (1) calculating the variation for each individual observation in the sample, (2) squaring that calculated value for each individual observation, and (3) summing the squared values across all n observations in the sample. Doing so provides the following important values.

Our aggregate measure of the total variation present in the sample data is referred to as the **total sum of squares (TSS)** and is calculated as

$$TSS = \sum_{i=1}^{n}(y_i - \bar{y})^2 \qquad \textbf{4.7.1}$$

Our aggregate measure of the explained variation present in the sample data is referred to as the **explained sum of squares (ESS)** and is calculated as

$$ESS = \sum_{i=1}^{n}(\hat{y}_i - \bar{y})^2 \qquad \textbf{4.7.2}$$

Note that while "explained sum of squares" is our preferred terminology, this value is called the "regression sum of squares" in Excel or the "model sum of squares" in other statistical programs.

Our aggregate measure of unexplained variation present in the sample data is referred to as the **unexplained sum of squares (USS)** and is calculated as

$$USS = \sum_{i=1}^{n}(y_i - \hat{y}_i)^2 \qquad \textbf{4.7.3}$$

Note that while "unexplained sum of squares" is our preferred terminology, this value is called the "residual sum of squares" in Excel and the "error sum of squares" in other statistical programs.

From the preceding discussion, it should be clear that within the observed sample

$$TSS = ESS + USS \qquad \textbf{4.7.4}$$

To calculate these values, we need to calculate the predicted value of y for each observation and sample mean value of y before using those values to calculate the TSS, ESS, and USS. For our 150-observation city property crime sample the calculations look like Table 4.7.

TABLE 4.7 Calculated Values Required to Determine the TSS, ESS, and USS for Our 150-Observation City Property Crime Sample

Metro Area	Property Crimes/ 100,000 (y_i)	Unemployment Rate (x_i)	($\hat{y}_i$)	$(y_i - \bar{y})^2$	$(\hat{y}_i - \bar{y})^2$	$(y_i - \hat{y}_i)^2$
Santa Barbara-Santa Maria-Goleta	2.528	0.076	4473.36	4,091,250.44	5,911.25	3,786,135.05
Honolulu	3,679	0.057	4322.66	758.697.46	51,795.83	414,022.02
Fort Smith	5,861	0.070	4425.77	1,717,756.02	15,493.99	2,059,531.43
Hattiesburg	4,568	0.063	4370.25	310.83	32,398.84	39,056.49
Billiings	4,360	0.042	4203.68	36,054.28	120,105.58	24,549.52
Rome	5,198	0.103	4687.51	419,552.91	18.843.42	260,567.08
Napa	2,554	0.085	4544.74	3,983,689.45	30.24	3,961,767.33
Reno-Sparks	3,814	0.110	4743.04	542,580.59	37,169.24	863,773.11
Davenport-Moline-Rock Island	4,914	0.065	4386.11	132,329.34	26,939.76	278,683.01
Chico	2,776	0.124	4854.08	3,147,678.68	92,316.97	4,318,112.83
Sebastian-Vero Beach	3,216	0.119	4814.42	1,779,846.86	69,790.32	2,554,523.19
Texarkana	6,911	0.052	4283.00	5,572,183.12	71,420.15	6.905,294.47
Midland	3,637	0.045	4227.48	834,897.96	104,178.80	349,233.84
St. George	2,043	0.066	4394.04	6,287,850.20	24,398.96	5,528,879.52

TSS
$\sum(y_i - \bar{y})^2 = 335{,}294{,}649.93$

ESS
$\sum(\hat{y}_i - \bar{y})^2 = 8{,}725{,}496.72$

USS
$\sum(y_i - \hat{y}_i)^2 = 326{,}569{,}153.21$

In words, based on the preceding calculations, we conclude that for our sample of U.S. cities, the estimated TSS, ESS, and USS are

$$TSS = 335{,}294{,}649.93$$
$$ESS = 8{,}725{,}496.72 \qquad \textbf{4.7.5}$$
$$USS = 326{,}569{,}153.21$$

Unfortunately, because these measures depend on the chosen units of measurement, we are unable to judge the goodness-of-fit of our estimated sample regression function by looking at these values alone (i.e., it is impossible to tell whether 335,294,649.93 is a relatively large or relatively small TSS). Instead, we must convert these numbers into values that are more meaningful.

Two Potential Measures of the Relative Goodness-of-Fit of Our Estimated Sample Regression Function

Generally speaking, the estimated sample regression function is a better fit for the observed sample data if (1) the aggregate explained variation in y is a larger percentage of the aggregate total variation in y (i.e., the *ESS* is a larger percentage of the *TSS*) or if (2) the aggregate unexplained variation in y is relatively smaller (i.e., the *USS* is smaller).

coefficient of determination (or the R^2) The total variation in y that can be explained by x. It is the square of the correlation coefficient between y and $\hat{y}$.

Notation:

R^2 Coefficient of determination

These facts form the basis for our two preferred measures of the relative goodness-of-fit of our estimated sample regression function.

The Coefficient of Determination (R^2)

Our first measure of the relative goodness-of-fit of an estimated sample regression function is the percentage of the total observed variation in y (the TSS) that is explained by the observed joint variation between y and x (the ESS). We refer to this value as the **coefficient of determination,** or the R-squared (R^2) of the estimated sample regression function. We calculate this value as

$$R^2 = \frac{ESS}{TSS} = \frac{\sum(\hat{y}_i - \bar{y}_i)^2}{\sum(y_i - \bar{y}_i)^2} \qquad \textbf{4.7.6}$$

To make sense of this value, we need to consider the range of potential outcomes that can be observed for this calculation. As long as the regression equation has an intercept, the calculated values must fall between 0 and 1 because (1) calculated variations can never be negative, meaning that the quotient of the calculated ESS and TSS values can never be less than 0, and (2) the observed joint variation between y and x can never explain more than the total observed variation in y, meaning that the ESS can never exceed the TSS and therefore the quotient of their values can never exceed 1.

As is often the case, the lower and upper bounds of the range of possible outcomes have specific interpretations. To see this, start by considering that the calculated R^2 can only equal 0 if the calculated ESS equals 0, an event that can only occur if there is no statistical relationship between y and x (in which case all observed data points lie on the horizontal line $\bar{y}$). Conversely, the calculated R^2 can only equal 1 if the calculated ESS equals the calculated TSS, an event that can only occur if the observed joint variation between y and x perfectly explains the total variation in y (in which case all observed data points lie on the line $\hat{y}_i = \hat{\beta}_0 + \hat{\beta}_1 x_i$).

Because we are unlikely to ever observe a sample for which there is either no relationship or a perfectly defined relationship between y and x, we need to focus on the interpretation of calculated R^2 values that fall between 0 and 1. As might be expected, the closer the calculated R^2 falls to a particular bound, the more similar the data are to the interpretation of that bound. As a general rule then, we interpret calculated R^2 values closer to 1 as indicating that the estimated sample regression function does a better job explaining the underlying relationship between y and x, while we interpret calculated R^2 values closer to 0 as indicating that the estimated sample regression function does a poorer job explaining the underlying relationship between y and x.

Visually, this interpretation can be depicted as shown in Figure 4.17.

For our 150-observation city property crime sample, the coefficient of determination is calculated as

$$R^2 = \frac{ESS}{TSS} = \frac{8{,}725{,}496.72}{335{,}294{,}649.93} = 0.0260 \qquad \textbf{4.7.7}$$

We interpret this value as saying that within our sample of 150 cities, 2.60 percent of the total observed variation in property crimes rates is explained by the observed joint variation between property crime rates and unemployment rates. Is this value relatively large or relatively small? Unfortunately, as we discuss next, there is no set decision rule for answering this question.

The Importance of the Calculated R^2

As discussed earlier, if we calculate $R^2 = 1$, then we have fully explained the total observed variation in y through the observed joint variation between y and x. Does this mean that we should always strive for a calculated R^2 value of 1? No! In fact, we could always generate a calculated R^2 value of 1 by including the dependent variable (or some multiple of the dependent variable) as an independent variable in the estimated sample

FIGURE 4.17
Using the Ratio of the *ESS* to the *TSS* (the R^2) to Define the Relative Goodness-of-Fit of the Estimated Sample Regression Function

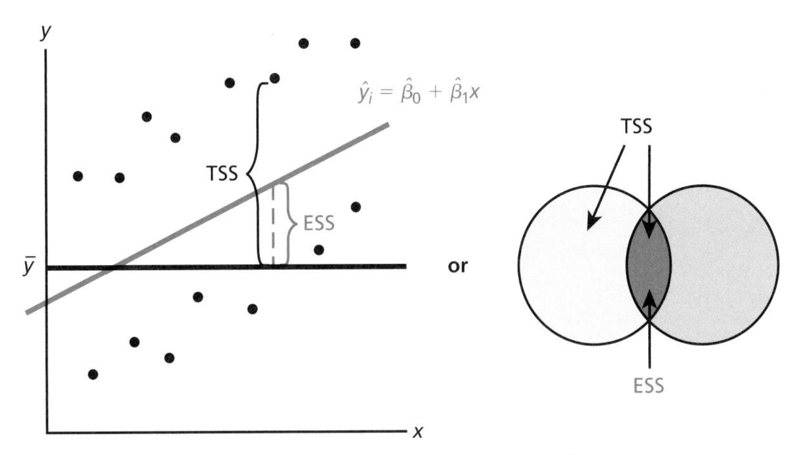

ESS **smaller percentage of *TSS* ∴ R^2 smaller**
→Estimated Sample Regression Function is a Worse Fit for Observed Sample Data

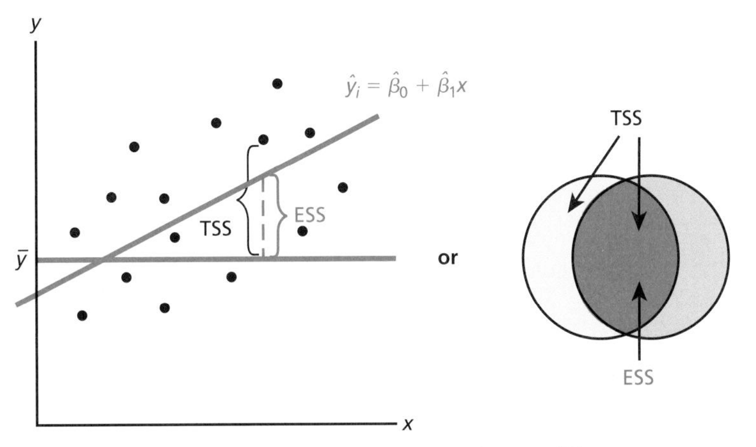

ESS **larger percentage of *TSS* ∴ R^2 larger**
→Estimated Sample Regression Function is a Better Fit for Observed Sample Data

regression function. As an example, suppose that we estimate $\hat{y}_i = \hat{\beta}_0 + \hat{\beta}_1(y_i + 5)$. Because the observed variation in $y + 5$ perfectly explains the observed variation in y, we calculate that $R^2 = 1$.

For this reason, we caution that it is incorrect to argue that the goal of regression analysis is to achieve a calculated R^2 that is as close to 1 as possible. In point of fact, the correct interpretation of the calculated R^2 is much more nuanced, especially given that (for reasons that will be discussed later) with cross-section data (such as those in our city property crime example), it is likely that the estimated coefficient of determination is closer to 0 than to 1. In summary, we strongly caution against considering this statistic the only measure of the relative quality of the estimated sample regression function. We return to this issue in later chapters.

The Standard Error of the Estimated Sample Regression Function ($s_{y|x}$)

Our second measure of the relative goodness-of-fit of our estimated sample regression function is a function of the aggregate distance that individual observations tend to fall from the estimated sample regression function. We refer to this measure as the **standard error of the sample regression function, ($s_{y|x}$)**, and we calculate its value as

standard error of the sample regression function
A measure of how far, on average, the points fall away from the line.

$$s_{y|x} = \sqrt{\frac{USS}{n-k-1}} = \sqrt{\frac{\sum(y_i - \hat{y}_i)^2}{n-k-1}} \qquad \textbf{4.7.8}$$

Notation:

$s_{y|x}$ Standard error of sample regression function

degrees of freedom
The number of values in the final calculation that are free to vary.

Notation:

$(n - k - 1)$ Degrees of freedom in a simple linear regression

k Number of independent variables in the regression model (not including the intercept)

The term in the numerator of formula 4.7.8 makes sense because the unexplained sum of squares (the *USS*) represents the total vertical distance that each observed data point falls from the estimated sample regression function. The term in the denominator, $n - k - 1$, is the number of **degrees of freedom** of the estimated sample regression function, a value that indicates the number of independent pieces of information that remain after the model is estimated. As the formula 4.7.8 value indicates, the number of degrees of freedom depends on two factors: the number of observations in the sample (n) and the number of variables being estimated ($k + 1$). In this notation, k represents the number of independent variables included in the estimated sample regression function and $+1$ represents the intercept of the estimated sample regression function. Accordingly, in the case of simple linear regression, because we are only considering one independent variable, it follows that $k = 1$ and $(n - k - 1) = n - 2$.

As will be discussed in later chapters, a sample regression function cannot be estimated if the number of independent variables (k) is greater than the number of observations (n). More generally, the greater the difference between n and k, the more pieces of information go into estimating the sample regression function. As such, we are faced with an important trade-off between the number of observations and the number of independent variables. In particular, looking at formula 4.7.8, it should be clear that the number of degrees of freedom is a positive function of the number of observations (n) and a negative function of the number of independent variables included in the estimated sample regression function (k), meaning that increases in the sample size increase the number of degrees of freedom, while increases in the number of independent variables decrease the number of degrees of freedom. The larger the $n - k - 1$ term is, the smaller the standard error of the regression. This implies that the more independent pieces of information that we use to estimate the regression function, the better we do fitting a line through the data.

We interpret the calculated value of the standard error of the estimated sample regression function, $s_{y|x}$, as follows. Because we are dividing the unexplained variation in y by a function of the number of observations in the sample, we can interpret the value as indicating the degree to which each individual observation falls from the estimated sample regression function, on average. Note that this calculated value must fall between 0 and ∞. Why? Because calculated variations can never be less than 0, quotient in formula 4.7.8 can never be less than 0. On the other hand, because the calculated value of the *USS* does not have a clearly defined upper bound, the maximum value it can take on is ∞. With these boundaries in mind, we can interpret the calculated value of $s_{y|x}$ as follows. As determined earlier, we know that the larger the calculated *USS,* the further the observed data points tend to fall from the estimated sample regression function, while the smaller the calculated *USS,* the closer the observed data points tend to fall to the estimated sample regression function. Accordingly, as a general rule, the larger the calculated value of $s_{y|x}$, the worse the fit of the estimated sample regression function, while the smaller the calculated value of $s_{y|x}$, the better the fit of the estimated sample regression function.

Visually, this interpretation can be depicted as shown in Figure 4.18.

For our 150-observation city property crime sample, the standard error of the sample regression function is calculated as

$$s_{y|x} = \sqrt{\frac{326{,}569{,}153.21}{150 - 1 - 1}} = \sqrt{2{,}206{,}548.33} = 1{,}485.45 \qquad \textbf{4.7.9}$$

This calculation indicates that, on average, observed property crime rates per 100,000 citizens in our 150-city sample fall 1,485.45 away from the estimated sample regression function. Again, because the calculated value depends on the chosen unit of denomination, there is no definitive answer to whether this calculated value is relatively small or relatively large.

Now that we have learned how to calculate and correctly interpret the preceding statistics. we can take advantage of modern technology to reduce our workload by asking statistical programs—such as Excel, Stata, and SAS—to calculate the estimated sample regression function for us.

With this in mind, we turn to discussing Excel regression output.

FIGURE 4.18
Using the Relative Size of the *USS* (the $s_{y|x}$) to Define the Relative Goodness-of-Fit of the Estimated Sample Regression Function

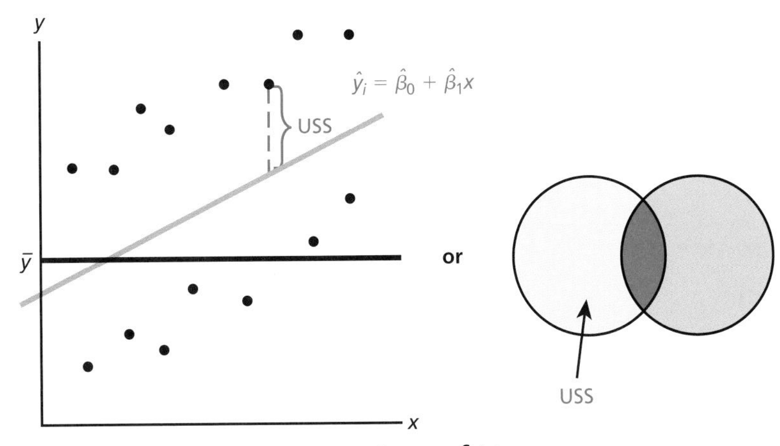

***USS* larger ∴ $s_{y|x}$ larger**
→Estimated Sample Regression Function is a Worse Fit for Observed Sample Data

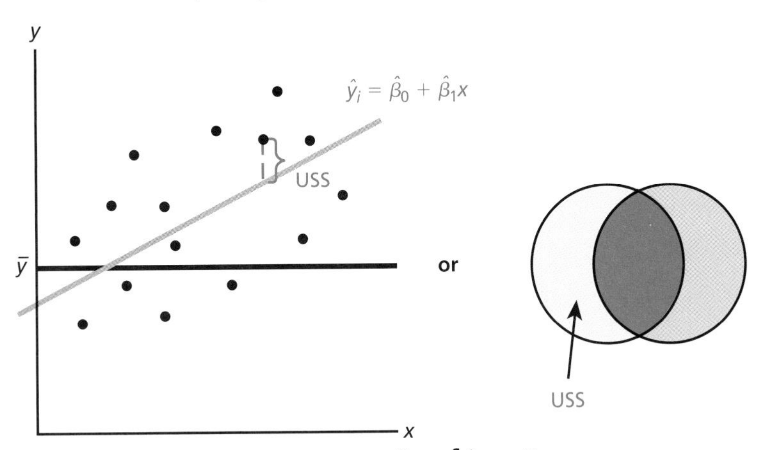

***USS* smaller ∴ $s_{y|x}$ smaller**
→Estimated Sample Regression Function is a Better Fit for Observed Sample Data

EMPIRICAL RESEARCH TOOL 4.4: ASSESSING THE GOODNESS-OF-FIT OF THE ESTIMATED SAMPLE SIMPLE LINEAR REGRESSION FUNCTION

Goal:
Numerically assess how well the estimated sample regression function fits the observed sample data.

Tools:
The coefficient of determination and the standard error of the estimated sample regression function.

Notation:
R^2 Coefficient of determination
$s_{y|x}$ Standard error of the estimated sample regression function

Formulas:

Coefficient of determination $$R^2 = \frac{ESS}{TSS} = \frac{\sum(\hat{y}_i - \bar{y}_i)^2}{\sum(y_i - \bar{y}_i)^2}$$

Standard error of the estimated sample regression function

$$s_{y|x} = \sqrt{\frac{USS}{n-k-1}} = \sqrt{\frac{\sum(y_i - \hat{y}_i)^2}{n-k-1}}$$

4.8 UNDERSTAND HOW TO READ REGRESSION OUTPUT IN EXCEL

After running a simple linear regression in Excel, we receive output in a table that looks like Table 4.8.

TABLE 4.8 Regression Output in Excel for the Simple Linear Regression for Our 150-Observation City Property Crime Sample

SUMMARY OUTPUT	
Regression Statistics	
Multiple R	0.161317606
R Square	0.02602337
Adjusted R Square	0.019442447
Standard Error	1485.4455
Observations	150

ANOVA

	df	SS	MS	F	Significance F
Regression	1	8725496.72	8725496.72	3.954364648	0.048593895
A	148	326569153.2	2206548.333		
Total	149	335294649.9			

	Coefficients	Standard Error	t Stat	p-value	Lower 95%	Upper 95%
Intercept	3870.548736	362.683323	10.67197881	4.48367E-20	3153.842076	4587.25540
April 2009 Jobless Rate	7931.702382	3988.669503	1.98855844	0.048593895	49.60298894	15813.80178

Once we learn to read such output tables, we see that they contain all of the values calculated in this chapter. In particular, we have Table 4.9.

Given that everything we have discussed in this chapter is presented here in a simple, compact form that is generated in a matter of seconds, this is clearly our preferred method for performing simple linear regression analysis (as opposed to performing the calculations by hand).

TABLE 4.9 Explanation of the Regression Output in Excel for the Simple Linear Regression for Our 150-Observation City Property Crime Sample

SUMMARY OUTPUT		
Regression Statistics		
Multiple R	0.161317606	
R Square	0.02602337	← *Coefficient of Determination* (R^2)
Adjusted R Square	0.019442447	
Standard Error	1485.4455	← *Standard Error of the Sample Regression Function* ($s_{y\|x}$)
Observations	150	← *Number of Observations* (n)

ANOVA

	df	SS	MS	F	Significance F
Regression	1	*ESS* → 8725496.7	8725496.72	3.954364648	0.048593895
Residual	$(n-k-1)$ → 148	*USS* → 326569153.2	2206548.33		
Total	$(n-1)$ → 149	*TSS* → 335294649.9			

	Coefficients	Standard Error	t Stat	p-value	Lower 95%	Upper 95%
Intercept $\hat{\beta}_0$ →	3870.548736	362.683323	10.67197881	4.48367E-20	3153.842076	4587.25540
Unemployment Rate $\hat{\beta}_1$ →	7931.702382	3988.669503	1.98855844	0.048593895	49.60298894	15813.80178

EXCEL EXAMPLE 4.2

Using the regression analysis tool to estimate the sample regression function by OLS

Regression Analysis in Excel's Toolpak:

1. In the "Data" tab, click the "Data Analysis" toolpak.

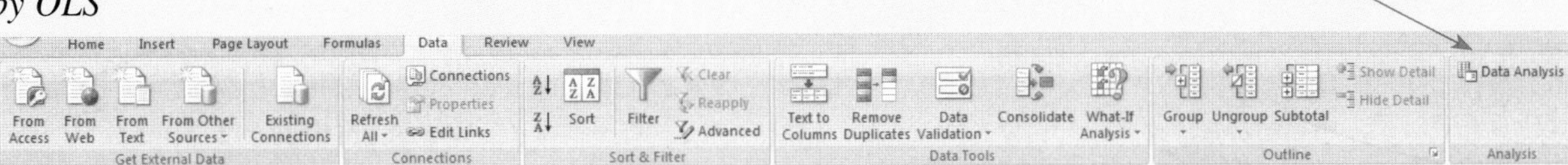

2. In the "Data Analysis" window, highlight "Regression" and click "OK".

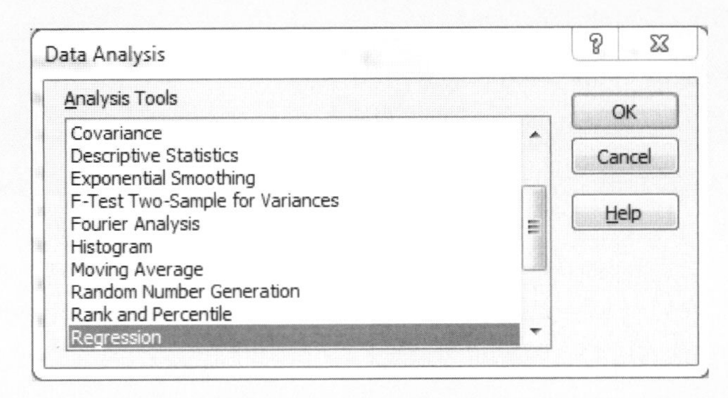

3. Click the tab next to the "Input Y Range" window, and highlight the observations for the dependent variable, including the variable name (**$C$1:$C$201**).
4. Click the tab next to the "Input X Range" window, and highlight the observations for the dependent variable, including the variable name (**$D$1:$D$201**).
5. Check the "Labels" box because we included the variable name in the preceding steps.
6. Check the "Output Range" tab, and highlight the desired first cell for the output (**$F$3**).

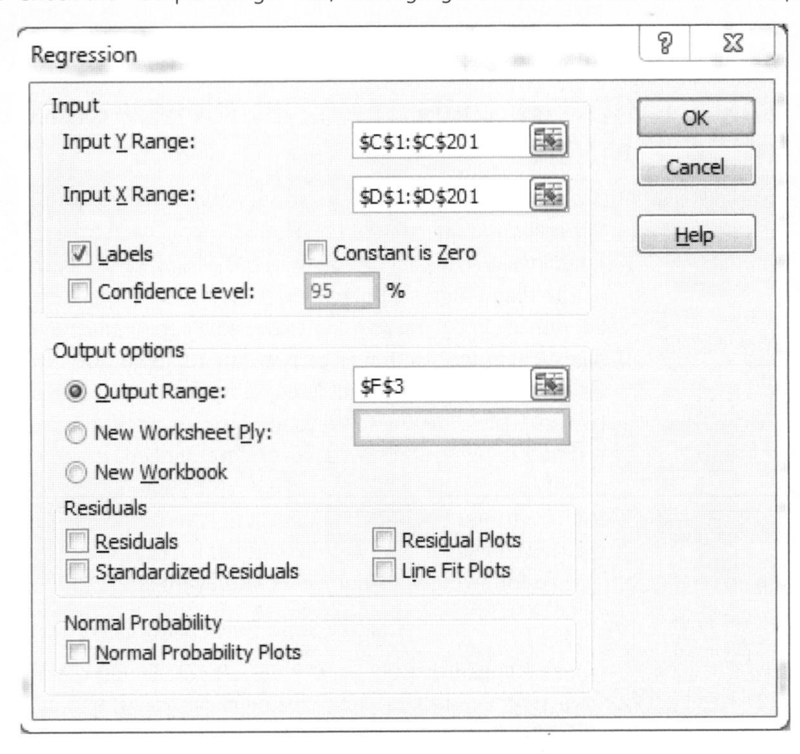

7. Click "OK" to run the regression.

SUMMARY OUTPUT

Regression Statistics	
Multiple R	0.39238316
R Square	0.153964544
Adjusted R Square	0.149691638
Standard Error	6262440.007
Observations	200

ANOVA

	df	SS	MS	F	Significance F
Regression	1	1.41314E+15	1.41314E+15	36.03274498	9.11178E−09
Residual	198	7.76519E+15	3.92182E+13		
Total	199	9.17833E+15			

	Coefficients	Standard Error	*t* Stat	*p*-value	Lower 95%	Upper 95%
Intercept	10792308.27	463406.70	23.28906398	1.29914E−58	9878462.178	11706154.36
Profits ($ millions)	1015.443772	169.16371	6.002728128	9.11178E−09	681.8499832	1349.037561

Based on these results, we conclude that the estimated sample regression function is

$$\widehat{Compensation}_i = \$10{,}792{,}308.27 + \$1{,}015.44\widehat{Profit}$$

which indicates that (1) for a firm with 0 profit, we would expect the CEO to receive $10,792,308.27 in compensation and (2) on average, we would expect each additional $1 million in profit to be associated with $1,015.44 more in CEO compensation.

The tools introduced in this chapter provide an indication of the degree to which linear correlation exists between two random varables of interest. There is an important question related to the concept of statistical correlation: How should we react to that fact that two random variables are linearly correlated? Should we actively change our behavior? If not, why not?

4.9 UNDERSTAND THE DIFFERENCE BETWEEN CORRELATION AND CAUSATION

causation
Said to exist between two random variables if changes in the value of one is responsible for changes in the value of the other.

spurious correlation
Occurs when there is correlation between two random variables that does not result from a relationship between those two variables but from their relationship to other variables.

Statisticians refer to the question of what to make of observed correlation between two variables as a question of correlation versus **causation.** To see why this question is important, consider that according to Lucas et al. (2003), married people are happier and in better health than unmarried people. On the basis of this knowledge, should we recommend that an unmarried person propose to the next person that he or she meets (or to his or her current significant other) in hopes of becoming happier and healthier? Not necessarily. Why not? Because it is entirely possible that despite the observed statistical correlation between these two variables, they actually have little or no true relationship to each other (a situation referred to as **spurious correlation**). Indeed, the high divorce rate in the United States might suggest that it is not marriage itself that makes married people happier and healthier. Rather, it might be that healthier and happier people are more likely to get and to remain married (in which case there would not be a causal relationship between the two variables).

The following well-known examples illustrate this important point:

Can the Super Bowl help you corner the market?

In 33 of the first 42 years (or 80 percent of the time) after the first Super Bowl was played in 1967, the stock market increased in calendar years following a National Football Conference (NFC) victory and decreased in calendar year following an American Football Conference (AFC) victory. (Source: International Dairy Foods Association)

Does education pay?

Cheesman, Day, and Newburger (2002) estimate that lifetime earnings (from ages 25 through 64) increase from an average of $1.2 million for high school graduates to an average of $2.1 million for college graduates to an average of $2.5 million for master's degree recipients to an average of $3.4 million for PhD recipients to an average of $4.4 million for professional degree recipients.

Is ice cream deadly?

Nearly two-thirds of the 3,600 annual accidental drownings in the United States occur in June, July, and August, while nearly 80 percent of the $23 billion in annual U.S. ice cream sales occur during those same three months. (Sources: eMedicineHealth; International Dairy Foods Association)

Does it matter what time you drive home?

According to the National Traffic Scorecard calculated by INRIX about the traffic in Honolulu, Hawaii, "If you happen to be driving on a Thursday from 5 p.m. to 6 p.m. on its (Honolulu's) main highways, you're no longer in the Aloha State, you're in the worst place and worst hour of any single roadway in the U.S., taking 88 percent more time to get where you're going than if there were no congestion." (Source: *Honolulu Star-Bulletin,* June 18, 2008)

The random variables in all four examples exhibit statistical correlation. While true, the more important question to ask is whether we should alter our behavior on the basis of the observed correlations. Namely, should we convert all of our assets to stocks if an NFC team wins this year's Super Bowl? Should we invest in a college education to increase our lifetime earnings? Should the government ban ice cream to reduce accidental drowning? Should we avoid rush hour if at all possible in order to reduce our travel time?

In order, the answers to these questions are: no, yes, no, yes. Why? Consider first the no answers. While it may be true that more often than not the stock market moves in a certain direction depending on the identity of the Super Bowl champion, there is no rational reason to believe that the conference affiliation of the Super Bowl champion actually *causes* the stock market to increase or decrease. Likewise, while the positive correlation between ice cream sales and accidental drowning in the summer months is no coincidence (warmer weather increases both the number of swimmers and the number of ice cream eaters), there is no rational reason to believe that eating ice cream *causes* swimmers to drown accidentally (even if consumed within a half-hour prior). In both cases, the presence of correlation between the two random variables provides no information as to the root causes of the observed outcomes (stock market movement and accidental drowning).

Consider next the "yes" answers. We might choose to alter our behavior on the basis of the observed correlations between education and earnings and congestion and travel time because it seems reasonable that additional education actually does *cause* increased earnings and that increased congestion actually does *cause* increased travel time. We refer to relationships in which changes in one random variable *cause* changes in another random variable as relationships exhibiting causation.

It is important to note that the presence of correlation does not imply causation and that the presence of causation does not imply correlation. Indeed, as the Super Bowl winner and accidental drowning examples illustrate, it is possible for two random variables to be linearly correlated without being causally related. Likewise, it is possible for two random variables to be causally related while having an estimated correlation that is either very small or zero because the relationship may be nonlinear.

This discussion introduces the obvious question, "If two random variables are determined to be correlated, how can we be certain that changes in one random variable actually cause changes in the other random variable?" We return to this very important question in later chapters.

The upshot of this chapter's discussion is that we should be careful in placing too much importance on the mere presence of correlation between two random variables. Rather, once we determine that statistical correlation exists, we should think carefully about whether that correlation might reasonably suggest causation. If it does, then we should explore the potential correlation and causation further. If it does not, then we should likely focus our research elsewhere.

ADDITIONS TO OUR EMPIRICAL RESEARCH TOOLKIT

In this chapter we have introduced a number of tools that will prove valuable when performing empirical research. They include:

- The population regression model and the sample regression function.
- The estimated sample regression function.
- Predicting outcomes based on our estimated sample regression function.
- Assessing the goodness-of-fit of the estimated sample regression function.
- Reading regression output in Excel.

OUR NEW EMPIRICAL TOOLS IN PRACTICE: USING WHAT WE HAVE LEARNED IN THIS CHAPTER

Using the tools discussed in this chapter, our former student was able to determine that the estimated slope coefficient and estimate intercept were

$$\hat{\beta}_1 = \frac{\sum_{i=1}^{n}(x_i - \bar{x})(y_i - \bar{y})}{\sum_{i=1}^{n}(x_i - \bar{x})^2} = \frac{-118.48}{3{,}060.67} = -0.0387$$

and

$$\hat{\beta}_0 = \bar{y} - \hat{\beta}_1\bar{x} = 3.0693 - (-0.0387)(4.6667) = 3.2500$$

Superimposing this estimated sample regression function over the scatter diagram between college GPA and hours of video games played per week, results in Figure 4.19.

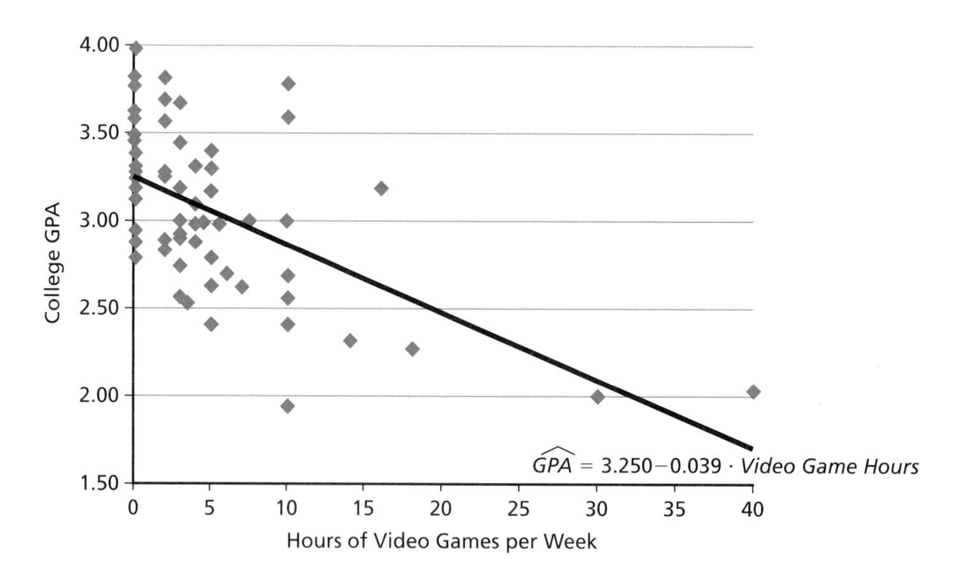

FIGURE 4.19
Scatter Diagram with Estimated Sample Regression Function for Our Student's Empirical Research Project

On the basis of these values, the student concluded that his roommate was likely performing worse in college due to the number of hours he spent playing video games rather than studying. As a result of his analysis, our student was able to report to his roommate that each additional hour spent playing video games likely decreased his overall GPA by 0.039 point on a 4-point scale. Combined with the fact that the roommate admitted to playing 25 hours of video games a week, our student was able to suggest that student's GPA is nearly 1 full point lower than it might have been had he chosen to play 0 hours of video games, a result the student determined as follows:

Predicted GPA with Video Game Hours = *25*

$$\widehat{GPA} = 3.250 - 0.039 \cdot 25 = 3.250 - 0.968 = 2.282$$

Predicted GPA with Video Game Hours = *0*

$$\widehat{GPA} = 3.250 - 0.039 \cdot 0 = 3.250$$

Difference between Predicted GPAs

$$3.250 - 2.282 = 0.968$$

Our student was also able to assess the relative goodness-of-fit his estimated sample regression function. For this application, the relevant calculated sums of squares are

$$TSS = \sum_{i=1}^{n}(y_i - \bar{y})^2 = 14.094$$

$$ESS = \sum_{i=1}^{n}(\hat{y}_i - \bar{y})^2 = 4.587$$

$$USS = \sum_{i=1}^{n}(y_i - \hat{y}_i)^2 = 9.057$$

and the calculated coefficient of determination and the calculated standard error of the estimated sample regression function are

$$R^2 = \frac{ESS}{TSS} = \frac{4.587}{14.094} = 0.3255$$

and

$$s_{y|x} = \sqrt{\frac{USS}{n-k-1}} = \sqrt{\frac{9.057}{64}} = 0.3854$$

The first of these measures suggested that in the student's sample, the variation in hours of video game play per week explain nearly 33 percent of the total variation in student GPA. The second suggested that the individual data points fall an average of 0.3854 away from the estimated sample regression function.

Based on this analysis, our former student was well on his way to producing a successful simple linear regression empirical research project.

LOOKING AHEAD TO CHAPTER 5

We have now learned how to determine the estimated sample regression function and how to assess the degree to which that function explains the linear relationship between y and x that is observed in our specific sample drawn from the population of interest. While providing valuable information, these tools do not yet tell us anything about the unobserved population parameters. Chapter 5 introduces hypothesis testing in linear regression analysis, which is the primary tool we use to gather such information.

Problems

4.1 Explain in the following examples why the two variables may be spuriously correlated.

a. Men who have beards tend to be happier than men who don't have beards.

b. House fires that have a lot of firemen at them tend to have more monetary damage than those house fires with fewer firemen.

c. People who are married tend to report being happier than those who are not married.

d. People who go to bed with their shoes on tend to wake up with a headache.

4.2 Consider the following scatterplot:

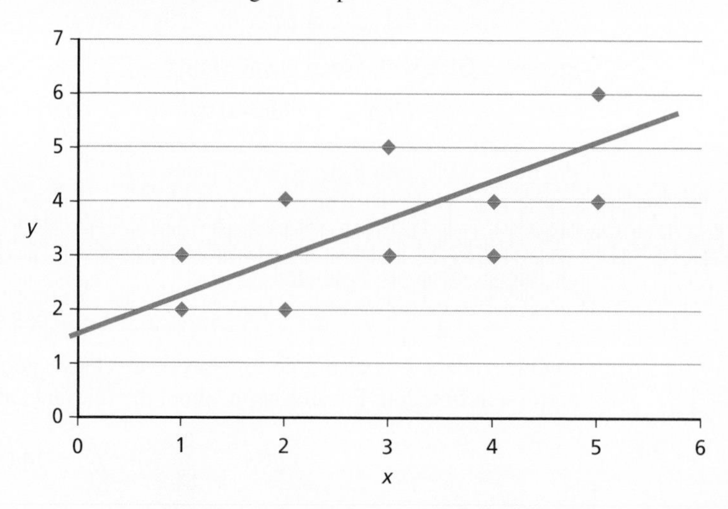

Using simple linear regression analysis, the equation for a line through the data is estimated to be $\hat{y} = 1.9 + 0.55x$. For each of the x values, calculate the observed y, the predicted y, and the residual.

4.3 For the following four regression equations, explain what the slope and intercept mean.

a. $\widehat{wage} = 2.05 + 1.32 education$, where wage is dollars earned per hour and education is number of years the person went to school.

b. $\widehat{GPA} = 1.14 + 0.23 hours\ study$, where GPA is measured in points and hours study is the number of hours spent studying in a week.

c. $\widehat{sleep} = 10.33 - 0.44 work$, where sleep is hours spent sleeping per night and work is the number of hours worked per day.

d. $\widehat{savings} = 586 + 0.15 salary$, where savings is dollars saved in the bank and the salary is the number of dollars earned in a year.

4.4 Name the type of error that has occurred in each of the following circumstances.

a. You specified the equation as $wage = \beta_0 + \beta_1 education + \varepsilon$, but wage is also determined by the ability of the person.

b. You specified the equation as a linear function, but the scatterplot has a quadratic shape.

c. When collecting data to determine the relationship between GPA and hours spent studying every week, most students do not know the exact hours they spent studying each week and have to give an estimate.

d. You eat lunch at the same cafeteria every day. Some days you choose to eat a hamburger and other days you choose to eat a taco, even though these choices cost the same amount and you have the same income to spend each day.

4.5 For the following four regressions, predict the value of the y variable for the value of the x variable given.

a. $\widehat{wage} = 2.05 + 1.32 education$, where wage is dollars earned per hour and education is number of years the person went to school. Predict the wage if a person has 15 years of education.

b. $\widehat{GPA} = 1.14 + 0.23 hours\ study$, where GPA is measured in points and hours study is the number of hours spent studying in a week. Predict the GPA for a student who studies 11 hours a week.

c. $\widehat{sleep} = 10.33 - 0.44 work$, where sleep is hours spent sleeping per night and work is the number of hours worked per day. Predict the amount of sleep a person gets a night if they work 7 hours a day.

d. $\widehat{savings} = 586 + 0.15salary$, where savings is dollars saved in the bank and the salary is the number of dollars earned in a year. Predict the amount of savings a person has if they earn $25,000 a year.

4.6 Grinfield Service Company's marketing director is interested in analyzing the relationship between her company's sales and the advertising dollars spent. In the course of her analysis, she selected a random sample of 20 weeks and recorded the sales for each week and the amount spent on advertising. The summary statistics are for 20 observations.

	Sales ($)	**Advertising ($)**
Sample mean	3,353	298
Standard deviation	1,408	133

$$Cov(X, Y) = 170{,}436.10$$

a. Find the correlation coefficient between sales and advertising. What does it mean?

b. Find the least squares line that shows how weekly sales (y) is related to advertising dollars (x).

c. According to the least squares line, how is weekly sales related to advertising dollars? What does the intercept mean?

4.7 What is the standard error of the regression model in the following scenarios?

a. $SSUnexplained = 83$, $n - 2 = 58$.

b. $SSTotal = 1234$, $SSExplained = 865$, $n = 145$.

c. $SSExplained = 56$, $SSTotal = 78$, $n = 78$.

Exercises

E4.1 For each of the following three data sets, create a scatterplot, calculate the regression line, determine the R^2, and explain what the slope means.

a. x	y	b. x	y	c. x	y
1	5	3	36	3	3
2	3	4	30	4	2
3	4	6	17	6	2
5	7	9	16	7	2
6	10	9	24	9	1
7	9	10	12	10	3
8	12	11	20	11	3
8	9	12	15	12	2

E4.2 Consider the two data sets listed in **house.xls.** In the first data set, the prices of houses are listed in dollars and the square-footage is listed in feet, while the second data set lists the prices of houses in hundreds of dollars and the square footage in yards. Calculate the covariance and the correlation coefficient for both data sets, and comment on the similarities and differences between your findings. Is this what you expected?

E4.3 A business owner is interested in how the cost of shipping a package is related to the distance a package is shipped. To this end, data have been collected and are contained in **ship.xls.**

a. Calculate a correlation coefficient, and explain what it means about the relationship between shipping cost and distance.

b. Now calculate the estimated sample regression function. What do the slope and intercept mean?

c. If the company is going to ship a package 1,200 miles, how much do you estimate it will cost?

E4.4 A manager of a trucking company is interested in determining how the maintenance cost of the company's trucks is related to the age of the truck. Data are contained in truck.xls, which contains information on maintenance costs and the age of each truck in the fleet.

a. Calculate a correlation coefficient, and explain what it means about the relationship between maintenance cost and age.
b. Now calculate the estimated sample regression function, assuming that maintenance cost is the dependent variable. What do the slope and intercept mean?
c. If a truck is 7 years old, what are the estimated maintenance costs?

References

Lewis, Al. "A Super Bowl Prediction: Stock Market Will Be Up in 2007." www.Denverpost.com, January 30, 2007.

Lucas, Richard E., Andrew E. Clark, Yannis Georgellis, and Ed Diener. "Reexaming Adaptation and the Set Point Model of Happiness: Reactions to Changes in Marital Status." *Journal of Personality and Social Psychology* 84, no. 3 (2003).

EMedicineHealth, www.emedicinehealth.com

International Dairy Foods Association, www.idfa.org

http://archives.starbulletin.com/2008/06/18/news/story02.html

http://usgovinfo.about.com/gi/dynamic/offsite.htm?site=http://www.census.gov/prod/2002pubs/p23-210.pdf

Chapter Five

Hypothesis Tests for Linear Regression Analysis

CHAPTER OBJECTIVES

After reading this chapter, you will be able to

1. Construct sampling distributions.
2. Understand desirable properties of simple linear regression estimators.
3. Understand the simple linear regression assumptions required for OLS to be the best linear unbiased estimator.
4. Understand how to conduct hypothesis tests in linear regression analysis.
5. Conduct hypothesis tests for the overall statistical significance of the sample regression function.
6. Conduct hypothesis tests for the statistical significance of the estimated slope coefficient, $\hat{\beta}_1$.
7. Understand how to read regression output in Excel for the purposes of hypothesis testing.
8. Construct confidence intervals around the predicted value of y.

A STUDENT'S PERSPECTIVE

Recall our student who collected sample data on the college GPA and hours of video game play per week for 66 classmates. At the end of Chapter 4, we saw that the student's estimated sample simple linear regression function was:

$$\widehat{GPA} = 3.250 - 0.039 Video\ game\ hours$$

At this point, the student was faced with a most basic question: What information did the estimates for this sample provide about the unobserved population from which the sample was drawn (i.e., what information did the estimates for these 66 students provide about the population of all college students)? In this chapter, we introduce our primary empirical tool for answering this most important question.

BIG PICTURE OVERVIEW

How can we use observed sample statistics to learn about unobserved population parameters? This is the fundamental question underlying all statistical analysis. The answer is complicated by the fact that because the population is unobserved, we can never know for certain the true value of the unobserved population parameter that we are attempting

hypothesis testing
A method in which sample data are used to learn about population parameters.

null hypothesis
A statement about the assumed value of the unobserved population parameter.

alternative hypothesis
A statement that directly contradicts the null hypothesis and is used to test whether the null hypothesis is true.

Notation:

H_0 Null hypothesis
H_A Alternative hypothesis

to estimate. Instead, we are forced to develop a framework through which the information that we gather from a specific observed sample can be used to learn something valuable about the unobserved population parameter that we are attempting to estimate. The framework that we develop to accomplish this task is referred to as **hypothesis testing.**

While this description might sound complicated, the basic idea underlying hypothesis testing is actually rather simple. Namely, while we cannot directly observe the population parameter that we are trying to estimate, we can (1) make an assumption as to its likely value (i.e., determine a **null hypothesis, H_0**), (2) calculate statistics for a specific sample drawn from the population, and (3) ask ourselves "is it statistically likely to observe the sample statistic that we *actually* observe if the unobserved population parameter is indeed equal to the hypothesized value?" If the answer to this final question is no, then we can conclude that the hypothesized value is not a reasonable estimate of the unobserved population parameter and we reject the null hypothesis (H_o) in favor of an **alternative hypothesis** (H_A). If the answer is yes, then we can conclude that the hypothesized value is a reasonable estimate of the unobserved population parameter and we "fail to reject the null hypothesis (H_o)."

Figure 5.1 depicts the empirical research tool introduced in this chapter.

FIGURE 5.1
A Visual Depiction of the Empirical Research Tool Introduced in This Chapter

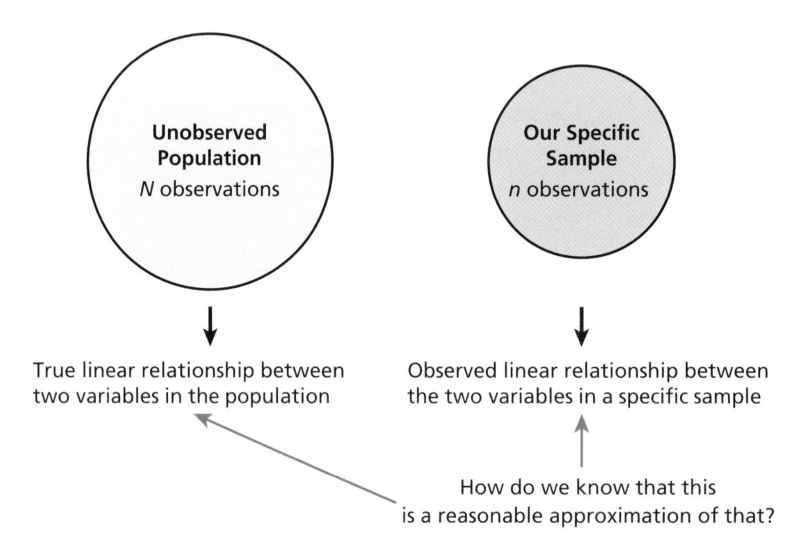

right-tailed test
A test of whether a parameter is greater than a given value.

left-tailed test
A test of whether a parameter is less than a given value.

two-tailed test
A test of whether a parameter equals a given value.

It is important to note that while we couch our discussion of hypothesis testing in terms of conclusions that we can draw about the null hypothesis, the alternative hypothesis is actually the hypothesis that we are testing. In practice, this means that to perform hypothesis tests we first need to determine the alternative hypothesis that we wish to test. In a first econometrics course, we generally wish to test hypotheses that are one of three types: (1) a **right-tailed test** determines whether the unobserved population parameter is likely to be greater than a specific value, (2) a **left-tailed test** determines whether the unobserved population parameter is likely to be less than a specific value, and (3) a **two-tailed test** determines whether the unobserved population parameter is likely to be different

EMPIRICAL RESEARCH TOOL 5.1: HYPOTHESIS TESTING IN LINEAR REGRESSION ANALYSIS

Goal:
To gain insight into specific parameters that exist for a population.

Problem:
Because the population is unobserved, the specific population parameters are unobserved.

Approach:

1. Draw a specific random sample from the population, and *calculate* sample statistics for that observed sample.
2. Use the *observed* sample statistics as the best estimate of the *unobserved* population parameters.
3. Ask whether it is statistically likely to observe the sample statistics *actually observed* if the unobserved population parameter equals the null hypothesis.

Intuition:
All we know for certain is the value of the observed sample statistics. Hence, we must figure out a way to use those observed values to learn something about the unobserved population parameters that they are trying to estimate. The way we do so is to hypothesize a value for the unobserved population parameters and ask whether it is statistically likely to observe the sample statistics that we *actually observed* if the hypothesized population parameter is indeed true. If it is not statistically likely to do so, then we conclude that the fact that we did actually observe the sample statistics is sound statistical evidence that the unobserved population parameter likely does not equal the hypothesized value (because if the hypothesized value were true, it would be statistically very unlikely to observe the sample statistics that we did actually observe). If it is statistically likely to do so, then we conclude that the unobserved population parameter *could* equal the hypothesized value (but not that it necessarily does).

from a specific value. In point of fact, determining the nature of the alternative hypothesis that we wish to test also determines the null hypothesis. For instance, if we wish to test whether the unobserved population parameter is greater than 0, then we would define our null and alternative hypotheses as

$$H_0\colon \beta_1 = 0$$

$$H_A\colon \beta_1 > 0 \qquad 5.1$$

and we would perform a right-sided hypothesis test.

Empirical Research Tool 5.1 summarizes hypothesis testing in linear regression analysis.

Before discussing the how-tos of hypothesis testing in linear regression analysis, we first need to introduce a number of empirical tools that help us make the calculations necessary to perform our desired tests. For the sake of continuity, the remainder of the chapter focuses on the 150-observation city property crime sample and the 200-observation CEO compensation sample that we introduced in Chapter 4.

5.1 CONSTRUCT SAMPLING DISTRIBUTIONS

When performing hypothesis tests, we must first confront the facts that (1) many, many samples other than the one that was actually collected could have been collected from the population and (2) the sample regression functions will differ (perhaps dramatically) for most of those sample regression functions. To drive home these points, note that the estimated sample regression function for our specific 150-observation city property crime sample is

$$Property\ \widehat{crime}/100{,}000 = 3{,}870.55 + 7{,}931.70 Unemployment\ rate \qquad 5.1.1$$

Suppose that instead of drawing that specific random sample from the population, we had drawn 150-observation random sample 2, for which the sample regression function is

$$\widehat{Property\ crime}/100{,}000 = 4{,}379.11 + 5{,}107.27\,Unemployment\ rate \quad \textbf{5.1.2}$$

or 150-observation random sample 3, for which the sample regression function is

$$\widehat{Property\ crime}/100{,}000 = 4{,}805.74 - 4{,}426.01\,Unemployment\ rate \quad \textbf{5.1.3}$$

In each case, we would have been presented with different information as to the likely value of the unobserved population parameter that we are attempting to estimate. Considering that rather than only these three samples, there are actually $359^{150} = 1.837 \times 10^{383}$ different 150 observations samples that can be drawn from the 359-observation population, we might ask: "How can we possibly hope to learn anything about the unobserved population parameter on the basis of the sample regression function for only one specific observed sample?" The answer to this very important question is that we are able to gain valuable information in large part due to our knowledge of what the resulting **sampling distribution** would look like if we were to collect and calculate sample statistics for all potential samples of a given size that could be drawn from the population.

sampling distribution The distribution of a sample statistic based on random sampling.

In practice, constructing a sampling distribution is a multistage process consisting of: (1) collecting all possible independent random samples of size n from the population of size N, (2) calculating a value of the desired sample statistic for each of those samples, and (3) placing the calculated values in order from smallest to largest to create a distribution. Figure 5.2 presents a visual example that helps set this important process in our minds.

FIGURE 5.2 A Depiction of the Construction of a Sampling Distribution

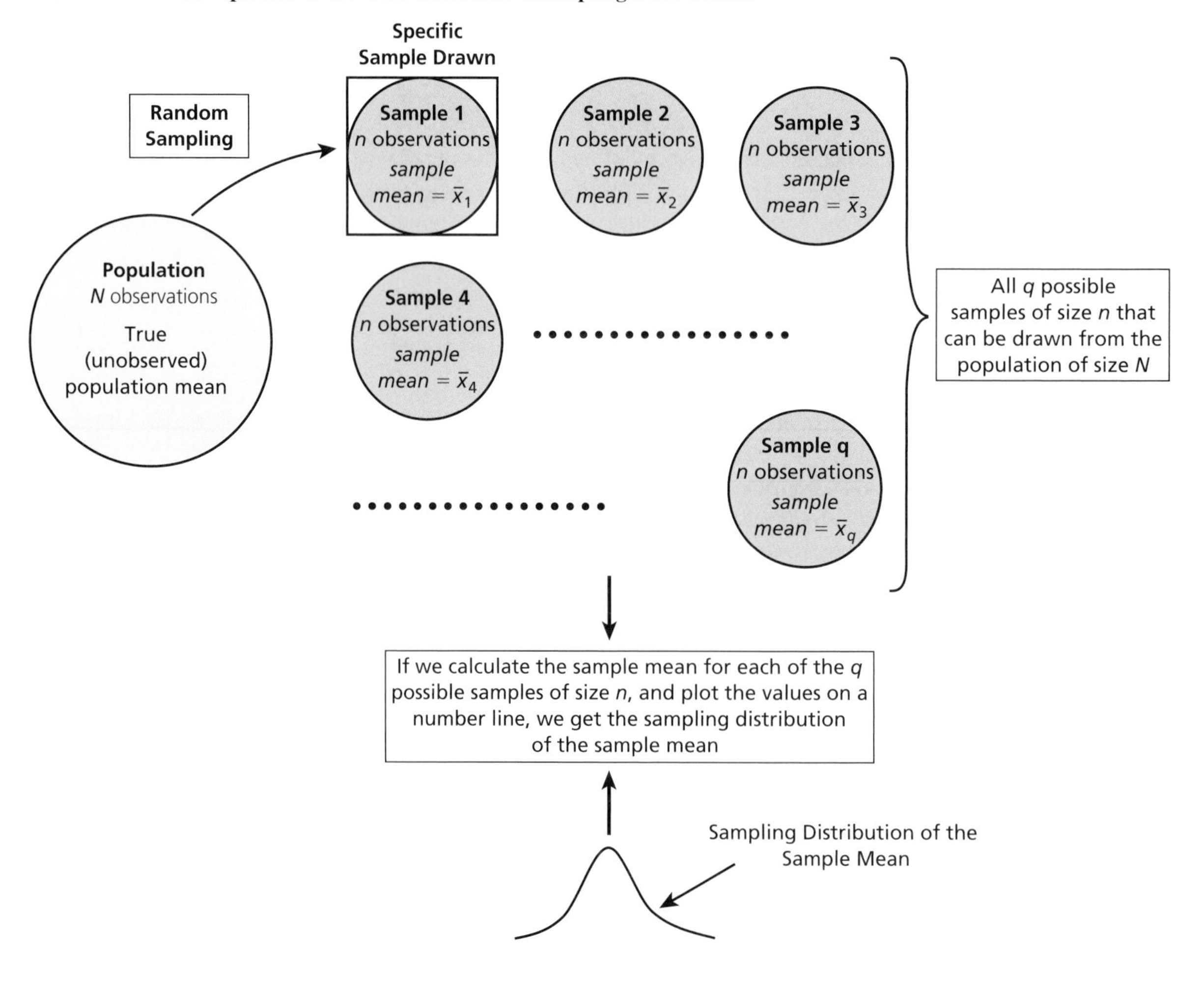

To provide a sense of how this process works, the file **Property Crime Data 100 Samples.xlsx** contains the estimated slope coefficients ($\hat{\beta}_1$) for 100 different 150-observations samples that could be randomly drawn from the 359-observation city property crime population. Constructing the histogram in Figure 5.3 starts to develop the sampling distribution of the estimated slope coefficient $\hat{\beta}_1$.

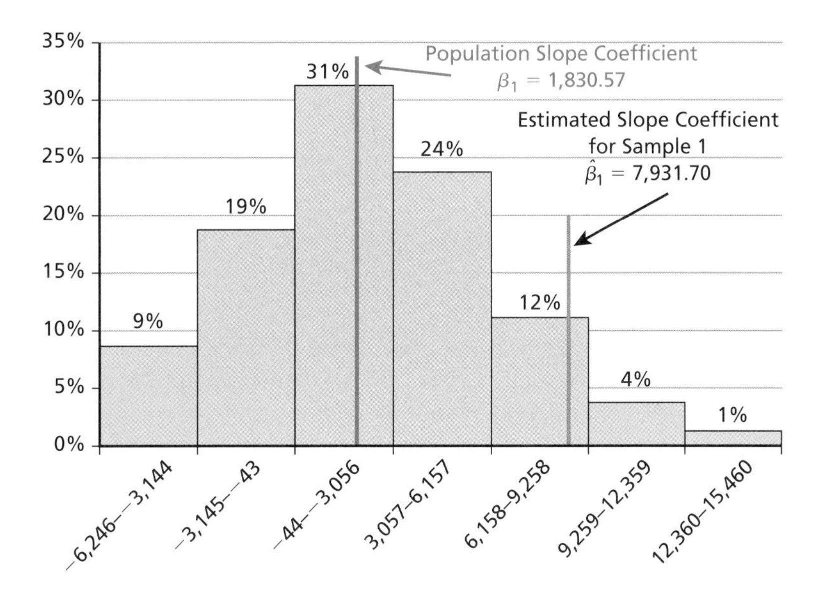

FIGURE 5.3
Histogram of Relative Frequencies for the 100 Different 150-Observation Samples Drawn from the 359-Observation City Property Crime Population

Note that due to our approach to data collection (i.e., treating the initial 359-observation data set as the population and drawing a specific 150-observation random sample from that data set), we are fortunate enough to know the exact value of the population parameter that these random samples are intended to estimate. Adding that value ($\beta_1 = 1{,}830.57$) to Figure 5.3 adds context to the importance of understanding sampling distributions of calculated sample statistics. Namely, imagine that we continue drawing samples until we have collected all $(359)^{150}$ possible independent random samples from the population [expanding our Excel file to include $(359)^{150}$ different worksheets]. What will we see? While we will occasionally observe estimated values of $\hat{\beta}_1$ that fall well away from the true unobserved population value that we are trying to estimate (i.e., $\beta_1 = 1{,}830.57$) we will collect many, many more that fall close (or even equal to) that value. As a result, upon adding additional samples, our histogram will become more clearly centered around a specific value that, under certain conditions, should be the true unobserved population parameter β_1.

As with all distributions of random variables, sampling distributions possess means and standard deviations of their own. While there is not a special name associated with the mean of the sampling distribution, the standard deviation of the sampling distribution is known as the **standard error** of the point estimate. This value plays such an important role throughout the remainder of the text that it is vitally important to understand what the value represents (i.e., that the standard error is the standard deviation of the sampling distribution for a given statistic).

standard error
The standard deviation of the sampling distribution.

Empirical Research Tool 5.2 summarizes the appropriate method for constructing a sampling distribution.

While understanding how sampling distributions are constructed is very important, think about what it would take to actually construct one in practice. To construct the sampling distribution of 20 observation samples that could be drawn from a 100-observation population, we would need to collect and calculate sample statistics for $100^{20} = 1 \times 10^{40}$ different samples. Imagine how difficult and time-consuming this process would be. Now imagine constructing a sampling distribution in which the unobserved population is the population of the United States, which currently exceeds 300 million individuals. As much as we might desire to, there is simply no way we could construct that distribution.

EMPIRICAL RESEARCH TOOL 5.2: CONSTRUCTING SAMPLING DISTRIBUTIONS

Goal:
To gain insight into the sampling distribution of a statistic.

Problem:
Because the population is unobserved, the specific population parameters in which we are interested are unobserved.

Approach:
1. Draw every possible sample of size *n* from the population of size *N*, and calculate the sample statistic of interest for each of those samples.
2. Plot the value of every calculated sample statistic on the number line to generate the sampling distribution for that sample statistic.

Intuition:
Because every possible sample of size *n* that we can draw from a population of size *N* will contain different observations, the calculated sample statistics will differ across samples. To get a sense of what our specific sample tells us about the unobserved population parameter that we are trying to estimate, we need some idea of how similar (or different) our specific sample is to the other samples that we could have potentially drawn from the population instead.

Usefulness:
In practice, we never actually construct a sampling distribution (mathematics has proven what the distributions will look like in most relevant cases). Nonetheless, to correctly understand statistical inference and hypothesis testing it is important to understand the theory behind what a sampling distribution represents.

theoretical probability distribution
A mathematical function that assigns either a probability to each outcome or a probability to a range of outcomes.

Fortunately for us, mathematicians have determined what the sampling distributions of important sample statistics should like look in specific theoretical situations. We refer to such distributions as **theoretical probability distributions,** and we rely on them to help us answer the fundamental question whether it is "statistically likely" to observe the specific sample statistic that we did observe if the unobserved population parameter was indeed equal to the null hypothesis. The fact that these distributions exist is very important because it allows us to perform hypothesis testing without having to construct our own sampling distribution. For a detailed review of the theoretical probability distributions used most frequently in the text, see the appendix to this chapter.

Before we can hope to learn anything from our observed sample statistics, we must first make sure that our chosen estimators possess a number of desirable properties.

5.2 UNDERSTAND DESIRABLE PROPERTIES OF SIMPLE LINEAR REGRESSION ESTIMATORS

The first property that we value is unbiasedness. By definition, an estimator is considered unbiased if its expected value is equal to the population parameter that it is trying to estimate. Figure 5.4 depicts this property.

FIGURE 5.4
Visual Depiction of the Sampling Distribution of an Unbiased Estimator of the Unobserved Population Slope Coefficient, β_1

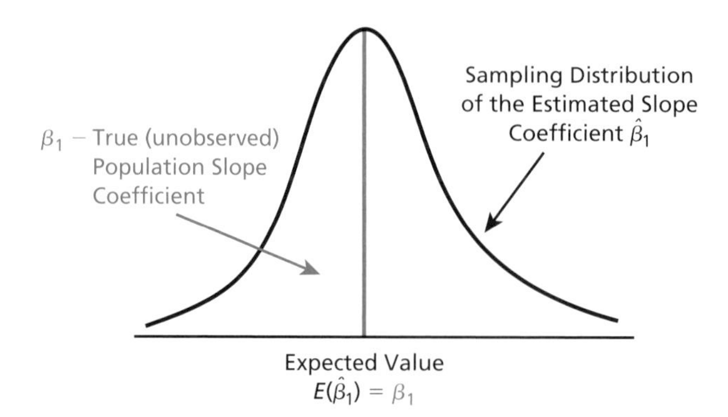

unbiased estimator
The expected value of the estimator is equal to the population parameter being estimated (i.e., $E(\hat{\beta}_1) = \beta_1$).

It is important to correctly interpret what it means for an estimator to be **unbiased.** Does the fact that the observed slope coefficient, $\hat{\beta}_1$, is an unbiased estimator of the unobserved population slope coefficient, β_1, imply that the observed value of $\hat{\beta}_1$ will equal β_1 for every possible sample that can be drawn from the population? Absolutely not! As demonstrated in the preceding discussion of sampling distributions, the observed point estimates of β_1 will differ (potentially by large amounts) across all possible samples of size n. Accordingly, it would be incorrect to claim that the value of the unbiased estimator observed for a given random sample is necessarily equal to the true unobserved population parameter being estimated. Rather, defining a point estimator as unbiased simply implies that the observed point estimate is correct *on average.*

If being unbiased does not mean that the estimators for all potential samples drawn from the population necessarily equal the unobserved population parameter, then why do we consider it a desirable property? Because unbiasedness means that if we collected many, many samples, computed the observed sample statistic for each sample, then averaged those calculated values, the average of all of the calculated value would equal the population parameter we are attempting to estimate. In other words, the average value of all potential estimators contained in the sampling distribution is equal to the true value of the unobserved population parameter, β_1. Does this property in any way guarantee correct inferences concerning the unobserved population parameter? No. But, given the nature of sampling distributions, this result is the best we can hope for.

biased estimator
The expected value of the estimator is not equal to the population parameter being estimated (i.e., $E(\hat{\beta}_1) \neq \beta_1$).

What if the expected value of the sampling distribution of a given estimator is not equal to the true unobserved population parameter being estimated? Then we refer to the estimator as being **biased.** As an example, Figure 5.5 presents the sampling distribution for an alternative estimator Z, which is a biased estimator of β_1 because the expected value of Z is not equal to β_1 (i.e. $E(Z) \neq \beta_1$).

FIGURE 5.5
A Visual Depiction of the Sampling Distribution of a Biased Estimator of the Unobserved Population Slope Coefficient, β_1

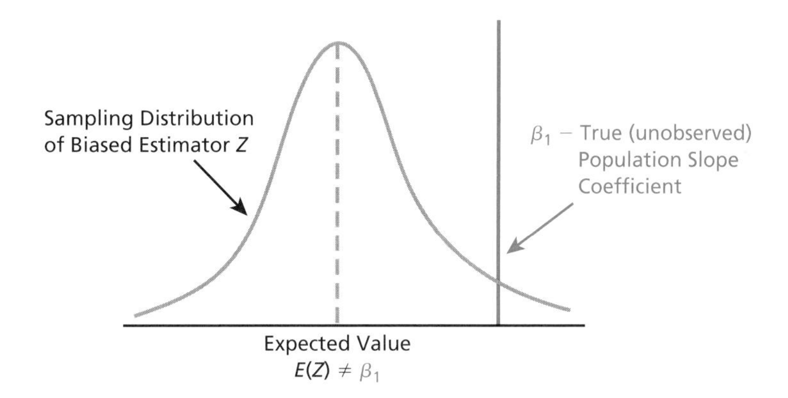

A comparison of Figures 5.4 and 5.5 demonstrates that the difference between biased and unbiased estimators is that for an unbiased estimator, the mass of the sampling distribution is centered on the true value of the unobserved population parameter, β_1, while for a biased estimator, the mass of the sampling distribution is centered on a different value.

This comparison should further illustrate why unbiasedness is considered a desirable property for an estimator. The fact that the mass of the sampling distribution for $\hat{\beta}_1$ is centered on the true (unobserved) value of β_1 while the mass of the sampling distribution for Z is not suggests that the observed value of $\hat{\beta}_1$ for a sample drawn at random from the population should be closer to the true value of β_1 than the observed value of $\hat{\beta}_1$.

bias
The difference between the expected value of the estimator and the population parameter that is being estimated.

By definition, the **bias** associated with an estimator is the degree to which the expected value of the estimator differs for the population parameter that is being estimated. Its value is calculated as

$$Bias = E(Estimator) - \beta_1 \qquad \textbf{5.2.1}$$

Note that if an estimator is unbiased, then the calculated bias of the estimator must equal 0. Hence, a potential method for determining whether an estimator is biased or unbiased is calculating the bias of the estimator and asking whether it is equal to 0.

Is unbiasedness the only desirable property for an estimator to possess (i.e., should our only deciding factor in determining the best possible estimator be whether the estimator is unbiased)? No. We demonstrate why by considering the following questions:

1. Is it possible for more than one estimator of a given population parameter to be unbiased?
2. If multiple estimators are unbiased, how can we decide which one is most preferred?

The answer to the first question is a resounding yes. In fact, there are potentially many different unbiased estimators for each given population parameter. If so, then how do we decide whether one unbiased estimator is more desirable than another unbiased estimator? By comparing the calculated variances of the set of unbiased estimators and choosing the one that provides the minimum variance. Throughout this text, we define a given unbiased estimator as being relatively **efficient** compared to another unbiased estimator if it has a smaller variance relative to the other estimator. Figure 5.6 demonstrates by comparing the sampling distributions $\hat{\beta}_1$ and V, which are both unbiased estimators of the unobserved population slope coefficient.

efficient
Estimator X is considered relatively efficient to estimator Y if X and Y are both unbiased and X has a lower variance than Y.

FIGURE 5.6
A Visual Comparison of the Sampling Distributions of Two Unbiased Estimators of the Unobserved Population Slope Coefficient, β_1

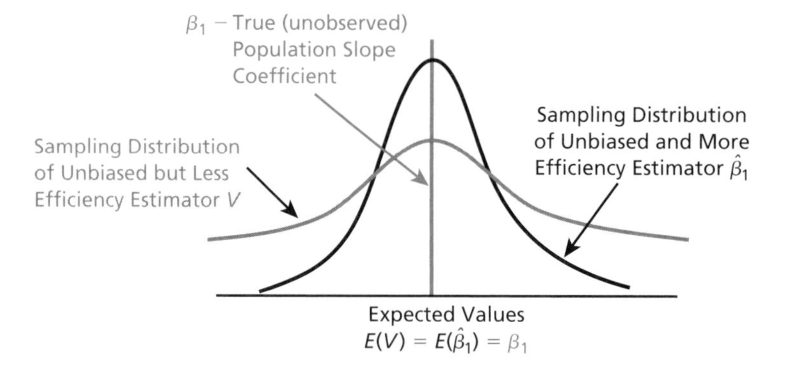

While both estimators in Figure 5.6 are centered on the true unobserved population mean and are therefore unbiased, the question is whether they do an equally good job estimating β_1 or whether one might clearly outperform the other. Looking at the figure, we can see that values of $\hat{\beta}_1$ are more closely concentrated around the true value of β_1, while the values of V are more widely spread around the true value of β_1. In statistical terms, this means that the variance of $\hat{\beta}_1$ is smaller than the variance of V. How does this difference affect the likelihood that the individual sample we draw from the population provides a point estimate that is close to the true unobserved population parameter? Due to its lower variance, we know that estimator $\hat{\beta}_1$ is more likely than estimator V to provide such estimates because the smaller variance means that a greater percentage of all possible samples provide point estimates that are closer to the true value of the unobserved population slope coefficient. In other words, among all unbiased estimators, the one that is most preferred is the one that has the minimum variance.

As defined earlier, the property that compares the variances of two unbiased estimators is called *efficiency* and the estimator with the lower variance is said to be the most efficient estimator of the population parameter. Accordingly, when comparing the estimators depicted previously, we would say that $\hat{\beta}_1$ is a more *efficient* estimator than V.

Now that we know that unbiasedness and efficiency are our two most preferred properties, we need to consider the theoretical conditions under which the OLS sample regression function is the most efficient unbiased estimator of the unobserved population regression model.

5.3 UNDERSTAND THE SIMPLE LINEAR REGRESSION ASSUMPTIONS REQUIRED FOR OLS TO BE THE BEST LINEAR UNBIASED ESTIMATOR

best linear unbiased estimator (BLUE)
Among all estimators that are linear and unbiased an estimator that is BLUE has the minimum variance.

If an estimator is both unbiased and minimum variance among all unbiased estimators, then it is considered the **best linear unbiased estimator (BLUE).** BLUE, in many ways, is the gold standard for estimators, because, by definition, no other unbiased estimator can have a lower variance. This brings us to one of the main reasons that we start our discussion of econometrics with ordinary least squares (OLS): If the following six assumptions hold, then OLS is the best linear unbiased estimator of the unobserved population regression model $y_i = \beta_0 + \beta_1 x_i + \varepsilon_i$.

Assumption S1: The model is linear in the parameters.

Assumption S1 states that for OLS to be an unbiased estimator, the population simple linear regression model must be correctly specified as linear in the parameters. This means that the dependent variable, y, must be related to the independent variable, x, and the error term, ε, as

$$y_i = \beta_0 + \beta_1 x_i + \varepsilon_i \qquad \textbf{5.3.1}$$

where β_0 is the population intercept and β_1 is the population slope parameter.

There are actually two important parts to this assumption. The first part, that the population regression model is linear in the parameters, is fairly innocuous. It simply means that OLS would not be an unbiased estimator of population regression models, such as $y_i = (\beta_0 \cdot \beta_1)x_i + \varepsilon_i$ and $y_i = \beta_0 + \beta_1^2 x_i + \varepsilon_i$, because such models do not define a linear relationship between y and x. Note that being linear in the parameters does not mean that the value of the independent variable must be linear. As an example, suppose that we wish to estimate the relationship $y_i = \beta_0 + \beta_1 x_i^2 + \varepsilon_i$. Even though x_i^2 is nonlinear, the population regression model does not violate assumption S1 because the model does define a linear relationship between y and x. To see why, think of setting x_i^2 equal to z_i and estimating the relationship $y_i = \beta_0 + \beta_1 z_i + \varepsilon_i$, which is clearly linear in the parameters.

The second part of the assumption, that the population regression model is *correctly specified* as $y_i = \beta_0 + \beta_1 x_i + \varepsilon_i$, is likely of greater concern. As an example, suppose that the true relationship between y and x is $\ln y_i = \beta_0 + \beta_1 \ln x_i = \varepsilon_i$ but we instead estimate $y_i = \beta_0 + \beta_1 x_i + \varepsilon_i$. Given that the model we estimate by OLS does not correctly describe the true relationship among y, x, and ε, it is not correctly specified, meaning that assumption S1 is violated and our estimates are not unbiased. Unfortunately, given that the true unobserved population relationship is unobserved, we may never know for certain whether our estimated relationship is indeed specified correctly. Nonetheless, we should make every attempt to specify the relationship as accurately as possible by considering the variables in detail, turning to the existing literature to see how others have specified similar relationships in previous empirical work. We return to this point in more detail in later chapters.

Assumption S2: The data are collected through independent, random sampling.

Assumption S2 states that for OLS to be an unbiased estimator of the population simple linear regression model $y_i = \beta_0 + \beta_1 x_i + \varepsilon_i$, the sample data must be obtained through random sampling.

As discussed in previous chapters, random sampling ensures that the data points are statistically independent across the units of observation, a fact that is required for OLS to be unbiased. Note that statistical independence across the units of observation does not mean that x_i and y_i are statistically unrelated for a given observation i. Indeed, estimating a nonzero value for $\hat{\beta}_1$ requires x_i and y_i to be statistically related for individual observations. Instead, assumption S2 means that x_i and y_i are not statistically related to x_j and y_j for two different units of observation i and j. Perhaps, the most obvious example for how this assumption might be violated is time-series analysis, in which the units of observation are collected for one individual, firm, country, etc., over time. In such cases, because the data are collected for the same individual, firm, country, etc., the data are by design not collected randomly and are therefore not statistically independent. To deal with this problem, when discussing time-series analysis in Chapters 10 and 11, we replace this assumption with one concerning how the error terms for time series variables are related to each other.

Note that it is possible for assumption S2 to be violated for cross-section data if the data across observations are somehow related to each other. As an example, suppose that we collect data on the unemployment rate in every county in Texas at one particular point in time. Because adjacent counties likely share the same labor market, the unemployment rates in adjacent counties may well be statistically related to each other (i.e., counties surrounding Austin might have statistically related unemployment rates and counties surrounding Dallas might have statistically related unemployment rates). In such a case, the data are not randomly distributed across observations, assumption S2 is violated, and our estimates are not unbiased.

Assumption S3: There must be sample variation in the independent variable.

Assumption S3 states that for OLS to be an unbiased estimator of the population simple linear regression model $y_i = \beta_0 + \beta_1 x_i + \varepsilon_i$, values of the independent variable must vary (i.e., the values of x_i cannot be the same for all i).

Recall from formula 5.7.2 that the estimated slope coefficient $\hat{\beta}_1$ is calculated as $\hat{\beta}_1 = \sum_{i=1}^{n}(x_i - \bar{x})(y_i - \bar{y})/\sum_{i=1}^{n}(x_i - \bar{x})^2$. If assumption S3 is violated, by definition, all of the x_i observations have the exact same value, meaning that each $x_i = \bar{x}$. If so, it would be the case that $\sum_{i=1}^{n}(x_i - \bar{x})^2 = \sum_{i=1}^{n}(\bar{x} - \bar{x})^2 = 0$, which would make it impossible to calculate an estimated value for $\hat{\beta}_1$ because the denominator would also take on the value of 0. In other words, if x does not vary, then we cannot calculate an estimated slope coefficient for the linear relationship between y and x.

Note, however, that if assumption S2 holds, it is unlikely for assumption S3 to be violated. To see why, consider the scatter plot in Figure 5.7, which demonstrates how a scatter diagram would look if there were no sample variation in the independent variable x_i.

FIGURE 5.7
A Visual Depiction of a Violation of Assumption S3

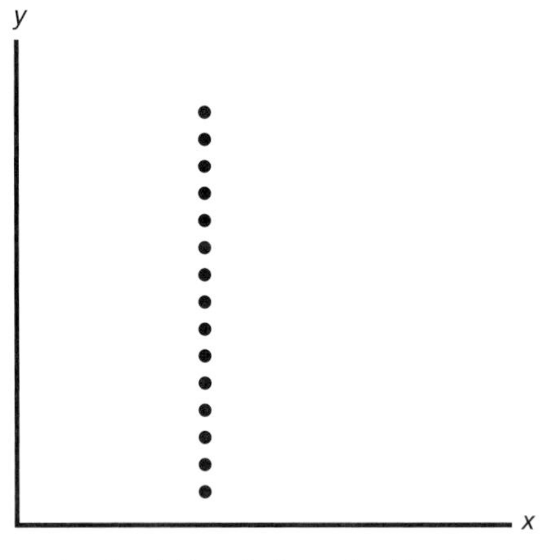

As should be obvious, in this situation, there is no way to estimate a linear relationship between y and x because y does not vary with x.

Notice that thinking about assumption S3 in this way provides additional intuition into how linear regression works: It does so by using the variation in the independent variable x to explain the variation in dependent variable y. In other words, if there is no variation in x, then it is impossible to use its variation to explain the variation in y.

Assumption S4: The error term has zero mean, or $E(\varepsilon_i) = 0$.

Assumption S4 states that for OLS to be an unbiased estimator of the population simple linear regression model $y_1 = \beta_0 + \beta_1 x_i + \varepsilon_i$, the error term ε_i must have an expected value of 0, [i.e., $E(\varepsilon_i) = 0$]. Note that this assumption pertains to the error term, ε_i, which resides in the population, and not the residual, e_i, which resides in the sample.

Fortunately, regardless of whether assumption S4 holds in theory, including the intercept term β_0 in the population regression model guarantees that it holds in practice. This follows from the fact that if the average value in the error term in the population happens to equal another value other than 0, then the intercept term serves to re-scale the data either up or down so that the average value equals 0.

This assumption highlights an important point. Attempting to interpret the estimated intercept is generally not that informative because if the expected value of the error term is truly different from 0, then the value of the estimated intercept automatically changes to recalibrate the regression function. This recalibration serves to change the interpretation of the estimated intercept as well. This is yet another reason that the value of the estimated intercept does not provide an accurate picture of the value of the dependent variable when the independent variable is equal to 0, thereby rendering the traditional interpretation uninformative.

Assumption S5: The error term is not correlated with the independent variable or any function of the independent variable, or $E(\varepsilon_i|x_i) = 0$.

Assumption S5 is sometimes referred to as the zero conditional mean assumption. It states that for OLS to be an unbiased estimator of the population simple linear regression model $y_i = \beta_0 + \beta_1 x_i + \varepsilon_i$, the values of the error term and the independent variable, or any function of the independent variable (i.e., x_i^2 or $\sqrt{x_i}$), must not be correlated.

The notation $E(\varepsilon_i/x_i) = 0$ bears additional explanation. The mathematical symbol "|" is read as "given," meaning that $E(\varepsilon_i|x_i) = 0$ should be read as "the expected value of the error term, ε_i, given the independent variable, x_i, is equal to 0."

This assumption is required for OLS to provide an unbiased estimate of the true marginal effect that x has on y (i.e., the effect that changes in x have on y, *holding all else constant*). To see why, suppose that assumption S5 is violated such that x is correlated with something in the error term. In such a case, $\hat{\beta}_1$ would not provide an unbiased estimate of the effect that a change in x has on y, *holding all else constant*, because every change in the value of x would also cause a change in the value of the error term, meaning that all else was not being held constant. As an example, suppose that we are interested in estimating the marginal effect that education has on earnings. While many, many things besides education are likely to affect an individual's earnings, one prominent factor is likely the individual's motivation. Notice that because we will not be including motivation in the simple linear regression of education on earnings, it will be part of the error term. To see why this might be problematic, consider the fact that we might expect individuals with greater motivation to acquire more education. In such a case, the independent variable education will be correlated with the error term, thereby violating the *all else constant* condition.

Unfortunately, because we do not observe the error term, we can't just calculate the correlation coefficient between the independent variable (or a function of the independent variable) and the error term to see whether its value is different from 0. Instead, we must attempt to verify assumption S5 using common sense. A valuable starting point for doing so is to make a list of different factors that are likely to be contained in the error term. As an example, in our property crime example in addition to the independent variable "unemployment rate," we might expect the property crime in a city to depend on factors such as income and education, demographics, police force per capita, concealed carry laws, etc. Because these factors are not explicitly included in our simple linear regression of property crime rates on unemployment rates, they end up in the error term. Accordingly, we need to determine whether any of the factors in our list are likely to be correlated with the independent variable. For the property crime example, it is likely that many of these other factors are correlated with the unemployment rate. As such, we might be afraid that assumption S5 fails for that example. As we discuss in Chapter 6, we refer to the preceding situation as a case of omitted variable bias, and it is one of the main reasons that, in practice, we normally perform multiple linear regression analysis rather than simple linear regression analysis when examining questions of economic interest.

The Importance of Assumptions S1 through S5

If assumptions S1 through S5 hold, then OLS provides an unbiased estimate of the population simple linear regression model $y_i = \beta_0 + \beta_1 x_i + \varepsilon_i$. Again, it is important to consider what this means. The fact that an estimator is unbiased means that it provides a correct estimate of the true (unobserved) population parameter, *on average,* across all potential samples and not that the estimate for each particular sample necessarily provides a correct estimate.

Note that the opposite of this conclusion is also true. If any one of assumptions S1 through S5 are violated, then OLS does not provide an unbiased estimate of the population simple linear regression model $y_i = \beta_0 + \beta_1 x_i + \varepsilon_i$.

Our final assumption relates to the efficiency rather than the unbiasedness of the OLS estimates.

Assumption S6: The error term has constant variance, or $Var(\varepsilon_i) = \sigma^2$.

Assumption S6 states that for OLS to have the minimum variance among all potential unbiased estimators of the population simple linear regression model $y_i = \beta_0 + \beta_1 x_i + \varepsilon_i$, the error term ε_i must have the same variance for every given value of the independent variable [i.e., it must be the case that $Var(\varepsilon) = \sigma^2$ for all x].

As far as new terminology goes, regression models for which the error term ε_i has a constant variance for every given value of the independent variable are referred to as being **homoskedastic,** while regression models for which the error term ε_i has a non-constant variance for given values of the independent variable are referred to as being **heteroskedastic.**

homoskedastic
The variance of the error term given the independent variable, x, is constant, or $Var(\varepsilon|x) = \sigma^2$.

heteroskedastic
The variance of the error term given the independent variable, x, is not constant, or $Var(\varepsilon|x) = \sigma_i^2$.

Note that being heteroskedastic does not mean that an estimator is biased. Instead, heteroskedasticity results in the calculated standard errors that are incorrect. In other words, in the presence of heteroskedasticity, OLS estimates remain unbiased but they no longer have minimum variance among all possible estimators. As such, they are no longer BLUE. Chapter 9 discusses the potential causes and consequences of heteroskedasticity in detail.

To further understand what it means to have a heteroskedastic error term, suppose that we are attempting to explain a family's monthly expenditure on meals by its monthly income. Because they lack the means to spend lavishly on food, we might expect families with lower monthly income to have relatively low monthly meal expenditures meaning that the variance in monthly meal expenditures is likely relatively small in lower-income families. At the same time, because families with higher monthly incomes can afford to spend more lavishly on food but because not all choose to do so, then we might observe the scatter diagram in Figure 5.8, in which the variance in monthly meal expenditures is larger for higher-income families than for lower-income families.

FIGURE 5.8
A Visual Depiction of Heteroskedastic Data

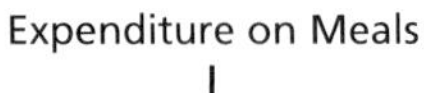

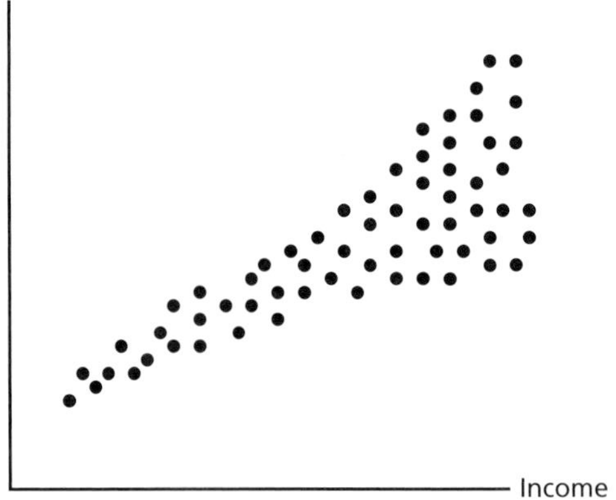

Because the data fan out as the value of the independent variable increases, the variance of the error term increases as the value of the independent variable increases, clearly indicating that the variance of the error term is nonconstant, or that these data exhibit heteroskedasticity. In such a case, OLS would be unbiased but the standard errors and all hypothesis testing are wrong.

The Importance of Assumptions S1 through S6

It is important to note that assumption S6 is not required for OLS to be unbiased. Rather, it is required for OLS to be the unbiased estimator with the minimum variance, which is required for OLS to be the *best linear unbiased estimator (BLUE).* If assumptions S1 through S5 hold but assumption S6 is violated, then OLS estimates are unbiased but not BLUE.

The six assumptions required for OLS to be BLUE are summarized in the following box.

Assumptions Required for OLS to Be the Best Linear Unbiased Estimator (BLUE) of the Population Simple Linear Regression Model $y_i = \beta_0 + \beta_1 x_i + \varepsilon_i$

Assumptions Required for OLS to Be Unbiased

Assumption S1: The model is linear in the parameters.
Assumption S2: The data are collected through independent, random sampling.
Assumption S3: There must be sample variation in the independent variable.
Assumption S4: The error term has zero mean, or $E(\varepsilon_i) = 0$.
Assumption S5: The error term is uncorrelated with the independent variable and all functions of the independent variable, or $E(\varepsilon_i|x_i) = 0$.

Additional Assumption Required for OLS to be BLUE

Assumption S6: The error term has constant variance, or $Var(\varepsilon_i) = \sigma^2$.

We now possess all of the tools required to conduct hypothesis testing in linear regression analysis.

5.4 UNDERSTAND HOW TO CONDUCT HYPOTHESIS TESTS IN LINEAR REGRESSION ANALYSIS

There are three different methods for performing hypothesis tests in linear regression analysis. Before discussing the three methods, recall that we perform hypothesis tests by (1) assuming a value for the unobserved population parameter that we are trying to estimate, (2) asking whether it is "statistically likely" to observe the sample statistic that we actually observed if the hypothesis about the unobserved population parameter is indeed true, and (3) rejecting the null hypothesis if we find statistically significant evidence that the null hypothesis is unlikely to be true. With this in mind, we note that the primary difference among the three methods lies in the way that each determines "statistical likely."

Method 1: Construct Confidence Intervals around the Population Parameter

confidence interval Indicates the degree to which we might expect the true unobserved population mean to fall within the interval if many, many intervals are calculated.

Our first method for performing hypothesis tests involves calculating a **confidence interval** around our observed sample statistics and asking whether that calculated interval contains the null hypothesis. If the interval does not contain the null hypothesis, then we conclude that it is statistically unlikely to observe the sample statistic that we did observe if the null hypothesis is indeed true, and therefore, we conclude that the null hypothesis is likely untrue, and we reject H_0. If it does, then we conclude that the observed sample

margin of error
The value added or subtracted from the sample mean that determines the length of the interval.

critical value
Is determined by the level of confidence and is the value that the standard error is multiplied by to obtain the margin of error.

level of significance
Determines the level of confidence; a measure of how willing you are to be wrong.

statistic does not provide clear statistical evidence against the likelihood that the null hypothesis is true, then we conclude the opposite, and we fail to reject H_0.

To calculate the appropriate confidence interval around a given point estimate, we add and subtract a value, called the **margin of error,** to the point estimate

$$\text{Point estimate} \pm \underbrace{\text{Critical value} \cdot \text{Standard error}}_{\text{Margin of Error}} \tag{5.4.1}$$

As formula 5.4.1 indicates, the confidence interval has three components: (1) the point estimate of the population parameter that the confidence interval is trying to bracket, (2) the **critical value,** and (3) the standard error of the point estimate. By definition, the appropriate critical value is one that satisfies a given **level of significance,** α, which is defined as the total percentage of observations in the sampling distribution that are more extreme than the critical value. Figure 5.9 depicts this concept for a two-sided test.

FIGURE 5.9
A Visual Depiction of Determining the Desired Level of Significance for the Sampling Distribution of a Given Estimator

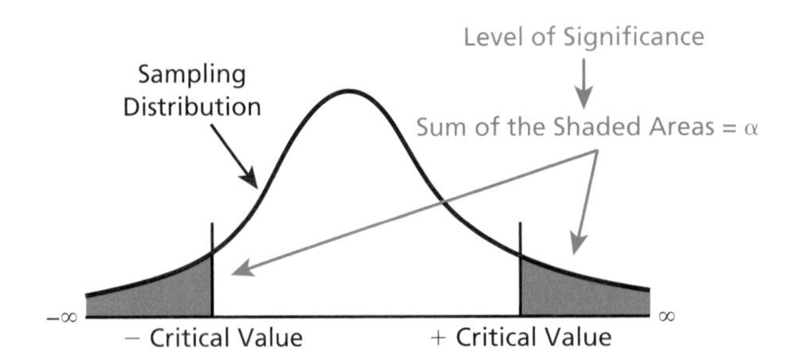

Notation:
α Level of significance

confidence level
The number of times out of 100 if a method is repeated many times; contains the true unobserved population mean.

There are two important points that we should note here. First, while we could theoretically choose any significance level, economists generally focus on the 10 percent, 5 percent, and 1 percent levels. Second, we refer to the **confidence level** as being $1 - \alpha$, meaning that the 10 percent, 5 percent, and 1 percent significance levels are equivalent to the 90 percent, 95 percent, and 99 percent confidence levels, respectively. Given the frequency with which we use these confidence levels, it is useful to become familiar with their values. Table 5.1 presents the critical values for these three confidence levels in the case that the number of observations in our sample is large (i.e., $n \geq 100$).

TABLE 5.1
Critical Values for the Most Commonly Used Confidence Levels from the Normal Probability Distribution ($n \geq 100$)

Confidence Level	α	$\alpha/2$	$Z_{\alpha/2}$
90%	0.10	0.05	1.645
95%	0.05	0.025	1.96
99%	0.01	0.005	2.576

Notation:
$(1 - \alpha)$ Confidence level

Note that it is impossible to construct a similar table for cases in which the number of observations in our sample is not large (i.e., $n < 100$) because values for the Student's-t distribution (discussed later in the appendix to this chapter) depend not only on the chosen confidence level but also on the number of observations, meaning that the critical values take on different values for each different confidence level and each different sample size. Accordingly, we will always need to consult the Student's-t table to determine the exact critical value to use when constructing confidence intervals for smaller samples.

Significant care must be taken when interpreting and using calculated confidence intervals. To start, consider Figure 5.10, which depicts the 90 percent, 95 percent, and 99 percent confidence intervals for a given sample.

FIGURE 5.10 **A Comparison of 90 Percent, 95 Percent, and 99 Percent Confidence Intervals**

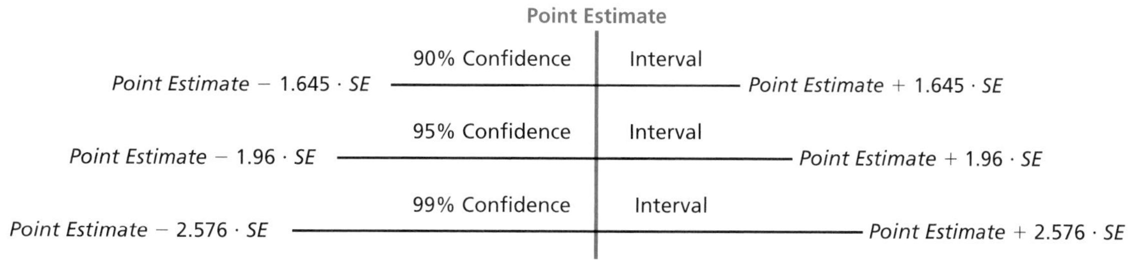

The most important thing to learn from this figure is that the greater the desired confidence level, the wider must be the associated confidence interval. This makes sense because, in the context of statistical inference, increased confidence refers to being more certain that the given confidence interval contains the true value of the unobserved population parameter. The only way to be more certain that a confidence interval contains a certain value is to make the interval wider.

With this in mind, to correctly interpret calculated confidence intervals, note that the preceding confidence intervals are calculated around the sample mean for the specific random sample that was drawn from the population. As we have discussed many times, this is not the only sample that can be drawn from the population. This realization is important because it implies that all of the different possible samples of size n that we could draw from the population of size N will have different point estimates, different standard errors, and therefore different confidence intervals. Accordingly, just like there will be a sampling distribution of the point estimates, there will also be a sampling distribution of the confidence intervals around the point estimates.

To get a better idea of how the concept of a sampling distribution of calculated confidence intervals affects our ability to perform valid statistical inference, consider Figure 5.11, which contains the 95 percent confidence intervals calculated around the estimated sample slope coefficients for the 100 different samples in the file **Property Crime Data 100 Samples.xlsx.**

As Figure 5.11 demonstrates, not all of the calculated confidence intervals contain the value of the unobserved population parameter. Indeed, among the 100 different random samples, the 5 highlighted with stars do not contain the true value. What should we make of this fact? And how does it help us understand the correct interpretation of the information contained within a given confidence interval?

Perhaps the easiest way to answer these questions is to note that a confidence interval is much like a weather forecast. To see how, suppose that the latest forecast calls for a 95 percent chance of rain tomorrow. Does such a forecast mean that come tomorrow it will 95 percent rain? No. Tomorrow it will either rain or it will not rain (it will not 95 percent rain—that is impossible). Accordingly, the appropriate interpretation a 95 percent chance of rain is that if the same atmospheric conditions were to be repeated multiple times, on 95 percent of those occasions it would rain and on 5 percent it would not. Does this provide any information as to the specific days on which it will rain? No. It simply provides information as to the likelihood that any one given day with a specific set of atmospheric conditions will see rain.

The correct interpretation of a confidence interval is similar. Once a confidence interval is calculated around an observed point estimate, the true unobserved population parameter either falls within that interval or it does not. As such, the correct interpretation of a 95 percent confidence interval is that if we were to calculate confidence intervals around every sample mean in the sampling distribution (as we started to do in Figure 5.11), then 95 percent of the constructed confidence intervals would contain the true value of the unobserved population parameter.

Does this interpretation imply that the probability that any one given 95 percent confidence interval contains the true unobserved population parameter is equal to 95 percent? Absolutely not! This is a very significant point, and in terms of the larger picture of

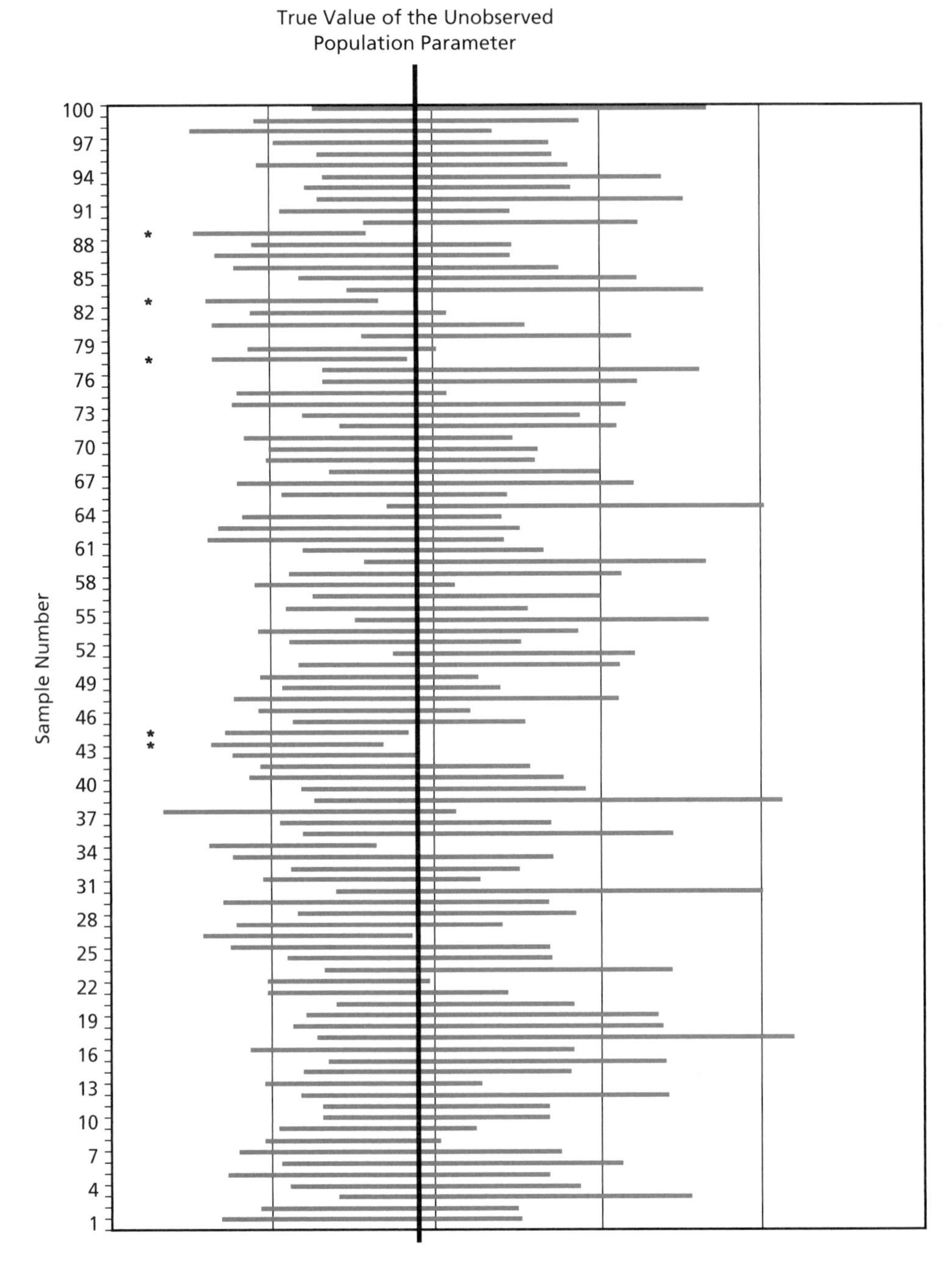

FIGURE 5.11
A Visual Depiction of 95 Percent Confidence Intervals for 100 Different Samples Drawn from a Population

statistical inference, it is important to consider what this implies about our ability to estimate an unknown population parameter on the basis of a sample statistic that is observed for a specific independent random sample that is drawn from the population. Namely, it is important to note that a confidence interval will never be able to indicate for sure whether the point estimate is truly equal to the true unobserved population parameter (or necessarily that close to the true unobserved population parameter). Instead, it provides information on a range of values that should be considered more likely for the unknown population parameter based on the observed sample drawn from the population.

After this rather lengthy introduction to confidence intervals, the obvious question is how can we use confidence intervals to perform hypothesis tests? We can do so by (1) formulating a hypothesis as to the true value of the unobserved population parameter, (2) calculating the value of our point estimate and constructing a confidence interval, and (3) rejecting the null hypothesis if the value in the null hypothesis falls outside the calculated confidence interval.

rejection rule
A statement that is used to determine whether the null hypothesis is rejected.

At this point, we stop to stress the importance of point 3. We commonly refer to such a statement as a **rejection rule** because it provides the key to drawing the correct conclusions to our hypothesis test. To understand why, consider the following question: If all but 5 percent of all possible 95 percent confidence intervals contain the true value of the unobserved population parameter being estimated, then what do we make of observing a sample for which the calculated 95 percent confidence interval does not contain the null hypothesis? The answer is that that the null hypothesis is most likely not true. Accordingly, in such a situation, we have statistical evidence to reject the null hypothesis.

Based on the preceding discussion, we define the appropriate rejection rule for the confidence interval method of hypothesis testing as

$$\text{Reject } H_0 \text{ if } H_0 \text{ is outside the calculated confidence interval.} \qquad \textbf{5.4.2}$$

Empirical Research Tool 5.3 summarizes hypothesis testing using the confidence interval method.

EMPIRICAL RESEARCH TOOL 5.3: HYPOTHESIS TESTING USING CALCULATED CONFIDENCE INTERVALS

Goal:

To gain insight into the likely value of a specific parameter that exists for a population of interest.

Problem:

Because the population is unobserved, we can never know the true value of the unobserved population parameter for certain.

Process:

1. Collect a specific sample of size *n* from the population, and calculate the value of the sample statistic of interest.
2. Construct a confidence interval around the observed sample statistic.
3. Determine whether the value of the null hypothesis H_0 falls inside the constructed confidence interval.
4. If H_0 falls *outside* the constructed confidence interval, then reject H_0.

Intuition:

By definition, 90 percent confidence intervals are constructed such that if we collect all possible samples of size *n* from the population, 90 percent of the calculated confidence intervals will contain the true value of the unobserved population parameter of interest. Hence, if the confidence interval we construct for our specific observed sample does not contain our null hypothesis, then we conclude that it is unlikely for that hypothesis to be true because if it were true it would have been statistically unlikely to observe a calculated confidence interval that did not contain the hypothesized value.

Method 2: Compare Calculated Test Statistics with Predetermined Critical Values

test-statistic (*t*-stat)
A value calculated from the sample data and used to determine the validity of the hypothesis being tested.

critical value
A number obtained from a table that is the value the test statistic is compared to when deciding whether to reject or fail to reject a hypothesis.

Our second method for hypothesis testing in linear regression analysis involves (1) formulating a hypothesis as to the true value of the unobserved population parameter, (2) calculating a ***test*-statistic** (or *t*-stat) based on the observed sample statistic and comparing that value to a predetermined **critical value** that indicates the likelihood of observing a given sample statistic if the null hypothesis is indeed true, and (3) rejecting the null hypothesis if the calculated test statistic is greater than the critical value.

For linear regression analysis, the *t*-statistic for the significance of an estimated slope coefficient is

$$t\text{-stat} = \frac{\hat{\beta}_j - H_0}{\textit{Standard error}_j} \qquad \textbf{5.4.3}$$

In general, we employ the following rejection rule for this hypothesis test:

$$\text{Reject } H_0 \text{ if the } |\textit{Test}\text{-statistic}| > \textit{Critical value} \qquad \textbf{5.4.4}$$

Note the intuition behind this test. The *test*-statistic is a measure of how far the observed estimated slope coefficient falls from the hypothesized population parameter, adjusted for the standard error. The critical value is the point beyond which we decide that those two values are different enough to merit rejection of the null hypothesis.

While formula 5.4.3 presents the general rejection rule for this type of test, in practice, the appropriate decision rule to employ depends on the type of question being tested in the null hypothesis. For a right-tailed test, the appropriate rejection rule is

$$\text{Reject } H_0 \text{ if } t\text{-stat} > t_{\alpha,n-1}$$

which is depicted in Figure 5.12.

FIGURE 5.12
Rejection Region for a Right-Tailed Test

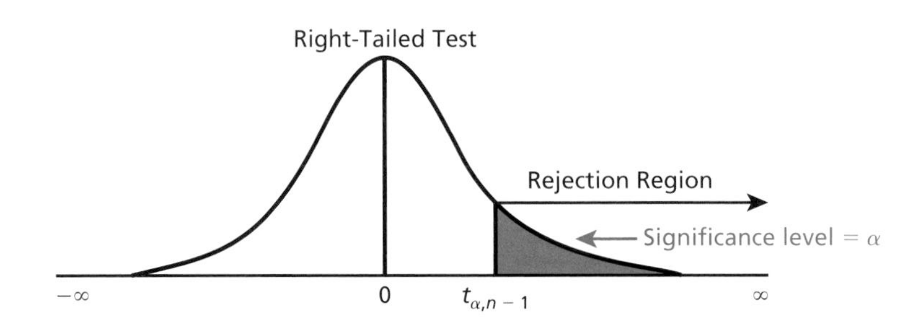

For a left-tailed test, the appropriate rejection rule is

$$\text{Reject } H_0 \text{ if } t\text{-stat} < -t_{\alpha,n-1}$$

which is depicted in Figure 5.13.

FIGURE 5.13
Rejection Region for a Left-Tailed Test

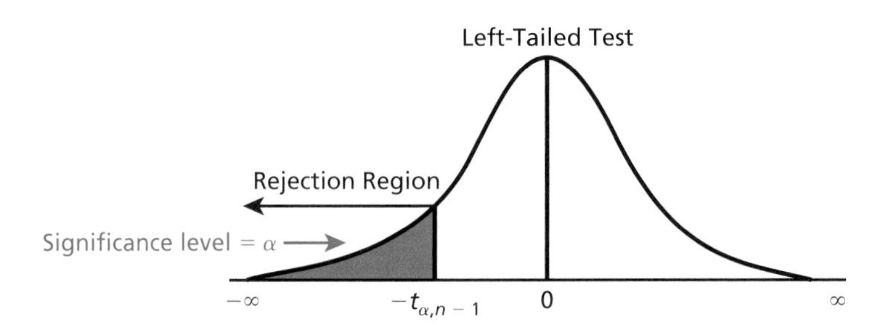

For a two-tailed test, the appropriate rejection rule is

$$\text{Reject } H_0 \text{ if } t\text{-stat} > t_{\alpha/2,n-1} \text{ or if } t\text{-stat} < -t_{\alpha/2,n-1}$$

which is depicted in Figure 5.14.

FIGURE 5.14
Rejection Regions for a Two-Tailed Test

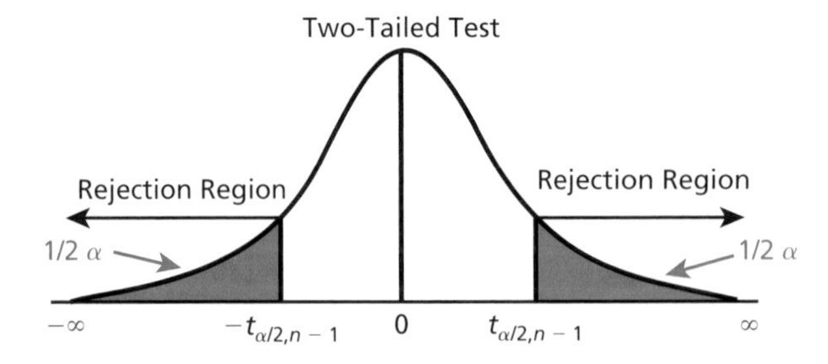

Looking across the rejection rules in Figures 5.12, 5.13, and 5.14, notice that the significance level, α, is kept whole when determining the critical value for both the right-tailed and left-tailed tests, while the significance level is divided by 2 for the two-tailed test. In the following chapters, we focus almost exclusively on two-tailed tests, but you should be aware that the other two types of tests are possible.

Empirical Research Tool 5.4 summarizes hypothesis testing using the critical value method.

EMPIRICAL RESEARCH TOOL 5.4: HYPOTHESIS TESTING BY COMPARING CALCULATED TEST-STATISTICS TO PREDETERMINED CRITICAL VALUES

Goal:

To gain insight into the likely value of a specific parameter that exists for a population of interest.

Problem:

Because the population is unobserved, we can never know the true value of the unobserved population parameter for certain.

Process:

1. Collect a specific sample of size n from the population, and calculate the value of the sample statistic of interest.
2. Calculate a test-statistic for the sample statistic of interest.
3. Compare the calculated test-statistic to a predetermined critical value.
4. If the absolute value of the calculated test-statistic is greater than the predetermined critical value, then reject H_0.

Intuition:

By definition, calculated test statistics measure how far an observed sample statistic falls away from a given hypothesized value. Hence, if the absolute value of the calculated test statistic is sufficiently large (as measured by the predetermined critical value), then we conclude that it is unlikely for the hypothesis to be true because, if it were true, it would have been statistically unlikely to observe such a large calculated test statistic.

Method 3: Calculate and Compare *p*-Values with Predetermined Levels of Significance

Our third method for hypothesis testing in linear regression analysis involves (1) formulating a hypothesis as to the true value of the unobserved population parameter, (2) calculating the probability of obtaining a test statistic that is either equal to or more extreme than the calculated test-statistic if the null hypothesis is indeed true, and (3) rejecting the null hypothesis if the calculated **p-value** is less than a predetermined confidence level.

p-value
The probability of obtaining a t-statistic at least as extreme as the one calculated using the sample statistics assuming the null hypothesis is true.

Again, the calculated p-value depends on the type of hypotheses being tested as follows:

$$\text{For a right-tailed test:} \quad p\text{-value} = P(Z > t\text{-stat}) \qquad 5.4.5$$

$$\text{For a left-tailed test:} \quad p\text{-value} = P(Z < t\text{-stat}) \qquad 5.4.6$$

$$\text{For a two-tailed test:} \quad p\text{-value} = 2P(Z > |t\text{-stat}|) \qquad 5.4.7$$

While the calculation of the p-value differs depending on the type of hypothesis being tested, the appropriate decision rule is the same in all three cases: We should

$$\text{Reject } H_0 \text{ if } p\text{-value} < \alpha \qquad 5.4.8$$

which makes intuitive sense because the preceding condition would only hold if, in the case that the null hypothesis were actually true, the probability of observing the test statistic that we actually observed was less than α (which is normally assumed to be 0.05), meaning that the condition would only hold if it were statistically very unlikely to observe the sample test statistic that we actually observed if the hypothesized value of the unobserved population parameter were indeed true.

Empirical Research Tool 5.5 summarizes hypothesis testing using the p-value method.

EMPIRICAL RESEARCH TOOL 5.5: HYPOTHESIS TESTING BY COMPARING CALCULATED P-VALUES TO PREDETERMINED LEVELS OF SIGNIFICANCE

Goal:

To gain insight into the likely value of a specific parameter that exists for a population of interest.

Problem:

Because the population is unobserved, we can never know the true value of the unobserved population parameter for certain.

Process:

1. Collect a specific sample of size *n* from the population, and calculate the value of the sample statistic of interest.
2. Calculate a *p*-value for the sample statistic of interest.
3. Compare the calculated *p*-value to the desired level of significance α.
4. If the calculated *p*-value $< \alpha$, then reject H_0.
5. If the calculated *p*-value $> \alpha$, then fail to reject H_0.

Intuition:

By definition, *p*-values measure the likelihood of observing a calculated test statistic as large as or larger than the test-statistic that is calculated for the observed sample *if the null hypothesis were indeed true.* Hence, if the calculated *p*-value is sufficiently large (smaller than the desired level of significance α), then we conclude that it is unlikely for the hypothesis to be true because, if it were true, it would have been statistically unlikely to observe such a small calculated *p*-value.

Differences among the Three Methods of Hypothesis Testing

Given that there are three possible methods for conducting hypothesis tests, an obvious question might be which one is preferred. The big picture answer is that so long as we are conducting a two-tailed test (which will be the usual case throughout the remainder of the text), it does not really matter because all three methods provide the same conclusion as to whether we reject or fail to reject the null hypothesis. That being said, there are differences among the information provided by the three methods. Most prominently, the *p*-value method not only provides a conclusion as to whether we should fail to reject or reject the null hypothesis, but it also attaches a probability to the likelihood that we observe the sample statistics that we actually do observe if the hypothesized values of the unobserved population parameters are in indeed true.

Excel Example 5.1 demonstrates how to calculate confidence intervals for our 200-observation CEO compensation sample.

EXCEL EXAMPLE 5.1

Commands for calculating confidence intervals for our CEO compensation sample

Using the "Descriptive Statistics" Command to Help Calculate Confidence Intervals

1. Determine the sample mean:
   In an empty cell (**F3**), type=**average(C2:C51).**
2. Determine the standard deviation:
   In an empty cell (**F5**), type=**stdev(C2:C51).**
3. Determine the margin of error:
   In an empty cell (**F7**), type **confidence(.05,F5,50),** where 0.05 is the desired confidence level, f5 is the sample standard deviation, and 50 is the sample size ($n = 50$).
4. Determine the upper and lower bounds of the confidence interval:
   In an empty cell (**F9**), type=**F3−F7.**
   In an empty cell (**F10**), type=**F3+F7.**

id	State	Tax Rate Per 20-Pack		
1	Alabama	\$0.43		
2	Alaska	\$2.00	**Mean**	\$1.4255
3	Arizona	\$2.00		
4	Arkansas	\$1.15	**Standard Deviation**	\$0.9317
5	California	\$0.87		
6	Colorado	\$0.84	**Margin of Error**	\$0.2583
7	Connecticut	\$3.00		
8	Delaware	\$1.60	**Lower Bound**	\$1.1672
9	Florida	\$1.34		
10	Georgia	\$0.37	**Upper Bound**	\$1.4255

This can be interpreted as indicating that the sample mean cigarette tax per 20-pack is \$1.43, that the sample standard deviation is \$0.93 per 20-pack, that the margin of error for a 95 percent confidence interval is \$0.26 per 20-pack, and that the 95 percent confidence interval for the true cigarette tax per 20-pack is (\$1.17, \$1.43) in billions.

This brings us to the point that we can test for the statistical significance of the sample regression function:

$$Property\ \widehat{crime}/100{,}000 = 3{,}870.55 + 7{,}931.70 Unemployment\ rate \qquad \textbf{5.4.9}$$

for our 150-observation city property crime sample.

Throughout the remainder of the text, we add new types of hypothesis tests as the need arises. For now, we introduce two of the most commonly used in linear regression analysis.

5.5 CONDUCT HYPOTHESIS TESTS FOR THE OVERALL STATISTICAL SIGNIFICANCE OF THE SAMPLE REGRESSION FUNCTION

***F*-test for the overall significance of the sample regression function**
A test that determines if the coefficients are jointly equal to 0.

The first hypothesis test that we consider is referred to as the ***F*-test for the overall significance of the regression function.** In the case of simple linear regression analysis, because we are only dealing with one independent variable, we can determine whether the sample regression function achieves overall statistical significance by determining whether the estimated slope coefficient, $\hat{\beta}_1$, suggests that the population parameter, β_1, is statistically different from 0. To see why, consider that if $\beta_1 \neq 0$, then the population regression model is correctly specified as $y_i = \beta_0 + \beta_1 x_i + \varepsilon_i$, meaning that x does explain some of the variation in y. Conversely, if $\beta_1 = 0$, then the population regression model is correctly specified as $y_i = \beta_0 + \varepsilon_i$, and x does not explain any of the variation in y. Hence, testing whether $\beta_1 \neq 0$ also tests whether the estimated sample simple linear regression function is statistically significant.

To conduct the hypothesis test, we start by defining our null and alternative hypotheses as

$$H_0\colon \beta_1 = 0$$
$$H_1\colon \beta_1 \neq 0 \qquad \textbf{5.5.1}$$

Based on the preceding discussion, it should be clear that there are three possible methods for testing these hypotheses. While we only need pursue one of these methods in practice, for illustrations purposes, throughout the remainder of the chapter, we present all three. In the particular case of testing for overall significance, however, the confidence interval approach is typically not used.

***F*-statistic for the overall regression (*F*-stat)**
The ratio of the mean squared regression to the mean squared error.

The first step in the critical value method is calculating the appropriate test statistic. In this case, the test statistic is referred to as the ***F*-statistic for the overall regression** (or the regression ***F*-stat**), which is calculated as

$$F\text{-}statistic = \frac{MSExplained}{MSUnexplained} \qquad \textbf{5.5.2}$$

where

$$\text{MSExplained} = \text{Mean square of regression} = \frac{ESS}{k}$$

$$k = \text{Number of independent variables}$$

$$\text{MSUnexplained} = \text{Mean square unexplained} = \frac{USS}{n-k-1} \qquad \textbf{5.5.3}$$

There is a fairly simple intuition underlying this calculation. As we learned in Chapter 4, the better the fit of the sample regression function to the observed sample data, the greater the calculated explained sum of squares (*ESS*) relative to the calculated unexplained sum of squares (*USS*). Accordingly, because the *MSExplained* depends directly on the calculated *ESS* and because the *MSUnexplained* depends directly on the calculated *USS*, the larger the calculated F-statistic, the greater the percentage of the explained variation in y relative to the unexplained variation in y. Accordingly, the larger the calculated F-statistic, the more likely we are to reject the null hypothesis that $\beta_1 = 0$ in favor of the alternative hypotheses that $\beta_1 \neq 0$.

After completing this step, we need to determine whether the sample regression function fits the observed data well enough to possess overall significance by comparing the calculated F-statistic for the overall regression to a given **critical value** that is determined by looking up the value for $F_{\alpha,k,n-k-1}$ in the F-table in Appendix C. As always, our rejection rule is to reject H_0 if the calculated F-statistic exceeds the predetermined critical value.

critical value
The value beyond which the null hypothesis is rejected.

The appropriate p-value for testing the overall significance of the sample regression function is difficult to calculate by hand; fortunately, standard statistical programs (Excel, Stata, SAS, etc.) provides the calculated p-value in a value referred to as the **significance *F* of sample regression function.** As always with the p-value approach, we test the null hypothesis by asking whether the calculated p-value is smaller than a predetermined threshold value (0.10 for 10 percent significance, 0.05 for 5 percent significance, etc.). Our rejection rule is to reject H_0 if the significance F is less than the predetermined threshold.

significance *F* of the sample regression function
The calculated p-value of F-test for the overall significance of the overall regression model.

Because all of our methods for conducting this particular hypothesis test yield the same conclusion, we can choose whichever method we most prefer. As discussed in the previous section, because it provides a specific probability while the others do not, our personal preference is to use the p-value method.

With this in mind, Hypothesis Testing 5.1 presents the F-test for the overall significance of the regression function for our 150-observation city property crime sample.

Hypothesis Testing 5.1: Testing for the Overall Significance of the Sample Regression Function

Hypothesis: H_0: $\beta_1 = 0$
H_A: $\beta_1 \neq 0$

***p*-Value Method:**

Test-Statistic

Significance $F = 0.0030$

Significance level: $\alpha = 0.05$

Rejection Rule

Reject H_0 if significance $F < 0.05$.

Conclusion:

Because the significance F is less than the significance level of 0.05 we reject H_0 at $\alpha = 0.05$ and conclude that the regression model does explain a significant portion of the observed variation in property crime rates (i.e., there is statistical evidence that unemployment rates affect property crime rates).

* *A visual representation is presented on the next page.*

Visual Depiction:

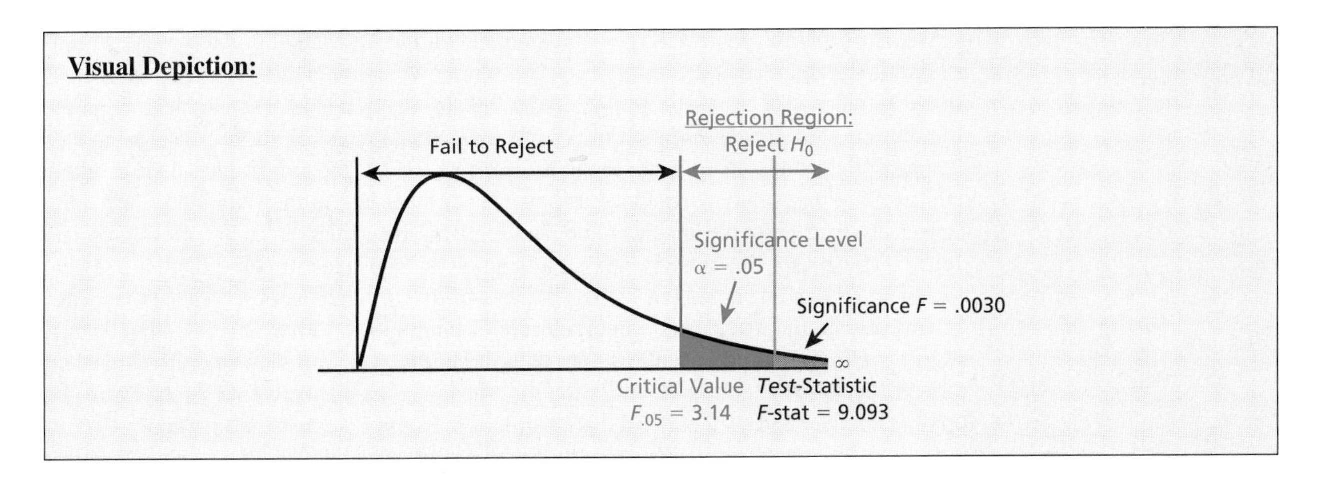

5.6 CONDUCT HYPOTHESIS TESTS FOR THE STATISTICAL SIGNIFICANCE OF THE SLOPE COEFFICIENT

t-test for the individual significance of the slope coefficient Determines whether the slope on the variable is statistically different from 0.

standard error of the slope coefficient The average deviation away from the observed slope.

Notation:
$s_{\hat{\beta}_1}$ Standard error of estimated slope coefficient

The second hypothesis test that we consider is referred to as the **t-test for the individual significance of the slope coefficient.** Before discussing that test, we need to discuss a value that plays an important role in the test.

Calculate the Standard Error of the Estimated Slope Coefficient

The **standard error of the slope coefficient,** $s_{\hat{\beta}_1}$, is calculated as

$$s_{\hat{\beta}_1} = \frac{s_{y|x}}{\sqrt{\sum_{i=1}^{n}(x_i - \bar{x})^2}} \qquad 5.6.1$$

Note that the numerator in formula 5.6.1, the calculated standard error of the sample regression function, provides an indication of how far each observed value of y falls from the sample regression function, on average, while the denominator, which is the numerator from the calculation for the variance of the independent variable, provides an indication of how spread out the observed values of x are from the sample mean.

Looking at formula 5.6.1, it should be clear that (1) as the explanatory power of the sample regression function increases, the calculated value of $s_{\hat{\beta}_1}$ decreases because the more precise the estimates, the smaller the value of $s_{y|x}$, and (2) as the amount of observed variation in the independent variable increases, the calculated value of $s_{\hat{\beta}_1}$ decreases because the greater the variation in x, the larger the sum in the denominator of the calculation.

This second fact merits further explanation. Consider Figure 5.15.

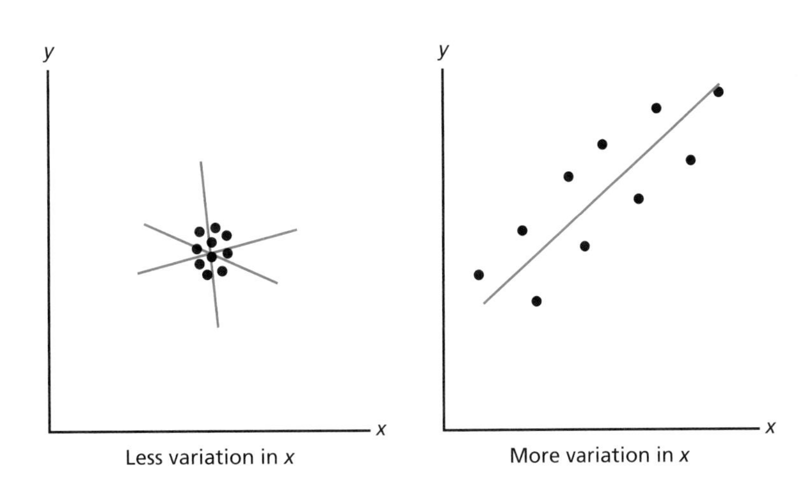

FIGURE 5.15
Fitting a Better Line When There Is More Variation in *x*

The left panel in Figure 5.15 depicts a sample with less variation in the observed x values, while the right panel depicts a sample with more variation in the observed x values. As should be clear, it is easier to fit a regression line through the observed sample data on the right because the greater variation in the observed x values allows for a clearer picture of the appropriate slope coefficient for the sample regression function. In fact, there is likely only one line that can be envisioned as being the best-fit line in the situation on the right. Conversely, because of the lower variation in the observed x values on the left, the appropriate slope coefficient for the sample regression function is not as clear because there are several possible lines that one could envision as the best-fit line through the observed sample data.

This discussion provides an important rule of thumb to follow when collecting data. If given the choice, we prefer collect data with more observed variation in the independent variable, because the greater the variation in x, the lower the standard error of the estimated slope coefficient and the greater the precision of the sample regression function.

For our 150-observation city property crime sample, we calculate the standard error of the estimated slope coefficient as

$$s_{\hat{\beta}_1} = \frac{s_{y|x}}{\sqrt{\sum(x_i - \bar{x})^2}} = \frac{1{,}485.45}{\sqrt{0.138694}} = 3{,}988.67 \qquad \textbf{5.6.2}$$

We interpret this value as indicating that on average the individual observations fall 3,988.67 away from the sample regression function.

Test for the Individual Significance of the Slope Coefficient

Armed with the preceding knowledge, we can now consider the t-test for the individual significance of the slope coefficient. In this case, we wish to test whether the slope coefficient for a given independent variable is statistically different from 0. Again, the reason for this is that if $\beta_1 = 0$, then the population regression model is correctly specified as $y_i = \beta_0 + \varepsilon_i$, and x does not explain any of the variation in y; whereas if $\beta_1 \neq 0$, then the population regression function model is correctly specified as $y_i = \beta_0 + \beta_1 x_i + \varepsilon_i$, and x does explain at least some of the variation in y. Note that while we are usually far more interested in the statistical significance of the slope coefficient, we can also use this test to determine if the estimated intercept is statistically different from 0 by testing whether $\beta_0 \neq 0$.

Because there is only one slope coefficient in simple linear regression, we start by defining our null and alternative hypotheses as

$$H_0\colon \beta_1 = 0 \qquad H_1\colon \beta_1 \neq 0 \qquad \textbf{5.6.3}$$

For illustration purposes, we again work through the three potential methods for performing this hypothesis tests. The confidence interval for the estimated slope coefficient is calculated the same way as any other confidence interval:

$$\textit{Parameter estimate} \pm \textit{Critical value} \cdot \textit{Standard error} \qquad \textbf{5.6.4}$$

In the case of large samples ($n \geq 100$), the 95 percent confidence interval is calculated as

$$\hat{\beta}_1 \pm 1.96 \cdot s_{\hat{\beta}_1} \qquad \textbf{5.6.5}$$

Note that this confidence interval is calculated around the estimated slope coefficient but that we are using it to learn about the unobserved population parameter. To do so, we simply ask whether the hypothesized population parameter (which, in this case, is 0) falls within the confidence interval calculated around the estimated slope coefficient. If it does not, then we conclude that it is statistically unlikely to observe the specific sample statistic that we did observe if the null hypothesis is indeed true, and we reject H_0.

The calculated test-statistic for the critical value method is referred to as a t-statistic (or t-stat) because the sampling distribution of the estimated slope coefficient is assumed to follow the Student's-t distribution. The formula for calculating the t-statistic for the estimated slope coefficient (assuming that the null hypothesis is that $\beta_1 = 0$) is

$$t\text{-statistic} = \frac{\hat{\beta}_1 - 0}{s_{\hat{\beta}_1}} \qquad \textbf{5.6.6}$$

Microsoft Example

$H_0: \beta_1 = 1$
$H_1: \beta_1 \neq 1$

Hypothesis states that Microsoft's risk premium moves in perfect step with the market risk premium

$t\text{-stat} = \frac{\hat{\beta}_1 - H_0}{s_{\hat{\beta}_1}} = \frac{1.3189 - 1}{0.16608} = 1.983$

$\alpha = 0.05$
critical value = 1.96
pg 516

$1.983 > 1.96$, we reject $H_0: \beta_1 = 1$ and conclude that Microsoft is not in perfect step with the market

The intuition behind this test statistic is fairly straightforward. Because the estimated slope coefficient $\hat{\beta}_1$ indicates the average relationship between y and x in the observed sample while the estimated standard error of the slope coefficient $s_{\hat{\beta}_1}$ indicates the average distance that each observed data point falls from that average relationship, it follows that the larger the calculated t-statistic, the greater the likelihood that $\beta_1 \neq 0$, and the smaller the calculated t-statistic, the smaller the likelihood that $\beta_1 \neq 0$. To determine whether the calculated t-statistic is larger or smaller in a statistical sense, we compare the calculated t-statistic to the critical value $t_{\alpha/2, n-k-1}$ in the Student's-t table and we implement the rejection rule reject H_0 if the calculated t-statistic exceeds the critical value.

The methodology for determining the p-value for the estimated slope coefficient depends on the number of observations in the sample. If the sample size is large ($n \geq 100$), then the appropriate calculation for a two-tailed test is

$$p\text{-value} = 2P(Z > |t\text{-stat}|) \qquad \textbf{5.6.7}$$

If sample size is not large ($n < 100$), then the calculation of the p-value is much more difficult because it is determined through probabilities that are generally not presented in the standard t-table. Fortunately, as with the significance F, the **p-value for individual significance** is included in the typical regression output table, meaning that we do not have to attempt to determine the value ourselves. As always with the p-value method, our rejection rule is reject H_0 if the calculated p-value is less than a predetermined threshold value that depends on the chosen level of significance.

p-value for individual significance
The probability that the test statistic is as large or larger in absolute value, assuming the null hypothesis is true.

With this in mind, Hypothesis Testing 5.2 presents the t-test for the individual significance of an estimated slope coefficient for our 150-observation city property crime sample.

Hypothesis Testing 5.2: Testing for the Individual Significance of the Slope Coefficient

Hypothesis:

H_0: $\beta_1 = 0$
H_A: $\beta_1 \neq 0$

p-Value Method:

p-value = 0.0486 (found on the Excel output at the end of the chapter)
Significance level: $\alpha = 0.05$

Rejection Rule
Reject H_0 if p-value < 0.05.

Conclusion:

Because $0.0486 < 0.05$, we reject H_0 at $\alpha = 0.05$ and conclude that unemployment rates are statistically related to property crime rates.

Visual Depiction:

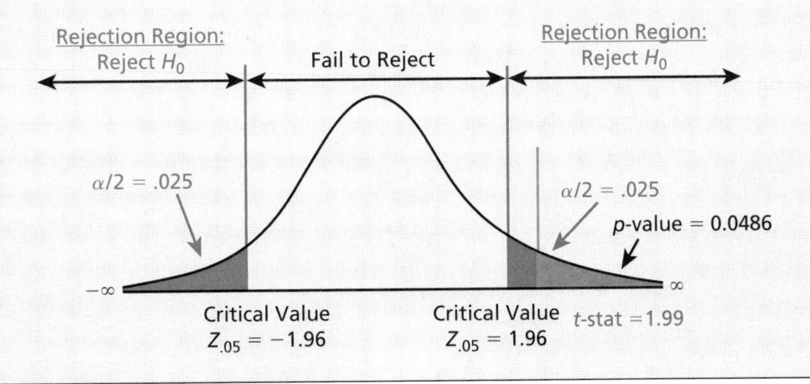

As a final point, we note that for simple linear regression, the F-test for the overall significance of the sample regression function and the t-test for the individual significance of the slope coefficient always come to the same conclusion and, in fact, have the same calculated p-value. This is because a special relationship exists between these two tests when the number of explanatory variables is equal to 1 (when $k = 1$). In such a case, it is true that F-statistic $=$ (t-statistic)^2. If so, then why take the time to introduce the two tests separately when they do the exact same thing? It turns out that this relationship only holds in the case of simple linear regression. In the case of multiple linear regression (i.e., when $k > 1$), the two tests become different and may reach different conclusions because the F-test for the overall significance of the sample regression function will test if the $k > 1$ estimated slope coefficients are all simultaneously equal to zero while the t-test for the individual significance of a slope coefficients will test whether each of the $k > 1$ estimated slope coefficients are individually equal to zero.

5.7 UNDERSTAND HOW TO READ REGRESSION OUTPUT IN EXCEL FOR THE PURPOSE OF HYPOTHESIS TESTING

In Chapter 4, we demonstrated how to read Excel regression output to determine the sample regression function as well as the different measures of the relative goodness-of-fit of those estimates. We now discuss how to read Excel regression output for the values required to perform the hypothesis tests introduced in this chapter. Table 5.2 highlights the location of these values.

TABLE 5.2 Explanation of Regression Output in Excel for Hypothesis Testing

SUMMARY OUTPUT	
Regression Statistics	
Multiple R	0.16131761
R Square	0.02602337
Adjusted R Square	0.01944245
Standard Error	1485.4455
Observations	150

ANOVA	df	SS	MS	F	Significance F
Regression	1	8725496.72	8725496.72	3.954364648	0.048593895
Residual	148	326569153.2	2206548.33	↗	↗
Total	149	335294649.9		*F-statistic*	*p-value for F-statistic*

	Coefficients	Standard Error	*t* Stat	*p*-value	Lower 95%	Upper 95%
Intercept	3870.548736	362.683323	10.67197881	4.48367E-20	3153.842076	4587.255397
Unemployment Rate	7931.702382	3988.669503	1.988558435	0.048593895	49.60298894	15813.80178
	↑ $\hat{\beta}_1$	↑ $s_{\hat{\beta}_1}$	↑ *t-stat for* $\hat{\beta}_1$	↑ *p-value for* $\hat{\beta}_1$	↖ *95% Confidence Interval for* $\hat{\beta}_1$	↗

As discussed earlier, one of the most important things to do with our estimates once we have calculated our sample regression function is to test whether each of the independent variables achieve individual statistical significance. Through experience, we have found that when interpreting regression results (particularly in the case of multiple linear regression), it is helpful to highlight those variables achieving statistical significance so that our eyes are drawn to the estimates that will be the focus of our analysis. We personally like to highlight variables achieving individual significance at the 5 percent level in red and variables achieving individual significance at the 10 percent level in orange. In a similar vein, for reasons that will become clear as we work through different examples, we have also learned that it is valuable to highlight the number of observations in the given sample being studied. Finally, we also find it informative to include notes below our estimates that call the reader's attention to information that is important for interpreting the results provided, such as what the dependent variable for the analysis is and what the highlighted rows indicate.

With these points in mind, Excel Regression Output 5.1 demonstrates the manner in which we present Excel regression output throughout the remainder of the text.

Excel Regression Output 5.1: The Sample Regression Function for our 150-Observation City Property Crime Sample

SUMMARY OUTPUT

Regression Statistics	
Multiple R	0.16131761
R Square	0.02602337
Adjusted R Square	0.01944245
Standard Error	1485.4455
Observations	**150**

ANOVA

	df	**SS**	**MS**	**F**	**Significance F**
Regression	1	8725496.72	8725496.72	3.954364648	0.048593895
Residual	148	326569153.2	2206548.333		
Total	149	335294649.9			

	Coefficients	**Standard Error**	***t* Stat**	***P*-value**	**Lower 95%**	**Upper 95%**
Intercept	3870.548736	362.683323	10.67197881	4.48367E-20	3153.842076	4587.255397
Unemployment Rate	7931.702382	3988.669503	1.988558435	0.048593895	49.60298894	15813.80178

Note: Highlighted variables are significant at the 5 percent level.

Again, with a little practice, reading such output tables becomes old-hat and the results of the preceding statistical tests can be determined quite easily.

Excel Example 5.2 demonstrates how to use the regression wizard to calculate the sample regression function for our 200-observation CEO compensation sample.

EXCEL EXAMPLE 5.2

Using the Regression Analysis Tool to estimate the sample regression function by OLS

Regression Analysis in Excel's Toolpak

1. In the "Data" tab, click the "Data Analysis" toolpak.

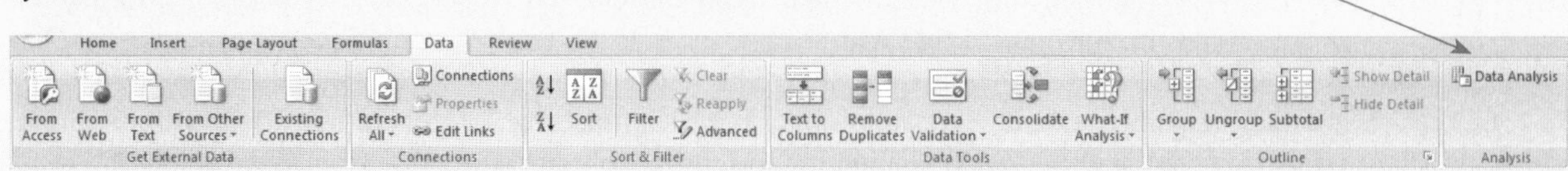

2. In the "Data Analysis" window, highlight "Regression" and click "OK".

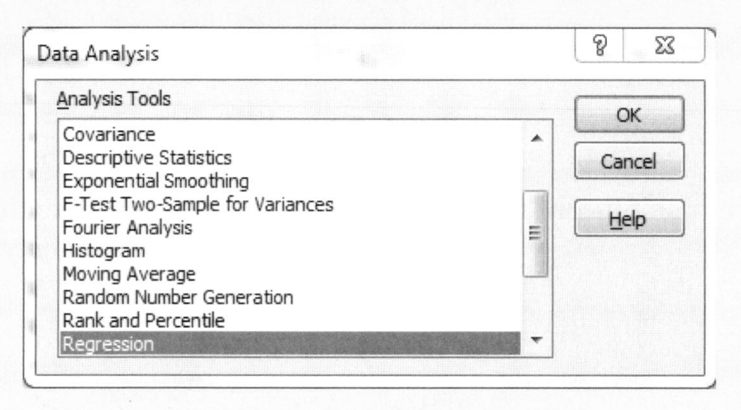

3. Click the tab next to the "Input Y Range" window, and highlight the observations for the dependent variable, including the variable name (**$C$1:$C$201**).
4. Click the tab next to the "Input X Range" window, and highlight the observations for the dependent variable, including the variable name (**$D$1:$D$201**).
5. Check the "Labels" box because we included the variable name in the preceding steps.
6. Check the "Output Range" tab, and highlight the desired first cell for the output (**$F$3**).

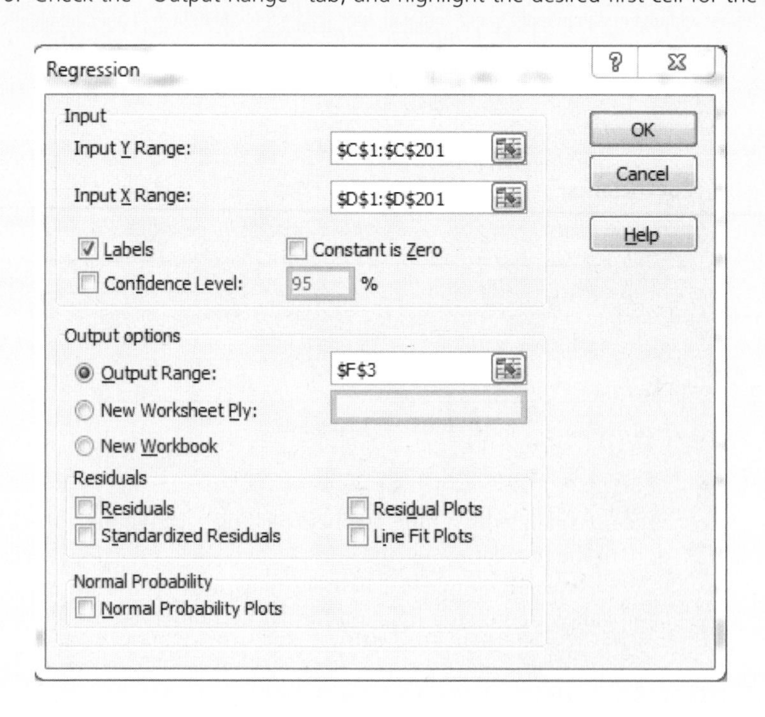

7. Click "OK" to run the regression.

SUMMARY OUTPUT

Regression Statistics	
Multiple R	0.39238316
R Square	0.153964544
Adjusted R Square	0.149691638
Standard Error	6262440.007
Observations	200

ANOVA

	df	SS	MS	F	Significance F
Regression	1	1.41314E+15	1.41314E+15	36.0324498	9.11178E-09
Residual	198	7.76519E+15	3.92182E+13		
Total	199	9.17833E+15			

	Coefficients	Standard Error	*t* Stat	*P*-value	Lower 95%	Upper 95%
Intercept	10792308.27	463406.70	23.28906398	1.29914E-58	9878462.178	11706154.36
Profits ($ millions)	1015.443772	169.16371	6.002728128	9.11178E-09	681.8499832	1349.037561

Note: Highlighted variables are significant at the 5 percent level.

The first thing to notice about this regression is that the *p*-value for overall significance (the entry in the "Significance *F*" column) is very, very small, meaning that for any reasonable level of significance, we reject the null hypothesis that $\beta_1 = 0$ and we conclude that, at least for this sample, firm profits help explain CEO compensation. Because this is a simple linear regression, the *F*-test for overall significance and the *t*-test for individual significance are exactly the same. This can be verified by noticing that the *p*-value in the Profits row equals the *p-value* in the "Significance *F*" column. With regard to the Profits variable, the calculated confidence interval (681.853, 1349.04) does not include 0, the calculated *t*-statistic (6.003) is greater than 1.96, and the calculated *p*-value (9.11*E*-09) is less than 0.05, all of which indicate that the Profits variable is statistically significant at the 5 percent level. The coefficient estimate on the Profits variable indicates that, on average, every $1 million increase in firm profits is associated with a $1,015.44 in CEO compensation. The estimated intercept indicates that within this sample, the CEO of a firm with 0 profit would be expected to receive $10,792,303.27 in compensation. Finally, the calculated *R*-square of 0.1540 means that 15.40 percent of the total variation in CEO compensation can be explained by the variation in firm profits.

5.8 CONSTRUCT CONFIDENCE INTERVALS AROUND THE PREDICTED VALUE OF *y*

We know that the predicted value of y associated with a given value of x is $\hat{y} = \hat{\beta}_0 + \hat{\beta}_1 x$. Is this predicted value definitely correct? No. As with any prediction, some degree of error will be associated with this value. Accordingly, we need to develop some sense of the likely error that is associated with the prediction. We do this by calculating a confidence interval around the predicted value of y.

As we learned earlier, a confidence interval consists of three components: a point estimate, a critical value, and a standard error of the prediction. As discussed earlier, the point estimate in this case will be the predicted value of y (i.e., $\hat{y}$). The appropriate critical value for the predicted value of y will be the one used to calculate the confidence interval around the slope coefficient (i.e., $t_{\alpha/2,n-k-1}$). The standard error of the predicted value of y is less obvious because it depends on the type of prediction being calculated. We discuss the different types of predictions that can be calculated later, but for now, we simply define the standard error of the prediction as $s_{\hat{p}}$. Accordingly, the formula for the confidence interval around the predicted value of y is

$$\hat{y} \pm t_{\frac{\alpha}{2},n-k-1} s_{\hat{p}} \qquad \textbf{5.8.1}$$

There are two types of predicted values of y that can be calculated:

1. Predictions about the mean value of y.
2. Predictions about a specific value of y.

As an example of the distinction between these types of predictions, suppose that your best friend is considering moving to a city with an unemployment rate of 8 percent. Being a concerned friend, you are interested in predicting the property crime rate in that city. There are two ways to calculate this prediction: (1) by calculating the predicted mean annual property crime rates for all cities with unemployment rates of 8 percent and (2) by calculating the predicted the property crime rate for one specific city with an unemployment rate of 8 percent out of all cities with unemployment rates of 8 percent. Which calculated value should be more precise? The first. Why? Because it is easier to predict the mean value for a distribution of multiple observations than to predict the specific value for a given observation drawn from the distribution of multiple observations. For this reason, the calculated standard error of the prediction is smaller for predictions about the mean value of y than for predictions about a specific value of y.

Before we present the formulas for calculating the standard errors for each of these types of predictions, we present the intuition behind the shape of the confidence interval for a prediction and the difference between a confidence interval for a mean and an individual. Figure 5.16 summarizes this intuition by depicting the calculated confidence intervals for different potential values of x.

FIGURE 5.16
Prediction Intervals for Individual and Mean Values

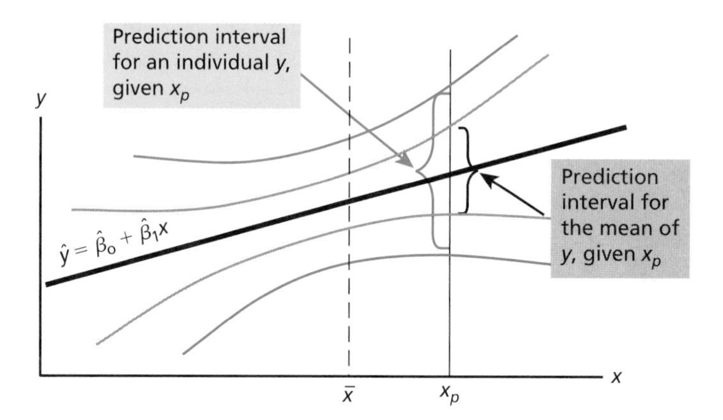

Figure 5.16 demonstrates two important facts regarding confidence intervals for predicted values of y. The first is that the widths of both types of prediction intervals increase as the x value for which the prediction is calculated moves away from the mean value $\bar{x}$. The reason for this is that the sample regression function is most precise for the mean value of x, and therefore, predictions for the mean value of x are more precise than predictions for other values of x; this difference increases as the value of x falls farther from the mean. A useful analogy is the forecast track of a hurricane. As a hurricane advances toward landfall, weather forecasters often present a map of the storm's "forecast cone," which indicates the path that the storm can most likely be expected to follow in the coming days. For example, Figure 5.17 traces the path forecast by the National Oceanic and Atmospheric Administration (NOAA) after Tropical Storm Dean formed in the Atlantic Ocean in August 2007.

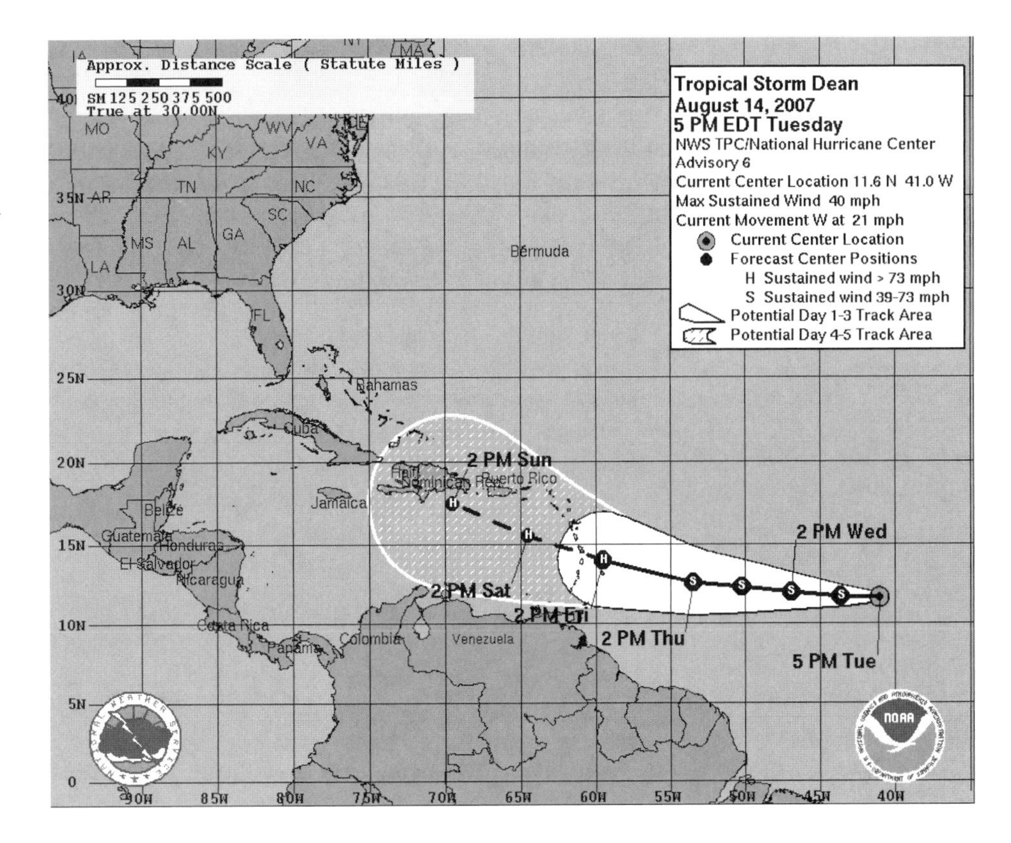

FIGURE 5.17
Diagram of the Path of a Hurricane

Source: National Oceanic and Atmospheric Administration, www.nhc.noaa.gov/aboutcone.shtml.

Why is the forecast a cone as opposed to a forecast line? Because the forecasters realize that there is likely to be error associated with the predicted path and that this error is likely to increase the farther away the time period is from the present. NOAA's website explains the cone as follows, "The cone represents the probable track of the center of a tropical cyclone, and is formed by enclosing the area swept out by a set of circles (not shown) along the forecast track (at 12, 24, 36 hours, etc). The size of each circle is set so that two-thirds of historical official forecast errors over a 5-year sample fall within the circle." Put another way, forecasters realize that the predictions made by their computer models are most precise in the near future when there is less variability in the hurricane path and less precise in the more distant future when there is greater variability in the hurricane path. For this reason, the confidence interval (or the cone) around the forecast path is smaller in the short term and larger in the long term. In this sense, the hurricane "forecast cone" is similar to the prediction interval for y given either the mean value of x or an individual value of x.

The second fact demonstrated in Figure 5.17 is that for each possible value of x, the prediction interval for a specific value of y given that particular value of x is larger than the confidence interval for the mean value of y given that particular value of x. A useful analogy is fishing with a net. Suppose that we desire to catch a fish of one specific size out of the many fish living in the body of water in which we are fishing. Will they need a larger or smaller net to accomplish this task than the one they would need to catch an average size fish? They will need a larger net because it is much easier to gather an average than a fish of a specific size.

These facts are demonstrated in the following calculations. The formula for the standard error for a mean prediction is

$$s_{\hat{p},m} = \sqrt{(s_{y|x})^2 \left\{ \frac{1}{n} + \frac{(x_{\hat{p}} - \bar{x})^2}{\sum_{i=1}^{n} (x_i - \bar{x})^2} \right\}} \quad \textbf{5.8.2}$$

This is one of the more complicated formulas that we are going to present in this book. Despite the fact that it looks scary, we have already discussed almost all of its components.

The $(s_{y|x})^2$ term is the standard error of the regression function squared, n is the number of observations in the sample, and $\sum_{i=1}^{n}(x_i - \bar{x})^2$ is the numerator of the sample variance of the independent variable and is also the denominator of the slope coefficient estimate. The only component that is not familiar is $(x_{\hat{p}} - \bar{x})^2$, which is the square of the value for which the prediction is calculated, $x_{\hat{p}}$, less the mean of x. The intuition behind this component is that the further the predicted value falls from the mean value of x, the larger the standard error of the prediction and the lower the accuracy of the prediction.

To see how this formula is used, suppose that we are interested in constructing a 95 percent confidence interval (5 percent significance level) around our prediction for the mean property crime rate for a city with an unemployment rate of 8 percent. The point estimate of the calculated prediction is

$$\hat{y} = \hat{\beta}_0 + \hat{\beta}_1 x_{\hat{p}} = 3{,}870.55 + 7{,}931.70 \cdot (0.08) = 4{,}505.09 \qquad \textbf{5.8.3}$$

the appropriate critical value is

$$t_{\propto/2,n-k-1} = t_{0.25,148} = 1.96 \qquad \textbf{5.8.4}$$

and the calculated standard error of the prediction is

$$s_{\hat{p},m} = \sqrt{(s_{y|x})^2\left\{\frac{1}{n} + \frac{(x_{\hat{p}} - \bar{x})^2}{\sum_i^n (x_i - \bar{x})^2}\right\}} = \sqrt{(1{,}485.45)^2\left\{\frac{1}{150} + \frac{(0.08 - 0.085769)^2}{0.138693893}\right\}}$$

$$= 123.29 \qquad \textbf{5.8.5}$$

Accordingly, the calculated confidence interval around the predicted mean property crime rate for a city with an unemployment rate of 8 percent (which we refer to as the confidence interval for the mean of y given x_p) is

$$\hat{y} \pm t_{\frac{\alpha}{2},n-2} S_{\hat{p},m} = 4{,}505.09 \pm 1.96 \cdot 123.29$$

$$4{,}505.09 \pm 241.85$$

$$(4{,}263.23, 4{,}746.94) \qquad \textbf{5.8.6}$$

Because it is calculated at a 95 percent confidence level, the appropriate interpretation of this interval is that on average, if we take many, many samples and create confidence intervals in the preceding manner, the true mean predicted property crime rate for a city with an unemploy ment rate of 8 percent will fall within the interval (4,263.23, 4,746.94) 95 out of 100 times.

Suppose that instead of predicting the *mean* property crime rate for *all* cities with unemployment rates of 8 percent, we wish to predict the property crime rate for one *specific* city with an unemployment rate of 8 percent. In this case, we want to construct a confidence interval around one specific city with an unemployment rate of 8 percent instead of the mean value across all cities with unemployment rates of 8 percent. The only thing that changes in our calculated confidence interval is the calculated standard error of the prediction. The one change we make is to add a 1 to the calculated standard error in formula 5.8.2. Accordingly, the calculated standard error for the individual prediction is

$$S_{\hat{p},i} = \sqrt{(s_{y|x})^2\left\{1 + \frac{1}{n} + \frac{(x_{\hat{p}} - \bar{x})^2}{\sum_i^n (x_i - \bar{x})^2}\right\}} \qquad \textbf{5.8.7}$$

To see how this formula is used, suppose that we are interested in constructing a 95 percent confidence interval (5 percent significance level) around our prediction for the mean property crime rate for a city with an unemployment rate of 8 percent. The point estimate of the calculated prediction is the same as earlier:

$$\hat{y} = \hat{\beta}_0 + \hat{\beta}_1 x_{\hat{p}} = 3{,}870.55 + 7{,}931.70 \cdot (0.08) = 4{,}505.09 \qquad \textbf{5.8.8}$$

while the appropriate critical value is

$$t_{\propto/2,n-k-1} = t_{.025,148} = 1.96 \qquad \textbf{5.8.9}$$

Confidence Intervals around predicted value of Y

$$\hat{Y} \pm t_{\frac{\alpha}{2}, n-k-1}(S_{\hat{p}})$$

Two types - Prediction about mean value of Y
" " specific " " "

Mean prediction formula = $S_{\hat{p},m} = \sqrt{(S_{Y|X})^2 \left\{ \frac{1}{n} + \frac{(X_p - \bar{X})^2}{\sum (X_i - \bar{X})^2} \right\}}$

X_p = Value used for the prediction

$(S_{Y|X})^2 = \frac{USS}{(n-k-1)}$

$(S_{Y|X})^2 = MS\,Unexplained$

$S_{Y|X} = \sqrt{MS\,Unexplained}$

If we do this many, many times, 95 out of 100 times the mean predicted value will fall within this interval

Specific prediction formula = $S_{\hat{p},i} = \sqrt{(S_{Y|X})^2 \left\{ 1 + \frac{1}{n} + \frac{(X_p - \bar{X})^2}{\sum (X_i - \bar{X})^2} \right\}}$

Sample f-stat problem

$$\text{f-stat} = \frac{MS\,Explained}{MS\,Unexplained} = \frac{6331}{20} = 316.55$$

significance level = $\alpha = 0.05$

Rejection Rule: Reject H_0 if p-value < 0.05

p-value = 2.46 E-57

Because 2.46 E-57 is less than 0.05, we reject H_0 & conclude that GPA is related to class attendance

n = # of observations in a samp

N = # of observations in a population

s = sample standard deviation = $\sqrt{s^2}$

$$s^2 = \text{sample variance} = \frac{\sum_{i=1}^{n}(x_i - \bar{x})^2}{n-1}$$

$$Var(x) = (Stdev\,x)^2 = s^2$$

Covariance between X + Y

$$cov(x,y) = S_{xy} = \frac{\sum_{i=1}^{n}(x_i - \bar{x})(y_i - \bar{y})}{n-1}$$

Correlation coefficient between x + y

$$r_{xy} = \frac{cov(x,y)}{Stdev(x)\,Stdev(y)} = \frac{S_{xy}}{S_x S_y}$$

if $S_{xy} > 0$ and/or $r_{xy} > 0$, then we conclude that the estimated linear relationship is positive.

Covariance = unit based measure of the degree of linear relationship between Y + X

Correlation Coefficient = Unitless measure of the degree of linear relationship between Y + X

The larger the covariance relative to the standard deviations, the larger the correlation coefficient, r_{xy}

correlation coefficient falls between -1 + 1. Negative = negative slope line

1 = stronger relationship

Marginal effect = the effect that a one-unit change in the independent variable has on the dependent variable, holding all else constant

Deterministic = A relationship in which an exact linear relationship exists between two variables

Probabilistic = A relationship in which an exact linear relationship does not exist between two variables

Error term measures
1) Omitted variables
2) Measurement errors
3) Incorrect functional form - fit the wrong model to the data

---

Coefficient of determination = r^2 = The percentage of the variation in Y that can be explained by X
- Goodness of fit measure

$$r^2 = \frac{ESS}{TSS} = \frac{\sum^{n}(\hat{Y}_i - \bar{Y})^2}{}$$

r^2 can only = 0 if ESS = 0

ESS can only = 0 if there is no statistical relationship between Y + X

r^2 = 1 if ESS = TSS which

Lin

Y =

X =

e =

$\hat{Y}_i$ =

resid

Popu

Y

Y_i

X_i

B_0

B_1

and the calculated standard error of the prediction is

$$s_{\hat{p},m} = \sqrt{(s_{y|x})^2 \left\{ 1 + \frac{1}{n} + \frac{(x_{\hat{p}} - \bar{x})^2}{\sum_{i}^{n}(x_i - \bar{x})^2} \right\}}$$

$$= \sqrt{(1{,}485.45)^2 \left\{ 1 + \frac{1}{150} + \frac{(0.08 - 0.085769)^2}{0.138693893} \right\}} = 1490.56 \qquad \textbf{5.8.10}$$

Now the calculated confidence interval around the property crime rate for a specific city with an unemployment rate of 8 percent (which we refer to as the confidence interval for an individual y given x_p) is

$$\hat{y} \pm t_{\frac{\alpha}{2},n-2} s_{\hat{p},m} \; or \; 4{,}505.09 \pm 1.96 \cdot 1{,}490.56$$
$$4{,}505.09 \pm 2{,}921.50$$
$$(1{,}583.583,\ 7{,}426.59)$$

Because it is calculated at the 95 percent confidence level, the appropriate interpretation of this interval is that on average, if we take many, many samples and create confidence intervals in the preceding manner, the true individual predicted property crime rate for a city with an unemployment rate of 8 percent will fall within the interval (1,583.583, 7,426.59) 95 out of 100 times. Notice that the confidence interval for the predicted property crime rate of a specific city with an unemployment rate of 8 percent is much wider than the confidence interval for the predicted mean property crime rate of all cities with unemployment rates of 8 percent.

ADDITIONS TO OUR EMPIRICAL RESEARCH TOOLKIT

In this chapter we have introduced a number of tools that will prove valuable when performing empirical research. They include:

- Construct sampling distributions.
- Understand desirable properties of simple linear regression estimators.
- Understand the simple linear regression assumptions required for OLS to be the best linear unbiased estimator.
- Understand how to conduct hypothesis tests in linear regression analysis.
- Conduct hypothesis tests for the overall statistical significance of the sample regression function.
- Conduct hypothesis tests for the statistical significance of the estimated slope coefficient, $\hat{\beta}_1$.
- Understand how to read regression output in Excel.
- Construct confidence intervals around the predicted value of y.

OUR NEW EMPIRICAL TOOLS IN PRACTICE: USING WHAT WE HAVE LEARNED IN THIS CHAPTER

As noted at the end of Chapter 4, the estimated sample simple linear regression function for our student's hours of video games played data was

$$\widehat{GPA}_i = 3.25 - 0.039 \cdot Video\ game\ hours_i$$

and the predicted GPA for a student who played 25 hours of video games a week was

$$\widehat{GPA} = 3.250 - 0.039 \cdot 25 = 3.250 - 0.968 = 2.282$$

On the basis of the information presented in this chapter, our student was able to learn about the unobserved population parameters in which he was interested by performing hypothesis tests for the overall significance of the sample regression function and the individual significance of the estimated slope coefficient. To demonstrate what he learned, the student started with the Excel output presented in Table 5.3.

TABLE 5.3 Excel Regression Output for Our Former Student's Hours of Video Games Played Data

SUMMARY OUTPUT	
Regression Statistics	
Multiple R	0.570478014
R Square	0.325445164
Adjusted R Square	0.314905245
Standard Error	0.385420065
Observations	66

ANOVA

	df	SS	MS	F	Significance F
Regression	1	4.58679337	4.586793369	30.87738666	5.71131E-07
Residual	64	9.50711208	0.148548626		
Total	65	14.09390544			

	Coefficients	Standard Error	*t* Stat	*P*-value	Lower 95%	Upper 95%
Intercept	3.250004865	0.05751274	56.50930296	2.44138E-56	3.13510996	3.364899771
Video Game Hours	−0.038712086	0.00696668	−5.55674245	5.71131E-07	−0.05262964	−0.024794529

Note: Highlighted variables are significant at the 5 percent level.

Given that this is a simple linear regression, the student performed both desired hypothesis tests in the same way. Because the p-value for the overall significance of the sample regression function and the p-value for the individual significance of the estimated slope coefficient are both less than 0.05, the student failed to reject the null hypothesis that $\beta_1 = 0$, and we conclude that, for this sample, video game hours have a significant explanatory effect on GPA.

Combined with the work discussed in Chapter 4, and with an effective write-up, this analysis formed the basis of a successful empirical research project for our former student.

LOOKING AHEAD TO CHAPTER 6

So far, we have learned how to estimate the linear relationship between a dependent variable and a single independent variable through simple linear regression analysis. While valuable, this tool only allows us to answer the rather limited question of how a given variable is linearly related to only one other variable. In most real-world situations, economists are actually interested in learning about the linear relationship between a dependent variable and multiple independent variables. For instance, a health economist might be interested in learning how obesity rates are related to age, sex, race/ethnicity, income, education, exercise, and a number of other potentially important factors. In Chapter 6, we introduce multiple linear regression analysis, which is the primary tool by which we investigate such relationships.

Problems

5.1 In which of the following two scenarios is the goodness-of-fit measure better?

a. In a scatter plot of the data the dots are extremely close to the line or in the scatter plot the dots are very are far from the line.

b. The correlation coefficient is 0.92 or the correlation coefficient is 0.12.

c. The sum of squares unexplained is large relative to the total sum of squares or the sum of squares unexplained is small relative to the total sum of squares.

5.2 Calculate the SSTotal, SSExplained, and the SSUnexplained for each of the points on the graph.

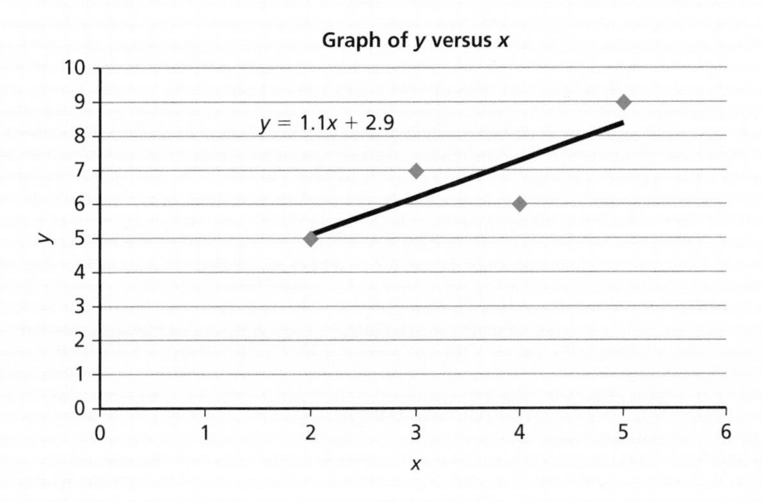

5.3 Given the following data set calculate the SSTotal, SSExplained, and SSUnexplained.

x	y
1	5
2	3
3	4
5	7
6	10
7	9
8	12
8	9

5.4 For the data in problem 5.3, calculate the R^2 and explain what it means.

5.5 What does the R^2 mean in the following scenarios?

a. The dependent variable is salary, the independent variable is education, and the R^2 is 0.23.

b. The dependent variable is GPA, the independent variable is numbers of hours spent studying, and the R^2 is 0.43.

c. The dependent variable is GDP, the independent variable is productivity, and the R^2 is 0.93.

5.6 Fill in the rest of the following ANOVA table if the number of observations is 56, there is one independent variable, the SSExplained is 45.63, and the MSUnexplained is 12.44.

ANOVA

	df	SS	MS	F	Significance F
Regression					0.0005
Residual					
Total					

5.7 For the following values, calculate the R^2.

a. *SSTotal* = 1234, *SSExplained* = 865.

b. *SSTotal* = 32, *SSUnexplained* = 18.

c. *SSTotal* = 16,467, *SSUnexplained* = 1,156.

5.8 For the data in problem 5.3, calculate the standard error of the slope coefficient.

5.9 If you are trying to explain savings rates using incomes, would you rather your sample contain a wide range of incomes or a small range of incomes? Why or why not?

5.10 For the data in problem 5.3, calculate the F-statistic and comment on the overall significance of the regression.

5.11 For the data in problem 5.3, calculate the t-statistic and comment on the significance of the independent variable.

5.12 For the data in problem 5.3, calculate the confidence interval for the slope and comment if the slope coefficient is statistically significant.

5.13 The sleep study lab at San Diego State University is trying to find factors that explain the number of minutes people sleep. It has collected data from 706 individuals. Sleep is number of minutes of sleep a person gets during the night per week and age is the age in years of an individual.

The summary statistics are

	Sleep (in minutes)	Age (in years)
Sample mean	32,663.56	38.81586
Standard deviation	444.41	11.34264

$$\sum_{i=1}^{706}(x_1 - \bar{x})(y_i - \bar{y}) = 321{,}165.20$$

a. Find the covariance between *Sleep* and *Age.*

b. Find the correlation coefficient for *Sleep* and *Age.*

c. Find the least squares line that shows how *Sleep (y)* is related to *Age (x).*

d. According to the least squares line, how is *Sleep* related to *Age?*

e. What is the coefficient of determination from the regression? What does it mean?

f. Use the estimated regression equation developed in part (c) to calculate a 95 percent confidence interval for the expected the expected number of minutes of sleep per week for someone who is 23 years old. The mean squared unexplained is 196,168.5056 and

$$\sum_{i-1}^{706}(x_1 - \bar{x})^2 = 90{,}702.06$$

5.14 The Transactional Records Access Clearinghouse at Syracuse University reported data showing the odds of an Internal Revenue Service audit. The data show the average adjusted gross income reported and the percentage of returns that were audited for 20 selected IRS districts.

The summary statistics are

	Gross Income ($)	Percent Audited
Sample mean	33,636	.83
Standard deviation	2,696.14	.2238

$$\sum_{i=1}^{706}(x_1 - \bar{x})(y_i - \bar{y}) = 5{,}623.11$$

a. Find the covariance between *Gross Income* and *Percent Audited.*

b. Find the correlation coefficient for *Gross Income* and *Percent Audited.*

c. Find the least squares line that shows how Percent Audited *(y)* is related to Gross Income *(x).*

d. According to the least squares line, how is *Percent Audited* related to *Gross Income?*

e. What is the coefficient of determination from the regression? What does it mean?

f. Use the estimated regression equation developed in part (c) to calculate a 95 percent confidence interval for the expected percentage audited for districts with an average adjusted gross income of \$35,000. The mean squared unexplained is 0.0436 and

$$\sum_{i=1}^{20}(x_1 - \bar{x})^2 = 145{,}383{,}319$$

5.15 A professor would like to explain the number of classes a student attended out of 32 possible classes. The professor decides to run a simple linear regression and determines that the students' GPA is the factor that has the most explanatory power.

ANOVA

	df	SS	MS	F	Significance F
Regression	1	6,331	6331		2.46E-57
Residual	678	13,874	20		
Total	679	20,205			

	Coeff.	Std. Error	*t* Stat	*P*-value	Lower 95%	Upper 95%
Intercept	15.36	0.64	24.12	2.88E-93	14.11	16.62
GPA	4.15	0.24	17.59	2.46E-57	3.68	4.61

a. What is the R^2 and what does it mean?

b. What is the *F*-statistic? Test the overall significance of the regression model.

c. What is the standard error of the regression, and what does it mean?

d. Test the significance of GPA using a *t*-test.

e. If a student has a GPA of 3.3, how many classes is he or she predicted to have attended?

Exercises

E5.1 Obtain scatterplots for y_1 against x_1 and y_2 against x_2 in the data set **scatterplot.xls**. Choose which graph has a lower R^2.

E5.2 The file **facebook.xls** contains information on number of times a person has been tagged in a photo and the number of friends the person has on Facebook. The variable that you are trying to explain is the number of times a person has been tagged.

a. Compute the R^2, standard error of the regression, and standard error of the slope without using the regression analysis tool in Excel.

b. Now use the regression analysis tool and check your work.

E5.3 Refer to exercise 5.2.

a. Test the overall significance of the regression using an *F*-test.

b. Test the significance of number of friends using a *t*-test.

E5.4 The file **baseball.xls** contains information on Major League Baseball players' salaries and the number of years they have been in the major leagues. The dependent variable is salaries.

a. Create a scatterplot with salaries on the *y*-axis.

b. Calculate the R^2 and explain what it means.

c. Calculate the *F*-statistic and test the overall significance of the regression model.

d. Calculate the standard error of the regression function and explain what it means.

e. Compute the standard error of the slope coefficient and perform a *t*-test.

E5.5 The file **work.xls** contains information on a student's GPA and the number of hours they work a week. The dependent variable is GPA.

a. Create a scatterplot with GPA on the y-axis.

b. Calculate the R^2 and explain what it means.

c. Calculate the F-statistic and test the overall significance of the regression model.

d. Calculate the standard error of the regression function and explain what it means.

e. Compute the standard error of the slope coefficient and perform a t-test.

E5.6 You are hired by Bob's Pizza to compute a prediction interval for total receipts in Maine because they are thinking of locating there. The data are contained in **Bobs.xls**.

a. Using the regression function in Excel, perform a regression analysis and write out the estimated regression equation.

b. Predict the total receipts for Maine.

c. Compute a prediction interval for a mean of total receipts for Maine and explain what the interval means.

d. Compute a prediction interval for an individual of total receipts for Maine and explain what the interval means.

e. If the manager needs $15,000 worth of receipts for the restaurant to be profitable, would you suggest locating in Maine? Explain your answer.

Appendix 5A

Common Theoretical Probability Distributions

standard normal probability distribution
A normal probability distribution function with a population mean of 0 and a population standard deviation of 1. It is denoted by a Z.

There are three primary theoretical probability distributions that are used in this text: the standard normal probability distribution, the Student's-t probability distribution, and the F-distribution.

The Standard Normal Probability Distribution

The **standard normal probability distribution** is a normal probability distribution with a mean of 0 and a standard deviation of 1 that looks like Figure 5A.1.

FIGURE 5A.1
The Standard Normal Probability Distribution

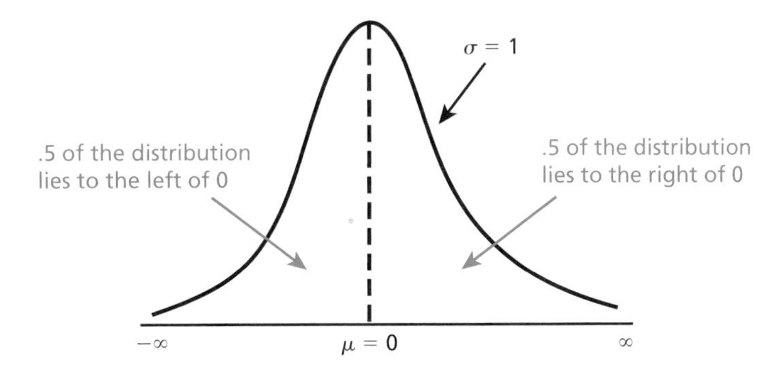

The standard normal probability distribution is special because any normal probability distribution, regardless of its population mean and standard deviation, can be converted to the standard normal probability distribution through the following relatively simple transformation: For each observed value in a normal probability distribution (x) the corresponding value in the standard normal probability distribution (z) is

$$z = \frac{x - \mu}{\sigma} \qquad \text{5A.1}$$

This proves extremely useful, because it allows us to list the area under the curve between 0 and z in one convenient table that can then be used to solve statistical problems. As an example that we commonly encounter, suppose that we would like to determine a critical value z for the 95 percent confidence level. To use the standard normal table to determine this value, we start by noting that due to the symmetry of the distribution, we only need to focus on one side of the distribution (i.e., because of symmetry, the area to the right of 0 must equal the area to the left of 0). Accordingly, we limit our focus to one side of the distribution, and we divide all of the values by 2 (because we are only dealing with half of the distribution). Hence, to determine the critical value z for the 95 percent confidence level, we need to determine the value z for which exactly $0.05/2 = 0.025$ of the distribution lies to the right of z. Visually, we want to determine the value z in Figure 5A.2.

FIGURE 5A.2
Determining the Critical Value for the 95 Percent Confidence Level in the Standard Normal Probability Distribution

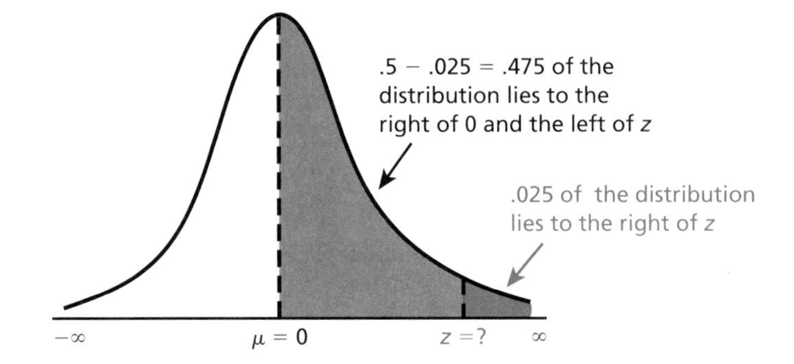

How do we use the standard normal table to determine this value? We first need to recognize that the values listed in the standard normal table in Appendix C represent the percentage of the distribution that lies between 0 and z (i.e., the values represent the gray area in Figure 5A.2). Hence, to determine the critical value z for the 95 percent confidence level, we need to search the interior of the table for the value 0.475. Once we find that value in the table, we look for the row heading to find the first two digits of our desired critical value, and we look for the column heading to find the third digit of our desired critical value. For the 95 percent confidence level, we do so by following the blue lines in Table 5A.1.

TABLE 5A.1
Using the Standard Normal Table to Determine the Appropriate Critical Values for the 95 Percent and 90 Percent Confidence Levels

Area under the Normal Curve from 0 to X

			1.6 + (0.04 + 0.05)/2				1.9 + 0.06			
X	0.00	0.01	0.02	0.03	0.04	0.05	0.06	0.07	0.08	0.09
0.0	0.00000	0.00399	0.00798	0.01197	0.01595	0.01994	0.02392	0.02790	0.03188	0.03586
0.1	0.03983	0.04380	0.04776	0.05172	0.05567	0.05962	0.06356	0.06749	0.07142	0.07535
0.2	0.07926	0.08317	0.08706	0.09095	0.09483	0.09871	0.10257	0.10642	0.11026	0.11409
0.3	0.11791	0.12172	0.12552	0.12930	0.13307	0.13683	0.14058	0.14431	0.14803	0.15173
0.4	0.15542	0.15910	0.16276	0.16640	0.17003	0.17364	0.17724	0.18082	0.18439	0.18793
0.5	0.19146	0.19497	0.19847	0.20194	0.20540	0.20884	0.21226	0.21566	0.21904	0.22240
0.6	0.22575	0.22907	0.23237	0.23565	0.23891	0.24215	0.24537	0.24857	0.25175	0.25490
0.7	0.25804	0.26115	0.26424	0.26730	0.27035	0.27337	0.27637	0.27935	0.28230	0.28524
0.8	0.28814	0.29103	0.29389	0.29673	0.29955	0.30234	0.30511	0.30785	0.31057	0.31327
0.9	0.31594	0.31859	0.32121	0.32381	0.32639	0.32894	0.33147	0.33398	0.33646	0.33891
1.0	0.34134	0.34375	0.34614	0.34849	0.35083	0.35314	0.35543	0.35769	0.35993	0.36214
1.1	0.36433	0.36650	0.36864	0.37076	0.37286	0.37493	0.37698	0.37900	0.38100	0.38298
1.2	0.38493	0.38686	0.38877	0.39065	0.39251	0.39435	0.39617	0.39796	0.39973	0.40147
1.3	0.40320	0.40490	0.40658	0.40824	0.40988	0.41149	0.41308	0.41466	0.41621	0.41774
1.4	0.41924	0.42073	0.42220	0.42364	0.42507	0.42647	0.42785	0.42922	0.43056	0.43189
1.5	0.43319	0.43448	0.43574	0.43699	0.43822	0.43943	0.44062	0.44179	0.44295	0.44408
1.6	0.44520	0.44630	0.44738	0.44845	0.44950	0.45053	0.45154	0.45254	0.45352	0.45449
1.7	0.45543	0.45637	0.45728	0.45818	0.45907	0.45994	0.46080	0.46164	0.46246	0.46327
1.8	0.46407	0.46485	0.46562	0.46638	0.46712	0.46784	0.46856	0.46926	0.46995	0.47062
1.9	0.47128	0.47193	0.47257	0.47320	0.47381	0.47441	0.47500	0.47558	0.47615	0.47670
2.0	0.47725	0.47778	0.47831	0.47882	0.47932	0.47982	0.48030	0.48077	0.48124	0.48169
2.1	0.48214	0.48257	0.48300	0.48341	0.48382	0.48422	0.48461	0.48500	0.48537	0.48574
2.2	0.48610	0.48645	0.48679	0.48713	0.48745	0.48778	0.48809	0.48840	0.48870	0.48899
2.3	0.48928	0.48956	0.48983	0.49010	0.49036	0.49061	0.49086	0.49111	0.49134	0.49158
2.4	0.49180	0.49202	0.49224	0.49245	0.49266	0.49286	0.49305	0.49324	0.49343	0.49361
2.5	0.49379	0.49396	0.49413	0.49430	0.49446	0.49461	0.49477	0.49492	0.49506	0.49520
2.6	0.49534	0.49547	0.49560	0.49573	0.49585	0.49598	0.49609	0.49621	0.49632	0.49643
2.7	0.49653	0.49664	0.49674	0.49683	0.49693	0.49702	0.49711	0.49720	0.49728	0.49736
2.8	0.49744	0.49752	0.49760	0.49767	0.49774	0.49781	0.49788	0.49795	0.49801	0.49807
2.9	0.49813	0.49819	0.49825	0.49831	0.49836	0.49841	0.49846	0.49851	0.49856	0.49861
3.0	0.49865	0.49869	0.49874	0.49878	0.49882	0.49886	0.49889	0.49893	0.49896	0.49900
3.1	0.49903	0.49906	0.49910	0.49913	0.49916	0.49918	0.49921	0.49924	0.49926	0.49929
3.2	0.49931	0.49934	0.49936	0.49938	0.49940	0.49942	0.49944	0.49946	0.49948	0.49950
3.3	0.49952	0.49953	0.49955	0.49957	0.49958	0.49960	0.49961	0.49962	0.49964	0.49965
3.4	0.49966	0.49968	0.49969	0.49970	0.49971	0.49972	0.49973	0.49974	0.49975	0.49976
3.5	0.49977	0.49978	0.49978	0.49979	0.49980	0.49981	0.49981	0.49982	0.49983	0.49983
3.6	0.49984	0.49985	0.49985	0.49986	0.49986	0.49987	0.49987	0.49988	0.49988	0.49989
3.7	0.49989	0.49990	0.49990	0.49990	0.49991	0.49991	0.49992	0.49992	0.49992	0.49992
3.8	0.49993	0.49993	0.49993	0.49994	0.49994	0.49994	0.49994	0.49995	0.49995	0.49995
3.9	0.49995	0.49995	0.49996	0.49996	0.49996	0.49996	0.49996	0.49996	0.49997	0.49997
4.0	0.49997	0.49997	0.49997	0.49997	0.49997	0.49997	0.49998	0.49998	0.49998	0.49998

The black lines in Table 5A.1 present another example that we will encounter throughout the text—the critical value for the 90 percent confidence level. To determine this critical value, we searched the interior of the table for the value 0.45. Given that 0.45 itself is not listed in the table, we determine the critical value by finding the values that bracket 0.45, which in this case are 0.44950 and 0.45053. Because both of these values are in the row headed 1.6, we know that our desired critical value must start with 1.6. The bigger issue is determining the correct column heading. In this case, we look to the column headings for 0.44950 and 0.45053, which are 0.04 and 0.05, respectively, and because 0.45 is almost exactly between the two values in the table, we split the difference between the column headings and determine that our desired critical is 1.645. We can visually summarize these values as shown in Figure 5A.3.

FIGURE 5A.3 **Critical Values for the 95 Percent and 90 Percent Confidence Levels in the Standard Normal Probability Distribution**

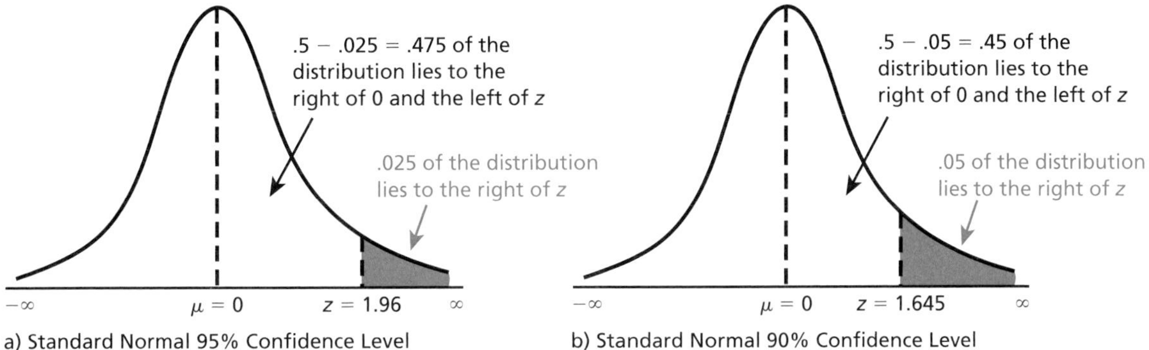

Note that these two values—1.96 for the 95 percent confidence level and 1.645 for the 90 percent confidence level—will become so important in future chapters that it is best to simply commit them to memory.

The Student's-*t* Probability Distribution

Student's-*t* probability distribution (*t*-distribution)
A symmetric distribution with fatter tails than the normal distribution.

The **Student's-*t* probability distribution** (or the ***t*-distribution**) is similar to the normal probability distribution in that it is a symmetric distribution for which the mean and the median are equal. It differs from the normal probability distribution in that the tails of the Student's-*t* probability distribution are fatter than the tails of the normal probability distribution.

Another important difference between the Student's-*t* and the normal probability distribution is that the Student's-*t* probability distribution depends on the degrees of freedom associated with the statistical problem at hand, while the normal probability distribution does not. The reason for this is that the Student's-*t* distribution changes depending on the sample size, while the normal distribution is the same regardless of the sample size.

How do differences in the number of degrees of freedom affect the shape of the Student's-*t* probability distribution? As demonstrated in Figure 5A.4, Student's-*t* probability distributions with smaller sample sizes have fatter the tails, while Student's-*t* probability distributions with larger sample sizes have skinnier tails.

Note that as the sample size increases, the tails of the Student's-*t* probability distribution become skinnier and the distribution begins to more closely resemble the normal probability distribution. Why? As the sample size increases, the number of degrees of freedom increases and with greater degrees of freedom more information goes into the estimation of the sample mean. In point of fact, the influence of the estimated standard deviation decreases with an increasing sample size to the extent that once the degrees of freedom exceed 120, the Student's-*t* distribution becomes the normal distribution (as can be seen in the bottom row of the Student's-*t* table presented in Appendix C at the back of the text).

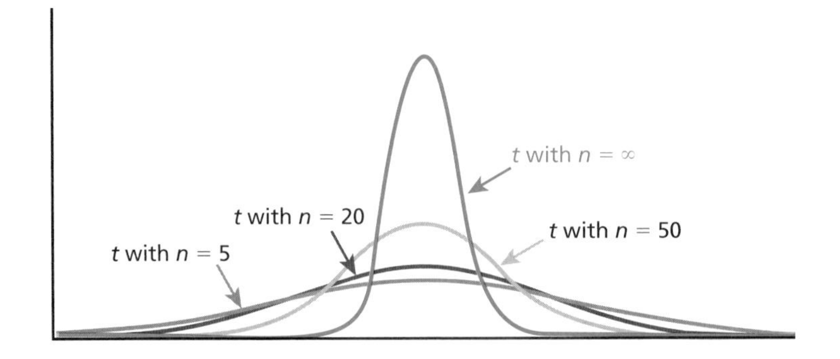

FIGURE 5A.4
A Comparison of Student's-*t* Probability Distributions with Different Sample Sizes

As with the standard normal distribution, the Student's-t distribution is extremely valuable because the area under the curve between 0 and t can be listed in one convenient table that can be used to solve statistical problems. The Student's-t table is read in much the same way as the standard normal table except that in addition to the desired percentage of all observations exceeding t, the threshold value will also depend on the degrees of freedom. As an example, suppose that we are interested in determining the threshold value for the 95 percent confidence level for a 27-observation sample. Because we are looking for the 2.5 percent threshold, we would search down the $p = 0.025$ column and because there are $n - 1 = 26$ degrees of freedom, we would search across the 26 degrees of freedom row. Similarly, to determine the threshold value for the 90 percent confidence level, we would need to determine the threshold value such that only 5.0 percent of the observations exceed t. These two problems would result in the threshold values shown in Table 5A.2.

TABLE 5A.2
Using the Student's-*t* Table to Determine the Appropriate Critical Values for the 95 Percent and 90 Percent Confidence Levels

Degrees of Freedom	p=0.05	p=0.025	p=0.01	p=0.005
1	12.71	25.45	63.66	127.32
2	4.30	6.20	9.92	14.09
3	3.18	4.17	5.84	7.45
4	2.78	3.50	4.60	5.60
5	2.57	3.16	4.03	4.77
6	2.45	2.97	3.71	4.32
7	2.36	2.84	3.50	4.03
8	2.31	2.75	3.36	3.83
9	2.26	2.68	3.25	3.69
10	2.23	2.63	3.17	3.58
11	2.20	2.59	3.11	3.50
12	2.18	2.56	3.05	3.43
13	2.16	2.53	3.01	3.37
14	2.14	2.51	2.98	3.33
15	2.13	2.49	2.95	3.29
16	2.12	2.47	2.92	3.25
17	2.11	2.46	2.90	3.22
18	2.10	2.44	2.88	3.20
19	2.09	2.43	2.86	3.17
20	2.09	2.42	2.84	3.15
21	2.08	2.41	2.83	3.14
22	2.07	2.41	2.82	3.12
23	2.07	2.40	2.81	3.10
24	2.06	2.39	2.80	3.09
25	2.06	2.38	2.79	3.08
26 →	2.06 →	2.38	2.78	3.07
27	2.05	2.37	2.77	3.06
28	2.05	2.37	2.76	3.05
29	2.04	2.36	2.76	3.04
30	2.04	2.36	2.75	3.03
40	2.02	2.33	2.70	2.97
60	2.00	2.30	2.66	2.92
120	1.98	2.27	2.62	2.86
infinity	1.96	2.24	2.58	2.81

We can visually summarize these values as shown in Figure 5A.5.

FIGURE 5A.5 Critical Values for the 95 Percent and 90 Percent Confidence Levels in the Student's-*t* Probability Distribution

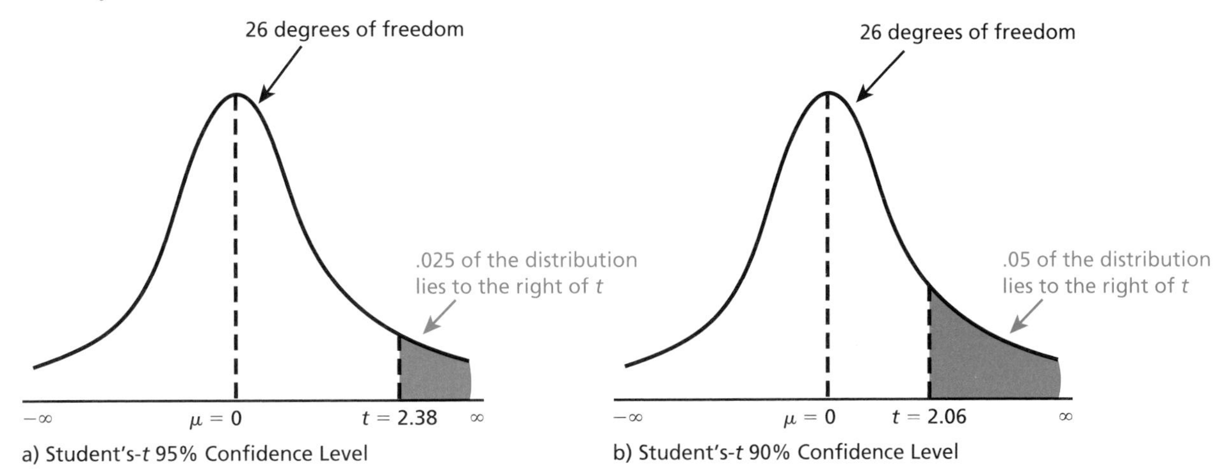

When working with actual data, an obvious question is whether the normal probability distribution or the Student's-*t* probability distribution provides a more accurate description of the true sampling distribution in which we are interested. As a general rule, if the sample size is relatively small (i.e., $n \leq 120$), we use the Student's-*t* probability distribution; if the sample size is relatively large (i.e., $n > 120$), we use the normal probability distribution.

The F-probability Distribution

F-probability distribution
A symmetric distribution with fatter tails than the normal distribution.

The **F-probability distribution** differs from the standard normal and Student's-*t* distributions in a number of ways. First, the F-probability distribution is restricted to contain only positive values, and therefore, the distribution is bounded to fall between 0 and ∞ rather than $-\infty$ and ∞. Second, the F-probability distribution is asymmetric, with more of the mass falling closer to 0 and progressively less falling toward ∞. The general shape of the F-probability distribution is given in Figure 5A.6.

FIGURE 5A.6 The F-probability Distribution

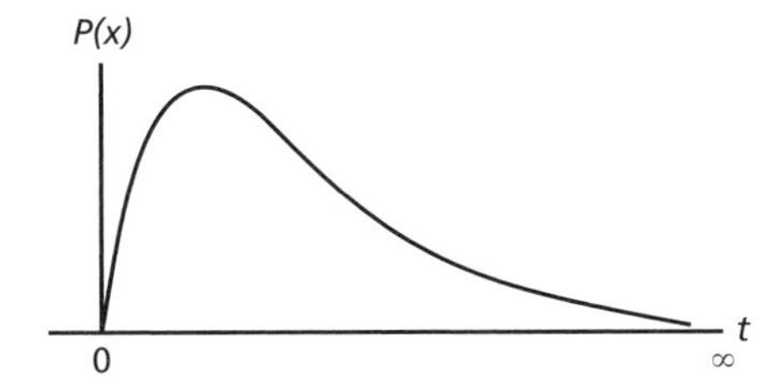

Third, because the F-probability distribution is calculated as a ratio, it has two different degrees of freedom: one for the numerator and one for the denominator. Note that the exact calculations of the respective degrees of freedom will differ depending on the specific hypothesis being tested. Finally, because the distribution is asymmetric, we do not divide the area to the right of the appropriate critical value by 2, meaning that for the 95 percent confidence level, the appropriate critical value is the one for which 5 percent of the distribution lies to the right. Visually, we depict this last fact as shown in Figure 5A.7.

Given that the F-probability distribution has two different degrees of freedom, working with the F-table is a little different that the standard normal and S-*t* tables. First, because the table must list values corresponding to two different degrees of freedom, it cannot list values for different levels of significance. Instead, there is a separate F-table for each different level of significance. In general, we focus on the 5 percent significance level

FIGURE 5A.7
Determining the Critical Value for the 95 Percent Confidence Level in the *F*-probability Distribution

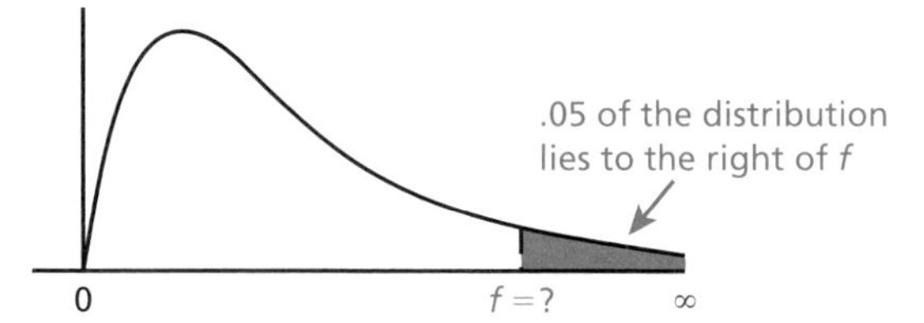

($\alpha = 0.05$). We then need to look down the row headings to find the one corresponding to the denominator degrees of freedom and across the column headings to find the one corresponding to the numerator degrees of freedom. Tracing across and down those specific rows and columns determines the appropriate critical value.

As an example, when determining the critical value for an F-test of the overall significance of a given sample regression function. The numerator degrees of freedom (numerator DF) is the number of independent variables in the regression (k) and the denominator degrees of freedom (denominator DF) is the degrees of freedom of the regression, ($n - k - 1$). Accordingly, for a regression with 2 independent variables and 23 observations, the appropriate critical value would be determined as shown in Table 5A.3.

TABLE 5A.3
Using the *F*-Table to Determine the Appropriate Critical Value for the 5 Percent Significance Level

CRITICAL VALUES for the F Distribution, ALPHA = .05

Denominator	Numerator DF									
DF	1	2	3	4	5	6	7	8	9	10
1	161.448	199.500	215.707	224.583	230.162	233.986	236.768	238.883	240.543	241.882
2	18.513	19.000	19.164	19.247	19.296	19.330	19.353	19.371	19.385	19.396
3	10.128	9.552	9.277	9.117	9.013	8.941	8.887	8.845	8.812	8.786
4	7.709	6.944	6.591	6.388	6.256	6.163	6.094	6.041	5.999	5.964
5	6.608	5.786	5.409	5.192	5.050	4.950	4.876	4.818	4.772	4.735
6	5.987	5.143	4.757	4.534	4.387	4.284	4.207	4.147	4.099	4.060
7	5.591	4.737	4.347	4.120	3.972	3.866	3.787	3.726	3.677	3.637
8	5.318	4.459	4.066	3.838	3.687	3.581	3.500	3.438	3.388	3.347
9	5.117	4.256	3.863	3.633	3.482	3.374	3.293	3.230	3.179	3.137
10	4.965	4.103	3.708	3.478	3.326	3.217	3.135	3.072	3.020	2.978
11	4.844	3.982	3.587	3.357	3.204	3.095	3.012	2.948	2.896	2.854
12	4.747	3.885	3.490	3.259	3.106	2.996	2.913	2.849	2.796	2.753
13	4.667	3.806	3.411	3.179	3.025	2.915	2.832	2.767	2.714	2.671
14	4.600	3.739	3.344	3.112	2.958	2.848	2.764	2.699	2.646	2.602
15	4.543	3.682	3.287	3.056	2.901	2.790	2.707	2.641	2.588	2.544
16	4.494	3.634	3.239	3.007	2.852	2.741	2.657	2.591	2.538	2.494
17	4.451	3.592	3.197	2.965	2.810	2.699	2.614	2.548	2.494	2.450
18	4.414	3.555	3.160	2.928	2.773	2.661	2.577	2.510	2.456	2.412
19	4.381	3.522	3.127	2.895	2.740	2.628	2.544	2.477	2.423	2.378
20	4.351	3.493	3.098	2.866	2.711	2.599	2.514	2.447	2.393	2.348
21	4.325	3.467	3.072	2.840	2.685	2.573	2.488	2.420	2.366	2.321
22	4.301	3.443	3.049	2.817	2.661	2.549	2.464	2.397	2.342	2.297
23	4.279	3.422	3.028	2.796	2.640	2.528	2.442	2.375	2.320	2.275
24	4.260	3.403	3.009	2.776	2.621	2.508	2.423	2.355	2.300	2.255
25	4.242	3.385	2.991	2.759	2.603	2.490	2.405	2.337	2.282	2.236

It is important to note that Table 5A.3 is an abbreviated version of the actual F-table. For illustrative purposes, we only included 25 rows in the table, whereas the actual F-table contains many additional rows, the number of which depends on the source publishing the table.

Chapter Six

Multiple Linear Regression Analysis

CHAPTER OBJECTIVES

After reading this chapter, you will be able to:

1. Understand the goals of multiple linear regression analysis.
2. Understand the "holding all other independent variables constant" condition in multiple linear regression analysis.
3. Understand the multiple linear regression assumption required for OLS to be BLUE.
4. Interpret multiple linear regression output in Excel.
5. Assess the goodness-of-fit of the sample multiple linear regression function.
6. Perform hypothesis tests for the overall significance of the sample regression function.
7. Perform hypothesis tests for the individual significance of a slope coefficient.
8. Perform hypothesis tests for the joint significance of a subset of slope coefficients.
9. Perform the Chow test for structural differences between two subsets of data.

A STUDENT'S PERSPECTIVE

Suppose that your dream job after college lands you in a very small town with a limited social scene. Suppose further that after a few years establishing your career you realize that starting a family is equally important to your life's goals. How would you handle this situation? Would you simply resign yourself to your current circumstance, or would you try to find a more suitable location for meeting a life partner?

This is exactly the situation encountered by one of our former students. As an economist with sound econometrics training, this individual took it upon himself to collect data on major U.S. metropolitan statistical areas (MSAs) and to estimate the linear relationship between a key marriage indicator and several important demographic factors. To collect appropriate data, the individual turned to U.S. census data that he located on the Internet. As a starting point for his analysis, the student calculated the summary statistics in Table 6.1.

These summary statistics indicated to the student that while the mean ratio of unmarried women to unmarried men in these 90 MSAs is 118.7, the values range from a minimum of 98.0 to a maximum of 133.7. Turning to the independent variables, in terms of individuals 18 years of age and older, the smallest MSA in the sample had 343,932 residents, while the largest MSA had 14,613,326 residents. At the same time, the least college-educated MSAs had 14.7 and 15.3 percent of men and women who had obtained a BA degree or higher, respectively, while the most college-educated MSAs had a maximum of 48.2 and 45.5 percent of men and women, respectively. Finally, the minimum median income in the sample is \$33,732, while the maximum median income is \$84,523. Although these

TABLE 6.1 **Summary Statistics for Our Former Student's MSA Marriage Data**

	Ratio of Unmarried Women/100 Unmarried Men	Population 18 and Over in MSA	Percentage of Males With BA or higher	Percentage of Females With BA or higher	Median Income (Thousands)
Mean	118.682	1,580,854.04	29.682	28.576	$50.74
Standard Deviation	8.270	2,072,403.92	6.338	6.032	$ 7.92
Minimum	98.039	343,932.00	14.700	15.300	$33.73
25th Percentile	113.846	511,773.00	26.150	25.600	$45.41
Median	120.423	849,974.50	29.650	27.800	$49.89
75th Percentile	124.758	1,614,302.25	32.850	32.225	$55.17
Maximum	133.741	14,613,326.00	48.200	45.500	$84.52
Observations	90	90	90	90	90

summary statistics are informative as to the empirical distributions of the individual variables, they do not provide any indication of the linear relationship existing between the ratio of unmarried women to unmarried men and the independent variables.

BIG PICTURE OVERVIEW

multiple linear regression analysis
Occurs when one dependent variable is regressed on more than one independent variable.

The primary tool that empirical economists use to gather information as to the linear relationship that exists between a dependent variable and a series of independent variables is **multiple linear regression analysis.** In this chapter, we introduce the method by which we calculate the multiple linear regression function, we discuss how to correctly interpret our estimated slope coefficients, and we detail how to perform statistical inference in multiple linear regression analysis.

Figure 6.1 depicts the empirical research tools introduced in this chapter.

FIGURE 6.1
A Visual Depiction of the Empirical Research Tools Introduced in This Chapter

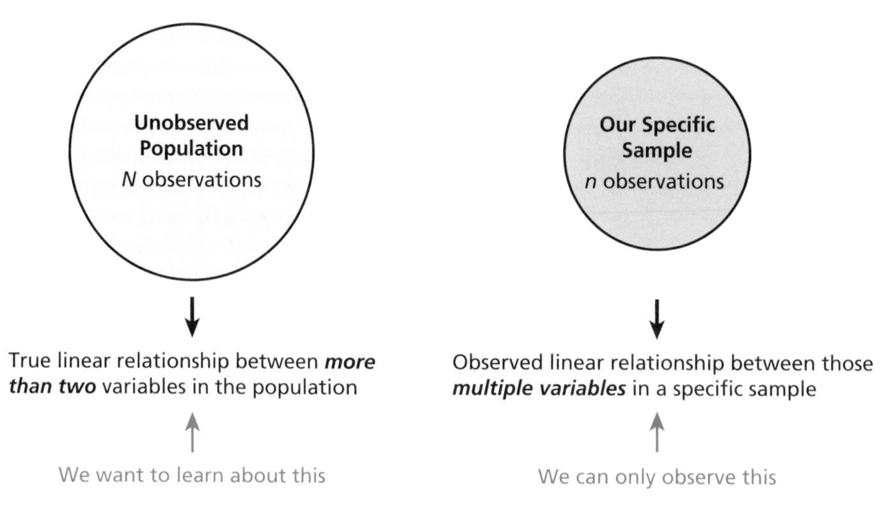

Before proceeding with our discussion, we need to introduce the data sets that will be the focus of our analysis in this chapter.

DATA TO BE ANALYZED: OUR MLB POSITION PLAYER AND INTERNATIONAL GDP SAMPLES

Multiple linear regression analysis is a powerful tool that allows us to quantify the linear relationship between a given dependent variable and potentially large numbers of independent variables. While true, to make our exposition as clear and clear as possible, in this chapter we focus on the simplest possible multiple linear relationship—that between a given dependent variable and exactly two independent variables. The examples on which we focus are as follows.

Data Analyzed in the Text

Labor economic theory suggests that a worker's salary should be a function of his or her marginal productivity. To empirically test this theory, we need to collect data on both an individual's salary and his or her measured marginal productivity. Obtaining such information is often complicated by the fact that (1) we will generally not have access to salary data for private firms and (2) even if we have access to salary data, we will, in many cases, be unable to accurately measure individual marginal productivity.

Important exceptions to these concerns are professional sports leagues, for which annual salaries and marginal productivity measures are easily collected. It is for this very reason that academic economists have devoted enough empirical attention to the salaries of professional athletes for Hakes and Sauer (2006) to argue that "a case can be made that more is known about pay and quantified performance in (major league baseball) than in any other labor market in the American economy."

After collecting usable salary data, we must identify and collect usable marginal productivity data. For our MLB example, a first productivity measure that we might consider is years of work experience because that measure serves as a proxy for the specific human capital that a player accumulated in his career. A second productivity measure that we

Moneyball: The Art of Winning an Unfair Game

by Michael Lewis (2003)

In the early 2000s, Oakland A's general manager Billy Beane was able to assemble one of the most successful teams in baseball, despite having one of the lowest payrolls. How did he do it? By hiring statistical analysts to identify exploitable inefficiencies in the market for MLB players, which was a state-of-the-art empirical approach that no other teams were using at the time. As a result of this practice, Beane and his statisticians were able to identify and sign players who were relatively "undervalued" by other teams in the market and identify and trade players who were relatively "overvalued" by other teams. Oakland A's President Sandy Alderson summarized the ingenuity of this approach by stating that "I couldn't do a regression analysis, but I knew what one was, and the results made sense to me" (p. 57). After completing your current course, you should not only be able to perform regression analysis, but you should be able to correctly interpret and make sense of your results. With luck, you will be able to find an application that proves as fruitful as the one identified by Billy Beane (and eventually copied by other teams).

Addendum: After losing in the first round of the playoffs in several consecutive seasons, Beane was quoted as saying that "My s*** doesn't work in the playoffs. My job is to get us to the playoffs. What happens after that is f***ing luck." This analysis makes perfect sense because, as we discuss in future chapters, linear regression analysis is based on average values, which tend to hold over a 162-game season but not necessarily over a 5-game playoff series.

Source: Lewis, Michael, *Moneyball: The Art of Winning an Unfair Game,* W.W. Norton & Company, 2011

might consider is the player's offensive productivity on the playing field. While offensive productivity takes on many different dimensions (home runs, batting average, runs batted in, etc.), to make our initial analysis as simple as possible, we represent a player's offensive productivity strictly by the number of home runs hit during the previous season.

With these facts in mind, following the procedure outlined in Appendix A, we collect data on MLB position players (i.e., all MLB players except pitchers) who were on opening-day rosters during the 2009 MLB season. To highlight the importance of understanding sampling distributions, we again generate a specific 200-player sample that we analyze throughout the chapter.

As first discussed in Chapter 4, an important question that must be addressed at the start of any empirical research project is: "What is the dependent variable and what are the independent variables in our multiple linear regression analysis?" In this case, we are interested in determining the role that a position player's experience and offensive productivity play in explaining his annual salary. Accordingly, the dependent variable in our analysis is the player's annual salary, and the independent variables are the player's experience and the number of home runs he hit in the previous season (which is our simple measure of offensive productivity).

Table 6.2 presents summary statistics for our specific 200-observation MLB position player sample.

TABLE 6.2
Summary Statistics for Our Specific 200-Observation MLB Position Player Sample

	Salary	Experience	Home Runs
Mean	$ 3,699,375.00	4.25	10.76
Standard Deviation	$ 4,877,217.16	3.89	10.50
Minimum	$ 400,000.00	0.00	0.00
25th Percentile	$ 419,375.00	1.00	2.00
Median	$ 2,000,000.00	3.00	8.00
75th Percentile	$ 4,621,875.00	6.00	17.00
Maximum	$23,854,494.00	20.00	48.00
Observations	200	200	200

As these data indicate, the league minimum and maximum salaries in our sample of position players on opening-day rosters in 2009 were $400,000 and nearly $24 million, respectively, while the mean salary was nearly $3.7 million. At the same time, the minimum and maximum years of experience in the sample were 0 (for all rookies) and 20, respectively, while the mean value was 4.25. Finally, the minimum and maximum number of home runs in the sample were 0 and 48, respectively, while the mean was 10.76. The fact that the median salary, experience, and home runs are so much closer to the minimum values than the maximum values might suggest that the empirical distributions for all three of these variables are skewed to the right.

Data Analyzed in the Excel Boxes

The data that we analyze in the Excel boxes in this chapter are related to a different example of interest to economists. Macroeconomic theory suggests that a country's GDP should be a function of both the size and the productivity of its labor force. In this chapter, we consider a simple measure of the size of a country's labor force to be its population and a simple measure of a country's productivity to be its life expectancy. Following the process outlined in Appendix A, we collect a 63-observation sample of international GDPs, population, and life expectancies.

In this case, we are interested in determining the role that a country's population and life expectancy play in determining its GDP. Accordingly, the dependent variable in our analysis is the country's GDP, and the independent variables are the country's population and life expectancy.

Table 6.3 presents summary statistics for these data.

TABLE 6.3
Summary Statistics for Our 63-Observation International GDP Sample

	GDP/1,000,000,000	Population/1,000,000	Life Expectancy
Mean	1,177.79	76.00	72.51
Standard Deviation	2,859.62	238.24	9.34
Minimum	0.90	0.03	41.84
25th Percentile	11.90	2.38	70.35
Median	119.50	10.21	75.63
75th Percentile	703.10	40.81	78.89
Maximum	14,290.00	1,338.61	82.51
Observations	63	63	63

As these data indicate, the mean GDP for countries in our sample is nearly \$1.18 trillion, while the minimum GDP is \$900 million and the maximum is nearly \$14.3 trillion. At the same time, the mean population is 76 million, while the minimum is 300,000 and the maximum is 1.34 billion. Finally, the mean life expectancy is 72.5 years, while the minimums and maximums are 41.84 and 82.5 years, respectively. The fact that the median GDP of nearly \$120 billion and the median population of roughly 10 million are so much closer to the minimum values than the maximum values might suggest that the distributions for both of these variables are skewed to the right.

6.1 UNDERSTAND THE GOALS OF MULTIPLE LINEAR REGRESSION ANALYSIS

Suppose that we are interested in determining the linear relationship between a given dependent variable, y, and a series of k independent variables, $x_1, x_2, \ldots, x_k$ in a given population of interest. We start by writing the true linear relationship that exists in the population, which is known as the population multiple linear regression model, as

$$y_i = \beta_0 + \beta_1 x_{1,i} + \beta_2 x_{2,i} + \cdots + \beta_k x_{k,i} + \varepsilon_i \qquad 6.1.1$$

Because we cannot directly observe the entire population, we will not know for certain the true values of the unobserved population parameters in formula 6.1.1. Instead, the best that we can do is to collect a sample from the population and use observed values for that sample as our best estimates of the unobserved population parameters. We write the estimated sample multiple regression function for our observed sample as

$$\hat{y}_i = \hat{\beta}_0 + \hat{\beta}_1 x_{1,i} + \hat{\beta}_2 x_{2,i} + \cdots + \hat{\beta}_k x_{k,i} \qquad 6.1.2$$

To understand the method by which we estimate formula 6.1.2, it is important to be able to visualize what we are attempting to accomplish. To make our visual depiction tractable, we return to the simplest possible example, which is the one in which we are estimating the linear relationships between the dependent variable y and exactly two independent variables, x_1 and x_2. Because we are now in three-dimensional space, the shape that best fits the data is a plane. Figure 6.2 depicts the multiple linear regression function $\hat{y} = \hat{\beta}_0 + \hat{\beta}_1 x_1 + \hat{\beta}_2 x_2$ that best fits our observed sample data.

Note that each individual observation in our sample will now have three dimensions, y, x_1, x_2. How do we determine the plane that best fits our sample data? To answer this question, we find it helpful to visualize the calculation for a single observation in our sample. Doing so, we have the depiction in Figure 6.3.

Again, in reality, rather than having only one observation, we will have many, many observations in our specific sample. Accordingly, rather than the single residual in Figure 6.3, we will possess many, many different residuals, such as those in Figure 6.4.

As might be expected based on our previous discussions, the best-fit plane will be the one that is closest on average to all of the individual observations. Accordingly, to determine the best-fit plane, we must minimize some measure of the aggregate residuals for all of the many, many observations in the sample. Because the best-fit plane will perfectly balance the individual positive deviations with the individual negative residuals, we must square the individual

FIGURE 6.2
A Visual Depiction of the Multiple Linear Regression Function

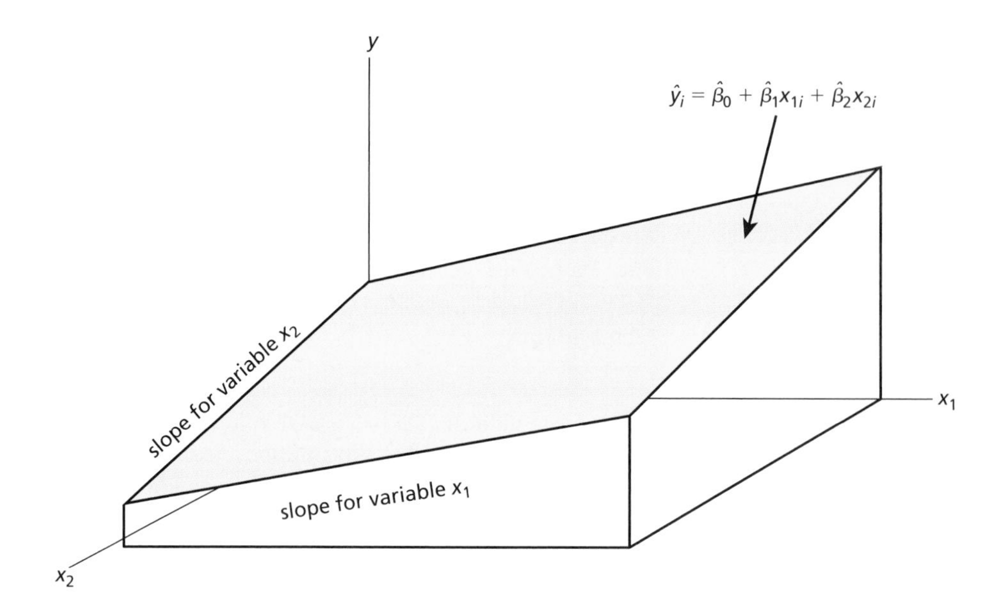

FIGURE 6.3
A Visual Depiction of the Predicted Value of *y* and the Calculated Residual for a Given Observation

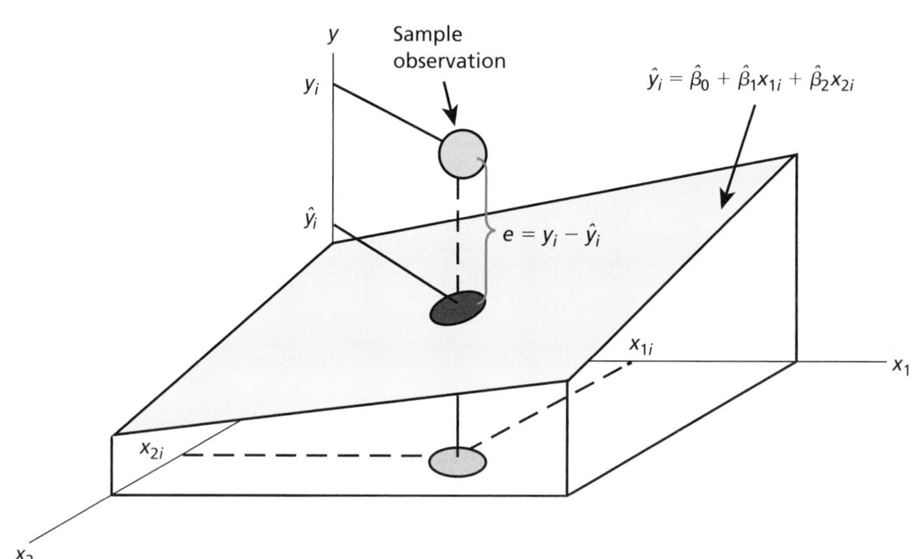

FIGURE 6.4
A Visual Depiction of the Predicted Values of *y* and the Calculated Residuals for Multiple Observations

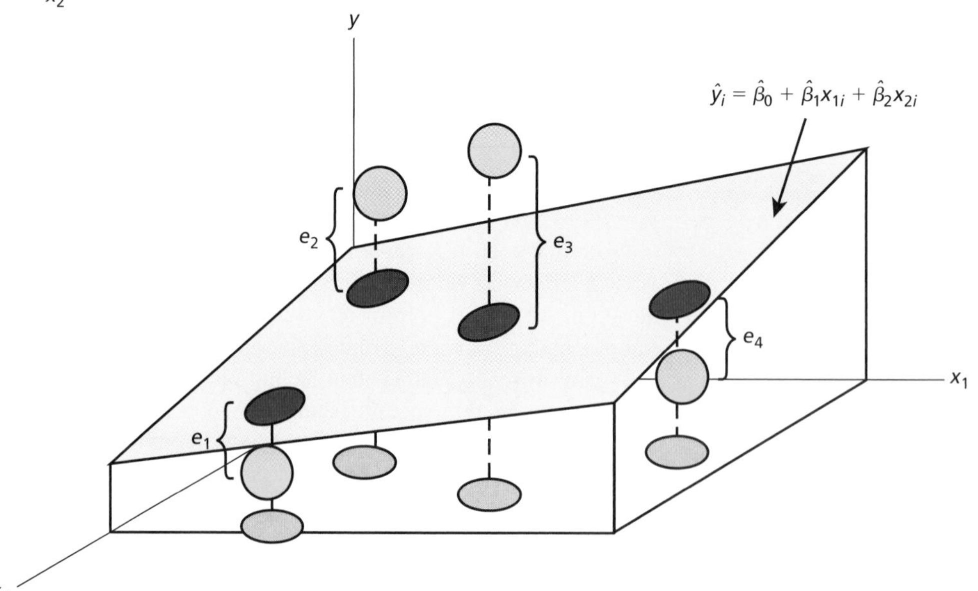

residuals before summing them. The best-fit plane will then be the one that minimizes. Formally, we determine this plane by solving the objective function in formula 6.1.3.

$$\textit{Minimize} \sum_{i=1}^{n} e_i^2 = \sum_{i=1}^{n}(y_i - \hat{y}_i)^2 = \sum_{i=1}^{n}(y_i - (\hat{\beta}_0 + \hat{\beta}_1 x_{1i} + \hat{\beta}_2 x_{2i}))^2 \qquad 6.1.3$$

Suppose that our multiple linear regression analysis were to include k independent variables rather than two independent variables. This would affect our analysis in a number of ways. First, we would be moving from three-dimensional space to multidimensional space, meaning that we would not be able to present a visual depiction of our sample regression function because we would be moving from a plane to some multidimensional figure. Second, we would now solve the objective function in formula 6.1.4.

$$\textit{Minimize} \sum_{i=1}^{n} e_i^2 = \sum_{i=1}^{n}(y_i - \hat{y}_i)^2 = \sum_{i=1}^{n}(y_i - (\hat{\beta}_0 + \hat{\beta}_1 x_{1i} + \hat{\beta}_2 x_{2i} + \cdots + \hat{\beta}_k x_{ki}))^2 \qquad 6.1.4$$

Solving this objective function results in the multiple linear regression sample regression function

$$\hat{y}_i = \hat{\beta}_0 + \hat{\beta}_1 x_1 + \hat{\beta}_2 x_2 + \cdots + \hat{\beta}_k x_k \qquad 6.1.5$$

where $\hat{\beta}_0$ is the predicted value of y when the values of the independent variables are all equal to 0; $\hat{\beta}_1$ is the estimated marginal effect that a change in x_1 has on y, holding *all other independent variables constant;* $\hat{\beta}_2$ is the estimated marginal effect that a change in x_2 has on y, *holding all other independent variables constant;* and so on. Because we solve for this function by minimizing the sum of squared residuals, we once again refer to the process as ordinary least squares (OLS).

Empirical Research Tool 6.1 summarizes the multiple linear regression function.

EMPIRICAL RESEARCH TOOL 6.1: THE MULTIPLE LINEAR REGRESSION FUNCTION

Goal:

Estimate the linear relationship between y and a series of independent variables, $x_1, x_2, \ldots, x_k$, that best fits the observed sample data.

Tools:

Minimizing the sum of squared residuals by solving the problem

$$\text{Minimize} \sum_{i=1}^{n} e_i^2 = \sum_{i=1}^{n}(y_i - \hat{y}_i)^2 = \sum_{i=1}^{n}(y_i - (\hat{\beta}_0 + \hat{\beta}_1 x_{1,i} + \hat{\beta}_2 x_{2,i} + \cdots + \hat{\beta}_k x_{k,i}))^2$$

Formulas:

The multiple linear regression function is

$$\hat{y}_i = \hat{\beta}_0 + \hat{\beta}_1 x_{1,i} + \hat{\beta}_2 x_{2,i} + \cdots + \hat{\beta}_k x_{k,i}$$

Given the obvious importance of the "holding all other independent variables constant" condition in the correct interpretation of the sample regression function, it is important to consider the meaning of the condition as it applies to multiple linear regression analysis.

6.2 UNDERSTAND THE "HOLDING ALL OTHER INDEPENDENT VARIABLES CONSTANT" CONDITION IN MULTIPLE LINEAR REGRESSION ANALYSIS

Recall from prior economics courses that economists are most frequently interested in identifying the marginal effect that a given independent variable is expected to have on the dependent variable, *holding all other independent variables constant.* Note that the phrase "holding all other independent variables constant" is italicized because of the important role it plays in correctly determining the estimated marginal effect. To see this, consider the case in which our dependent variable is related to exactly two independent variables, x_1 and x_2. In such a case, a linear regression of y on only x_1 provides an incorrect estimate of the true marginal effect that changes in x_1 are expected to have on y because x_2 (i.e., all other independent variables) is not be being held constant.

To see why not, we use Venn diagrams to describe the joint variation between our variables of interest. To start, consider only the relationship between the dependent variable y and one of the independent variables x_1. Figure 6.5 depicts the estimated marginal effect resulting from the sample regression function $\hat{y}_i = \hat{\beta}_0 + \hat{\beta}_1 x_i$ in this case.

FIGURE 6.5
A Venn Diagram of the Estimated Linear Relationship between y and x_1

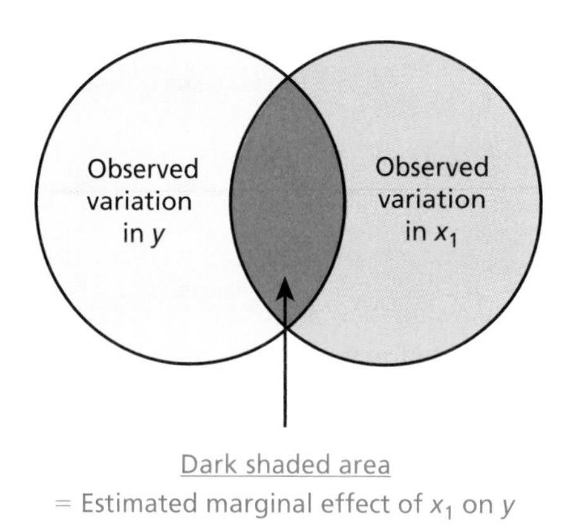

If the dependent variable is actually related to both x_1 and x_2, does the dark area in Figure 6.5 represent the true marginal effect of x_1 on y? No, because the estimated marginal effect in Figure 6.5 does not hold the effect that x_2 has on y constant. To see this, Figure 6.6 presents the Venn diagram for the true relationship between the dependent variable y and the independent variables x_1, and x_2.

FIGURE 6.6
A Venn Diagram of the Estimated Multiple Linear Relationship among y and x_1 and x_2

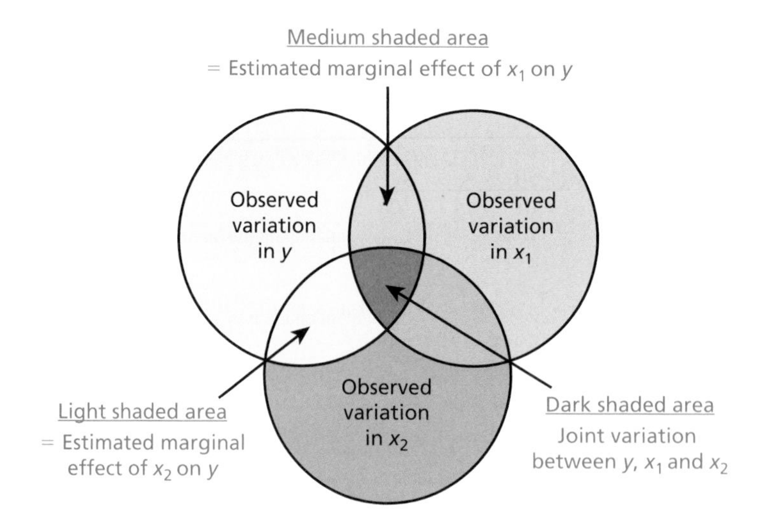

To demonstrate the importance of the holding all other independent variables constant condition, Figure 6.7 compares the estimated marginal effects in Figures 6.5 and 6.6.

FIGURE 6.7
A Comparison of the Estimated Marginal Effect of x_1 and y in the Venn Diagrams in Figures 6.5 and 6.6

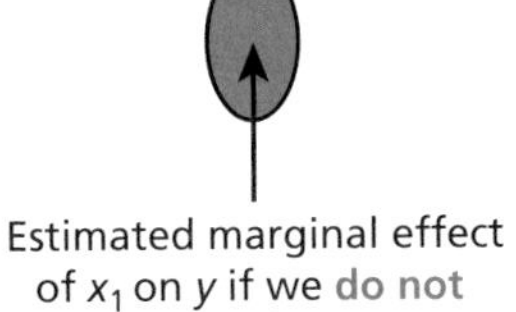

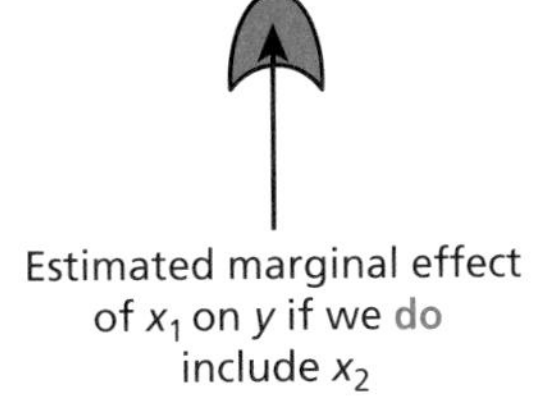

Notice that the difference between the two estimated marginal effects of experience on salary is the dark shaded area in Figure 6.6. What does this area represent? It represents the joint variation between y and x_1 and x_2, or the area in which both x_1 and x_2 vary with y. In other words, the linear regression of y on x_1 alone fails to provide the correct estimate of the true marginal effect of x_1 on y because it fails to account for the joint variation between x_1 and x_2 and therefore it does not hold the effect of x_2 (i.e., all else) constant.

omitted variable bias Results in coefficient estimates being wrong on average when a variable that explains y is not included in the regression function and that variable is linearly related to one or more of the included independent variables.

Econometricians refer to this as a problem of **omitted variable bias** and argue that if the dependent variable is theoretically related to multiple independent variables, then all of those independent variables must be included in the regression analysis to ensure correct estimation of the marginal effects associated with each individual independent variable.

Now that we know how to estimate our multiple linear regression function, we need to consider desirable properties that we would like our multiple linear regression estimates to possess.

6.3 UNDERSTAND THE MULTIPLE LINEAR REGRESSION ASSUMPTIONS REQUIRED FOR OLS TO BE BLUE

The two desirable properties of estimators that we consider are unbiasedness and efficiency. By definition, an estimator is said to be *unbiased* if the expected value of the estimator is equal to the value of the unobserved population parameter that is attempting to estimate. Likewise, by definition, an estimator is said to be *efficient* if it has the minimum variance among all unbiased estimators of a given population parameter. Estimators that are both unbiased and have the minimum variance among all unbiased estimators are said to be the best linear unbiased estimator (BLUE) and are considered to be the gold standard of all estimators. Accordingly, our goal is to always identify estimators that are BLUE for every given empirical situation.

Fortunately, we know that if a number of assumptions are met, then our estimated multiple linear sample regression function is BLUE.

Assumption M1: The model is linear in the parameters.

Assumption M1 states that for OLS to be an unbiased estimator, the population multiple linear regression model must be correctly specified as linear in the parameters, meaning that the dependent variable, y, must be related to the independent variables, $x_1, x_2, \ldots, x_k$ and the error term, u, as ε

$$y_i = \beta_0 + \beta_1 x_{1,i} + \beta_2 x_{2,i} + \cdots + \beta_k x_{k,i} + \varepsilon_i \qquad \textbf{6.3.1}$$

where β_0 is the population intercept and $\beta_1, \beta_2, \ldots, \beta_k$ are the population slope parameters. As with simple linear regression analysis, there are two important parts to this assumption: (1) Each individual independent variable must enter the estimated regression function linearly, and (2) the population regression model must be *correctly specified* as $y_i = \beta_0 + \beta_1 x_{1,i} + \beta_2 x_{2,i} + \cdots + \beta_k x_{k,i} + \varepsilon_i$. Again, while we may never know the true population relationship, we should make every attempt to specify the relationship as accurately as possible by studying the variables in detail using the tools outlined in previous chapters and/or by considering how others have specified similar relationships in previous empirical work.

Assumption M2: The data are collected through independent, random sampling.

Assumption M2 states that for OLS to be an unbiased estimator of the population multiple linear regression model, $y_i = \beta_0 + \beta_1 x_{1,i} + \beta_2 x_{2,i} + \cdots + \beta_k x_{k,i} + \varepsilon_i$, the sample data must be obtained through random sampling. After our discussion in previous chapters, this assumption should be fairly well understood.

Assumption M3: The data are not perfectly multicollinear.

Assumption M3 states that for OLS to be an unbiased estimator of the population multiple linear regression model $y_i = \beta_0 + \beta_1 x_{1,i} + \beta_2 x_{2,i} + \cdots + \beta_k x_{k,i} + \varepsilon_i$, values of the independent variable must vary (i.e., the values of x_i cannot be the same for all i) and that none of the independent variables are linear combinations of each other. As discussed in the case of simple linear regression, this assumption is required for us not to be dividing by 0 when we estimate individual slope coefficients.

Assumption M4: The error term has zero mean, or $E(\varepsilon_i) = 0$.

Assumption M4 states that for OLS to be an unbiased estimator of the population multiple linear regression model $y_i = \beta_0 + \beta_1 x_{1,i} + \beta_2 x_{2,i} + \cdots + \beta_k x_{k,i} + \varepsilon_i$, the error term ε_i must have an expected value of 0 (i.e., $E(\varepsilon_i) = 0$).

Note that in multiple linear regression, as in simple linear regression, if the residual takes on a constant value other than 0, the intercept is automatically rescaled, meaning that the interpretation of the estimated intercept might lack informative value.

Assumption M5: The error term is uncorrelated with each independent variable and all functions of each independent variable, $E(\varepsilon_i | x_{ij}) = 0$ for all j.

Assumption M5 states that for OLS to be an unbiased estimator of the population multiple linear regression model $y_i = \beta_0 + \beta_1 x_{1,i} + \beta_2 x_{2,i} + \cdots + \beta_k x_{k,i} + \varepsilon_i$, the values of the error term and the independent variables and all functions of the independent variable must not be correlated [i.e., $Corr(\varepsilon, x_j) = 0$ and $Corr(\varepsilon, f(x_j)) = 0$ for all j independent variables.]

As with simple linear regression, if this assumption is violated, $\hat{\beta}_j$ does not provide an unbiased estimate of the effect that a change in x_j has on y, holding all other independent variables constant, because every time x_j changes the error term also changes, meaning that all else is not being held constant.

The Importance of Assumptions M1 through M5

If assumptions M1 through M5 hold, then OLS is an unbiased estimator of the population multiple linear regression model $y_i = \beta_0 + \beta_1 x_{1,i} + \beta_2 x_{2,i} + \cdots + \beta_k x_{k,i} + \varepsilon_i$. Again, consider what this means. The fact that an estimator is unbiased means that it provides a correct estimate of the true (unobserved) population parameter, on average, across all potential samples. It does not mean that any particular estimate equals the true population parameter.

Conversely, if any one of assumptions M1 through M5 are violated, then OLS does not provide unbiased estimates of the population multiple linear regression function $y = \beta_0 + \beta_1 x_1 + \beta_2 x_2 + \cdots + \beta_k x_k + \varepsilon$. Many of the more advanced econometrics techniques have actually been developed to generate unbiased estimates in such cases.

Assumption M6: The error term has constant variance, or $Var(\varepsilon_i) = \sigma^2$.

Assumption M6 states that for OLS to have the minimum variance of all potential unbiased estimators of the population multiple linear regression function $y_i = \beta_0 + \beta_1 x_{1,i} + \beta_2 x_{2,i} + \cdots + \beta_k x_{k,i} + \varepsilon_i$, the error term ε_i must have the same variance for every given value of the independent variable (i.e., $Var(\varepsilon) = \sigma^2$ for all x). This means that for all values of the independent variables the variance of the error term remains constant.

The Importance of Assumption M6

Note that this assumption is not required for OLS to be unbiased. Rather, it is required for OLS to be the unbiased estimator with the minimum variance of all unbiased estimators, or the best linear unbiased estimator. For an estimator to be BLUE, it must possess the smallest variance among all of the unbiased estimators of the unobserved population parameters.

The six assumptions required for OLS to be BLUE for multiple linear regression are summarized in the following box.

Assumptions Required for OLS to Be the Best Linear Unbiased Estimator (BLUE) of the Population Multiple Linear Regression Model
$y_i = \beta_0 + \beta_1 x_{1,i} + \beta_2 x_{2,i} + \cdots + \beta_k x_{k,i} + \varepsilon_i$

Assumptions Required for OLS to Be Unbiased
Assumption M1: The model is linear in the parameters.
Assumption M2: The data are collected through independent, random sampling.
Assumption M3: The data are not perfectly multicollinear.
Assumption M4: The error term has zero mean, or $E(\varepsilon_i) = 0$.
Assumption M5: The error term is uncorrelated with each independent variable and all functions of each independent variable, or $E(\varepsilon_i | x_{ij}) = 0$ for all j.

Additional Assumption Required for OLS to be BLUE
Assumption M6: The error term has constant variance, *or* $Var(\varepsilon_i) = \sigma^2$.

Once we know that our multiple linear regression function provides estimates that are BLUE, we need to correctly interpret the estimated intercept and the estimated slope coefficients.

6.4 INTERPRET MULTIPLE LINEAR REGRESSION OUTPUT IN EXCEL

Using preprogrammed linear algebra formulas, statistical programs easily calculate and provide the multiple linear regression function. Excel Regression Output 6.1 presents the output from estimating the multiple linear relationship between salary and experience and home runs for our specific 200-observation MLB position player sample.

Excel Regression Output 6.1: Estimating the Multiple Linear Regression Function for Our 200-Observation MLB Position Player Sample

SUMMARY OUTPUT

Regression Statistics	
Multiple R	0.729038463
R Square	0.531497080
Adjusted R Square	0.526740705
Standard Error	3355225.154
Observations	200

ANOVA

	df	SS	MS	F	Significance F
Regression	2	2.51593E+15	1.25796E+15	111.7441539	3.67419E-33
Residual	197	2.21773E+15	1.12575E+13		
Total	199	4.73366E+15			

		Coefficients	Standard Error	*t* Stat	*P*-value	Lower 95%	Upper 95%
Intercept	$\hat{\beta}_0 \rightarrow$	−1,003,204.933	394,238.700	−2.5446637	0.01170467	−1,780,674.790	−225,735.070
Experience	$\hat{\beta}_1 \rightarrow$	569,508.462	63,560.106	8.9601559	2.48239E-16	444,162.912	694,854.012
HR	$\hat{\beta}_2 \rightarrow$	212,460.856	23,578.026	9.0109687	1.78871E-16	165,963.126	258,958.587

↑ Estimated Slope Coefficients

How do we interpret these results? A useful first step is to write the multiple linear regression function as

$$\hat{y}_i = \hat{\beta}_0 + \hat{\beta}_1 x_{1i} + \hat{\beta}_2 x_{2i} \qquad \textbf{6.4.1}$$

where

$\hat{\beta}_0$ = Estimated intercept represents the predicted value for y when x_{1i} and x_{2i} are both equal to 0

$\hat{\beta}_1$ = Estimated slope coefficient for the estimated linear relationship between y and x_1, *holding* x_2 *constant*

$\hat{\beta}_2$ = Estimated slope coefficient for the estimated linear relationship between y and x_2, *holding* x_1 *constant*

For our 200-observation MLB position player sample, our multiple linear regression function is

$$\underset{y_i}{\underset{\downarrow}{\widehat{Salary}}} = \underset{\hat{\beta}_0}{\underset{\downarrow}{-\$1{,}003{,}204.93}} + \underset{\hat{\beta}_1}{\underset{\downarrow}{\$569{,}508.46}}\underset{x_{1i}}{\underset{\downarrow}{Experience}} + \underset{\hat{\beta}_2}{\underset{\downarrow}{\$212{,}460.86}}\underset{x_{2i}}{\underset{\downarrow}{Home\ runs}}$$

For our estimated intercept, we conclude that

$$\hat{\beta}_0 = -\$1{,}003{,}204.93$$

meaning that for our observed sample, we estimate a position player with 0 years experience and 0 home runs to earn a salary of $-\$1{,}003{,}204.93$.

Is this reasonable? Of course not. This demonstrates an important fact. If the mean value of the error term is different from 0, then the intercept automatically rescales our estimates to adjust for this, thereby rendering our estimated intercept essentially meaningless. Accordingly, when interpreting our results, we often pay no attention to the estimated intercept because it is nonsensical.

Moving on to our estimated coefficients, we conclude that

$$\hat{\beta}_1 = \$569{,}508.46$$

meaning that for our observed sample, we estimate each additional year of experience to be associated with a \$569,508.46 increase in salary, *holding all other independent variables* (i.e, home runs) *constant.* In addition,

$$\hat{\beta}_2 = \$212{,}460.86$$

meaning that for our observed sample, we estimate each additional home run to be associated with a \$212,460.86 increase in salary, *holding all other independent variables* (i.e., experience) *constant.*

As with simple linear regression analysis, a valuable benefit of multiple linear regression analysis is that once we have estimated our sample regression function, we can calculate predicted values for the dependent variable by plugging different values for the independent variables into the sample regression function. As an example, suppose that we wish to predict the annual salary for a position player with 4 years of experience and 23 home runs. Based on our above estimates, the player's predicted annual salary would be

$$\begin{aligned}\widehat{Salary} &= -\$1{,}003{,}204.93 + \$569{,}508.46(Experience) \\ &\quad + \$212{,}460.86(Home\ Runs) \\ &= -\$1{,}003{,}204.93 + \$569{,}508.46(4) + \$212{,}460.86(23) \\ &= \$6{,}161{,}428.61\end{aligned} \qquad \textbf{6.4.2}$$

We should interpret this value as follows. Based on the observed sample data, we predict a position player with 4 years of experience and 23 home runs to earn a salary of \$6,161,428.61. Note that due to this being a predicted value based on the sample regression function, it is unlikely for any player to actually earn this exact amount (indeed, looking at our data confirms that no player in our sample actually does). Nonetheless, this estimate is valuable because it represents our best guess as to the value that we would expect to observe for the dependent variable given specific values of the independent variables. As an example, we note that within our specific sample, only Johnny Peralta of was actually observed having 4 years of experience and hitting 23 home runs, and his actual salary was only $3,650,000 rather than the $6,161,428.61 that we would have predicted for him. This may lead us to conclude that Peralta was underpaid for his performance (although we haven't controlled for other factors that likely influence his salary and doing so might change this conclusion).

Finally, Excel Example 6.1 demonstrates how to use the regression tool to estimate and interpret the sample regression function for our 63-observation international GDP sample.

EXCEL EXAMPLE 6.1

Using the regression tool to estimate the multiple linear regression function by OLS for our international GDP sample

Make sure that the independent variables we want to include in the regression are in columns next to each other. Then we will use the "Regression" tool in the "Data Analysis" toolpak to perform the regression.

1. Click on the "Data" tab.
2. Click the "Data Analysis" tab, which is the furthest tab on the right.
3. In the "Analysis Tools" menu, highlight "Regression" and click "OK".
4. In the "Regression" box

   Click the "Input Y Range" tab, and highlight the dependent variable (**B1:B64**).
   Click the "Input X Range" tab, and highlight the dependent variable (**C1:D64**).
   Click the "Labels" box to include variable names in the output.
   Click the "Output Range," and highlight an empty cell (**F3**).
   Click "OK".

SUMMARY OUTPUT

Regression Statistics	
Multiple R	0.638582448
R Square	0.407787543
Adjusted R Square	0.388047128
Standard Error	2237.003564
Observations	63

ANOVA

	df	SS	MS	F	Significance F
Regression	2	206747858.1	103373929	20.65749571	1.49392E-07
Residual	60	300251096.7	5004184.946		
Total	62	506998954.8			

	Coefficients	Standard Error	*t* Stat	*P*-value	Lower 95%	Upper 95%
Intercept	−2,781.879	2,224.247	−1.250705872	0.21589722	−7,231.035	1,667.278
Population/ 1,000,000	7.394403415	1.19286431	6.198863833	5.70441E-08	5.00831956	9.780487271
Life Expectancy	46.85515323	30.43221581	1.539656314	0.128901828	−14.01834124	107.7286477

According to these results, the estimated regression equation is

$$\widehat{GDP} = -2{,}781.8789 + 7.3944 Population + 46.8552 Life\ expectancy$$

The coefficient on Population can be interpreted as suggesting that, on average, for every 1 million increase in population, GDP is expected to increase by $7.394, holding life expectancy constant. The coefficient on Life Expectancy can be interpreted as suggesting that, on average, for every 1 year increase in life expectancy, GDP is expected to increase by $46.8552 billion, holding Population/1,000,000 constant.

Once we have calculated and correctly interpreted our sample regression function, we need to answer two important questions:

1. How well does our sample regression function fit the observed sample data?
2. What can we learn about the unobserved population parameters of interest from our sample regression function?

We answer the first of these questions by assessing the goodness-of-fit of our sample regression function.

6.5 ASSESS THE GOODNESS-OF-FIT OF THE SAMPLE MULTIPLE LINEAR REGRESSION FUNCTION

There are two potential measures of the goodness-of-fit of the sample multiple linear regression function that we consider here: (1) the percentage of the total variation in y that is explained by the joint variation between y and all of our independent variables, $x_1, x_2, \ldots, x_k$, and (2) the overall percentage of unexplained variation in y that is present in the sample regression function.

The Coefficient of Determination (R^2)

The formula and the intuition for calculating the R-squared of the sample regression function is the same for multiple linear regression as for simple linear regression. There is one practical difference, however. In the case of multiple linear regression analysis, the joint variation that "explains" the total variation in y is the joint variation between y and all of the independent variables, $x_1, x_2, \ldots, x_n$. We discuss the importance of this fact next.

We interpret the calculated R^2 in multiple linear regression analysis the same way that we did for simple linear regression analysis: Possible values for the calculated R^2 are bounded by 0 and 1, with a value of 0 indicating that the observed variation in the x values explain *none* of the observed variation in y and a value of 1 indicating that the observed variation in the x values explain *all* of the observed variation in y.

The regression output in Excel displays the values used to calculate R^2 as well as the calculated value itself. Excel Regression Output 6.2 presents these values for our specific 200-observation MLB position player sample.

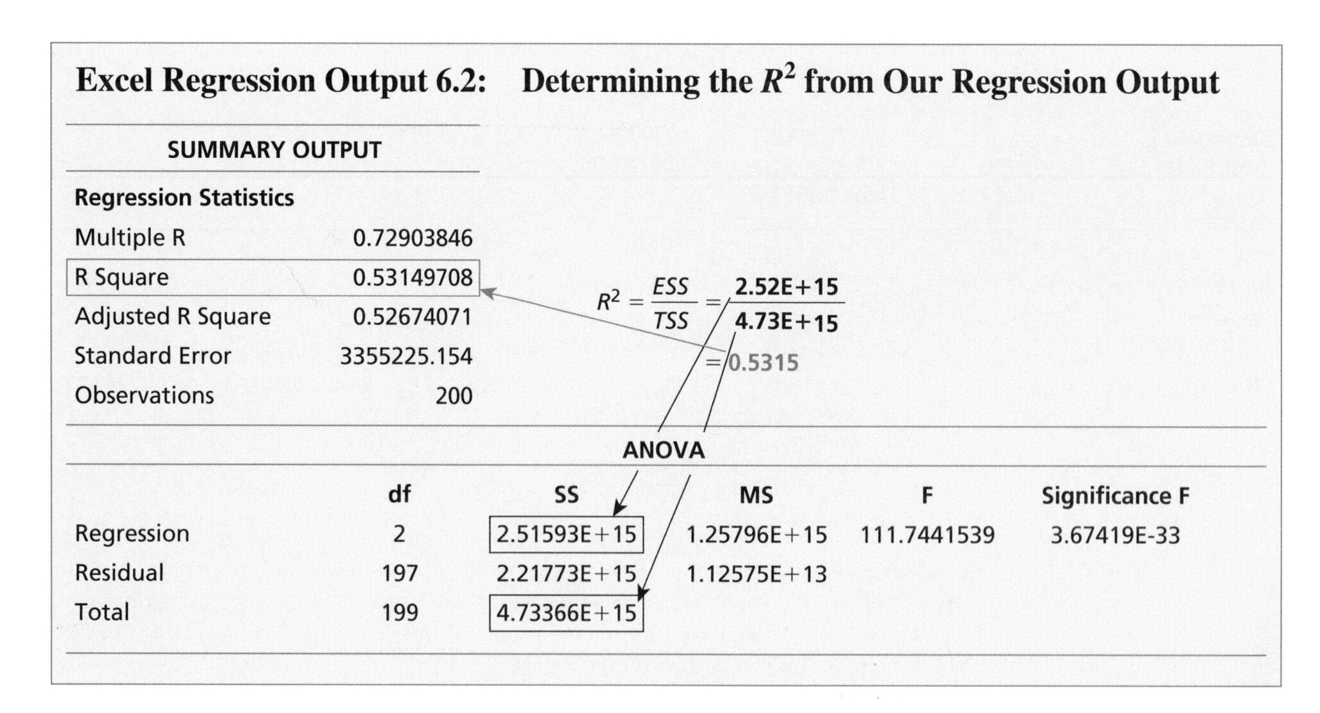

Excel Regression Output 6.2: Determining the R^2 from Our Regression Output

SUMMARY OUTPUT

Regression Statistics	
Multiple R	0.72903846
R Square	0.53149708
Adjusted R Square	0.52674071
Standard Error	3355225.154
Observations	200

$$R^2 = \frac{ESS}{TSS} = \frac{2.52E+15}{4.73E+15} = 0.5315$$

ANOVA

	df	SS	MS	F	Significance F
Regression	2	2.51593E+15	1.25796E+15	111.7441539	3.67419E-33
Residual	197	2.21773E+15	1.12575E+13		
Total	199	4.73366E+15			

As we learned in Chapter 4, in general, the greater the percentage of the observed variation in the dependent variable that is explained by the observed joint variation between the dependent and the independent variables, the better the "fit" of the sample regression function. This general rule of thumb tends to hold in the case of multiple linear regression analysis. An important caveat to this rule does exist, however. As mentioned earlier, given the nature of economic data, nearly all independent variables exhibit at least some relationship with the dependent variable. Accordingly, adding an independent variable to our analysis must increase the calculated R^2 because, by definition, every independent variable that is related to the dependent variable increases the explained sum of squares (ESS) of the sample regression function. Figure 6.8 demonstrates this fact using Venn diagrams.

FIGURE 6.8
A Visual Depiction of How the Addition of an Independent Variable Affects the Calculated R^2 of the Sample Regression Function

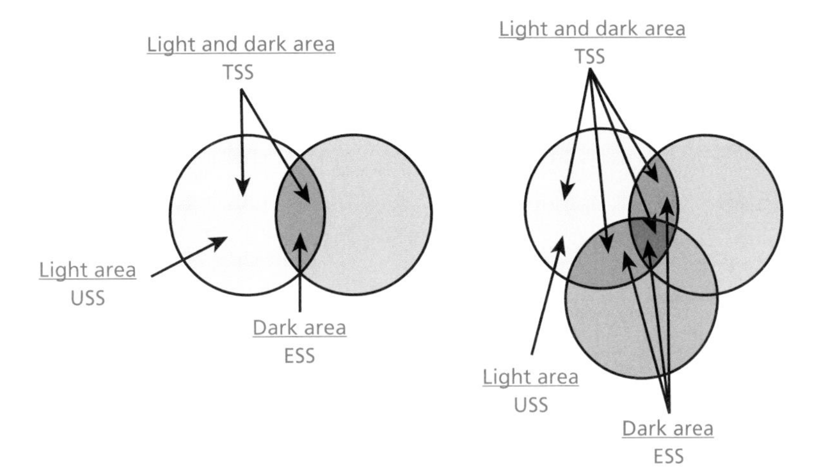

Figure 6.8 demonstrates that as we add independent variables that are correlated with the dependent variable, the *ESS* of our sample regression function increases (and the *USS* decreases). Accordingly, because the *TSS* does not change, when we calculate the R^2 of the sample regression function as the ratio of the *ESS* to the *TSS*, adding such variables necessarily increases the calculated R^2.

In terms of our interpretation of the calculated values, this means that we can potentially increase the value of the calculated R^2 simply by adding as many independent variables as possible to our multiple linear regression analysis. If so, would it be appropriate to conclude that sample regression function is the most appropriate specification simply because it has the highest possible calculated R^2? No.

The Adjusted R^2 ($\bar{R}^2$)

adjusted R^2 ($\bar{R}^2$) A modified version of the R^2 that is weighted for the degrees of freedom on the unexplained sum of squares and the total sum of squares.

We can account for the preceding fact by calculating the **adjusted R^2** (or $\bar{R}^2$), which is a value that weights the calculated R^2 for the number of independent variables included in the sample regression function. This weighted value is calculated as

$$\bar{R}^2 = 1 - \frac{USS/(n-k-1)}{TSS/(n-1)} = 1 - (1 - R^2)\left(\frac{n-1}{n-k-1}\right) \qquad 6.5.1$$

where n is the number of observations in the specific random sample drawn from the population and k is the number of independent variables included in the sample regression function.

This conversion is potentially informative because it penalizes the excessive use of independent variables that have little statistical relationship with the dependent variable. To see how, consider what happens when an independent variable is added to the sample regression function. As discussed earlier, adding an independent variable has two effects: (1) It increases the *ESS* and decreases the *USS* of the sample regression function, and (2) it increases the value of k, which necessarily decreases the degrees of freedom of the sample regression function ($n - k - 1$). Notice that these two terms make up the numerator of the fraction in the initial formula. Accordingly, whether the fraction increases or decreases (and whether the calculated $\overline{R}^2$ increases or decreases) depends on whether the change in the *USS* is greater than or less than the change in the degrees of freedom. If the *USS* decreases by more than the degrees of freedom, then the value of the numerator decreases and the R_A^2 increases. If, on the other hand, the *USS* decreases by less than the degrees of freedom, then the value of the numerator increases and the $\overline{R}^2$ decreases.

The regression output in Excel displays the values used to calculate the adjusted R^2 as well as the calculated value itself. Excel Regression Output 6.3 presents these values for our specific 200-observation MLB position player sample.

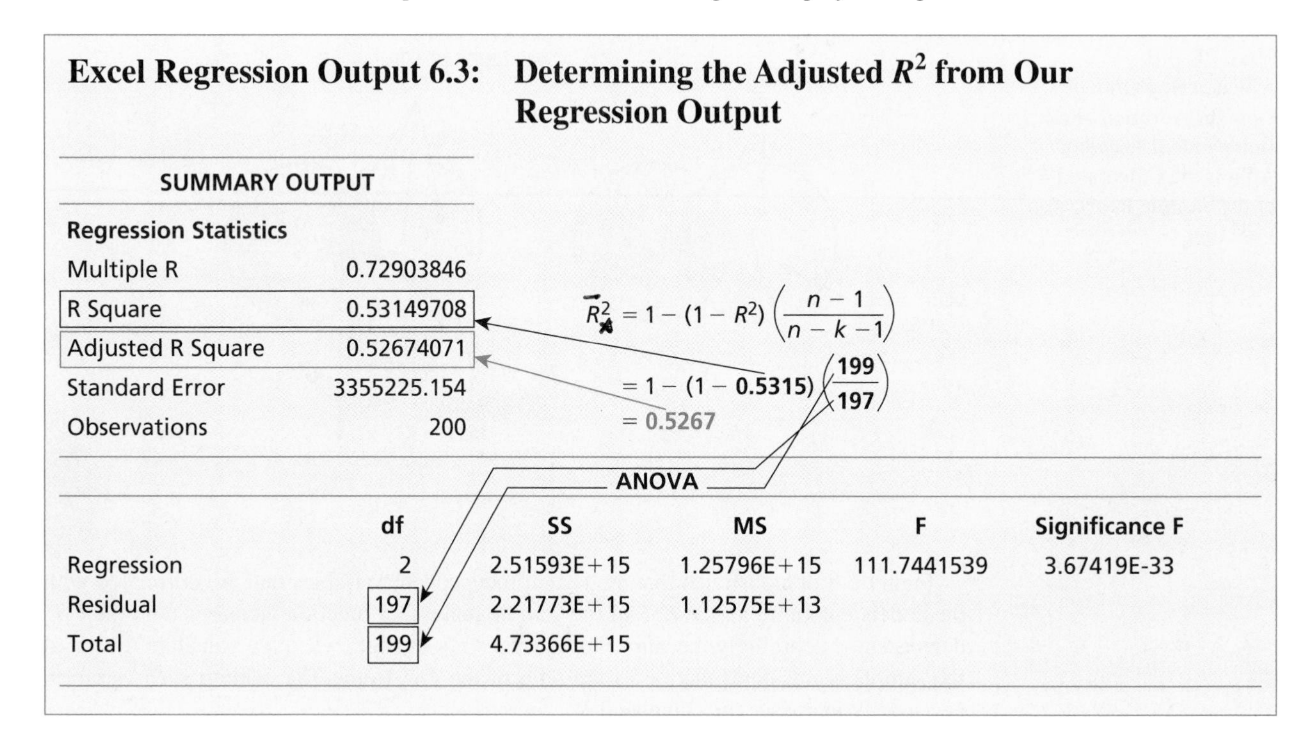

Excel Regression Output 6.3: Determining the Adjusted R^2 from Our Regression Output

SUMMARY OUTPUT

Regression Statistics	
Multiple R	0.72903846
R Square	0.53149708
Adjusted R Square	0.52674071
Standard Error	3355225.154
Observations	200

$$\overline{R}_A^2 = 1 - (1 - R^2)\left(\frac{n-1}{n-k-1}\right)$$

$$= 1 - (1 - \mathbf{0.5315})\left(\frac{\mathbf{199}}{\mathbf{197}}\right)$$

$$= 0.5267$$

ANOVA

	df	SS	MS	F	Significance F
Regression	2	2.51593E+15	1.25796E+15	111.7441539	3.67419E-33
Residual	197	2.21773E+15	1.12575E+13		
Total	199	4.73366E+15			

We should interpret this value as follows. Using the degrees of freedom correction, the $\overline{R}^2$ is the percentage of variation of the dependent variable y that can be explained by the independent variables, $x_1, x_2, \ldots, x_k$. Because of the degrees of freedom correction, the interpretation is not as straightforward as the regular R^2. The adjusted R^2 becomes a useful tool in later chapters that will allow us to compare goodness of fit between more complex models.

Standard Error of the Sample Regression Function

standard error of the sample regression function
The variation left in the dependent variable after the effects of the independent variables have been taken out.

The calculation of the **standard error of the sample regression function** is almost exactly the same for multiple linear regression as for simple linear regression, with the lone difference being that $k > 1$ for multiple linear regression. Excel Regression Output 6.4 presents the values needed for the calculation as well as the calculated value itself for our specific 200-observation MLB position player sample.

As with simple linear regression, this calculated value provides a general indication of the average distance each observed salary tends to fall from the salary predicted by the sample regression function. In other words, on average, observed annual salaries in our specific 200-observation MLB position player sample fall \$3,355,225.15 away from the sample regression function. As before, because this calculated value depends on the chosen unit of denomination, there is no rule for determining whether this number is relatively large or relatively small. Some sense might be gleaned by comparing the value to the minimum and maximum values in the sample, but beyond that we cannot conclude very much from the calculated value itself.

Excel Regression Output 6.4: Determining the Standard Error of the Regression Model from Our Regression Output

SUMMARY OUTPUT

Regression Statistics	
Multiple R	0.72903846
R Square	0.53149708
Adjusted R Square	0.52674071
Standard Error	3355225.154
Observations	200

$$S_{y|x} = \sqrt{\frac{UnexplainedSS}{n-k-1}} = \sqrt{MSUnexplained}$$

$$= \sqrt{1.13E+13}$$

$$= 3355225.15$$

ANOVA

	df	SS	MS	F	Significance F
Regression	2	2.51593E+15	1.25796E+15	111.7441539	3.67419E-33
Residual	197	2.21773E+15	1.12575E+13		
Total	199	4.73366E+15			

Empirical Research Tool 6.2 summarizes the potential measures of the goodness-of-fit of our multiple linear regression function.

EMPIRICAL RESEARCH TOOL 6.2: ASSESSING THE GOODNESS-OF-FIT OF OUR MULTIPLE LINEAR REGRESSION FUNCTION

Goal:
Numerically assess how well the sample regression function fits the observed sample data.

Tools:
The coefficient of determination, the adjusted R^2, and the standard error of the sample regression function.

Notation:
R^2 Coefficient of determination
$\bar{R}^2$ Adjusted R^2
$S_{y|x}$ Standard error of the sample regression function

Formulas:

$$\bar{R}^2 == 1 - \frac{USS/(n-k-1)}{TSS/(n-1)} = 1 - (1 - R^2)\left(\frac{n-1}{n-k-1}\right)$$ Adjusted R^2

$$R^2 = \frac{ESS}{TSS} = \frac{\sum(\hat{y}_i - \bar{y}_i)^2}{\sum(y_i - \bar{y}_i)^2}$$ Coefficient of determination

$$S_{y|x} = \sqrt{\frac{USS}{n-k-1}} = \sqrt{\frac{\sum(y_i - \hat{y}_i)^2}{n-k-1}}.$$ Standard error of the sample regression function

Finally, Excel Example 6.2 demonstrates how to assess the relative goodness-of-fit for the sample regression function for our 63-observation international GDP sample.

EXCEL EXAMPLE 6.2

Assessing the goodness-of-fit of the sample regression function for our international GDP sample

For our GDP example, the regression results are

SUMMARY OUTPUT		
Regression Statistics		
Multiple R	0.638582448	
R Square	0.407787543	← (R^2)
Adjusted R Square	0.388047128	← ($\bar{R}^2$)
Standard Error	2237.003564	← ($s_{y\|x}$)
Observations	63	

The calculated R^2 says that 41 percent of the variation in GDP can be explained by population and life expectancy. The adjusted R^2 says that given the degrees of freedom adjustment 39 percent of the variation in GDP can be explained by population and life expectancy. The standard error of the regression model, 2237.003, is the variability that remains in GDP after the effects of population and life expectancy are taken out.

Having answered our first question concerning the practical value of our multiple linear regression function, we now turn to the question of what our estimates tell us about the unobserved population parameters that we are attempting to estimate.

6.6 PERFORM HYPOTHESIS TESTS FOR THE OVERALL SIGNIFICANCE OF THE SAMPLE REGRESSION FUNCTION

The first hypothesis test that we perform seeks to identify whether the sample regression function itself explains a significant enough portion of the total variation in y for us to say that the function "has explanatory power" over the dependent variable.

Consider the general form of the population multiple linear regression model, which is written as

$$y_i = \beta_0 + \beta_1 x_{1,i} + \beta_2 x_{2,i} + \cdots + \beta_k x_{k,i} \quad \textbf{6.6.1}$$

In this case, for the regression model as a whole to have absolutely no explanatory power on the dependent variable, *all* of the true unobserved slope parameters would have to be 0 (so that $y_i = \beta_0 + \varepsilon_i$). Conversely, for the independent variables as a whole to have some explanatory power on the dependent variable, at least one of the true unobserved slope parameters would have to be statistically different from 0. Based on these facts, the null and alternative hypotheses for the F-test for the overall significance of the multiple linear regression function are

$$\begin{aligned} &H_0: \beta_1 = \beta_2 = \cdots = \beta_k = 0 \\ &H_A: \text{At least one of } \beta_1, \beta_2, \ldots, \beta_k \text{ are not equal to } 0 \end{aligned} \quad \textbf{6.6.2}$$

Because a confidence interval is not easily calculated for overall significance, we focus only on the critical value and p-value methods for testing this hypothesis. For the test of the overall significance of the multiple linear regression model, the appropriate test statistic is calculated as

$$F = \frac{\frac{ESS}{k}}{\frac{USS}{n-k-1}} = \frac{MSExplained}{MSUnexplained} \quad \textbf{6.6.3}$$

and the appropriate critical value is found by looking in the F-table for the value $F_{\frac{\alpha}{2}, k, n-k-1}$. In this case, the appropriate p-value is difficult to calculate by hand; instead, we simply rely on Excel output to provide the value for us.

Excel Regression Output 6.5 presents the F-test statistic and the significance F for our specific 200-observation MLB position player sample.

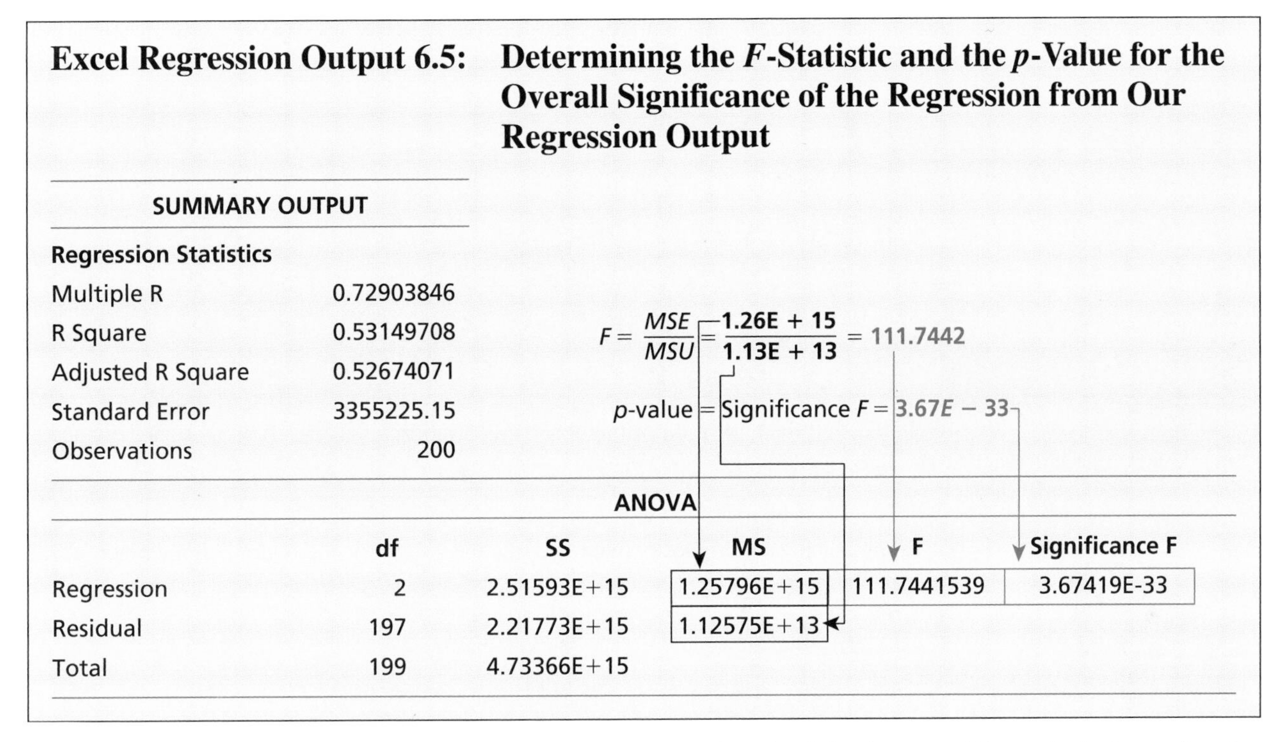

Excel Regression Output 6.5: Determining the *F*-Statistic and the *p*-Value for the Overall Significance of the Regression from Our Regression Output

SUMMARY OUTPUT

Regression Statistics	
Multiple R	0.72903846
R Square	0.53149708
Adjusted R Square	0.52674071
Standard Error	3355225.15
Observations	200

$F = \frac{MSE}{MSU} = \frac{1.26E+15}{1.13E+13} = 111.7442$

p-value = Significance $F = 3.67E-33$

ANOVA

	df	SS	MS	F	Significance F
Regression	2	2.51593E+15	1.25796E+15	111.7441539	3.67419E-33
Residual	197	2.21773E+15	1.12575E+13		
Total	199	4.73366E+15			

While it is valuable to understand each of the three possible methods for performing hypothesis tests, in reality, we only need to perform one. For reasons explained in Chapter 5 (i.e., because it is the only one that has a probability attached), we generally prefer conducting the p-value whenever possible. Hypothesis Testing 6.1 presents the F-test for the overall significance of the multiple linear regression function for our 200-observation MLB position player sample.

Hypothesis Testing 6.1: Hypothesis Tests for the Overall Significance of the Multiple Linear Regression Model

Question:
All else equal, does the regression model explain a significant portion of the observed variation in salaries?

Population Regression Function:

$y_i = \beta_0 + \beta_1\, Experience_i + \beta_2\, Home\ runs + \varepsilon_i$

Hypothesis:

H_0: $\beta_1 = \beta_2 = 0$

H_A: ($\beta_1 \neq 0$ or $\beta_2 \neq 0$) or ($\beta_1 \neq 0$ and $\beta_2 \neq 0$)

***p*-Value Method:**

Test-Statistic

p-value = 3.67419E-33

Significance level: $\alpha = 0.05$

Rejection Rule

Reject H_0 if p-value < 0.05.

Conclusion:
Because 3.67419E-33 < 0.05, we reject H_0 at $\alpha = 0.05$ and conclude that at least one of the independent variables experience and/or home runs are statistically related to salary.

* A visual representation is presented on the next page.

Visual Depiction:

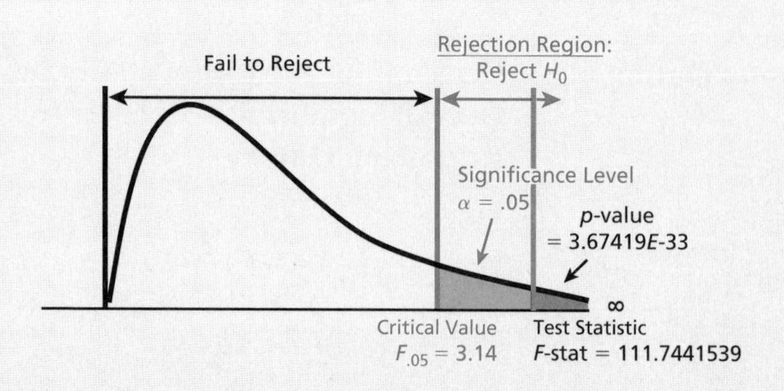

Inference:
The regression model does explain a significant portion of the observed variation in salaries (i.e., there is evidence that at least one independent variable affects y).

Empirical Research Tool 6.3 summarizes the F-test for the overall significance of the multiple linear regression function.

EMPIRICAL RESEARCH TOOL 6.3: HYPOTHESIS TESTS FOR THE OVERALL SIGNIFICANCE OF THE MULTIPLE LINEAR REGRESSION FUNCTION

Goal:
To determine whether the independent variables as a group explain a statistically significant portion of total variation in the dependent variable.

Hypothesis:
$H_0: \beta_1 = \beta_2 = \cdots = \beta_k = 0$
H_A: at least one of $\beta_1, \beta_2, \ldots, \beta_k \neq 0$

Process:

1. Collect a specific sample of size n from the population, and estimate the sample regression function.
2. Calculate the F-statistic for the overall significance of the sample regression function.
3. Compare the calculated p-value for the calculated F-statistic to the desired level of significance α.
4. If the calculated p-value $< \alpha$, then **reject H_0 and conclude that at least one of the explanatory variables help explain the dependent variable.**

When We Might Use It:
Every time we estimate a sample regression function.

Instead of asking whether the entire or overall multiple linear regression model has significant explanatory power as a whole, we might wish to ask whether each individual independent variable has explanatory power over the dependent variable.

6.7 PERFORM HYPOTHESIS TESTS FOR THE INDIVIDUAL SIGNIFICANCE OF A SLOPE COEFFICIENT

To perform a hypothesis test for the individual significance of an slope coefficient, we start again with the general form of the population multiple regression model

$$y_i = \beta_0 + \beta_1 x_{1,i} + \beta_2 x_{2,i} + \cdots + \beta_k x_{k,i} + \varepsilon_i \qquad 6.7.1$$

If an individual independent variable has absolutely no explanatory power over the dependent variable, then the true unobserved slope parameter for that variable equals 0. If, on the other hand, the individual independent variable has at least some explanatory power over the dependent variable, then the true unobserved slope parameter is different from 0. Accordingly, the null and alternative hypotheses for the *t*-test for the individual significance of a slope parameter are

$$H_0: \beta_j = 0$$
$$H_1: \beta_j \neq 0 \qquad 6.7.2$$

where *j* is one of the *k* independent variables in the multiple regression model.

In this case, we can use each of our three potential methods for hypothesis testing. The confidence interval around the slope parameter is calculated as

$$\hat{\beta}_j \pm z_{\alpha/2} s_{\hat{\beta}_j} \quad \text{if } n \text{ is large } (n \geq 100)$$
$$\hat{\beta}_j \pm t_{\alpha/2, n-k-1} s_{\hat{\beta}_j} \quad \text{if } n \text{ is not large } (n < 100) \qquad 6.7.3$$

The test statistic for individual significance (i.e., whether for the null hypothesis that $\beta_j = 0$) is calculated as

$$t\text{-stat} = \frac{\hat{\beta}_j - H_0}{s_{\hat{\beta}_j}} = \frac{\hat{\beta}_j - 0}{s_{\hat{\beta}_j}} = \frac{\hat{\beta}_j}{s_{\hat{\beta}_j}} \qquad 6.7.4$$

while the appropriate table value is found by looking in the student's-*t* table for the value representing $t_{\frac{\alpha}{2}, n-k-1}$.

Finally, the appropriate *p*-value is calculated as

$$p\text{-value} = 2 \times P(Z > |t\text{-stat}|) \qquad 6.7.5$$

Excel Regression Output 6.6 presents the appropriate confidence interval, *t*-statistic, and *p*-value for our specific 200-observation MLB position player sample.

Excel Regression Output 6.6: Determining the Values for Hypothesis Testing about a Single Parameter from Our Regression Output

<u>t-Statistic</u>

$t\text{-stat} = \hat{\beta}_1 / s_{\hat{\beta}_1}$

$= \frac{569508.46}{63560.11} = 8.96$

<u>p-value</u>

p-value

$= 2 \times P(Z > |t\text{-stat})$

$= 2.48E-16$

<u>Confidence interval</u>

$\hat{\beta}_1 \pm z_{\frac{\alpha}{2}} s_{\hat{\beta}_1} =$

$569508.46 \pm (1.96) \times (63560.11)$

$= (444{,}162.91, 694{,}854.01)$

	Coefficients	Standard Error	*t* Stat	*p*-value	Lower 95%	Upper 95%
Intercept	−1,003,204.933	394,238.700	−2.544663759	0.011704679	−1,780,674.790	−225,735.076
Experience	569,508.462	63,560.106	8.960155911	2.48239E-16	444,162.912	694,854.012
HR	212,460.856	23,578.026	9.010968688	1.78871E-16	165,963.126	258,958.587

Hypothesis Testing 6.2 presents the *t*-test for the individual significance of an estimated slope coefficient for our 200-observation MLB position player sample.

Empirical Research Tool 6.4 summarizes the individual significance of the population slope coefficient.

Hypothesis Testing 6.2: Testing for the Individual Significance of a Slope Coefficient

Question:
All else equal, is experience statistically related to salary (i.e., does experience belong in the population regression function)?

Population Regression Function:

$$y_i = \beta_0 + \beta_1\ Experience_i + \beta_2\ Home\ runs + \varepsilon_i$$

Hypothesis:

H_0: $\beta_1 = 0$
H_A: $\beta_1 \neq 0$

***p*-value Method:**

Test Statistic

p-value = 2.48239E-16
Significance level: $\alpha = 0.05$

Rejection Rule

Reject H_0 if p-value < 0.05

Conclusion:
Because 2.48239E-16 < 0.05, we reject H_0 at $\alpha = 0.05$ and conclude that experience is statistically related to salary.

Visual Depiction:

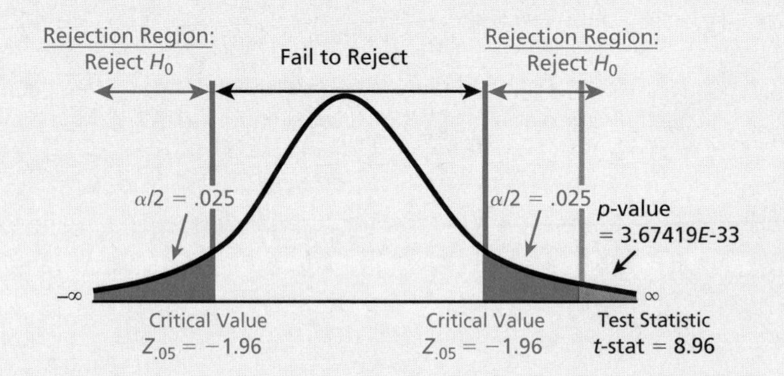

Inference:
β_1 is statistically different from 0 at the 5 percent level. These results suggest that experience is statistically related to salary or that salary belongs in the population regression model.

experience

EMPIRICAL RESEARCH TOOL 6.4: HYPOTHESIS TESTS FOR THE INDIVIDUAL SIGNIFICANCE OF THE POPULATION SLOPE COEFFICIENT

Goal:
To determine whether a single independent variables explains a statistically significant portion of total variation in the dependent variable.

Hypothesis:
For any independent variable j

$$H_0: \beta_j = 0$$
$$H_A: \beta_j \neq 0$$

Process:

1. Collect a specific sample of size n from the population, and estimate the sample regression function.
2. Compare the calculated p-value for the estimated slope coefficient for the independent variable of interest to the desired level of significance α.

If the calculated p-value $< \alpha$, then reject H_0 and conclude that the dependent variable j helps explain the independent variable.

When We Might Use It:
Every time we estimate a sample regression function.

Finally, Excel Example 6.3 demonstrates how to test for the overall and for our 63-observation international GDP sample.

EXCEL EXAMPLE 6.3

Testing for the overall and individual significance for our international GDP sample

For our GDP example, the regression results are

SUMMARY OUTPUT

Regression Statistics	
Multiple R	0.638582448
R Square	0.407787543
Adjusted R Square	0.388047128
Standard Error	2237.003564
Observations	63

ANOVA

	df	SS	MS	F	Significance F
Regression	2	206747858.1	103373929	20.65749571	1.49392E-07
Residual	60	300251096.7	5004184.946		
Total	62	506998954.8			

	Coefficients	Standard Error	*t* Stat	*p*-value	Lower 95%	Upper 95%
Intercept	−2781.87889	2224.247084	−1.250705872	0.21589722	−7231.03545	1667.27767
Population/ 1,000,000	7.394403415	1.192864308	6.198863833	5.70441E-08	5.00831956	9.78048727
Life Expectancy	46.85515323	30.43221581	1.539656314	0.128901828	−14.01834124	107.728648

Because the significance F less than 0.05, we reject the null hypothesis that $\beta_1 = \beta_2 = 0$ at the 5 percent level and conclude that at least one of Population or Life Expectancy is related to GDP. The p-value on Population of 5.70E-08 is less than 0.01, which means we conclude that population is related to GDP at the 1 percent level. The p-value on Life Expectancy is 0.1289, which is greater than 0.1 and suggests that Life Expectancy is not related to GDP at the 10 percent level.

In the two hypothesis tests introduced so far, we have asked whether the *entire* set of independent variables jointly explain a statistically significant portion of the observed variation in the dependent variable or whether an *individual* independent variable explains a statistically significant portion of the observed the variation in the

exclusion restriction
A restriction in which a subset of the independent variables are left out of the model.

dependent variable. Suppose instead that we wish to ask whether a *subset* of independent variables jointly explains a statistically significant portion of the observed variation in the dependent variable. We can answer such questions by performing **exclusion restriction** tests.

6.8 PERFORM HYPOTHESIS TESTS FOR THE JOINT SIGNIFICANCE OF A SUBSET OF SLOPE COEFFICIENTS

unrestricted regression model
The initial model with no variables left out.

restricted regression model
The regression model where a subset of the independent variables are left out.

Exclusion restriction tests are performed by running two separate regressions: one that includes the entire set of independent variables (referred to as the **unrestricted regression model**) and one that excludes the subset of independent variables for which we wish to test joint significance (referred to as the **restricted regression model**). We then compare either the R^2 or the unexplained sum of squares (USS) from the two regressions to determine the relative effect that omitting the subset of independent variables has on the overall fit of the multiple linear regression function.

To demonstrate, suppose that we expand our multiple linear regression analysis to include the number of runs scored and the number of runs batted in (RBIs) in addition to the number of home runs hit and the years of experience. In this case, we would estimate the population regression model

$$Salary_i = \beta_0 + \beta_1\, Experience_i + \beta_2\, Home\ runs + \beta_3\, Runs_i + \beta_4\, RBIs + \varepsilon_i \quad \textbf{6.8.1}$$

and test whether the subset of offensive productivity parameters, β_2, β_3, and β_4, jointly explain the observed variation in salary. In such a case, for tβ_2, β_3, and β_4 to jointly have no explanatory power over the dependent variable, all three parameters would have to equal 0, while β_2, β_3, and β_4 to jointly have some explanatory power over the dependent variable, at least one of the three parameters would have to be different from 0. As such, we write the null and alternative hypotheses for this test as

$$\begin{aligned} &H_0\colon \beta_2 = \beta_3 = \beta_4 = 0 \\ &H_A\colon \text{At least one of } \beta_2, \beta_3, \beta_4 \text{ not equal to } 0 \end{aligned} \quad \textbf{6.8.2}$$

To perform the test, we estimate two different sample multiple linear regression functions: the unrestricted regression model in formula 6.8.1 and the restricted regression model that imposes the exclusion restriction in the null hypothesis, which is written as

$$Salary_i = \beta_0 + \beta_1\, Experience_i + \varepsilon_i \quad \textbf{6.8.3}$$

The appropriate test statistic compares the results of these two sample regression functions and is written as either

$$F = \frac{\dfrac{(USS_{restricted} - USS_{unrestricted})}{q}}{\dfrac{USS_{unrestricted}}{n-k-1}} \quad \text{or} \quad F = \frac{\dfrac{(R^2_{unrestricted} - R^2_{restricted})}{q}}{\dfrac{(1 - R^2_{unrestricted})}{n-k-1}} \quad \textbf{6.8.4}$$

where q is equal to the number of restrictions in the null hypothesis and $n - k - 1$ is calculated from the unrestricted regression model. Note that an easy way to determine q, the number of restrictions in the null hypothesis, is to simply count the number of equal signs in the null hypothesis. In this case, it is 3.

Excel Regression Output 6.7 presents the sample regression function for the unrestricted model for our specific 200-observation MLB position player sample.

Excel Regression Output 6.8 presents the sample regression function for the restricted model for our specific 200-observation MLB position player sample.

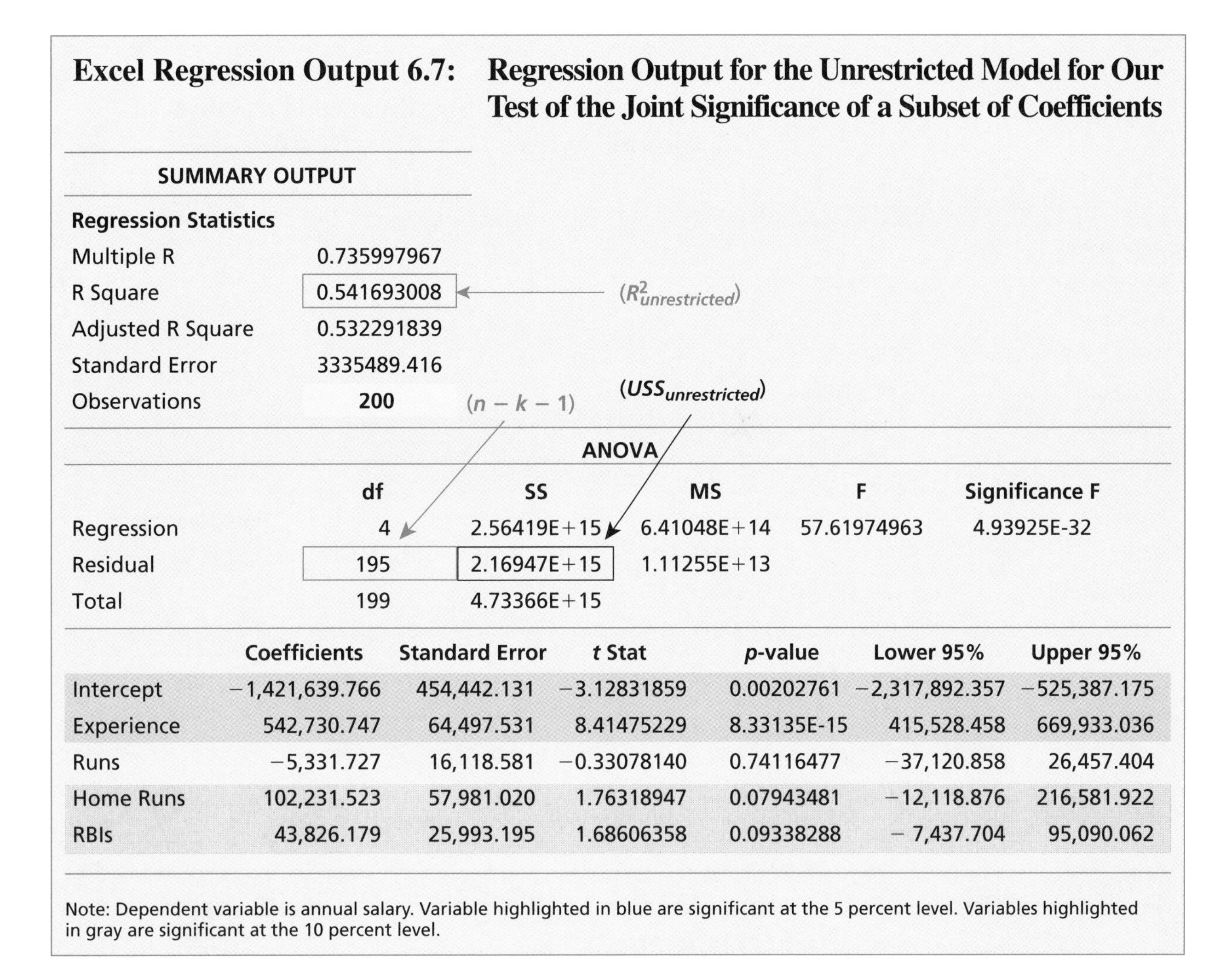

Excel Regression Output 6.7: Regression Output for the Unrestricted Model for Our Test of the Joint Significance of a Subset of Coefficients

SUMMARY OUTPUT

Regression Statistics	
Multiple R	0.735997967
R Square	0.541693008
Adjusted R Square	0.532291839
Standard Error	3335489.416
Observations	200

($R^2_{unrestricted}$) ($n-k-1$) ($USS_{unrestricted}$)

ANOVA

	df	SS	MS	F	Significance F
Regression	4	2.56419E+15	6.41048E+14	57.61974963	4.93925E-32
Residual	195	2.16947E+15	1.11255E+13		
Total	199	4.73366E+15			

	Coefficients	Standard Error	*t* Stat	*p*-value	Lower 95%	Upper 95%
Intercept	−1,421,639.766	454,442.131	−3.12831859	0.00202761	−2,317,892.357	−525,387.175
Experience	542,730.747	64,497.531	8.41475229	8.33135E-15	415,528.458	669,933.036
Runs	−5,331.727	16,118.581	−0.33078140	0.74116477	−37,120.858	26,457.404
Home Runs	102,231.523	57,981.020	1.76318947	0.07943481	−12,118.876	216,581.922
RBIs	43,826.179	25,993.195	1.68606358	0.09338288	− 7,437.704	95,090.062

Note: Dependent variable is annual salary. Variable highlighted in blue are significant at the 5 percent level. Variables highlighted in gray are significant at the 10 percent level.

Hypothesis Testing 6.3 presents the test for the joint significance of a subset of coefficients in our multiple linear regression function.

Empirical Research Tool 6.5 summarizes the F-test for the joint significance of a subset of coefficients for our multiple linear regression function.

Instead of testing whether a subset of independent variables has explanatory power over our dependent variable, suppose we have reason to believe that the population parameters in which we are interested are structurally different for two distinct subsets of our data.

6.9 PERFORM THE CHOW TEST FOR STRUCTURAL DIFFERENCES BETWEEN TWO SUBSETS OF DATA

Chow test
A test of whether the coefficients in two different data sets are equal.

As an example of the **Chow test** for structural differences between two subsets of data, suppose that due to the designated hitter rule, we suspect that the salaries of American League position players might be determined in ways that are structurally different than those for National League position players.

The Chow test is based on comparing the calculated unexplained sum of squares from a "pooled" regression containing both subsets of data (USS_{pooled}) to the sum of the unexplained sum of squares from separate regressions (regressions 1 and 2) containing only the different subsets of data ($USS_1 + USS_2$). The intuition behind this test is that if the subsets are structurally equivalent, then $USS_{pooled} = USS_1 + USS_2$; however, if the

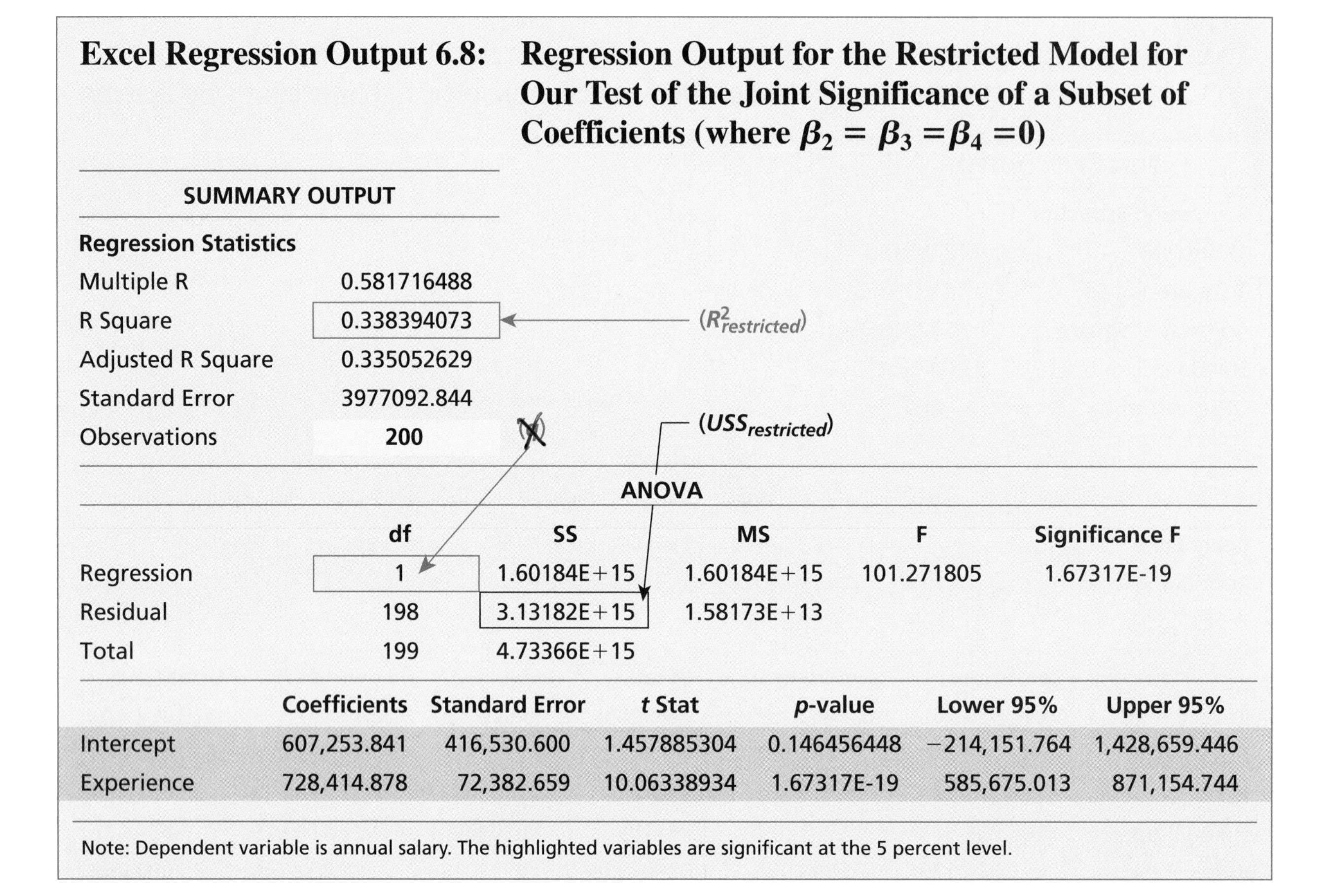

Excel Regression Output 6.8: Regression Output for the Restricted Model for Our Test of the Joint Significance of a Subset of Coefficients (where $\beta_2 = \beta_3 = \beta_4 = 0$)

SUMMARY OUTPUT

Regression Statistics	
Multiple R	0.581716488
R Square	0.338394073
Adjusted R Square	0.335052629
Standard Error	3977092.844
Observations	200

ANOVA

	df	SS	MS	F	Significance F
Regression	1	1.60184E+15	1.60184E+15	101.271805	1.67317E-19
Residual	198	3.13182E+15	1.58173E+13		
Total	199	4.73366E+15			

	Coefficients	Standard Error	t Stat	p-value	Lower 95%	Upper 95%
Intercept	607,253.841	416,530.600	1.457885304	0.146456448	−214,151.764	1,428,659.446
Experience	728,414.878	72,382.659	10.06338934	1.67317E-19	585,675.013	871,154.744

Note: Dependent variable is annual salary. The highlighted variables are significant at the 5 percent level.

Hypothesis Testing 6.3 Testing for the Joint Significance of a Subset of Coefficients

Question:

Does the subset of offensive productivity measures (home runs, runs scored, RBIs) jointly explain the variation in salary?

Population Regression Function:

$$Salary_i = \beta_0 + \beta_1 Experience_i + \beta_2 Home\ runs + \beta_3 Runs_i + \beta_4 RBIs + \varepsilon_i$$

Hypothesis:

H_0: $\beta_2 = \beta_3 = \beta_4 = 0$

H_A: At least one of β_2, β_3, β_4 not equal to 0

For this test, we will use the critical value method.

Critical Value Method:

Test-Statistic

$$Test\text{-Statistic: either } F = \frac{(3.13E + 15 - 2.17E + 15)/3}{2.17E + 15/195} = 28.8331$$

$$\text{or } F = \frac{(.5417 - .3384)/3}{(1 - .5417)/195} = 28.8331$$

Critical Value: $F_{\alpha,q,n-k-1} = F_{.05,3,195} = 3.0$

Rejection Rule

Reject H_0 if $F > F_{\alpha,q,n-k-1}$.

Conclusion:

Because = 28.8331 > 3.0, we reject H_0 at $\alpha = 0.05$ and conclude that the subset of offensive productivity measures (home runs, runs scored, RBIs) does jointly explain the variation in salary.

EMPIRICAL RESEARCH TOOL 6.5: HYPOTHESIS TESTS FOR THE JOINT SIGNIFICANCE OF A SUBSET OF COEFFICIENTS

Goal:

To determine whether a subset of independent variables jointly explain a statistically significant portion of total variation in the dependent variable.

Hypothesis:

For a subset of independent variable $j, k, \ldots, l$

$$H_0: \beta_j = \beta_k = \cdots = \beta_l = 0$$
$$H_A: \text{At least one of } \beta_j, \beta_k, \ldots, \beta_l \neq 0$$

Process:

1. Estimate the unrestricted model that contains all of the independent variables, and calculate the unexplained sum of squares USS_{UR}.
2. Estimate the restricted model that omits the subset of independent variables that we are testing, and calculate the unexplained sum of squares USS_R.
3. Calculate the test statistic $F = \dfrac{\dfrac{(USS_R - USS_{UR})}{q}}{\dfrac{USS_{UR}}{n-k-1}}$
4. Compare the calculated *test*-statistic to the predetermined critical value $F_{\alpha,q,n-k-1}$.
5. If the calculated *test*-statistic is greater than $F_{\alpha,q,n-k-1}$, then reject H_0.

Why It Works:

The intuition behind the test of the joint significance of coefficients has to do with the residuals. Look closely at the numerator of the *test*-statistic. If the unexplained sum of squares, USS_R, is equal to the unexplained sum of squares unrestricted, USS_{UR}, then the *F*-statistic will be equal to zero, and we would fail to reject the null hypothesis and conclude that the coefficients are not statistically different from 0. When would this happen? These two values would be exactly equal if none of the independent variables associated with the coefficients that we are testing are related to the dependent variable, *y*, at all. Even if USS_R is not exactly equal to USS_{UR} but they are relatively close to each other, we would still fail to reject the null hypothesis and conclude that the independent variables associated with the coefficients don't jointly add enough to the model to merit their inclusion. On the other hand, if USS_R is very different from USS_{UR}, then we should reject the null hypothesis that the coefficients are jointly equal to 0 and conclude that the independent variables jointly add enough to the model to merit inclusion.

When We Might Use It:

When we suspect that a group of variables might jointly explain a statistically significant portion of the total variation in the dependent variable even though some of the variables might not achieve individual significance.

subsets are structurally different, then $USS_{pooled} \neq USS_1 + USS_2$. Accordingly, a test based on comparing USS_{pooled} with $USS_1 + USS_2$ should provide statistical evidence as to the degree to which the sample regression functions are structurally equivalent/structurally different.

The appropriate test statistic for a Chow test adjusts for the degrees of freedom in the different sample regression functions and is written as

$$F\text{-stat} = \frac{\dfrac{USS_{pooled} - (USS_1 + USS_2)}{k+1}}{\dfrac{USS_1 + USS_2}{n - 2(k+1)}} \qquad \textbf{6.9.1}$$

where k is the number of independent variables in each regression and n is the number of observations in the pooled regression.

The critical value for conducting the Chow hypothesis test is the table value $F_{\infty, k+1, n-2(k+1)}$, and the rejection rule is to reject H_0 if the calculated F-statistic is greater than the critical value.

To perform our Chow test for structural differences between the salaries of American and National League position players, we estimate the population regression model

$$Salary_i = \beta_0 + \beta_1\, Experience_i + \beta_2\, Home\ runs_i + \varepsilon_i \qquad 6.9.2$$

for (1) the pooled regression that includes both American and National League position players, recording the unexplained sum of squares as USS_{pooled}; (2) the subset of only National League position players, recording the unexplained sum of squares as USS_1; and (3) the subset of only American League position players, recording the unexplained sum of squares as USS_2.

Excel Regression Output 6.9 presents results for the three different regressions for our specific 200-observation MLB position player sample.

Excel Regression Output 6.9: Statistics for the Pooled and Separate League Salary Regression for the Chow Test

Pooled Regression (USS_{pooled})

ANOVA	df	SS
Regression	2	2.52E+15
Residual	197	2.22E+15
Total	199	4.73E+15

National League Only (USS_1)

ANOVA	df	SS
Regression	2	1.88E+15
Residual	112	1.06E+15
Total	114	2.94E+15

American League Only (USS_2)

ANOVA	df	SS
Regression	2	6.95E+14
Residual	82	1.1E+15
Total	84	1.79E+15

Based on these results, we test for structural differences between American and National League position player salaries using the Chow test as follows.

Hypothesis Testing 6.4 presents the Chow test for structural differences between the American and National Leagues for our multiple linear regression function.

Hypothesis Testing 6.4: Chow Test for Structural Differences in American League and National League Position Player Salaries

Question:

Is there a structural difference between American League and National League position player salaries?

Population Regression Function:

$Salary_i = \beta_0 + \beta_1 Experience_i + \beta_2 Home\ runs_i + \varepsilon_i$

Hypothesis:

H_0: $\beta_0, \beta_1, \beta_2$ are structurally similar for American and National League position players

H_A: At least one of $\beta_0, \beta_1, \beta_2$ are structurally different for American and National League position players

For this test, we will use the critical value method.

Critical Value Method:

Test-Statistic

$$F = \frac{(USS_{pooled} - (USS_1 + USS_2))/k + 1}{(USS_1 + USS_2)/(n - 2(k + 1))} = \frac{(2.22E + 15 - (1.06E + 15 + 1.10E + 15))/3}{(1.06E + 15 + 1.10E + 15)/194} = 1.729$$

Critical Value

$$F_{\alpha,k+1,(n-2(k+1))} = F_{.05,3,194} = 3.0$$

Rejection Rule

Reject H_0 if $F > F_{\alpha,k+1,(n-2(k+1))}$

Conclusion:

Because $= 1.729 < 3.0$, we *fail to reject* H_0 at $\alpha = 0.05$ and conclude that there is no structural difference between the salaries of American and National League position players, and we continue to analyze the pooled regression results.

Empirical Research Tool 6.6 summarizes the Chow test for structural differences between two subsets of data.

EMPIRICAL RESEARCH TOOL 6.6: THE CHOW TEST FOR STRUCTURAL DIFFERENCES BETWEEN TWO SUBSETS OF DATA

Goal:

To determine whether the sample regression functions for two or more subsets of the data are structurally different.

Hypothesis:

H_0: There is no structural difference in the sample regression functions

H_0: There is a structural difference in the sample regression functions

Why It Works:

The intuition behind the Chow test is based on a simple fact: If the two subsets of data are structurally equivalent, then the sum of their unexplained sum of squares ($USS_1 + USS_2$) would exactly equal the unexplained sum of squares for the pooled regression (USS_{pooled}). Hence, comparing the unexplained sum of squares for the pooled regression to the sum of the unexplained sums of squares from the separate regressions $[USS_{pooled} - (USS_1 + USS_2)]$ should provide an indication of the degree to which the subsets of data are structurally equivalent. If $USS_{pooled} - (USS_1 + USS_2)$ were close to 0; then the calculated *test*-statistic would be "small," and we would conclude that the subsets appear to be structurally equivalent. If $USS_{pooled} - (USS_1 + USS_2)$ is far from 0, then the calculated *test*-statistic would be "large," and we would conclude that the subsets appear to be structurally different and that they should be estimated separately. The appropriate threshold for determining whether the calculated *test*-statistic is "small" or "large" is the table value for $F_{\alpha,k+1,n-2(k+1)}$.

When We Might Use It:

When we suspect that the estimated intercepts and slopes are different between two or more subsets within a given data set.

ADDITIONS TO OUR EMPIRICAL RESEARCH TOOLKIT

In this chapter, we have introduced a number of tools that will prove valuable when performing empirical research:

- The correlation matrix for the linear relationship between more than two random variables.
- The multiple linear regression assumption required for OLS to be BLUE.
- The multiple linear regression function.

- Measures of the goodness-of-fit of the multiple linear regression function.
- Hypothesis tests for the overall significance of the multiple linear regression function.
- Hypothesis tests for the individual significance of an estimated slope coefficient.
- Hypothesis tests for the joint significance of a subset of estimated slope coefficients.
- The Chow test for structural differences between two subsets of data.

OUR NEW EMPIRICAL TOOLS IN PRACTICE: USING WHAT WE HAVE LEARNED IN THIS CHAPTER

Using the tools introduced in this chapter, our former student estimated the sample multiple linear regression function for his 90-observation sample of the ratios of unmarried women to unmarried men in U.S. MSAs. Doing so produced the output in Table 6.4.

TABLE 6.4 **The Excel Regression Output for Our Student's Marriage Data**

SUMMARY OUTPUT	
Regression Statistics	
Multiple R	0.412821156
R Square	0.170421307
Adjusted R Square	0.131382310
Standard Error	7.707934381
Observations	**90**

ANOVA					
	df	**SS**	**MS**	**F**	**Significance F**
Regression	4	1037.435836	259.3589589	4.365411988	0.002934458
Residual	85	5050.041455	59.41225241		
Total	89	6087.477291			

	Coefficients	**Standard Error**	***t* Stat**	***p*-value**	**Lower 95%**	**Upper 95%**
Intercept	140.2074364	5.572587349	25.16020434	3.77344E-41	129.12764	151.2872328
Population 18 and over	3.24965E-07	4.33548E-07	0.749549108	0.455595823	−5.37043E-07	1.18697E-06
Males BA or higher	−0.480654659	0.434809070	−1.105438438	0.272088778	−1.345171562	0.383862244
Females BA or higher	0.719126615	0.470456045	1.528573441	0.130083213	−0.216266022	1.654519252
Median Income (Thousands)	−0.558203085	0.173715321	−3.213320974	0.001854499	−0.903595677	−0.212810494

Note: Dependent variable is the ratio of unmarried women per 100 unmarried men in an MSA. Variables highlighted in red are significant at the 5 percent level.

Based on the fact that the calculated p-value for the significance of the overall sample regression function, 0.002934458, was less than 0.05, our former student concluded that this particular sample regression function did indeed explain a statistically significant portion of the total variation in MSA unmarried women rates. Likewise, given that the calculated p-value for the individual significance of median income, 0.001854499, was less than 0.05 and that the calculated p-values for all or the remaining independent variables are greater than 0.05, he further concluded that only the median income of an MSA achieved individual significance at the 5 percent level. The estimated slope coefficient for this variable suggested to the student that for every \$1,000 increase in the median income of a given MSA, there were fewer unmarried females per 100 unmarried males in the MSA. In other words, based on this sample regression function, it appeared to the student that if he wanted to live in an MSA in which marriage was relatively more prevalent, he would need to relocate to an MSA with a lower median income (which likely also indicates a lower cost-of-living).

Based on these findings, our former student was well on his way to completing a successful empirical research project.

LOOKING AHEAD TO CHAPTER 7

While this chapter has introduced multiple linear regression analysis, there are still a number of issues that need to be addressed if we are to get the maximum value out of this very valuable tool. First, suppose that we are interested in determining the linear relationship between the dependent variable and a quality, such as a person's sex, rather than a quantity, such as years of work experience. Second, suppose that we suspect that the true relationship between the dependent variable and a given independent variable is actually quadratic rather than linear. Finally, suppose that we are interested in estimating the elasticity between the dependent variable and a given independent variable, which is defined as the percentage change in the dependent variable that results from a given percentage change in the independent variable. Chapter 7 introduces methods for dealing with such concerns in multiple linear regression analysis.

Problems

6.1 Suppose that you have a data set that has student-level information on college GPA, hours studied, SAT score, and high school GPA and that you obtain the following correlation matrix.

	College GPA	Hours Studied	SAT Score	HS GPA
College GPA	1			
Hours Studied	0.7817	1		
SAT score	0.4433	0.1848	1	
HS GPA	0.3957	0.3275	0.1376	1

a. What information does this matrix tell you about these data? Be as specific as possible.

b. What information is not available in this correlation matrix?

6.2 Suppose you run the following three regressions with intercepts:

- A simple regression of *IQ* on *education* to obtain the slope coefficient $\hat{\delta}_1$.
- A simple regression of *log(wage)* on *education* to obtain the slope coefficient $\widetilde{\beta}_1$.
- A multiple regression of *log(wage)* on *education* and *IQ* to obtain the slope coefficients $\hat{\beta}_1$ and $\hat{\beta}_2$, respectively.

a. Under what two conditions are $\widetilde{\beta}_1$ and $\hat{\beta}_1$ equal? Put the conditions in terms of a subset of $\hat{\delta}_1$, $\widetilde{\beta}_1$, $\hat{\beta}_1$, and $\hat{\beta}_2$.

b. Draw two Venn diagrams that illustrate your answer to part (a).

c. Draw a Venn diagram to explain why $\widetilde{\beta}_1$ and $\hat{\beta}_1$ are generally not equal.

6.3 Suppose you are interested in estimating the ceteris paribus relationship between y and x_1. For this purpose, you can collect data on two control variables, x_2 and x_3. Let $\widetilde{\beta}_1$ be the simple linear regression estimate from y on x_1, and let $\hat{\beta}_1$ be the multiple regression estimate from y on x_1, x_2, and x_3.

a. Assume that x_1 is not correlated with x_2 but that x_2 and x_3 have a large partial effect on y. Would you expect $\widetilde{\beta}_1$ and $\hat{\beta}_1$ to be similar or very different? Explain, and draw a Venn diagram to illustrate your answer.

b. If x_1 is highly correlated with x_2 and x_3 but x_2 and x_3 have no partial effect on y, would you expect $\tilde{\beta}_1$ and $\hat{\beta}_1$ to be similar or very different? Explain, and draw a Venn diagram to illustrate your answer.

6.4 I know that y depends linearly on x, but I am not sure whether or not it also depends on another variable z. A friend suggests that I should regress y on x first, calculate the residuals, and then see whether they are correlated with z. What advice would you offer your friend?

6.5 Medicorp Company, which sells medical supplies to health care providers, is reviewing its new bonus program. The program provides bonuses to salespeople based on performance. Medicorp management wants to know whether bonuses paid in 1995 had an effect on 1996 sales. You have been asked to help them develop a regression model to explain sales. You have a random sample of 50 of Medicorp's sales territories containing the following information on each territory:

ADV	Amount spent on advertising in 1996 ($1,000)
BONUS	Total amount of bonuses paid in 1995 ($1,000)
RELPRICE	Medicorp's average price relative to the industry average
COMPET	Largest competitor's sales ($1,000)
SALES	Medicorp's sales in 1996 ($1,000)

The partial Excel results are shown here:

SSExplained = 1,237,904

MSUnexplained = 24,665

ANOVA

	df	SS	MS	F	Significance F
Regression	____	____	____	____	0.0001
Residual	____	____	____		
Total	____	____			

	Coefficients	Standard Error	*t* Stat	*p*-value
Intercept	889.1	162.1		0.0001
ADV	10.8	1.8		0.0001
BONUS	11.6	3.02		0.0003
RELPRICE	−122	71.65		0.0955
COMPET	−0.18	0.15		0.2364

a. Complete the ANOVA table.

b. Find R^2. Explain what the number tells you about this regression model.

c. What should R^2 be if all variations in SALES have been explained by our model?

d. Test whether SALES is related to any of the X's (the overall significance of the model). Use a significance level of 0.01.

e. Test whether SALES is related to BONUS. Use a significance level of 0.05.

f. Explain in the context of this problem what the numbers for the following coefficients mean: ADV, BONUS, RELPRICE.

g. Find a 95 confidence interval for BONUS. What parameter does this confidence interval bracket?

h. Management expects the following in 1997 for the Raleigh sales territory:

Amount spent on advertising: 60 ($1,000)

Amount paid in bonuses in 1997: 45 ($1,000)

Average price relative to the industry average: 0.7

Largest competitor's sales: 100 ($1,000)

Forecast 1997 sales for the Raleigh sales territory.

6.6 Suppose you are interested in predicting the price of a laptop computer based on its various features.

Price: the price of the laptop in dollars
Speed: speed of the laptop in megahertz
Charge: time (in minutes) the battery takes to charge

The partial Excel results are shown here:

SSUnexplained = 1698387.21
MSExplained = 554446.062

ANOVA

	df	SS	MS	F	Significance F
Regression	____	____	____	____	0.00479
Residual	____	____	____		
Total	21	____			

	Coefficients	Standard Error	*t* Stat	*p*-value
Intercept	1500.6007	1085.6889		
Speed	10.1506	14.5019		
Charge	1.6284	4.4568		

a. Complete the ANOVA table.
b. Find R^2. Explain what the number tells you about this regression model.
c. Test whether risk is related to any of the X's (the overall significance of the model). Use a significance level of 0.05.
d. Test whether price is related to speed. Use a significance level of 0.05. What does this result imply?
e. Explain in the context of this problem what the numbers for the following coefficients mean: speed and charge.
f. Find a 95 confidence interval for speed. What parameter does this confidence interval bracket?
g. What is the standard error of the regression?
h. Write out the regression equation.
i. Estimate the price of a laptop with a speed of 33 megahertz and the charge lasts 305 minutes.

6.7 Management proposed the following regression model to predict sales at a fast-food outlet.

$$y_i = \beta_0 + \beta_1 x_{1,i} + \beta_2 x_{2,i} + \beta_3 x_{3,i} + \varepsilon_i$$

where $x_{1,i}$ = Number of competitors within one mile
$x_{2,i}$ = Population within one mile (1000s)
$x_{3,i}$ = Population beyond one mile but within five miles (1000s)
y_i = Sales ($1000s)

The following sample regression function was developed after 20 outlets were surveyed.

$$\hat{y}_i = 10.1 - 4.2x_{1,i} + 6.8x_{2,i} + 2.3x_{3,i}$$

a. How does the number of competitors within one mile affect sales?
b. How does the population within 1 mile affect sales?
c. How does the population beyond 1 mile but within 5 miles affect sales?
d. Predict sales for a store with two competitors, a population of 8,000 within 1 mile, and population beyond 1 mile but within 5 miles of 13,000.

6.8 A 10-year study conducted by the American Heart Association provided data on how age, blood pressure, and smoking relate to the risk of strokes. Assume that the regression results pertain to data on the following.

Risk: the probability that the patient will have a stroke over the next 10-year period
Age: age of the person
Pressure: blood pressure
Family: number of strokes the person's parents have had

The partial Excel results are shown here:

ANOVA

	df	SS	MS	F	Significance F
Regression	3	3660.74	1220.25	36.82	2.06E-07
Residual	16	530.21	33.14		
Total	19	4190.95			

	Coefficients	Standard Error	*t* Stat	*p*-value
Intercept	−91.76	15.22		
Age	1.08	0.17		
Pressure	0.25	0.05		
Family	8.74	3		

b. This is the variation left in risk when the effects of age, pressure, & family have been removed.

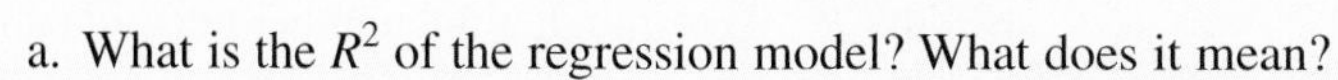

a. What is the R^2 of the regression model? What does it mean?

b. What is the standard error of the regression? What does it mean?

c. Explain in the context of this problem what the numbers for the following coefficients mean: Age, Pressure, Family.

d. Test the overall significance of the regression model at a 5 percent significance level.

e. Is pressure statistically significant in explaining risk? Test this hypothesis at a 10 percent significance level.

f. Find a 95 percent confidence interval for age. What does this interval mean, and what parameter does it bracket?

g. Estimate the risk of a heart attack for a person who is 70 years old, with a blood pressure of 165, and whose parents have had one stroke.

h. Can you see a potential problem with predicting using this regression model?

6.9 You are trying to determine how the price of a home in Florida is related to the square footage of the house, the number of bathrooms, how nice the house is, and whether the house has a pool. Because you have taken Econ 301, you propose the following model

$$y_i = \beta_0 + \beta_1 x_{1,i} + \beta_2 x_{2,i} + \beta_3 x_{3,i} + \varepsilon_i$$

where x_1 = Square footage

x_2 = Number of bathrooms

x_3 = A niceness rating expressed as an integer from 1 to 7

y = Price of the house ($1000s)

The following estimated regression equation was developed after a sample of 80 homes was taken.

$$\hat{y}_i = 24.9760 + 0.0526 \times x_{1,i} + 10.0430 \times x_{2,i} + 10.0420 \times x_{3,i} + \varepsilon_i$$

a. How much does the number of bathrooms add to the average sales price?

b. If it costs $32,500 to increase the niceness rating from 5 to 7, what percentage of this increase in rating can a customer buying a pool expect to recoup when selling his or her home?

c. If it costs $24,000 to increase the niceness rating from 2 to 4, what percentage of this increase in rating can a customer buying a pool expect to recoup when selling his or her home?

d. Consider your answers to parts (b) and (c). Can you see a problem with the niceness rating?

e. Predict the price of a home that has 3,200 square feet, 3 bathrooms, a niceness rating of 3.

6.10 The following is a multiple regression model with two explanatory variables and 70 observations.

$$y_i = \beta_0 + \beta_1 x_{1,i} + \beta_2 x_{2,i} + \varepsilon_i$$

a. Explain how you would test the hypothesis that β_1 and β_2 are equal. Be as specific as possible.

b. Say you want to generate a confidence interval around a prediction when $x_{1,i} = 6$ and $x_{2,i} = 12$. Explain in detail how you would generate this confidence interval.

6.11 The athletic director of San Diego State University is interested in developing a multiple regression model that might be used to explain variations in attendance at football games at his school. We have the following data:

y = Game attendance

x_1 = Team win/loss percentage to date

x_2 = Opponent win/loss percentage to date

x_3 = Games played this season

x_4 = Temperature at game time

	Coefficients	Standard Error
Intercept	14122.2409	4335.79
Team Win/Loss Percentage	63.1533	14.9388
Opponent Win/Loss Percentage	10.0958	14.314
Games Played	31.5062	177.129
Temperature	10.4609	62.0937

a. What is the sample regression function?

b. Explain in the context of this problem what the number for the temperature coefficient means.

c. Predict the average attendance if the team's win/loss percentage is 60, the opponent's win/loss percentage is 40, the number of games played this season is 50, and the temperature is 70 degrees.

d. If the athletic director wants to increase attendance, what should he do?

Exercises

E6.1 Use the dataset **Compu.xls** to show that the two-step regression provides equivalent results to a multiple linear regression. First, regress experience on education and save the residuals; then regress wage on those residuals. Compare these results to the multiple linear regression of wage on experience and education.

E6.2 In dataset **facebook.xls,** you have information on individuals on Facebook that include the number of pictures individuals have been tagged in, the number of friends, the age of the people, and how long they have been a member of Facebook. The dependent variable is the number of pictures individuals have been tagged in.

a. Run a regression, and explain what each of the coefficients mean.
b. Test the overall significance of the regression model.
c. Test the individual significance of each of the explanatory variables.
d. What is the R^2? What does it tell us about the regression model?
e. What is the predicted value of Facebook friends if an individual has 250 friends, they are 25 years old, and they have been a member of Facebook for 1.5 years?
f. What is a 95 percent mean prediction interval for your prediction in part (e)?
g. What is a 95 percent individual prediction interval?

E6.3 You are interested in examining how a person's body mass index (BMI) is related to their age, number of hours spent working per week, number of hours spent exercising per week, and number of times he or she is sick in a year. Use the dataset **BMI.xls** to complete the following questions.

a. Run a regression, and explain what each of the coefficients mean.
b. Test the overall significance of the regression model.
c. Test the individual significance of each of the explanatory variables.
d. What is the R^2? What does it tell us about the regression model?
e. What is the predicted value of BMI if a person is 35 years old, works 45 hours a week, exercises 3 hours per week, and is sick 2 times a year.
f. What is a 95 percent mean prediction interval for your prediction in part (e)?
g. What is a 95 percent individual prediction interval?

Chapter Seven

Qualitative Variables and Nonlinearities in Multiple Linear Regression Analysis

CHAPTER OBJECTIVES

After reading this chapter, you will be able to:

1. Construct and use qualitative independent variables.
2. Construct and use interaction effects.
3. Control for nonlinear relationships.
4. Estimate marginal effects as percent changes and elasticities.
5. Estimate a more fully specified model.

A STUDENT'S PERSPECTIVE

Recall our former student who was interested in empirically determining the U.S. city in which he was most likely to find a significant other. After collecting data on 90 different MSAs, the student was able to use the tool of multiple linear regression analysis to determine the sample regression function

$$\begin{aligned}\widehat{\textit{Unmarried women ratio}} = {} & 140.21 + .000000325 - 07 \times \textit{Population} \\ & -0.481 \times \textit{\%Males BA or higher} \\ & +0.719 \times \textit{\%Females BA or higher} \\ & -0.558 \times \textit{Median income (thousands)} \qquad 7.1\end{aligned}$$

While the student felt that these estimates were a good start, he suspected that regional differences existed in the proclivity of young adults to marry in the United States (i.e., that individuals in certain regions were either more or less likely to marry than those in other regions). How could he control for such potential differences in his multiple linear regression analysis? Likewise, suppose he also suspects that the relationship between the dependent variable and an area's population increases at an increasing rate up to a point before increasing at a decreasing rate beyond that point. How could he control for such a potential nonconstant estimated marginal effect in his analysis? Finally, suppose the student wishes to calculate estimated marginal effects either in terms of percentage changes or elasticities. How could he do so? This chapter provides an answer to these important questions by introducing methods for dealing with qualitative variables, nonlinear estimated relationships, and percent changes and elasticities in multiple linear regression analysis.

BIG PICTURE OVERVIEW

Chapter 6 introduced multiple linear regression analysis, which is a powerful tool that enables us to estimate the linear relationship between a dependent variable and a series of independent variables in a manner that provides the estimated marginal effects in which economists are most often interested. In this chapter, we increase the power of this tool by learning how to (1) work with qualitative independent variables, such as race, sex, education level, etc.; (2) allow our estimated marginal effects to differ at different values of an independent variable; and (3) calculate our estimated marginal in terms of percentage changes and elasticities. Figure 7.1 depicts the empirical research tools introduced in this chapter.

FIGURE 7.1
A Visual Depiction of the Empirical Tools Introduced in This Chapter

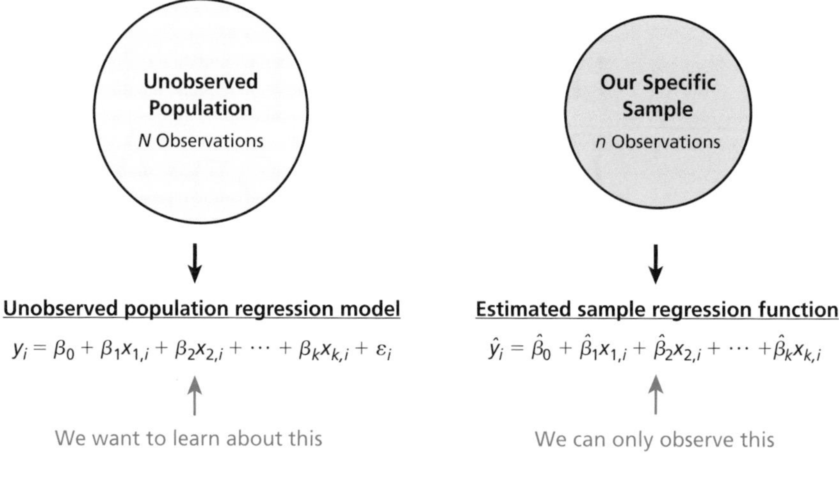

For the sake of continuity, the remainder of the chapter focuses on the same two data sets introduced in Chapter 5: our 200-observation MLB position player sample and our 63-observation international GDP sample.

7.1 CONSTRUCT AND USE QUALITATIVE INDEPENDENT VARIABLES

In 2010, Ozzie Guillen, then manager of the Chicago White Sox, made headlines by claiming that Major League Baseball favored Japanese players while discriminating against Latin American players. Suppose that we wish to examine whether this alleged favoritism for Japanese players extends to annual salaries. How might we do so? While simply adding a variable indicating whether a player was Japanese to our multiple linear regression analysis might seem straightforward, it is complicated by the fact that a player's nationality is defined by a specific quality (Japanese or non-Japanese) rather than a specific quantity (years of experience, home runs, etc.). Accordingly, before we can minimize the sum of squared residuals to determine the best-fit linear relationship, we must convert the qualitative values to quantitative values that can be included in the multiple linear regression.

The manner in which we convert qualitative values to quantitative values depends on the number of potential outcomes that can be observed for the qualitative variable.

Binary Dummy Variables

binary dummy variable A variable that takes on the value of 1 if a condition is true and 0 if a condition is false. These variables may also be called indicator variables.

If there are only two possible outcomes for a given independent variable (male/female, college graduate/noncollege graduate, etc.), we solve the problem presented by the qualitative nature of the data by creating a **binary dummy variable** that takes on the value 1 whenever one possible outcome is observed and 0 whenever the other possible outcome is observed. As an example, for our 200-observation MLB position player sample, we create the dummy variable $Japanese_i$ that is equal to 1 if the player is Japanese and 0 if the player is non-Japanese. Doing so produces the data in Table 7.1.

TABLE 7.1 Creating the Dummy Variable $Japanese_i$ for Our 200-Observation MLB Position Player Sample

id	Player	Salary	Experience	Japanese
1	Tracy, Chad	$ 5,000,000	4	0
2	Buscher, Brian	$ 412,500	0	0
3	Bautista, Jose A.	$ 2,400,000	3	0
4	Roberts, Ryan	$ 400,000	0	0
5	Matsui, Hideki	$13,000,000	6	1

We then use this variable to test the hypothesis that salaries differ for Japanese and non-Japanese players, holding all other independent variables constant, by estimating the population multiple linear regression model

$$Salary_i = \beta_0 + \beta_1 Experience_i + \beta_2 Japanese_i + \varepsilon_i \qquad 7.1.1$$

As with any multiple linear regression, we determine the sample regression function by minimizing the sum of squared residuals in exactly the same way that we did in previous chapters. The main thing to understand in this case is that the correct interpretation of the estimated slope coefficient for a binary dummy variable differs from the correct interpretation for a quantitative variable. To see how, consider that because the dummy variable $Japanese_i$ takes on only two possible values, either $Japanese_i = 0$ or $Japanese_i = 1$, we have two different sample regression functions:

<u>If the player is in the National League, and $Japanese_i = 0$, then</u>

$$\begin{aligned}\widehat{Salary}_i &= \hat{\beta}_0 + \hat{\beta}_1 Experience_i + \hat{\beta}_2(Japanese_i)\\ &= \hat{\beta}_0 + \hat{\beta}_1 Experience_i + \hat{\beta}_2(0)\\ &= \hat{\beta}_0 + \hat{\beta}_1 Experience_i \end{aligned} \qquad 7.1.2$$

<u>If the player is in the National League, and $Japanese_i = 1$, then</u>

$$\begin{aligned}\widehat{Salary}_i &= \hat{\beta}_0 + \hat{\beta}_1 Experience_i + \hat{\beta}_2(Japanese_i)\\ &= \hat{\beta}_0 + \hat{\beta}_1 Experience_i + \hat{\beta}_2(1)\\ &= (\hat{\beta}_0 + \hat{\beta}_2) + \hat{\beta}_1 Experience_i \end{aligned} \qquad 7.1.3$$

Table 7.2 presents a dummy variable worksheet that aids in correctly interpreting these estimates.

TABLE 7.2 A Worksheet to Help Understand the Correct Interpretation of a Binary Dummy Variable

	Intercept	Slope
Japanese	$\hat{\beta}_0 + \hat{\beta}_2$	$\hat{\beta}_1$
Not Japanese	$\hat{\beta}_0$	$\hat{\beta}_1$

What are we to make of this information? Our answer depends on the sign of the estimated slope coefficient for the variable $Japanese_i$. If $\hat{\beta}_2 > 0$, then the correct depiction is shown in Figure 7.2.

FIGURE 7.2
Visual Depiction of the Sample Regression Function, Including Binary Dummy Variable $Japanese_i$ if $\hat{\beta}_2 > 0$

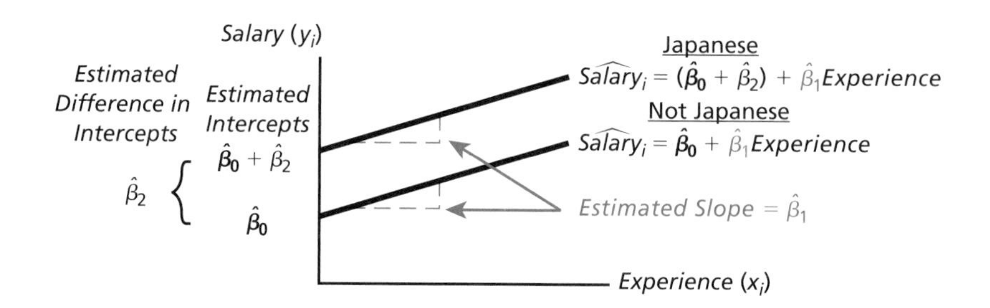

If $\hat{\beta}_2 < 0$, then the correct depiction is shown in Figure 7.3.

FIGURE 7.3
Visual Depiction of the Sample Regression Function, Including Binary Dummy Variable $Japanese_i$ if $\hat{\beta}_2 < 0$

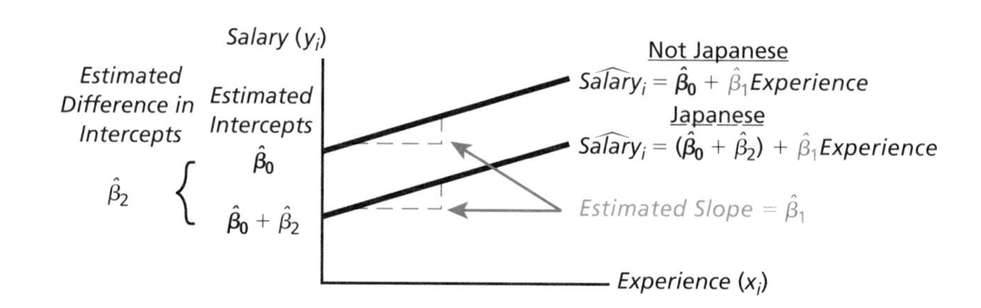

The visual depictions in Figures 7.2 and 7.3 demonstrate two important points concerning the correct interpretation of binary dummy variables: (1) including a binary dummy variable defines a different intercept for each of the possible values of the binary dummy variable and (2) including a binary dummy variable does not affect the slope of the sample regression function (i.e., the estimated marginal effect of experience on salary). In other words, for our MLB position player sample, we estimate the marginal effect of experience on salary ($\hat{\beta}_1$) to be the same for both Japanese and non-Japanese players but we estimate the intercept for Japanese players ($\hat{\beta}_0 + \hat{\beta}_2$) to differ from the intercept for non-Japanese players, ($\hat{\beta}_0$).

For our 200-observation MLB position player sample, we estimate the sample regression function:

$$\widehat{salary}_i = \hat{\beta}_0 + \hat{\beta}_1 Experience_i + \hat{\beta}_2 Japanese_i \quad \textbf{7.1.4}$$

and get Excel Regression Output 7.1.

Interpreting Regression Output 7.1 demonstrates the correct interpretation for these estimates.

Excel Regression Output 7.1: Estimated Marginal Effects for the Binary Dummy Variable *$Japanese_i$*

SUMMARY OUTPUT	
Regression Statistics	
Multiple R	0.614560974
R Square	0.377685191
Adjusted R Square	0.371367274
Standard Error	3866968.07
Observations	200

ANOVA

	df	SS	MS	F	Significance F
Regression	2	1.78783E+15	8.93917E+14	59.78001922	5.1286E-21
Residual	197	2.94583E+15	1.49534E+13		
Total	199	4.73366E+15			

	Coefficients	Standard Error	*t* Stat	*P*-value	Lower 95%	Upper 95%
Intercept	490006.553	406359.173	1.20584592	0.229323182	−311365.834	1291378.942
Experience	733199.171	70391.473	10.41602257	1.61177E-20	594381.626	872016.7163
Japanese	9693796.346	2748645.017	3.52675456	0.000523310	4273251.262	15114341.43

Note: Dependent variable is annual salary. Highlighted variables are significant at the 5 percent level.

We can present these results in a more formal way by writing the sample regression function, with standard errors in parentheses to enable the reader to determine the statistical significance of each estimated value, as

$$\widehat{Salary}_i = \underset{(406,359.17)}{490,006.55} + \underset{(70,391.47)}{733,199.17}Experience_i + \underset{(2,748,645.02)}{9,693,796.35}Japanese_i$$

Interpreting the Regression Output 7.1: The Binary Dummy Variable *Japanese*$_i$

Binary Dummy Variable Worksheet

	Intercept	Coefficient
Japanese	$\hat{\beta}_0 + \hat{\beta}_2 = \$490,006.53 + \$9,693,796.35 = \$10,183,802.90$	$\hat{\beta}_1 = \$733,199.17$
Not Japanese	$\hat{\beta}_0 = \$490,006.53$	$\hat{\beta}_1 = \$733,199.17$

Estimated Sample Regression Functions

Japanese: $\widehat{Salary}_i = \$10,183,802.90 + \$733,199.17 Experience_i$

Non-Japanese: $\widehat{Salary}_i = \$490,006.53 + \$733,199.17 Experience_i$

Visual Depiction

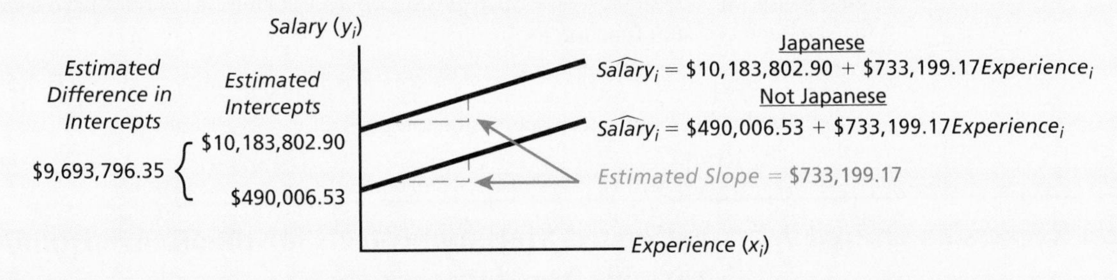

In Words

Holding experience constant,

1. A Japanese position player with 0 years of experience is prediced to earn a salary of $10,183,802.90.
2. A non-Japanese position player with 0 years of experience is prediced to earn a salary of $490,006.53.
3. A Japanese position player is predicted to earn $9,693,796.35 more than a non-Japanese position player.

Holding a player's nationality constant,

1. Each additional year of experience is estimated to increase a position player's salary by $733,199.17.

Hypothesis Testing 7.1 presents the t-test for the individual significance of the estimated slope coefficient for the binary dummy variable $Japanese_i$.

Hypothesis Testing 7.1: Testing the Individual Significance of the Binary Dummy Variable $Japanese_i$

Question:
Holding experience constant, are the salaries of Japanese players statistically different from the salaries of other players in our sample?

Population Regression Function:

$$Salary_i = \beta_0 + \beta_1 Experience_i + \beta_2 Japanese_i + \varepsilon_i$$

Hypothesis:

$H_0{:}\beta_2 = 0$

$H_A{:}\beta_2 \neq 0$

Hypothesis Testing:
We can use all three methods to test this hypothesis. The necessary values are in the AL row in the Excel Regression Output 7.1.

p-value $= 0.00052331$

Conclusion:
Because 0.0.00052331 < 0.05 we reject H_0 at $\alpha = 0.05$ and conclude that, holding experience constant, Japanese position players receive salaries that are statistically higher than non-Japanese position players in our sample.

Note that after practicing a few of times, we will quickly get the hang of the correct interpretation and hypothesis testing techniques. At that point, we will be able to combine the preceding techniques into one step, as we demonstrate in the Excel examples that follow.

An obvious question at this point might be why we chose to define the binary dummy variable $Japanese_i$ as equal to 1 if the player was Japanese and 0 if he was non-Japanese. No particular reason, actually. We could just as easily have chosen to define the variable $non\text{-}Japanese_i$ to equal 1 for non-Japanese players and 0 for Japanese players. If we had done so for our 200-observation MLB position player sample, we would have estimated the sample regression function as

$$\widehat{salary}_i = \hat{\beta}_0 + \hat{\beta}_1 Experience_i + \hat{\beta}_2 non\text{-}Japanese_i \quad \text{7.1.5}$$

and gotten the results in Excel Regression Output 7.2.

Excel Regression Output 7.2: Estimated Marginal Effects for the Binary Dummy Variable *Non-Japanese*$_i$

SUMMARY OUTPUT	
Regression Statistics	
Multiple R	0.614560974
R Square	0.377685191
Adjusted R Square	0.371367274
Standard Error	3866968.07
Observations	200

ANOVA

	df	SS	MS	F	Significance F
Regression	2	1.78783E+15	8.93917E+14	59.78001922	5.1286E-21
Residual	197	2.94583E+15	1.49534E+13		
Total	199	4.73366E+15			

	Coefficients	Standard Error	*t* Stat	*P*-value	Lower 95%	Upper 95%
Intercept	10183802.9	2745436.082	3.70935712	0.000270182	4769586.088	15598019.71
Experience	733199.1714	70391.473	10.41602257	1.61177E-20	594381.6266	872016.7163
Not Japanese	−9693796.346	2748645.017	−3.52675456	0.00052331	−15114341.43	−4273251.26

Note: Dependent variable is annual salary. Highlighted variables are significant at the 5 percent level.

Interpretation

Estimated Sample Regression Functions

Japanese: $\widehat{Salary}_i = \$10{,}183{,}802.90 + \$733{,}199.17 Experience_i$

Non-Japanese: $\widehat{Salary}_i = \$490{,}006.53 + \$733{,}199.17 Experience_i$

which is exactly the same as in the result that we found in Excel Regression Output 7.1.

Notice that regardless of whether we control for a player's league with the binary dummy variable $Japanese_i$ or the binary dummy variable $non\text{-}Japanese_i$, we calculate the same sample regression functions for Japanese and non-Japanese players. The only practical difference between the two approaches is that the estimated coefficients for the $Japanese_i$ and $non\text{-}Japanese_i$ variables are exactly the same number but are negatives of each other. This makes sense because no matter which specification of the binary dummy variable we include, the remaining salary and experience data are the same, meaning that the estimated slope coefficient and the estimated intercept should be the same magnitude. The upshot of this discussion is that in cases where we wish to define binary variables (male/female, college graduate/noncollege graduate, etc.), the way we assign the binary values does not matter so long as we take care to interpret the sample regression functions correctly.

Empirical Research Tool 7.1 summarizes the use of binary dummy variables.

EMPIRICAL RESEARCH TOOL 7.1: BINARY DUMMY VARIABLES

Goal:

Estimate the intercept for qualitative variables.

Process:

1. Define a binary dummy variable, BDV_i, such that

$BDV_i = 1$ if the individual possess a given quality

$BDV_i = 0$ if the individual does not possess the given quality

2. Estimate the sample regression function

$$\hat{y}_i = \hat{\beta}_0 + \hat{\beta}_1 x_{1,i} + \hat{\beta}_2 BDV_i + \cdots + \hat{\beta}_k x_{k,i}$$

Interpretation:

The estimated slope coefficient, $\hat{\beta}_2$, shifts the intercept for observations possessing the quality so that

If $BDV_i =$	then Estimated Intercept
0	$\hat{\beta}_0$
1	$\hat{\beta}_0 + \hat{\beta}_2$

Note:
Even though the qualities in this case take on two possible values, you should only include a binary dummy variable for one of the two qualities (if you also include an intercept in the equation), and the binary variable should only take on values of 0 and 1.
Example:
For the sample regression function

$$\text{Test score}_i = 67.23 + 2.48\text{Hours studied}_i + 4.37\text{Blue eyes}_i$$

We would conclude that, with 0 hours of studying,

- An individual *without* blue eyes would average a test score of 67.23.
- An individual *with* blue eyes would average a test score of 67.23 + 4.37 = 71.60.

Holding eye color constant,

- An individual studying one more hour would average a test score 2.48 higher than a student studying one less hour.

Finally, Excel Example 7.1 demonstrates how to include and interpret a binary dummy variable for our 63-observation international GDP sample.

EXCEL EXAMPLE 7.1

Estimating our sample regression function with the binary dummy variable

Top Education Quartile

For our GDP data, based on data indicating education expenditures as a percentage of GDP for all countries our 227-observation population, we create a new variable

$$\text{Top education quartile}_i = 1 \text{ for countries in the top quartile of the population}$$
$$\text{Top education quartile}_i = 0 \text{ for countries not in the top quartile of the population}$$

and estimate the following multiple linear regression model for our 63-observation sample

$$GDP/1{,}000{,}000{,}000_i = \beta_0 + \beta_1 Population/1{,}000{,}000_i + \beta_2 Top\ education\ quartile_i + \varepsilon_i$$

SUMMARY OUTPUT

Regression Statistics	
Multiple R	0.687258345
R Square	0.472324033
Adjusted R Square	0.454734835
Standard Error	2111.599566
Observations	63

ANOVA

	df	SS	MS	F	Significance F
Regression	2	239467791.3	119733895.6	26.85307253	4.68834E-09
Residual	60	267531163.5	4458852.726		
Total	62	506998954.8			

	Coefficients	Standard Error	*t* Stat	*P*-value	Lower 95%	Upper 95%
Intercept	77.11658482	326.698454	0.236048209	0.814199189	−576.3776155	730.6107851
Population/ 1,000,000	6.174802339	1.19479589	5.168081333	2.84977E-06	3.784854742	8.564749935
Top Ed. Quartile	1,894.175	599.031	3.162066107	0.002457269	695.935	3,092.415

Statistical Inference:

For the variable $Population/1{,}000{,}000_i$

- Because the calculated p-value $= 2.85E-06 < 0.05$, we reject $H_0{:}\beta_1 = 0$ and conclude that, holding education quartile constant, every 1,000,000 person increase in population is estimated to increase *GDP* by 6.17 billion (i.e., $6.17 \times 1{,}000{,}000{,}000$)

For the variable *Top education quartile*$_i$

- Because the calculated *p*-value = 0.002 < 0.05, we reject H_0:$\beta_2 = 0$ and conclude that, holding population constant, countries in the top education quartile have *GDPs* that are 1.89418 trillion greater than those for countries not in the top education quartile.

While the preceding techniques work for qualitative variables that are binary in nature, economists frequently encounter situations in which qualitative variables have more than two possible outcomes.

Categorical Variables

categorical variable
A variable that has two or more categories but for which there is no intrinsic ordering associated with the categories.

Consider the position that a MLB position player plays. In a general sense, a position player can be defined as playing catcher, infielder, outfielder, or designated hitter. We can deal with this situation by creating a **categorical variable** in which each possible outcome is assigned a specific numerical value (starting from 0). For our 200-observation MLB position player sample, we create the categorical variable *Position*$_i$ that is equal to 0 if the player is a catcher, 1 if the player is an infielder, 2 if the player is an outfielder, and 3 if the player is a designated hitter. Doing so produces the data in Table 7.3.

TABLE 7.3
Creating the Categorical Variable Position$_i$ for Our 200-Observation MLB Position Player Sample

id	Player	Salary	Experience	Position Name	Position
1	Tracy, Chad	$ 5,000,000	4	Infielder	1
2	Buscher, Brian	$ 412,500	0	Infielder	1
3	Bautista, Jose A.	$ 2,400,000	3	Infielder	1
4	Roberts, Ryan	$ 400,000	0	Infielder	1
5	Matsui, Hideki	$13,000,000	6	Outfielder	2
6	Kotsay, Mark	$ 1,500,000	11	Outfielder	2
7	Rasmus, Colby	$ 400,000	0	Outfielder	2
8	Chavez, Endy	$ 2,050,000	4	Outfielder	2
9	Cabrera, Asdrubal	$ 416,700	1	Infielder	1
10	Rios, Alex	$ 6,400,000	4	Outfielder	2

We use this variable to test the hypothesis that the linear relationship between salary and experience differs depending on a player's position by estimating the population multiple linear regression model:

$$Salary_i = \beta_0 + \beta_1 Experience_i + \beta_2 Position_i + \varepsilon_i \qquad \textbf{7.1.6}$$

For our 200-observation MLB position player sample, we estimate the sample regression function and get the results in Excel Regression Output 7.3.

Excel Regression Output 7.3: Estimated Marginal Effects for the Categorical Variable *Position$_i$*

SUMMARY OUTPUT

Regression Statistics	
Multiple R	0.6000
R Square	0.3600
Adjusted R Square	0.3535
Standard Error	3921580.42
Observations	200

ANOVA					
	df	SS	MS	F	Significance F
Regression	2	1.70E+15	8.52E+14	55.4023	8.13E-20
Residual	197	3.03E+15	1.54E+13		
Total	199	4.73E+15			

	Coefficients	Standard Error	*t* Stat	*P*-value	Lower 95%	Upper 95%
Intercept	−633,716.577	632,796.902	−1.0015	0.3178	−1,881,642.050	614,208.897
Experience	729,953.088	71,374.833	10.2270	5.78E-20	589,196.280	870,709.897
Position	979,714.854	380,051.352	2.5778	0.0107	230,223.569	1,729,206.139

Note: Dependent variable is annual salary. Highlighted variables are significant at the 5 percent level.

Interpreting the Regression Output 7.2 demonstrates the correct interpretation for these sample regression functions.

Interpreting the Regression Output 7.2: The Categorical Variable $Position_i$

Categorical Variable Worksheet

	Intercept	Slope
Catcher	$\hat{\beta}_0 = -\$633,716.58$	$\hat{\beta}_1 = \$729,953.09$
Infielder	$\hat{\beta}_0 + \hat{\beta}_2 = -\$633,716.58 + (\$979,714.85) = \$345,998.28$	$\hat{\beta}_1 = \$729,953.09$
Outfielder	$\hat{\beta}_0 + 2\hat{\beta}_2 = -\$633,716.58 + (2 \cdot \$979,714.85) = \$1,325,713.13$	$\hat{\beta}_1 = \$729,953.09$
Designated Hitter	$\hat{\beta}_0 + 3\hat{\beta}_2 = -\$633,716.58 + (3 \cdot \$979,714.85) = \$2,305,427.99$	$\hat{\beta}_1 = \$729,953.09$

Estimated Sample Regression Functions

Catcher: $\widehat{Salary}_i = -\$633,716.58 + \$729,953.09 Experience_i$

Infielder: $\widehat{Salary}_i = \$345,998.28 + \$729,953.09 Experience_i$

Outfielder: $\widehat{Salary}_i = \$1,325,713.13 + \$729,953.09 Experience_i$

Designated Hitter: $\widehat{Salary}_i = \$2,305,427.99 + \$729,953.09 Experience_i$

Visual Depiction

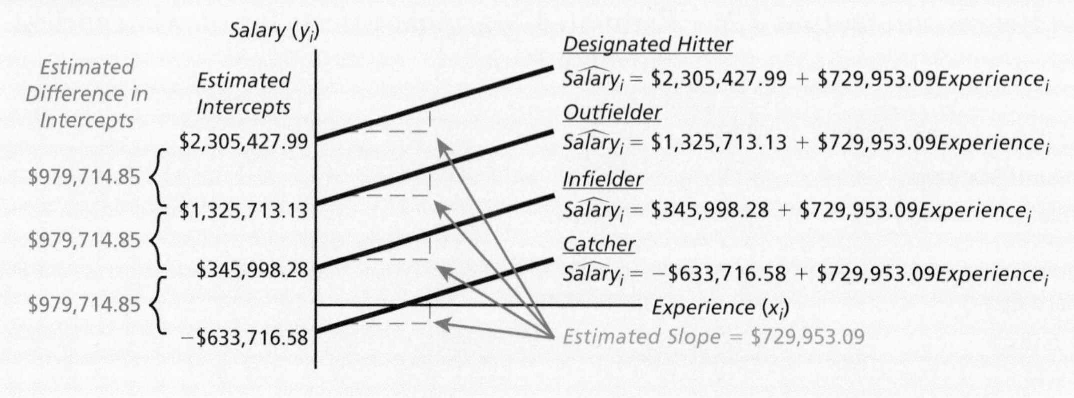

In Words

Holding experience constant,

1. A catcher with 0 years of experience would be predicted to earn −\$633,716.58.
2. An infielder with 0 years of experience would be predicted to earn \$345,998.28.
3. An outfielder with 0 years of experience would be predicted to earn 1,325,713.13.
4. A designated hitter with 0 years of experience would be predicted to earn \$2,305,427.99.
5. The estimated difference between the predicted salary for a player at each position differs by exactly \$979,714.15.

Holding position constant,

1. Each additional year of experience is estimated to increase a position player's salary by \$729,953.09.

Empirical Research Tool 7.2 summarizes the use of categorical variables as independent variables.

EMPIRICAL RESEARCH TOOL 7.2: CATEGORICAL VARIABLES

Goal:

Estimate different intercepts for each possible outcome for a qualitative variable that takes on j different possible outcomes.

Process:

1. Define a categorical variable, Cat_i, such that

$$j \text{ possible outcomes} \begin{cases} Cat_i = j \text{ if the individual possesses the jth possible outcome} \\ \vdots \\ Cat_i = 2 \text{ if the individual possesses the 2nd possible outcome} \\ Cat_i = 1 \text{ if the individual possesses the 1st possible outcome} \\ Cat_i = 0 \text{ if the individual does not possess any of the possible outcomes} \end{cases}$$

2. Estimate the sample regression function

$$\hat{y}_i = \hat{\beta}_0 + \hat{\beta}_1 x_{1,i} + \hat{\beta}_2 Cat_i + \cdots + \hat{\beta}_k x_{k,i}$$

Interpretation:

The estimated slope coefficient, $\hat{\beta}_2$, shifts the intercept for observations possessing each specific outcome, so that

If	$Cat_i =$	then	Estimated Intercept
	0		$\hat{\beta}_0$
	1		$\hat{\beta}_0 + \hat{\beta}_2$
	2		$\hat{\beta}_0 + (2 \cdot \hat{\beta}_2)$
	$\vdots$		$\vdots$
	$j - 1$		$\hat{\beta}_0 + ((j-1)\hat{\beta}_2)$

Note:

This approach constrains the difference in estimated intercepts to be the same across all possible outcomes of the qualitative variable.

Example:

For the sample regression function,

$$\widehat{Test\ score}_i = 66.48 + 2.31 Hours\ studied_i + 3.36 Grade\ level_i$$

Holding hours studying constant,

- An individual with an additional grade level will average a test score that is 3.36 higher than that of a student with one grade level lower (i.e., the test score of a sophomore will average 3.36 higher than that of a freshman, the test score of a junior will average 2 × 3.36 = 6.72 higher than that of a freshman, and the test score of a senior will average 3 × 3.36 = 10.08 higher than that of a freshman).

Holding grade level constant,

- An individual studying one more hour would average a test score that is 2.31 higher than that of a student studying one less hour.

Finally, Excel Example 7.2 demonstrates how to include and interpret a categorical variable for our 63-observation international GDP sample.

EXCEL EXAMPLE 7.2

Estimating our sample regression function with the categorical variable $Continent_i$

For our GDP data, based on the continent in which each country is located, we create a new variable

$Continent_i = 0$ if the country is in Asia
$Continent_i = 1$ if the country is in Africa
$Continent_i = 2$ if the country is in Europe
$Continent_i = 3$ if the country is in North America
$Continent_i = 4$ if the country is in South America

and estimate the multiple linear regression model

$$GDP/1{,}000{,}000{,}000_i = \beta_0 + \beta_1 Population/1{,}000{,}000_i + \beta_2 Continent_i + \varepsilon_i$$

SUMMARY OUTPUT

Regression Statistics	
Multiple R	0.646228201
R Square	0.417610888
Adjusted R Square	0.398197918
Standard Error	2218.372793
Observations	63

ANOVA

	df	SS	MS	F	Significance F
Regression	2	211728283.9	105864141.9	21.51195206	9.04477E-08
Residual	60	295270670.9	4921177.849		
Total	62	506998954.8			

	Coefficients	Standard Error	*t* Stat	*P*-value	Lower 95%	Upper 95%
Intercept	−75.78635131	473.8115271	−0.159950417	0.873457399	−1023.550509	871.9778061
Population/ 1,000,000	7.896028984	1.2077730	6.537676249	1.52881E-08	5.480123265	10.3119347
Continent	420.0954024	227.0764182	1.850017741	0.069237004	−34.12505847	874.3158632

Statistical Inference:

For the variable $Continent_i$

- Because the calculated p-value $= .0692 > .005$, we fail to reject $H_0{:}\beta_2 = 0$ at a significance level of 5 percent and conclude that, holding population constant, GDP does not differ significantly in a constant fashion across continents.

The interpretation of the estimated marginal effect for the categorical variable $Position_i$ demonstrates an important concern regarding the desired treatment of categorical variables in multiple linear regression analysis. Simply entering the categorical variable as one variable with multiple possible outcomes imposes the restrictive assumption that each one-unit increase in value results in a constant increase in the dependent variable. Specifically, for our MLB position player sample, the nature of the categorical variable $Position_i$ constrains us to estimate that, holding experience constant, the salaries of infielders are exactly \$979,714.15 greater than the salaries of catchers, the salaries of outfielders are exactly \$979,714.15 greater than the salaries of infielders, and the salaries of designated hitters are exactly \$979,714.15 greater than the salaries of outfielders. Do we really believe that the differences in salary between positions are constant? No. For this reason, directly entering the categorical variable is generally not our preferred approach.

Categorical Variables as a Series of Dummy Variables

We can relax the restriction of a constant estimated marginal difference between each given categorical outcome by converting the categorical variable into a series of dummy variables and including *all but one* of those variables in our multiple linear regression analysis. Note the importance of the italicized phrase. If we did attempt to include every single binary dummy variable, then we could not estimate our model because it would suffer from perfect collinearity.

For our 200-observation MLB position player sample, we create the dummy variables $\boldsymbol{Infielder_i}$, $\boldsymbol{Outfielder_i}$, and $\boldsymbol{DH_i}$. Doing so produces the data in Table 7.4.

TABLE 7.4 Creating the Dummy Variables $Infielder_i$, $Outfielder_i$, and DH_i for Our 200-Observation MLB Position Player Sample

id	Player	Salary	Experience	Position Name	Infielder	Outfielder	DH
1	Tracy, Chad	$ 5,000,000	4	Infielder	1	0	0
2	Buscher, Brian	$ 412,500	0	Infielder	1	0	0
3	Bautista, Jose A.	$ 2,400,000	3	Infielder	1	0	0
4	Roberts, Ryan	$ 400,000	0	Infielder	1	0	0
5	Matsui, Hideki	$13,000,000	6	Outfielder	0	1	0
6	Kotsay, Mark	$ 1,500,000	11	Outfielder	0	1	0
7	Rasmus, Colby	$ 400,000	0	Outfielder	0	1	0
8	Chavez, Endy	$ 2,050,000	4	Outfielder	0	1	0
9	Cabrera, Asdrubal	$ 416,700	1	Infielder	1	0	0
10	Rios, Alex	$ 6,400,000	4	Outfielder	0	1	0

We can use this series of dummy variables to test the hypothesis that the linear relationship between salary and experience differs depending on a player's position by estimating the population multiple linear regression model

$$Salary_i = \beta_0 + \beta_1 Experience_i + \beta_2 Infielder_i + \beta_3 Outfielder_i + \beta_4 DH_i + \varepsilon_i \quad \textbf{7.1.8}$$

base group
The category that is not explicitly included in the regression model.

Note that because we do not include the binary dummy variable for catchers, catchers are by definition the omitted, or **base group**. When interpreting our results, we must be careful to interpret the estimated coefficients for the remaining dummy variables as being relative to the (omitted) base group.

For our 200-observation MLB position player sample, we estimate the sample regression function as

$$\widehat{Salary}_i = \hat{\beta}_0 + \hat{\beta}_1 Experience_i + \hat{\beta}_2 Infielder_i + \hat{\beta}_3 Outfielder_i + \hat{\beta}_4 DH_i \quad \textbf{7.1.9}$$

and get Excel Regression Output 7.4.

Excel Regression Output 7.4: Estimated Marginal Effects for a Series of Dummy Variables Instead of the Categorical Variable $Position_i$

SUMMARY OUTPUT

Regression Statistics	
Multiple R	0.6143
R Square	0.3774
Adjusted R Square	0.3646
Standard Error	3887652.24
Observations	**200**

ANOVA

	df	SS	MS	F	Significance F
Regression	4	1.79E+15	4.47E+14	29.55012452	3.26E-19
Residual	195	2.95E+15	1.51E+13		
Total	199	4.73E+15			

	Coefficients	Standard Error	*t* Stat	*P*-value	Lower 95%	Upper 95%
Intercept	−1,594,144.289	771,745.839	−2.0656	0.0402	−3,116,184.525	−72,104.053
Experience	732,041.070	71,258.202	10.2731	4.60E-20	591,505.358	872,576.781
Infielder	2,607,475.123	811,428.149	3.2134	0.0015	1,007,173.277	4,207,776.969
Outfielder	2,497,002.798	827,859.617	3.0162	0.0029	864,294.746	4,129,710.851
DH	4,288,829.422	2,360,686.786	1.8168	0.0708	−366,926.516	8,944,585.359

Note: Dependent variable is annual salary. Catchers are the omitted group. Variables highlighted in blue are significant at the 5 percent level. Variables highlighted in light gray are significant at the 10 percent level.

Interpreting the Regression Output 7.3 demonstrates the correct interpretation for these estimates.

Interpreting the Regression Output 7.3: Entering a Categorical Variable as a Series of Dummy Variables

Series of Binary Dummy Variables Worksheet

	Intercept	Slope
Catcher:	$\hat{\beta}_0 = -\$1,594,144.29$	$\hat{\beta}_1 = \$732,041.07$
Infielder:	$\hat{\beta}_0 + \hat{\beta}_2 = -\$1,594,144.29 + \$2,607,475.12 = \$1,013,330.83$	$\hat{\beta}_1 = \$732,041.07$
Outfielder:	$\hat{\beta}_0 + \hat{\beta}_3 = -\$1,594,144.29 + \$2,497,002.80 = \$902,858.51$	$\hat{\beta}_1 = \$732,041.07$
Designated Hitter:	$\hat{\beta}_0 + \hat{\beta}_4 = -\$1,594,144.29 + \$4,288,829.42 = \$2,694,685.13$	$\hat{\beta}_1 = \$732,041.07$

Estimated Sample Regression Functions

Catcher: $\widehat{Salary}_i = -\$1,594,144.29 + \$732,041.07 Experience_i$

Infielder: $\widehat{Salary}_i = \$1,013,330.83 + \$732,041.07 Experience_i$

Outfielder: $\widehat{Salary}_i = \$902,858.51 + \$732,041.07 Experience_i$

Designated Hitter: $\widehat{Salary}_i = \$2,694,685.13 + \$732,041.07 Experience_i$

Visual Depiction

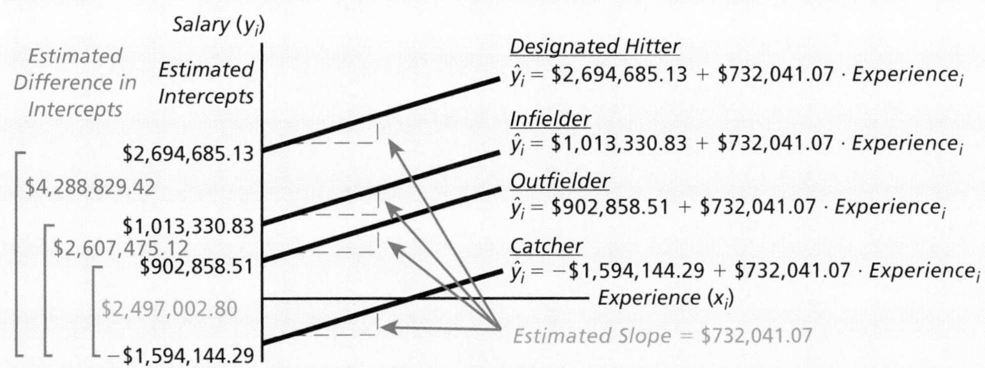

In Words

Holding experience constant,

1. A catcher with 0 years of experience would be predicted to earn −$1,594,144.29.
2. An infielder with 0 years of experience would be predicted to earn $1,013,330.83.
3. An outfielder with 0 years of experience would be predicted to earn $902,858.51.
4. A designated hitter with 0 years of experience would be predicted to earn $2,694,685.13.
5. The estimated difference between the predicted salary for an outfielder and a catcher is $2,497,002.80.
6. The estimated difference between the predicted salary for an infielder and a catcher is $2,607,475.12.
7. The estimated difference between the predicted salary for a DH and a catcher is $4,288,829.42.

Holding position constant,

1. Each additional year of experience is estimated to increase a position player's salary by $732,041.07.

Hypothesis Testing 7.2 presents the t-test for the individual significance of the estimated slope coefficients for our series of binary dummy variables.

Hypothesis Testing 7.2: Testing the Individual Significance of the Series of Binary Dummy Variables

Question:

We start with the first dummy variable $Infielder_i$ and ask whether, holding experience constant, infielder salaries are statistically different than catcher salaries in our sample.

Population Regression Function:

$$Salary_i = \beta_0 + \beta_1 Experience_i + \beta_2 Infielder_i + \beta_3 Outfielder_i + \beta_4 DH_i + \varepsilon_i$$

Hypothesis:

H_0: $\beta_2 = 0$
H_A: $\beta_2 \neq 0$

Hypothesis Testing:

We can use all three methods to test this hypothesis. The necessary values are in the Infielder row in Excel Regression Output 7.4.

p-value $= 0.0015$

Conclusion:

Because $0.0015 < 0.05$. we reject H_0 at $\alpha = 0.05$ and conclude that, holding experience constant, infielder salaries are statistically different than catcher salaries in our sample.

Note: We could do the same thing for outfielders (β_3) and designated hitters (β_4). Looking at the estimated p-values for these variables, it should be clear that we would reject H_0:$\beta_3 = 0$ at $\alpha = 0.05$ and we would fail to reject H_0:$\beta_4 = 0$ at $\alpha = 0.05$ (although we would reject that hypothesis at $\alpha = 0.10$).

Empirical Research Tool 7.3 summarizes the use of estimating categorical variables as a series of binary dummy variables.

EMPIRICAL RESEARCH TOOL 7.3: CATEGORICAL VARIABLES AS A SERIES OF BINARY DUMMY VARIABLES

Goal:

Allow the estimated intercepts to differ across the different possible outcomes of a qualitative variable that takes on j different possible outcomes.

Process:

1. Define a series of $j - 1$ binary dummy variables, such that

$BDV_{1,i} = 1$ if the individual possesses the 1st possible outcome, 0 otherwise

$BDV_{2,i} = 1$ if the individual possesses the 2nd possible outcome, 0 otherwise

$\vdots$

$BDV_{j-1,i} = 1$ if the individual possesses the jth possible outcome, 0 otherwise

2. Estimate the sample regression function

$$\hat{y}_i = \hat{\beta}_0 + \hat{\beta}_1 BDV_{1,i} + \hat{\beta}_2 BDV_{2,i} \cdots + \hat{\beta}_{j-1} BDV_{j-1,i} + \hat{\beta}_j x_{j,i} + \ldots + \hat{\beta}_k x_{k,i}$$

Interpretation:

The estimated slope coefficients, $\hat{\beta}_1, \hat{\beta}_2, \ldots, \hat{\beta}_{j-1}$ shift the intercept for observations possessing the different possible outcomes so that

		Estimated Intercept
If "omitted group"	then	$\hat{\beta}_0$
If $BDV_{1,i} = 1$	then	$\hat{\beta}_0 + \hat{\beta}_1$
If $BDV_{2,i} = 1$	then	$\hat{\beta}_0 + \hat{\beta}_2$
$\vdots$		$\vdots$
If $BDV_{j-1,i=1}$	then	$\hat{\beta}_0 + \hat{\beta}_{j-1}$

Note:

This approach allows the difference in estimated intercepts to differ across all possible outcomes of the qualitative variable. Be sure to omit one outcome!

Example:

For the sample regression function,

$$\widehat{Test\ score}_i = 65.18 + 2.15 Hours\ studied_i + 2.18 Sophomore_i + 3.45 Junior_i + 4.99 Senior_i$$

Note that **Freshman** is the omitted grade level. As a result, we would conclude that with 0 hours of studying:

- A freshman would average a test score of 65.18.
- A sophomore would average a test score of 65.18 + 2.18 = 67.36.
- A junior would average a test score of 65.18 + 3.45 = 68.63.
- A sophomore would average a test score of 65.18 + 4.99 = 70.17.

Holding grade level constant,

- An individual studying one more hour would average a test score that is 2.15 higher than a student studying one less hour.

Finally, Excel Example 7.3 demonstrates how to include and interpret a series of dummy variables for our 63-observation international GDP sample.

The one feature that the preceding techniques have in common is that they all shift the estimated intercepts in the sample regression function without shifting the estimated slope coefficients. In doing so, the values do not directly answer the question of whether the estimated marginal effects might differ for different values of a qualitative variable (i.e., that the marginal effect of experience on salary might differ by nationality). We can answer this question by constructing variables that allow not only for different intercepts but also for different slopes of the sample regression function and including them as additional variables in our multiple linear regression analysis.

EXCEL EXAMPLE 7.3

Estimating our sample regression function with a series of dummy variables instead of the categorical variable $Continent_i$

For our GDP data, based on the continent in which each country is located, we create four new dummy variables.

$Africa_i = 1$ if the country is in Africa, 0 otherwise
$Europe_i = 1$ if the country is in Europe, 0 otherwise
$North\ America_i = 1$ if the country is in North America, 0 otherwise
$South\ America_i = 1$ if the country is in South America, 0 otherwise

with the omitted variable being Asia, and estimate the multiple linear regression model as

$$GDP/1{,}000{,}000{,}000_i = \beta_0 + \beta_1(Population/1{,}000{,}000)_i + \beta_2 Africa_i + \beta_3 Europe_i + \beta_4 North\ America_i + \beta_5 South\ America_i + \varepsilon_i$$

SUMMARY OUTPUT

Regression Statistics	
Multiple R	0.688448875
R Square	0.473961853
Adjusted R Square	0.427818156
Standard Error	2163.090668
Observations	63

ANOVA

	df	SS	MS	F	Significance F
Regression	5	240298164.3	48059632.85	10.27143214	4.71433E-07
Residual	57	266700790.6	4678961.238		
Total	62	506998954.8			

	Coefficients	Standard Error	*t* Stat	*P*-value	Lower 95%	Upper 95%
Intercept	97.572	537.044	0.181684122	0.856475185	−977.840	1,172.985
Pop./1,000,000	7.643	1.198	6.379835711	3.40887E-08	5.244	10.042
Africa	−263.132	891.000	−0.295322372	0.768820727	−2,047.329	1,521.065
Eur	455.420	715.362	0.636628408	0.526915409	−977.068	1,887.908
NA	2,265.999	829.883	2.730502654	0.008399641	604.186	3,927.812
SA	−51.925	1,203.151	−0.043157110	0.965727123	−2,461.193	2,357.344

Statistical Inference:

Because the calculated *p*-values are greater than 0.05 for Africa, Europe, and South America, we fail to reject that $\beta_2 = 0$, $\beta_3 = 0$, and $\beta_5 = 0$, and we conclude that, holding population constant, *GDP* is not statistically different for countries on those continents than for countries in Asia.

Because the calculated *p*-value $= 0.01 < 0.05$ for North America, we reject $H_0{:}\beta_4 = 0$, and we conclude that, holding population constant, *GDP* is statistically different by $2.2660 trillion for North American countries than for Asian countries.

7.2 CONSTRUCT AND USE INTERACTION EFFECTS

interaction term
A variable in a regression model that takes account of the joint variation between two variables.

Interaction terms are the product of two different independent variables. In practice, the nature and interpretation of interaction terms differs depending on whether they are constructed as the product of a quantitative variable and a binary dummy variable or as the product of two quantitative variables. We start here with the former.

For our 200-observation MLB position player sample, we create the interaction term $(\textbf{\textit{Experience}} \cdot \textbf{\textit{Japanese}})_i$ by multiplying the quantitative variable $Experience_i$ with the qualitative variable $Japanese_i$ for each individual observation. Doing so produces the data in Table 7.5.

TABLE 7.5
Creating the Interaction Term $Experience \cdot Japanese_i$ for Our 200-Observation MLB Position Player Sample

id	Player	Salary	Experience	Japanese	Experience · Japanese
1	Tracy, Chad	\$ 5,000,000	4	0	0
2	Buscher, Brian	\$ 412,500	0	0	0
3	Bautista, Jose A.	\$ 2,400,000	3	0	0
4	Roberts, Ryan	\$ 400,000	0	0	0
5	Matsui, Hideki	\$13,000,000	6	1	6

We use this variable to test the hypothesis that the estimated marginal effect of experience on salary differs for Japanese and non-Japanese players by estimating the population model

$$Salary_i = \beta_0 + \beta_1 Experience_i + \beta_2 Japanese_i + \beta_3(Experience \cdot Japanese)_i + \varepsilon_i \quad \textbf{7.2.1}$$

To see how this model allows us to test our null hypothesis, we construct the interaction term worksheet in Table 7.6.

TABLE 7.6
Interaction Term Worksheet

	Intercept	Slope
Japanese	$\hat{\beta}_0 + \hat{\beta}_2$	$\hat{\beta}_1 + \hat{\beta}_3$
Not Japanese	$\hat{\beta}_0$	$\hat{\beta}_1$

As Table 7.6 demonstrates, including an interaction term allows the estimated slop coefficient to differ for the two possible outcomes of our binary dummy variable. In particular, the estimated slope coefficient for Japanese players, holding all other independent variables constant, is now $\hat{\beta}_1 + \hat{\beta}_3$, while the estimated slope coefficient for Japanese players, holding all other independent variables constant, is now $\hat{\beta}_1$.

Excel Regression Output 7.5 presents the sample regression function for our 200-observation MLB position player sample regression function.

Excel Regression Output 7.5: Estimated Marginal Effects for the Interaction Term $(\textbf{\textit{Experience}} \cdot \textbf{\textit{Japanese}})_i$

SUMMARY OUTPUT

Regression Statistics	
Multiple R	0.61542533
R Square	0.37874834
Adjusted R Square	0.36923939
Standard Error	3873507.26
Observations	200

ANOVA

	df	SS	MS	F	Significance F
Regression	3	1.79287E+15	5.97622E+14	39.83070561	3.82538E-20
Residual	196	2.9408E+15	1.50041E+13		
Total	199	4.73366E+15			

	Coefficients	Standard Error	*t* Stat	*P*-value	Lower 95%	Upper 95%
Intercept	478807.0504	407505.4296	1.174970971	0.241431772	−324851.187	1282465.288
Experience	735832.7839	70656.98986	10.41415415	1.70374E-20	596487.224	875178.343
Japanese	11921192.95	4729911.979	2.520383678	0.012520142	2593138.775	21249247.120
Experience · Japanese	−635832.7839	1097869.343	−0.579151598	0.563151895	−2800986.121	1529320.554

Note: Dependent variable is annual salary. Variables highlighted in blue are significant at the 5 percent level.

When interpreting these results, we need to be careful about the "holding all other independent variables constant" condition. Namely, when interpreting the estimated marginal effect of experience on salary, we are holding the Japanese variable constant at either 0 or 1, depending on the player's nationality. When interpreting the estimated marginal effect of being Japanese on salary, we are holding the number of years of experience constant. With this in mind, Interpreting the Regression Output 7.4 demonstrates the correct interpretation for these estimates.

Interpreting the Regression Output 7.4: The Interaction Term $(Experience \cdot Japanese)_i$

	Intercept	Coefficient
Japanese	$\hat{\beta}_0 + \hat{\beta}_2$ = \$478,807.05 + \$11,921,192.95 = 12,400,000.00	$\hat{\beta}_1 + \hat{\beta}_3$ = \$735,832.78 − \$635,832.78 = \$100,000.00
Not Japanese	$\hat{\beta}_0$ = \$478,807.05	$\hat{\beta}_1$ = \$735,832.78

Estimated Sample Regression Functions

Japanese: $\widehat{Salary}_i = \$12{,}400{,}000.00 + \$100{,}000.00 \cdot Experience_i$

Non-Japanese: $\widehat{Salary}_i = \$478{,}807.05 + \$735{,}832.78 \cdot Experience_i$

Visual Depiction

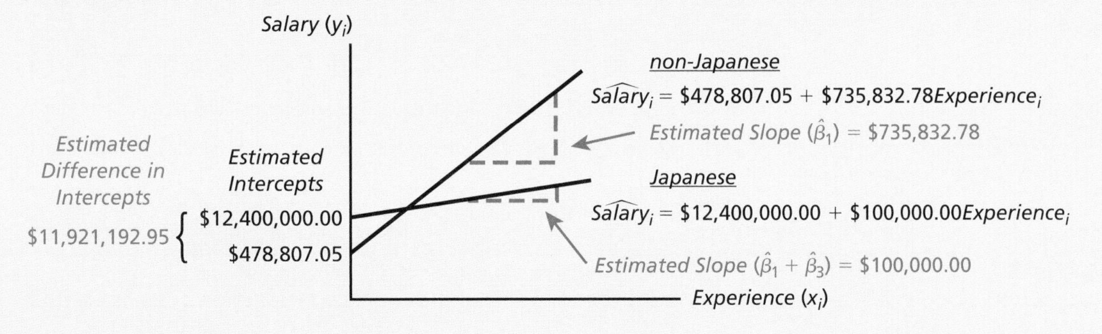

In Words

Holding experience constant,

1. A Japanese position player with 0 years of experience would be predicted to earn \$12,400,000.00, on average.
2. A non-Japanese position player with 0 years of experience would be predicted to earn \$478,807.05, on average.

Holding nationality constant,

1. A Japanese position player would be predicted to earn \$100,000.00 more for each additional year of experience, on average.
2. A non-Japanese position player would be predicted to earn \$735,832.78 more for each additional year of experience, on average.

Hypothesis Testing 7.3 present the t-test for the individual significance of the estimated slope coefficient for our interaction term.

Hypothesis Testing 7.3: Testing for the Individual Significance of the Interaction Term $(Experience \cdot Japanese)_i$

Question:
All other independent variables equal, does the marginal effect of experience on salary differ between the ~~two leagues?~~ Japanese + non-Japanese

Population Regression Function:

$$Salary_i = \beta_0 + \beta_1 Experience_i + \beta_2 Japanese_i + \beta_3 (Experience \cdot Japanese)_i + \varepsilon_i$$

Hypothesis:
$H_0: \beta_3 = 0$
$H_A: \beta_3 \neq 0$

Hypothesis Testing:
We can use all three methods to test this hypothesis. The necessary values are in the $Experience \cdot Japanese_i$ row in Excel Regression Output 7.5.

$$p\text{-value} = 0.5632$$

Conclusion:
Because $0.5632 > 0.05$, we fail to reject H_0 at $\alpha = 0.05$ and conclude that, holding all other independent variables constant, the marginal effect of experience on salary is the same ~~between~~ for Japanese and non-Japanese players.

Empirical Research Tool 7.4 summarizes the use of interaction terms between quantitative and binary dummy variables.

EMPIRICAL RESEARCH TOOL 7.4: INTERACTION TERMS BETWEEN A QUANTITATIVE VARIABLE AND A BINARY DUMMY VARIABLE

Goal:
Allow the estimated *marginal effect* of a given independent variable to differ for different values of another independent variable.

Process:
1. Define an interaction term, Int_i, that is the product of a quantitative independent variable x_{1i} and a binary dummy variable x_{2i}, such that $Int_i = x_{1i} \cdot x_{2i}$
2. Estimate the sample regression function

$$\hat{y}_i = \hat{\beta}_0 + \hat{\beta}_1 x_{1,i} + \hat{\beta}_2 x_{2,i} + \hat{\beta}_3 Int_i + \cdots + \hat{\beta}_k x_{k,i}$$

Interpretation:
The estimated slope coefficient, $\hat{\beta}_3$, shifts the slope of the sample regression function for observations possessing quality x_{2i} so that

			Estimated Slope
If	$X_{2,i} = 0$	then	$\hat{\beta}_1$
If	$X_{2,i} = 1$	then	$\hat{\beta}_1 + \hat{\beta}_3$

Example:
For the sample regression function

$$Test\ score_i = 68.13 + 2.29 \cdot Hours\ studied_i - 0.37 Blue\ eyes_i + 1.21 (Hours\ studied \cdot Blue\ eyes)_i$$

For the estimated intercept, if $Hours\ studied_i = 0$, then we would estimate:

- An individual *without* blue eyes (i.e., $Blue\ Eyes_i = 0$) to average a test score of 68.13.
- An individual *with* blue eyes (i.e., $Blue\ Eyes_i = 1$) to average a test score of $68.13 - 0.37 = 67.76$.

For the estimated slope, we would estimate:

- An individual *without* blue eyes (i.e., $Blue\ Eyes_i = 0$) who studied one more hour to average a test score 2.29 higher than a student who studied one less hour.
- An individual *with* blue eyes (i.e., $Blue\ Eyes_i = 1$) who studied one more hour to average a test score 3.50 higher than a student who studied one less hour.

Finally, Excel Example 7.4 demonstrates how to include and interpret an interaction term for our 63-observation international GDP sample.

EXCEL EXAMPLE 7.4

Estimating our sample regression function with the interaction term (Population/1,000,000 · Top education quartile)$_i$

For our GDP data, we create a new variable

$$(Population/1{,}000{,}000 \cdot Top\ education\ quartile)_i$$

and estimate the multiple linear regression model

$$GDP/1{,}000{,}000{,}000_i = \beta_0 + \beta_1 Population/1{,}000{,}000_i + \beta_2 Top\ Education\ Quartile_i + \beta_3(Population/1{,}000{,}000 Top\ education\ quartile)_i + \varepsilon_i$$

SUMMARY OUTPUT

Regression Statistics	
Multiple R	0.687737754
R Square	0.472983219
Adjusted R Square	0.446185755
Standard Error	2128.088811
Observations	63

ANOVA

	df	SS	MS	F	Significance F
Regression	3	239801997.5	79933999.16	17.65029811	2.70271E-08
Residual	59	267196957.3	4528761.989		
Total	62	506998954.8			

	Coefficients	Standard Error	t Stat	P-value	Lower 95%	Upper 95%
Intercept	24.220	382.520	0.063315845	0.949729023	−741.202	789.641
Population/1,000,000	8.825	9.830	0.897785641	0.372948960	−10.844	28.494
Ed. Top Quartile	1,954.666	643.466	3.037716083	0.003547508	667.094	3,242.237
Population/1,000,000 · Ed. Top Quartile	−2.691	9.904	−0.271654876	0.786835711	−22.509	17.128

Statistical Inference:

For the variable (*Population*/1,000,000*Top education quartile*)

- Because the calculated p-value $= 0.7868 > 0.05$, we fail to reject $H_0{:}\beta_3 = 0$, and we conclude that the marginal effect of population on *GDP* is not statistically different for countries in the top education quartile than for countries in the bottom education quartile.

Suppose that instead of interacting a quantitative variable with a binary dummy variable, we wish to interact two different quantitative variables. For instance, suppose that we wish to test whether the estimated marginal effects of home runs differs according to the number of years of experience that a player has accumulated. While the construction of interaction terms between two quantitative independent variables is straightforward, the interpretation of the results is not because the estimated relationship will be nonlinear rather than linear. For this reason, we choose to leave the discussion of the interaction between two different quantitative independent variables until later in the chapter.

7.3 CONTROL FOR NONLINEAR RELATIONSHIPS

Not all questions of interest to economists can be addressed by creating variables that allow for different estimated intercepts and/or different estimated slopes. Some important questions require construction of variables that allow us to estimate nonlinear relationships between the dependent variable and certain independent variables.

As an example, labor economic theory suggests that the economic return to additional years of work experience might follow an inverted U-shape with the return to additional years of experience increasing early in the career before hitting a maximum and then decreasing later in the career.

Quadratic Effects

Suppose that the economic return to additional years of experience does follow this hypothesized relationship. Figure 7.4 presents the scatter diagram between salary and experience in such a case.

FIGURE 7.4
A Quadratic Relationship between *y* and *x*

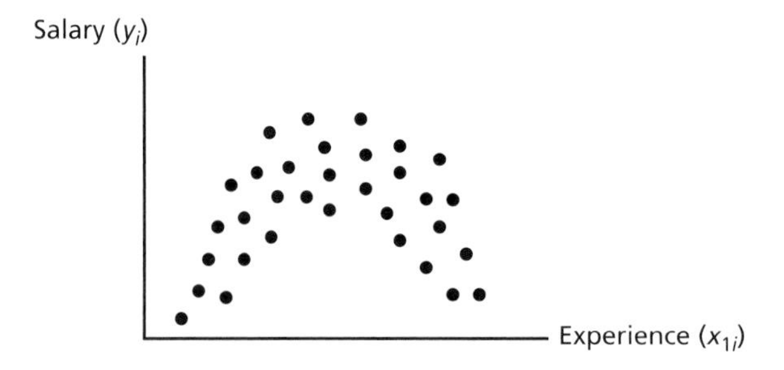

If we attempted to estimate a linear relationship between salary and experience in such a case, our best-fit sample regression function would look like Figure 7.5.

FIGURE 7.5
Fitting a Line through a Quadratic Relationship between *y* and *x*

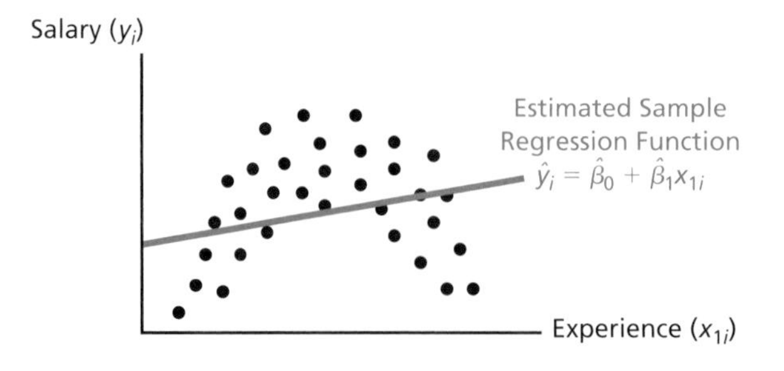

quadratic term
A variable that is entered into a regression model that is squared. Its role is to take account of a quadratic relationship between y and x.

Because the sample regression function in Figure 7.5 does not explain the true relationship between salary and experience well, we need to develop a different method for estimating the relationship. We can do so by including a **quadratic term** equal to the square of experience for each individual in our multiple linear regression analysis. Adding such a term produces a sample regression function that better explains the true relationship between salary and experience because it allows the estimated marginal effect that experience has on salary to differ for different levels of experience, thereby fitting a parabola through the sample data as in Figure 7.6.

FIGURE 7.6
Fitting a Curve through a Quadratic Relationship between *y* and *x*

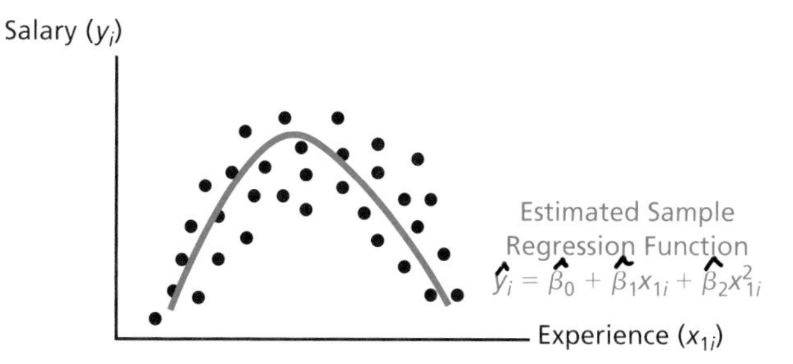

For our 200-observation MLB position player sample, we create the quadratic experience term $Experience_i^2$ by squaring the number of years of experience for each individual observation. Doing so produces the data in Table 7.7.

TABLE 7.7
Creating the Quadratic Term $Experience_i^2$ for Our 200-Observation MLB Position Player Sample

id	Player	Salary	Experience	Experience Squared
1	Tracy, Chad	\$ 5,000,000	4	16
2	Buscher, Brian	\$ 412,500	0	0
3	Bautista, Jose A.	\$ 2,400,000	3	9
4	Roberts, Ryan	\$ 400,000	0	0
5	Matsui, Hideki	\$13,000,000	6	36

We use this variable to test whether the economic return to additional years of experience follows the hypothesized parabolic shape by specifying the population regression model as

$$Salary_i = \beta_0 + \beta_1 Experience_i + \beta_2 Experience_i^2 + \varepsilon_i \qquad \textbf{7.3.1}$$

We must take care when interpreting the results of sample regression function. Because experience enters the sample regression function in two different places, the correct interpretation of the marginal effect of experience on salary is a little more complicated than we have encountered before. Specifically, by definition, a one-year increase in experience affects both the variable $Experience_i$ and the variable $Experience_i^2$. Accordingly, to correctly determine the estimated marginal effect of experience on salary, we must take the partial derivative of the sample regression function with respect to experience:

$$\frac{\partial Salary_i}{\partial Experience_i} = \hat{\beta}_1 + (2\hat{\beta}_2 Experience_i) \qquad \textbf{7.3.2}$$

Formula 7.3.2 demonstrates a number of important facts about the estimated relationship between the dependent variable and the independent variable for which the quadratic term is included. For one, the estimated marginal effect depends on the specific value at which it is being interpreted. (Note: This fact is what makes the estimated effect nonlinear.) As examples, consider that the estimated marginal effect of an additional year of experience for MLB position players with one year of experience is

$$\frac{\partial Salary_i}{\partial Experience_i} = \hat{\beta}_1 + (2\hat{\beta}_2 0) = \hat{\beta}_1 \qquad \textbf{7.3.3}$$

while the estimated marginal effect of an additional year of experience for MLB position players with six years of experience is

$$\frac{\partial Salary_i}{\partial Experience_i} = \hat{\beta}_1 + (2\hat{\beta}_2 5) = \hat{\beta}_1 + 10\hat{\beta}_2 \qquad \textbf{7.3.4}$$

Particular attention should be paid to a number of issues associated with these estimated marginal effects. First, for a player currently possessing one year of experience, the marginal change in experience was from 0 to 1, and therefore, the appropriate base year to plug into formula 7.3.3 is 0. Likewise, for a player currently possessing six years of experience, the marginal change in experience was from to 6, and therefore, the appropriate base year to plug into formula 7.3.4 is 5.

Second, notice that the exact nature of the estimated quadratic relationship depends on the signs of $\hat{\beta}_1$ and $\hat{\beta}_2$. The two most frequently encountered cases are those in which $\hat{\beta}_1 > 0$ and $\hat{\beta}_2 < 0$, which results in an estimated relationship that follows the inverted-U shape in Figure 7.7,

FIGURE 7.7
A Hypothetical Quadratic Function with $\hat{\beta}_1 > 0$ and $\hat{\beta}_2 < 0$

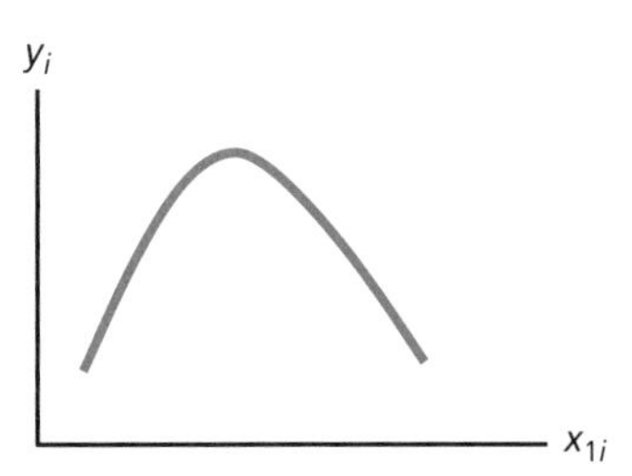

and those in which $\hat{\beta}_1 < 0$ *and* $\hat{\beta}_2 > 0$, which results in an estimated relationship that follows a regular U shape as in Figure 7.8.

FIGURE 7.8
A Hypothetical Quadratic Function with $\hat{\beta}_1 < 0$ and $\hat{\beta}_2 > 0$

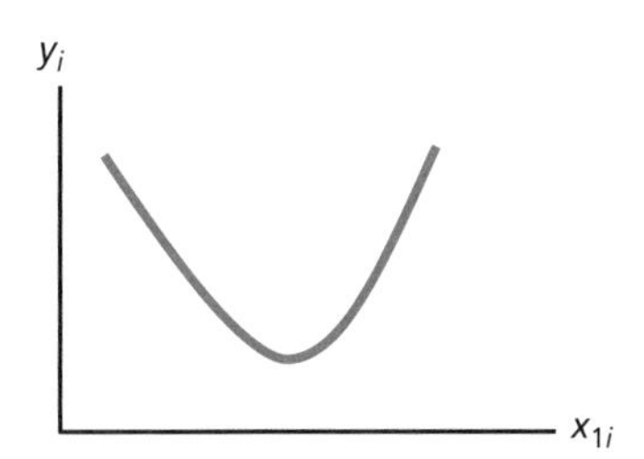

Third, notice that we can solve for the inflection point of the estimated quadratic relationship by solving for the value of the independent variable that sets the derivative equal to 0, which we do as follows

$$\beta_1 + (2\beta_2 Experience_i) = 0 \qquad 7.3.5$$

$$Experience_i^* = \frac{-\beta_1}{2\beta_2} \qquad 7.3.6$$

Excel Regression Output 7.6 presents the sample regression function for our 200-observation MLB position player sample regression function.

Excel Regression Output 7.6: Estimated Marginal Effects Allowing for the Quadratic Effects of *Experience*$_i$

SUMMARY OUTPUT

Regression Statistics	
Multiple R	0.612733874
R Square	0.375442801
Adjusted R Square	0.369102118
Standard Error	3873928.738
Observations	200

ANOVA

	df	SS	MS	F	Significance F
Regression	2	1.77722E+15	8.8861E+14	59.21173574	7.30909E-21
Residual	197	2.95644E+15	1.50073E+13		
Total	199	4.73366E+15			

	Coefficients	Standard Error	*t* Stat	*P*-value	Lower 95%	Upper 95%
Intercept	−391,475.534	499,968.441	−0.783000489	0.434567082	−1,377,452.793	594,501.724
Experience	1,323,920.958	187,928.766	7.044802048	3.03789E-11	953,310.587	1,694,531.330
Experience Squared	−46,178.286	13,508.408	−3.418484793	0.000765151	−72,817.933	−19,538.639

Note: Dependent variable is annual salary. Highlighted variables are significant at the 5 percent level.

Interpreting the Regression Output 7.5 demonstrates the correct interpretation for these sample regression functions.

Interpreting the Regression Output 7.5: The Quadratic Terms $Experience_i$ and $Experience_i^2$

Derivative with Respect to Experience

$$\frac{\partial Salary_i}{\partial Experience_i} = \beta_1 + (2\beta_2 Experience_i)$$

$$= \$1{,}323{,}920.96 + (2 \cdot \text{-}\$46{,}178.29 Experience_i)$$

$$= \$1{,}323{,}920.96 - (\$92{,}356.57 Experience_i)$$

Estimated Marginal Effect of Experience on Salary

$Experience_i$	Estimated Marginal Effect of Experience on Salary
1	\$1,323,920.96 − (\$92,356.57 · 0) = \$1,323,920.96
5	\$1,323,920.96 − (\$92,356.57 · 4) = \$954,494.67
10	\$1,323,920.96 − (\$92,356.57 · 9) = \$492,711.81
20	\$1,323,920.96 − (\$92,356.57 · 19) = \$−430,853.90

Inflection Point

$$Experience_i^* = \frac{-\beta_1}{2\beta_2} = \frac{-\$1{,}323{,}920.86}{2(-\$46{,}178.29)} = 14.33$$

meaning that the estimated relationship between experience and salary reaches its maximum at 14.33 years of experience, at which point a player is expected to earn

$$\widehat{Salary} = -\$391{,}475.53 + (\$1{,}323{,}920.96 \cdot 14.33) - (\$46{,}178.29 \cdot 14.33^2)$$

$$= \$9{,}097{,}650.77$$

Visual Depiction

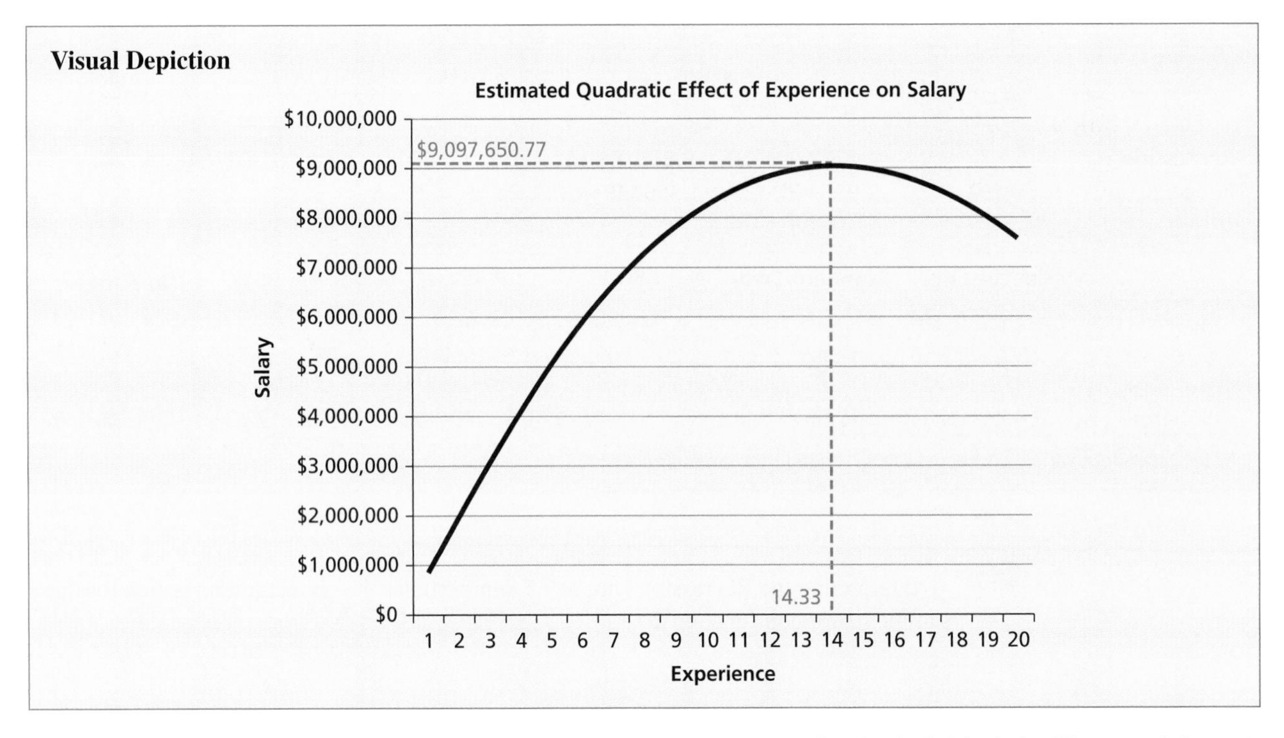

Hypothesis Testing 7.4 presents the t-test for the individual significance of the estimated slope coefficient for a quadratic term.

Hypothesis Testing 7.4: Testing the Individual Significance of the Quadratic Experience Term

Question:
All other independent variables equal, does experience exhibit a quadratic effect on salary in our sample?

Sample Regression Function:

$$Salary_i = \beta_0 + \beta_1 Experience_i + \beta_2 Experience_i^2 + \varepsilon_i$$

Hypothesis:

H_0: $\beta_2 = 0$
H_A: $\beta_2 \neq 0$

Hypothesis Testing:
We can use all three methods to test this hypothesis. The necessary values are in the Experience Squared row in Excel Regression Output 7.6.

p-value $= 0.0007652$

Conclusion:
Because $0.0007652 < 0.05$, we reject H_0 at $\alpha = 0.05$ and conclude that experience does exhibit a quadratic effect on salary in our sample.

Empirical Research Tool 7.5 summarizes the use of quadratic terms.

EMPIRICAL RESEARCH TOOL 7.5: QUADRATIC EFFECTS OF A QUANTITATIVE VARIABLE

Goal:
Allow the estimated marginal effect of a given independent variable to differ for different values of that variable.

Process:

1. Define a quadratic term, $x_{1,i}^2$, that is the square of the quantitative independent variable x_{1i}.
2. Estimate the sample regression function

$$\hat{y}_i = \hat{\beta}_0 + \hat{\beta}_1 x_{1,i} + \hat{\beta}_2 x_{1,i}^2 + \cdots + \hat{\beta}_k x_{k,i}$$

Interpretation:

The estimated marginal effect of $x_{1,i}$ is found by taking the derivative of the sample regression function with respect to $x_{1,i}$, which is

$$\frac{\partial \hat{y}_i}{\partial x_{1,i}} = \hat{\beta}_1 + (2\hat{\beta}_2 x_{1,i})$$

Note:

Care must be taken when performing this calculation. For instance, if we are interested in the estimated marginal effect of the fifth year of education we would plug 4 rather than 5 into this equation (because the marginal effect is the effect of changing from 4 to 5 and not the effect at 5).

Example:

For the sample regression function

$$\textit{Test score}_i = 68.12 + 2.52\textit{Hours studied}_i - 0.04\textit{Hours studied}_i^2$$

We would conclude that, with 0 hours of studying,

- An individual would average a test score of 68.12.

For the estimated marginal effect of hours studied, we would estimate that:

- An individual studying one hour would average a test score that is $2.52 + 2(-0.04)0 = 2.52$ higher than a student studying 0 hours.
- An individual studying two hours would average a test score that is $2.52 + 2(-0.04)1 = 2.44$ higher than a student studying for 1 hour.
- An individual studying three hours would average a test score that is $2.52 + 2(-0.04)2 = 2.36$ higher than a student studying for 2 hours.
- An individual studying ten hours would average a test score that is $2.52 + 2(-0.04)9 = 1.80$ higher than a student studying for 9 hours.

Finally, Excel Example 7.5 demonstrates how to include and interpret a quadratic term for our 63-observation international GDP sample.

EXCEL EXAMPLE 7.5

Estimating our sample regression function with the quadratic term Life Expectancy$_i^2$

For our GDP data, we create a new variable *Life Expectancy$_i^2$* and estimate the multiple linear regression model:

$$GDP/1{,}000{,}000{,}000_i = \beta_0 + \beta_1 \textit{ Life expectancy}_i + \beta_2 \textit{ Life expectancy}_i^2 + \varepsilon_i$$

SUMMARY OUTPUT

Regression Statistics	
Multiple R	0.169716966
R Square	0.028803849
Adjusted R Square	−0.003569356
Standard Error	2864.7147430
Observations	63

ANOVA

	df	SS	MS	F	Significance F
Regression	2	14603521.15	7301760.575	0.889743496	0.416110411
Residual	60	492395433.7	8206590.561		
Total	62	506998954.8			

	Coefficients	Standard Error	*t* Stat	*P*-value	Lower 95%	Upper 95%
Intercept	−4,573.299	15,271.017	−0.299475724	0.765612064	−35,119.881	25,973.283
Life Expectancy	114.688	473.712	0.242104355	0.809524918	−832.878	1,062.254
Life Expectancy Squared	−0.480	3.599	−0.133398461	0.894324679	−7.678	6.718

Statistical Inference:

Because the calculated *p*-value = 0.8943 > 0.05, we fail to reject H_0: $\beta_3 = 0$ and conclude that the marginal effect of life expectancy on *GDP* is *not* estimated to follow a quadratic relationship.

Interaction Effects between Two Quantitative Variables

Suppose that we are interested in testing whether the estimated marginal effect that home runs have on salary differs depending on a player's years of experience. We can test this hypothesis by constructing an interaction term that is the product of those two variables and including it in our multiple linear regression analysis.

For our 200-observation MLB position player sample, we create the interaction term $Experience_i \cdot HR_i$ by multiplying the value of those two variables together for each individual observation. Doing so produces the data in Table 7.8.

TABLE 7.8
Creating the Interaction Term ($Experience \cdot HR_i$) for Our 200-Observation MLB Position Player Sample

id	Player	Salary	Experience	HR	Experience · HR
1	Tracy, Chad	$ 5,000,000	4	5	32
2	Buscher, Brian	$ 412,500	0	4	0
3	Bautista, Jose A.	$ 2,400,000	3	15	45
4	Roberts, Ryan	$ 400,000	0	0	0
5	Matsui, Hideki	$13,000,000	6	9	54

We use this variable to test the hypothesis that the estimated marginal effect of home runs on salary differs depending on a player's experience by estimating the population multiple linear regression model

$$\widehat{Salary}_i = \hat{\beta}_0 + \hat{\beta}_1 Experience_i + \hat{\beta}_2 Home\ runs_i + \hat{\beta}_3 (Experience \cdot Home\ runs)_i + \varepsilon_i \quad \textbf{7.3.7}$$

Two things make the estimated marginal effect of home runs on salary nonlinear in formula 7.3.7: (1) The variable $Experience_i$ enters the population regression function twice, meaning that a change in home runs affects both the variable $Experience_i$ and the variable $(Experience \cdot Home\ runs)_i$; and (2) the variable $Experience_i$ is a quantitative variable, meaning that the estimated effect of the other quantitative variable, $Home\ Runs_i$, will differ depending on the years of experience that the player has accumulated. To correctly determine the estimated marginal effect for the quantitative variable $Experience_i$ we must take the derivative of population regression model with respect to experience:

$$\frac{\partial Salary_i}{\partial Experience_i} = \hat{\beta}_1 + (\hat{\beta}_3 Home\ runs_i) \quad \textbf{7.3.8}$$

We can now determine the estimated marginal effect that one additional year of experience has on salary by plugging different numbers of home runs into formula 7.3.8. As examples, for players hitting 6 and 32 home runs, respectively, the estimated marginal effect that one additional year of experience has on salary is

Player with 6 home runs: $$\frac{\partial Salary_i}{\partial Experience_i} = \hat{\beta}_1 + (\hat{\beta}_3 \cdot 6) \quad \textbf{7.3.9}$$

Player with 32 home runs: $$\frac{\partial Salary_i}{\partial Experience_i} = \hat{\beta}_1 + (\hat{\beta}_3 \cdot 32) \quad \textbf{7.3.10}$$

Similarly, to determine the estimated marginal effect that one additional home run has on salary we must take the derivative of population regression model with respect to home runs and plugging different years of experience into the resulting expression. As examples, for players with 4 and 11 years experience, respectively, the estimated marginal effect that one additional home run has on salary is

Player with 4 years experience: $$\frac{\partial Salary_i}{\partial Home\ Runs_i} = \hat{\beta}_2 + (\hat{\beta}_3 \cdot 4) \quad \textbf{7.3.11}$$

Player with 11 years experience: $$\frac{\partial Salary_i}{\partial Home\ Runs_i} = \hat{\beta}_2 + (\hat{\beta}_3 \cdot 11) \quad \textbf{7.3.12}$$

Notice that unlike the quadratic effect, where we subtract 1 from the value of the independent variable before substituting in for the equation, with interaction effects the exact value is put in for the independent variable. In this case, when we want to determine the marginal effect of the number of homeruns on salary for a player with four years of experience we put 4 into the calculation instead of 3 like we would have for a quadratic effect.

Excel Regression Output 7.7 presents the sample regression function for our 200-observation MLB position player sample regression function.

Excel Regression Output 7.7: Estimated Marginal Effects for the Interaction Term $(Experience \cdot HR)_i$

SUMMARY OUTPUT

Regression Statistics	
Multiple R	0.779582356
R Square	0.60774865
Adjusted R Square	0.601744802
Standard Error	3077888.048
Observations	200

ANOVA

	df	SS	MS	F	Significance F
Regression	3	2.87688E+15	9.58959E+14	101.2265351	1.29512E-39
Residual	196	1.85679E+15	9.47339E+12		
Total	199	4.73366E+15			

	Coefficients	Standard Error	*t* Stat	*P*-value	Lower 95%	Upper 95%
Intercept	252,146.164	414,912.991	0.60770853	0.544084272	−566,120.830	1,070,413.158
Experience	261,804.916	76,711.269	3.41286124	0.000780949	110,519.464	413,090.367
HR	62,282.864	32,553.814	1.91322788	0.057176291	−1,917.852	126,483.580
Experience · HR	29,256.559	4,739.724	6.17262943	3.78759E-09	19,909.155	38,603.964

Note: Dependent variable is annual salary. Variables highlighted in blue are significant at the 5 percent level. Variables highlighted in light gray are significant at the 10 percent level.

See corrected page 212

Interpreting the Regression Output 7.6 demonstrates the correct interpretation for these sample regression functions.

Interpreting the Regression Output 7.6: The Interaction Term $(Experience \cdot HR)_i$

For *Experience*:
Derivative with respect to $Experience_i$

$$\frac{\partial Salary_i}{\partial Experience_i} = \hat{\beta}_1 + (\hat{\beta}_3 Home\ runs_i)$$

$$= \$261{,}804.92 + (\$29{,}256.56 Home\ run_i)$$

and the estimated marginal effect of *Experience* on *Salary* is

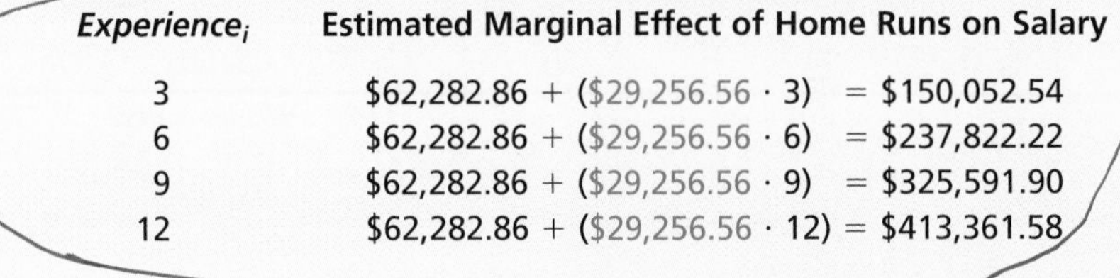

$Experience_i$	Estimated Marginal Effect of Home Runs on Salary
3	$62,282.86 + ($29,256.56 · 3) = $150,052.54
6	$62,282.86 + ($29,256.56 · 6) = $237,822.22
9	$62,282.86 + ($29,256.56 · 9) = $325,591.90
12	$62,282.86 + ($29,256.56 · 12) = $413,361.58

For *Home runs*:
Derivative with respect to $Home\ runs_i$

$$\frac{\partial Salary_i}{\partial Home\ runs_i} = \hat{\beta}_2 + (\hat{\beta}_3 \cdot Experience_i)$$

$$= \$62{,}282.86 + (\$29{,}256.56 \cdot Experience_i)$$

and the estimated marginal effect of *Home runs* on *Salary* is

$Home\ Runs_i$	Estimated Marginal Effect of Experience on Salary
5	$261,804.92 + ($29,256.56 · 5) = $408,087.71
10	$261,804.92 + ($29,256.56 · 10) = $554,370.51
15	$261,804.92 + ($29,256.56 · 15) = $700,653.31
20	$261,804.92 + ($29,256.56 · 20) = $846,936.10

Hypothesis Testing 7.5 presents the *t*-test for the individual significance of the estimated slope coefficient for an interaction term between two quantitative variables.

Hypothesis Testing 7.5: Testing the Individual Significance of the Interaction Term $(Experience \cdot HR)_i$

Question:
All other independent variables equal, does the marginal effect of experience on salary differ depending on the number of home runs (and vice versa)?

Sample Regression Function:

$$Salary_i = \beta_0 + \beta_1 Experience_i + \beta_2 HR_i + \beta_3(Experience_i \cdot HR_i) + \varepsilon_i$$

Hypothesis:

$H_0: \beta_3 = 0$
$H_A: \beta_3 \neq 0$

Hypothesis Testing:
We can use all three methods to test this hypothesis. The necessary values are in Experience · HR row in Excel Regression Output 7.7.

p-value = 3.7876E-09

Conclusion:
Because 3.7876E − 09 < 0.05, we reject H_0 at $\alpha = 0.05$ and conclude that the marginal effect of experience on salary does differ depending on the number of home runs (and vice versa).

Empirical Research Tool 7.6 summarizes the use of interaction terms between two quantitative variables.

EMPIRICAL RESEARCH TOOL 7.6: INTERACTION TERMS BETWEEN TWO QUANTITATIVE VARIABLES

Goal:
Allow the estimated marginal effect of a given quantitative independent variable to differ for different values of another quantitative independent variable.

Process:
1. Define an interaction term, Int_i, that is the product of a quantitative independent variables x_{1i} and x_{2i}, such that $Int_i = x_{1i} \cdot x_{2i}$
2. Estimate the sample regression function

$$\hat{y}_i = \hat{\beta}_0 + \hat{\beta}_1 x_{1,i} + \hat{\beta}_2 x_{2,i} + \hat{\beta}_3 Int_i + \cdots + \hat{\beta}_k x_{k,i}$$

Interpretation:
The estimated marginal effect of $x_{1,i}$ now depends on the value of $x_{2,i}$, estimated marginal effect of $x_{1,i}$ now depends on the value of $x_{2,i}$ so that

The marginal effect of $x_{1,i}$ is

$$\frac{\partial \hat{y}_i}{\partial x_{1,i}} = \hat{\beta}_1 + (\not{2}\hat{\beta}_3 x_{2,i})$$

The marginal effect of $x_{2,i}$ is

$$\frac{\partial \hat{y}_i}{\partial x_{2,i}} = \hat{\beta}_2 + (\not{2}\hat{\beta}_3 x_{1,i})$$

Example:

For the sample regression function

$$\widehat{Test\ score}_i = 67.23 + 2.87 Hours\ studied_i + 2.43 Grade\ level_i + 1.36\ Hours\ studied_i \cdot Grade\ level_i$$

For the estimated marginal effect of *Hours studied*, we must set grade level to a specific value

- If $Grade\ level_i$ = **0** (i.e., the student is a freshman), then for each additional hour studied, we would estimate average test scores to increase by 2.87 + (1.36 · **0**) = 2.87.
- If $Grade\ level_i$ = **1** (i.e., the student is a sophomore), then for each additional hour studied, we would estimate average test scores to increase by 2.87 + (1.36 · **1**) = 4.23.
- If $Grade\ level_i$ = **2** (i.e., the student is a junior), then for each additional hour studied, we would estimate average test scores to increase by 2.87 + (1.36 · **2**) = 5.59.

For the estimated marginal effect of *Grade Level*, we must set hours studied to a specific value

- If $Hours\ studied_i$ = **0**, then for each higher grade level, we would estimate average test scores to increase by 2.43 + (1.36 · **0**) = 2.43.
- If $Hours\ studied_i$ = **3**, then for each higher grade level, we would estimate average test scores to increase by 2.43 + (1.36 · **3**) = 6.51.
- If $Hours\ studied_i$ = **10**, then for each higher grade level, we would estimate average test scores to increase by 2.43 + (1.36 · **10**) = 16.03.

Finally, Excel Example 7.6 demonstrates how to include and interpret an interaction term between two quantitative variables for our 63-observation international GDP sample.

EXCEL EXAMPLE 7.6

Estimating the sample regression function with the interaction term (Population/1,000,000Life Expectancy)$_i$

For our GDP data, we create a new variable (*Population*/1,000,000*Life Expectancy*)$_i$ and estimate the multiple linear regression model:

$$GDP/1{,}000{,}000{,}000_i = \beta_0 + \beta_1 Population/1{,}000{,}000_i + \beta_2 Life\ Expectancy_i + \beta_3(Population/1{,}000{,}000 Life\ Expectancy)_i + \varepsilon_i$$

SUMMARY OUTPUT

Regression Statistics	
Multiple R	0.693703509
R Square	0.481224559
Adjusted R Square	0.454846147
Standard Error	2111.38402
Observations	63

ANOVA

	df	SS	MS	F	Significance F
Regression	3	243980348.4	81326782.81	18.24312071	1.7115E-08
Residual	59	263018606.4	4457942.481		
Total	62	506998954.8			

	Coefficients	Standard Error	*t* Stat	*P*-value	Lower 95%	Upper 95%
Intercept	1,561.792	2,581.917	0.604896369	0.547567365	−3,604.612	6,728.197
Population/1,000,000	−109.718	40.539	−2.706457629	0.008879189	−190.837	−28.599
Life Expectancy	−12.661	35.343	−0.358222445	0.721455382	−83.382	58.061
Population/1,000,000 · Life Expectancy	1.594	0.551	2.889973181	0.005382921	0.490	2.697

Statistical Inference:

Because the calculated *p*-value = 0.01 < 0.05, we reject $H_0{:}\beta_3 = 0$ and conclude that the marginal effect of population on *GDP does* differ for different life expectancies, and vice versa.

For Life Expectancy:

Derivative with respect to *Life expectancy*$_i$

$$\frac{\partial GDP/1{,}000{,}000{,}000_i}{\partial Life\ expectancy_i} = \hat{\beta}_2 + (\hat{\beta}_3 Population/1{,}000{,}000_i)$$

$$= -12.66 + (1.59 Population/1{,}000{,}000_i)$$

and the estimated marginal effect of *Life expectancy* on *GDP*/1,000,000,000 is

Population/ 1,000,000,000	Estimated Marginal Effects of Life Expectancy on GDP/1,000,000,000
10	$= -12.66 + (1.59 \cdot 10) = 3.24$
30	$= -12.66 + (1.59 \cdot 30) = 35.04$
80	$= -12.66 + (1.59 \cdot 80) = 114.54$
150	$= -12.66 + (1.59 \cdot 150) = 225.84$

7.4 ESTIMATE MARGINAL EFFECTS AS PERCENT CHANGES AND ELASTICITIES

In all of the preceding cases, we interpret the estimated slope coefficients as representing the estimated marginal effect that *unit changes* in a given independent variable are estimated to have on the dependent variable. In addition to such marginal effects, we are often interested in estimating relationships in terms of either percentage changes or elasticities (which are calculated as the percentage change in the dependent variable due to a given percentage change in the independent variable).

We can use multiple linear regression analysis to estimate such relationships by replacing the dependent variable (and potentially some of the independent variables of interest) with their natural logs to rescale the estimated marginal effects into percentage change or elasticity terms.

The Log-Linear Model

log-linear model
A regression model in which the dependent variable is logged and the independent variable is not logged. This model is estimated to take account of a nonlinear relationship between y and x.

We are able to generate estimates of the percentage change in the dependent variable that is likely to result from a unit change in a given independent variable by including the natural log of the dependent variable in our multiple linear regression. We refer to doing so as estimating a **log-linear model,** because the dependent variable is in log form while the independent variable remains in linear form.

For our 200-observation MLB position player sample, we create the variable ln($Salary_i$) for each observation. Doing so produces the data in Table 7.9.

TABLE 7.9
Creating ln($Salary_i$) for Our 200-Observation MLB Position Player Sample

id	Player	Salary	ln(Salary)	Experience	HR
1	Tracy, Chad	$ 5,000,000	$15.42	4	8
2	Buscher, Brian	$ 412,500	$12.93	0	4
3	Bautista, Jose A.	$ 2,400,000	$14.69	3	15
4	Roberts, Ryan	$ 400,000	$12.90	0	0
5	Matsui, Hideki	$13,000,000	$16.38	6	9

We use this variable to estimate the percentage change in salary that is likely to be associated with additional years of experience or additional home runs (holding the other variable constant) by estimating the population multiple linear regression model as

$$ln(Salary_i) = \beta_0 + \beta_1 Experience_i + \beta_2 Home\ run_i + \varepsilon_i \qquad 7.4.1$$

Excel Regression Output 7.8 presents the sample regression function for our 200-observation MLB position player sample regression function.

Excel Regression Output 7.8: Estimated Marginal Effects for the Log-Linear Model

SUMMARY OUTPUT

Regression Statistics	
Multiple R	0.818964203
R Square	0.670702366
Adjusted R Square	0.667359243
Standard Error	0.733714820
Observations	200

ANOVA

	df	SS	MS	F	Significance F
Regression	2	216.0041209	108.0020604	200.6214931	3.03723E-48
Residual	197	106.0524751	0.538337437		
Total	199	322.056596			

	Coefficients	Standard Error	*t* Stat	*P*-value	Lower 95%	Upper 95%
Intercept	12.96712138	0.086211436	150.4106886	2.9252E-205	12.79710562	13.13713714
Experience	0.181687091	0.013899214	13.07175305	1.59269E-28	0.154276744	0.209097439
HR	0.05648589	0.005156002	10.95536642	4.06856E-22	0.046317847	0.066653933

Note: Dependent variable is log annual salary. Highlighted variables are significant at the 5 percent level.

Statistical Inference:

For the *Experience* variable:

- Because *p*-value = 1.59*E*-28 < 0.05, we reject H_0: $\beta_1 = 0$ and conclude that holding home runs constant, each additional year of experience is expected to increase salary by 18.17 percent.
  For the *Home run* variable:
- Because *p*-value = 4.07*E*-22 < 0.05, we reject H_0: $\beta_2 = 0$ and conclude that holding experience constant, each additional home run is expected to increase salary by 5.65 percent.

Empirical Research Tool 7.7 summarizes the log-linear model.

EMPIRICAL RESEARCH TOOL 7.7: THE LOG-LINEAR MODEL

Goal:

Calculate the estimated marginal effects of the independent variables in percentage change terms.

Process:

1. Calculate the natural log of the dependent variable, $\log y_i$.
2. Estimate the sample regression function

$$\widehat{\log y_i} = \hat{\beta}_0 + \hat{\beta}_1 x_{1,i} + \hat{\beta}_2 x_{2,i} + \cdots + \hat{\beta}_k x_{k,i}$$

Interpretation:

The estimated slope coefficients, $\hat{\beta}_1, \hat{\beta}_2, \ldots, \hat{\beta}_k$ are denominated so that they indicate the percentage change in y_i resulting from a one-unit increase in the given independent variable. In other words, if $x_{1,i}$ increases by one unit, then y increase by an average of $(\hat{\beta}_1 \cdot 100)\%$ all other independent variables constant.

Example:

$$\log \widehat{Test\ score_i} = 12.96 + 0.0716 Hours\ studied_i + 0.1264 GPA_i$$

We would conclude that:

- Holding *GPA* constant, we estimate that if hours studied increases by 1 unit, then average test score increases by $(0.0716 \cdot 100)\% = 7.16$ percent.
- Holding *Hours studied* constant, we estimate that if GPA increases by 1 unit, then test score increases by $(0.1264 \cdot 100)\% = 12.64$ percent.

Finally, Excel Example 7.7 demonstrates how to estimate and interpret a log-linear model for our 63-observation international GDP sample.

EXCEL EXAMPLE 7.7

Estimating the sample regression function for a log-linear model

For our GDP data, we create a new variable $ln(GDP/1{,}000{,}000{,}000_i)$ and estimate the multiple linear regression model:

$$ln(GDP/1{,}000{,}000{,}000_i) = \beta_0 + \beta_1 Population/1{,}000{,}000_i + \beta_2 Life\ Expectancy_i + \varepsilon_i$$

SUMMARY OUTPUT

Regression Statistics	
Multiple R	0.533152346
R Square	0.284251424
Adjusted R Square	0.260393138
Standard Error	2.31225486
Observations	63

ANOVA

	df	SS	MS	F	Significance F
Regression	2	127.3986451	63.6993225	11.91415955	4.39354E-05
Residual	60	320.7913524	5.34652254		
Total	62	448.1899975			

	Coefficients	Standard Error	*t* Stat	*P*-value	Lower 95%	Upper 95%
Intercept	−1.751760992	2.299069261	−0.76194354	0.449078516	−6.350584187	2.847062204
Pop./1,000,000	0.005025241	0.001232991	4.07564932	0.000136887	0.002558891	0.007491591
Life Expectancy	0.081180144	0.031455935	2.58075760	0.012321851	0.018258906	0.144101382

Statistical Inference:

For the *Population*/1,000,000 variable:

- Because *p*-value = 0.00 < 0.05, we reject H_0: $\beta_1 = 0$ and conclude that, holding life expectancy constant, each increase of 1,000,000 in *Population*/1,000,000 is estimated to increase *GDP*/1,000,000,000 by 0.5 percent.

For the *Life Expectancy* variable:

- Because *p*-value = 0.01 < 0.05, we reject H_0: $\beta_2 = 0$ and conclude that, holding population constant, each one ~~percent~~ year increase in *Life expectancy* is estimated to increase *GDP*/1,000,000,000 by 8.12 percent.

The Log-Log Model

Economists are often interested in estimating different elasticities (i.e., the price elasticity of demand, the income elasticity of demand, the cross-price elasticity of demand etc.). We can calculate such estimates by including both the log of the dependent variable and the log of the independent variable of interest in our multiple linear regression analysis. When we do so, we are said to be calculating a **log-log model,** because both the dependent and the independent variable are entered in log form.

log-log model
A regression model in which both the dependent and independent variable are logged. Under this circumstance, the slope coefficient on the independent variable is an elasticity.

There is an important issue associated with estimating a log-log model. Because it is impossible to calculate the natural log of 0, we cannot estimate a log-log model for variables for which observations are assigned a value of 0. In other words, we cannot calculate a log-log model for binary dummy variables. This fact is of little concern, however, because the concept of an elasticity does not apply to qualitative variables, and therefore, we would never want to estimate a log-log model for such variables. Of greater concern are quantitative variables that take on the value of 0. For example, in our 200-observation MLB position player sample, a significant percentage of players are rookies, meaning that they have 0 years of experience and hit 0 home runs. What if we wish to estimate a log-log model to determine the estimated elasticities of experience and home runs? There are two possibilities: (1) either drop all observations for which the value is 0 and estimate the elasticity for the remaining non-zero values or (2) convert the 0 values to values very close but not equal to 0, such as 0.0000000001, for which we are able to calculate the natural log. While both approaches are occasionally employed, we do not recommend their use because they are both rather arbitrary. Instead, in such cases, we recommend estimating a log-linear model.

Given that due to the presence of rookies, we cannot estimate a log-log model for our MLB position player sample, we turn to our 63-observation GDP sample and estimate the population multiple linear regression model:

$$ln(GDP/1{,}000{,}000{,}000)_i = \beta_0 + \beta_1 ln(Population/1{,}000{,}000)_i + \beta_2 ln(Life\ expectancy)_i + \varepsilon_i \quad 7.4.2$$

Empirical Research Tool 7.8 summarizes the log-log model.

EMPIRICAL RESEARCH TOOL 7.8: THE LOG-LOG MODEL

Goal:

Calculate the estimated marginal effects of given independent variables so that they represent estimated elasticities.

Process:

1. Calculate the natural log of the dependent variable, $\ln y_i$.
2. Calculate the natural log of the desired independent variables, say $\ln x_{2,i}$.
3. Estimate the sample regression function.

$$\widehat{\ln y_i} = \hat{\beta}_0 + \hat{\beta}_1 x_{1,i} + \hat{\beta}_2 \ln x_{2,i} + \cdots + \hat{\beta}_k x_{k,i}$$

Interpretation:

The estimated slope coefficient, $\hat{\beta}_2$, is denominated so that it indicates the percentage change in y_i resulting from a percentage change in $x_{2,i}$, or the estimated elasticity between y_i and $x_{2,i}$.

Example:

For the sample regression function

$$\ln \widehat{Tests\ Scores_i} = 2.34 + 2.98 \ln Hours\ studied_i + 1.36 \ln GPA_i$$

We would conclude that:

- Holding *GPA* constant, we estimate that if hours studied increases by 1 percent, then average test score increases by 2.98 percent.
- Holding *Hours studied* constant, we estimate that if GPA increase by 1 percent, then average test score increases by 1.36 percent.

Finally, Excel Example 7.8 demonstrates how to estimate and interpret a log-log model for our 63-observation international GDP sample.

EXCEL EXAMPLE 7.8

A log-log regression

For our GDP data, we create new variables *ln(Population/1,000,000$_i$)* and *ln(Life Expectancy$_i$)* and estimate the multiple linear regression model:

$$ln(GDP/1{,}000{,}000{,}000_i) = \beta_0 + \beta_1\ ln(Population/1{,}000{,}000_i) + \beta_2\ ln(Life\ Expectancy_i) + \varepsilon_i$$

SUMMARY OUTPUT

Regression Statistics	
Multiple R	0.962322684
R Square	0.926064948
Adjusted R Square	0.923600446
Standard Error	0.743157127
Observations	63

ANOVA

	df	SS	MS	F	Significance F
Regression	2	415.0530466	207.5265233	375.7615307	1.16282E-34
Residual	60	33.13695091	0.552282515		
Total	62	448.1899975			

	Coefficients	Standard Error	*t* Stat	*P*-value	Lower 95%	Upper 95%
Intercept	−27.2282786	2.786441016	−9.77170466	5.08643E-14	−32.80199053	−21.65456684
ln(Population/ 1,000,000)	0.96581453	0.036907717	26.16836281	1.63051E-34	0.89198810	1.03964095
ln(Life Expectancy)	6.97096513	0.649592838	10.73128386	1.38038E-15	5.67158600	8.27034426

Statistical Inference:

For the *Population*/1,000,000 variable:

- Because *p*-value = 1.63*E*-34 < 0.05, we *reject* H_0: $\beta_1 = 0$ and conclude that, holding life expectancy constant, each 1 percent increase in *Population*/1,000,000 is estimated to increase *GDP*/1,000,000,000 by 0.9658 percent.

For the *Life Expectancy* variable:

- Because *p*-value = 1.28*E*-15 < 0.05, we *reject* H_0: $\beta_2 = 0$ and conclude that, holding population constant, each 1 percent increase in *Life expectancy* is estimated to increase *GDP*/1,000,000,000 by 6.971 percent.

7.5 ESTIMATE A MORE FULLY SPECIFIED MODEL

Previous chapters focused on incremental changes to a fairly limited sample regression function in order to highlight the common approaches available for dealing with different types of data. In reality, rather than pursuing such an incremental approach, we would start our analysis by estimating a more fully specified model that is predicted by theory, such as:

$$\begin{aligned} ln(salary_i) = \beta_0 &+ \beta_1 Experience_i + \beta_2 Experience_i^2 + \beta_3 Home\ runs_i \\ &+ \beta_4 (Experience \cdot HomeRun)_i + \beta_5 Japanese_i \\ &+ \beta_6 (Experience \cdot Japanese)_i + \beta_7 Infielder_i + \beta_8 Outfielder_i \\ &+ \beta_9 DH_i + \varepsilon_i \end{aligned} \quad \textbf{7.5.1}$$

Excel Regression Output 7.9 presents the sample regression function for our 200-observation MLB position player sample regression function.

Excel Regression Output 7.9: Estimated Marginal Effects for the More Fully Specified Model

SUMMARY OUTPUT

Regression Statistics	
Multiple R	0.90110888
R Square	0.811997214
Adjusted R Square	0.803091818
Standard Error	0.564509743
Observations	200

ANOVA

	df	SS	MS	F	Significance F
Regression	9	261.5090585	29.05656206	91.18036878	4.21322E-64
Residual	190	60.54753743	0.31867125		
Total	199	322.056596			

	Coefficients	Standard Error	*t* Stat	*P*-value	Lower 95%	Upper 95%
Intercept	12.31757779	0.12825721	96.03809628	5.526E-163	12.06458685	12.57056874
Experience	0.44662410	0.02932681	15.22920842	9.41829E-35	0.38877614	0.50447205
Experience Squared	−0.02084327	0.00211184	−9.86970839	8.24865E-19	−0.02500894	−0.01667760
Home Runs	0.03919094	0.00639030	6.13287687	4.89983E-09	0.02658589	0.05179597
Experience × Home Runs	0.00136559	0.00092219	1.48080665	0.140314475	−0.00045346	0.00318464
Japanese	3.16062486	0.69194803	4.56771997	8.85182E-06	1.79573789	4.52551183
Experience × Japanese	−0.29705606	0.16059172	−1.84975956	0.065901332	−0.61382774	0.01971562
Infielder	0.37531797	0.11950524	3.14059854	0.001955645	0.13959053	0.61104541
Outfielder	0.32874647	0.12284486	2.67611087	0.008098866	0.08643153	0.57106142
DH	0.57075983	0.35408587	1.61192487	0.108638142	−0.12768452	1.26920418

Note: Dependent variable is log annual salary. Catchers are the omitted group. Variables highlighted in blue are significant at the 5 percent level. Variables highlighted in gray are significant at the 10 percent level.

Statistical Inference:

Overall significance:

- Because p-value = 4.21322*E*-64 < 0.05, we reject H_0: $\beta_1 = \beta_2 = \cdots = \beta_9 = 0$ and conclude that at least one of the explanatory variables help explain salary.

Individual significance:

- Because p-value *is* < 0.05 for *Experience, Experience Squared, Home Runs, Japanese, Infielder,* and *Outfielder,* we conclude that all of those variables are statistically significant at the 5 percent level.
- Because 0.05 < p-value *is* < 0.10 for *Experience* × *Japanese* and *DH,* we conclude that those variables are statistically significant at the 10 percent level.

Finally, Excel Example 7.9 demonstrates how the interpretion of a more fully specified model for our 63-observation international GDP sample.

EXCEL EXAMPLE 7.9

Estimating a more fully specified model for our international GDP data

For our GDP data, we estimate the multiple linear regression model:

$$
\begin{aligned}
ln(GDP/1{,}000{,}000{,}000_i) &= \beta_0 + \beta_1(Population/1{,}000{,}000)_i \\
&+ \beta_2 Top\ education\ quartile_i + \beta_3\left(\frac{Population}{1{,}000{,}000} \cdot Top\ education\ quartile\right)_i \\
&+ \beta_4 Log(Life\ expectancy) + \beta_5 Life\ Expectancy_i^2 \\
&+ \beta_6(Population/1{,}000{,}000 \cdot Life\ expectancy)_i + \beta_7 Africa_i \\
&+ \beta_8 Europe_i + \beta_9 North\ America_i + \beta_{10} South\ America_i + \varepsilon_i
\end{aligned}
$$

SUMMARY OUTPUT

Regression Statistics	
Multiple R	0.89513296
R Square	0.80126302
Adjusted R Square	0.76304437
Standard Error	1.30878631
Observations	63

ANOVA

	df	SS	MS	F	Significance F
Regression	10	359.1180741	35.91180741	20.965237	6.67212E-15
Residual	52	89.07192344	1.712921605		
Total	62	448.1899975			

	Coefficients	Standard Error	*t* Stat	*P*-value	Lower 95%	Upper 95%
Intercept	−10.25625574	8.788512424	−1.167007025	0.248531399	−27.89169572	7.379184251
Population/ 1,000,000	−0.076445959	0.029025964	−2.633709567	0.011097974	−0.134690816	−0.018201103
Top Ed. Quartile	3.926061175	0.453525269	8.656763905	1.18424E-11	3.015996164	4.836126186
Population/ 1,000,000 · Top Ed. Quartile	−0.068663706	0.008485677	−8.091718345	9.12066E-11	−0.085691461	−0.05163595
Life Expectancy	0.351807572	0.259973965	1.353241552	0.181832415	−0.169868343	0.87348348
Life Expectancy^2	−0.002527090	0.001927749	−1.310901789	0.195650868	−0.006395402	0.00134122
Population/ 1,000,000 · Life Expectancy	0.002010206	0.00045893	4.380196028	5.764E-05	0.001089294	0.002931117
Africa	1.279038591	0.75085068	1.703452664	0.09445363	−0.227653493	2.785730676
Eur	0.684256453	0.50709555	1.349363927	0.18306612	−0.333305206	1.701818112
NA	−0.062627778	0.53244456	−0.117623094	0.90681946	−1.131055947	1.005800391
SA	−0.118920278	0.75967679	−0.156540621	0.87621309	−1.643323263	1.4054S2707

Statistical Inference:

Overall significance:

- Because *p*-value = 6.67*E*-15 < 0.05, we reject H_0: $\beta_1 = \beta_2 = \cdots = \beta_{10} = 0$ and conclude that at least one of the explanatory variables help explain salary.

Individual significance:

- Because *p*-value *is* < 0.05 for *Population*/1,000,000, *Top education quartile*, *Population*/1,000,000 × *Top education quartile*, *Population*/1,000,000 · *Life expectancy*, we conclude that all of those variables are statistically significant at the 5 percent level.
- Because *p*-value *is* < 0.10 for *Africa*, we conclude that this variable is statistically significant at the 10 percent level.

ADDITIONS TO OUR EMPIRICAL RESEARCH TOOLKIT

In this chapter we have introduced a number of tools that will prove valuable when performing empirical research:

- Binary dummy variables and categorical variables.
- Interaction terms.
- Quadratic terms.
- Log-linear and log-log models.

OUR NEW EMPIRICAL TOOLS IN PRACTICE: USING WHAT WE HAVE LEARNED IN THIS CHAPTER

Because our former student suspected that there are potentially significant regional differences in the proclivity of young adults to marry in the United States, he classified his 90 different MSAs according to the nine different census regions in which they were located. To start developing an idea of whether the suspected cross-regional differences exist, the former student calculated the separate summary statistics for each of the nine census regions, producing Table 7.10.

Looking at the summary statistics in Table 7.10, our student concluded that the Mountain and Pacific census regions had by far the lowest relative ratios of unmarried women to unmarried men. Given such apparent geographical differences, the student included dummy variables for eight of the nine census regions (New England omitted) in his analysis, producing the sample regression function in Table 7.11.

Based on these results, our student concluded that, all other independent variables equal, cities with lower median incomes in the Mountain or Pacific region are locations in which women are relatively less likely to be married (perhaps suggesting that they are more likely to desire to be married than otherwise similar women in the Northeast). As a result, the student chose to switch jobs and relocate to a city in the Northwest that had a lower cost of living (and lower median income), and within a year he was engaged to his future wife, which we consider to be evidence of a successful empirical research project.

LOOKING AHEAD TO CHAPTER 8

While this chapter has introduced multiple linear regression analysis, there are still a number of issues that need to be addressed if we are to get the maximum value out of this very valuable tool. First, suppose that we are interested in determining the linear relationship between the dependent variable and a quality, such as a person's sex, rather than a quantity, such as years of work experience. Second, suppose that we suspect that the true relationship between the dependent variable and a given independent variable is actually quadratic rather than linear. Finally, suppose that we are interested in estimating the elasticity between the dependent variable and a given independent variable, which is defined as the percentage change in the dependent variable that results from a given percentage change in the independent variable. How might we address each of these situations? Chapter 8 introduces methods for dealing with such concerns in multiple linear regression analysis.

TABLE 7.10 **Summary Statistics by Census Region for Our Former Student's MSA Marriage Data**

	New England	Middle Atlantic	South Atlantic	East North Central	East South Central	West North Central	West South Central	Mountain	Pacific
Ratio Unmarried Women/100 Unmarried Men	125.787	124.519	120.865	119.295	126.655	118.648	118.733	107.332	109.415
	(3.455)	(2.959)	(5.372)	(5.847)	(4.831)	(6.154)	(9.467)	(6.548)	(5.013)
Population 18 and Over	1,345,141	2,222,538	1,453,892	1,779,435	766,963	1,274,459	1,505,309	1,110,123	2,212,774
	(1,292,671.0)	(4,284,281.0)	(1,322,469.0)	(1,934,038.0)	(315,612.1)	(898,705.2)	(1,503,246.0)	(907,060.4)	(2,685,320.0)
Percentage of Males BA or Higher	33.340	29.373	29.721	30.900	26.900	32.367	27.000	31.967	28.164
	(6.336)	(5.046)	(6.713)	(5.223)	(2.539)	(3.894)	(6.164)	(5.722)	(9.935)
Percentage of Females BA or Higher	34.140	27.736	28.600	29.445	26.586	31.783	26.055	28.756	27.864
	(5.529)	(5.331)	(6.607)	(5.614)	(2.437)	(3.349)	(5.922)	(4.520)	(8.879)
Median Income (thousands)	57.760	51.375	49.470	49.349	44.307	53.677	46.844	51.417	56.307
	(7.784)	(6.770)	(9.991)	(4.934)	(1.979)	(5.312)	(7.051)	(4.785)	(9.197)
Observation	5	11	19	11	7	6	11	9	11
Percentage of Observations	.056	.122	.211	.122	.078	.067	.122	.100	.122

TABLE 7.11 The Estimated Sample Multiple Linear Regression Function for Our Former Student's MSA Marriage Data

SUMMARY OUTPUT

Regression Statistics	
Multiple R	0.78652700
R Square	0.61862473
Adjusted R Square	0.55918962
Standard Error	5.49097641
Observations	90

ANOVA

	df	SS	MS	F	Significance F
Regression	12	3765.863998	313.8219998	10.40840611	7.64956E-12
Residual	77	2321.613293	30.15082198		
Total	89	6087.477291			

	Coefficients	Standard Error	*t* Stat	*P*-value	Lower 95%	Upper 95%
Intercept	145.6934038	5.84256044	24.93656766	1.26908E-38	134.0593798	157.3274278
Population 18 and Over	2.69285E-07	3.18025E-07	0.84674350	0.39976212	−3.63983E-07	9.02554E-07
Males BA or Higher	0.216659721	0.361877859	0.59870952	0.55112389	−0.50393114	0.93725053
Females BA or Higher	−0.35091428	0.38075257	−0.92163339	0.35959854	−1.10908949	0.40726093
Median Income (Thousands)	−0.26855983	0.15324922	−1.75243846	0.08367919	−0.57371801	0.03659835
Middle Atlantic	−4.60654988	3.21854429	−1.43125259	0.15640414	−11.0154902	1.80239048
South Atlantic	−8.33746687	2.98125542	−2.79662949	0.00651837	−14.2739047	−2.40102899
East North Central	−9.98665914	3.22990836	−3.09193265	0.00276895	−16.4182282	−3.55509002
East South Central	−3.84498164	3.48623390	−1.10290409	0.27350395	−10.7869601	3.09699682
West North Central	−8.83138504	3.39387337	−2.60244979	0.01109798	−15.5904502	−2.07431988
West South Central	−11.4926589	3.23117373	−3.55680625	0.00064611	−17.9267477	−5.05857016
Mountain	−21.6866804	3.46825714	−6.25290443	2.07684E-08	−28.5928626	−14.7804983
Pacific	−18.0767946	3.15172388	−5.73552611	1.81637E-07	−24.3526786	−11.8009107

Note: Dependent variable is ratio of unmarried women to 100 unmarried men in an MSA. New England is the omitted census region. Highlighted variables in blue are significant at the 5 percent level. Variable highlighted in light gray are significant at the 10 percent level.

Problems

7.1 The Polk Utility corporation is developing a multiple linear regression model that it plans to use to predict customers' utility usage. The analyst currently has three quantitative variables in the model (x_1, x_2, and x_3) but she is dissatisfied with the *R*-squared and the size of the standard error. Two variables that she thinks might be useful are whether a house has a gas or an electric water heater and whether a house was constructed before or after the 1974 energy crisis.

a. How many dummy variables would you set up to handle this situation?

b. Provide the model she should use to predict customers' utility usage.

c. What values do the new variables assume, and what does each coefficient on the dummy variable represent?

7.2 The June 1997 issue of *Management Accounting* gave the following rule for predicting your current salary if you are a managerial accountant. Take $31,865. Next add $20,811 if you are top management, add $3,604 if you are senior management, or subtract $11,419 if you are entry management. Then add $1,105 for every year you have been a managerial accountant. Add $7,600 if you have a master's degree or subtract $12,467 if you have no college degree. Add $11,527 if you have a professional certification. Finally, add $8,667 if you are male.

a. How do you think the journal derived this method of estimating an accountant's current salary? Be specific.

b. How could a managerial accountant use this information to determine whether he or she is significantly underpaid? Be as specific as possible.

7.3 Management proposed the following regression model to predict sales at a fast-food outlet:

$$y_i = \beta_0 + \beta_1 x_{1,i} + \beta_2 x_{2,i} + \beta_3 x_{3,i} + \varepsilon_i$$

where y_i = sales ($1000s)
$x_{1,i}$ = number of competitors within one mile
$x_{2,i}$ = population within one mile (1000s)
$x_{3,i}$ = 1 if a drive up window is present and 0 otherwise

The following estimated regression equation was developed after 20 outlets were surveyed:

$$\hat{y}_i = 10.1 - 4.2x_{1,i} + 6.8x_{2,i} + 15.3x_{3,i}$$

a. What is the expected amount of sales attributable to the drive-up window?

b. Predict sales for a store with two competitors, a population of 8,000 within one mile, and no drive-up window.

c. Predict sales for a store with one competitor, a population of 3,000 within one mile, and a drive-up window.

7.4 The white male professors at the University of Shucks Corner (USC) are threatening to sue the university for sexual discrimination. The kingpin behind the threatened suit regressed annual salaries (in thousands of dollars) of all the university professors (S) on the following variables:

D_{MA} = 1 if the professor is male, 0 otherwise

D_A = 1 if the professor is an associate professor, 0 otherwise

D_F = 1 if the professor is a full professor, 0 otherwise

And they obtained the following results (standard errors are in parentheses):

$$\hat{S} = \underset{(10.0)}{44.5} - \underset{(1.0)}{2.2}D_{MA} + \underset{(3.0)}{3.2}D_A + \underset{(5.2)}{18.4}D_F$$

where $n = 120$
$R^2 = 0.82$

Note: There are three ranks of professors (assistant, associate, and full professors listed from junior to senior) at USC.

a. Formally test the hypothesis that there is no sexual discrimination at USC. State your hypothesis clearly, show all work, etc. Use the tables provided if needed. Based on this formal test, what conclusion would you draw?

b. What assumptions are you implicitly making when you conducted the test in part (a)? Offer all assumptions you are making.

c. What, if anything, can you say about the average salary of male assistant professors relative to a male full professor based on the regression results?

d. Another fast-thinking professor thinks that the preceding model is not the most appropriate model to estimate. She thinks that either one of the following models will be much easier to interpret and help get at the issue more directly.

(1) $S_i = \beta_0 + \beta_1 D_{MA,i} + \beta_2 D_{FE,i} + \beta_3 D_{A,i} + \beta_4 D_{F,i} + \beta_5 D_{AT,i} + \varepsilon_i$

(2) $S_i = \beta_1 D_{MA,i} + \beta_2 D_{FE,i} + \beta_3 D_{F,i} + \beta_4 D_{AT,i} + \varepsilon_i$

where all variables are as defined earlier and

D_{FE} = 1 if the professor is female, 0 otherwise

D_{AT} = 1 if the professor is an assistant professor, 0 otherwise

Discuss the feasibility of the two proposed options and their advantages and disadvantages over the original model (if any).

e. Suppose you have been hired by the university to defend USC. What would be your approach in terms of trying to discredit the analysis of those suing the university?

7.5 The following table contains the OLS coefficient estimates of the *Income* model, where $Income_i$ is a dependent variable. Estimated standard errors are reported in parentheses below the coefficient estimates.

$Income_i$ = Annual income of individual i, measured in thousands of dollars

Age_i = Age of individual i, measured in years

$Experience_i$ = Work experience of individual i, measured in years

$Female_i$ = 1 if individual i is female, 0 otherwise

	(1)	(2)
Intercept	9.6849	45.667
	(3.826)	(16.220)
Age	0.40762	−1.4581
	(.103)	(.938)
Age Squared	—	0.0118
		(.012)
Experience	—	1.1994
		(.454)
Female	—	−57.737
		(30.090)
Female × Age	—	2.9376
		(1.679)
Female × Age Squared	—	−0.0317
		(.022)
Female × Experience	—	−0.967
		(.803)
R-squared	0.168	0.5926
SSR	5,207.7	2,549.9
Observations	80	80

a. According to regression (1), explain how age is related to income.

b. Is age statistically significant in regression (1)? Be as specific as possible when answering this question.

c. The results of regression (2) conflict with these results. Why?

d. There is one formal test to see whether regression (2) or regression (1) is preferable. State your null and alternative hypotheses. Calculate the required test statistic, state the decision rule you use, and the inference you draw from the test. Test the hypothesis at a 5 percent significance level.

e. In regression (2), what is the marginal effect of being female on income?

7.6 Suppose that we are trying to explain wage using gender and years of education.

a. Write out a model that allows the intercept between males and females to differ. Define your dummy variable, and explain what the coefficients mean.

b. Now write out a model that allows the slopes to differ as well. Now explain what the coefficients mean.

c. If women with no education started out at a lower salary than men with no education, but then had larger returns to education, what sign would you expect your coefficients from part (b) to have? Draw the relevant picture for the above scenario.

7.7 Suppose you are interested in estimating how a faculty member's salary is related to whether they have moved to a different university during their career and whether they moved to or from California. Regressions are given in the accompanying table. The dependent variable is the natural log of annual salary. The independent variables are a 1 if the person moved and 0 otherwise; number of years since last moved is a 1 if the person moved to California and 0 otherwise; number of years since moved to California is 1 if the person moved from California and 0 otherwise; number of years since moved from California, number of years of experience, number of years of experience squared, Male is 1 if the person is male and 0 otherwise, the number of top 5 articles the faculty member has published, the number of top 36 articles the faculty member has published, and number of other articles published. Standard errors are in the parentheses below the coefficient estimates.

	(1) All Faculty	(2) All Faculty
Moved	0.1134	0.0490
	(0.0203)	(0.0215)
Years since last move	−0.0063	−0.0058
	(0.0010)	(0.0010)
Moved to CA	—	0.1271
	—	(0.0562)
Years since move to CA	—	−0.0022
	—	(0.0031)
Moved from CA	—	0.1265
	—	(0.0399)
Years since move from CA	—	−0.0017
	—	(0.0020)
Experience	0.0113	0.0115
	.0029)	(0.0028)
Experience squared	−0.00015	−0.00015
	(0.00007)	(0.00006)
Male	0.0066	0.0141
	(0.0190)	(0.0190)
Top 5 articles	0.0357	0.0308
	(0.0034)	(0.0033)
Top 36 articles	0.0056	0.0063
	(0.0029)	(0.0028)
Other articles	0.0035	0.0037
	(0.0008)	(0.0008)
R-square	0.4794	0.5025
Observations	1024	1024

a. Consider the regression results contained in column 1. Explain the marginal effects of moved, experience, male, and top 5 articles, and comment if the coefficient estimates are statistically significant at the 5 percent level.

b. Now consider the results contained in column 2. Explain what the marginal effects on moved to California and moved from California mean, and comment if each of these are statistically significant.

c. Is regression (1) or regression (2) statistically preferred at the 5 percent level? Provide the hypothesis, test statistic, rejection rule, and your decision.

d. Where does the experience term reach a maximum? What does this number mean to a faculty member?

e. If you were going to give advice to a faculty member on how to maximize their salary using your preferred model from part (d), what would you tell them?

Exercises

E7.1 Suppose you think that there are diminishing returns to studying. Test this hypothesis by opening up the file survey **data.xls** and creating a new variable *Hours study squared.*

a. Regress *GPA* on *Hours studied* and *Hours studied squared.* Explain how *Hours studied* affects *GPA,* and comment on the statistical significance of the independent variables at the 5 percent level.

b. Where does *Hours studied* reach a maximum?

c. Now estimate a more fully specified model by regressing *GPA* on *Hours studied, Hours studied squared, Work, Video game, Texts,* and *Male.* Interpret the marginal effect of *Hours studied,* and comment on the statistical significance of all of the independent variables at the 5 percent level.

E7.2 A human resources manager at ABC Inc. is trying to determine the variable that best explains the variation of employee salaries using the sample of 52 full-time employees in the file **ABC.xls**. Create a table of correlation coefficients to help this manager identify whether the employee's (a) gender, (b) age, (c) number of years of relevant work experience prior to employment at Beta, (d) the number of years of employment at Beta, or (e) the number of years of postsecondary education has the strongest linear relationship with annual salary. Which of these variables has the weakest linear relationship with annual salary?

E7.3 The National Basketball Association (NBA) records a variety of statistics for each team. Four of these statistics are the proportion of games won (*PCT*), the proportion of field goals made by the team (*FG%*), the proportion of three-point shots made by the team's opponent (*OPP 3 PT%*), and the number of turnovers committed by the team's opponent (*Opp TO*). The data contained in **NBA.xls** show the values of these statistics for the 29 teams in the NBA for a portion of the 2004 season (www.nba.com, January 3, 2004).

a. Determine the estimated regression equation that can be used to predict the proportion of games won given the proportion of field goals made by the team.

b. Provide an interpretation for the slope of the estimated regression equation developed in part (a).

c. Determine the estimated regression equation that can be used to predict the proportion of games won given the proportion of field goals made by the team, the proportion of three-point shots made by the team's opponent, and the number of turnovers committed by the team's opponent.

d. Discuss the implications of the estimated regression equations developed in part (c).

e. Estimate the proportion of games won for a team with the following values for the three independent variables: $FG\% = 0.45$, $Opp\ 3\ Pt\% = 0.34$, and $Opp\ TO = 17$.

f. Does the estimated regression equation provide a good fit for the data? Explain.

g. Use the *F*-test to determine the overall significance of the relationship. What is your conclusion at the 0.05 level of significance?

h. Use the *t*-test to determine the significance of each independent variable. What is your conclusion at the 0.05 level of significance?

E7.4 The National Football League rates prospects by position on a scale that ranges from 5 to 9. The ratings are interpreted as follows: 8–9 should start the first year; 7–7.9

should start; 6–6.9 will make the team as backup; and 5–5.9 can make the club and contribute. The file **Football.xls** shows the position, weight, speed (for 40 yards), and ratings for 25 NFL prospects (*USA Today,* April 14, 2000).

a. Develop a dummy variable that will account for the player's position.

b. Develop an estimated regression equation to show how rating is related to position, weight, and speed.

c. At the 0.05 level of significance, test whether the estimated regression equation indicates a significant relationship between the independent variables and the dependent variable.

d. Does the estimated regression equation provide a good fit for the data? Explain.

e. Is position a significant factor in the payer's rating? Use a significance level of 0.05. Explain.

f. Suppose that a new offensive tackle prospect who weighs 300 pounds ran the 40 yards in 5.1 seconds. Use the estimated regression equation developed in part (b) to estimate the ratings for this player. What will this player's role be on the team next year?

E7.5 Open file **Housing price.xls**.

a. Regress housing price on square feet, bedrooms, lot size, and pool. Explain what each of the coefficients mean, and comment on the statistical significance for each coefficient at a 5 percent significance level.

b. Now suppose that you think that an interaction effect exists between bedrooms and lot size. Create a new variable in Excel to reflect this, and add this variable to your regression you estimated in part (a). Comment on the statistical significance of all of the variables at a 5 percent level, and explain the marginal effects of both bedrooms and square feet.

E7.6 Open file **Housing price.xls**.

a. Create a new variable log housing price by using the ln function in Excel. Regress log housing price on square feet, bedrooms, lot size, and pool. Explain what each of the coefficients mean, and comment on the statistical significance for each coefficient at a 5 percent significance level.

b. Create another new variable log square feet. Regress log housing price on log square feet, bedrooms, lot size, and pool. Explain what each of the coefficients mean, and comment on the statistical significance for each coefficient at a 5 percent significance level.

E7.7 Open file **Video game xls**. Regress units sold on time since announcement, PS3 consoles sold, average rating, online MP, sequel, part of series, and multi-platform. Comment on the statistical significance of each variable at the 5 percent level. What variables would you suggest keeping, and which ones would you not include? Why? Using an F-test, test whether the variables you would omit are jointly significantly significant at a 5 percent level.

Chapter Eight

Model Selection in Multiple Linear Regression Analysis

CHAPTER OBJECTIVES

After reading this chapter, you will be able to:

1. Understand the problem presented by omitted variable bias.
2. Understand the problem presented by including an irrelevant variable.
3. Understand the problem presented by missing data.
4. Understand the problem presented by outliers.
5. Perform the reset test for the inclusion of higher-order polynomials.
6. Perform the Davidson-MacKinnon test for choosing among non-nested alternatives.
7. Consider how to implement the "eye test" to judge the sample regression function.
8. Consider what it means for a *p*-value to be just above a given cutoff.

A STUDENT'S PERSPECTIVE

Continuing with our former student who was interested in empirically determining the U.S. city in which he was most likely to find a significant other, at the end of Chapter 7, we learned that his sample regression function was

$$\begin{aligned}\widehat{Unmarried\ women\ ratio} = {} & 140.21 + 3.25E - 07Population \\ & - 0.481 \times \%Males\ BA\ or\ higher \\ & + 0.719 \times \%Females\ BA\ or\ higher \\ & - 0.558 \times Median\ income\ (thousands) \qquad \textbf{8.1}\end{aligned}$$

While we have learned how to correctly interpret these estimates and how to use them to learn about the unobserved population regression model, we have not yet to considered whether the sample multiple linear regression function in formula 8.1 is actually the most preferred specification for this analysis. While correct model specification is much more art than science, this chapter introduces some factors that should be considered and some tools that might be employed when choosing a most preferred model.

BIG PICTURE OVERVIEW

Recall that in Section 7.5, we estimated the more fully specified population regression model:

$$\begin{aligned} Log\ Salary_i = {} & \beta_0 + \beta_1 Experience_i + \beta_2 Experience_i^2 + \beta_3 Home\ runs_i \\ & + \beta_4 (Experience \cdot Home\ run)_i + \beta_5 Japanese_i \\ & + \beta_6 (Experience \cdot Japanese)_i + \beta_7 Infielder_i \\ & + \beta_8 Outfielder_i + \beta_9 DH_i + \varepsilon_i \end{aligned} \qquad \textbf{8.2}$$

for our 200-observation MLB position player sample, with Excel Regression Output 8.1 repeating the results.

Excel Regression Output 8.1: Estimated Marginal Effects for the More Fully Specified Model

SUMMARY OUTPUT

Regression Statistics	
Multiple R	0.90110888
R Square	0.811997214
Adjusted R Square	0.803091818
Standard Error	0.564509743
Observations	200

ANOVA

	df	SS	MS	F	Significance F
Regression	9	261.5090585	29.05656206	91.18036878	4.21322E-64
Residual	190	60.54753743	0.31867125		
Total	199	322.056596			

	Coefficients	Standard Error	*t* Stat	*p*-value	Lower 95%	Upper 95%
Intercept	12.31757779	0.12825721	96.03809628	5.526E-163	12.06458685	12.57056874
Experience	0.44662410	0.02932681	15.22920842	9.41829E-35	0.38877614	0.50447205
Experience Squared	−0.02084327	0.00211184	−9.86970839	8.24865E-19	−0.02500894	−0.01667760
Home Runs	0.03919094	0.00639030	6.13287687	4.89983E-09	0.02658589	0.05179597
Experience × Home Runs	0.00136559	0.00092219	1.48080665	0.140314475	−0.00045346	0.00318464
Japanese	3.16062486	0.69194803	4.56771997	8.85182E-06	1.79573789	4.52551183
Experience × Japanese	−0.29705606	0.16059172	−1.84975956	0.065901332	−0.61382774	0.01971562
Infielder	0.37531797	0.11950524	3.14059854	0.001955645	0.13959053	0.61104542
Outfielder	0.32874647	0.12284486	2.67611087	0.008098866	0.08643153	0.57106142
DH	0.57075983	0.35408587	1.61192487	0.108638142	−0.12768452	1.26920418

Note: Dependent variable is log annual salary. Catchers are the omitted group. Variables highlighted in blue are significant at the 5 percent level. Variables highlighted in gray are significant at the 10 percent level.

Statistical Inference:

Overall significance:

- Because *p*-value = 4.21322E – 64 – 63 < 0.05, we reject $H_0{:}\beta_1 = \beta_2 = \cdots = \beta_9 = 0$ and conclude that at least one of the explanatory variables help explain salary.

Individual significance:

- Because *p*-value *is* < 0.05 for *Experience, Experience Squared, Home Runs, Japanese, Infielder,* and *Outfielder,* we conclude that all of those variables are statistically significant at the 5 percent level.
- Because 0.05 < *p*-value *is* < 0.10 for *Experience* × *Japanese* and *DH,* we conclude that those variables are statistically significant at the 10 percent level.

As mentioned earlier, we are unlikely to ever be certain that we have included every single independent variable that is correlated with the dependent variable. This in no way means that we should simply accept our best effort as fact because there is no way to prove that ours is the absolutely "correct" model. Instead, we should perform due diligence to make sure that we have identified and included all potentially important independent variables in our analysis. This is exactly the reason that we encourage a thorough literature review after writing out the model motivated by our intuition and training. From experience, we know that turning to the skills and insights of others often identifies potentially important independent variables that we had not initially considered.

Figure 8.1 visually summarizes the empirical tools introduced in this chapter.

FIGURE 8.1
A Visual Depiction of the Empirical Tools Introduced in This Chapter

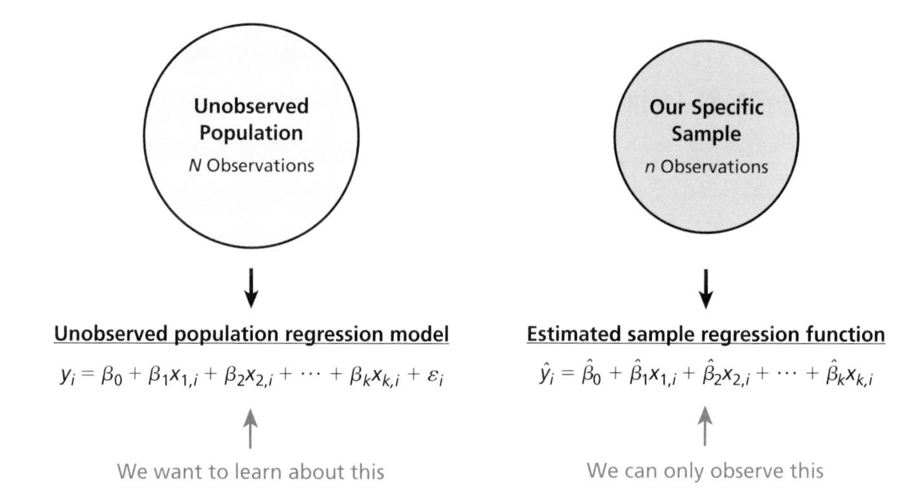

Question: How do we know that the population regression model is correctly specified?

Answer: We should consider a number of things

(1) Omitted variable bias
(2) Inclusion of irrelevant variables
(3) Missing data
(4) Outliers
(5) The inclusion of higher-order polynomials } The Reset Test
(6) Choosing among non-nested alternatives } The Davidson-MacKinnon Test

For the sake of continuity, we continue to focus the discussion in this chapter on our 200-observation MLB position player sample and our 63-observation international GDP sample.

8.1 UNDERSTAND THE PROBLEM PRESENTED BY OMITTED VARIABLE BIAS

As an example of why it is important to make sure that we have identified and included all potentially important independent variables in our estimation, suppose we fail to identify and include the variables Home Run and Home Run · Experience. We would then estimate the model

$$\begin{aligned} Log\ salary_i = \beta_0 &+ \beta_1 Experience_i + \beta_2 Experience_i^2 + \beta_3 Japanese_i \\ &+ \beta_4 (Experience \cdot Japanese)_i + \beta_5 Infielder_i \\ &+ \beta_6 Outfielder_i + \beta_7 DH_i + \varepsilon_i \end{aligned} \quad \textbf{8.1.1}$$

and get Excel Regression Output 8.2.

Excel Regression Output 8.2: Regression Output for Our MLB Position Player Sample with the Home Run Variables Omitted

SUMMARY OUTPUT	
Regression Statistics	
Multiple R	0.827483651
R Square	0.684729193
Adjusted R Square	0.673234945
Standard Error	0.72720585
Observations	200

ANOVA

	df	SS	MS	F	Significance F
Regression	7	220.5215532	31.50307902	59.57146425	8.34234E-45
Residual	192	101.5350428	0.528828348		
Total	199	322.056596			

	Coefficients	Standard Error	*t* Stat	*p*-value	Lower 95%	Upper 95%
Intercept	12.363387460	0.154999148	79.76422849	3.7696E-149	12.05766769	12.66910723
Experience	0.555158477	0.035637509	15.57792613	6.57598E-36	0.48486718	0.62544977
Experience Squared	−0.025474442	0.002570865	−9.90889807	5.89799E-19	−0.03054521	−0.02040368
Japanese	3.260945435	0.891038722	3.65971237	0.000326219	1.50346383	5.01842705
Experience × Japanese	−0.368993243	0.206666433	−1.78545319	0.075766296	−0.77662138	0.03863490
Infielder	0.493556314	0.151820949	3.25091047	0.001358594	0.19410521	0.79300742
Outfielder	0.556215517	0.155528625	3.57629033	0.000441021	0.24945141	0.86297962
DH	1.064636556	0.444886112	2.39305415	0.017672509	0.18714477	1.94212834

Note: The dependent variable is log annual salary. Catcher is the omitted position. Variables highlighted in blue are significant at the 5 percent level. Variables highlighted in gray are significant at the 10 percent level

omitted variable bias
The bias that results in the coefficient estimates when a variable is omitted from the model that explains the dependent variable and is also related to one or more of the explanatory variables.

When comparing the results in Excel Regression Output 8.1 with the results in Excel Regression Output 8.2, we should notice that the estimated slope coefficients and the estimated statistical significance have changed for some variables. This highlights the importance of taking steps to avoid **omitted variable bias** because, if we do not, the OLS estimates are on average wrong and we will likely draw incorrect inferences from our results.

For this reason, we encourage devoting our full effort to researching and identifying all independent variables that economic theory (and previous research) suggests should be included in our econometric specification.

8.2 UNDERSTAND THE PROBLEM PRESENTED BY INCLUDING AN IRRELEVANT VARIABLE

On a somewhat similar note, suppose that rather than omitting a theoretically justified independent variable, we include a variable that, in actuality, has no reasonable theoretical relation to the dependent variable. This also has the potential to negatively affect our ability to perform statistical inference. As an extreme example, suppose that we create a new variable, *Letter B,* which is equal to 1 if the first letter in a player's last name starts with B and 0 otherwise. Does it make sense that, all other independent variables constant, a player whose last name starts with B earns a statistically different salary than a player whose last name does not end with B? Most likely not. Yet, if we estimate the population following regression model

$$\begin{aligned} ln(Salary_i) = {} & \beta_0 + \beta_1 Experience_i + \beta_2 Experience_i^2 + \beta_3 Home\ runs_i \\ & + \beta_4 (Experience \cdot Home\ runs)_i + \beta_5 Japanese_i \\ & + \beta_6 (Experience \cdot Japanese)_i + \beta_7 Infielder_i \\ & + \beta_8 Outfielder_i + \beta_9 DH_i + \beta_{10} Letter\ B_i + \varepsilon_i \end{aligned} \qquad 8.2.1$$

we get the results shown in Excel Regression Output 8.3.

Excel Regression Output 8.3: Regression Output for Our MLB Position Player Sample with the Irrelevant Variable, Letter B, Included

SUMMARY OUTPUT

Regression Statistics	
Multiple R	0.904095079
R Square	0.817387912
Adjusted R Square	0.807725896
Standard Error	0.557827549
Observations	200

ANOVA

	df	SS	MS	F	Significance F
Regression	10	263.2451684	26.32451684	84.59807707	2.72324E-64
Residual	189	58.81142758	0.311171574		
Total	199	322.056596			

	Coefficients	Standard Error	*t* Stat	*p*-value	Lower 95%	Upper 95%
Intercept	12.33384557	0.12692599	97.1735199	2.711E-163	12.08347199	12.58421916
Experience	0.45332352	0.02911813	15.5684295	1.04307E-35	0.39588525	0.51076179
Experience Squared	−0.02134480	0.00209762	−10.17573247	1.13492E-19	−0.02548255	−0.01720705
Home Runs	0.03885548	0.00631626	6.15166354	4.47612E-09	0.02639607	0.05131491
Experience × Home Runs	0.00144107	0.00091184	1.580405353	0.115686154	−0.00035761	0.00323975
Japanese	3.14162601	0.68380464	4.594332679	7.91697E-06	1.79275637	4.49049564
Experience × Japanese	−0.30097608	0.15869944	−1.89651628	0.059417142	−0.61402581	0.01207366
Infielder	0.38462210	0.11815631	3.2551973	0.001342754	0.15154755	0.61769665
Outfielder	0.33179940	0.12139761	2.73316256	0.006868521	0.09233108	0.57126772
DH	0.63968325	0.35110911	1.82189304	0.070051928	−0.05291284	1.33227933
Letter B	−0.29009513	0.12281511	−2.36204759	0.019191153	−0.53235961	−0.04783066

Note: The dependent variable is log annual salary. Catcher is the omitted position. Variables highlighted in blue are significant at the 5 percent level. Variables highlighted in gray are significant at the 10 percent level.

inclusion of an irrelevant variable
Occurs when variable is included in the regression model but is unrelated to the dependent variable.

When comparing the results in Excel Regression Output 8.1 with the results in Excel Regression Output 8.3, we see that the included irrelevant variable is estimated to achieve statistical significance even though it makes absolutely no economic sense. We refer to this issue as the **inclusion of an irrelevant variable,** which does not lead to biased estimates but may cause larger the standard errors. Again, the potential that such an issue exists highlights the importance of seriously considering the theoretical underpinnings of our chosen empirical specification before estimating our population regression model.

8.3 UNDERSTAND THE PROBLEM PRESENTED BY MISSING DATA

When collecting data, we often encounter cases in which we are unable to collect data for some of the observations in the sample. One of the advantages of our MLB position player data, and one of the reasons that "more is known about pay and quantified performance in this market than in any other labor market in the American economy" (Hakes and Sauer, 2006) is that due to the nature of baseball statistics, there are almost no variables for which data are not recorded. For this reason, we cannot rely on our MLB sample as an example in which missing data exist. Instead, we turn to our international GDP sample, which is a prime example of missing data because some countries are either unable to or fail to report data for a number of our desired independent variables. As an example, while macroeconomic theory predicts that investments in human capital are an important component of economic growth, a common measure of human capital investment—educational expenditures as a percentage of GDP—is missing for 11 of the 63 countries in our specific international GDP random sample. Table 8.1 presents the data for these countries, as well as the data for several countries with nonmissing data.

TABLE 8.1
Variables with Missing Education Expenditure Data for Our 63-Observation International GDP Sample

id	Country	Ln(GDP/1,000,000,000)	Education Expenditure % of GDP
21	Greenland	0.10	—
25	Jersey	1.63	—
27	Korea, South	7.15	—
33	Liberia	0.43	—
37	Morocco	4.92	—
39	New Caledonia	1.15	—
41	Northern Mariana Island	−0.11	—
48	San Marino	0.51	—
53	Suriname	1.45	—
56	Taiwan	6.61	—
58	Timor-Leste	1.00	—
2	Andorra	1.30	2.3
3	Aruba	0.81	4.8
4	Bahamas, The	2.17	3.6
5	Belarus	4.74	6.1
6	Burkina Faso	2.88	4.2

Given that Excel will not estimate regressions for data with missing values, we must somehow correct for these missing observations. Empirically, we have two options for doing so:

1. If we do not believe the data to be missing due to some sort of systematic process, we could simply drop the observations with missing data and estimate the model for the observations with non-missing data.
2. We could create a new dummy variable, which is equal to 1, if the data are missing for a given observation, and we could set the value of the variable for which the data are missing equal to 0 for those observations with missing data (and for which the "data missing" dummy variable is equal to 1).

Following the first approach, we would estimate the population regression model

$$\begin{aligned} ln(GDP/1{,}000{,}000{,}000_i) = {} & \beta_0 + \beta_1(Population/1{,}000{,}000)_i + \beta_2 Top\ education\ quartile_i \\ & + \beta_3\left(\frac{Population}{1{,}000{,}000} \cdot Top\ education\ quartile\right)_i \\ & + \beta_4 Log(Life\ expectancy) + \beta_5 Life\ expectancy_i^2 \\ & + \beta_6(Population/1{,}000{,}000 \cdot Life\ expectancy)_i \end{aligned}$$

$$+ \beta_7 Africa_i + \beta_8 Europe_i + \beta_9 North\ America_i + \beta_{10} South\ America_i + \beta_{11} Education\ expenditure\ \%\ of\ GDP_i + \varepsilon_i \quad \mathbf{8.3.1}$$

for the 51 out of 63 observations with nonmissing data, and we would get Excel Regression Output 8.4.

Excel Regression Output 8.4: Regression Output for Our International GDP Sample with the Missing Observations Deleted

SUMMARY OUTPUT

Regression Statistics	
Multiple R	0.906239068
R Square	0.821269249
Adjusted R Square	0.770858011
Standard Error	1.182065974
Observations	51 ⟵ We dropped the 12 observations with missing values

ANOVA

	df	SS	MS	F	Significance F
Regression	11	250.3999979	22.76363617	16.29139235	2.48319E-11
Residual	39	54.49391872	1.397279967		
Total	50	304.8939166			

	Coefficients	Standard Error	*t* Stat	*p*-value	Lower 95%	Upper 95%
Intercept	−0.98368875	14.67201214	−0.06704525	0.946888219	−30.6606342	28.6932567
Pop./1,000,000	−0.06404479	0.031584149	−2.02775104	0.049457049	−0.12792976	−0.00015982
Top Ed. Quartile	3.49171439	0.490284961	7.12180595	1.45907E-08	2.50001942	4.48340928
Population/ 1,000,000 × Top Ed. Quartile	−0.05686613	0.008586185	−6.62298039	7.08622E-08	−0.07423333	−0.03949894
Life Expectancy	0.06810047	0.422018738	0.16136837	0.87263635	−0.78551299	0.92171394
Life Expectancy^2	−0.00052589	0.003026809	−0.17374453	0.86296495	−0.00664819	0.00559641
Population/ 1,000,000 × Life Expectancy	0.00168872	0.000490211	3.44487697	0.00138058	0.00069717	0.00268026
Africa	0.97944184	0.887848228	1.10316359	0.27671690	−0.81640070	2.77528437
Europe	0.58426368	0.551545059	1.05932175	0.29597024	−0.53134149	1.69986885
North America	−0.20845167	0.601664286	−0.34645844	0.73086055	−1.42543255	1.00852921
South America	0.35338032	0.820206791	0.43084296	0.66895453	−1.30564449	2.01240513
Education Expend % of GDP	0.24917576	0.152150532	l.63769234	0.10953058	−0.05857774	0.55692926

Note: The dependent variable is log real GDP. Asia is the omitted continent. Highlighted variables are significant at the 5 percent level.

Following the second approach, we would first create the new dummy variable *Missing*, which is equal to 1 if a country's educational expenditure data are missing, and we would replace the missing observation with a 0 for all observations for which the variable *Missing* equals 1. Doing so produces the data in Table 8.2.

TABLE 8.2 Constructing the Dummy Variable for Missing Data and Setting the Missing Observations to 0 for Our International GDP Data

id	Country	Ln(GDP/1,000,000,000)	Education Expenditure % of GDP	Education Expenditure Missing
21	Greenland	0.10	0	1
25	Jersey	1.63	0	1
28	Korea, South	7.15	0	1
33	Libería	0.43	0	1
37	Morocco	4.92	0	1
39	New Caledonia	1.15	0	1
41	Northern Mariana Island	−0.11	0	1
48	San Marino	0.51	0	1
53	Suriname	1.45	0	1
56	Taiwan	6.61	0	1
58	Timor-Leste	1.00	0	1
2	Andorra	1.30	2.3	0
3	Aruba	0.81	4.8	0
4	Bahamas, The	2.17	3.6	0
5	Belarus	4.74	6.1	0

After creating the new dummy variable and setting the missing values of the independent variable to 0, we would control for the potential effects of the missing data by estimating the following population regression model:

$$\begin{aligned} ln(GDP/1{,}000{,}000{,}000_i) = {} & \beta_0 + \beta_1(Population/1{,}000{,}000)_i + \beta_2 Top\ education\ quartile_i \\ & + \beta_3\left(\frac{Population}{1{,}000{,}000}\cdot Top\ education\ quartile\right)_i \\ & + \beta_4 log(Life\ expectancy) + \beta_5 Life\ expectancy_i^2 \\ & + \beta_6(Population/1{,}000{,}000 \cdot Life\ expectancy)_i \\ & + \beta_7 Africa_i + \beta_8 Europe_i + \beta_9 North\ America_i \\ & + \beta_{10} South\ America_i \\ & + \beta_{11} Education\ expenditure\ \%\ of\ GDP_i \\ & + \beta_{12} Education\ expenditure\ missing_i + \varepsilon_i \end{aligned} \quad \text{8.3.2}$$

for all 63 observations in our sample, and we would get the results shown in Excel Regression Output 8.5.

Excel Regression Output 8.5: Regression Output for Our International GDP Sample with the Missing Observation Dummy Variable Included and the Missing Values Set to 0

SUMMARY OUTPUT	
Regression Statistics	
Multiple R	0.90440498
R Square	0.817948369
Adjusted R Square	0.774255977
Standard Error	1.277448396
Observations	**63**

ANOVA

	df	SS	MS	F	Significance F
Regression	12	366.5962773	30.54968977	18.72061335	1.74233E-14
Residual	50	81.5937202	1.63187441		
Total	62	448.1899975			

	Coefficients	Standard Error	*t* Stat	*p*-value	Lower 95%	Upper 95%
Intercept	−7.46390993	8.87982942	−0.84054654	0.40460372	−25.2995719	10.37175202
Population/ 1,000,000	−0.06624490	0.02908885	−2.27732928	0.02707798	−0.12467158	−0.00781822
Top Ed. Quaitile	3.47510003	0.50178184	6.92551976	7.84795E-09	2.46724157	4.48295849
Population/ 1,000,000 × Top Ed. Quartile	−0.06605682	0.00841076	−7.85384999	2.80051E-10	−0.082950315	−0.04916332
Life Expectancy	0.22260519	0.26491894	0.84027664	0.40475356	−0.309500138	0.75471053
Life Expectancy^2	−0.00143054	0.00198530	−0.72056263	0.47453411	−0.005418135	0.00255706
Population/ 1,000,000 × Life Expectancy	0.00184298	0.00045731	4.03005343	0.00019000	0.000924448	0.00276151
Africa	1.22250493	0.73495716	1.66336897	0.10249509	−0.25369994	2.69870980
Europe	0.22881540	0.54495444	0.41987987	0.67637204	−0.86575778	1.32338858
North America	−0.51376109	0.56105123	−0.91571156	0.36421365	−1.64066563	0.61314344
South America	0.00239690	0.74407462	0.00322131	0.99744258	−1.49212093	1.49691472
Education Expend % of GDP	0.29154938	0.16018458	1.82008395	0.07473470	−0.03019081	0.61328957
Ed. Exp. Missing	0.52459602	0.77281349	0.67881322	0.50038632	−1.02764553	2.07683757

Note: The dependent variable is log real GDP. Asia is the omitted continent. Highlighted variables are significant at the 5 percent level. Variables highlighted in gray are significant at the 5 percent level

Given that we estimate a statistically insignificant effect for the Ed. Exp. Missing dummy variable, we can conclude that omitting the data with missing values, as we have been doing, does not have any significant effect on our results.

8.4 UNDERSTAND THE PROBLEM PRESENTED BY OUTLIERS

In previous chapters, we have seen that outliers can significantly affect the calculated values of sample statistics, such as the sample mean. The same potential holds for the slope coefficients estimated by OLS. To determine the potential outliers in our 200-observation MLB position player, we create the scatterplot in Figure 8.2.

Figure 8.2 indicates that five players earn salaries that are more than 3 standard deviations above the mean, while one player's home runs were more than 3 standard deviations above the mean. Our question is whether these potential outliers exert undue influence over our results, thereby rendering our OLS estimated biased.

While some researchers are undoubtedly tempted to deal with this situation by simply dropping the observations that are suspected to be outliers, we believe that it is never an acceptable option to simply delete data that might cause problems with our estimation. Instead, steps should be taken to control for the potential problems without dropping the suspect data (which would bias our results).

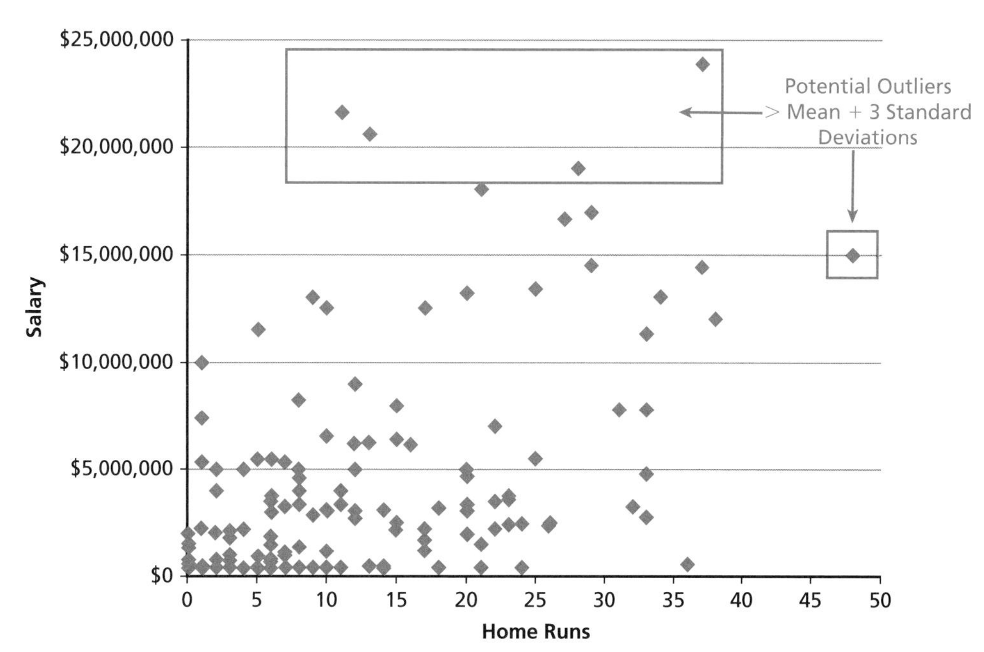

FIGURE 8.2 **Scatter Diagram of Salary versus Home Runs Indicating Potential Outliers for Both Variables**

In this case, we might control for the effect that potential outliers have on our estimates by constructing the binary dummy variables *Salary Outlier* and *HR Outlier.* Doing so produces the data in Table 8.3.

TABLE 8.3 **Constructing the Outlier Dummy Variables for Our 200-Observation MLB Position Player Sample**

id	Player	Salary	Salary Outliers	HR	HR Outliers
13	Lee, Carlos	$19,000,000	1	28	0
14	Flores, Jesus	$415,500	0	8	0
15	Jeter, Derek	$21,600,000	1	11	0
16	Ausmus, Brad	$1,000,000	0	3	0
17	Crawford, Carl	$8,250,000	0	8	0
18	Quintanilla, Omar	$408,000	0	2	0
19	Helms, Wes	$950,000	0	5	0
20	Scott, Luke	$2,400,000	0	23	0
21	Johnson, Reed	$3,000,000	0	6	0
22	Howard, Ryan	$15,000,000	0	48	1

We would then estimate the population regression model:

$$\begin{aligned} ln(Salary_i) = \beta_0 &+ \beta_1 Experience_i + \beta_2 Experience_i^2 + \beta_3 Home\ runs_i \\ &+ \beta_4 (Experience \times Home\ runs)_i + \beta_5 Japanese_i \\ &+ \beta_6 (Experience \times Japanese)_i + \beta_7 Infielder_i \\ &+ \beta_8 Outfielder_i + \beta_9 DH_i + \beta_{10} Salary\ outlier_i \\ &+ \beta_{11} HR\ outlier_i + \varepsilon_i \end{aligned} \quad (8.4.1)$$

and obtain Excel Regression Output 8.6.

Excel Regression Output 8.6: Regression Output for Our MLB Position Player Sample with the Outlier Dummy Variables Included

SUMMARY OUTPUT

Regression Statistics	
Multiple R	0.90687101
R Square	0.822415028
Adjusted R Square	0.812024418
Standard Error	0.551556847
Observations	200

ANOVA

	df	SS	MS	F	Significance F
Regression	11	264.8641844	24.07856222	79.14983083	1.91846E-64
Residual	188	57.19241153	0.304214955		
Total	199	322.056596			

	Coefficients	Standard Error	*t* Stat	*p*-value	Lower 95%	Upper 95%
Intercept	12.33091563	0.12570763	98.09202149	2.0999E-163	12.08293688	12.57889437
Experience	0.45008403	0.02871410	15.67467165	5.77321E-36	0.39344080	0.50672725
Experience Squared	−0.02112336	0.00207083	−10.20043701	1.00547E-19	−0.02520840	−0.01703831
Home Runs	0.03945229	0.00660610	5.97209786	1.14839E-08	0.02642068	0.05248390
Experience × Home Runs	0.00072238	0.00095089	0.75968971	0.448391639	−0.00115340	0.00259816
Japanese	3.15892448	0.67610333	4.67225101	5.66417E-06	1.82520069	4.49264827
Experience × Japanese	−0.29284287	0.15693981	−1.86595660	0.063605043	−0.60243216	0.01674643
Infielder	0.36287053	0.11698372	3.10188913	0.002219209	0.13210111	0.59363994
Outfielder	0.31353458	0.12022234	2.60795605	0.009840192	0.07637646	0.55069271
DH	0.67932104	0.34785114	1.95290734	0.052315006	−0.00687191	1.36551399
Salary Outlier	0.85375685	0.27426790	3.11285741	0.002142298	0.31271882	1.39479488
HR Outlier	0.67190007	0.58613149	1.14632994	0.253115604	−0.48433962	1.82813976

Note: The dependent variable is log annual salary. Catcher is the omitted position. Highlighted variables are significant at the 5 percent level. Variables highlighted in gray are significant at the 10 percent level.

By way of interpretation, notice that the dummy variable indicating our five potential salary outliers is estimated to be positive and statistically significant, suggesting that holding all other independent variables constant, the salaries of these five position players were 90 percent higher than the salaries of otherwise similar players. Conversely, the dummy variable indicating our one potential home run outlier is estimated to be statistically insignificant, suggesting that, holding all other variables constant, the salary of that player is not statistically different than otherwise similar players.

8.5 PERFORM THE RESET TEST FOR THE INCLUSION OF HIGHER-ORDER POLYNOMIALS

While the previous sections discuss reasons that we should make every effort to identify the "correct" econometric specification, there are some statistical tests that potentially help us make that identification. We introduce two such tests in the following sections.

reset test
A method that is used to detect if higher order polynomial terms should be included in the model.

If Ho fails rejection: conclude that the squares and the cubes of the predicted value of Y are not significant, therefore, powers of the original independent variables are not needed as additional variables to enhance the original model.

Chapter 7 introduced the possibility of allowing for potential non-linearities in independent variables by including higher-order polynomials of the independent variables. While possible, an obvious question is how to know whether we should include such terms. The **reset test** for the inclusion of higher-order polynomials is a method of determining whether we should include such terms in our estimated sample regression function by estimating the linear sample regression function by OLS, calculating the predicted values squared, predicted values cubed and the predicted values raised to the fourth power from that regression, and including those terms along with the original linear terms in a new regression. The intuition behind this test is that the predicted values squared, predicted values cubed and the predicted values raised to the fourth power of the initial OLS regression contain polynomial measures of the independent variables and thus if those values are jointly significant in the new regression then polynomial measures of the independent variables should be included in the model.

In steps, the reset test is performed as follows

1. Estimate the original linear population regression model

$$y_i = \beta_0 + \beta_1 x_{1,i} + \beta_2 x_{2,i} + \cdots + \beta_k x_{k,i} + \varepsilon_i \qquad \textbf{8.5.1}$$

and calculate the predicted values.

For our 200-observation MLB position player sample, we would estimate the population regression model

$$\begin{aligned} ln(Salary_i) = {} & \beta_0 + \beta_1 Experience_i + \beta_2 Experience_i^2 + \beta_3 Home\ Runs_i \\ & + \beta_4 (Experience \cdot Home\ Runs)_i + \beta_5 Japanese_i \\ & + \beta_6 (Experience \cdot Japanese)_i + \beta_7 Infielder_i \\ & + \beta_8 Outfielder_i + \beta_9 DH_i + \varepsilon_i \qquad \textbf{8.5.2} \end{aligned}$$

which provides the results in Excel Output 8.1 then calculating the predicted values from the regression.

2. Create new variables by squaring the predicted values ($\hat{y}_i^2$), by cubing the predicted values ($\hat{y}_i^3$), and by raising the predicted values to the fourth power ($\hat{y}_i^4$),

For our 200-observation MLB position player sample, this looks as

TABLE 8.4
Calculating the Residuals Squared and the Residuals Cubed for the Reset Test for Our 200-Observation MLB Position Player Sample

Observation	Predicted Log Salary ($\hat{y}_i$)	Residuals $\hat{y}_i^2$	Residuals Squared $\hat{y}_i^3$	Residuals Cubed $\hat{y}_i^4$
1	14.50312622	210.3406701	3050.597287	44243.1975
2	12.84965954	165.1137503	2121.655477	27262.55054
3	14.49449424	210.0903633	3045.153561	44137.96076
4	12.69289577	161.1096029	2044.947397	25956.30416
5	16.38045992	268.319467	4395.196274	71995.33639

3. Estimate the linear regression

$$y_i = \beta_0 + \beta_1 x_{1,i} + \beta_2 x_{2,i} + \cdots + \beta_k x_{k,i} + \beta_{k+1}\hat{y}_i^2 + \beta_{k+2}\hat{y}_i^3 + \beta_{k+3}\hat{y}_i^4 + \varphi_i. \qquad \textbf{8.5.3}$$

For our MLB position player example, we would estimate the equation

$$\begin{aligned} ln(Salary_i) = {} & \beta_0 + \beta_1 Experience_i + \beta_2 Experience_i^2 + \beta_3 Home\ Runs_i \\ & + \beta_4 (Experience \cdot Home\ Runs)_i + \beta_5 Japanese_i \\ & + \beta_6 (Experience \cdot Japanese)_i + \beta_7 Infielder_i \\ & + \beta_8 Outfielder_i + \beta_9 DH_i + \beta_{10}\hat{y}_i^2 + \beta_{11}\hat{y}_i^3 + \beta_{12}\hat{y}_i^4 + \varepsilon_i \qquad \textbf{8.5.4} \end{aligned}$$

and get Excel Regression Output 8.7.

Excel Regression Output 8.7 Regression Output for the Reset Test for Our MLB Position Player Sample

SUMMARY OUTPUT

Regression Statistics	
Multiple R	0.908695724
R Square	0.825727919
Adjusted R Square	0.814544684
Standard Error	0.547846894
Observations	200

ANOVA

	df	SS	MS	F	Significance F
Regression	12	297.9311229	22.16092691	73.83622992	3.06954E-64
Residual	187	56.12547305	0.30013622		
Total	199	322.056596			

	Coefficients	Standard Error	*t* Stat	*p*-value	Lower 95%	Upper 95%
Intercept	77.43052391	20.35096019	3.80476023	0.00019216	37.28355405	117.5774938
Experience	−0.56200861	0.69219877	−0.81191795	0.41787102	−1.92753058	0.80351336
Experience Squared	−0.02589830	0.03196756	0.81014304	0.41888772	−0.03716510	0.08896169
Home Runs	−0.05049899	0.06470094	−0.78049852	0.43608435	−0.17813654	0.07713856
Experience × Home Runs	−0.00288211	0.00570824	−0.50490390	0.61422083	− 0.01414292	0.00837870
Japanese	−3.68315436	4.50813346	−0.81700207	0.41496689	−12.57648895	5.21018023
Experience × Japanese	0.37338514	0.47559780	0.78508593	0.43339670	−0.56484138	1.31161166
Infielder	−0.50586328	0.57162615	−0.88495476	0.37731750	−1.63352790	0.62180134
Outfielder	−0.42788416	0.51314118	−0.83385269	0.40542786	−1.44017367	0.58440536
DH	−0.63437294	0.99133640	−0.63991693	0.52300984	−2.59001297	1.32126709
Predicted Squared	−2.20824064	0.63795776	−3.46110791	0.00066652	−3.46655968	−0.94952160
Predicted Cubed	0.21361923	0.06305630	3.38775387	0.00085916	0.08922611	0.33801236
Predicted Fourth	−0.00559338	0.00169348	−3.30288742	0.00114656	−0.00893417	−0.00225260

Note: The Dependent variable is log salary. Catcher is the position. Highlighted variables are significant at the 5 percent level.

4. Perform an F-test of the joint significance of $\hat{y}_i^2$, $\hat{y}_i^3$ and $\hat{y}_i^4$.
The appropriate null and alternative hypotheses for this test are

$$H_o{:}\beta_{10} = \beta_{11} = \beta_{12} = 0$$
$$H_A{:}\beta_{10}, \beta_{11} \text{ and } \beta_{12} \text{ are jointly significant} \quad \textbf{8.5.5}$$

For our 200-observation MLB position player sample, the F-statistic for the joint significance of β_{10} and β_{11} is 68.68, which far exceeds the table value of 3, meaning that we should reject the null hypothesis and conclude that β_{10} and β_{11} are jointly significant and that polynomial terms should be included in our model.

Empirical Research Tool 8.1 summarizes the reset test.

EMPIRICAL RESEARCH TOOL 8.1: THE RESET TEST FOR THE INCLUSION OF HIGHER-ORDER POLYNOMIALS

How to Do It:

1. Estimate the original regression $y_i = \beta_0 + \beta_1 x_{1,i} + \beta_2 x_{2,i} + \cdots + \beta_k x_{k,i} + \varepsilon_i$.
2. Create new variables by squaring the predicted values $\hat{y}_i^2$, cubing the predicted values, $\hat{y}_i^3$, and raising the predicted values to the fourth power, $\hat{y}_i^4$
3. Estimate the regression $y_i = \beta_0 + \beta_1 x_{1,i} + \beta_2 x_{2,i} + \cdots + \beta_k x_{k,i} + \beta_{k+1}\hat{y}_i^2 + \beta_{k+2}\hat{y}_i^3 + \beta_{k+3}\hat{y}_i^4 + \varphi_i$.
4. Perform an *F*-test for the joint significance of $\hat{y}_i^2$, $\hat{y}_i^3$ and $\hat{y}_i^4$.

Why It Works:

The residuals squared and the residuals cubed of the initial OLS regression contain polynomial measures of the independent variables. Hence, if those values are jointly significant, then polynomial measures of the independent variables should be included in the model.

8.6 PERFORM THE DAVIDSON-MACKINNON TEST FOR CHOOSING AMONG NON-NESTED ALTERNATIVES

tests of non-nested alternatives
Tests for models that are not subsets of each other.

Davidson-MacKinnon test
A test for models that are not nested within each other.

Besides testing for higher-order polynomials, we can also test for whether certain independent variables in our model should be entered in log form rather than in linear form. Technically, we refer to a test between linear models and log-log or linear-log models as a **test of non-nested alternatives.** The basic test for such differences is the **Davidson-MacKinnon test,** which we outline here.

Note that as with our discussion of log-log models in Chapter 7, we cannot perform the Davidson-MacKinnon test on data for which variables take on values of 0. Again, due to the presence of rookies in our sample, this precludes us from performing such a test on our MLB position player data. Instead, we again focus on our international GDP data because there are several independent variables with only non-0 values in those data.

Suppose that we are choosing between two potential models: one that is linear in all parameters (potential model 1) and one that is logarithmic in some parameters (potential model 2). These two potential models can be written as

Potential model 1:

$$y_{1,i} = \beta_0 + \beta_1 x_{1,i} + \beta_2 x_{2,i} + \cdots + \beta_k x_{k,i} + \varepsilon_i \quad \text{8.6.1}$$

Potential model 2:

$$y_{2,i} = \beta_0 + \beta_1 \ln x_{1,i} + \beta_2 x_{2,i} + \cdots + \beta_k \ln x_{k,i} + \varepsilon_i \quad \text{8.6.2}$$

For our international GDP data, we might define our potential models as

Potential model 1:

$$\begin{aligned} \ln(GDP/1{,}000{,}000{,}000)_i = \beta_0 &+ \beta_1(Population/1{,}000{,}000)_i \\ &+ \beta_2(Population/1{,}000{,}000)_i^2 \\ &+ \beta_3(Life\ expectancy)_i \\ &+ \beta_4(Life\ expenctancy)_i^2 + \varepsilon_i \end{aligned} \quad \text{8.6.3}$$

Potential model 2:

$$\begin{aligned} \ln(GDP/1{,}000{,}000{,}000)_i = \beta_0 &+ \beta_1 \ln(Population/1{,}000{,}000)_i \\ &+ \beta_2 \ln(Life\ expectancy)_i + \varepsilon_i \end{aligned} \quad \text{8.6.4}$$

The steps for conducting the Davidson-MacKinnon test are as follows.

1. Estimate potential model 2 and calculate the predicted value $\hat{y}_{2,i}$.

For our 63-observation international GDP sample, we run the regression for model 2, calculate the predicted values (by clicking the "residuals" tab in the regression window), and get Excel Regression Output 8.8.

Excel Regression Output 8.8: Regression Output for Our International GDP Sample for the First Stage of the Davidson-Mackinnon Test

SUMMARY OUTPUT	
Regression Statistics	
Multiple R	0.962322684
R Square	0.926064948
Adjusted R Square	0.923600446
Standard Error	0.743157127
Observations	63

ANOVA

	df	SS	MS	F	Significance F
Regression	2	415.0530466	207.5265233	375.7615307	1.16282E-34
Residual	60	33.1369509	0.55228251		
Total	62	448.1899975			

	Coefficients	Standard Error	*t* Stat	*p*-value	Lower 95%	Upper 95%
Intercept	−27.2282787	2.78644102	−9.77170467	5.08643E-14	−32.80199053	−21.65456684
Ln (Population/ 1,000,000)	0.96581453	0.03690772	26.16836281	1.63051E-34	0.89198811	1.03964096
Log (Life Expectancy)	6.97096514	0.64959284	10.73128386	1.38038E-15	5.67158601	8.27034427

Note: The dependent variable is log real GDP. Highlighted variables are significant at the 5 percent level.

and

Observation	Predicted Log GDP ($\hat{y}_{2,i}$)	Residuals (ε_i)
1	1.140477501	0.156985646
2	1.140477501	0.156985646
3	0.700044393	0.114435073
4	0.820604457	1.351758049
5	4.639605633	0.097469624

2. Add the predicted value $\hat{y}_{2,i}$ to potential model 1 and estimate the model

$$y_{1,i} = \beta_0 + \beta_1 x_{1,i} + \beta_2 x_{2,i} + \cdots + \beta_k x_{k,i} + \beta_{k+1}\hat{y}_{2,i} + \varepsilon_i \quad \textbf{8.6.5}$$

For our 63-observation international GDP sample, we estimate the population regression model

$$\begin{aligned} Ln(GDP/1{,}000{,}000{,}000)_i = {} & \beta_0 + \beta_1(Population/1{,}000{,}000)_i \\ & + \beta_2(Population/1{,}000{,}000)_i^2 \\ & + \beta_3(Life\ expectancy)_i \\ & + \beta_4(Life\ expectancy)_i^2 + \beta_5\hat{y}_{2,i} + \varepsilon_i \end{aligned} \quad \textbf{8.6.6}$$

and get Excel Regression Output 8.9.

3. Perform a *t*-test of the individual significance of the estimated slope coefficient β_5. The appropriate null and alternative hypotheses for this test are

$$\begin{aligned} H_o&: \beta_5 = 0 \\ H_A&: \beta_5 \neq 0 \end{aligned} \quad \textbf{8.6.7}$$

Excel Regression Output 8.9: Regression Output for the Second Stage of the Davidson-Mackinnon Test for Our International GDP sample

SUMMARY OUTPUT

Regression Statistics	
Multiple R	0.972328802
R Square	0.9454233
Adjusted R Square	0.94063587
Standard Error	0.655084448
Observations	63

ANOVA

	df	SS	MS	F	Significance F
Regression	5	423.7292664	84.74585327	197.4803454	1.13757E-34
Residual	57	24.4607312	0.42913563		
Total	62	448.1899975			

	Coefficients	Standard Error	*t* Stat	*p*-value	Lower 95%	Upper 95%
Intercept	8.751381	3.55874098	2.45912278	0.01698665	1.62512516	15.87763684
Population/ 1,000,000	0.00671117	0.00227499	2.94997802	0.00460371	0.00215558	0.01126675
Population/ 1,000,000 Squared	−4.99209E-06	1.60723E-06	−3.10601241	0.00295362	−8.21052E-06	−1.77366E-06
Life Expectancy	−0.28089753	0.11039464	−2.54448516	0.01367750	−0.50195899	−0.05983607
Life Expectancy Squared	0.00220179	0.00083624	2.63296905	0.01087456	0.00052725	0.00387634
Predicted Ln (GDP)	0.92220681	0.04888591	18.86446959	3.50748E-26	0.82431446	1.02009916

Note: The dependent variable is log real GDP. Highlighted variables are significant at the 5 percent level.

For our 63-observation international GDP sample, the t-statistic for the individual significance of β_5 is 18.87, which far exceeds the critical value of 1.96, meaning that we should reject the null hypothesis and conclude that β_5 is statistically significant and that the non-nested alternative measures should be included in our model.

Empirical Research Tool 8.2 summarizes the Davidson-MacKinnon test.

EMPIRICAL RESEARCH TOOL 8.2: THE DAVIDSON-MACKINNON TEST FOR CHOOSING AMONG NON-NESTED ALTERNATIVES

How to Do It:

1. Estimate potential model 2 and calculate the predicted value $\hat{y}_{2,i}$.
2. Add the predicted value $\hat{y}_{2,i}$ to potential model 1.
3. Perform a t-test of the individual significance of the predicted value included in the regression.

Why It Works:

The Davidson-MacKinnon test works for a reason similar to the reset test for the inclusion of higher-order polynomial works. The predicted value of y from the non-nested alternative model contains the non-nested measures of the included independent variables. Hence, if the predicted value of y from the non-nested alternative model is individually significant in the initial model, then the non-nested measures of the independent variables should be included in the model.

8.7 CONSIDER HOW TO IMPLEMENT THE "EYE TEST" TO JUDGE THE SAMPLE REGRESSION FUNCTION

As with all powerful tools if not used correctly, multiple linear regression analysis can prove quite dangerous. In particular, once we have learned the basic tools, it is tempting to accept all estimated sample regression functions as gospel truth without considering how peculiarities in the underlying data, rather than any true causal relationships between variables, might be responsible for the estimated significance of given results. For this reason, we always strongly encourage our students to take a step back and carefully consider whether the conclusions suggested by their results are truly reasonable. If any results do not pass this so-called eye test, then we encourage them to further explore their sample data to determine whether their estimates are the result of obvious data issues.

As an example, consider the more fully specified estimated sample regression function for our 200-observation MLB position player sample that we calculated in Chapter 6, which is repeated in Excel Regression Output 8.10.

Most of the estimated coefficients seem reasonable—all other variables constant, it is believable that each additional home run adds 4 percent to an individual's annual salary,

Excel Regression Output 8.10: Estimated Marginal Effects for the More Fully Specified Model for Our MLB Position Player Sample

SUMMARY OUTPUT

Regression Statistics	
Multiple R	0.901108880
R Square	0.811997214
Adjusted R Square	0.803091818
Standard Error	0.564509743
Observations	200

ANOVA

	df	SS	MS	F	Significance F
Regression	9	261.5090585	29.05656206	91.18036878	4.21322E-64
Residual	190	60.54753743	0.31867125		
Total	199	322.056596			

	Coefficients	Standard Error	*t* Stat	*p*-value	Lower 95%	Upper 95%
Intercept	12.31577790	0.12825721	96.03809628	5.526E-163	12.06458685	12.57056874
Experience	0.44662410	0.02932681	15.22920842	9.41829E-35	0.38877614	0.50447205
Experience Squared	−0.02084327	0.00211184	−9.86970839	8.24865E-19	−0.02500894	−0.01667760
Home Runs	0.03919094	0.00639030	6.13287687	4.89983E-09	0.02658589	0.05179599
Experience × Home Runs	0.00136559	0.00092219	1.48080665	0.140314475	−0.00045346	0.00318464
Japanese	3.16062486	0.69194803	4.56771997	8.85182E-06	1.79573789	4.52551183
Experience × Japanese	−0.29705606	0.16059172	−1.84975956	0.06590133	−0.61382774	0.01971562
Infielder	0.37531797	0.11950524	3.14059854	0.00195565	0.13959053	0.61104542
Outfielder	0.32874647	0.12284486	2.67611087	0.00809887	0.08643153	0.57106142
DH	0.57075983	0.35408587	1.61192487	0.10863814	−0.12768452	1.26920418

Note: Dependent variable is log annual salary. Catcher is the omitted position. Variables highlighted in blue are significant at the 5 percent level. Variables highlighted in gray are significant at the 10 percent level.

TABLE 8.5 **The 15 Highest-Paid Position Players in Our Sample Sorted by Descending Annual Salary**

Obs.	Player	Salary	Experience	Experience Squared	Home Runs	Experience · Home Runs	Japanese
1	Ramirez, Manny	$23,854,494	15	225	37	555	0
2	Jeter, Derek	$21,600,000	12	144	11	132	0
3	Teixeira, Mark	$20,625,000	6	36	13	78	0
4	Lee, Carlos	$19,000,000	10	100	28	280	0
5	Hunter, Torii	$18,000,000	10	100	21	210	0
6	Soriano, Alfonso	$17,000,000	8	64	29	232	0
7	Ramirez, Aramis	$16,650,000	9	81	27	243	0
8	Howard, Ryan	$15,000,000	3	9	48	144	0
9	Berkman, Lance	$14,500,000	9	81	29	261	0
10	Cabrera, Miguel	$14,383,049	5	25	37	185	0
11	Beltre, Adrian	$13,400,000	10	100	25	250	0
12	Lee, Derrek	$13,250,000	10	100	20	200	0
13	Matsui, Hideki	$13,000,000	6	36	9	54	1
14	Thome, Jim	$13,000,000	16	256	34	544	0
15	Fukudome, Kosuke	$12,500,000	1	1	10	10	1

that infielders and outfielders earn 37.5 and 32.9 percent more, respectively, than catchers (who are generally not as famous), and so on. There is, however, one estimate that should stand out as being suspicious: Holding all other independent variables constant, does it seem reasonable that a Japanese player earn an annual salary that is 316 percent higher than the annual salary earned by an observably similar non-Japanese player? Probably not.

For this reason, we suggest looking at the data for Japanese players in more detail. Doing so, we find that only 2 of the 200 MLB position players in our specific sample are Japanese. Looking at where these two Japanese players fall in the annual salary distribution for our sample is potentially revealing. In particular, sorting our sample from highest to lowest salary produces the results shown in Table 8.5.

Looking at Table 8.5, we notice that the 2 Japanese players are among the 15 highest-paid position players in our specific 200-observation MLB position player sample. At the same time, their six and one years of prior MLB experience, respectively, are among the lowest in the sample. This fact is not surprising, given that Japanese players usually come to the United States after first proving themselves over multiple years in the Japanese league. Accordingly, when they arrive in MLB, they have relatively little prior MLB experience but are paid relatively high salaries given their proven worth in the other league. Nonetheless, it is reasonable to expect the combination of relatively lower observed prior MLB experience and relatively higher observed annual salaries to combine to produce our estimate that Japanese players earn far more than non-Japanese players, holding all other variables constant.

As further proof of this possibility, we note that if we estimate a sample regression function that omits the variables $Japanese_i$ and $(Experience \cdot Japanese)_i$ and we predict individual annual salaries on the basis of the estimated results, for our two Japanese players produces the results shown in Table 8.6.

TABLE 8.6
A Comparison of Predicted and Actual Annual Salaries for the Two Japanese Players in Our 200-Observation LB Position Player Sample

id	Player	Predicted Salary	Actual Salary	Difference
5	Matsui, Hideki	$1,647,743.68	$13,000,000	−$11,352,256
195	Fukudome, Kosuke	$376,326.35	$12,500,000	−$12,123,674

Given the preceding evidence, we have reason to believe that our very large estimated coefficient on the variable $Japanese_i$ is likely due to our specific sample lacking sufficient numbers of Japanese players to enable us to accurately the marginal effect associated with being Japanese rather than non-Japanese. What should we do in a case such as this in which our sample regression function violates the eye test? At the very least, we should mention the fact whenever presenting our results.

8.8 CONSIDER WHAT IT MEANS FOR A *p*-value TO BE JUST ABOVE A GIVEN SIGNIFICANCE LEVEL

There is a final issue to discuss that is at least somewhat related to the eye test. What should we make of an estimated slope coefficient that is only slightly above the predetermined threshold value? As an example, suppose that when estimating the population regression model,

$$Speeders_i = \beta_0 + \beta_1 Police_i + \beta_2 Speeding\,fine_i + \beta_3 Drivers_i + \varepsilon_i \qquad 8.8.1$$

we find the estimated p-values in Table 8.7.

TABLE 8.7
A Comparison of Hypothetical Estimated *p*-values

	p-value
Intercept	0.030
Number of Police	0.049
Speeding Fine	0.051
Number of Drivers	0.101

Based on these values, we would conclude that (1) the intercept and the number of police are *statistically significant* , (2) the fine charged for speeding is *marginally significant,* and the number of drivers on the road is *statistically insignificant.*

Think about these conclusions for a moment. Are the values 0.049 and 0.051 that far apart? No. Yet our conclusion that one estimate is *statistically significant* and the other is only *marginally significant* suggests a rather large difference between the two. Likewise, it is perhaps a more significant concern that we consider a coefficient with an estimated p-value of 0.099 to be marginally significant while we consider a coefficient with an estimated p-value of 0.101 to be statistically insignificant. Unfortunately, strictly interpreting the 0.05 and 0.10 cutoffs forces us to draw such conclusions.

An amusing restatement of this concern is offered by Ralph Rosnow and Robert Rosenthal who write that

> *"Surely, God loves the 0.06 nearly as much as the 0.05".*
>
> —*R. L. Rosnow & R. Rosenthal, "Statistical Procedures and the Justification of Knowledge in Psychological Science,"* American Psychologist 44 (1989) 1276–1284.

The visual depiction in Figure 8.3 addresses our concern about the black-and-white nature of the rejection rules that we typically employ when evaluating the statistical significance of our estimates.

Should our "belief" in an estimate with a p-value just slightly above 0.10 (just slightly in the blue area in Figure 8.3) really be that much stronger than our "belief" in an estimate with a p-value just slightly below 0.10 (i.e. just slightly in the yellow area)? Not really. Yet, we generally totally discount the former estimate as being statistically insignificant, while we accept the latter are being statistically significant at the 10 percent level.

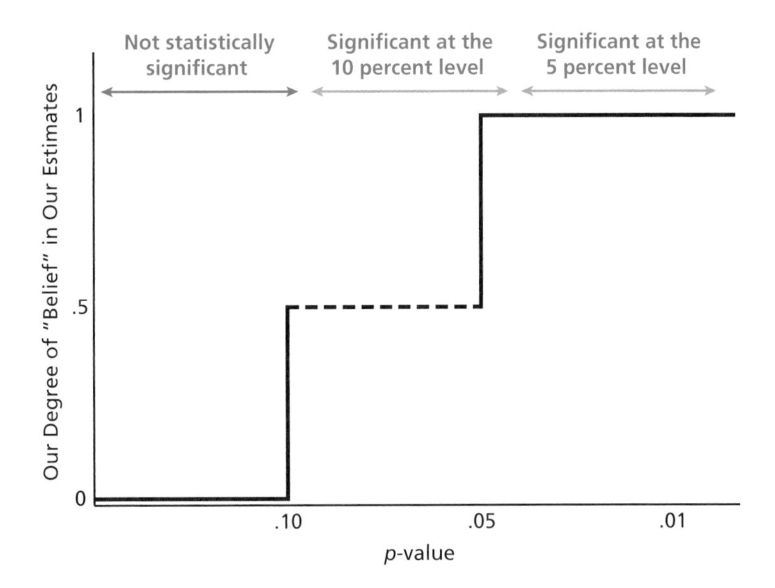

FIGURE 8.3 A Visual Depiction of Our Degree of "Belief" in Our Estimates

What should we make of the discussion in this section? That it is probably not accurate to be so black and white in our interpretation of what qualifies a given estimate to be statistically significant at the 5 percent or 10 percent level. Most importantly, we suggest that one not simply dismiss a variable as having no significance whatsoever if its estimated *p*-value is only slightly above 0.10.

ADDITIONS TO OUR EMPIRICAL RESEARCH TOOLKIT

In this chapter, we have introduced a number of tools that will prove valuable when performing empirical research:

- The reset test for the inclusion of higher-order polynomials.
- The Davidson-MacKinnon test for the choice among non-nested alternatives.
- The eye test for judging our sample regression function.

OUR NEW EMPIRICAL TOOLS IN PRACTICE: USING WHAT WE HAVE LEARNED IN THIS CHAPTER

To verify that his sample regression function was correctly specified, our former student considered several different possible specifications and satisfied himself that there were no obvious omitted variables for which he had access to data and that there were no obvious irrelevant variables that he was mistakenly including in his chosen specification. One concern that the student did have is that certain quantitative variables might more accurately be estimated with quadratic terms. To statistically test for this possibility, the student performed the reset test, obtaining the results in Table 8.8.

TABLE 8.8 The Results of Our Former Student's Reset Test for the Inclusion of Higher-Order Polynomials

SUMMARY OUTPUT	
Regression Statistics	
Multiple R	0.93521342
R Square	0.87462414
Adjusted R Square	0.85122064
Standard Error	3.19003183
Observations	90

ANOVA					
	df	SS	MS	F	Significance F
Regression	14	5324.254559	380.303897	37.37151826	4.57961E-28
Residual	75	763.2227323	10.1763031		
Total	89	6087.477291			

	Coefficients	Standard Error	*t* Stat	*p*-value	Lower 95%	Upper 95%
Intercept	430.1885462	743.1427666	0.57887739	0.5644298	−1050.55718	1910.93281
Population 18 and Over	−1.30705E-07	3.19276E-07	−0.40937971	0.68344358	−7.66877E-07	5.05467E-07
Males BA or Higher	−0.00836217	0.34815173	−0.02401875	0.98090230	−0.70206962	0.68534528
Females BA or Higher	0.07115195	0.37930548	0.18758483	0.85171552	−0.68463070	0.82693461
Median Income (thousands)	0.03949513	0.174454947	0.22639157	0.82152107	−0.30811394	0.38710419
Middle Atlantic	0.82122294	3.44434181	0.23842667	0.81220920	−6.04177783	7.68422371
South Atlantic	0.40618590	4.051229714	0.10026237	0.92040717	−7.6660654	8.47843719
East North Central	0.69834296	4.640794869	0.15047917	0.88079601	−8.54864253	9.94532845
East South Central	1.25733317	3.59016356	0.35021612	0.72717140	−5.89622378	8.41089011
West North Central	0.43279591	4.451446377	0.09722591	0.92280985	−8.43690448	9.30249630
West South Central	1.94987605	5.116611609	0.38108737	0.70423034	−8.24519497	12.14494708
Mountain	8.82933746	9.190174308	0.96073667	0.33981335	−9.48248430	27.14115923
Pacific	7.12785926	7.657494612	0.93083438	0.35496609	−8.13003159	22.38575012
Predicted Values Squared	−0.21568759	0.323694465	−0.66633079	0.50727178	−0.86066288	0.42928770
Predicted Values Cubed	0.002776522	0.003673401	0.75584528	0.45214133	−0.00454289	0.01009593
Predicted Values Fourth	−9.67311E-06	1.1706E-05	−0.82633474	0.41127064	−3.29979E-05	1.36517E-05

Note: Dependent variable is ratio of unmarried women to 100 unmarried men in an MSA. New England is the omitted census region. Variables highlighted in blue are significant at the 5 percent level. Variables highlighted in gray are significant at the 10 percent level.

Given that *Predicted Values Squared, Predicted Values Cubed,* and *Predicted Values Fourth* terms are all statistically insignificant at the 10 percent level, our student concluded that he should not include higher-ordered polynomials in his chosen population regression model. Based on these results, our student felt comfortable with his original specification of his regression model.

LOOKING AHEAD TO CHAPTER 9

So far, we have only been considering issues related to estimating sample regression functions by OLS. As discussed in Chapter 6, in order for OLS to provide estimates that are BLUE, six different assumptions must hold for the data in our specific sample drawn from the population. Unfortunately, it is not always reasonable to assume that all six of these assumptions hold. Chapter 9 examines the case in which assumption M6, that the covariance of the error term is constant across all values of the independent variables, is violated. This violation is referred to as heteroskedasticity, and we discuss methods to test for heteroskedasticity and steps to take to correct for heteroskedasticity.

Problems

8.1 You are interested in modeling the determinants of NBA basketball salaries. To do this you propose the following model:

$$ln(Salary_i) = \beta_0 + \beta_1 Yrs_i + \beta_2 PPG_i + \beta_3 RPG_i + \beta_4 F_i + \beta_5 G_i + \varepsilon_i$$

where

Yrs_i = Number of years the player has been in the NBA
PPG_i = The player's average points scored per game over the past year
RPG_i = The player's average rebounds collected per game over the past year
F_i = A dummy variable equal to 1 if the player plays the Forward position and 0 otherwise
G_i = A dummy variable equal to 1 if the player plays the Guard position and 0 otherwise

a. Suppose that you estimate $\beta_1 = 0.16$. Explain the meaning of this coefficient to a non-econometrician.

b. The third position on a basketball team is the Center. Suppose you thought that Centers got paid more to rebound than other positions. Explain how you would adjust the model above to test the hypothesis that rebounds per game has a bigger effect on the salary paid to a Center than the salaries paid to both Forwards and Guards.

c. Suppose you want to test for any difference in salaries between U.S.-born and foreign players. Show how you could augment the regression model to answer this question, and write down the form of the test statistic you would use to answer this question.

d. Another researcher proposes a slightly different model:

$$ln(Salary) = \beta_0 + \beta_1 ln(Yrs) + \beta_2 ln(PPG) + \beta_3 ln\,(RPG) + \beta_4 F + \beta_5 G + \varepsilon_i$$

Describe the steps you would take in choosing between this model and the original specification. What are the limitations of the test you would use to choose between these two models?

8.2 A public health researcher is trying to estimate the determinants of fertility rates in developing countries. She proposes the following model:

$$FR_i = \beta_0 + \beta_1 Age_i + \beta_2 Education_i + \beta_3 Urban_i + u_i$$

where

FR_i = The fertility rate for individual i (measured as the number of children ever born)
Age_i = The age in years for individual i
$Education_i$ = The number of years of education for individual i
$Urban_i$ = 1 if individual i lives in an urban area

Natural log is nonlinear and estimates are biased without transformation even if the true model is non linear

a. Briefly explain how you would test the null hypothesis that both *Education* and *Urban* status were jointly insignificant. In other words, how would you test the hypothesis that *Age* is the only relevant variable in explaining fertility rates?

b. Explain how you would test if the coefficients on age and education were equal.

c. The researcher is concerned about nonlinearities in this model and proposes the following semi-log specification:

$$lnFR_i = \beta_0 + \beta_1 Age_i + \beta_2 Education_i + \beta_3 Urban_i + u_i$$

Briefly explain why estimating this semi-log model is *more* likely to lead to biased estimates than the linear model, even if the true model is nonlinear. Explain the reasons you may choose to use a semi-log model and how you would interpret the coefficient estimates.

8.3 Suppose that you estimate the following model relating a country's air pollution ($Poll_i$) to its per capita GDP (GDP_i):

$$Poll_i = \beta_0 + \beta_1 GDP_i + \beta_2 GDP_i^2 + \varepsilon_i$$

a. You estimate $\hat{\beta}_1 = 4{,}000$ and $\hat{\beta}_2 = -0.25$. Given these estimates, at what income level is air pollution maximized?

b. Suppose you are concerned that your model suffers from heteroskedasticity. If indeed it does, what would be the consequences of estimating this model with OLS?

c. Briefly describe how you would test for heteroskedasticity in the preceding model if you were unsure of its exact form.

d. Suppose you found evidence of heteroskedasticity in part (c). Briefly explain how you would adjust the model given this result.

e. Another researcher proposes an alternative model:

$$Poll_i = \beta_0 + \beta_1 ln(GDP_i) + \beta_2 ln(GDP_i^2) + \varepsilon_i$$

Briefly explain how you would choose between this model and the original. Identify one potential problem with this procedure.

8.4 Consider the regression model $y_i = \beta_0 + \beta_1 x_{1,i} + \beta_2 x_{2,i} + \varepsilon_i$.

a. Show that the OLS estimator for β_1 can be written as $\hat{\beta}_1 = \dfrac{\sum_i \hat{r}_{i1} y_i}{\sum_i \hat{r}_{i1}^2}$, where $\hat{r}_1$ is the residual from a regression of x_1 on x_2: $\hat{x}_1 = \hat{\alpha}_0 + \hat{\alpha}_1 x_2$. Show your work.

b. The variance of the OLS estimator $\hat{\beta}_1$ can be written as $Var(\hat{\beta}_1) = \dfrac{\sum_i \hat{u}_i^2/(n-k-1)}{TSS_1(1-R_1^2)}$, where TSS_1 is the total variation in x_1 and R_1^2 is the R-squared from a regression of x_1 on all other explanatory variables. Using this expression, explain why our estimates improve when each explanatory variable (x_1, x_2, etc.) has a large amount of variation *independent* of other explanatory variables.

Including irrelevant variables does not cause bias

c. Consider the regression $Wage_i = \beta_0 + \beta_1 Married_i + \beta_2 Height_i + \varepsilon_i$, where you are regressing a man's wage on his marital status and height. Assume that there is no relationship between a man's height and wages ($\beta_2 = 0$), but you include this variable in the regression anyway. Does including this irrelevant variable in your regression bias your estimate of β_1? Prove that including height in the regression causes $Var(\hat{\beta}_1)$ to increase, assuming again that height has no correlation with wages.

8.5 Suppose that you are interested in modeling the determinants of Major League Baseball position player salaries. To do this, you propose the following model:

$$ln(Salary_i) = \beta_0 + \beta_1 Exp_i + \beta_2 BA_i + \beta_3 RBI_i + \beta_4 HR_i + \beta_3 INF_i + \beta_4 AllStar_i + \varepsilon_i$$

where

Exp = The player's years in the league
BA = The player's batting average
RBI = The number of runs batted in by the player
HR = The number of home runs hit by the player
Inf = 1 if the player is an infielder and 0 otherwise
$AllStar$ = 1 if the player made the All Star team and 0 otherwise

a. Suppose you think that infielders get paid less to hit homeruns than outfielders. However, infielders get paid more to have a high batting average. How would you test these hypotheses?

b. Suppose you could differentiate players by birthplace, into natives and foreigners. You want to test for the presence of any nativity discrimination in baseball. How would you go about testing for any differences? Write down the form of the test statistic you would use.

c. A fellow sports economist offers a competing model to your own. She proposes that the true model should in fact be:

$$ln(Salary_i) = \beta_0 + \beta_1 ln(Exp)_i + \beta_2 BA_i + \beta_3 INF_i + \beta_4 BA_i^2 + \beta_4 RBI_i^2 + \varepsilon_i$$

Describe how you would choose between your model and your colleague's model. What are the limitations of the specification test used to choose between the two models?

Exercises

E8.1 Suppose you are investigating the factors that affect college GPA. You perform a survey, and the data are contained in the Excel file **Survey 1.xls** and then regress GPA on hours studied, work, video game, texts, and male.

a. Suppose you think that you have omitted an important variable, ability, that is correlated with many of your independent variables. What are the consequences of this omission on the coefficient estimates and hypothesis tests?

b. Perform the same regression that you did in part (a), but then add the additional variable, eye color. What are the consequences of including this irrelevant variable on your coefficient estimates and hypothesis tests?

larger standard error is better than biased estimator

c. Would you rather omit a relevant variable such as ability or include an irrelevant variable such as eye color? Explain your reasoning.

E8.2 Suppose you are interested in investigating how housing prices in San Diego are related to distance to the beach. Unfortunately, you were not able to collect data on distance to beach for all of your observations. The data for this problem are contained in the Excel file **Housing price 1.xls**.

a. Add observations to the distance to the beach column to account for the missing observations, and add an additional variable called missing data that also accounts for the missing observations.

b. Regress housing price on square feet, bedrooms, lot size, pool, distance to the beach, and missing data. What do you conclude about the missing data and the distance to the beach variables?

c. One of the assumptions about missing data is that there isn't a special reason that the data are missing. Compare the sample mean for the distance to beach variable to the average distance to beach for houses in the city of San Diego of 15 miles. Do you think that the distance to beach variable portrays an accurate depiction of houses in San Diego?

E8.3 Suppose you are interested in how video games sales are related to time since announcement, PS3 consoles sold, average rating, online MP, sequel, part of series, and multiplatform, but you think that the online MP contains outliers.

a. Create a scatter plot of video game sales on online MP, and inspect the graph for outliers.

b. Run a regression that accounts for the two outliers in these data. What do you conclude?

c. Do you believe that the outliers in online MP are there for a special reason, or are they just an artifact of the data?

E8.4 Open file **Housing price.xls**.

a. Create a new variable log housing price by using the ln function in Excel. Regress log housing price on square feet, bedrooms, lot size, and pool.

b. Create another new variable log square feet. Regress log housing price on log square feet, bedrooms, lot size, and pool.

c. Use the Davidson-MacKinnon test to see if model (a) or model (b) is statistically preferred.

E8.5 Suppose you want to investigate if higher-order polynomials are appropriate in the **gpa.xls** data. Use the reset test on all variables to test this hypothesis.

Chapter **Nine**

Heteroskedasticity

CHAPTER OBJECTIVES

After reading this chapter, you will be able to:

1. Understand methods for detecting heteroskedasticity.
2. Correct for heteroskedasticity.

A STUDENT'S PERSPECTIVE

Suppose that after seeing a report on CNN, you become interested in the United Nation's Human Development Index, which according to the UN's website, is "a new way of measuring development by combining indicators of life expectancy, educational attainment and income into a composite human development index, the HDI. The breakthrough for the HDI was the creation of a single statistic which was to serve as a frame of reference for both social and economic development. The HDI sets a minimum and a maximum for each dimension, called goalposts, and then shows where each country stands in relation to these goalposts, expressed as a value between 0 and 1." Suppose further that given your interest in social and economic development, you decide to investigate the degree to which different independent factors are correlated with a country's HDI score.

This is exactly the situation encountered by one of our former students. For her econometric research project, she collected data on several variables from the UN's Human Development Reports website for the 155 different countries for which data was reported in 2005 (the most recent year in which data was recorded for all of the variables for a large number of countries). Table 9.1 presents the simple summary statistics that she reported for her data.

TABLE 9.1 **Summary Statistics for Our Former Student's 2005 HDI Data**

	Human Development Index (HDI) Value	GDP per Capita in PPP Terms (constant 2005 international $)	Forest Area (% of total land area)	Adolescent Fertility Rate (births per 1,000 women aged 15–19)	Maternal Mortality Ratio (deaths of women per 100,000 live births)	Shares in Parliament, Female-Male Ratio	Carbon Dioxide Emissions per Capita (tonnes)
Mean	0.635	11,453.01	29.97	61.37	225.99	0.207	17.74
Standard Deviation	0.182	12,950.69	22.27	52.14	310.38	0.160	22.37
Minimum	0.260	266.00	0.00	2.20	2.00	0.000	0.10
25th Percentile	0.484	1,853.50	10.35	18.35	19.00	0.103	2.15
Median	0.667	6,200.00	29.10	43.60	70.00	0.158	8.70
75th Percentile	0.782	16,751.50	44.90	93.40	355.00	0.260	26.55
Maximum	0.938	68,319.00	94.70	230.60	1,500.00	0.828	122.10
Observations	155	155	155	155	155	155	155

The student interpreted these values as indicating that the distribution of HDI scores was fairly symmetric, with the mean being 0.635 and the median being 0.667. She also noted that in 2005 the country with the highest HDI of 0.938 was Norway, while the country with the lowest HDI of 0.260 was the Democratic Republic of Congo. Turning to the independent variables, she was struck by the large variances between the lowest and highest values for each of the independent variables. For instance, the minimum GDP per capita was $266 (Democratic Republic of Congo) while the maximum was $68,319 (Luxembourg), and the minimum percentage of forested land area was 0 (Oman) while the maximum was 94.70 (Suriname).

The student's sample regression function for these data is presented in Table 9.2.

TABLE 9.2 **Sample Regression Function for Our Former Student's 2005 HDI Data**

SUMMARY OUTPUT	
Regression Statistics	
Multiple R	0.945028056
R Square	0.893078026
Adjusted R Square	0.888743352
Standard Error	0.060802975
Observations	155

ANOVA	df	SS	MS	F	Significance F
Regression	6	4.570185289	0.761697548	206.031157	3.22824E-69
Residual	148	0.547156259	0.003697002		
Total	154	5.117341548			

	Coefficients	Standard Error	*t* Stat	*p*-value	Lower 95%	Upper 95%
Intercept	0.650741304	0.014087424	46.19306721	8.26553E-90	0.62290283	0.678579778
GDP per capita in PPP terms (constant 2005 international $)	6.62304E-06	7.43293E-07	8.910407855	1.72526E-15	5.1542E-06	8.09188E-06
Forest area (% of total land area)	0.000413302	0.000234014	1.766144133	0.079433423	−4.91379E-05	0.000875743
Adolescent fertility rate (births per 1,000 women aged 15–19)	−0.000583509	0.000160855	−3.627543946	0.000393171	−0.000901378	−0.000265639
Maternal mortality ratio (deaths of women per 100,000 live births)	−0.0003042	2.57163E-05	−11.8290841	3.82119E-23	−0.000355018	−0.000253381
Shares in parliament, female-male ratio	0.054969406	0.03464241	1.586766241	0.114699824	−0.013488238	0.123427049
Carbon Dioxide Emissions per capita (tonnes)	−0.000603142	0.000403933	−1.493173035	0.137520678	−0.001401364	0.000195079

Note: Dependent variable is Human Development Index. Variables highlighted in blue are significant at the 5 percent level. Variables highlighted in light gray are significant at the 10 percent level.

She interpreted these results as indicating that, all other independent variables constant, richer countries and countries with greater percentages of forest area tend to score significantly higher on the HDI, while countries with higher adolescent fertility and maternal mortality rates tended to score significantly lower. Conversely, she concluded that the percentage of women holding seats in parliament and the level of carbon dioxide emissions were not significantly correlated with the HDI.

Our former student was not completely satisfied with these results, however. Based on her training, she was concerned as to whether the six assumptions required for OLS to provide estimates that are BLUE (best linear unbiased estimates) held for these data. How might she go about testing whether the assumptions all hold? If she finds that one does not, then what can she do about it? This chapter answers these questions for one of the most commonly encountered violations for cross-section data.

BIG PICTURE OVERVIEW

Recall from Chapter 5 that there the six assumptions required for ordinary least squares (OLS) to provide best linear unbiased estimates (BLUE). These assumptions are listed in the following box.

Assumptions Required for OLS to be the Best Linear Unbiased Estimator

Assumption M1: The model is linear in the parameters.
Assumption M2: The data are collected through independent, random sampling.
Assumption M3: The data are not perfectly multicollinear.
Assumption M4: The error term has zero mean, or $E(\varepsilon_i) = 0$.
Assumption M5: The error term is uncorrelated with each independent variable and all functions of each independent variable, or $E(\varepsilon_i|x_{ij}) = 0$ for all j.
Assumption M6: The error term has constant variance, or $Var(\varepsilon_i) = \sigma^2$.

In reality, because the population is unobserved, we can never know for certain whether these assumptions hold. Instead, we have to rely on our intuition and training to determine whether they are likely a reasonable approximation of the truth. While we will often have no reason to believe that any of the assumptions are clearly violated, there are certain situations in which one will clearly stand out as being suspect. The rest of econometrics (and the remainder of this text) deals in large part with identifying and addressing such situations.

homoskedasticity
Occurs when the error terms have a constant variance.

heteroskedasticity
Occurs when the error term has a nonconstant variance.

Perhaps the most obvious violation of the six assumptions occurs when assumption M6 is violated by data for which the error term does not have a constant variance. Figure 9.1 visually depicts the difference between cross-sectional data for which the error term has a constant variance (**homoskedasticity**) and cross-sectional data for which it does not (**heteroskedasticity**).

FIGURE 9.1
Scatter Diagrams of Hypothetical Homoskedastic and Heteroskedastic Data

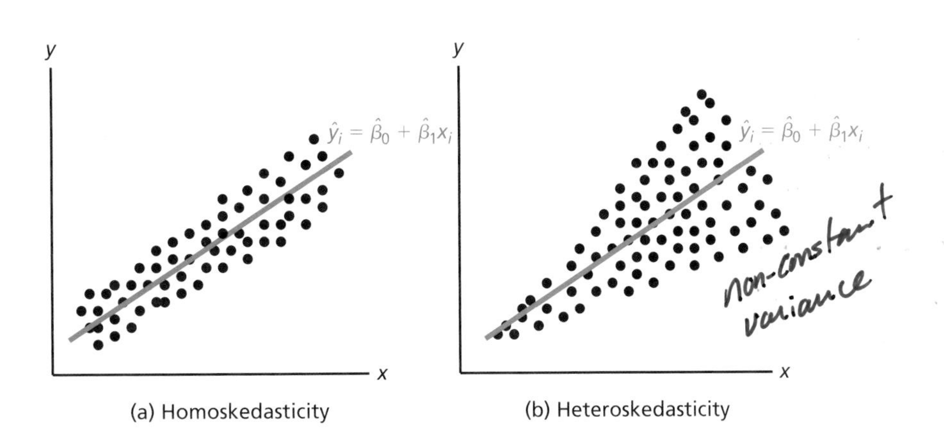

The difference between these two situations should be clear. In the first panel of Figure 9.1, the data are randomly distributed around the sample regression function, and the residuals do not appear to systematically vary with the value of the independent variable, x_i. In the second panel, the data are not randomly distributed around the sample regression function, and the residuals do appear to systematically vary with the value of the independent variable, with the variance being relatively small for lower values of x_i and relatively large for larger values of the x_i.

In the presence of heteroskedasticity, while still being unbiased, our OLS estimates no longer have the minimum variance among all unbiased estimators, meaning that they are no longer BLUE. To understand why, consider that, by definition, the OLS estimator gives the same relative weight to each observation in the estimation process. While this equal weighting makes sense when there is no systematic variance in the error term (Figure 9.1a), equal weighting does not make sense where there is systematic variance across observations (Figure 9.1b). As might be expected then, in the presence of heteroskedasticity, an unbiased estimator with minimum variance would be one that gives more weight to observations that are closely scattered around the sample regression function and less weight to observations that are widely scattered around the sample regression function.

In addition to not being the unbiased estimator with the minimum variance, in the presence of heteroskedasticity, the calculated standard errors for the OLS estimated slope coefficients are incorrect because the formulas for calculating those standard errors are derived under the assumption of homoskedasticity. This is an important concern because all of our statistical measures of confidence (t-statistics, p-values, confidence intervals, and F-tests) involve the calculated standard error, meaning that if the estimated standard error is incorrect, then all of the values calculated on the basis of that estimate are also incorrect.

Based on this discussion, we summarize the issues and consequences associated with heteroskedasticity in the following box.

The Issues and Consequences Associated with Heteroskedastic Data

Problem:
Heteroskedasticity violates assumption *M6*, which states that the error term must have constant variance.

Consequences:
Under heteroskedasticity,
1. Parameter estimates are unbiased.
2. Parameter estimates are not minimum variance among all unbiased estimators.
3. Estimated standard errors are incorrect, and all measures of precision based on the estimated standard errors are also incorrect.

Figure 9.2 visually summarizes the empirical tools introduced in this chapter.

Before introducing our preferred methods for detecting and correcting for potential heteroskedasticity, we need to introduce the data that we analyze in the remainder of the chapter.

Our Empirical Example: The Relationship between Income and Expenditures

Perhaps the most well-known example in which data are likely to be heteroskedastic is the relationship between income and expenditures, such as total food expenditures. Such data are likely to be heteroskedastic because (1) due to their limited financial capacity, low-income individuals tend to spend a similar fraction of their incomes on food, leading to low variances in food expenditures, and (2) due to their greater financial capacity, high-income

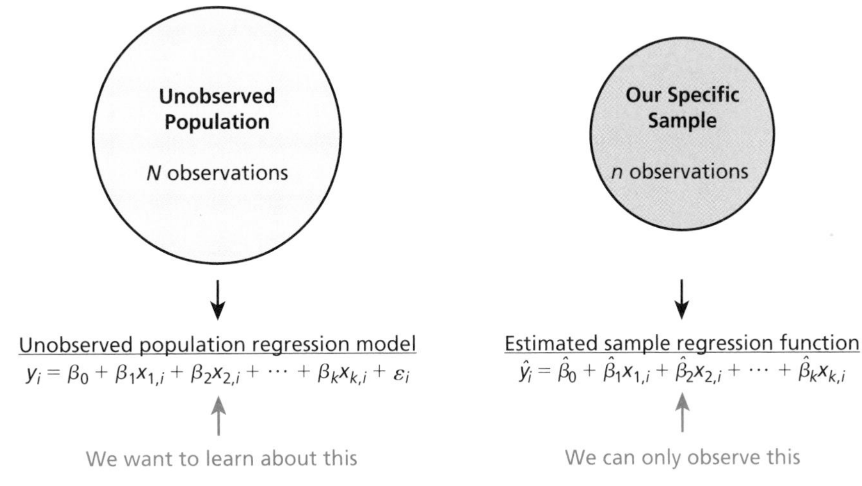

Question: How do we know that assumption M6 holds?

Answer: We can test for heteroskedasticity.
- The Breusch-Pagan Test
- The General White's Test
- The Modified White's Test
- The Goldfeld-Quandt Test

Question: What do we do if our data are heteroskedastic?

Answer: We can correct for the heteroskedasticity.
- Weighted Least Squares
- White's Heteroskedastic Consistent Standard Errors

FIGURE 9.2
A Visual Depiction of the Empirical Tools Introduced in This Chapter

individuals *can* afford to spend large amounts on food, with some choosing to do so and some choosing not to do so, leading to higher variances in food expenditures. Based on this intuition, Figure 9.3 presents a likely scatter diagram of food expenditures versus income.

FIGURE 9.3
Hypothetical Scatter Diagram of Food Expenditures versus Income

As demonstrated in Figure 9.3, the variance of food expenditures increases with increasing income, meaning that the data are likely to violate assumption M6 that the error term has constant variance across different values of the independent variable. Accordingly, we would conclude that OLS is no longer BLUE and that the calculated standards of the OLS estimated slope coefficients are incorrect. In the remainder of this chapter, we introduce methods for determining whether our data are indeed heteroskedastic as well as procedures for ensuring that our estimates are BLUE and our calculated standard errors are correct in the presence of heteroskedasticity.

DATA TO BE ANALYZED: OUR CALIFORNIA HOME MORTGAGE APPLICATION SAMPLE

With the previous discussion in mind, in this chapter we analyze the relationship between requested home mortgage amounts and applicant income for a very large number of Californians. We choose these particular data for the following reasons: (1) housing is one of the primary expenditures that an individual makes; (2) as with food, it is likely that individuals with higher incomes have higher variances in their housing expenditures than individuals with lower incomes; and (3) the government collects and makes available individual home mortgage application data.

Following the procedure outlined in Appendix B, we collected from the Home Mortgage Disclosure Act database a sample of 73,046 mortgage applications filed in the state of California in 2007. (Note: These data are potentially available for all 50 states and the District of Columbia, but given the size of just the California sample, we quickly realized that the full national sample would be far too large and unwieldy to use here.) Basic summary statistics for our California home mortgage application data are given in Table 9.3.

TABLE 9.3
Simple Summary Statistics for Our California Home Mortgage Application Data

	Loan Amount	Applicant Income
Mean	$ 411,614.20	$ 174,287.97
Standard Deviation	$ 385,799.44	$ 208,602.19
Minimum	$ 2,000.00	$ 1,000.00
25th Percentile	$ 188,000.00	$ 88,000.00
Median	$ 360,000.00	$ 133,000.00
75th Percentile	$ 520,000.00	$ 192,000.00
Maximum	$20,100,000.00	$8,795,000.00
Observation	73,046	73,046

These simple summary statistics suggest that there is wide variation in both the requested loan amount and applicant income. This is evident in the fact that the standard deviation for requested loan amount is almost as large as the sample mean, and the standard deviation for applicant income is larger than the sample mean. Requested loan amounts range from as little as $2,000 to as much as $20 million, while applicant income ranges from as low as $1,000 to as high as almost $9 million. To get a better idea of how requested loan amounts vary with applicant income, Figure 9.4 presents a scatter diagram

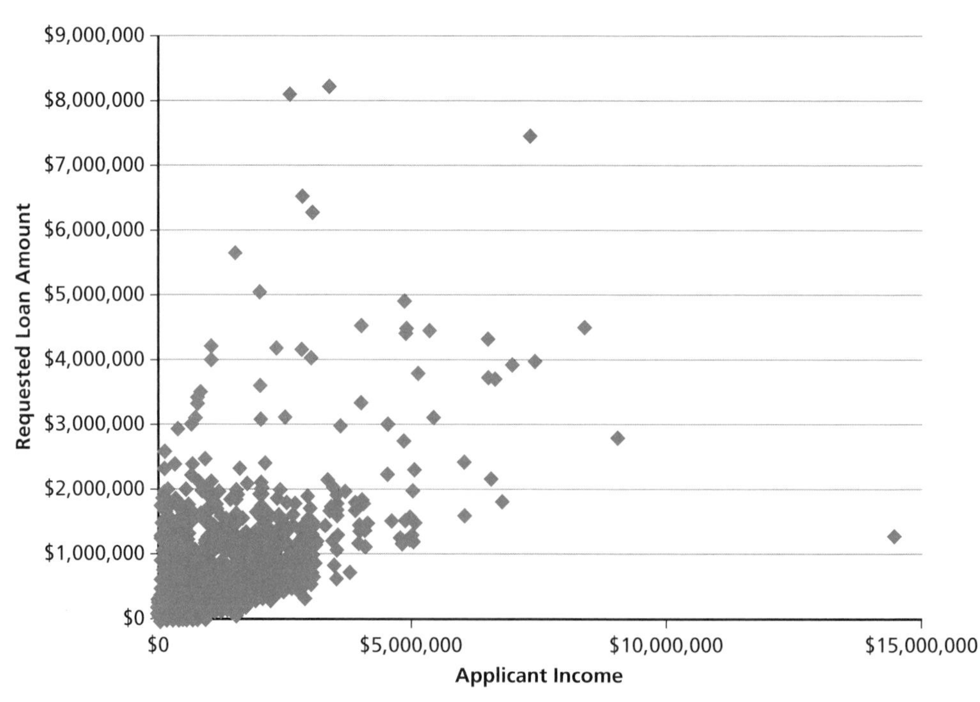

FIGURE 9.4
Scatter Diagram of Requested Loan Amount versus Applicant Income for the First 32,000 Observations in Our California Mortgage Application Data

of the two variables (note that because Excel limits scatter diagrams to only the first 32,000 observations, not all observations in our sample are represented).

The fact that requested loan amounts fan out as observed applicant incomes increase suggests that these data may well be heteroskedastic.

As a baseline for our empirical analysis, we estimate the population regression model

$$Loan\ amount_i = \beta_0 + \beta_1 Applicant\ income + \varepsilon_i \qquad 9.1$$

and get Excel Regression Output 9.1.

Excel Regression Output 9.1: Estimated Marginal Effects for Our California Home Mortgage Application Data

SUMMARY OUTPUT

Regression Statistics	
Multiple R	0.627106328
R Square	0.393262347
Adjusted R Square	0.393254040
Standard Error	300514.2314
Observations	73,046

← Number of observations in our California mortgage application data set

ANOVA

	df	SS	MS	F	Significance F
Regression	1	4.27559E+15	4.27559E+15	47344.11113	0
Residual	73044	6.59652E+15	90308803262		
Total	73045	1.08721E+16			

	Coefficients	Standard Error	*t* Stat	*p*-value	Lower 95%	Upper 95%
Intercept	209,474.635	1,448.923	144.5725987	0	206634.7505	212314.5202
Applicant Income	1.160	0.005	217.5870197	0	1.149354828	1.170249531

Note: Dependent variable is the requested loan amount. Highlighted variables are significant at the 5 percent level.

These results suggest that, on average, each additional $1 of applicant income is estimated to be associated with a $1.16 increase in the requested loan amount. For context, this implies that an individual with $100,000 more income would request a $116,000 larger loan. Of course, our focus in this chapter is not these particular estimates but whether these data satisfy the six assumptions required for the OLS estimates to be BLUE and how to deal with cases in which they do not.

An Important Caveat before Continuing

As with many other facets of modern life, the treatment of potential heteroskedasticity has benefited greatly from computer power. Accordingly, rather than taking the time to test whether data is indeed heteroskedastic before implementing a relatively clunky approach to correcting for it, modern researchers include a very simple command asking their chosen statistical program to provide estimates with White's heteroskedastic consistent standard errors (which we introduce in Section 9.2) as a default when working with cross-section data.

Nonetheless, we believe that in order to understand the intuition behind what that simple command is doing and why, it is important to first work through the more "old-school" examples that we do next before learning how to calculate White's heteroskedastic consistent standard errors.

We start our discussion by introducing four of the most popular methods for detecting whether heteroskedasticity is present in our data. Before doing so, the preceding box makes an important point about the information that we are about to introduce.

9.1 UNDERSTAND METHODS FOR DETECTING HETEROSKEDASTICITY

The various methods for detecting heteroskedasticity essentially represent different ways of determining whether the data being analyzed are more similar to the graphical representation of homoskedastic data in Figure 9.1a or to the graphical representation of heteroskedastic data in Figure 9.1b. If the data are determined to be more like the former, then we conclude that assumption M6 is not violated, that our OLS estimates are BLUE, and that our estimated standard errors are likely correct. If they are determined to be more like the latter, then we conclude the opposite and we must take steps to correct our OLS estimates to ensure that they are BLUE and that our estimated standard errors are correct. Note that throughout this chapter, we are assuming that assumptions M1 through M5 hold and that we only need be concerned with whether assumption M6 is violated.

The Informal Method for Detecting Heteroskedasticity

The first method for detecting heteroskedasticity is an informal graphical method. While this informal method does not provide a definitive answer as to whether the data are heteroskedastic, it does provide some idea as to the likelihood that the problem exists and whether the calculated error variance is likely to be increasing or decreasing with the value of the independent variable.

The informal method consists of (1) creating scatter diagrams of the estimated residuals from the original OLS regression versus the independent variable suspected of being heteroskedastic and (2) assessing whether the residuals appear to vary with the observed values of the independent variable. Visually, we want to determine whether these **residual plots** look more like the one in Figure 9.5a or the one in Figure 9.5b.

residual plots
Graphs that have the residuals plotted against other variables.

FIGURE 9.5
Hypothetical Residual Plots for Homoskedastic and Heteroskedastic Data

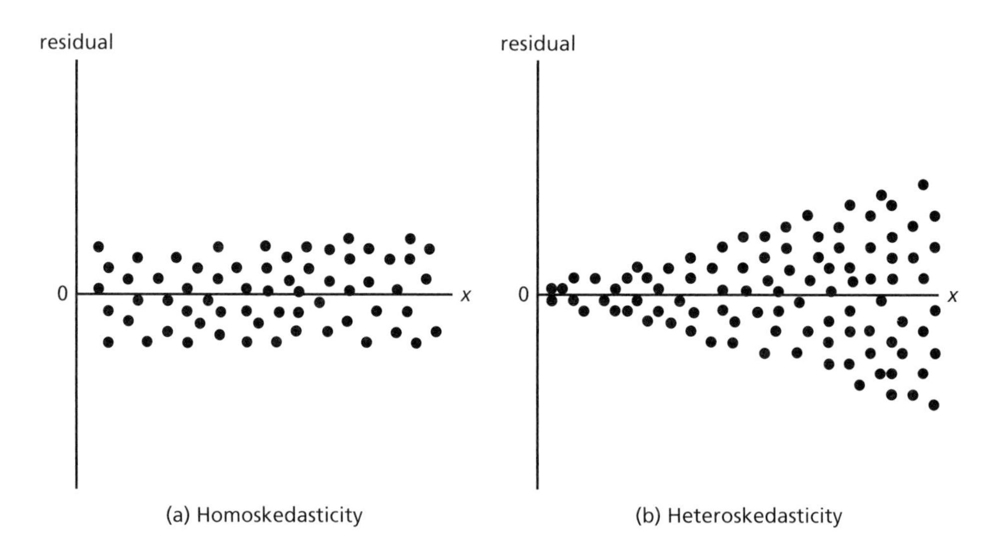

If the actual residual plots look more like Figure 9.5b, then we conclude that the data possess nonconstant error variance and that assumption M6 is likely violated.

Note that it is easiest to determine the residuals and the resulting residual plots by asking Excel to make the calculations for us by checking the "Residual Plots" box when running the OLS regression (as we do in Excel Example 9.1).

EXCEL EXAMPLE 9.1

Using the Regression Wizard to generate a residual plot

To get Excel to include the calculated residuals as well as a graph of the residuals versus a given independent variable, simply check the box next to "Residual Plots" which for our example looks as follows

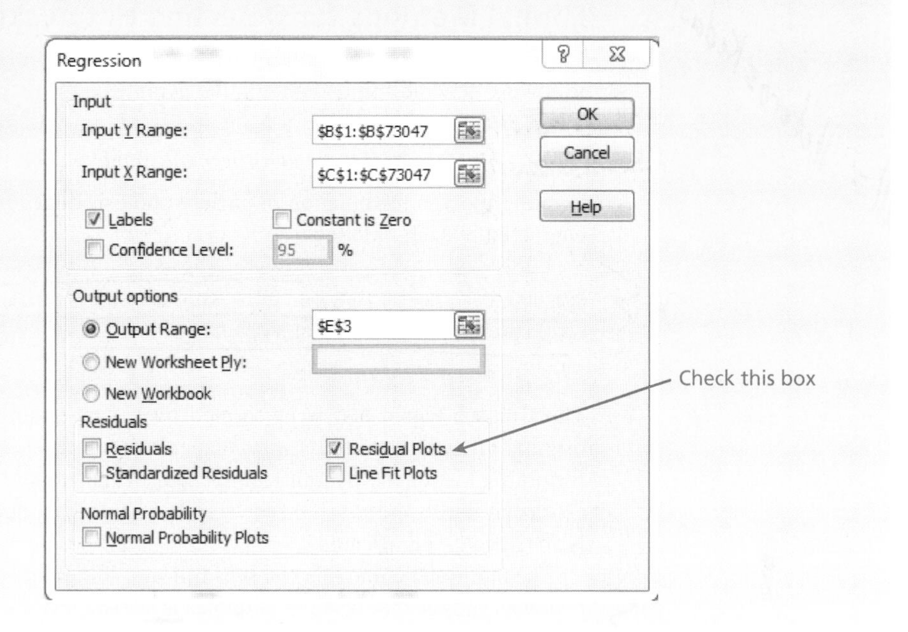

Figure 9.6 presents the resulting residual plot for our California mortgage application sample (note that just like for scatter diagrams, Excel limits all residual plots to a maximum of 32,000 observations, meaning that not all of our observations are included).

FIGURE 9.6 **Residual Plot versus Applicant Income for the First 32,000 Observations in Our California Mortgage Application Data**

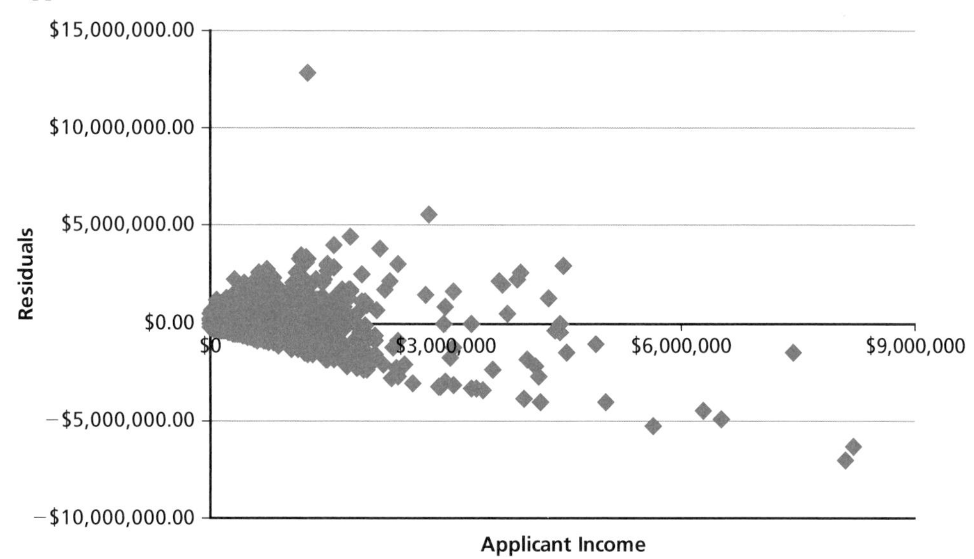

The data points in Figure 9.6 appear to fan out as applicant income increases, suggesting that the variance of the calculated residuals increases with applicant income. If true, then assumption M6 is violated, and our data are heteroskedastic. While this informal method is quite simple, it suffers in practice from its informality—individuals looking at the same picture may well come to different conclusions as to whether apparent heteroskedasticity exists or not. Instead, the informal method is often used as a simple first check to see if more formal detection methods should be employed.

Formal Methods for Detecting Heteroskedasticity

The four formal methods introduced in this section are all based on statistical tests of the following general null and alternative hypotheses:

$$H_0\text{: the error term has constant variance}$$
$$H_A\text{: the error term has nonconstant variance} \quad \textbf{9.1.1}$$

with the specific formulation of each hypothesis depending on the empirical specification employed in each individual test.

Under this framework, if we reject the null hypothesis, then we conclude that our data are heteroskedastic, that our OLS estimates are not BLUE, that our calculated standard errors are incorrect, and that steps must be taken to obtain more efficient estimates.

The Breusch-Pagan Test

The Breusch-Pagan test is performed by (1) regressing the squared residuals from the original OLS regression on the independent variables from that regression and (2) performing a test of the overall significance of the sample regression function to see if the estimated linear relationship between the squared residuals and the independent variables is statistically significant.

The intuition behind this test is as follows. If the linear relationship between the squared residuals and the independent variables is statistically significant, then we should conclude that the error variance (the squared residuals) systematically changes with the value of the independent variables, implying that the error variance is nonconstant, that assumption M6 is violated, and that the data are heteroskedastic. If the relationship is not statistically significant, then we should conclude the opposite.

The individual steps for conducting the Breusch-Pagan test are

1. Estimate the population regression model,

$$y_i = \beta_0 + \beta_1 x_{1i} + \beta_2 x_{2i} + \cdots + \beta_k x_{ki} + \varepsilon_i$$

and obtain the estimated residuals,

$$e_i = y_i - \hat{y}_i$$

For our California home mortgage application data, we estimate the population regression model as

$$Loan\ amount_i = \beta_0 + \beta_1 Applicant\ income + \varepsilon_i \quad \textbf{9.1.2}$$

and calculate the estimated residuals as shown in Table 9.4.

TABLE 9.4 **Predicted Requested Loan Amounts and Residuals for Our California Home Mortgage Application Data**

Observation	Predicted Loan Amount ($\hat{y}_i$)	Residuals (e_i)
1	\$261,665.73	−\$ 73,665.73
2	\$306,898.02	−\$260,898.02
3	\$266,304.94	−\$131,304.94
4	\$376,486.15	−\$223,486.15
5	\$424,038.04	\$169,961.96

2. Square the residuals to get e_i^2.

For our California home mortgage application data, we do so as shown in Table 9.5.

TABLE 9.5 **Calculation of the Squared Residuals e_i^2 for Our California Home Mortgage Application Data**

Observation	Predicted Loan Amount ($\hat{y}_i$)	Residuals (e_i)	Squared Residuals (e_i^2)
1	\$261,665.73	−\$ 73,665.73	\$ 5,426,640,289.79
2	\$306,898.02	−\$260,898.02	\$68,067,776,054.87
3	\$266,304.94	−\$131,304.94	\$17,240,987,847.05
4	\$376,486.15	−\$223,486.15	\$49,946,058,920.81
5	\$424,038.04	\$169,961.96	\$28,887,068,305.10

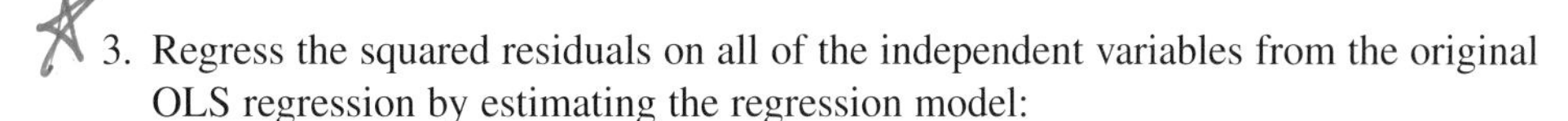

3. Regress the squared residuals on all of the independent variables from the original OLS regression by estimating the regression model:

$$e_i^2 = \gamma_0 + \gamma_1 x_{1i} + \gamma_2 x_{2i} + \cdots + \gamma_k x_{ki} + \varphi_i \qquad \textbf{9.1.3}$$

For our California home mortgage application data, we estimate the model

$$e_i^2 = \gamma_0 + \gamma_1 Applicant\ income_i + \varphi_i \qquad \textbf{9.1.4}$$

and get Excel Regression Output 9.2.

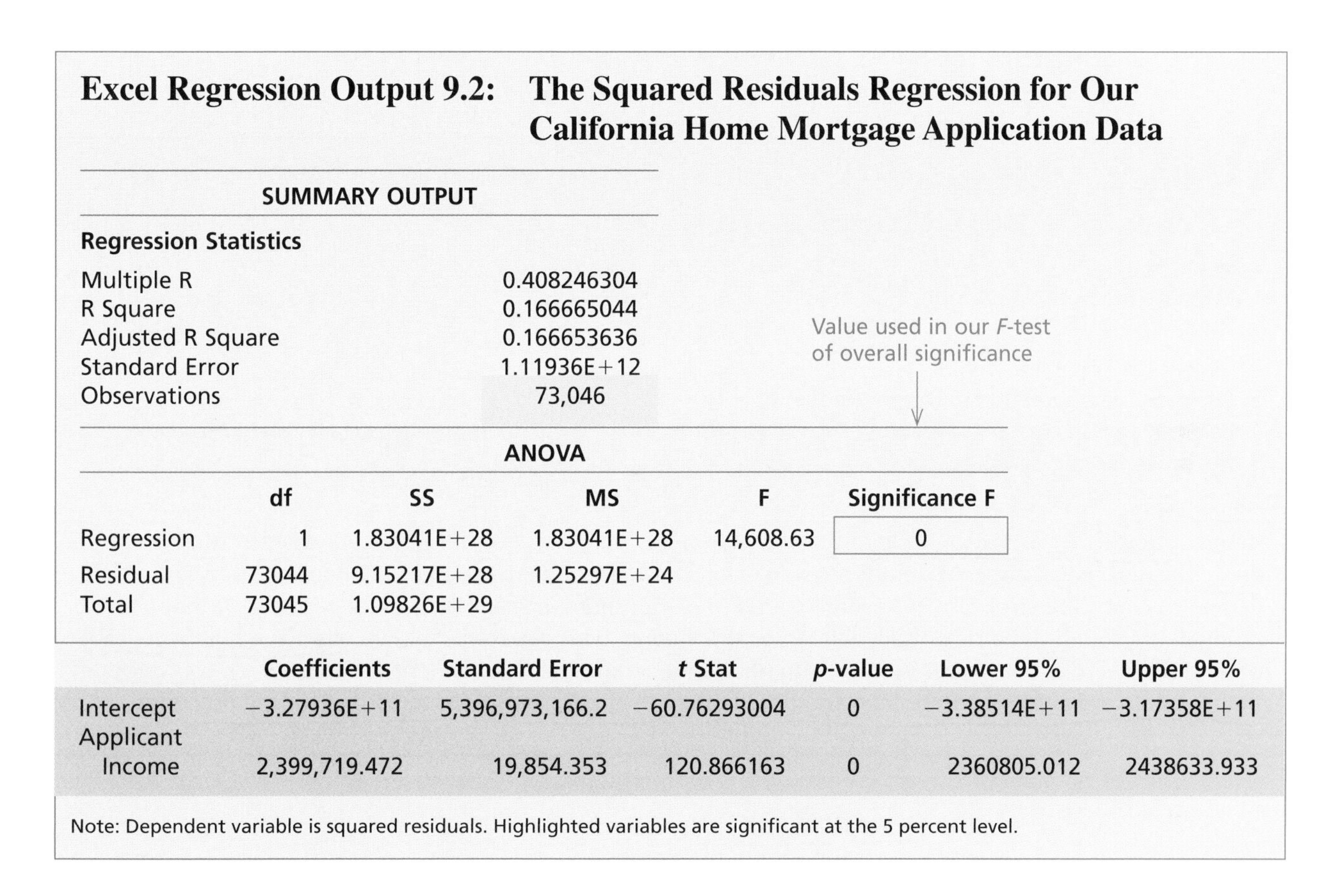

Excel Regression Output 9.2: The Squared Residuals Regression for Our California Home Mortgage Application Data

SUMMARY OUTPUT

Regression Statistics	
Multiple R	0.408246304
R Square	0.166665044
Adjusted R Square	0.166653636
Standard Error	1.11936E+12
Observations	73,046

ANOVA

	df	SS	MS	F	Significance F
Regression	1	1.83041E+28	1.83041E+28	14,608.63	0
Residual	73044	9.15217E+28	1.25297E+24		
Total	73045	1.09826E+29			

Value used in our *F*-test of overall significance

	Coefficients	Standard Error	*t* Stat	*p*-value	Lower 95%	Upper 95%
Intercept	−3.27936E+11	5,396,973,166.2	−60.76293004	0	−3.38514E+11	−3.17358E+11
Applicant Income	2,399,719.472	19,854.353	120.866163	0	2360805.012	2438633.933

Note: Dependent variable is squared residuals. Highlighted variables are significant at the 5 percent level.

4. Perform an F-test for the overall significance of the sample regression function to determine whether the squared residuals are statistically related to the independent variables. Formally, the null and alternative hypotheses for this test are

$$H_0\colon \gamma_1 = \gamma_2 = \cdots = \gamma_k = 0$$
$$H_A\colon \textit{at least on } \gamma_i \neq 0 \qquad \textbf{9.1.5}$$

To see why, look back at formula 9.1.3 and notice that the γ_i terms are the coefficients on the linear relationship between the squared residuals and the independent variables. Hence, if we reject the null hypothesis, because, for example, we estimate that $\gamma_3 \neq 0$, then we would conclude that $e_i^2 = \gamma_0 + \gamma_3 x_{3i}$, that assumption *M*6 is violated and that the error term is heteroskedastic.

Note that the F-statistic and the p-value of the F-statistic are automatically calculated and presented in Excel Regression Output 9.2. To perform the desired hypothesis test at the 95 percent level then, all we need do is check whether the significance F is less than 0.05.

For our California home mortgage application data, the null and alternative hypotheses are

$$H_0\colon \gamma_1 = 0$$
$$H_1\colon \gamma_i \neq 0 \qquad \textbf{9.1.6}$$

Because the estimated significance F of 0 is less than 0.05, we reject the null hypothesis and conclude that assumption M6 is violated, that our data are heteroskedastic, and that the calculated standard errors for the OLS estimated slope coefficients are incorrect.

As a final point, note that while the preceding method involves an F-test of the overall significance of all of the included independent variables, t-tests of the individual significance of each of the independent variables can also prove valuable. In particular, if there is more than one independent variable, then the t-tests of individual significance offer information about which particular variables are potentially responsible for the heteroskedasticity.

Empirical Research Tool 9.1 summarizes the Breusch-Pagan test.

EMPIRICAL RESEARCH TOOL 9.1: THE BREUSCH-PAGAN TEST FOR THE PRESENCE OF HETEROSKEDASTICITY

How to Do It:

1. Estimate the population regression model $y_i = \beta_0 + \beta_1 x_{1i} + \beta_2 x_{2i} + \cdots + \beta_k x_{ki} + \varepsilon_i$ and obtain the residuals, e_i.
2. Square the residuals, or e_i^2.
3. Estimate the population regression model $e_i^2 = \gamma_0 + \gamma_1 x_{1i} + \gamma_2 x_{2i} + \cdots + \gamma_k x_{ki} + \varphi$.
4. Perform an F-test for overall significance to see if the squared residuals are statistically related to any of the independent variables.

Why It Works:

Heteroskedasticity exists if the residuals of the OLS regression vary with the observed values of the independent variables. Regressing the squared residuals on the independent variables provides a direct test of the degree to which the error term is linearly related to one or more of the independent variables. If the squared residuals are found to be statistically related to the independent variables (i.e., we reject the null hypothesis of no statistical relationship between the squared residuals and the independent variables), then we conclude that the data are heteroskedastic, and we should take the appropriate steps to correct for the problem.

The General White's Test

The general White's test for heteroskedasticity is in many ways similar to the Breusch-Pagan test, with the primary difference being that instead of regressing the squared residuals from the original OLS regression on only the independent variables, we regress them on the independent variables, the independent variables squared, and the cross-products of the independent variables. In particular, for the population regression model

$$y_i = \beta_0 + \beta_1 x_{1i} + \beta_2 x_{2i} + \beta_3 x_{3i} + \beta_4 x_{4i} + \varepsilon \qquad \textbf{9.1.7}$$

the general White's test would consist of calculating the squared residuals from the OLS estimation and using those values as the dependent variables in the population regression model

$$\begin{aligned} e_i^2 = {} & \theta_0 + \theta_1 x_{1i} + \theta_2 x_{2i} + \theta_3 x_{3i} + \theta_4 x_{4i} + \theta_5 x_{1i}^2 + \theta_6 x_{2i}^2 + \theta_7 x_{3i}^2 + \theta_8 x_{4i}^2 + \\ & \theta_9 (x_{1i} \times x_{2i}) + \theta_{10}(x_{1i} \times x_{3i}) + \theta_{11}(x_{1i} \times x_{4i}) + \theta_{12}(x_{2i} \times x_{3i}) + \\ & \theta_{13}(x_{2i} \times x_{4i}) + \theta_{14}(x_{3i} \times x_{4i}) + \varepsilon_i^* \end{aligned} \qquad \textbf{9.1.8}$$

As this simple example suggests, a potential drawback to the general White's test for heteroskedasticity is that adding independent variables to the OLS regression quickly increases the degrees of freedom required to perform the test because it forces us to include so many additional variables. In this case, with only four independent variables, the general White's test uses up 14 degrees of freedom. For this reason, rather than the general White's test, we prefer to use a modified version of White's test for heteroskedasticity.

The Modified White's Test

In the modified White's test, we (1) regress the squared residuals from the original OLS regression on the predicted value of the dependent variable and the predicted value of the dependent variable squared and (2) perform a test of joint significance of the to see if the estimated linear relationship between the squared residuals and the independent variables is statistically significant. The reason this approach works is that the predicted value of the dependent variable is a linear function of the independent variables, while the predicted value of the dependent variable squared is a linear function of the squared and the cross-product terms for the independent variables. Accordingly, by including those terms in our regression, we are controlling for all of the linear, squared, and cross-product terms of the independent variables that are included in the general version of White's test, but we are only sacrificing two additional degrees of freedom rather than the many, many that would have been sacrificed in the general White's test.

The individual steps for conducting the modified White's test for heteroskedasticity are

1. Estimate the population regression model

$$y_i = \beta_0 + \beta_1 x_{1i} + \beta_2 x_{2i} + \cdots + \beta_k x_{ki} + \varepsilon_i \qquad \textbf{9.1.9}$$

obtain the residuals,

$$e_i = y_i - \hat{y}_i \qquad \textbf{9.1.10}$$

and the predicted value of the dependent variable

$$\hat{y}_i = \hat{\beta}_0 + \hat{\beta}_1 x_{1i} + \hat{\beta}_2 x_{2i} + \cdots + \hat{\beta}_k x_{ki} \qquad \textbf{9.1.11}$$

(both of which we obtain by checking the "Residuals" box in the regression wizard in Excel).

2. Square the residuals (e_1^2) and the predicted value of the dependent variable ($\hat{y}_i^2$).
3. Regress the squared residuals on the predicted value of the dependent variable and the predicted value of the dependent variable squared by estimating the population regression model

$$e_i^2 = \delta_0 + \delta_1 \hat{y}_i + \delta_2 \hat{y}_i^2 + u_i \qquad \textbf{9.1.12}$$

For our California home mortgage application data, we estimate the population regression model

$$e_i^2 = \delta_0 + \delta_1 \widehat{Loan\ amount} + \delta_{21} \widehat{Loan\ amount^2} + u_i \qquad \textbf{9.1.13}$$

and get Excel Regression Output 9.3.

Excel Regression Output 9.3: The Modified White's Test for Heteroskedasticity Regression for Our California Home Mortgage Application Data

SUMMARY OUTPUT	
Regression Statistics	
Multiple R	0.489896076
R Square	0.239998166
Adjusted R Square	0.239977356
Standard Error	1.06898E+12
Observations	73,046

ANOVA

	df	SS	MS	F	Significance F
Regression	2	2.6358E+28	1.3179E+28	11,532.989	0.000
Residual	73043	8.34679E+28	1.14272E+24		
Total	73045	1.09826E+29			

← Value used in our *F*-test of overall significance

	Coefficients	Standard Error	*t* Stat	*p*-value	Lower 95%	Upper 95%
Intercept	−1.1425E+11	10969931423	−10.41481901	2.21075E-25	−1.35751E+11	−92748824142
Predicted Loan Amount	249,831.637	27,145.089	9.20356663	3.55068E-20	196627.3597	303035.9142
Predicted Loan Amount Squared	0.446	0.005	83.95219706	0	0.435810963	0.456646796

Note: Dependent variable is squared residuals. Highlighted variables are significant at the 5 percent level.

4. Perform an *F*-test of the joint significance of the predicted loan amount and the predicted loan amount squared to see if they are statistically related to the dependent variable and the dependent variable squared, in which case the error term would have nonconstant variance because it would systematically vary with the linear, the squared, and the cross-product terms of the independent variables. Formally, the null and alternative hypotheses for this test would be

$$H_0: \delta_1 = \delta_2 = 0$$
$$H_A: \textit{either } \delta_1 \textit{ or } \delta_2 \neq 0 \qquad \textbf{9.1.14}$$

To see why, look back at formula 9.1.9 and notice that the δ_1 and δ_2 terms are the coefficients on the linear relationship between the squared residuals and the predicted value of the dependent variable and the predicted value of the dependent variable squared, respectively. Hence, if we reject the null hypothesis, because, for example, we estimate that $\delta_1 \neq 0$, then we would conclude that $\hat{e}_i^2 = \delta_0 + \delta_1 y_i$, meaning that assumption M6 is violated, that the error term is heteroskedastic, and that the calculated standard errors of the estimated slope coefficients are incorrect.

For our California home mortgage application data, even though we are performing a simple linear regression, our null and alternative hypotheses are specified as in formula 9.1.11. Looking at Excel Regression Output 9.3, we see that either because the calculated F-statistic of 11,532.99 exceeds the table value of $F_{2,\infty,.05} = 3.00$ or because the estimated significance F of 0 is less than 0.05, we reject the null hypothesis and conclude that assumption M6 is violated and that our data are heteroskedastic.

Empirical Research Tool 9.2 summarizes the modified White's test.

EMPIRICAL RESEARCH TOOL 9.2: MODIFIED WHITE'S TEST FOR THE PRESENCE OF HETEROSKEDASTICITY

How to Do It:

1. Estimate the population regression model $y_i = \beta_0 + \beta_1 x_{1i} + \beta_2 x_{2i} + \cdots + \beta_k x_{ki} + \varepsilon_i$ and obtain the residuals, e_i.
2. Square the residuals.
3. Estimate the population regression model $e_i^2 = \delta_0 + \delta_1 \hat{y}_i + \delta_2 \hat{y}_i^2 + u_i$.
4. Perform an *F*-test for overall significance to see if the squared residuals are statistically related to the $\hat{y}_i$ and $\hat{y}_i^2$ variables.

> Why It Works:
> This test works for the same reason that that Breusch-Pagan test works. The primary difference is that the $\hat{y}_i$ and $\hat{y}_i^2$ variables are a function of the independent variables, the independent variables squared, and the cross-products of the independent variables, meaning that including those terms in the squared residual regression test whether the squared residuals are a function of all of those terms rather than a function of the independent variables alone.

The final detection method that we introduce is based on a different approach that divides the data into groups and asks whether the estimated error variances differ across the groups.

The Goldfeld-Quandt Test

We generally use the Goldfeld-Quandt test when we think the error variance is nonconstant in such a way that it is large for some values (group *a*) and small for other values (group *b*) of a specific independent variable. In such a case, because the variance of the residuals for the observations in group *a* should be significantly larger than the variance of the residuals for the observations in group *b*, a comparison of the unexplained sums of squares from the OLS regressions for the separate groups of observations should represent an ideal test for the presence of such heteroskedasticity.

The first step in this test is to identify which of the independent variables is responsible for the heteroskedasticity. Once we have identified a suspect independent variable (if there are many possibilities, then we will need to repeat the test separately for each of the possibilities), the individual steps for performing the Goldfeld-Quandt test are:

1. Sort the entire data set from the lowest to the highest value of the suspect independent variable.

Table 9.6 presents the results of sorting our California home mortgage application data by applicant income.

TABLE 9.6
The First Five Observations of Our California Home Mortgage Application Data Sorted from Lowest to Highest Applicant Income

Observation	Loan Amount (y_i)	Applicant Income (x_i)
9711	$ 315,000	$1,000
19797	$ 700,000	$1,000
19798	$ 402,000	$1,000
19801	$ 724,000	$1,000
56719	$1,700,000	$1,000

2. Omit the middle *c* observations from the ordered data set to generate two separate groups of observations: the $(n - c)/2$ with the lowest values of the suspect independent variable and the $(n - c)/2$ with the highest values of the suspect independent variable. Note that there is no steadfast rule governing the appropriate choice of *c*. In general, if we possess enough observations, we prefer to divide our data into thirds, omitting the middle third of the observations and keeping the lowest and highest thirds for our test.

For our California home mortgage application data, because we have 73,046 observations, we delete the middle 24,348 observations, leaving us with groups containing the 24,349 lowest and the 24,349 highest values of the independent variable *Applicant income.*

3. Run two separate regressions with the remaining $(n - c)$ observations, with the first regression being for the $(n - c)/2$ observations with the lowest values of the suspect independent variable and the second regression being for the $(n - c)/2$ observations with the highest values of the suspect independent variable.

Excel Regression Output 9.4 presents the results of these regressions for our California home mortgage application data.

Excel Regression Output 9.4: The Goldfeld-Quandt Test for Our California Home Mortgage Application Data

Lowest Third

SUMMARY OUTPUT

Regression Statistics	
Multiple R	0.274434604
R Square	0.075314352
Adjusted R Square	0.075276373
Standard Error	122291.1032
Observations	24,349

Value used in calculation of Goldfeld-Quandt statistic: USS_1, USS_2

ANOVA

	df	SS	MS	F	Significance F
Regression	1	2.96564E+13	2.96564E+13	1983.029082	0
Residual	24347	3.64112E+14	14955113928		
Total	24348	3.93769E+14			

	Coefficients	Standard Error	*t*-Stat	*p*-value	Lower 95%	Upper 95%
Intercept	111,387.810	3,032.937	36.72605077	1.9263E-287	105443.0664	117332.5529
Applicant Income	1,714	0.038	44.53121469	0	1.638141362	1.788987996

Note: Dependent variable is the requested loan amount. Highlighted variables are significant at the 5 percent level.

Highest Third

SUMMARY OUTPUT

Regression Statistics	
Multiple R	0.559786436
R Square	0.313360854
Adjusted R Square	0.313332652
Standard Error	458699.0806
Observations	24,349

ANOVA

	df	SS	MS	F	Significance F
Regression	1	2.33785E+15	2.33785E+15	11111.21726	0
Residual	24347	5.12273E+15	2.10405E+11		
Total	24348	7.46058E+15			

	Coefficients	Standard Error	*t*-Stat	*p*-value	Lower 95%	Upper 95%
Intercept	345,839.124	4,127.623	83.78649981	0	337748.7287	353929.5194
Applicant Income	0.980	0.009	105,4097588	0	0.962263537	0.998727551

Note: Dependent variable is the requested loan amount. Highlighted variables are significant at the 5 percent level.

4. Obtain the unexplained sum of squares from each of the two separate regressions and form the test statistic

$$GQ = \frac{USS_2}{USS_1} \quad \textbf{9.1.15}$$

where USS_2 is the larger and USS_1 the smaller of the two sums of squares.

Note that depending on the nature of the suspected heteroskedasticity, either sample can have the larger unexplained sum of squares. If the heteroskedasticity is such that smaller values of the independent variable have greater error variance than larger values, then the sample of the smallest observed values will have the larger unexplained sum of squares, and that value will form the numerator of the test statistic. If the heteroskedasticity is such that larger values of the independent variable have greater error variance than smaller values, then the sample of the largest observed values will have the larger unexplained sum of squares, and that value will form the numerator of the test statistic. In other words, identifying which sample forms the numerator of the test statistic also identifies the underlying nature of any observed heteroskedasticity. Finally, note that the degrees of freedom for this test are $n_1 - k_1$ and $n_2 - k_2$, meaning that the table value to which we compare our calculated test statistic is $F_{n_1-k_1, n_2-k_2, .05}$ at the 95 percent confidence level.

Formally, the null and alternative hypotheses for this test would be

$$H_0\colon USS_1 = USS_2 \text{ or } \frac{USS_2}{USS_1} = 1$$

$$H_1\colon USS_1 \neq USS_2 \text{ or } \frac{USS_2}{USS_1} \neq 1 \quad \textbf{9.1.16}$$

To see why, recall that USS_1 and USS_2 are our numerical measures of the error variance of both equations. Hence, if we reject the null hypothesis, then it is appropriate to conclude that error variances do differ systematically across different observed values of the suspected independent variable, leading us to conclude that the error term is heteroskedastic.

For our California home mortgage application data, the calculated value of our test statistic is

$$GQ = \frac{USS_2}{USS_1} = \frac{5.12273E+15}{3.64112E+14} = 14.069 \quad \textbf{9.1.17}$$

In this case, because the calculated F-statistic of 14.069 exceeds the table value of $F_{\infty,\infty,.05} = 1$ (we use the ∞ for the degrees of freedom because our sample size far exceeds 1,000, which is the next-to-last value listed in the table), we reject the null hypothesis and conclude that assumption M6 is violated and that our data are heteroskedastic.

Empirical Research Tool 9.3 summarizes the Goldfeld-Quandt text.

EMPIRICAL RESEARCH TOOL 9.3: THE GOLDFELD-QUANDT TEST FOR THE PRESENCE OF HETEROSKEDASTICITY

How to Do It:

1. Identify which independent variable is suspected of contributing to heteroskedasticity, and sort the data from smallest to largest on that variable.
2. Omit the middle c observations.
3. Run two regressions with the remaining $(n - c)$ observations.
4. Form the test statistic $GQ = \frac{USS_2}{USS_1}$, where USS_2 is the larger value (because the F-statistic must be greater than or equal to 1).
5. Reject the null hypothesis of homoskedasticity if $GQ > F_{n_1-k_1, n_2-k_2, .05}$.

$k_1 = K+1$ $K =$ # of independent variables in the model being estimated for the 2 sets of observations
$k_2 = K+1$

> Why It Works:
> This test works when the suspected heteroskedasticity is of the type that the error variances either increase (or decrease) with the value of a given independent variable. In such cases, this test works by comparing the unexplained sum of squares (i.e., the total error variance) for the largest values of the suspect independent variable to the unexplained sum of squares (i.e., the total error variance) for the smallest values of the suspect independent variable. If we find that the unexplained sum of squares for the largest values is "large" relative to the unexplained sum of squares for the smallest values, then we conclude that the error variance changes significantly with the value of the independent variable, suggesting that the data are heteroskedastic.

After finding evidence pointing toward the presence of heteroskedasticity, we should take steps to correct the calculated standard errors of the estimated slope coefficients to ensure that our resulting estimates are BLUE. We address two potential adjustments next.

9.2 CORRECT FOR HETEROSKEDASTICITY

There are two primary ways to correct for the fact that the presence of heteroskedasticity in our data result in OLS estimates that are no longer the minimum variance unbiased estimator and estimated standard errors that are incorrect. The first method involves converting our observed data into a form for which the coefficient estimates from an OLS regression on the converted data are BLUE.

Weighted Least Squares

weighted least squares (WLS)
A method in which the variables are weighted such that the error term becomes homoskedastic.

In **weighted least squares (WLS)**, we transform the model that we estimate by re-weighting all variables to correct for the suspected nature of the heteroskedasticity, thereby "forcing" OLS to provide BLUE estimates for the re-weighted data. To perform, we first need to make an educated guess as to the exact form of heteroskedasticity that is present in our data.

As an example, suppose that our original population regression model is

$$y_i = \beta_0 + \beta_1 x_{1i} + \beta_2 x_{2i} + \beta_3 x_{3i} + \varepsilon_i \qquad 9.2.1$$

and that assumptions M1 through M5 hold but that we have found our data to be heteroskedastic, with the exact form of the heteroskedasticity being

$$Var(\varepsilon) = \sigma^2 x_{1i}^2 \qquad 9.2.2$$

Notice that the error variance in formula 9.2.2 is nonconstant because it depends on the observed value of x_{1i} for each individual observation. To "force" our data to satisfy assumption M6, we need to re-weight every single observation in the sample in a manner that removes the x_{1i}^2 term from the error variance in 9.2.2. Because all values in variance calculations are squared, we can make this transformation by dividing every single observation by x_{1i} (because $\sqrt{x_{1i}^2} = x_{1i}$). Doing so leaves us with the transformed model

$$\frac{y_i}{x_{1i}} = \beta_0 \frac{1}{x_{1i}} + \beta_1 \frac{x_{1i}}{x_{1i}} + \beta_2 \frac{x_{2i}}{x_{1i}} + \beta_3 \frac{x_{3i}}{x_{1i}} + \frac{\varepsilon_i}{x_{1i}} \qquad 9.2.3$$

or

$$y_i^* = \beta_0 x_0^* + \beta_1 x_{1i}^* + \beta_2 x_{2i}^* + \beta_3 x_{3i}^* + \varepsilon_i^* \qquad 9.2.4$$

where

$$(y_i^* = y_i/x_{1i}),\ (x_0^* = 1/x_{1i}),\ (x_{1i}^* = x_{1i}/x_{1i}),\ (x_{2i}^* = x_{2i}/x_{1i}),\text{ and }(x_{3i}^* = x_{3i}/x_{1i})$$

Note that when transforming the data, we must be sure to re-weight the intercept as well as the values of the independent variables and that, after this re-weighting, the transformed value of the intercept will still be a constant, but the value will be $1/x_{1i}$ rather than 1.

For our California home mortgage application data, the transformed population regression model is

$$\frac{\textit{Loan amount}_i}{\textit{Applicant income}_i} = \beta_0 \frac{1}{\textit{Applicant income}_i} + \beta_1 \frac{\textit{Applicant income}_i}{\textit{Applicant income}_i} + \frac{\varepsilon_i}{\textit{Applicant income}_i} \quad \textbf{9.2.5}$$

or

$$y_i^* = \beta_0 x_0^* + \beta_1 x_{1i}^* + \varepsilon_i^* \quad \textbf{9.2.6}$$

Table 9.7 demonstrates how we perform these calculations for the first five observations in our sample.

TABLE 9.7 Converted Data for the First Five Observations in Our California Home Mortgage Application for Weighted Least Squares under the Assumption That $Var(\varepsilon) = \sigma^2 x_i^2$

Observation	Loan Amount (y_i)	Applicant Income (x_i)	Weighted Loan Amount ($y_i^* = y_i/x_{1i}$)	Weighted Intercept ($x_0^* = 1/x_{1i}$)	Weighted Applicant Income ($x_{1i}^* = x_{1i}/x_{1i}$)
9711	$ 315,000	$1,000	$ 315.00	$0.001000	$1.00
19797	$ 700,000	$1,000	$ 700.00	$0.001000	$1.00
19798	$ 402,000	$1,000	$ 402.00	$0.001000	$1.00
19801	$ 724,000	$1,000	$ 724.00	$0.001000	$1.00
56719	$1,700,000	$1,000	$1,700.00	$0.001000	$1.00

Our desired WLS estimates are obtained by estimating the converted population regression model in formula 9.2.5 by OLS. Do not be surprised if the coefficient estimates change a little between the original model and the converted model, even though they are both unbiased. This happens when working with sample sizes that are not extremely large.

We note that, due to the way the Regression Wizard is programmed, a special issue is associated with estimating the transformed model in Excel. Namely, because we have to include the weighted intercept as an independent variable, we must ask Excel to suppress the normal intercept, which we do by checking the "Constant is Zero" box in the Regression Wizard (as we do in Excel Example 9.2).

EXCEL EXAMPLE 9.2

Constraining the intercept to be 0 in Excel

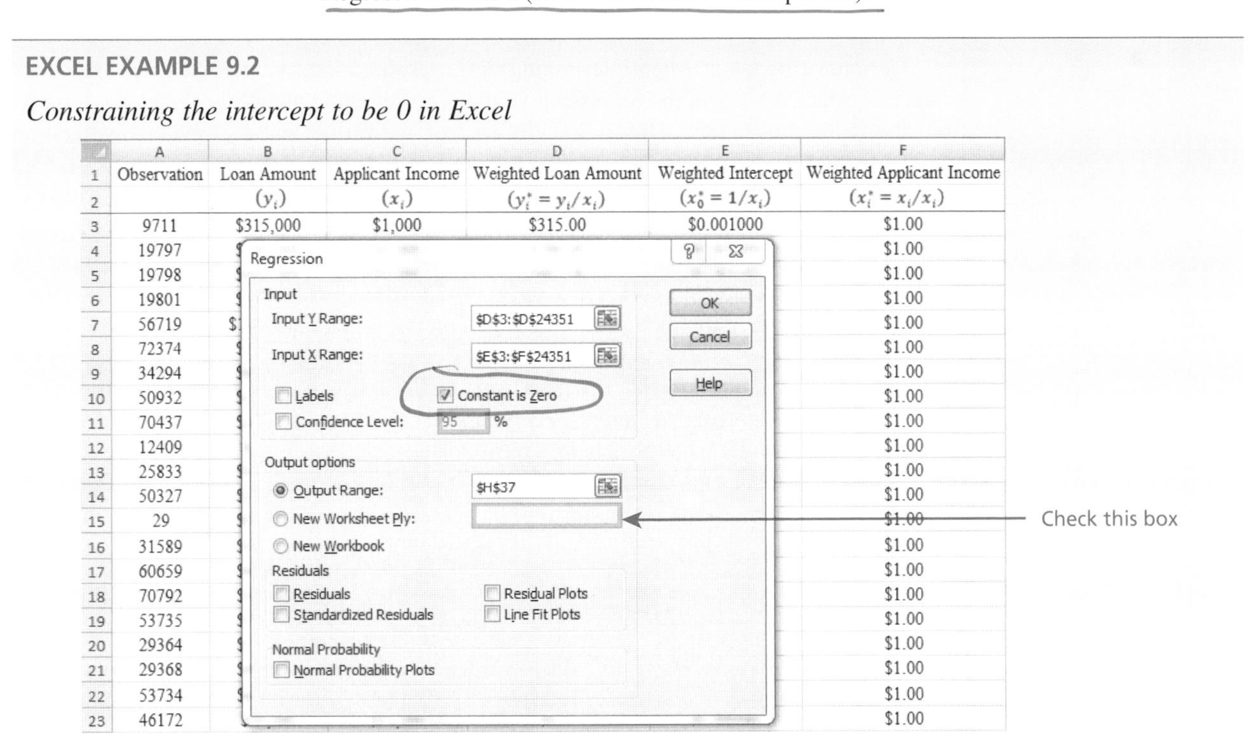

Excel Regression Output 9.5 presents the results of estimating our transformed weighted least squares regression.

Excel Regression Output 9.5: Weighted Least Squares Under the Assumption that $Var(\varepsilon) = \sigma^2 x_i^2$ for Our California Home Mortgage Application Data

SUMMARY OUTPUT

Regression Statistics	
Multiple R	0.753875325
R Square	0.568328005
Adjusted R Square	0.568308405
Standard Error	5.490485616
Observations	73046

ANOVA

	df	SS	MS	F	Significance F
Regression	2	2899020.236	1449510.118	48083.9055	0
Residual	73044	2201942.957	30.1454323		
Total	73046	5100963.192			

	Coefficients	Standard Error	*t* Stat	*p*-value	Lower 95%	Upper 95%
Intercept	0	#N/A	#N/A	#N/A	#N/A	#N/A
Weighted Intercept	522,950.212	1,877.212	278.5781237	0	519270.8831	526629.5408
Weighted Applicant Income	−1.813	0.026	−69.3650845	0	−1.864109575	−1.76165899

Note: Dependent variable is the requested loan amount. Highlighted variables are significant at the 5 percent level.

Care must be taken when interpreting these results. First, notice that when we check the "Constant is" box in the regression window, Excel automatically includes the top row in the regression output. This is Excel's way of indicating that the regular intercept is indeed suppressed in the regression (thus, a good check that we are performing weighted least squares correctly is to make sure that the first line of output appears this way). The remaining coefficient estimates should then be interpreted as follows. On average, if an individual applicant has an income of $0, then we would expect that individual to apply for a mortgage of $522,950.21. At the same time, for each additional dollar of applicant income, we estimate the requested mortgage amount to *decrease* by an average of $1.81. The fact that this estimated marginal effect seems nonsensical and changes so much from the original OLS estimates may well suggest that our initial assumption as to the form of the heteroskedasticity is likely incorrect.

How do we know whether this approach has succeeded in producing coefficient estimates that are BLUE and estimated standard errors that are correct? If (and it's a big if) our initial suspicion as to the true form of the heteroskedasticity is indeed correct, then the converted model should be homoskedastic. To see this, note that in our converted model

$$\varepsilon_i^* = \frac{\varepsilon_i}{x_{1i}} \qquad \textbf{9.2.7}$$

Taking the variance of this error term, we get

$$Var(\varepsilon_i^*) = Var\left(\frac{\varepsilon_i}{x_{1i}}\right) \qquad \textbf{9.2.8}$$

Because in order to factor a term out a variance calculation we must square it, we can rewrite formula 9.2.8 as

$$Var(\varepsilon_i^*) = \frac{1}{x_{1i}^2} Var(\varepsilon_i) \quad \textbf{9.2.9}$$

Based on our assumption that $Var(\varepsilon_i) = \sigma^2 x_{1i}^2$, we can rewrite formula 9.2.9 as

$$Var(\varepsilon^*) = \frac{1}{x_{1i}^2}\sigma^2 x_{1i}^2 = \sigma^2 \quad \textbf{9.2.10}$$

which is indeed homoskedastic.

Does this theoretical fact guarantee that our WLS approach accurately corrects for the underlying heteroskedasticity? No. To determine whether our chosen WLS approach comes anywhere close to producing estimates that are BLUE, we should perform one of the preceding statistical tests to see if we still reject the null hypothesis of homoskedasticity for our transformed data. If we do, then we will need to try different assumed forms of the suspected heteroskedasticity until we find the one that succeeds in our failing to reject the null hypothesis of homoskedasticity for the transformed data. If we do not, then we can move forward with our analysis.

Excel Regression Output 9.6 presents the results of performing the Goldfeld-Quandt test for our transformed California home mortgage application data.
For these results, the calculated value of our test statistic is

$$GQ = \frac{USS_2}{USS_1} = \frac{5.12273E+15}{3.64112E+14} = 14.0691 \quad \textbf{9.2.11}$$

In this case, because the calculated F-statistic of 14.0691 is greater than the table value of $F_{\infty,\infty,.05} = 1$, we reject the null hypothesis and conclude that assumption M6 is violated, that our converted data are still heteroskedastic, and that our estimated standard errors are still incorrect.

A Different Assumed Form of Heteroskedasticity

Suppose that our first attempt did not result in our failing to reject the null hypothesis of homoskedasticity. We would need to pursue a different possibility such as the assumption that we have the same model as used earlier but that the form of the heteroskedasticity is actually

$$Var(\varepsilon) = \sigma^2 x_i \quad \textbf{9.2.12}$$

To perform WLS in this case, we would follow the process outlined earlier, except that we would now re-weight the data so that the error variance in formula 9.2.12 no longer contains the x_i term, which we would do by dividing all variables (and the intercept) by $\sqrt{x_i}$. If this does not result in our failing to reject the null hypothesis of homoskedasticity, then would continue with different assumed forms of heteroskedasticity until we did finally fail to reject that null hypothesis.

Empirical Research Tool 9.4 summarizes weighted least squares.

White's Heteroskedastic Consistent Standard Errors

White's heteroskedastic consistent standard errors
Standard errors that are corrected for the heteroskedasticity that is inherent in the data.

While the preceding procedure theoretically provides estimates that are BLUE and estimated standard errors that are correct in the presence of heteroskedasticity, it can be rather time-consuming and difficult to perform. For this reason, by far the most popular correction for the presence of heteroskedasticity is a procedure known as **White's heteroskedastic consistent standard errors.** While the exact calculations of these

Excel Regression Output 9.6: The Goldfeld-Quandt Test of Weighted Least Squares Under the Assumption that $Var(\varepsilon) = \sigma^2 x_i^2$ for Our California Home Mortgage Application Data

Lowest Third

SUMMARY OUTPUT

Regression Statistics	
Multiple R	0.274434604
R Square	0.075314352
Adjusted R Square	0.075276373
Standard Error	122291.1032
Observations	24,349

Value used in calculation of Goldfeld-Quandt statistic: USS_1 (Residual SS, lowest third), USS_2 (Residual SS, highest third)

ANOVA

	df	SS	MS	F	Significance F
Regression	1	2.96564E+13	2.96564E+13	1983.029082	0
Residual	24347	3.64112E+14	14955113928		
Total	24348	3.93769E+14			

	Coefficients	Standard Error	*t*-Stat	*p*-value	Lower 95%	Upper 95%
Intercept	111,387.810	3,032.937	36.72605077	1.9263E-287	105443.0664	117332.5529
Applicant Income	1.714	0.038	44.53121469	0	1.638141362	1.788987996

Note: Dependent variable is the requested loan amount. Highlighted variables are significant at the 5 percent level.

Highest Third

SUMMARY OUTPUT

Regression Statistics	
Multiple R	0.559786436
R Square	0.313360854
Adjusted R Square	0.313332652
Standard Error	458699.0806
Observations	24,349

ANOVA

	df	SS	MS	F	Significance F
Regression	1	2.33785E+15	2.33785E+15	11111.21726	0
Residual	24347	5.12273E+15	2.10405E+11		
Total	24348	7.46058E+15			

	Coefficients	Standard Error	*t*-Stat	*p*-value	Lower 95%	Upper 95%
Intercept	345,839.124	4,127.623	83.78649981	0	337748.7287	353929.5194
Applicant Income	0.980	0.009	105.4097588	0	0.962263537	0.998727551

Note: Dependent variable is the requested loan amount. Highlighted variables are significant at the 5 percent level.

EMPIRICAL RESEARCH TOOL 9.4: WEIGHTED LEAST SQUARES

How to Do It:

1. Assume the form of heteroskedasticity, say, $Var(\varepsilon) = \sigma^2 h(x)$.
2. Create new variables by dividing through by the square root of $h(x)$ to get $y_i^* = y_i/\sqrt{h(x)}$, $x_0^* = 1/\sqrt{h(x)}$, $x_{1i}^* = x_{1i}/\sqrt{h(x)}$, $x_{2i}^* = x_{2i}/\sqrt{h(x)}$, $\cdots$, $x_{ki}^* = x_{ki}/\sqrt{h(x)}$.
3. Estimate the population regression model $y_i^* = \beta_0 x_0^* + \beta_1 x_{1i}^* + \varepsilon_i^*$.

Why It Works:

Weighted least squares changes the model from one that was initially heteroskedastic into one that is homoskedastic. This is accomplished because the new error term $\varepsilon^* = \varepsilon/\sqrt{h(x)}$ has variance $Var(\varepsilon^*) = \sigma^2 h(x)/(\sqrt{h(x)})^2 = \sigma^2$ as long as the assumed form of heteroskedasticity is correct.

standard errors are quite complicated, they do result in correct estimated standard errors in the presence of heteroskedasticity, meaning that all measures of precisions based on those values will also be correct.

In a theme that recurs throughout the remaining chapters of this text, while Excel does not have a canned option for estimating White's heteroskedastic consistent standard errors, more advanced statistical packages do. As an example, using the Stata command

```
reg loan amount appincome, robust
```

for our California home mortgage application data, we get Empirical Output 9.1.

Empirical Output 9.1: White's Heteroskedastic Consistent Standard Errors for Our California Home Mortgage Application Data

	Coefficent	Robust Standard Error	t	P > |t|	Lower 95%	Upper 95%
Intercept	209,474.60	9,763.69	21.45	0.000	190,337.80	228,611.40
Applicant Income	1.159802	0.0589456	19.68	0.000	1.044269	1.275335
Prob > F			0.0000			
R-Squared			.3933			
Observations			73,046			

Note: Dependent variable is the applied for loan amount. Highlighted variables are significant at the 5 percent level.

It is informative to compare the estimates in Empirical Output 9.1 with the regular OLS estimates in Excel Regression Output 9.1. Note that because OLS is unbiased in the presence of heteroskedasticity, the estimated coefficients are the same in both cases. While true, the estimated White's heteroskedastic consistent standard errors in Empirical Output 9.1 are much larger than the estimated OLS standard errors in Excel Regression Output 9.1, resulting in calculated t-statistics that are roughly one-tenth as large. Given that we have more than 73,000 observations in our sample, this difference does not alter the results of our hypothesis testing (we find applicant income to be statistically significant at the 5 percent level in both cases). Notice, however, that it could alter the estimated statistical significance, particularly for the much smaller samples that we often encounter. This is a primary reason that it is so important to control for potential heteroskedasticity. It is also the reason that many researchers routinely correct for heteroskedasticity without even testing for it (and why White's paper is the most cited of all papers in economic literature). In fact, we would not doubt that many researchers typically add the command for White's standard errors to their regressions without giving a second thought as to why they are doing so. The thinking behind this approach is that there is virtually no consequence to correcting the standard errors for heteroskedasticity if it is not present, but the consequence of not correcting the standard errors for heteroskedasticity if it is present is potentially immense because doing so could yield all statistical inference incorrect.

Empirical Research Tool 9.5 summarizes the process.

EMPIRICAL RESEARCH TOOL 9.5: WHITE'S HETEROSKEDASTIC CONSISTENT STANDARD ERRORS

How to Do It:

In a more advanced statistical package than Excel, ask the program to estimate the population regression model with White's heteroskedastic consistent standard errors.

Why It Works:

This method works because, unlike the usual OLS standard errors, White's heteroskedastic consistent standard errors standard errors are now adjusted for heteroskedasticity. The coefficient estimates have not changed because they are unbiased in the presence of heteroskedasticity.

ADDITIONS TO OUR EMPIRICAL RESEARCH TOOLKIT

In this chapter we have introduced a number of tools that will prove valuable when performing empirical research. They include:

- Statistical tests for the presence of heteroskedasticity, including the Breusch-Pagan, the modified White's, and the Goldfeld-Quandt tests.
- Empirical methods for correcting the estimated standard errors in the presence of heteroskedasticity, including weighted least squares and White's heteroskedastic consistent standard errors.

OUR NEW EMPIRICAL TOOLS IN PRACTICE: USING WHAT WE HAVE LEARNED IN THIS CHAPTER

Understanding the potential consequences of not controlling for heteroskedasticity when it is indeed present, our former student decided to test whether assumption M6 held for her data. She started by examining residual plots for each of her independent variables, finding that the one presented in Figure 9.7 stood out as more suspicious than the others.

On the basis of Figure 9.7, our former student decided to test whether her data were heteroskedastic with respect to maternal mortality. Employing the Breusch-Pagan test, the student produced the sample regression results in Table 9.8.

FIGURE 9.7
Residual Plot versus Maternal Mortality in Our Former Student's Human Development Index Data

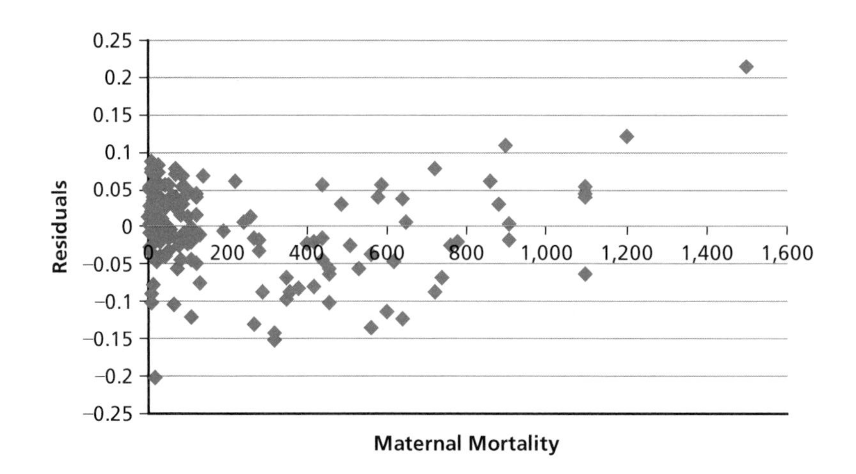

TABLE 9.8 Estimated Marginal Effects for Residuals Squared Regression for the Breusch-Pagan Test for Our Former Student's Human Development Index Data

SUMMARY OUTPUT	
Regression Statistics	
Multiple R	0.317938273
R Square	0.101084746
Adjusted R Square	0.095209482
Standard Error	0.005905373
Observations	155

ANOVA

	df	SS	MS	F	Significance F
Regression	1	0.000600002	0.000600002	17.20514363	5.54524E-05
Residual	153	0.005335636	3.48734E-05		
Total	154	0.005935638			

	Coefficients	Standard Error	*t* Stat	*p*-value	Lower 95%	Upper 95%	Lower 95.0%	Upper 95.0%
Intercept	0.002092866	0.000587401	3.562927534	0.000489374	0.000932403	0.003253329	0.000932403	0.003253329
Material mortality ratio	6.35954E-06	1.53319E-06	4.147908344	5.54524E-05	3.33058E-06	9.3885E-06	3.33058E-06	9.3885E-06

Note: Dependent variable is the residuals squared. Highlighted variables are significant at the 5 percent level.

On the basis of the estimated coefficient on maternal mortality being statistically significant at the 5 percent level, the student rejected the null hypothesis of homoskedasticity and concluded that her data were indeed heteroskedastic with respect to maternal mortality. Accordingly, she re-estimated her initial model with White's heteroskedastic consistent standard errors, producing the results in Table 9.9.

TABLE 9.9 Estimated Marginal Effects with White's Heteroskedastic Consistent Standard Errors for Our Former Student's Human Development Index Data

	Coefficent	Robust Standard Error	*t*	P > |*t*|	Lower 95%	Upper 95%
Intercept	0.6507413	0.0159586	40.78	0.000	0.6192052	0.6822774
GDP per capita in PPP terms (constant 2005 international $)	6.62E-06	9.11E-07	7.27	0.000	4.82E-06	8.42E-06
Forest area (% of total land area)	0.0004133	0.0002311	1.79	0.076	−0.0000434	0.00087
Adolescent fertility rate (births per 1,000 women aged 15–19)	−0.0005835	0.0001704	−3.42	0.001	−0.0009203	−0.0002467
Maternal mortality ratio (deaths of women per 100,000 live births)	−0.0003042	0.0000372	−8.18	0.000	−0.0003777	−0.0002307
Shares in parliament female-male ratio	0.0549694	0.0375786	1.46	0.146	−0.0192905	0.1292294
Carbon Dioxide Emissions per capita (tonnes)	−0.0006031	0.0003772	−1.60	0.112	−0.0013485	0.0001422
Prob > F			0.0000			
R-Squared			.8931			
Observations			155			

Note: Dependent variable is the Human Development Index. Standard errors are White's heteroskedastic consistent standard errors. Variables highlighted in blue are significant at the 5 percent level. Variables highlighted in gray are significant at the 10 percent level.

On the basis of this work, along with an effect write-up, our former student was judged to have conducted a successful empirical research project.

LOOKING AHEAD TO CHAPTER 10

The material covered so far in the text has focused exclusively on cross-section data. While such data are the focus of a vast number of empirical studies, there are certainly instances in which we wish to focus on time-series data. Chapter 10 begins our discussion of methods for dealing with such data.

Problems

9.1 The following equation models immigration to the United States:

$$I_i = \beta_0 + \beta_1 w_i + \beta_2 D_i + \beta_3 Lang_i + \varepsilon_i$$

I_i = Total immigrants from country i to the US

w_i = Wage differential between country i and the US

D_i = Distance between country i and the US

$Lang_i$ = Dummy variable equal to 1 if country i's official language is English

After estimating the model via OLS, you plot the residuals against distance:

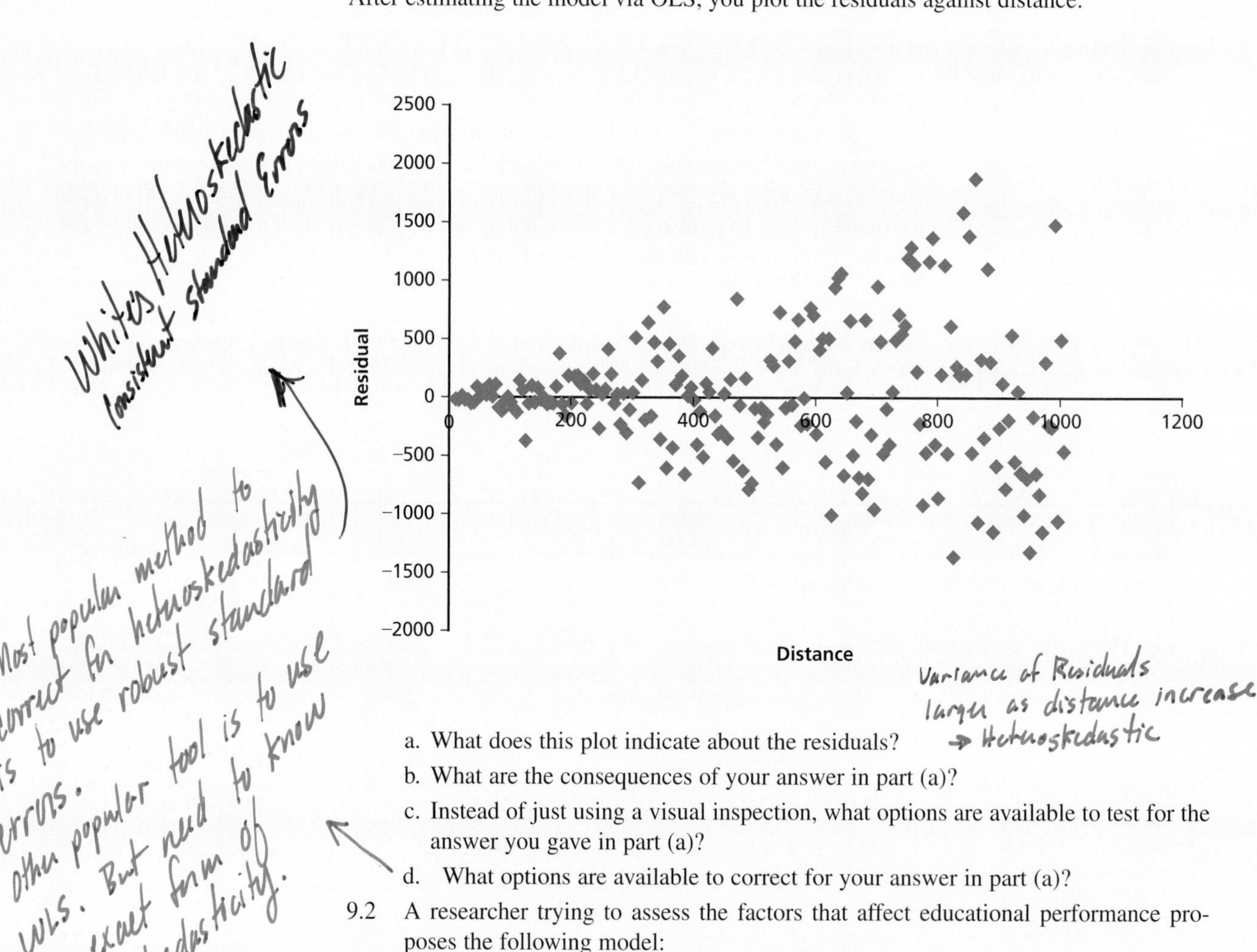

a. What does this plot indicate about the residuals?

b. What are the consequences of your answer in part (a)?

c. Instead of just using a visual inspection, what options are available to test for the answer you gave in part (a)?

d. What options are available to correct for your answer in part (a)?

9.2 A researcher trying to assess the factors that affect educational performance proposes the following model:

$$Test\ score_i = \beta_0 + \beta_1 Class\ size_i + \beta_2 Spending_i + \beta_3 Salary_i + \varepsilon_i$$

Student scores on a standardized test are predicted to be a function of the ratio of students to teachers (class size) in school district *i*, the expenditure per student in school district *i*, and the average salary paid to teachers in district *i*.

a. Suppose you estimated the preceding model and found a statistically positive coefficient for $\hat{\beta}_1$, implying that student test scores increase as classes get larger. Come up with an economic explanation for why students may do better in larger classes.

b. Suppose you found a statistically positive coefficient for $\hat{\beta}_2$, suggesting that student performance increases with expenditure per student. Explain why we might doubt the accuracy of this estimate of the effect on student expenditure on student performance.

c. Explain in detail the steps you would take to test the hypothesis that class size if the only variable that matters for student test scores.

d. You are interested in seeing if there are any regional differences in this educational production function. Specifically, you believe that students and schools in the northern part of the country are fundamentally different from those in the southern part of the country. Explain in detail how you would test for any differences between northern and southern schools.

e. You are concerned that your model is less accurate in school districts with higher average teacher salaries. If this is indeed the case, what effect(s) would this have on your estimates? Explain in detail how you would correct for this specific form of heteroskedasticity.

9.3 Consider the population regression model $y_i = \beta_0 + \beta_1 x_i + \varepsilon_i$.

a. You are concerned that this model suffers from heteroskedasticity. You are, however, sure that $E(\varepsilon_i) = 0$ and $Cov(x_i, \varepsilon_i) = 0$. What are the consequences of heteroskedasticity in your regression model? Will you be able to conduct hypothesis tests on your OLS estimate of β_1?

b. Describe the steps you would take to conduct White's generalization of the Breusch-Pagan test on this regression model. Be explicit about the form of the test and the test statistic.

c. Consider the population regression model $Price_i = \beta_0 + \beta_1 Area_i + \beta_2 Dist_i + \varepsilon_i$, where you are regressing the sale price of a house on its area in square feet and the square footage (*Area*) and its distance from the beach (*Dist*). You suspect that the heteroskedasticity in this regression is being caused specifically by the distance variable. Explain how you would test this hypothesis using the Goldfeld-Quandt test.

d. Suppose that you confirmed that distance was responsible for heteroskedasticity in part (c). Explain how you would correct for this specific form of heteroskedasticity.

9.4 Consider the population regression model $F_i = \beta_0 + \beta_1 Y_i + \beta_2 A_i + \varepsilon_i$, where F_i is the sales of a firm in the *i*th state, Y_i is total income in that state, and A_i is the amount of money spent by the company advertising in that state ($i = 1, 2, 3, \ldots, 50$).

a. You suspect that the error term ε_i is heteroskedastic with a standard deviation σ_i that depends on the size of the population P_i. Describe step-by-step how you will go about testing for this. Be sure to state the null and alternative hypotheses, the regression(s) that you will run, the test statistic you will compute and its distribution (including the degrees of freedom), and the criterion for acceptance or rejection of the null hypothesis.

b. Suppose you find that there is heteroskedasticity but ignore it and use OLS to estimate the model. Are your estimates (1) unbiased? (2) consistent? (3) efficient? Carefully justify your answer.

c. Assume that $\sigma_i = \sigma P_i$. Describe step-by-step how you will obtain estimates that are BLUE.

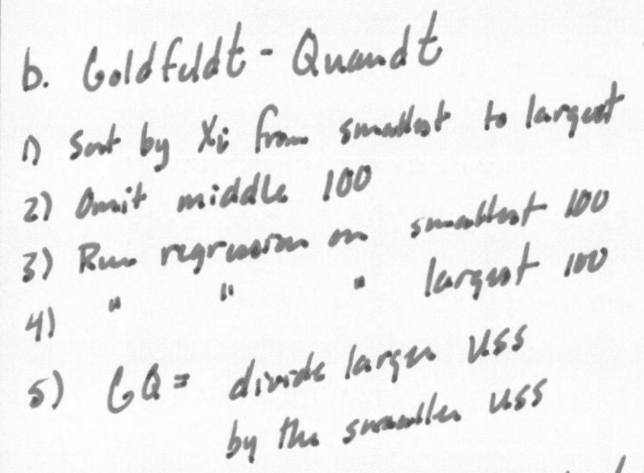

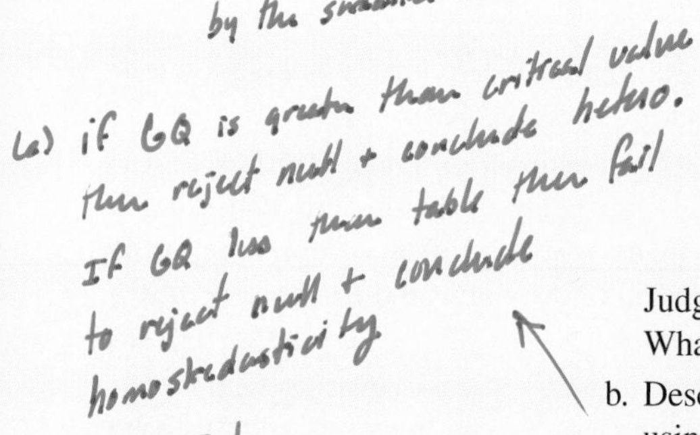

9.5 Consider the population regression model $y_i = \beta_0 + \beta_1 x_1 + \beta_2 x_2 + \varepsilon_i$.

a. You estimate the model and plot the residuals against x_1. This graph is given as follows:

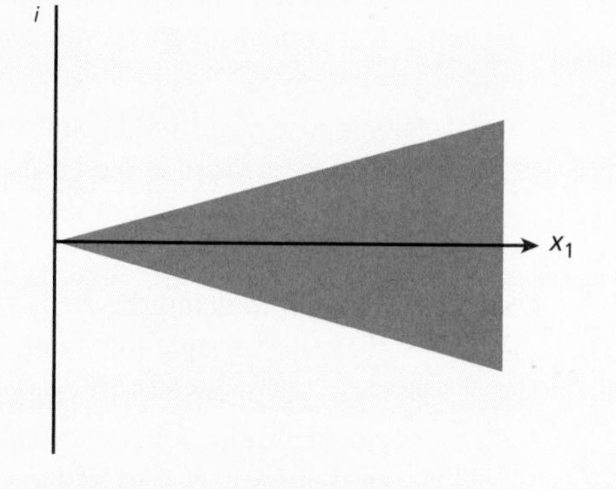

Judging by this graph, what potential problem does the regression suffer from? What are the consequences of this problem?

b. Describe how you would test for the presence of the problem described in part (a) using a Goldfeld-Quandt test assuming there are 300 observations.

c. Now suppose that the problem in part (a) is being caused by some function of the explanatory variables $h(x_1, x_2)$. Describe how you would test for the presence of the problem in part (a) with White's generalization of the Breusch-Pagan test.

d. Based on the information in the graph, what problem does this model suffer from? Will OLS estimates be consistent? Are hypothesis tests valid?

e. You believe that the error term has the following variance process: $Var(\varepsilon_i) = \sigma^2 D_i^2$. Using any of the methods discussed in this chapter, describe how you correct for heteroskedasticity.

f. Now suppose that the error term actually has the following variance process: $Var(\varepsilon_i) = \sigma^2(D_i/w_i^2)$. Using weighted least squares, describe how you would correct the model to deal with heteroskedasticity. Prove that the resulting transformed model has a constant variance.

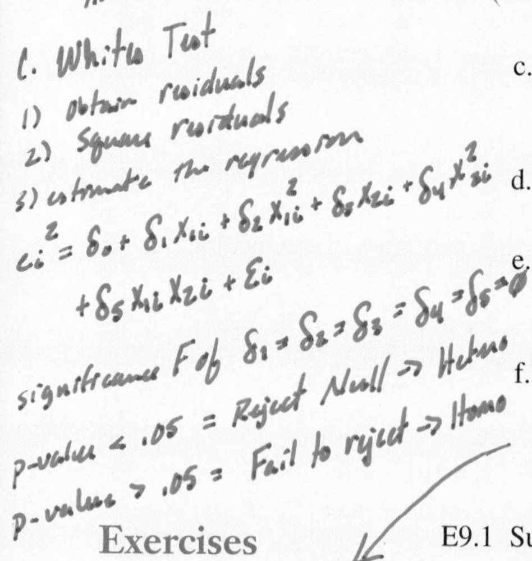

Exercises

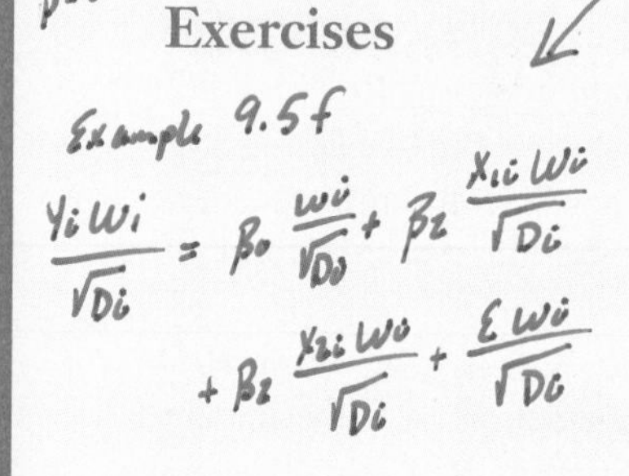

E9.1 Suppose you think that the relationship between the number of Olympic medals regressed on GDP per capita is likely heteroskedastic. Use the Excel file **Olympic medals heteroskedasticty.xls**.

a. First use informal graphical methods to investigate heteroskedasticity. Create a scatterplot graph with Olympic medals on the y-axis and GDP per capita on the x-axis.

b. Now use another graph to investigate the same issue. Regress Olympic medals on GDP per capita and save the residuals. Create a scatterplot with the residuals on the y-axis and GDP per capita on the x-axis.

c. Looking at the two scatterplots, do you think heteroskedasticity exists? What are the implications of heteroskedasticity on your regression analysis?

E9.2 Suppose you think that the relationship between the number of Olympic medals regressed on GDP per capita is likely heteroskedastic. Use the Excel file **Olympic medals heteroskedasticty.xls**.

a. Use the Breaush-Pagan test to formally test if heteroskedasticity exists in these data. What do you conclude?

b. Use the modified White's test to formally test if heteroskedasticity exists in these data. What do you conclude?

c. Use the Goldfeld-Quandt test to formally test if heteroskedasticity exists in these data. What do you conclude?

d. Do you think it is necessary to use three different tests to see if heteroskedasticity exists in these data? Comment on the conditions under which each of these three tests would be most preferable.

E9.3 Suppose you think that a relationship exists between the property value and the number of 2006 wins of a college football team. Use the Excel file **ap wins heteroskedasticty.xls**.

a. First use informal graphical methods to investigate heteroskedasticity. Create a scatterplot with property value on the y-axis and wins on the x-axis.

b. Now use another graph to investigate the same issue. Regress property values on wins and save the residuals. Create a scatterplot with the residuals on the y-axis and wins on the x-axis.

c. Looking at the two scatterplots, do you think heteroskedasticity exists? What are the implications of heteroskedasticity on your regression analysis?

E9.4 Suppose you think that a relationship exists between the property value and the number of 2006 wins of a college football team. Use the Excel file **ap wins heteroskedasticty.xls**.

a. Use the Breaush-Pagan test to formally test if heteroskedasticity exists in these data. What do you conclude?

b. Use the modified White's test to formally test if heteroskedasticity exists in these data. What do you conclude?

c. Use the Goldfeld-Quandt test to formally test if heteroskedasticity exists in these data. What do you conclude?

d. Do you think it is necessary to use three different tests to see if heteroskedasticity exists in these data? Comment on the conditions under which each of these three tests would be most preferable.

E9.5 Suppose you think that a relationship between the number of Olympic medals regressed on GDP per capita is heteroskedastic and that you want to correct for heteroskedasticity. Use the Excel file **Olympic medals heteroskedasticty.xls**.

a. Assume that the form of heteroskedasticity is $h(x)$ = GDP per capita squared. Use weighed least squares to correct for heteroskedasticity.

b. Use the Breusch-Pagan test to formally test if heteroskedasticity still exists in the weighted data. What do you conclude?

c. Now assume that the form of heteroskedasticity is $h(x)$ = GDP per capita. Use weighed least squares to correct for heteroskedasticity.

d. Use the Breusch-Pagan test to formally test if heteroskedasticity still exists in the weighted data in part (c). What do you conclude?

Chapter Ten

Time-Series Analysis

CHAPTER OBJECTIVES

After reading this chapter, you will be able to:

1. Understand the assumptions required for OLS to be the best linear unbiased estimator for time-series data.
2. Understand stationarity and weak dependence.
3. Estimate static time-series models.
4. Estimate distributed lag models.
5. Understand and account for time trends and seasonality.
6. Test for structural breaks in the data.
7. Understand the problem presented by spurious regression.
8. Learn to perform forecasting and out-of-sample prediction.

A STUDENT'S PERSPECTIVE

Suppose that after following the ongoing national debate concerning the debt ceiling and the size of U.S. national debt, you become interested in the degree to which certain institutional factors affect the country's annual budget surplus (deficit). What would you do?

This is exactly the situation encountered by one of our former students. To determine an answer, the student collected data on the real surplus (deficit) in the United States between 1940 and 2011, as well as data on a number of factors that might affect the annual surplus (deficits) in those same years. Table 10.1 presents the simple summary statistics that she calculated for these data.

While collecting these data, our former student realized that they seemed different than the cross-section data with which she had previously been working. Namely, the fact that the data varied over time struck her as being something new and different. To get a better sense of what the difference might be, she produced Figure 10.1 by plotting her dependent variable over time.

Looking at the entries in Figure 10.1, the student immediately noticed that the data seemed to follow a different pattern than cross-sectional data. In particular, rather than being randomly scattered throughout the figure, the data points seemed to follow a rather obvious up-and-down pattern. This raised an important question in the student's mind: Would the multiple linear regression analysis appropriate for these data be the same as it was for cross-section data?

BIG PICTURE OVERVIEW

time-series data
Data collected for a given individual, country, firm, etc., over many different time periods.

When dealing with **time-series data,** which is data for one individual (firm, nation, etc.) observed over a number of different time periods, we define the population regression model that we wish to estimate as

$$y_t = \beta_0 + \beta_1 x_{1,t} + \beta_2 x_{2,t} + \cdots + \beta_k x_{k,t} + \varepsilon_t \qquad \textbf{10.1}$$

FIGURE 10.1
Scatter Diagram of Our Former Student's Data on U.S. Annual Surpluses (Deficits) Over Time

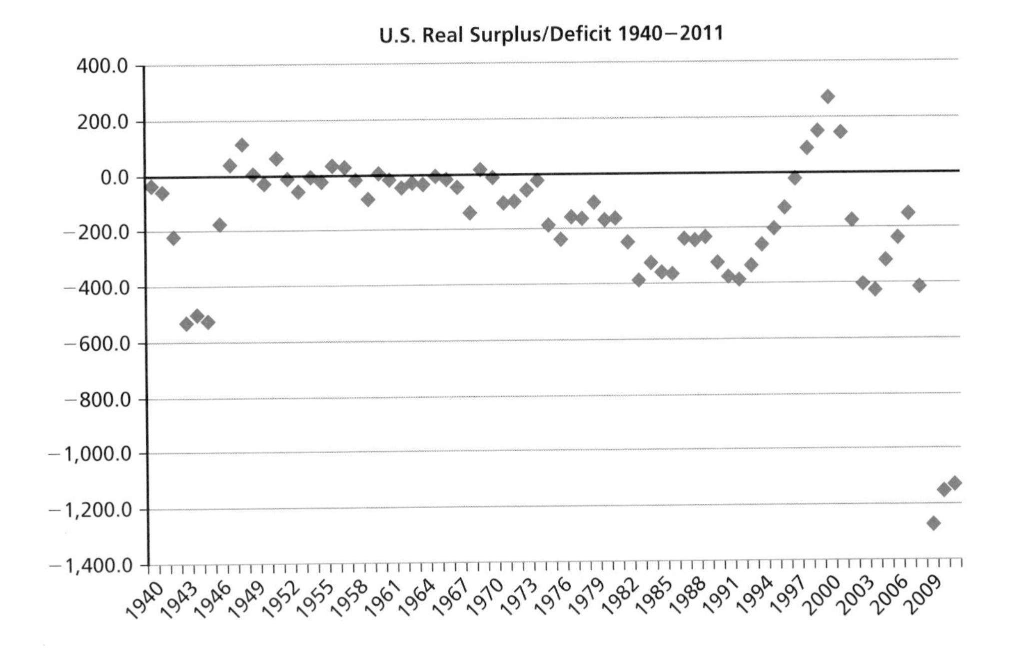

where the subscript t indicates that the unit of observation is the time period for a given individual, firm, nation, etc.

As we will discuss in this chapter and in Chapter 11, our preferred method for estimating the true linear relationship between y and x for time-series data is somewhat different than it is for cross-section data (in fact, time-series econometrics is a separate concentration in most PhD programs, owing to the vast differences between the types of analyses required to deal with the different types of data).

The first major difference that we are likely to notice between cross-section and time-series data is in the appearance of the observed data. Namely, while cross-section data are randomly scattered across the values of the independent variable, time-series data are non–randomly scattered over time, with values of the dependent variable in one time period being closely related to values of the dependent variable in previous time periods. Figure 10.2 provides a common visual depiction of time-series data.

FIGURE 10.2
A Visual Depiction of Hypothetical Time-Series Data

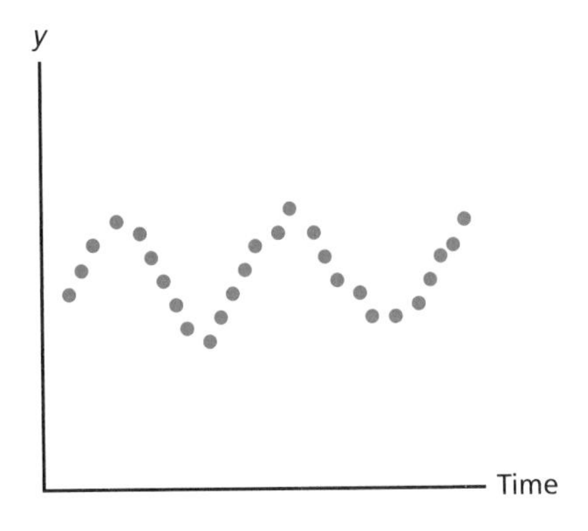

For economists, perhaps the most well-know time series is the U.S. business cycle, which is depicted in Figure 10.3 for the time period from 1977 to 2006.

The data depicted in Figures 10.2 and 10.3 hint at the empirical issues that we are likely to encounter when performing linear regression analysis for time-series data. Unlike cross-section data, for which the observed values are independent of each other due to the data being gathered through simple random sampling, in the case of time-series data, the observed values in any given time period are likely to be closely related to the observed values in immediate prior periods. Identifying and correcting for this **memory** in the

memory
In time-series data refers to the idea that what happens in one time period is affected by (or has memory of) what happened in previous time periods.

TABLE 10.1 Our Former Student's Data on U.S. Annual Surpluses (Deficits) from 1940–2011

	Real Surplus (billions)	Real GDP (billions)	Real Income Tax Receipts (millions)	Real Defense Expenditures (millions)
Mean	−185.39	5,919.61	472,212.87	340,163.77
Standard Deviation	270.16	3,730.58	311,887.00	142,934.76
Minimum	−1,274.40	1,111.37	10,241.10	19,058.55
25th Percentile	−275.40	2,552.88	197,417.74	265,274.81
Median	−136.90	4,927.65	393,522.30	318,250.06
75th Percentile	−22.25	8,465.14	655,988.89	393,406.27
Maximum	269.40	13,159.28	1,128,989.55	750,814.48
Observations	72	72	72	72

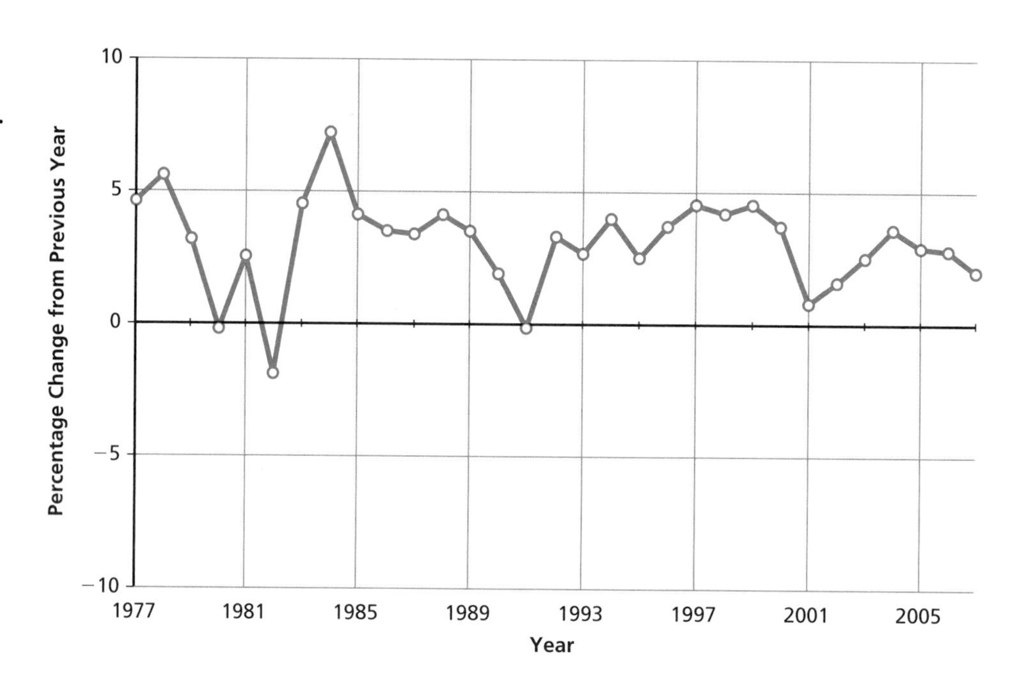

FIGURE 10.3 Line Graph of the Annual Percentage Change in U.S. Real GDP, 1977–2006

observed values presents the major challenge when performing time-series analysis. To see why, consider that Figure 10.4 represents the ordinary least squares (OLS) best-fit line through the observed time-series data.

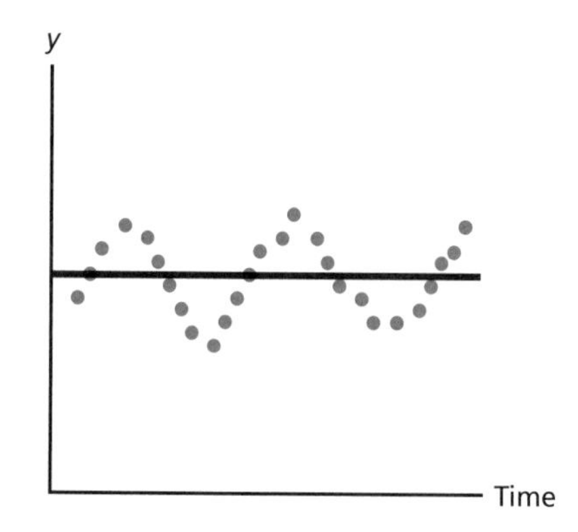

FIGURE 10.4 Scatterplot of Time-Series Data along with the OLS Best-Fit Line

Population (millions)	Democratic President	Democratic Senate	Democratic House	Recession
218,161.83	0.50	0.67	0.71	0.26
53,232.06	0.50	0.47	0.46	0.44
132,122.00	0.00	0.00	0.00	0.00
174,157.50	0.00	0.00	0.00	0.00
217,004.00	0.50	1.00	1.00	0.00
261,050.25	1.00	1.00	1.00	1.00
311,592.00	1.00	1.00	1.00	1.00
72	72	72	72	72

As Figure 10.4 demonstrates, the OLS best-fit line does not describe the observed data well. Accordingly, the remainder of the chapter introduces alternative estimation techniques that provide an improved fit to time-series data.

Figure 10.5 visually summarizes the empirical tools introduced in this chapter.

Before discussing the empirical issues confronted in time-series analysis, we must first introduce a new data set that will form the basis of our discussion in both the remainder of this chapter and in Chapter 11.

DATA TO BE ANALYZED: OUR U.S. HOUSES SOLD DATA, 1986Q2–2005Q4

Macroeconomic aggregates, such as U.S. gross domestic product (GDP), are one of the most commonly encountered examples of time-series data. Given that we have all

FIGURE 10.5
A Visual Depiction of the Empirical Tools Introduced in This Chapter

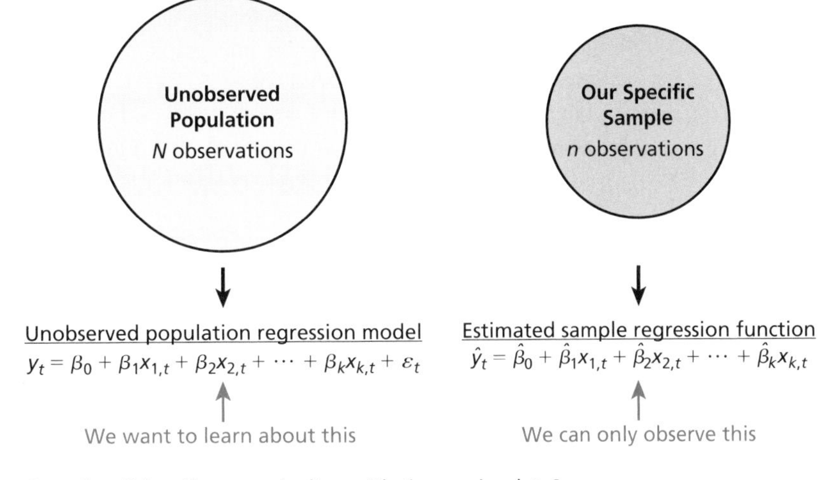

Question: What if we are dealing with time-series data?

Answer:

(1) We can estimate the population regression model with OLS. } Static Time-Series Models / Distributed Lag Model

(2) De-trend the data to deal with time-trends and seasonality.

(3) Test for structural breaks in the data.

(4) Forecast future outcomes. } Out-of-Sample Prediction

(5) Account for stationarity and weakly-dependent data.

likely worked extensively with U.S. GDP data in various Principles and Intermediate Macroeconomics courses, we choose to focus on a different macroeconomic variable: the total number of houses sold in the United States during different time periods. The reason for this focus is that (1) the housing sector is such an important component of the U.S. economy that measures of the performance of this sector are considered leading economic indicators as to the health of the U.S. economy and (2) the collapse of the housing bubble starting in 2006 received considerable media attention as an important contributor to the Great Recession (December 2007 to June 2009).

According to economic theory, several independent factors should be related to the number of houses sold in each quarter in the United States. These include the relative wealth of U.S. households, the relative price of U.S. homes, the mortgage rate U.S. citizens must pay for home loans, the number of U.S. households, and so on. For simplicity, we choose to focus on only one of these potential variables: the relative wealth of U.S. households, which we proxy for with quarterly U.S. GDP during our observed time period.

Following the procedure outlined in Appendix B, we collected data on the number of houses sold and the real GDP in each successive quarter from 1986Q2 through 2005Q4. The end date for our time-series deserves attention. While the data are clearly available up to the most recent quarter for which data are available, we decided to end our example data set with 2005Q4 because we suspected that a **structural break** occurred at that point in the time-series due to the collapse of the housing bubble and the onset of the Great Recession. Because, as we discuss in Section 10.6, structural breaks introduce empirical issues of their own, we limit the data analyzed in Sections 10.2 to 10.5 to the period before the suspected structural break occurred.

structural break
Occurs when we see an unexpected shift in time-series data.

As always, we recommend starting any empirical analysis with a simple summary analysis. With cross-section data, because the variation in the dependent and independent variables occurs across observations in a given time period, our initial analysis consists of summary measures of observed variation, such as the sample mean and sample standard deviation. With time-series data, because the observed variation in the dependent and independent variables occurs across time, such samplewide comparisons are largely uninformative. Instead, to consider the observed variation in different variables over time, we can compare line graphs of the dependent and independent variables over time. Figure 10.6 presents the line graph for the dependent variable in our U.S. houses sold data. Similarly, Figure 10.7 presents the line graph for the independent variable, real GDP (trillions), in our U.S. houses sold data.

Comparing these line graphs, we see that U.S. houses sold per quarter during this time period seem to move in the same general direction as U.S. real GDP per quarter. While

FIGURE 10.6
Line Graph of Our Dependent Variable: Number of Houses Sold in the United States, 1986Q2–2005Q4

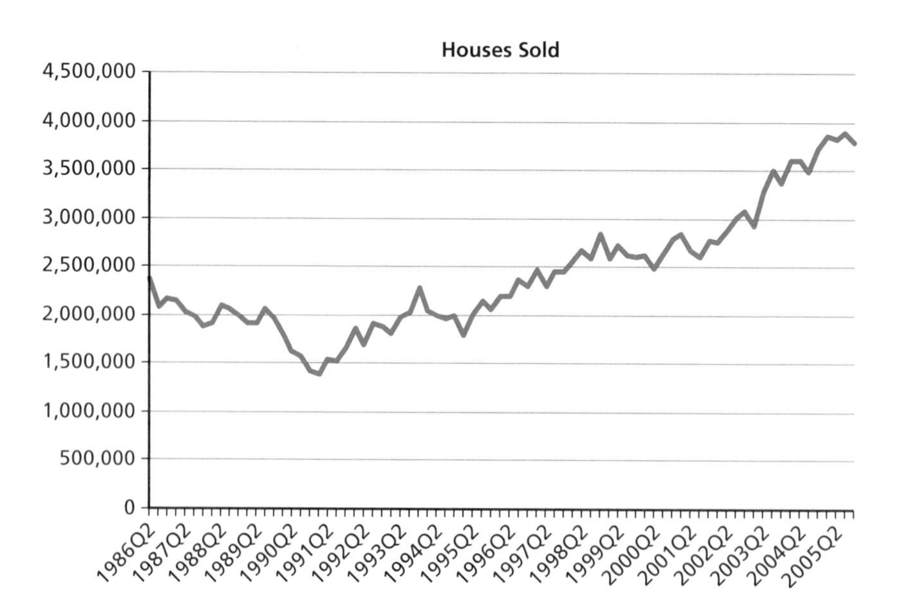

FIGURE 10.7
Line Graph of Our Independent Variable: U.S. Real GDP (billions), 1986Q2–2005Q4

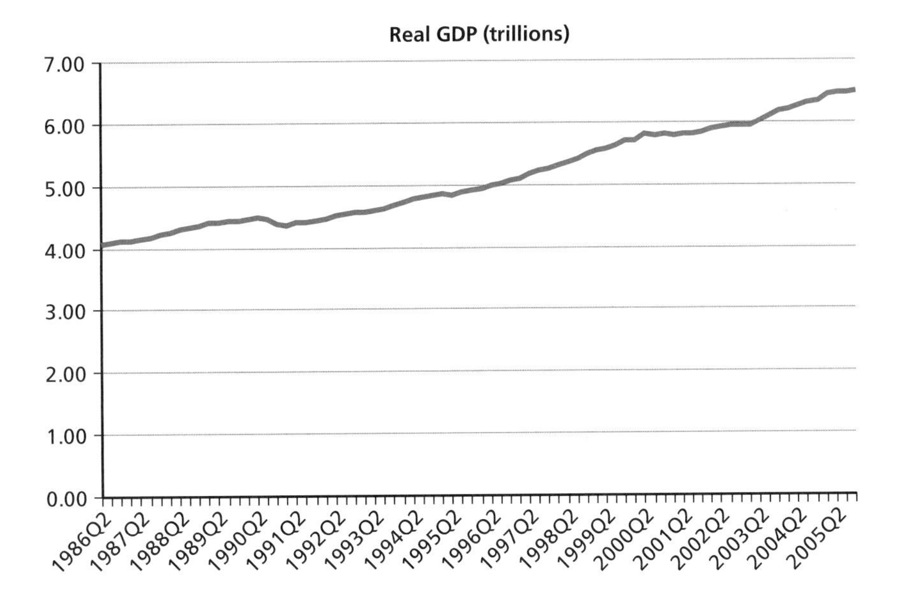

these two variables appear to move in the same direction, the obvious question is the degree to which observed changes in the independent variable correlate with observed changes in the dependent variable. Our goal is to use linear regression analysis to answer this question. Before we can do so, there are a number of assumptions that must be satisfied for OLS to provide estimates that are BLUE for time-series data.

10.1 UNDERSTAND THE ASSUMPTIONS REQUIRED FOR OLS TO BE THE BEST LINEAR UNBIASED ESTIMATOR FOR TIME-SERIES DATA

The six assumptions required for ordinary least squares (OLS) to provide best linear unbiased estimates (BLUE) for time-series data are presented in the following box.

Note that (1) if the first four of these assumptions hold, then our OLS estimates will be unbiased but not necessarily minimum variance among all unbiased estimators and (2) if all six of these assumptions hold, then our OLS estimates will be BLUE.

The first five of these assumptions should look familiar, as they are five of the six assumptions required for OLS estimates to be BLUE for cross-section data. The one cross-section assumption that is not included here is assumption M2, which states that the data must be collected through simple random sampling. Simple random sampling is inherently impossible for time-series data because time-series observations necessarily follow each other, meaning that they cannot be randomly sampled. This fact introduces the need for assumption T6. If the observation in this period is correlated with the observation in the

Assumptions Required for OLS to Be the Best Linear Unbiased Estimator (BLUE) for Time-Series Data

Assumption T1: The model is linear in the parameters.
Assumption T2: The data are not perfectly multicollinear.
Assumption T3: The error term has zero mean, or $E(\varepsilon_t) = 0$.
Assumption T4: The error term is uncorrelated with each independent variable and all functions of each independent variable, or $E(\varepsilon_t | x_{tj}) = 0$ for all j.
Assumption T5: The error term has constant variance, or $Var(\varepsilon_t) = \sigma^2$.
Assumption T6: The error term in one period is uncorrelated with the error term in any previous period, or $Cov(\varepsilon_t, \varepsilon_{t-j}) = 0$.

last period, then our OLS estimates are no longer BLUE because we are not incorporating all available information in our estimation process.

Of these six assumptions, the one most likely to be violated for time-series data is assumption T4, which is violated when an unobservable determinant of the variation in the dependent variable is also correlated with one or more of the independent variables. In such a case, our OLS estimates are biased because we are no longer holding all other independent variables constant when estimating the marginal effects of a given independent variable. To evaluate whether T4 is violated, we need to perform the thought experiment of asking ourselves whether any of the factors that are likely to be included in the error term are also likely to be correlated with any of the independent variables. The same is true for the remaining assumptions—the best way to determine whether any are likely to be violated is to thoroughly consider any and all potential violations.

While these assumptions are important for determining whether we can use OLS when dealing with time-series data, there is another important attribute that we must consider.

BIAS

10.2 UNDERSTAND STATIONARITY AND WEAK DEPENDENCE

Stationarity in Time Series

A stationary time series is one for which the probability distribution of the dependent variable does not change over time, meaning that if we start at time period t and shift forward h time periods, the probability distribution of the dependent variable in time period $t + h$ is exactly the same as it was in time period t. Note that in such a case, the joint probability distribution between the observations of the dependent variable in different time periods do not change over time. In other words, if the time-series process y_t is stationary, then each observation has the exact same properties (same mean, same variance, same probability distribution) for all time periods. Moreover, the joint distribution between y_t and y_{t+h} (for all $h > 0$) is the same for all time periods. Note that **stationarity** does not put any restrictions on the manner in which the observed values are related to each other; instead, it just requires that the relationship be the same across all time periods.

stationarity
Occurs when the probability distribution of a random variable does not change over time.

nonstationarity
Occurs when the probability distribution of a random variable does change over time.

The opposite of a stationary time series is one that is **nonstationary.** Such a time-series is one in which the probability distribution of the dependent variable does change over time and for which the preceding interpretation is exactly opposite. An obvious example of a nonstationary time series would be a time series with a statistically significant time trend because each observation in the time-trended data would have a different mean, and therefore, the data would not be stationary over time.

Why does stationarity matter? In more advanced courses, it is important because it simplifies proofs about the distributions and characteristics of the time-series data. For introductory courses, we prefer stationary time series because it is difficult to draw conclusions about how one time-series variable is related to another if the data is nonstationary. To see why, consider the following question. If the mean, variance, and/or probability distribution changes over time, how can we possibly hope to quantify the degree to which the independent variables help explain the dependent variable?

Unfortunately, in practice, it is extremely difficult to determine whether a specific time series is stationary or nonstationary because stationarity is a function of the underlying population distribution, which is unobserved, and not the realizations of that distribution that we observe in our sample. At best, we can sometimes spot time series that are most likely nonstationary, but it is extremely difficult to say for certain that a given time series is stationary.

Weakly Dependent Time Series

An additional attribute that we prefer our time-series data to possess is **weak dependence.** A stationary time series is said to be weakly dependent if y_t and y_{t+h} are almost independent as h increases. The term "almost independent" means that the observations of a given variable can be related to each other if they are close to each other in time, but the observations must become less and less related as the distance in time between

weakly dependent time-series
Occurs when the relationship between y_t and y_{t+h} goes to 0 as h approaches infinity.

them increases. As this statement might suggest, weak dependence is hard to technically define because there is no uniform definition that applies to all circumstances. For our purposes, we define "weak dependence" as existing when the correlation between y_t and y_{t+h} goes to 0 as h approaches infinity. Note that we can also refer to such data as being asymptotically uncorrelated.

Why does weak dependence matter? If our time series are not weakly dependent, then the correlation between x_t and x_{t+h} increases as h increases, meaning that events occurring long ago would have much greater influence on current observations of a time series than events happening more recently. If this were the case, we would need to develop different models than the ones traditionally used for time-series data. Again, while we can sometimes spot data that are likely to be weakly dependent, it is difficult to prove that the data are not; thus, we should be careful to fully consider whether this is a reasonable assumption. If it is, then we should be safe continuing with our more traditional estimation techniques.

10.3 ESTIMATE STATIC TIME-SERIES MODELS

static time-series model
When all variables in the model are measured at the same time period.

As a first pass at estimating the population regression model for our time-series data, we could estimate the relationship by OLS with all variables in the same time period. In its general form, we define the **static time-series** population regression model as

$$y_t = \beta_0 + \beta_1 x_{1,t} + \beta_2 x_{2,t} + \cdots + \beta_k x_{k,t} + \varepsilon_t \qquad \textbf{10.3.1}$$

Notice that the subscripts all refer to the same time-period, t, which is the defining fact of a static time-series model (i.e., the model is estimated with the data from the same time period).

For our U.S. houses sold data, we estimate the static time-series population regression model as

$$Houses\ sold_t = \beta_0 + \beta_1 Real\ GDP_t + \varepsilon_t \qquad \textbf{10.3.2}$$

and get Excel Regression Output 10.1.

Excel Regression Output 10.1: Static Time-Series Model for Our U.S. Houses Sold Data

SUMMARY OUTPUT

Regression Statistics	
Multiple R	0.911129439
R Square	0.830156855
Adjusted R Square	0.82795110
Standard Error	261775.2738
Observations	79

ANOVA

	df	SS	MS	F	Significance F
Regression	1	2.57905E+13	2.57905E+13	376.3594799	2.2565E-31
Residual	77	5.27652E+12	68526293956		
Total	78	3.1067E+13			

	Coefficients	Standard Error	*t* Stat	*p*-value	Lower 95%	Upper 95%
Intercept	−1,587,774.016	208,266.406	−7.6237644	5.37572E-11	−2002485.406	−1173062.627
Real GDP (trillions)	780,699.599	40,242.275	19.3999866	2.2565E-31	700566.993	860832.205

Note: Dependent variable is the number of houses sold in the U.S. in a given quarter. Highlighted variables are significant at the 5 percent level.

These estimates can be interpreted as follows. On average, if U.S. real GDP in a given period is 0, then we would expect a total of −1,587,774.02 houses to be sold in the United States. This, of course, makes no sense whatsoever because it is not possible to observe a negative number of houses sold. Then again, the United States will never have a real GDP of 0, so the thought experiment represented by the estimated intercept is meaningless. Again, this proves the potential folly of attempting to interpret the intercept in many instances. More relevantly, on average, for every $1 trillion increase in U.S. real GDP, the number of houses sold in the United States is estimated to increase by 780,699.60. Finally, notice that the number of observation for this regression is 79, owing to the fact that there are exactly 79 quarters between 1986Q2 and 2005Q4.

Empirical Research Tool 10.1 summarizes the static time-series model.

EMPIRICAL RESEARCH TOOL 10.1: STATIC TIME-SERIES ESTIMATION IN TIME-SERIES ANALYSIS

How to Do It:

Estimate the population regression model $y_t = \beta_0 + \beta_1 x_{1t} + \beta_2 x_{2t} + \cdots + \beta_k x_{kt} + \varepsilon_t$ by OLS.

Why It Works:

The static time-series model serves primarily as a baseline for learning about time-series data. It is important because it is the starting point for many methods for detecting and correcting for autocorrelation (which we discuss in Chapter 11). Its potential shortcoming is that it does not control for cross-time-period correlation in the data.

time dependence
When the error term from one period is correlated with the error term from another period.

While these results do provide rough estimates of the estimated linear relationship between the dependent and independent variables, they likely do not provide the best possible estimates because they ignore the **time dependence** of our time-series data. To generate estimates that are more accurate, we need to account for the time dependence, or memory, of the series.

10.4 ESTIMATE DISTRIBUTED LAG MODELS

distributed lag model
A model that includes the independent variables in addition to lagged values of one or more of the independent variables.

lagged independent variable
The value of an independent variable in a period prior to the current period.

A first pass at accounting for this possible correlation is to estimate a **distributed lag model,** which is a model that estimates the dependent variable as a function of the independent variables in addition to **lagged independent variables,** which are the values of the independent variables in previous periods.

By definition, if the value of an independent variable in the current period is t, then the value of that independent variable "lagged one period" is the value of that variable in the immediate prior period, or $t-1$; the value of that independent variable "lagged two periods" is the value of the variable two periods prior, $t-2$; and so on.

The distributed lag model consists of including different lagged independent variables in our regression analysis. To estimate a distributed lag model with one independent variable, x_1, we start by writing the population regression model to be estimated as

$$y_t = \beta_0 + \beta_1 x_{1,t} + \beta_2 x_{1,t-1} + \beta_3 x_{1,t-2} + \cdots + \beta_{k+1} x_{1,t-k} + \varepsilon_t \qquad \textbf{10.4.1}$$

The resulting coefficient estimates on the lagged independent variables, $\beta_2, \beta_3, \ldots, \beta_{k+1}$, provide an indication of whether the dependent variable in time-period t is correlated with the value of the independent variable in the immediate prior period, the value of the independent variable two periods prior, and so on.

Note that (1) the exact number of lags included for each independent variable is determined by either economic theory or by using t-tests and F-tests to determine the correct specifications and (2) for models with multiple independent variables, we could include lagged terms for any number of the independent variables.

Suppose that for our U.S. houses sold data, we wish to estimate a model that is lagged four periods (which is one full year for quarterly data). To do so, we would estimate the population regression model

$$\begin{aligned} \textit{Houses sold}_t = \beta_0 &+ \beta_1 \textit{Real GDP}_t + \beta_2 \textit{Real GDP}_{t-1} + \beta_3 \textit{Real GDP}_{t-2} \\ &+ \beta_4 \textit{Real GDP}_{t-3} + \beta_5 \textit{Real GDP}_{t-4} + \varepsilon_t \end{aligned} \qquad \textbf{10.4.2}$$

by OLS.

Before estimating the population regression model in formula 10.4.2, we need to calculate all of the lagged independent variables. Doing so produces the data in Table 10.2.

TABLE 10.2 Calculating Lagged Independent Variables for Our U.S. Houses Sold Data

Time	Quarter	Houses Sold	Real GDP (trillions)	Lagged 1Q	Lagged 2Q	Lagged 3Q	Lagged 4Q
1986	2	2,374,000	4.06				
1986	3	2,082,000	4.10	4.06			
1986	4	2,160,000	4.12	4.10	4.06		
1987	1	2,154,000	4.13	4.12	4.10	4.06	
1987	2	2,023,000	4.15	4.13	4.12	4.10	4.06
1987	3	1,981,000	4.17	4.15	4.13	4.12	4.10
1987	4	1,870,000	4.24	4.17	4.15	4.13	4.12

Note: We lose one observation for every time period that we lag.

We then estimate the population regression model in formula 10.4.2 by OLS and get Excel Regression Output 10.2.

Because the estimated intercept and the estimated slope coefficient have similar interpretations to those offered in the previous section, we do not present them here. Instead, we focus on the interpretation of the new lagged dependent variables. The fact that all of the estimated slope coefficients for these variables are statistically insignificant suggests that the number of houses sold in the current quarter is not statistically related to the real GDP in each of the previous four quarters.

Empirical Research Tool 10.2 summarizes the distributed lag model.

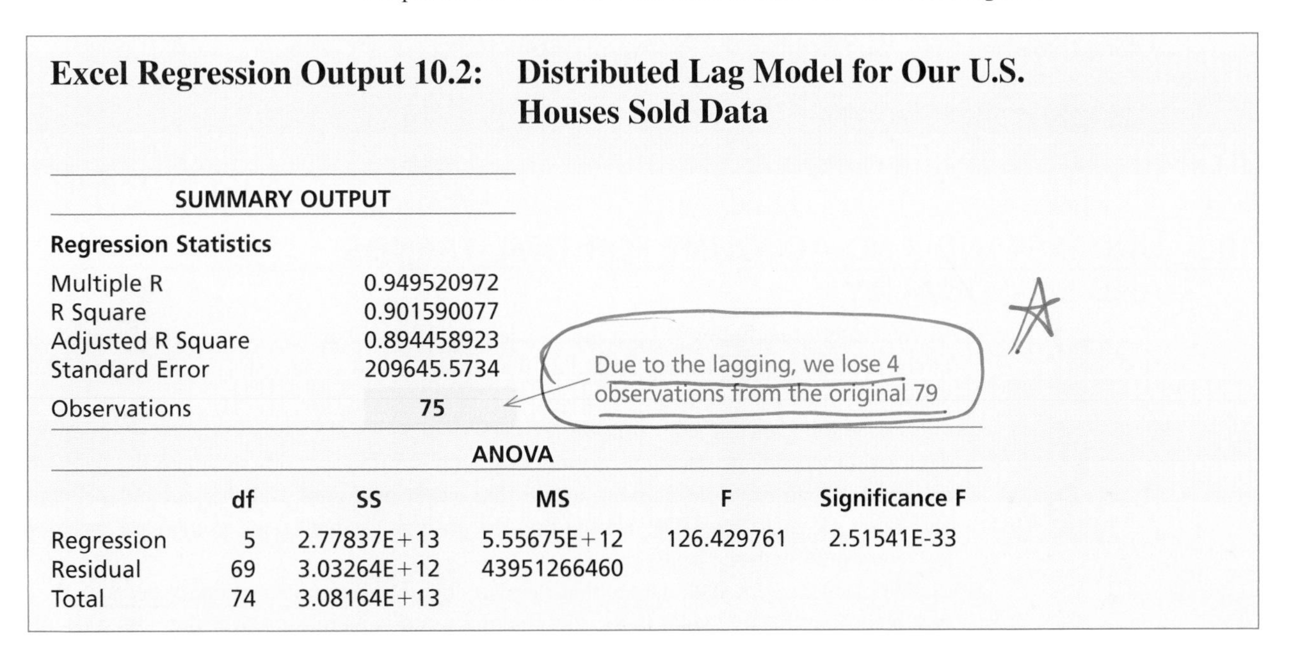

Excel Regression Output 10.2: Distributed Lag Model for Our U.S. Houses Sold Data

SUMMARY OUTPUT

Regression Statistics	
Multiple R	0.949520972
R Square	0.901590077
Adjusted R Square	0.894458923
Standard Error	209645.5734
Observations	**75**

Due to the lagging, we lose 4 observations from the original 79

ANOVA

	df	SS	MS	F	Significance F
Regression	5	2.77837E+13	5.55675E+12	126.429761	2.51541E-33
Residual	69	3.03264E+12	43951266460		
Total	74	3.08164E+13			

	Coefficients	Standard Error	*t* Stat	*p*-value	Lower 95%	Upper 95%
Intercept	−1,797,203.480	183,702.261	−9.783240925	1.14237E-14	−2163679.459	−1430727.5
Real GDP (trillions)	2,467,947.136	863,566.825	2.857853110	0.005633993	745178.4798	4190715.793
Lagged 1Q	−645,659.734	1,332,875.946	−0.484410973	0.629628365	−3304674.458	2013354.991
Lagged 2Q	131,908.049	1,314,737.839	0.100330305	0.920373050	−2490922.142	2754738.239
Lagged 3Q	237,075.884	1,331,886.669	0.178000043	0.859244495	−2419965.287	2894117.054
Lagged 4Q	−1,408,465.678	877,059.077	−1.605896016	0.112864068	−3158150.641	341219.2854

Note: Dependent variable is the number of houses sold in the U.S. in a given quarter. Highlighted variables are significant at the 5 percent level.

EMPIRICAL RESEARCH TOOL 10.2: DISTRIBUTED LAG MODELS IN TIME-SERIES ANALYSIS

How to Do It:

1. For a distributed lag model with one independent variable, x_1, estimate the population regression model as

$$y_t = \beta_0 + \beta_1 x_{1,t} + \beta_2 x_{1,t-1} + \beta_3 x_{1,t-2} + \cdots + \beta_{k+1} x_{1,t-k} + \varepsilon_t$$

   where $x_{1,t-1}$ is the value of the independent variable in the immediate prior period, $x_{1,t-2}$ the value of the independent variable two periods prior, and so on.

2. Perform *t*-tests for the individual significance or an *F*-test for the joint significance of the estimated slope coefficients, $\beta_2, \beta_3, \ldots, \beta_{k+1}$

Why It Works:

All other variables constant, the coefficient estimates $\beta_2, \beta_3, \ldots, \beta_{k+1}$ provide an indication of whether the dependent variable in time period *t* is correlated with the value of the independent variable in the immediate prior period, the value of the independent variable two periods prior, and so on, respectively.

Notes:

1. The exact number of lags included for each independent variable is determined by either economic theory or by using *t*-tests and *F*-tests to determine the correct specifications.
2. For models with more than one independent variable, we could include lagged terms for multiple or even for all of the independent variables.

10.5 UNDERSTAND AND ACCOUNT FOR TIME TRENDS AND SEASONALITY

Beyond simply including lagged independent variables, there are a number of empirical methods available for dealing with data that are observed to vary in specific ways either across or within time periods.

A potential concern with time-series data is that the observed values of the dependent and independent variables vary directly with the time periods in which the data are observed. As an example, looking at the line graph in Figure 10.8 for our independent variable, U.S. quarterly GDP, we see that the observed value seems to increase more or less constantly with the time period.

The problem with such data is that they are, by definition, nonstationary because they lack a constant mean, owing to the fact that the mean is increasing over time. As a result, we must take steps to remove the variation in the mean so that the data return to being stationary.

FIGURE 10.8
Line Graph of Our Independent Variable: U.S. Real GDP (billions), 1986Q2–2005Q4

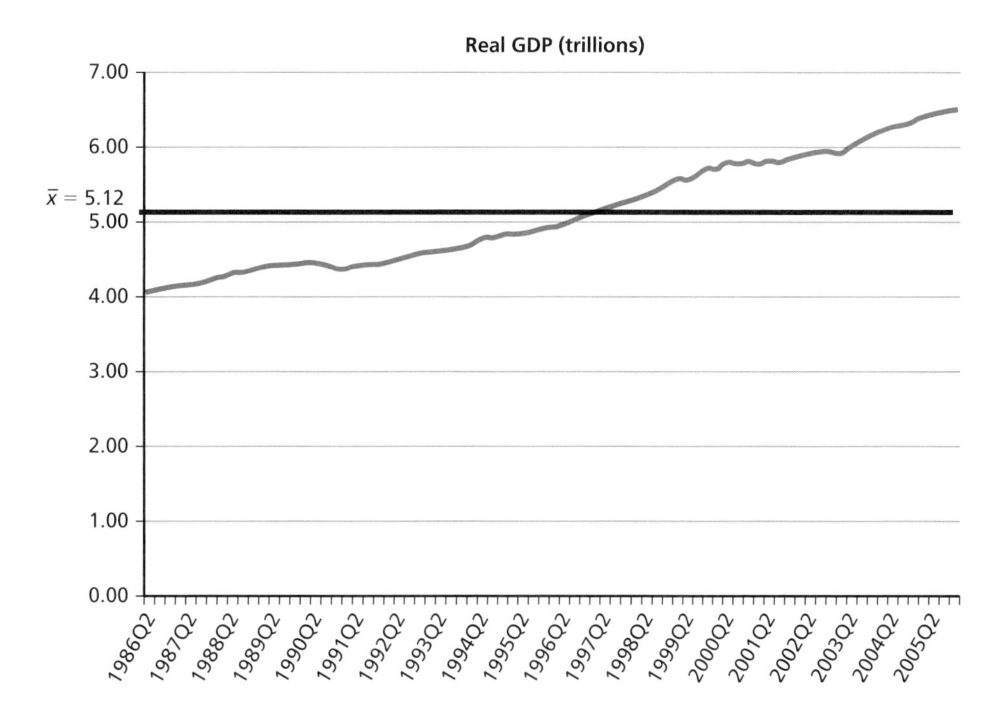

Time Trends

time trend
A method for estimating whether the data are trending up or down over time.

One method for dealing with this problem is to include a **time trend** as an independent variable and to estimate the population regression model:

$$y_t = \beta_0 + \beta_1 x_{1,t} + \beta_2 x_{2,t} + \cdots + \beta_k x_{k,t} + \beta_{k+1} t + \varepsilon_t \qquad 10.5.1$$

In formula 10.5.1, the independent variable t is a time trend that increases in incremental units from the first time period in our sample to the last, such that $t = 1, 2, \ldots, T$ with T being the last time period represented. Given this specification, the estimated slope coefficient for the time-trend variable, β_{k+1}, provides an indication of whether the data are trending up or down over time, holding all other independent variables constant.

Table 10.3 demonstrates how we construct the time trend for our U.S. houses sold data.

TABLE 10.3
Constructing the Time Trend for the First Five Observations for Our Houses Sold Data

Year	Quarter	Houses Sold	Real GDP (trillions)	Time Trend
1986	2	2,374,000	4.06	1
1986	3	2,082,000	4.10	2
1986	4	2,160,000	4.12	3
1987	1	2,154,000	4.13	4
1987	2	2,023,000	4.15	5

After constructing the time-trend variable, we estimate the population regression model

$$Houses\ sold_t = \beta_0 + \beta_1 Real\ GDP_t + \boldsymbol{\beta_2 t} + \varepsilon_t \qquad 10.5.2$$

by OLS and get Excel Regression Output 10.3.

Focusing on the new time-trend variables, we see that, holding U.S. real GDP constant, in each subsequent quarter we estimate the number of houses sold to decrease by nearly 35,500, a fact suggesting that these data trend down over time.

Note that as with other independent variables, it is possible to allow for nonlinear time trends by including the square of the time trend, the cube of the time trend, the log of the time trend, and so on, as additional independent variables.

Empirical Research Tool 10.3 summarizes the inclusion of a time trend.

Excel Regression Output 10.3: Time-Trended Model for Our U.S. Houses Sold Data

SUMMARY OUTPUT

Regression Statistics	
Multiple R	0.93741462
R Square	0.87874617
Adjusted R Square	0.87555528
Standard Error	222633.7027
Observations	79

ANOVA

	df	SS	MS	F	Significance F
Regression	2	2.73E+13	1.365E+13	275.3921633	1.51505E-35
Residual	76	3.767E+12	49565765565		
Total	78	3.1067E+13			

	Coefficients	Standard Error	*t* Stat	*p*-value	Lower 95%	Upper 95%
Intercept	−5,750,475.679	774,820.309	−7.421689408	1.39747E-10	−7293664.041	−4207287.317
Real GDP (trillions)	1,870,304.076	200,386.328	9.333491454	3.0748E-14	1471200.122	2269408.03
Time Trend	−35,491.832	6,431.303	−5.518606836	4.54476E-07	−48300.88184	−22682.78255

Note: Dependent variable is the number of houses sold in the U.S. in a given quarter. Highlighted variables are significant at the 5 percent level.

EMPIRICAL RESEARCH TOOL 10.3: INCLUDING A TIME TREND IN TIME-SERIES ANALYSIS

How to Do It:

1. Estimate the population regression model

$$y_t = \beta_0 + \beta_1 x_{1,t} + \beta_2 x_{2,t} + \cdots + \beta_k x_{k,t} + \beta_{k+1} t + \varepsilon_t$$

where t is a time trend that increases in incremental units from the first time period in our sample to the last, such that $t = 1, 2, \ldots, T$, with T being the last time period represented.

2. Perform t-tests for the individual significance of the slope coefficient, β_{k+1}.

Why It Works:

All other variables constant, the coefficient estimate β_{k+1} provides an indication of whether the data are trending up or down over time. Accordingly, if we reject the null hypothesis of no time trend, then we conclude that the observed values of the dependent and independent variables vary directly with the time periods in which the data are observed, and we should take steps to correct for the effects of the observed time trend.

de-trending
Occurs when the trend is removed from a time-series data set.

What should we do if we estimate our data to have a statistically significant time trend? We should either include a time trend in the regression model or we should **de-trend** the data. The steps for de-trending the data are as follows:

1. Separately regress the dependent variable *and* each of the independent variables on the time trend by estimating the population regression models

$$y_t = \beta_0 + \beta_1 t + \varepsilon_t$$

$$x_{1,t} = \delta_0 + \delta_1 t + \varepsilon_t$$
$$x_{2,t} = \varphi_0 + \varphi_1 t + \varepsilon_t$$
$$\vdots$$
$$x_{k,t} = \gamma_0 + \gamma_1 t + \varepsilon_t \qquad \textbf{10.5.3}$$

2. Calculate the residuals from each of those regressions

$$\tilde{y}_t = y_t - (\hat{\beta}_0 + \hat{\beta}_1 t)$$
$$\tilde{x}_{1,t} = x_{1,t} - (\hat{\delta}_0 + \hat{\delta}_1 t)$$
$$\tilde{x}_{2,t} = x_{2,t} - (\hat{\varphi}_0 + \hat{\varphi}_1 t)$$
$$\vdots$$
$$\tilde{x}_{k,t} = x_{k,t} - (\hat{\gamma}_0 + \hat{\gamma}_1 t) \qquad \textbf{10.5.4}$$

3. Estimate the de-trended population regression model

$$\tilde{y}_t = \beta_0 + \beta_1 \tilde{x}_{1,t} + \beta_2 \tilde{x}_{2,t} + \cdots + \beta_k \tilde{x}_{k,t} + \varepsilon_t \qquad \textbf{10.5.5}$$

For our U.S. houses sold data, we first estimate the population regression models

$$Houses\ sold_t = \beta_0 + \beta_1 t + \varepsilon_t \qquad \textbf{10.5.6}$$

and

$$Real\ GDP_t = \beta_0 + \beta_1 t + \varepsilon_t \qquad \textbf{10.5.7}$$

and get Excel Regression Output 10.4.

We then use the predicted values from Excel Regression Output 10.4 to calculate the predicted values $\widehat{Houses\ sold}_t$ and $\widehat{Real\ GDP}_t$, and we use those values to calculate the de-trended variables, which are just the residuals from the regression contained in Regression Output 10.4

Excel Regression Output 10.4: First-Stage Regression for De-Trending Our U.S. Houses Sold Data

Houses Sold (y_t):

SUMMARY OUTPUT

Regression Statistics	
Multiple R	0.860093288
R Square	0.739760463
Adjusted R Square	0.736380729
Standard Error	324034.4978
Observations	79

ANOVA

	df	SS	MS	F	Significance F
Regression	1	2.29822E+13	2.29822E+13	218.8812523	3.25609E-24
Residual	77	8.08487E+12	1.04998E+11		
Total	78	3.1067E+13			

	Coefficients	Standard Error	*t* Stat	*p*-value	Lower 95%	Upper 95%
Intercept	1465880.234	73611.21093	19.91381768	419476E-32	1319301.589	1612458.879
Time Trend	23652.67770	1598.733339	14.79463593	3.25609E-24	20469.19296	26836.16244

Note: Dependent variable is the number of houses sold in the U.S. in a given quarter. Variables highlighted in blue are significant at the 5 percent level.

Real GDP ($x_{1,t}$):

SUMMARY OUTPUT

Regression Statistics	
Multiple R	0.98530648
R Square	0.97082886
Adjusted R Square	0.97045001
Standard Error	0.12661276
Observations	79

ANOVA

	df	SS	MS	F	Significance F
Regression	1	41.08041941	41.08041941	2562.594844	7.31571E-61
Residual	77	1.23437082	0.01603079		
Total	78	42.31479023			

	Coefficients	Standard Error	t Stat	p-value	Lower 95%	Upper 95%
Intercept	3.858386454	0.028762735	134.1453277	4.93595E-93	3.801112534	3.915660375
Time Trend	0.031622938	0.000624687	50.62207862	7.31571E-61	0.030379028	0.032866848

Note: Dependent variable is U.S. real GDP in a given quarter. Highlighted variables are significant at the 5 percent level.

$$\widetilde{Houses\ sold}_t = Houses\ sold_t - \widehat{Houses\ sold}_t \qquad \textbf{10.5.8}$$

and

$$\widetilde{Real\ GDP}_t = Real\ GDP_t - \widehat{Real\ GDP}_t \qquad \textbf{10.5.9}$$

Table 10.4 demonstrates how we do so for our U.S. houses sold data.

TABLE 10.4 Constructing the De-Trended Values for Our Houses Sold Data

Year	Quarter	Houses Sold	Real GDP (trillions)	Predicted Houses Sold	Predicted Real GDP (trillions)	De-trended Houses Sold	De-trended Real GDP (trillions)
1986	2	2,374,000	4.06	1,489,532.91	3.890009393	884,467.088607595	0.170788406
1986	3	2,082,000	4.10	1,513,185.59	3.921632331	568,814.410905550	0.176627742
1986	4	2,160,000	4.12	1,536,838.27	3.953255269	623,161.733203505	0.163681937
1987	1	2,154,000	4.13	1,560,490.94	3.984878207	593,509.055501460	0.143664817
1987	2	2,023,000	4.15	1,584,143.62	4.016501145	438,856.377799415	0.132720583
1987	3	1,981,000	4.17	1,607,796.30	4.048124083	373,203.700097371	0.125677989
1987	4	1,870,000	4.24	1,631,448.98	4.079747021	238,551.022395326	0.158388615
1988	1	1,917,000	4.26	1,655,101.66	4.111369959	261,898.344693281	0.150358117
1988	2	2,100,000	4.31	1,678,754.33	4.142992897	421,245.666991236	0.164656068
1988	3	2,070,000	4.33	1,702,407.01	4.174615835	367,592.989289192	0.151386518

Finally, we estimate the de-trended population regression model

$$\widetilde{Houses\ sold}_t = \beta_0 + \beta_1 \widetilde{Real\ GDP}_t + \varepsilon_t \qquad \textbf{10.5.10}$$

by OLS and get Excel Regression Output 10.5.

These estimates can be interpreted as follows. On average, if the de-trended U.S. real GDP increases by $1 trillion, then the de-trended number of houses sold in the United States would be estimated to increase by 1.870 million. Notice that it is indeed correct for the intercept in the de-trended model to equal 0 (or a number very, very close to 0, which 3.10089E-09 certainly is) because the de-trending process removes the intercept term.

Excel Regression Output 10.5: De-Trended Model for Our U.S. Houses Sold Data

SUMMARY OUTPUT	
Regression Statistics	
Multiple R	0.73079982
R Square	0.534068377
Adjusted R Square	0.528017317
Standard Error	221183.3048
Observations	79

ANOVA

	df	SS	MS	F	Significance F
Regression	1	4.31788E+12	4.31788E+12	88.26030038	2.08553E-14
Residual	77	3.767E+12	48922054324		
Total	78	8.08487E+12			

close to Ø

	Coefficients	Standard Error	*t* Stat	*p*-value	Lower 95%	Upper95%
Intercept	3.10089E-09	24885.06601	1.24608E-13	1	−49552.49628	49552.49628
Detrended Real GDP (trillions)	1870304.076	199080.8653	9.394695332	2.08553E-14	1473883.4340	2266724.718

Note: Dependent variable is the de-trended number of houses sold in the U.S. in a given quarter. Highlighted variables are significant at the 5 percent level.

Moreover, notice that the estimated slope coefficient in Excel Regression Output 10.5 is the same as the estimated slope coefficient in Excel Regression Output 10.3. This is due to the fact that estimating the population regression model in formula 10.5.2 that includes the time-trend term has the same effect as following the process outlined described to de-trend the data. Empirical Research Tool 10.4 summarizes the de-trending process.

EMPIRICAL RESEARCH TOOL 10.4 DE-TRENDING TIME-SERIES DATA WITH A STATISTICALLY SIGNIFICANT TIME TREND

How to Do It:

1. Estimate the population regression models

$$y_t = \beta_0 + \beta_1 t + \varepsilon_t, x_{1,t} = \delta_0 + \delta_1 t + \varepsilon_t,\ x_{2,t} = \varphi_0 + \varphi_1 t + \varepsilon_t, \ldots, x_{k,t} = \gamma_0 + \gamma_1 t + \varepsilon_t.$$

2. Calculate the residuals from using the equations

$$\tilde{y}_t = y_t - (\hat{\beta}_0 + \hat{\beta}_1 t),\ \tilde{x}_{1,t} = x_{1,t} - (\hat{\delta}_0 + \hat{\delta}_1 t),\ \tilde{x}_{2,t} = x_{2,t} - (\hat{\varphi}_0 + \hat{\varphi}_1 t), \ldots, \tilde{x}_{k,t} = x_{k,t} - (\hat{\gamma}_0 + \hat{\gamma}_1 t).$$

Estimate the de-trended population regression model $\tilde{y}_t = \beta_0 + \beta_1\tilde{x}_{1,t} + \beta_2\tilde{x}_{2,t} + \cdots + \beta_k\tilde{x}_{k,t} + \varepsilon_t$.

Why It Works:

De-trending the data removes the effect of systematic changes over time from each of the variables, thereby providing variables that no longer exhibit a time trend.

Suppose that instead of increasing (or decreasing) across time periods, our data systematically increase (or decrease) only during specific time periods during the calendar year? As an example, suppose that we are interested in estimating the independent factors associated with quarterly turkey sales in the United States. In such a case, we would likely notice that the dependent variable is higher during the fourth quarter of each calendar year, owing to the American tradition of serving turkey during Thanksgiving and Christmas

seasonality
Occurs when the time series variable follows similar patterns depending on the season.

dinners. We refer to such cases as exhibiting **seasonality,** and we should take steps to control for this possibility.

Seasonality

quarterly seasonality
Occurs when a time-series differs during the same quarter every year.

The types of seasonality that we are likely to encounter depend in large part of the type of data that we are analyzing. Because macroeconomic data are often collected on a quarterly basis, one major type of seasonality that we are likely to encounter is **quarterly seasonality.** We can control for potential quarterly seasonality by adding dummy variables for three of the four quarters to our OLS regression (because we must omit one base group when including a series of dummy variables) and estimating the population regression model:

$$y_t = \beta_0 + \beta_1 x_{1,t} + \beta_2 x_{2,t} + \cdots + \beta_k x_{k,t} + \beta_{k+1}Q2 + \beta_{k+2}Q3 + \beta_{k+3}Q4 + \varepsilon_t \quad \textbf{10.5.11}$$

where *Q2, Q3,* and *Q4* are binary dummy variables indicating that the data are from the second, third, and fourth quarters of a given year, respectively. The resulting coefficient estimates, β_{k+1}, β_{k+2}, and β_{k+3}, provide an indication of whether the data are statistically different in the second, third, and fourth quarters of a given year than in the first quarter of that year, holding all other independent variables constant.

Table 10.5 demonstrates how we would construct the quarter dummies for our U.S. houses sold data.

TABLE 10.5
Constructing the Seasonality Terms for the First Five Observations for Our Houses Sold Data

Year	Quarter	Time	Houses Sold	Real GDP (trillions)	Q2	Q3	Q4
1986	2	1	2,374,000	4.06	1	0	0
1986	3	2	2,082,000	4.10	0	1	0
1986	4	3	2,160,000	4.12	0	0	1
1987	1	4	2,154,000	4.13	0	0	0
1987	2	5	2,023,000	4.15	1	0	0

After constructing these variables, we would estimate the population regression model

$$House\ sold_t = \beta_0 + \beta_1 Real\ GDP_t + \beta_2 Q2 + \beta_3 Q3 + \beta_4 Q4 + \varepsilon_t \quad \textbf{10.5.12}$$

and get Excel Regression Output 10.6.

seasonally adjusted data
Data that have had the effects of seasonality removed.

The results for our seasonality controls can be interpreted as follows. Holding real GDP constant, the number of houses sold in the second, third, and fourth quarters do not differ significantly from the number of houses sold in the first quarter. This is not at all surprising, given that the data provided by the U.S. Census Bureau are already **seasonally adjusted.**

Excel Regression Output 10.6: Our U.S. Houses Sold Data with Seasonality Terms Included

SUMMARY OUTPUT	
Regression Statistics	
Multiple R	0.911536886
R Square	0.830899494
Adjusted R Square	0.821758926
Standard Error	266444.3818
Observations	79

ANOVA					
	df	SS	MS	F	Significance F
Regression	4	2.58136E+13	6.4534E+12	90.90239271	8.77028E-28
Residual	74	5.25345E+12	70992608609		
Total	78	3.1067E+13			

	Coefficients	Standard Error	*t* Stat	*p*-value	Lower 95%	Upper 95%
Intercept	−1616003.341	218251.7492	−7.40430876	1.72062E-10	−2050879.438	−1181127.244
Real GDP (trillions)	780392.2761	40978.77469	19.04381676	3.02713E-30	698740.286	862044.266
Q2	34012.92492	85360.92831	0.39846011	0.69143844	−136072.435	204098.285
Q3	40935.87039	85360.11419	0.47956673	0.63294985	−129147.867	211019.608
Q4	42776.34071	85377.91881	0.50102347	0.61784172	−127342.874	212895.555

Note: Dependent variable is the number of houses sold in the U.S. in a given quarter. Highlighted variables are significant at the 5 percent level.

As a final note, when dealing with monthly data, we would control for potential seasonality in a similar way, although we would now add dummy variables for 11 of the 12 months to our estimated model.

Empirical Regression Tool 10.5 summarizes seasonality.

EMPIRICAL RESEARCH TOOL 10.5: INCLUDING SEASONALITY TERMS IN TIME-SERIES ANALYSIS

How to Do It:

1. Estimate the population regression model

$$y_t = \beta_0 + \beta_1 x_{1,t} + \beta_2 x_{2,t} + \cdots + \beta_k x_{k,t} + \beta_{k+1} Q2 + \beta_{k+2} Q3 + \beta_{k+3} Q4 + \varepsilon_t$$

where *Q2, Q3,* and *Q4* are binary dummy variables indicating that the data are from the second, third, and fourth quarters of a given year, respectively.

2. Perform *t*-tests for the individual significance of the estimated slope coefficients, $\beta_2, \beta_3, \ldots, \beta_{k+1}$.

Why It Works:

All other variables constant, the coefficient estimates, β_{k+1}, β_{k+2}, and β_{k+3}, provide an indication of whether the data are statistically different in the second, third, and fourth quarters of a given year than in the first quarter of that year. Accordingly, if we fail to reject the null hypothesis of no seasonality, then we conclude that the observed data systematically vary during specific periods in a given year, and we should take steps to correct for that fact.

10.6 TEST FOR STRUCTURAL BREAKS IN THE DATA

Rather than data that systematically increase or decrease across all time periods or data that differ at specific seasonal points within each time period, suppose that we are confronted with data that change drastically for all time periods after a significant event occurs. As an example, when introducing our U.S. houses sold data, we mentioned that we suspect a structural break to have occurred in the U.S. housing market after 2005Q4 when the U.S. housing bubble burst. Before attempting to statistically test for a structural break, we first need to add the data for the time periods 2006Q1–2011Q2 back into our sample (recall that we had initially dropped these data due to our concern about the potential existence of

FIGURE 10.9
Line Graph Demonstrating Where We Think a Structural Break Might Occur in U.S. Houses Sold Data

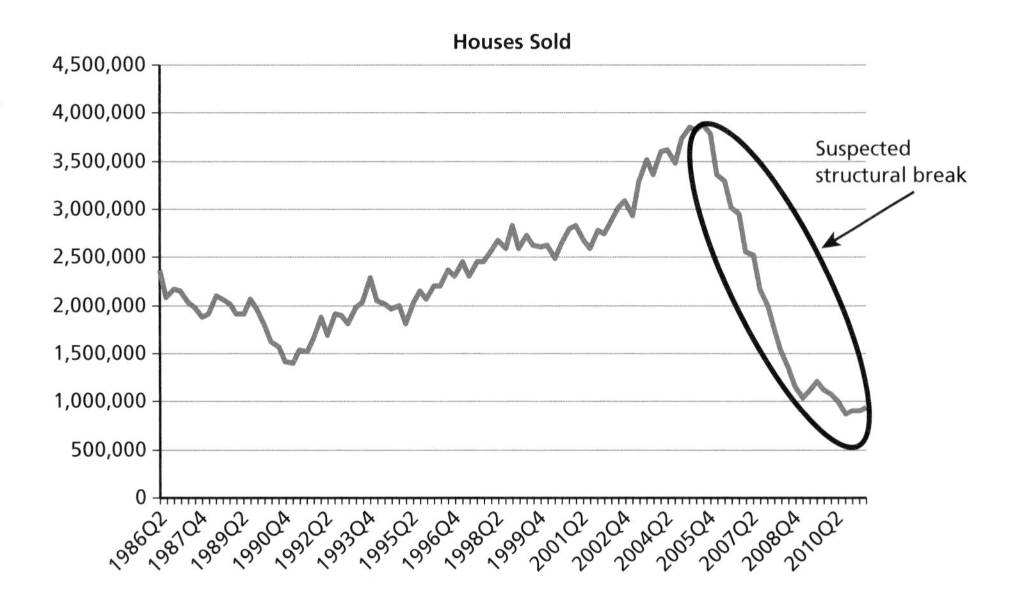

a structural break in our time series). After adding back in these data, Figure 10.9 presents the line graph for the number of houses sold in the United States between 1986Q2 and 2012Q4.

Based on the information in Figure 10.9, it should be clear why we suspect that the structural break started after 2005Q4.

To statistically test for a structural break, we: (1) construct a new variable SB_t that is equal to 1 for all time periods after the break is suspected to have occurred and 0 for all time periods before, (2) calculate interaction terms by multiplying SB_t by each of the independent variables in our model, (3) include SB_t and all of the interaction terms in the regression, by estimating the population regression model

$$y_t = \beta_0 + \beta_1 x_{1,t} + \beta_2 x_{2,t} + \cdots + \beta_k x_{k,t} + \beta_{k+1} SB_t + (\beta_{k+2} SB_t \cdot x_{1,t}) + (\beta_{k+3} SB_t \cdot x_{2,t}) + \cdots + (\beta_{2k+1} SB_t \cdot x_{k,t}) + \varepsilon_t \quad \textbf{10.6.1}$$

and (4) perform an F-test for the joint significance of the terms containing SB_t, because doing so will provide an indication of whether, all other independent variables constant, the values of the dependent variable are systematically statistically different after the onset of the suspected break than before.

Table 10.6 demonstrates these calculations for our U.S. houses sold data.

TABLE 10.6
Constructing the Variable for Testing Whether a Structural Break Occurs in Our Houses Sold Data

Year	Quarter	House Sold	Real GDP (trillions)	SB_t	SB_t × Real GDP (trillions)
1986	2	2,374,000	4.06	0	0
1986	3	2,082,000	4.10	0	0
1986	4	2,160,000	4.12	0	0
1987	1	2,154,000	4.13	0	0
1987	2	2,023,000	4.15	0	0

We then estimate the unrestricted population regression model

$$Houses\ sold_t = \beta_0 + \beta_1 Real\ GDP_t + \beta_2 SB_t + (\beta_3 SB_t \cdot Real\ GDP_t) + \varepsilon_t \quad \textbf{10.6.2}$$

by OLS, getting Excel Regression Output 10.7.

Excel Regression Output 10.7: Unrestricted Model for Our Test for a Potential Structural Break in Our U.S. Houses Sold Data

Unrestricted Regression

SUMMARY OUTPUT

Regression Statistics	
Multiple R	0.802035239
R Square	0.643260524
Adjusted R Square	0.632227344
Standard Error	448809.6823
Observations	101

ANOVA

	df	SS	MS	F	Significance F
Regression	3	3.52316E+13	1.17439E+13	58.30237005	1.24251E-21
Residual	97	1.95387E+13	2.0143E+11		
Total	100	5.47703E+13			

	Coefficients	Standard Error	*t* Stat	*p*-value	Lower 95%	Upper 95%
Intercept	−1587774.016	357069.5507	−4.446679963	2.32282E-05	−2296458.215	−879089.818
Real GDP (trillions)	780699.5988	68994.76209	11.31534591	1.99866E-19	643764.098	917635.099
SB_t	−12907850.3	6808049.503	−1.89596893	0.060940576	−26419943.7	604243.022
$SB_t \cdot$ Real GDP (trillions)	1657107.127	1024463.205	1.61753699	0.109009896	−376168.6978	3690382.952

Note: Dependent variable is number of houses sold in the U.S. in a given quarter. Variables highlighted in blue and gray are significant at the 5 percent and 10 percent levels.

To complete the F-test for the joint significance of the structural break terms, we then estimate the restricted population regression model

$$Houses\ sold_t = \beta_0 + \beta_1 Real\ GDP_t + \varepsilon_t \qquad \textbf{10.6.3}$$

by OLS, getting Excel Regression Output 10.8.

Excel Regression Output 10.8: Restricted Model for Our Test for a Potential Structural Break in Our U.S. Houses Sold Data

Restricted Regression

SUMMARY OUTPUT

Regression Statistics	
Multiple R	0.226734627
R Square	0.051408591
Adjusted R Square	0.041826859
Standard Error	724426.7789
Observations	101

ANOVA						
	df	SS	MS	F	Significance F	
Regression	1	2.81566E+12	2.81566E+12	5.365271549	0.022603402	
Residual	99	5.19546E+13	5.24794E+11			
Total	100	5.47703E+13				
	Coefficients	Standard Error	*t* Stat	*p*-value	Lower 95%	Upper 95%
Intercept	1253756.857	440677.5462	2.845066349	0.005396425	379357.0227	2128156.692
Real GDP (trillions)	184565.9477	79681.17382	2.316305582	0.022603402	26461.21597	342670.6794

Note: Dependent variable is number of houses sold in the U.S. in a given quarter. Highlighted variables are significant at the 5 percent level.

To determine whether a structural break did indeed occur, we calculate the *F*-statistic

$$F\text{-}statistic = \frac{(USS_R - USS_U)/2}{USS_U/n - k - 1} = \frac{16{,}207{,}949{,}471{,}377}{201{,}430{,}130{,}969.77} = 80.46 \quad \textbf{10.6.4}$$

Because the value of the calculated *F*-statistic exceeds the critical value of 3.09, we reject the null hypothesis of no structural break and conclude that a structural did indeed occur after 2005Q4.

Empirical Research Tool 10.6 summarizes how to test for structural breaks.

EMPIRICAL RESEARCH TOOL 10.6: TESTING FOR STRUCTURAL BREAKS IN THE TIME-SERIES DATA

How to Do It:

1. Estimate the population regression model

$$y_t = \beta_0 + \beta_1 x_{1,t} + \beta_2 x_{2,t} + \cdots + \beta_k x_{k,t} + \beta_{k+1} SB_t + (\beta_{k+2} SB_t \cdot x_{1,t}) + (\beta_{k+3} SB_t \cdot x_{2,t}) + \cdots + (\beta_{2k+1} SB_t \cdot x_{k,t}) + \varepsilon_t$$

where SB_t is a binary dummy variable equal to 1 if the observation is for a time period after the suspected structural break.

2. Perform an *F*-test for the joint significance of the slope coefficients $\beta_{k+1}, \beta_{k+2}, \ldots \beta_{2k+1}$.

Why It Works:

All other variables constant, the coefficient estimate $\beta_{k+1}, \beta_{k+2}, \ldots \beta_{2k+1}$ provides an indication of whether there are statistically different changes in the intercept and the slopes in the period after the suspected break than in the period before the suspected break. Accordingly, if we fail to reject the null hypothesis of no structural break, then we conclude that a structural break did occur, and we should take steps to correct for that fact.

10.7 UNDERSTAND THE PROBLEM PRESENTED BY SPURIOUS REGRESSION

spurious correlation
Occurs when a statistical relationship is found between two or more variables when none actually exits but the variables are related to another variable.

Turning to a different issue associated with time-series data, recall that as discussed in the final section of Chapter 4, there are many well-known situations in which correlation is observed between variables for which theory suggests that no causal relationship should exist. Such cases are referred to as exhibiting **spurious correlation**, and they are often encountered in time-series data. As an example, consider that in a March 25, 2011, column in the *New York Post,* Mike Vaccaro writes "Across the past 62 years, Kentucky has won six national championships. Tell me if any of these years ring a bell: 1949? 1951? 1958? 1978? 1996? 1998? Yes, you see the pattern, don't you? Since 1949, as surely as summer follows spring, whenever Kentucky wins a national championship, the Yankees follow suit with a World Series title seven months later. You can set your watch (or order your championship ring) by it."

In a similar vein, looking at the line graph in Figure 10.10, we notice that the number of houses sold in the United States seemed to trend down in the later 1980s/early 1990s before starting a steep uphill climb from the mid-1990s to early 2000s. Coincidentally, the New York Yankees suffered through a down period (at least for them) in the late 1980s and early 1990s before turning things around to win four World Series titles between 1996 and 2000. In fact, if we plot the number of wins per year for the Yankees between 1987 and 2005 versus the number of U.S. houses sold per year during the same period, we get Figure 10.10.

FIGURE 10.10
Line Graphs Comparing U.S. Houses Sold and NY Yankee Wins, 1987–2005

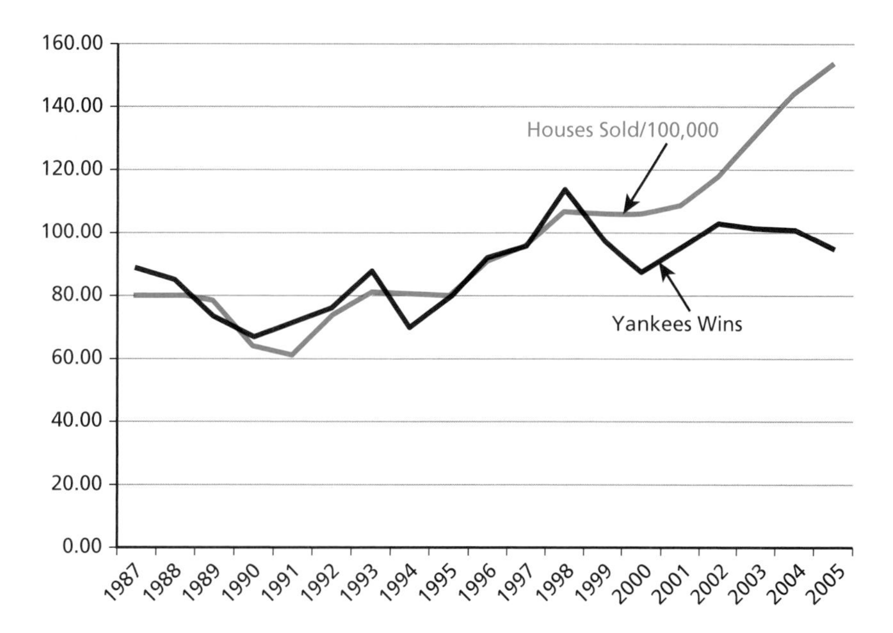

Notice that the respective line graphs seem to follow the same relative pattern, especially in the years between 1995 and 1998. To see whether these two variables are indeed statistically correlated, we estimate the population regression model

$$Houses\ sold_t = \beta_0 + \beta_1 Yankees\ wins_t + \varepsilon_t \qquad \textbf{10.7.1}$$

by OLS and get Excel Regression Output 10.9.

Excel Regression Output 10.9: Our U.S. Houses Sold Data Including Number of Wins per Year by the New York Yankees

SUMMARY OUTPUT	
Regression Statistics	
Multiple R	0.744325401
R Square	0.554020303
Adjusted R Square	0.527786203
Standard Error	1775333.726
Observations	19

Number of years between 1987 and 2005

Number of years between 1987 and 2005

ANOVA					
	df	SS	MS	F	Significance F
Regression	1	6.6561E+13	6.6561E+13	21.11832717	0.000257534
Residual	17	5.35808E+13	3.15181E+12		
Total	18	1.20142E+14			

	Coefficients	Standard Error	*t* Stat	*p*-value	Lower 95%	Upper 95%
Intercept	−3,500,613.328	2,897,074.984	−1.208326795	0.243461966	−9612907.203	2611680.546
Yankees Wins	148,984.327	32,419.837	4.595468113	0.000257534	80584.45041	217384.2031

Note: Dependent variable is the number of houses sold in the U.S. in a given quarter. Highlighted variables are significant at the 5 percent level.

These results can be interpreted as follows. Notice first that we now have 19 observations, owing to the fact that there are 19 years between 1987 and 2005. Second, holding all other independent variables constant, for our simple linear regression analysis, we estimate that each additional win in a given season by the New York Yankees is associated with a statistically significant increase in the number of houses sold in the United States of nearly 149,000. Does economic theory in any way justify this result (i.e., do we believe that the American public responds to a Yankees World Series victory by deciding to purchase more houses)? Of course not. This again highlights the importance of making sure that we let economic theory guide our chosen econometric specifications and that we be careful to make sure that our results pass the "eye test" before placing too much emphasis on them.

10.8 LEARN TO PERFORM FORECASTING

It is important to note that econometrics is a backward-looking rather than a forward-looking process. By this, we mean that we can only perform regression analysis on observed data that result from human behavior that has already occurred. We cannot look into the future and perform econometric analysis on data for human behavior that will eventually occur. Accordingly, when trying to use empirical analysis to inform our expectations about the future, the best we can do is to use lessons learned from observing past behavior to predict potential future behavior, which is a process referred to as **forecasting**.

forecasting
Predicting a value of the dependent variable that is not in the sample.

Unfortunately, performing accurate forecasting is notoriously difficult. As a nod to this inherent difficulty, in his *Newsweek* column of September 19, 1966, Nobel laureate Paul Samuelson joked, "Wall Street indexes predicted nine out of the last five recessions." Nonetheless, when dealing with important time series, such as a nation's GDP, one of the things that economists are most frequently asked to do is to forecast the future.

out-of-sample prediction
When the forecast is for a subset of the sample that is not used in the original regression and then compared to the true value of the dependent variable.

A common method for evaluating the accuracy of our forecast is referred to as **out-of-sample prediction.** For time-series data, out-of-sample prediction is performed by

1. Using the estimated coefficients from our sample regression function to predict outcomes of the dependent variable for a different set of observed values of the independent variables.

2. Comparing those predicted outcomes to the values of the dependent variable that are actually observed for the different set of data to assess the degree to which our estimated model is successful in forecasting unobserved events.

In many cases, this is done by estimating the desired econometric model for a subset of observations and using the results to predict outcomes for the remaining observations. As is sometimes the case, there are no hard-and-fast rules that govern the relative size of the estimated subsample and the relative size of the forecast subsample. Accordingly, the choice is generally a matter of feel left up to the researcher.

As an example of how to perform out-of-sample estimation, we first estimate the population regression model

$$Houses\ sold_t = \beta_0 + \beta_1 Real\ GDP_t + \varepsilon_t \qquad \textbf{10.8.1}$$

for the 51 quarters between 1986Q2 and 1998Q4, getting Excel Regression Output 10.10.

Excel Regression Output 10.10: In-Sample Regression for Our U.S. Houses Sold Data for the Period 1986Q2–1998Q4

SUMMARY OUTPUT

Regression Statistics	
Multiple R	0.648449173
R Square	0.42048633
Adjusted R Square	0.408659521
Standard Error	243145.8969
Observations	51

Number of quarters between 1986Q2 and 1998Q4 (points to Observations: 51)

ANOVA

	df	SS	MS	F	Significance F
Regression	1	2.10193E+12	2.10193E+12	35.55365693	2.67148E-07
Residual	49	2.89688E+12	59119927165		
Total	50	4.99881E+12			

	Coefficients	Standard Error	*t* Stat	*p*-value	Lower 95%	Upper 95%
Intercept	−460,867.049	420,654.795	−1.095594430	0.27861216	−1306204.493	384470.3943
Real GDP (trillions)	538,159.514	90,254.504	5.962688733	2.67148E-07	356786.3015	719532.7274

Note: Dependent variable is the number of houses sold in the U.S. in a given quarter. Highlighted variables are significant at the 5 percent level.

We then use the estimated marginal effects to predict the number of houses sold for the 28 quarters from 1999Q1 to 2011Q2 by plugging the observed real GDP in each of those quarters in the sample regression function

$$\widehat{Houses\ sold}_{t+k} = -460{,}867.049 + 538{,}159.514\ Real\ GDP_{t+k} + \varepsilon_{t+k} \qquad \textbf{10.8.2}$$

where $t + k$ are the 28 quarters from 1999Q1 to 2011Q2.

To generate an idea of how well our estimated values predict the values that are actually observed, we then compare the predicted values for the subsequent periods to the values that are actually observed in those periods by calculating the following equation for all 28 quarters that were omitted from the regression model

$$Difference = Houses\ sold - \widehat{Houses\ sold} \qquad \textbf{10.8.3}$$

Table 10.7 demonstrates the calculations for the first five observations in our U.S. houses sold sample.

TABLE 10.7
Calculating Number of Houses Sold for the First Five Observations Using Out-of-Sample Prediction

Year	Quarter	Houses Sold (y_t)	Real GDP (trillions) (x_t)	Predicted Houses Sold ($\hat{y}_t$)	Difference ($y_t - \hat{y}_t$)
1999	1	2,586,000	5.56	2,530,834.41	55,165.59
1999	2	2,729,000	5.58	2,542,358.56	186,641.04
1999	3	2,619,000	5.63	2,569,339.59	49,660.41
1999	4	2,608,000	5.71	2,611,948.49	−3,948.49
2000	1	2,629,000	5.71	2,614,080.08	14,919,92

Looking at the entries in Table 10.7, we see that the relative success of our model's predictions differs greatly by quarter. For instance, in 1999Q4, our model only underestimates the number of houses actually sold by roughly 4,000 units, while in 1999Q2 our model overestimates the number of houses actually sold by nearly 190,000 units. To judge our model based on the relative success of its out-of-sample predictions, we can calculate the root mean square error (MSE) of our prediction, which we do as follows

$$Root\ MSE = \sqrt{\frac{\Sigma(y_t - \hat{y}_t)^2}{l}} \tag{10.8.4}$$

where l is the number of observations omitted from the original regression model. For our U.S. houses sold data for the 28 quarters between 1999Q1 and 2011Q2, the root MSE is calculated as

$$Root\ MSE = \sqrt{\frac{\Sigma(y_t - \hat{y}_t)^2}{l}} = \sqrt{\frac{5{,}926{,}370{,}642{,}003.83}{28}} = 460{,}060.97 \tag{10.8.5}$$

What are we to make of this value? There is no hard-and-fast rule, but in general, we can say that the smaller the root MSE of a model the better.

Empirical Research Tool 10.7 summarizes the out-of-sample prediction process.

EMPIRICAL RESEARCH TOOL 10.7: OUT-OF-SAMPLE PREDICTION FOR TIME-SERIES DATA

How to Do It:

1. Estimate the population regression model $y_t = \beta_0 + \beta_1 x_{1t} + \beta_2 x_{2t} + \cdots + \beta_k x_{kt} + \varepsilon_t$ for the data from a certain time series covering time periods $t = 1, 2, \ldots, T$.
2. Use the estimated coefficients from that sample regression function to predict out-of-sample outcomes for subsequent time-periods $t = T + 1, T + 2, \ldots, T + k$.
3. Calculate the mean square error, $Root\ MSE = \sqrt{\frac{\Sigma(y_t - \hat{y}_t)^2}{l}}$, for the out-of-sample predictions.

Why It Works:

If our population regression model has true explanatory power, then the out-of-sample predictions for the subsequent time series should be close to the actual observed values. Accordingly, if the root MSE is small, then we conclude that our model provides accurate forecasts.

ADDITIONS TO OUR EMPIRICAL RESEARCH TOOLKIT

In this chapter we have introduced a number of tools that will prove valuable when performing empirical research. They include:

- Static time-series models.
- Distributed lag models.
- Methods for accounting for time trends and seasonality.
- Methods for testing for structural breaks in the data.
- Methods for performing forecasting and out-of-sample predictions.

OUR NEW EMPIRICAL TOOLS IN PRACTICE: USING WHAT WE HAVE LEARNED IN THIS CHAPTER

As a first pass, our former student estimated a static time-series model, which produced the sample regression function shown in Table 10.8.

TABLE 10.8 Estimated Marginal Effects for the Static Time-Series Regression for Our Former Student's U.S. Deficit Data

SUMMARY OUTPUT	
Regression Statistics	
Multiple R	0.932194502
R Square	0.86898659
Adjusted R Square	0.852349967
Standard Error	103.8101811
Observations	72

ANOVA

	df	SS	MS	F	Significance F
Regression	8	4503164.075	562895.5094	52.23335077	6.53338E-25
Residual	63	678922.8829	10776.5537		
Total	71	5182086.958			

	Coefficients	Standard Error	*t* Stat	*p*-value	Lower 95%	Upper 95%
Intercept	649.3974984	185.0572354	3.509171079	0.000835743	279.5901259	1019.204871
Real GDP (billions)	−0.156550175	0.022161725	−7.06398855	1.54578E-09	−0.200836849	−0.112263501
Real Income Tax Receipts (millions)	0.002172766	0.000203399	10.68229111	8.95067E-16	0.001766306	0.002579226
Real Defense Expenditures (millions)	−0.000990705	0.000114374	−8.661942184	2.4981E-12	−0.001219264	−0.000762146
Population (millions)	−0.002398064	0.001350336	−1.775902205	0.080578245	−0.005096494	0.000300366
Democratic President	−77.81236386	27.39808642	−2.840065641	0.006066424	−132.5630702	−23.06165753
Democratic Controlled Senate	37.46453695	38.27947228	0.978710905	0.331466297	−39.0308837	113.9599576
Democratic Controlled House	−50.98316103	35.78571732	−1.42467903	0.159185089	−122.4952101	20.52888801
Recession	−90.47031382	29.07439848	−3.11168308	0.002795174	−148.5708625	−32.36976518

Note: Dependent variable is annual U.S. surplus (deficit). Variables highlighted in blue are significant at the 5 percent level. Variables highlighted in gray are significant at the 10 percent level.

Because deficits are represented as negative numbers in these data, the student interpreted these estimates as follows. All other variables constant, U.S. annual deficits have been increasing over time with real GDP, defense expenditures, and population and decreasing with income tax receipts. At the same time, all other variables constant, deficits tend to be significantly higher under a Democratic president and during a recession.

Having learned about time-series data, our former student decided that it might be important to examine whether her U.S. deficit data exhibited a time trend. To test this possibility, the student estimated the sample regression function in Table 10.9.

TABLE 10.9 **Estimated Marginal Effects for Regression Including a Time Trend for Our Former Student's U.S. Deficit Data**

SUMMARY OUTPUT	
Regression Statistics	
Multiple R	0.943010927
R Square	0.889269608
Adjusted R Square	0.873195842
Standard Error	96.20328935
Observations	72

ANOVA					
	df	SS	MS	F	Significance F
Regression	9	4608272.439	512030.271	55.32428296	2.88271E-26
Residual	62	573814.5187	9255.072883		
Total	71	5182086.958			

	Coefficients	Standard Error	*t* Stat	*p*-value	Lower 95%	Upper 95%
Intercept	−1716.771684	722.7701321	−2.375266503	0.020642583	−3161.568578	−271.9747905
Real GDP (billions)	−0.178302213	0.021528184	−8.282268945	1.28289E-11	−0.22133644	−0.135267986
Real Income Tax Receipts (millions)	0.002272668	0.000190811	11.91055143	1.13391E-17	0.001891241	0.002654094
Real Defense Expenditures (millions)	−0.00097007	0.00010617	−9.136936717	4.33112E-13	−0.001182301	−0.000757839
Population (millions)	0.01649091	0.00574305	2.871457155	0.005584536	0.005010726	0.027971102
Democratic President	−94.01477248	25.84162906	−3.638113227	0.000560793	−145.6714524	−42.35809254
Democratic Controlled Senate	20.57163905	35.8268839	0.574195599	0.567912895	−51.04528072	92.18855883
Democratic Controlled House	−27.66659712	33.87750439	−0.816665738	0.417246412	−95.3867628	40.05356857
Recession	−92.8879686	26.95346484	−3.446234803	0.001025928	−146.7671766	−39.00876062
Time Trend	−45.93507534	13.63062331	−3.369990814	0.001297624	−73.18230282	−18.68784785

Note: Dependent variable is annual U.S. surplus(deficit). Highlighted variables are significant at the 5 percent level.

Given that the slope coefficient on the time-trend variable was estimated to be negative and statistically significant, our former student concluded that these data did exhibit a significant, negative time trend.

On the basis of the work presented here, in addition to having thought of an interesting question and having identified and collected appropriate data, our former student was well on her way to conducting a successful empirical research project.

LOOKING AHEAD TO CHAPTER 11

Just as we were worried about potential violations of assumption M6 for cross-section data, we should also be worried about violations of assumption T6 for time-series data. The discussion of autocorrelation in Chapter 11 proceeds much like the discussion of heteroskedasticity in Chapter 9, albeit we will be considering the problems associated with the errors being correlated with each other over time rather than the errors having a nonconstant variance.

Problems

10.1 Suppose you estimate the following distributed lag model with the independent variable lagged three times:

$$y_t = \beta_0 + \beta_1 x_{1,t} + \beta_2 x_{1,t-1} + \beta_3 x_{1,t-2} + \beta_4 x_{1,t-3} + \varepsilon_t$$

a. Assume that there is a random shock of size c to $x_{1,t}$, such that the shock was temporary (affected $x_{1,t}$ and then went away). Assume that no other shocks occur. What affect will this have on the y_t variable in the current period? Next period? Two periods from now? Three periods from now? Four periods from now? Five periods from now?

b. Now assume that the shock is permanent. How does this affect y_t in the current period? Next period? Two periods from now? Three periods for now? Four periods from now? Five periods from now?

10.2 How do the time-series assumptions differ from the multiple linear-regression assumptions? Why are they different?

10.3 Suppose you thought your data have a trend.

a. Describe how you would correct for it within the regression equation.

b. What transformation would you apply to the data to account for the trend?

10.4 What is seasonality? If you had monthly data and only a dependent variable, how would your correct for it? Section 10.5 explains how to de-trend data. How would you recommend you de-seasonalize data? Your answer should include a step-by-step explanation.

10.5 Suppose you thought your data had a structural break at a specific time period. What implications would this have on the coefficient estimates? How would you correct for the structural break?

10.6 Explain how a regression of y_t on x_t could result in a statistically significant relationship between the two variables when they are not actually related. What is this type of relationship called?

10.7 What is out-of-sample prediction? Say you had 500 time-series observations and would like to determine how well your model is performing. How would you suggest obtaining an out-of-sample prediction?

Exercises

E10.1 Use the data set **shipments.xls** for this problem. These data contain the number of shipments sent out for a shipping company each month and the number of calls they get each month.

a. Create two time-series graphs with shipments and calls as well as a scatterplot with shipments on the y-axis.

b. Estimate the static regression model of shipments against calls.

c. Create lagged version of calls with calls lagged one, two, and three periods.

d. Estimate distributed lagged model by regressing shipping on calls, calls lagged once, calls lagged twice, and calls lagged three times.

e. Compare and contrast the results from parts (b) and (d). Which model do you prefer?

E10.2 The file **beer.xls** has monthly beer sales for a beer manufacturer over a number of years.

a. Graph beer sales over time. Does it look like the series has a time trend or seasonality associated with it?

b. Run a regression that accounts for a time trend, and statistically test whether the time trend is statistically significant at a 5 percent level. What do you conclude now about whether these data have a time trend?

c. Run a regression that accounts for seasonality in these data, keeping in mind that these data are monthly. Statistically test if there is seasonality in these data at a 5 percent level. What do you conclude about if these data have seasonality?

d. Run a regression that accounts for a time trend and seasonality, and statistically test for them at a 5 percent level.

E10.3 The file **visit.xls** contains monthly visitor information for Exit Glacier in Alaska.

a. Create a time-series graph for these data. Explain why the graph looks like it does.

b. Run a regression that accounts for seasonality in these data, keeping in mind that these data are monthly. Statistically test whether there is seasonality in these data at a 5 percent level. What do you conclude now about whether these data have seasonality?

c. Seasonally adjust these data and graph your findings.

E10.4 Use the file **shipments.xls**.

a. Regress shipments on calls and a time trend.

b. Adjust both variables for the presence of a time trend, and regress the adjusted shipment variable on the adjusted calls variable. Comment on the similarities and differences from your results in part (a).

E10.5 Open file **dow jones.xls**.

a. Create a time-series graph for these data, and comment on what you see.

b. Regress stock price on housing starts and consumer confidence and comment on your results.

c. Assume that a structural break occurred in July 2006. Write out a regression model that would account for this, and estimate this model.

d. How did your results change between parts (a) and (b)?

E10.6 Suppose you are interested in forecasting beer sales for the next year. Open file **beer.xls** and regress beer on a time trend and monthly dummy variables.

a. Forecast beer sales for the next 12 months. Do you think that this is the best model to achieve an accurate forecast?

b. Do not include the last 12 observations in your model, run a regression and forecast 12 months into the future, and then compute the mean squared error for your forecast. Explain what this number means.

E10.7 You have been hired by the park management department in Alaska to forecast the number of visitors that will come to the Exit Glacier during the next year. Use **visit.xls** for this project.

a. Forecast visitor sales for the next 12 months. Do you think that this is the best model to achieve an accurate forecast?

b. Do not include the last 12 observations in your model, run a regression and forecast 12 months into the future, and then compute the mean squared error for your forecast. Explain what this number means.

Reference

www.nypost.com/p/sports/college/basketball/yankees_fans_should_pull_for_uk_Tpyf3jOGudixYF84tsTR8I#ixzz1b1DBmKfv

Chapter Eleven

Autocorrelation

CHAPTER OBJECTIVES

After reading this chapter, you will be able to:

1. Understand the autoregressive structure of the error term.
2. Understand methods for detecting autocorrelation.
3. Understand how to correct for autocorrelation.
4. Understand unit roots and cointegration.

A STUDENT'S PERSPECTIVE

Suppose that you are working with time-series data and, upon careful examination, become concerned that one of the six assumptions required for ordinary least squares (OLS) estimates to be best linear unbiased estimates (BLUE) for time-series data is violated. What should you do?

This is exactly the situation encountered by our former student who was interested in estimating the impact that several institutional factors have on U.S. annual budget surpluses (deficits). On the basis of her training, our former student was concerned as to whether the six assumptions required for OLS to provide estimates that are BLUE held for these time-series data. In particular, given the inherent nature of time-series data, the student was concerned that assumption T6, which states that the error term in a given time period is not correlated with the error term in any prior period, was potentially violated for her data.

BIG PICTURE OVERVIEW

Recall from Chapter 10 that there are six assumptions required for OLS to provide BLUE for time-series data, as listed in the following box.

Assumptions Required for OLS to Be the Best Linear Unbiased Estimator (BLUE) for Time-Series Data

Assumption T1: The model is linear in the parameters.
Assumption T2: The data are not perfectly multicollinear.
Assumption T3: The error term has zero mean, or $E(\varepsilon_t) = 0$.
Assumption T4: The error term is uncorrelated with each independent variable, and all functions of each independent variable, or $E(\varepsilon_t|x_{tj}) = 0$ for all j.
Assumption T5: The error term has constant variance, or $Var(\varepsilon_t) = \sigma^2$.
Assumption T6: The error term in one period is uncorrelated with the error term in any previous period, or $Cov(\varepsilon_t, \varepsilon_{t-j}) = 0$ for all j not equal to 0.

autocorrelation occurs when the error term in one time period is correlated with the error term from a previous time period.

As with cross-section data, we have to rely on our intuition and training to determine whether these assumptions can be considered reasonable. One of the main violations of the six time-series assumptions that we are likely to encounter, **autocorrelation,** occurs when the error term in a given time period t is in some way correlated with the error term from a previous time period, say, $t - 1$. In such a case, because assumption T6, $Cov(\varepsilon_t, \varepsilon_{t-1}) \neq 0$, is violated, our OLS estimates are no longer BLUE, and our estimated standard errors are incorrect.

As an example of the problems presented by autocorrelation, suppose that we wish to estimate the population regression model

$$y_t = \beta_0 + \beta_1 x_{1,t} + \beta_2 x_{2,t} + \cdots \beta_k x_{k,t} + \underbrace{\rho\varepsilon_{t-1} + u_t}_{\text{Composite error term, } \varepsilon_t} \qquad 11.1$$

Looking at the specification in formula 11.1, we can see that the composite error, ε_t, is a function of both this period's error term, u_t, and a previous period's error term, ε_{t-1}. Accordingly, assumption T6, which states that the error terms must not be correlated across time periods, is violated.

positive autocorrelation occurs when positive errors tend to follow positive errors and negative errors tend to follow negative errors.

negative autocorrelation occurs when positive errors tend to follow negative errors and negative errors tend to follow positive errors.

By definition, autocorrelation can either be positive or negative, with the difference being that in **positive autocorrelation,** above-average errors tend to follow other above-average errors and below-average errors tend to follow other below-average errors, resulting in a familiar cyclical pattern such as that observed for the U.S. business cycle. In **negative autocorrelation,** above-average errors tend to follow below-average errors and below-average errors tend to follow other above-average errors, resulting in the less common situation in which errors flip-flop from positive to negative and negative to positive and positive to negative and so on. Figure 11.1 presents these potential error patterns along with the baseline case of no autocorrelation.

FIGURE 11.1 A Visual Depiction of the Different Potential Types of Autocorrelation

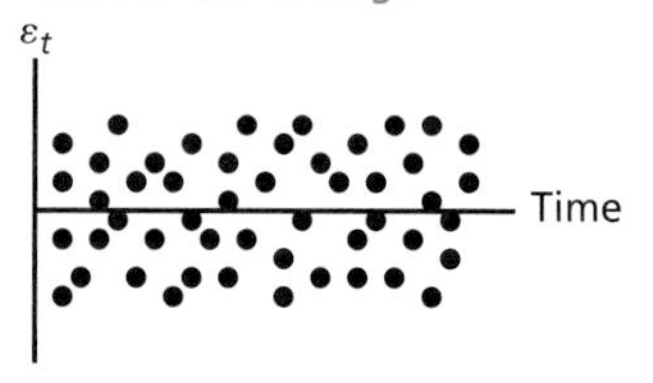

(a) No Autocorrelation

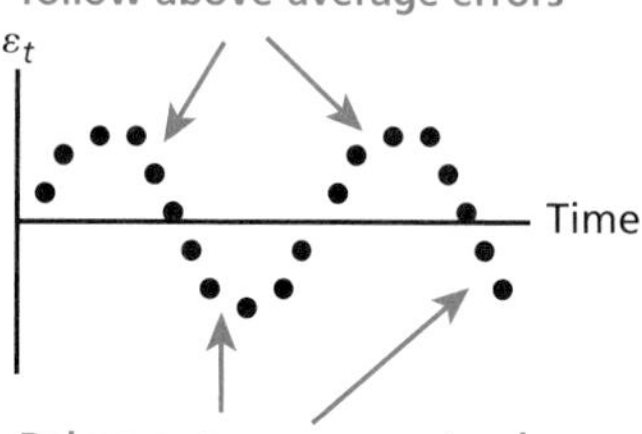

(b) Positive Autocorrelation

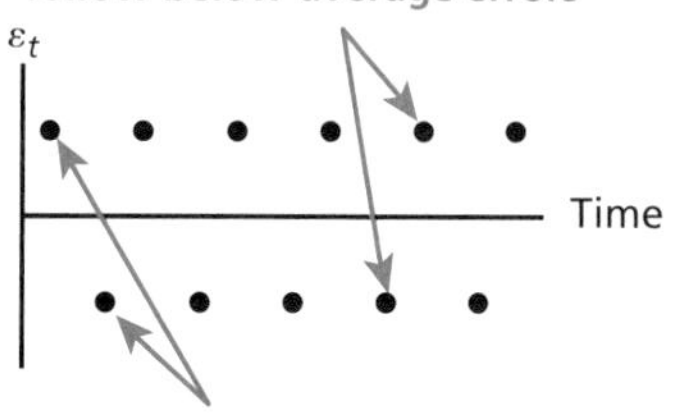

(c) Negative Autocorrelation

Autocorrelation is a potential problem because the composite error term has memory of the error terms in previous time periods. For this reason, the unexplained variation in the dependent variable in the current period, u_t, is correlated with the unexplained variation in the dependent variable in previous periods, ε_{t-1}. Unfortunately, because it assumes that autocorrelation does not exist, OLS does not account for this cross-period correlation and the resulting parameter estimates, while being unbiased, have greater variance than alternative unbiased estimators that do account for the memory in the error term. As with heteroskedasticity, because the OLS standard errors assume no autocorrelation, the calculated standard errors in the presence of autocorrelation are incorrect, thereby rendering all measures of precision based on those estimates incorrect.

Unbiased but have greater variance + standard errors are incorrect

Based on this discussion, we summarize the issues and consequences associated with autocorrelation in the following box.

The Issues and Consequences Associated with Autocorelated Data

Problem:
Autocorrelation violates time series assumption T6, which states that the error terms must not be correlated across time periods.

Consequences:
Under autocorrelation,
1. Parameter estimates are unbiased.
2. Parameter estimates are not minimum variance among all unbiased estimators.
3. Estimated standard errors are incorrect, and all measures of precision based on the estimated standard errors are also incorrect.

In this chapter, we introduce methods for determining whether our data suffer from autocorrelation and for correcting our estimates and standard errors if autocorrelation is detected. Figure 11.2 visually summarizes the goals of this chapter.

FIGURE 11.2
A Visual Depiction of the Empirical Tools Introduced in This Chapter

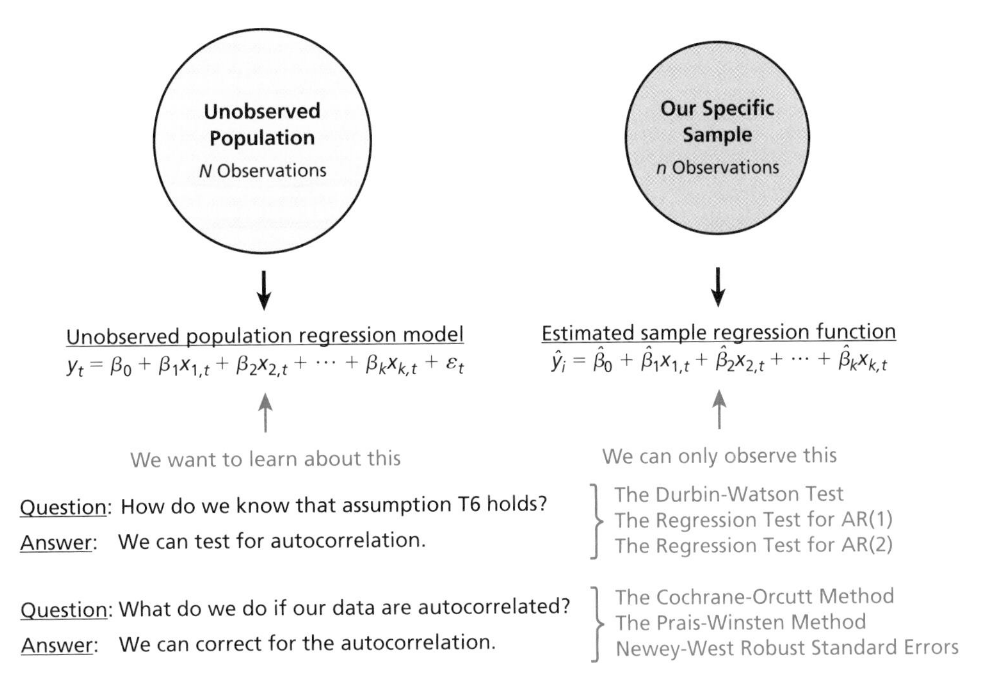

For consistency, we again analyze the U.S. houses sold data introduced in Chapter 9. Before starting to analyze those data, the following box introduces an important caveat concerning our treatment of autocorrelation.

An Important Caveat before Getting Started

As with heteroskedasticity, the treatment of potential autocorrelation in time-series data has benefited greatly from computer power. Accordingly, rather than taking the time to test whether data indeed exhibit autocorrelation before implementing a relatively clunky approach to correcting for it, modern researchers include a very simple command asking their chosen statistical program to provide estimates with Newey-West robust standard errors (which we introduce in Section 11.3) as a default when working with time-series data.

Nonetheless, we believe that in order to understand the intuition behind what that simple command is doing and why, it is important to first work through the more "old-school" examples before learning how to calculate Newey-West robust standard errors.

11.1 UNDERSTAND THE AUTOREGRESSIVE STRUCTURE OF THE ERROR TERM

autoregressive process
Occurs when future values of a time-series process are a function of past values.

To effectively deal with the memory embedded in the composite error term, we need to know something about the exact nature of the correlation, or the **autoregressive process,** between the current period's error and the prior period's error. When dealing with economic data, we are likely to encounter several different autoregressive processes.

The AR(1) Process

AR(1) process
Occurs when the error term in the current period depends on the error term in the previous period such that $\varepsilon_t = u_t + \rho\varepsilon_{t-1}$.

The **AR(1) process** assumes that the current period's error is related to the immediate prior period's error as follows:

$$\varepsilon_t = \rho\varepsilon_{t-1} + u_t \qquad \textbf{11.1.1}$$

where u_t is the error term for the current period, ε_{t-1} is the error term in the previous period, and ρ is the coefficient of autocorrelation, which describes the degree to which the errors in time periods t and $t-1$ are related.

This is the simplest possible autoregressive process and is the common starting point when using an old-school method to correct for the presence of autocorrelation in our data.

The AR(2) Process

AR(2) process
Occurs when the error term in the current period depends on the error term in the previous period such that $\varepsilon_t = u_t + \rho_1\varepsilon_{t-1} + \rho_2\varepsilon_{t-2}$.

A slightly more complex autoregressive structure that we sometimes encounter is the **AR(2) process,** in which we assume that the current period's error is related to the immediate prior period's error and the error two periods prior as follows:

$$\varepsilon_t = \rho_1\varepsilon_{t-1} + \rho_2\varepsilon_{t-2} + u_t \qquad \textbf{11.1.2}$$

where u_t is the error term for the current period, ε_{t-1} and ε_{t-2} are the composite error terms in the previous two time periods, respectively, and ρ_1 and ρ_2 are the coefficients of autocorrelation, which describe the degree to which the error in time-period t is related to the error in time period $t-1$.

The AR(1,4) Process

AR(1,4) process
Occurs when the error term in the current period depends on the error term in the previous period such that (insert equation 11.1.3 here)

While the preceding autoregressive processes are the easiest that can be formulated, they are not always the most realistic. As an example, consider U.S. consumer spending. While it is true that the unexplained variation in a given period is likely related to the unexplained variation in the immediate prior period, it is also true that consumer spending generally follows a somewhat predictable pattern throughout each calendar year, with spending traditionally peaking during the fourth quarter holiday season. Accordingly, we might expect the error in a given quarter to depend not only on the error in the immediate prior quarter, but also on the error in the same quarter in the immediate prior year. We can allow for such a memory structure by modeling the composite error term as

$$\varepsilon_t = \rho_1\varepsilon_{t-1} + \rho_4\varepsilon_{t-4} + u_t \qquad \textbf{11.1.3}$$

where ρ_1 and ρ_4 are defined as we would expect at this point. We refer to this formulation as the AR(1,4) process to acknowledge that we suspect this period's error to be affected by both the error 1 period prior and the error 4 periods prior.

Note that this formulation implicitly assumes we are dealing with quarterly data. Suppose we are dealing with monthly data instead. The appropriate expression of the composite error term would then be AR(1,12) or

$$\varepsilon_t = u_t + \rho_1\varepsilon_{t-1} + \rho_{12}\varepsilon_{t-12} \qquad \textbf{11.1.4}$$

where ρ_1 and ρ_{12} are defined as expected.

11.2 UNDERSTAND METHODS FOR DETECTING AUTOCORRELATION

There is a reason that our introduction to autocorrelation seems rather similar to our introduction to heteroskedasticity. The basic idea underlying these two situations is essentially the same: they both represent violations of the final assumption required for OLS to provide estimates that are BLUE and estimated standard errors that are correct. The only real difference between the two situations is that the exact natures of the violations differ because autocorrelation occurs primarily within time-series data, while the heteroskedasticity we discussed in Chapter 9 occurs primarily within cross-section data.

As with heteroskedasticity, the first step in dealing with potential autocorrelation is to determine whether the given assumption, in this case T6, is indeed violated. There are a number of methods for making this determination. In essence, these methods all represent different ways of determining whether the data being analyzed are more similar to the representation in Figure 11.1a or the representations in Figures 11.1b and 11.1c. If the data are determined to be more like the former, then we conclude that our data are unlikely to be autocorrelated. If they are more like the latter, then we conclude that our data are likely to be autocorrelated, that our OLS estimates are no longer BLUE, and that our OLS estimated standard errors are incorrect. In such cases, we need to develop alternative estimators that are BLUE. In the following discussions, we are assuming that assumptions T1 through T5 hold and that only assumption T6 is potentially violated.

Informal Methods for Detecting Autocorrelation

A first pass at identifying whether autocorrelation is likely present in our data is to construct and examine a simple residual plot for the estimated time-series model. Recall that we can easily obtain the residual plot in Excel by checking the "Residual Plots" box in the regression window.

For our U.S. houses sold data, we estimate the population regression model

$$\textit{Houses sold}_t = \beta_0 + \beta_1 \textit{Real GDP}_t + \varepsilon_t \qquad \textbf{11.2.1}$$

by OLS and get Excel Regression Output 11.1.

Excel Regression Output 11.1: Static Time-Series Regression for Our U.S. Houses Sold Data

SUMMARY OUTPUT

Regression Statistics	
Multiple R	0.911129439
R Square	0.830156855
Adjusted R Square	0.8279511
Standard Error	261775.2738
Observations	79

Number of quarters between 1986Q2 and 2005Q4 (refers to Observations)

ANOVA

	df	SS	MS	F	Significance F
Regression	1	2.57905E+13	2.57905E+13	376.3594799	2.2565E-31
Residual	77	5.27652E+12	68526293956		
Total	78	3.1067E+13			

	Coefficients	Standard Error	*t* Stat	*p*-value	Lower 95%	Upper 95%
Intercept	−1,587,774.016	208,266.406	−7.6237644	5.37572E-11	−2002485.406	−1173062.627
Real GDP (trillions)	780,699.599	40,242.275	19.3999866	2.2565E-31	700566.9928	860832.2048

Note: Dependent variable is the number of houses sold in the U.S. in a given quarter. Highlighted variables are significant at the 5 percent level.

Figure 11.3 presents the accompanying residual plot.

FIGURE 11.3
Residual Plot from the Time-Series Model Estimation for Our U.S. Houses Sold Data

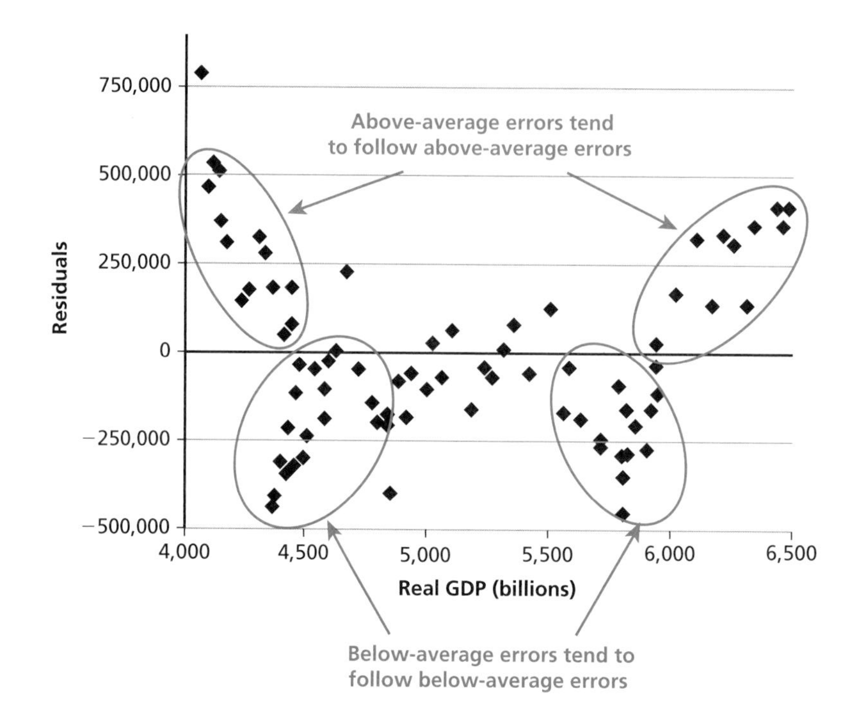

While far from being definitive, this informal method does at least provide some idea of whether autocorrelation is likely present in our data. In this case, while the relationship is certainly not exact, it does appear that above-average errors generally tend to follow above-average errors and below-average errors generally tend to follow below-average errors.

As with heteroskedasticity, the potential drawback to using the informal method to detect potential autocorrelation is its informality—individuals looking at the same picture may well come to different conclusions as to whether autocorrelation is apparent. Accordingly, the informal method is often employed as a simple first check to see if more formal detection methods should be considered.

Formal Methods for Detecting Autocorrelation

The formal methods that we consider for testing whether autocorrelation is present in our data are all based on statistical tests of the following general null and alternative hypotheses:

H_0: *the error terms are not correlated over time*
H_1: *the error terms are correlated over time* **11.2.2**

with the specific formulation of each hypothesis depending on the empirical specification employed in each individual test.

Under this framework, if we reject the null hypothesis, then we conclude that assumption T6 is violated, that our data are autocorrelated, that our time-series estimates are not BLUE, and that our calculated standard errors are incorrect. In such a case, we must take steps to obtain more efficient estimates.

The Durbin-Watson Test

The Durbin-Watson test is performed by (1) estimating the time-series model; (2) determining both the current-period residuals, e_t, and the residuals lagged one period, e_{t-1}; and (3) using those values to calculate the test statistic

$$d = \frac{\Sigma_{t=2}^{T}(e_t - e_{t-1})^2}{\Sigma_{t=1}^{T} e_t^2} \qquad \textbf{11.2.3}$$

which is then compared to a predetermined table value to determine whether the data are likely to be autocorrelated.

Mathematically, an approximation of the Durbin-Watson test statistic is

$$d \approx 2(1 - \rho) \quad \textbf{11.2.4}$$

Considering the possible extremes for the test statistic in formula 11.2.4 aids our interpretation. If autocorrelation is not present in our data, then $\rho = 0$ and $d = 2$; if perfect positive autocorrelation is present in our data, then $\rho = 1$ and $d = 0$; if perfect negative autocorrelation is present in our data, then $\rho = -1$ and $d = 4$. Accordingly, determining whether and which type of autocorrelation is present in our data is a matter of determining how close the calculated Durbin-Watson statistic falls to 0, 2, or 4.

The individual steps for conducting the Durbin-Watson test are as follows.

1. Estimate the population regression model

$$y_t = \beta_0 + \beta_1 x_{1,t} + \beta_2 x_{,t} + \cdots + \beta_k x_{k,t} + \varepsilon_t \quad \textbf{11.2.5}$$

and obtain the current-period residuals,

$$e_t = y_t - \hat{y}_t \quad \textbf{11.2.6}$$

For our U.S. houses sold data, we estimate the population regression model

$$Houses\ sold_t = \beta_0 + \beta_1 Real\ GDP_t + \varepsilon_t \quad \textbf{11.2.7}$$

and calculate the residuals. Doing so, for our U.S. houses sold data, we get Table 11.1.

TABLE 11.1
Calculating the Residuals from the Time-Series Estimation for the First Five Observations for Our U.S. Houses Sold Data

Observation (*t*)	Predicted Houses Sold ($\hat{y}_t$)	*Residuals* (e_t)
1	1,582,489.20	791,510.80
2	1,611,735.98	470,264.02
3	1,626,317.21	533,682.79
4	1,635,377.87	518,622.13
5	1,651,521.72	371,478.28

2. Calculate the terms required to determine the Durbin-Watson test statistic, which are e_t^2, e_{t-1}, and $(e_t - e_{t-1})^2$ for every period starting with $t = 2$.

Doing so for our U.S. houses sold data, we get Table 11.2.

3. Calculate the Durbin-Watson test statistic

$$d = \frac{\sum_{t=2}^{T}(e_t - e_{t-1})^2}{\sum_{t=1}^{T} e_t^2} \quad \textbf{11.2.8}$$

Doing so for our U.S. houses sold data, we get

$$d = \frac{\sum_{t=2}^{T}(e_t - e_{t-1})^2}{\sum_{t=1}^{T} e_t^2} = \frac{1{,}561{,}927{,}283{,}343.62}{5{,}276{,}524{,}634{,}637.01} = 0.2960 \quad \textbf{11.2.9}$$

4. Compare the calculated Durbin-Watson statistic to the Durbin-Watson tables in order to assess if the model suffers from first order autocorrelation.

For our U.S. houses sold data, the calculated Durbin-Watson statistic of 0.2960 is relatively close to 0, suggesting that positive autocorrelation likely exists in our data. To statistically confirm this fact, we turn to Durbin-Watson critical value tables. To use these tables, we need to identify the number of observations in our sample, which is denoted by *T*; the number of independent variables (including the intercept), which is denoted as *K*; and the desired level of significance. In this case, because $T = 79$, $K = 2$, and the desired level of significance is 5 percent, we should consult the Durbin-Watson table in Table 11.3.

Table 11.3 looks a little different than the critical value tables we have consulted previously. Namely, while the first two columns are the number of observations and the number of independent variables (including the intercept), the final two are new and different.

TABLE 11.2 **Calculating the Durbin-Watson Test Statistic for the First Five Observations for Our U.S. Houses Sold Data**

Observation (t)	Predicted Houses Sold ($\hat{y}_t$)	*Residuals* (e_t)	*Residuals Squared* (e_t^2)	*Lagged Residuals* (e_{t-1})	*Difference Squared* $(e_t - e_{t-1})^2$
1	1,582,489.20	791,510.80	626,489,353,161.92		
2	1,611,735.98	470,264.02	221,148,250,245.16	791,510.80	103,199,495,169.79
3	1,626,317.21	533,682.79	284,817,322,170.37	470,264.02	4,021,940,371.10
4	1,635,377.87	518,622.13	268,968,918,576.61	533,682.79	226,823,390.36
5	1,651,521.72	371,478.28	137,996,111,394.78	518,622.13	21,651,314,411.55

$$\sum_{t=2}^{T}(e_t - e_{t-1})^2 = 1{,}561{,}927{,}283{,}343.62$$

$$\sum_{t=1}^{T}e_t^2 = 5{,}276{,}524{,}634{,}637.01$$

$$d = 0.2960$$

TABLE 11.3 **Critical Values for the Durbin-Watson Test: 5 Percent Significance Level, $T = 6$ to 79, and $K = 2$ to 21 ($K \leq T - 4$)**

T	*K*	dL	dU	
6.	2.	0.61018	1.40015	
7.	2.	0.69955	1.35635	
7.	3.	0.46723	1.89636	
8.	2.	0.76290	1.33238	
8.	3.	0.55907	1.77711	
8.	4.	0.36744	2.28664	
9.	2.	0.82428	1.31988	
9.	3.	0.62910	1.69926	
9.	4.	0.45476	2.12816	
9.	5.	0.29571	2.58810	
10.	2.	0.87913	1.31971	
10.	3.	0.69715	1.64134	
⋮	⋮	⋮	⋮	
78.	20.	1.08756	2.25177	
78.	21.	1.05712	2.29011	
79.	2.	1.60887	1.66006	← Use this entry
79.	3.	1.58304	1.68667	
79.	4.	1.55679	1.71407	

Because of the way that the Durbin-Watson test statistic is calculated, there are actually two inconclusive regions in which we are neither able to reject nor fail to reject the null hypothesis. The dL and dU values reported in Table 11.3 are the lower and upper bounds for these regions, respectively. Recall that the Durbin-Watson test statistic is mathematically required to fall between 0 and 4, with the middle value of 2 representing no autocorrelation and the bounds of 0 and 4 representing perfect positive autocorrelation and perfect negative autocorrelation, respectively. Because our interpretations differ depending on the direction that we move away from the middle value of 2, we have two different inconclusive regions, one falling below 2 and one falling above 2. The fact that all of the entries in Table 11.3 are less than 2 indicates that these entries define the inconclusive region that lies to the left of 2 (i.e., if the calculated values lie between 1.60887 and 1.66006, the results are inconclusive). To find the inconclusive region that falls to the right of 2, we need to subtract both dL and dU from 4 (i.e., the inconclusive region to the right of 2 is bounded by 4 − 1.60887 = 2.39113 and 4 − 1.66006 = 2.33994).

Figure 11.4 visually depicts how to determine the inconclusive regions.

With this in mind, for our U.S. houses sold sample, because the calculated Durbin-Watson statistic of 0.2960 is less than the lower bound of 1.60887, we reject the null hypothesis and conclude that positive autocorrelation exists within our sample.

Empirical Research Tool 11.1 summarizes the Durbin-Watson test.

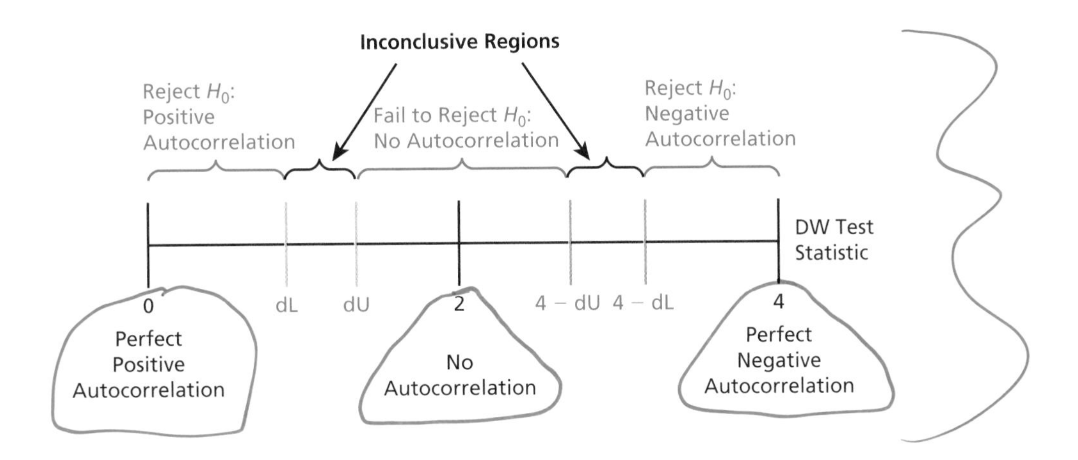

FIGURE 11.4
A Visual Depiction of How to Interpret the Durbin-Watson Test

EMPIRICAL RESEARCH TOOL 11.1: THE DURBIN-WATSON TEST FOR THE PRESENCE OF AUTOCORRELATION

How to Do It:

1. Estimate $y_t = \beta_0 + \beta_1 x_{1,t} + \beta_2 x_{,t} + \cdots + \beta_k x_{k,t} + \varepsilon_t$ and obtain the residuals, $e_t = y_t - \hat{y}_t$.
2. Determine the terms required to calculate the Durbin-Watson statistic, $(e_t)^2$, e_{t-1} and $(e_t - e_{t-1})^2$.
3. Calculate the Durbin-Watson statistic, $d = \frac{\Sigma_{t=2}^{T}(e_t - e_{t-1})^2}{\Sigma_{t=1}^{T} e_t^2}$.
4. Consult the appropriate Durbin-Watson table to determine whether to reject the null hypothesis of no autocorrelation.

Why It Works:

Under perfect positive autocorrelation, this period's error always equals last period's period error, meaning that $d = 0$. Under perfect negative autocorrelation, this period's error is always exactly opposite last period's error, meaning that $d = 4$. Accordingly, calculated values of the test statistic that are closer to 0 or closer to 4 indicate that autocorrelation is present in the data.

Potential Issues:

1. The test cannot be performed on models with lagged dependent variables.
2. The test can only be performed on models in which the suspected autocorrelation takes the form of AR(1).
3. The errors must be normally distributed.
4. The model must include an intercept.

The Regression Test for AR(1)

The regression test for AR(1) is performed by (1) calculating the residuals from the time-series model estimation, (2) regressing those residuals on the residuals lagged one period, and (3) performing a t-test for the individual significance of the resulting estimated slope coefficient. The intuition behind this test should be fairly clear. The estimated slope coefficient from the regression of the current residuals on the residuals lagged one period provides an estimate of the degree to which the current and the one-period lagged residuals are correlated. Accordingly, if the estimated slope coefficient is statistically significant, then we conclude that the residuals are correlated across time periods, that autocorrelation is present in our data, and that our OLS estimated standard errors are incorrect.

The individual steps for conducting the regression test for AR(1) are as follows.

1. Estimate the population regression model

$$y_t = \beta_0 + \beta_1 x_{1,t} + \beta_2 x_{,t} + \cdots + \beta_k x_{k,t} + \varepsilon_t \quad \textbf{11.2.10}$$

and obtain the residuals

$$e_t = y_t - \hat{y}_{t-1} \quad \textbf{11.2.11}$$

For our U.S. houses sold data, we estimate the population regression model as

$$Houses\ sold_t = \beta_0 + \beta_1 Real\ GDP_t + \varepsilon_t \quad \textbf{11.2.12}$$

2. Calculate the residuals e_t and the residuals lagged one-period e_{t-1} for every period starting with $t = 2$.

Table 11.4 presents the results of doing so for our U.S. houses sold data.

TABLE 11.4
Calculating the Terms Required to Perform the Regression Test for AR(1) for the First Five Observations for Our U.S. Houses Sold Data

Observation (t)	Predicted Houses Sold ($\hat{y}_t$)	Residuals (e_t)	Residuals Lagged One Period (e_{t-1})
1	1,582,489.20	791,510.80	
2	1,611,735.98	470,264.02	791,510.80
3	1,626,317.21	533,682.79	470,264.02
4	1,635,377.87	518,622.13	533,682.79
5	1,651,521.72	371,478.28	518,622.13

3. Estimate the population regression model

$$e_t = \rho e_{t-1} + u_t \quad \textbf{11.2.13}$$

Notice that there is no intercept in formula 11.2.13, and therefore, we need to ask Excel to constrain the intercept to 0 by checking the "Constant is 0" box in the regression window.

For our U.S. houses sold data, we do so and get Excel Regression Output 11.2.

There are two important facts to note about these results. First, when performing the regression test for AR(1), we lose one observation in our regression (i.e., our regression now has 78, rather than 79, observations). The reason for this is that the lagged residuals

Excel Regression Output 11.2: The Regression Test for AR(1) for Our U.S. Houses Sold Data

SUMMARY OUTPUT

Regression Statistics	
Multiple R	0.842516585
R Square	0.709834196
Adjusted R Square	0.696847183
Standard Error	132374.9704
Observations	78

We have to give up one observation when lagging residuals by one period

ANOVA					
	df	**SS**	**MS**	**F**	**Significance F**
Regression	1	3.30075E+12	3.30075E+12	188.3655222	2.87489E-22
Residual	77	1.34928E+12	17523132783		
Total	78	4.65004E+12			

	Coefficients	**Standard Error**	***t* Stat**	***p*-value**	**Lower 95%**	**Upper 95%**
Intercept	0	#N/A	#N/A	#N/A	#N/A	#N/A
Residuals Lagged One Period	0.797564044	0.058111871	13.72463195	2.19466E-22	0.681848527	0.913279561

Note: Dependent variable is the residual in a given quarter. Highlighted variables are significant at the 5 percent level.

cannot be calculated for the first time period, and therefore, the first observation must be dropped from the regression. Second, the positive estimated slope coefficient suggests that if autocorrelation exists, its memory structure is positive, meaning that above-average errors in one period tend to follow above-average errors in the immediate prior period and vice versa.

4. Perform a t-test for the individual significance of the estimated slope coefficient $\hat{\rho}$ to see if the residuals for the current period are statistically related to the residuals lagged one period.

   Formally, the null and alternative hypotheses for this test are

$$H_0: \rho = 0$$
$$H_1: \rho \neq 0 \qquad \textbf{11.2.14}$$

   To see why, look back at formula 11.2.13 and notice that $\hat{\rho}$ is the estimated slope coefficient between the residuals in the current period and the residuals lagged one period. Hence, if we reject the null hypothesis that $\rho = 0$, then we conclude that there is a statistically significant linear relationship between the current period residuals and the residuals lagged one period and that the data exhibit an AR(1) process.

   To perform the desired hypothesis test at the 95 percent level then, we simply need to check whether the estimated p-value for $\hat{\rho}$ is less than .05.

For our U.S. houses sold data, because the estimated p-value of $2.19E - 22$ is less than 0.05, we reject the null hypothesis and conclude that assumption T6 is violated, that autocorrelation is present in our data, and that our OLS estimated standard errors are correct.

Empirical Research Tool 11.2 summarizes the regression test for the presence of AR(1).

EMPIRICAL RESEARCH TOOL 11.2: THE REGRESSION TEST FOR THE PRESENCE OF AR(1) AUTOCORRELATION

How to Do It:

1. Estimate the population regression model $y_t = \beta_0 + \beta_1 x_{1,t} + \beta_2 x_{2,t} + \cdots + \beta_k x_{k,t} + \varepsilon$ and obtain the residuals, $e_i = y_t - \hat{y}_t$.
2. Calculate the residuals lagged one period e_{t-1} for each observation starting with $t = 2$.
3. Estimate the population regression model $e_t = \rho e_{t-1} + u_t$.
4. Perform a test of the individual significance of the estimated slope coefficient $\hat{\rho}$.

Why It Works:

Autocorrelation of the form AR(1) exists if the current period errors are correlated with immediate prior period errors. Hence, if a regression of the current period residuals on the residuals lagged one period yields a statistically significant coefficient, we would conclude that the errors are correlated and that an AR(1) process does exist.

The Regression Test for AR(2)

The regression test for AR(1) can be modified to test for higher-order autoregressive processes. As an example, suppose we suspect that the correct form of autocorrelation present in our data is AR(2). To modify the regression test, we would

1. Estimate the population regression model

$$y_t = \beta_0 + \beta_1 x_{1,t} + \beta_2 x_{,t} + \cdots + \beta_k x_{k,t} + \varepsilon_t \quad \textbf{11.2.15}$$

   and obtain the residuals

$$e_t = y_t - \hat{y}_t \quad \textbf{11.2.16}$$

Doing so for our U.S. houses sold data, we get the same results as in Excel Regression Output 11.2.

2. Calculate the residuals lagged one period, e_{t-1}, and the residuals lagged two-periods, e_{t-2}, for each observation starting with $t = 2$ (because we cannot calculate both values for the first two periods).

Doing so for our U.S. houses sold data, we get Table 11.5.

TABLE 11.5 Calculating the Terms Required to Perform the Regression Test for AR(2) for the First Five Observations for Our U.S. Houses Sold Data

Observation (t)	Predicted Houses Sold ($\hat{y}_t$)	Residuals (e_t)	Residuals Lagged One Period (e_{t-1})	Residuals Lagged Two Periods (e_{t-2})
1	1,582,489.20	791,510.80		
2	1,611,735.98	470,264.02	791,510.80	
3	1,626,317.21	533,682.79	470,264.02	791,510.80
4	1,635,377.87	518,622.13	533,682.79	470,264.02
5	1,651,521.72	371,478.28	518,622.13	533,682.79

3. Estimate the population regression model

$$e_t = \rho_1 e_{t-1} + \rho_2 e_{t-2} + u_t. \quad \textbf{11.2.17}$$

Doing so for our U.S. houses sold data, we get Excel Regression Output 11.3.

Excel Regression Output 11.3: The Regression Test for AR(2) for Our U.S. Houses Sold Data

SUMMARY OUTPUT

Regression Statistics	
Multiple R	0.848713011
R Square	0.720313774
Adjusted R Square	0.703251291
Standard Error	128514.523
Observations	77

We have to give up two observation when lagging residuals by one period

ANOVA

	df	SS	MS	F	Significance F
Regression	2	3.19019E+12	1.59509E+12	96.57882326	2.35056E-21
Residual	75	1.2387E+12	16515982627		
Total	77	4.42889E+12			

	Coefficients	**Standard Error**	***t* Stat**	***p*-value**	**Lower 95%**	**Upper 95%**
Intercept	0	#N/A	#N/A	#N/A	#N/A	#N/A
Residuals Lagged One Period	0.619612438	0.11069233	5.597609514	3.39154E-07	0.399102013	0.840122863
Residuals Lagged Two Periods	0.233936367	0.105572243	2.215888953	0.029732596	0.023625678	0.444247057

Note: Dependent variable is the number of houses sold in the U.S. in a given quarter. Highlighted variables are significant at the 5 percent level.

There are three important facts to note about these results. First, when performing the regression test for AR(2), we lose two observations in our regression owing to the fact that the desired lagged residual terms in this case cannot be calculated for the first and second time periods, meaning that both of those observations must be dropped from the regression. Second, the positive estimated slope coefficients suggest that if autocorrelation exists, its memory structure is positive, meaning that above-average errors in one period tend to follow above-average errors in the immediate prior period and vice versa. Finally, the fact that the estimated coefficient for the two-period lagged terms is so much smaller than the estimated coefficient for the one-period lagged terms suggests that the memory process likely dies out relatively quickly.

4. Perform an F-test for the joint significance of the two estimated slope coefficients, $\hat{\rho}_1$ and $\hat{\rho}_2$, to see if the residuals for the current period are statistically related to the residuals lagged one period and the residuals lagged two periods.

For our U.S. houses sold data, the null and alternative hypotheses would be

$$H_0: \rho_1 = 0 \text{ and } \rho_2 = 0$$
$$H_A: \rho_1 = 0 \text{ and/or } \rho_2 \neq 0 \qquad \textbf{11.2.18}$$

Based on Excel Regression Output 11.3, because the estimated p-value for overall significance is 2.35E-21 and the estimated p-values for the individual significance of ρ_1 and ρ_2 are all less than 0.05, we reject the null hypothesis and conclude that assumption T6 is violated, that autocorrelation of the form AR(2) is present in our data.

What should we do if we find evidence pointing toward the presence of autocorrelation in our data? While our OLS estimates are still unbiased, they are no longer minimum variance unbiased estimators, a fact that causes our estimated standard errors and the measures of precision based on those estimates to be incorrect. There are two primary ways to correct for this problem. The first is to convert our observed data into a form for which OLS estimates are BLUE (or nearly BLUE). The second is to rely on computer power to correct the standard errors in the initial model.

11.3 UNDERSTAND HOW TO CORRECT FOR AUTOCORRELATION

generalized least squares (GLS)
Applied when the variances of the observations are unequal or when there is a certain degree of correlation between the observations.

The first two methods for obtaining estimates that are BLUE (or nearly BLUE) in the presence of autocorrelation start with the assumption that we know the correct specification of the composite error term. As an example, suppose we know that the correct autoregressive process is AR(1) and that the error term is correctly specified as $\varepsilon_t = u_t + \rho\varepsilon_{t-1}$. In such a case, **generalized least squares (GLS)** would produce estimates that are BLUE by performing an unbiased estimate of $\hat{\rho}$ and then using that estimate to convert our data in such a way that running OLS on the converted data would result in estimates that are BLUE. There are two iterative processes for performing GLS in this case.

The Cochrane-Orcutt Method for AR(1) Processes

The Cochrane-Orcutt method is performed by (1) regressing the residuals from the time-series model estimation on the residuals lagged one period to generate an estimate of $\hat{\rho}$, (2) using that estimate to convert the values of the dependent and independent variables into values that account for the memory of the error terms, and (3) repeating the process until the estimate of $\hat{\rho}$ does not change across iterations (i.e., until the estimated value of $\hat{\rho}$ converges to a fixed value).

The steps for performing the Cochrane-Orcutt procedure are as follows.

Iteration 1:

1. Estimate the population regression model

$$y_t = \beta_0 + \beta_1 x_{1,t} + \beta_2 x_{2,t} + \cdots + \beta_k x_{k,t} + \varepsilon_t \quad \textbf{11.3.1}$$

and calculate the residuals, e_t, and the residuals lagged one-period e_{t-1}.

For our U.S. houses sold data, we estimate the population regression model

$$Houses\ sold_t = \beta_0 + \beta_1 Real\ GDP_t + \varepsilon_t \quad \textbf{11.3.2}$$

and obtain the residuals, e_t, by checking the "Residual Plot" box and then calculating the residuals lagged one period (e_{t-1}) by hand. Doing so, we get Table 11.6.

TABLE 11.6
Calculating the Residuals Lagged One Period for the First Iteration of the Cochrane-Orcutt Procedure for the First Five Observations for Our U.S. Houses Sold Data

Observation (t)	Predicted Houses Sold ($\hat{y}_t$)	Residuals (e_t)	Residuals Lagged One Period (e_{t-1})
1	1,582,489.20	791,511	
2	1,611,735.98	470,264	791,511
3	1,626,317.21	533,683	470,264
4	1,635,377.87	518,622	533,683
5	1,651,521.72	371,478	518,622

2. Estimate the population regression model $\varepsilon_t = \rho\varepsilon_{t-1} + u_t$ to generate an estimate of $\hat{\rho}$.

Doing so for our U.S. houses sold data, we get Excel Regression Output 11.4.

Excel Regression Output 11.4: Estimating $\hat{\rho}$ in the First Iteration of the Cochrane-Orcutt Procedure for Our U.S. Houses Sold Data

SUMMARY OUTPUT

Regression Statistics	
Multiple R	0.842516585
R Square	0.709834196
Adjusted R Square	0.696847183
Standard Error	132374.9704
Observations	78

We have to give up one observation when lagging residuals by one period

ANOVA

	df	SS	MS	F	Significance F
Regression	1	3.30075E+12	3.30075E+12	188.3655222	2.87489E-22
Residual	77	1.34928E+12	17523132783		
Total	78	4.65004E+12			

	Coefficients	Standard Error	*t* Stat	*p*-value	Lower 95%	Upper 95%
Intercept	0	#N/A	#N/A	#N/A	#N/A	#N/A
rho	0.797564044	0.058111871	13.72463195	2.19466E-22	0.681848527	0.913279561

Estimated value of $\hat{\rho}$

3. Convert the data using the estimated value of $\hat{\rho}$. Notice that in addition to the dependent and independent variables, we also need to convert the intercept for every observation. The converted values will then be $\tilde{y}_t = y_t - \hat{\rho}y_{t-1}$, $\tilde{\beta}_0 = 1 - \hat{\rho}$, and $\tilde{x}_{j,t} = x_{j,t} - \hat{\rho}x_{j,t-1}$ for all j independent variables.

Performing these calculations for our U.S. houses sold data, we make the conversions as shown in Table 11.7.

TABLE 11.7 Calculating the Converted Data for the First Iteration of the Cochrane-Orcutt Procedure for the First Five Observations for Our U.S. Houses Sold Data

Observation (t)	Houses Sold (y_t)	Real GDP (billions) (x_t)	Converted Houses Sold ($\tilde{y}_t = y_t - \hat{\rho}y_{t-1}$)	Converted Intercept ($\tilde{\beta}_0 = 1 - \hat{\rho}$)	Converted GDP ($\tilde{x}_{j,t} = x_{j,t} - \hat{\rho}x_{j,t-1}$)
1	2,374,000	4,061			
2	2,082,000	4,098	188,583	0.20	$859.51
3	2,160,000	4,117	499,472	0.20	$848.31
4	2,154,000	4,129	431,262	0.20	$845.02
5	2,023,000	4,149	305,047	0.20	$856.44

4. Estimate the population regression model

$$\tilde{y}_t = \tilde{\beta}_0 + \beta_1\tilde{x}_t + \varepsilon_t. \qquad 11.3.3$$

Doing so for our U.S. houses sold data, we get Excel Regression Output 11.5.

Excel Regression Output 11.5: Results from the First Iteration of the Cochrane-Orcutt Procedure for Our U.S. Houses Sold Data

SUMMARY OUTPUT

Regression Statistics	
Multiple R	0.970334201
R Square	0.941548463
Adjusted R Square	0.927621469
Standard Error	131713.4567
Observations	78

We have to give up one observation when lagging residuals by one period

ANOVA

	df	SS	MS	F	Significance F
Regression	2	2.12383E+13	1.06192E+13	612.1112143	3.56177E-47
Residual	76	1.31848E+12	17348434665		
Total	78	2.25568E+13			

	Coefficients	Standard Error	*t* Stat	*p*-value	Lower 95%	Upper 95%
Intercept	0	#N/A	#N/A	#N/A	#N/A	#N/A
Converted Intercept	−2,253,289.816	512,061.150	−4.40043111	3.4752E-05	−3273147.968	−1233431.665
Converted GDP	900.523	96.327	9.348569058	2.8776E-14	708.6700492	1092.374974

Note: Dependent variable is the number of houses sold in the U.S. in a given quarter. Highlighted variables are significant at the 5 percent level.

The goal of any iterative process is to repeat a given estimation process many, many times in hopes of generating a stable (or convergence) estimate of an unknown value. Accordingly, after completing this first iteration, we need to repeat the process to see how much the estimated value of $\hat{\rho}$ changes.

Iteration 2:

1. Obtain the residuals, e_t, and the residuals lagged one period, e_{t-1}, from the previous converted data regression.

Doing so for our U.S. houses sold data, we get Table 11.8.

TABLE 11.8
Calculating the Residuals and Residuals Lagged One Period for the Second Iteration of the Cochrane-Orcutt Procedure for the First Five Observations for Our U.S. Houses Sold Data

Observation (t)	Predicted Houses Sold ($\hat{y}_t$)	Residuals (e_t)	Residuals Lagged One Period (e_{t-1})
1	1,403,550.02	970,449.98	
2	1,437,285.64	644,714.36	970,449.98
3	1,454,104.82	705,895.18	644,714.36
4	1,464,556.12	689,443.88	705,895.18
5	1,483,177.75	539,822.25	689,443.88

2. Estimate the population regression model $e_t = \rho e_{t-1} + u_t$ to generate an estimate of $\hat{\rho}$.

Doing so for our U.S. houses sold data, we get Excel Regression Output 11.6.

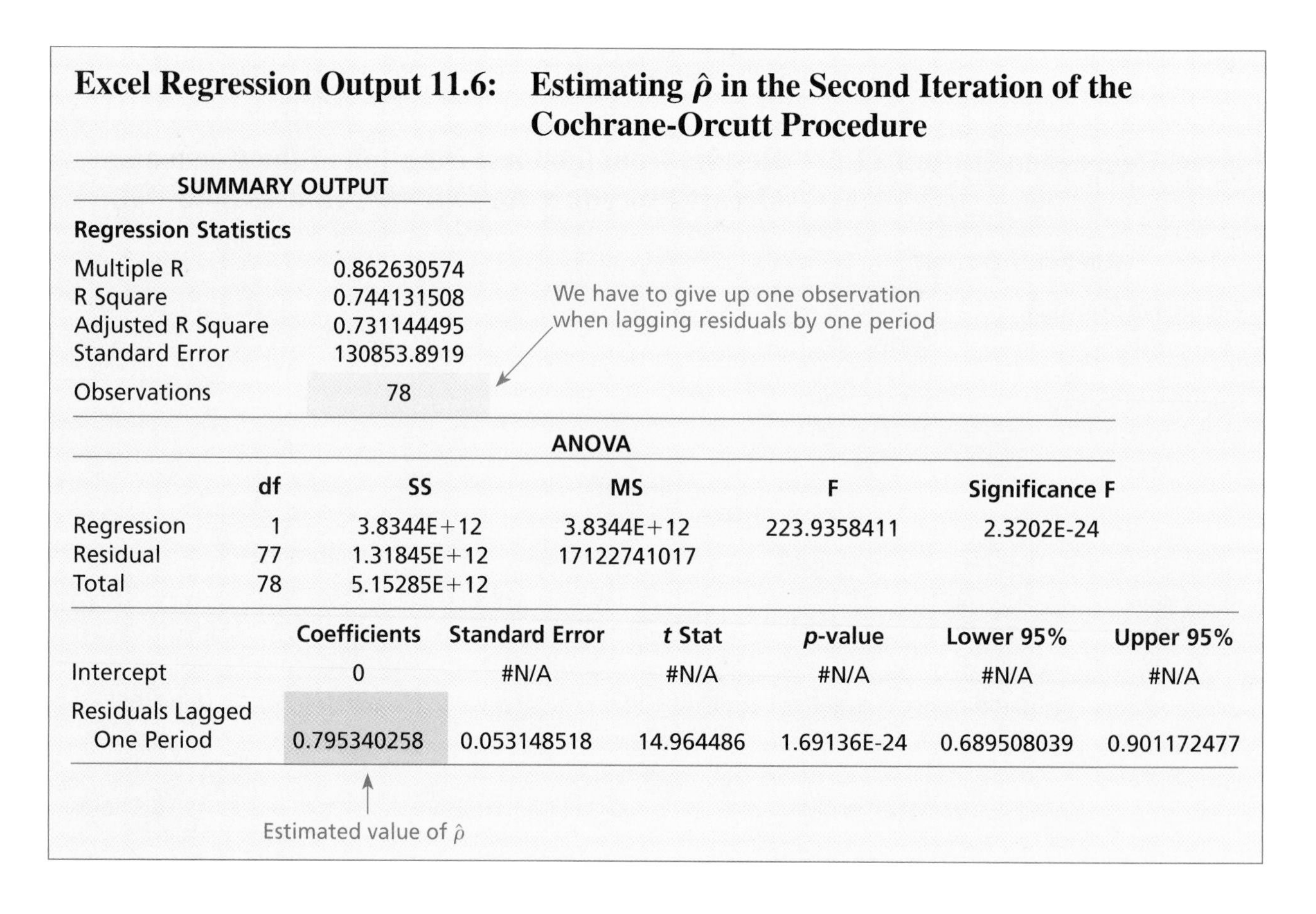

Excel Regression Output 11.6: Estimating $\hat{\rho}$ in the Second Iteration of the Cochrane-Orcutt Procedure

SUMMARY OUTPUT

Regression Statistics	
Multiple R	0.862630574
R Square	0.744131508
Adjusted R Square	0.731144495
Standard Error	130853.8919
Observations	78

ANOVA

	df	SS	MS	F	Significance F
Regression	1	3.8344E+12	3.8344E+12	223.9358411	2.3202E-24
Residual	77	1.31845E+12	17122741017		
Total	78	5.15285E+12			

	Coefficients	Standard Error	*t* Stat	*p*-value	Lower 95%	Upper 95%
Intercept	0	#N/A	#N/A	#N/A	#N/A	#N/A
Residuals Lagged One Period	0.795340258	0.053148518	14.964486	1.69136E-24	0.689508039	0.901172477

3. Convert y_t into $\tilde{y}_t = y_t - \hat{\rho}y_{t-1}$, the intercept into $\tilde{\beta}_0 = 1 - \hat{\rho}$, and x_t into $\tilde{x}_t = x_t - \hat{\rho}x_{t-1}$.

Doing so for our U.S. houses sold data, we get Table 11.9.

TABLE 11.9 Calculating the Converted Data for the Second Iteration of the Cochrane-Orcutt Procedure for the First Five Observations for Our U.S. Houses Sold Data

Observation (t)	Houses Sold (y_t)	Real GDP (billions) (x_t)	Converted Houses Sold ($\tilde{y}_t = y_t - \hat{\rho}y_{t-1}$)	Converted Intercept ($\tilde{\beta}_0 = 1 - \hat{\rho}$)	Converted GDP ($\tilde{x}_{j,t} = x_{j,t} - \hat{\rho}x_{j,t-1}$)
1	2,374,000	4,061			
2	2,082,000	4,098	193,862	0.20	$868.54
3	2,160,000	4,117	504,102	0.20	$857.43
4	2,154,000	4,129	436,065	0.20	$854.18
5	2,023,000	4,149	309,837	0.20	$865.63

4. Estimate the population regression model

$$\tilde{y}_t = \beta_0 + \beta_1\tilde{x}_t + \varepsilon_t. \quad \textbf{11.3.4}$$

Doing so for our U.S. houses sold data, we get Excel Regression Output 11.7.

Excel Regression Output 11.7: The Second Iteration of the Cochrane-Orcutt Procedure for Our U.S. Houses Sold Data

SUMMARY OUTPUT

Regression Statistics	
Multiple R	0.970920089
R Square	0.942685820
Adjusted R Square	0.928773792
Standard Error	131711.7969
Observations	78

We have to give up one observation when lagging residuals by one period

ANOVA

	df	SS	MS	F	Significance F
Regression	2	2.16854E+13	1.08427E+13	625.0121921	1.70374E-47
Residual	76	1.31845E+12	17347997442		
Total	78	2.30039E+13			

	Coefficients	Standard Error	*t* Stat	*p*-value	Lower 95%	Upper 95%
Intercept	0	#N/A	#N/A	#N/A	#N/A	#N/A
Converted Intercept	−2,246,985.498	506,738.077	−4.43421483	3.06929E-05	−3256241.83	−1237729.17
Converted GDP	899.427	95.357	9.432161125	1.99304E-14	709.5060986	1089.34778

Note: Dependent variable is the number of houses sold in the U.S. in a given quarter. Highlighted variables are significant at the 5 percent level.

Note that because the estimated value of $\hat{\rho}$ changed from the first iteration to the second (0.7976 to 0.7953), we do not yet have a stable estimate and we need to perform a third iteration. We do so be repeating the steps for the second iteration, ending up with Excel Regression Output 11.8.

Excel Regression Output 11.8: The Third Iteration of the Cochrane-Orcutt Procedure for Our U.S. Houses Sold Data

SUMMARY OUTPUT

Regression Statistics	
Multiple R	0.862253971
R Square	0.743481911
Adjusted R Square	0.730494898
Standard Error	130853.7128
Observations	78

We have to give up one observation when lagging residuals by one period

ANOVA

	df	SS	MS	F	Significance F
Regression	1	3.82134E+12	3.82134E+12	223.1737632	2.55677E-24
Residual	77	1.31845E+12	17122694162		
Total	78	5.13978E+12			

	Coefficients	Standard Error	*t* Stat	*p*-value	Lower 95%	Upper 95%
Intercept	0	#N/A	#N/A	#N/A	#N/A	#N/A
Residuals Lagged One Period	0.795097874	0.05322296	14.93900141	1.86559E-24	0.689117422	0.901078325

Estimated value of $\hat{\rho}$

Notice that the difference between the estimated value of $\hat{\rho}$ in the second and third iterations ($0.7953 - 0.7951 = 0.0001$) is much smaller than the difference between the estimated values of $\hat{\rho}$ in the first and second iterations ($0.7976 - 0.7953 = 0.0023$). Nonetheless, because the values are still different, we need to continue performing additional iterations until the estimated value of $\hat{\rho}$ converges to a stable value and the difference between successive iteration is 0. For our U.S. houses sold data, convergence occurs after six iterations, with Table 11.10 presenting a summary of the iterative process.

TABLE 11.10
Estimated Values of $\hat{\rho}$ from the Cochrane-Orcutt Procedure for Our U.S. Houses Sold Data

	Estimated rho ($\hat{\rho}$)
Iteration 1	0.797564
Iteration 2	0.795340
Iteration 3	0.795098
⋮	⋮
Convergence	0.795100

Once the process produces the convergence estimated value of $\hat{\rho}$, we use that value to calculate our converted data, and we perform OLS on those converted data to generate estimates that are BLUE and standard errors that are correct.

Doing so for our U.S. houses sold data, we get Regression Output 11.9.

Excel Regression Output 11.9: Results with the Convergence Value of $\hat{\rho}$ from the Cochrane-Orcutt Procedure for Our U.S. Houses Sold Data

SUMMARY OUTPUT

Regression Statistics	
Multiple R	0.970982297
R Square	0.942806621
Adjusted R Square	0.928896182
Standard Error	131711.7773
Observations	78

We have to give up one observation when lagging residuals by one period

ANOVA

	df	SS	MS	F	Significance F
Regression	2	2.1734E+13	1.0867E+13	626.4125693	1.57403E-47
Residual	76	1.31845E+12	17347992279		
Total	78	2.30524E+13			

	Coefficients	Standard Error	*t* Stat	*p*-value	Lower 95%	Upper 95%
Intercept	0	#N/A	#N/A	#N/A	#N/A	#N/A
Converted Intercept	−2,246,310.601	506,170.100	−4.43785716	3.02838E-05	−3254435.709	−1238185.493
Converted GDP	899.310	95.254	9.441179833	1.91564E-14	709.5949202	1089.024242

Note: Dependent variable is the number of houses sold in the U.S. in a given quarter. Highlighted variables are significant at the 5 percent level.

While the preceding process correctly implements the Cochrane-Orcutt method, it can be quite time-consuming, and with so many calculations required the potential for user error is greatly increased. As with White's heteroskedastic consistent standard errors, more-advanced statistical programs are programmed to calculate Cochrane-Orcutt estimates quite easily. After first setting the time period by typing "tsset time", using the Stata command

```
prais housessold real gdp, corc
```

we get Empirical Results 11.1.

Empirical Results 11.1: The Cochrane-Orcutt Correction for AR(1) for Our U.S. Houses Sold Data

Iterations:

Iteration 0: rho = 0.0000
Iteration 1: rho = 0.7976
Iteration 2: rho = 0.7953
Iteration 3: rho = 0.7951
Iteration 4: rho = 0.7951
Iteration 5: rho = 0.7951
Iteration 6: rho = 0.7951

Estimates:

	Coefficients	Standard Error
Intercept	−2,246,219.000	506,097.600
Real GDP	899.294	95.241
$\hat{\rho}$	0.7950685	
Significance F	0.0000	
R-Square	.5398	
Observations	78	

Durbin-Watson statistic (original) 0.296015
Durbin-Watson statistic (transformed) 2.396826

Note: Dependent variable is the number of houses sold in the U.S. in a given quarter.
Highlighted variables are significant at the 5 percent level.

Notice that this output contains all of the information in which we might be interested, including the coefficient estimates themselves, the number of iterations required to achieve convergence, the estimated convergence value of $\hat{\rho}$, and the value of the Durbin-Watson statistic (which is the same as we calculated in formula 11.2.9).

Empirical Research Tool 11.3 summarizes the Cochrane-Orcutt method.

EMPIRICAL RESEARCH TOOL 11.3: THE COCHRANE-ORCUTT METHOD FOR AR(1) PROCESSES

How to Do It:

1. Estimate the population regression model $y_t = \beta_0 + \beta_1 x_{1,t} + \beta_2 x_{2,t} + \cdots + \beta_k x_{k,t} + \varepsilon_t$, and obtain the residuals, $e_t = y_t - \hat{y}_t$, and the residuals lagged one period, $e_{1,t-1}$.
2. Estimate the population regression model $e_t = \rho e_{t-1} + u_t$ to generate an estimate of $\hat{\rho}$.
3. Convert the data using the estimated value of $\hat{\rho}$.
4. Estimate the population regression model $\tilde{y}_t = \beta_0 + \beta_1 \tilde{x}_t + \varepsilon_t$.

Why It Works:

In AR(1) processes, the current period error is related to the immediate prior period error according the equation $e_t = \rho e_{t-1} + u_t$. Accordingly, OLS estimates are not BLUE because they do not account for this correlation across time periods. This method accounts for the correlation by using the observed data to estimate the value of ρ and using that estimate to convert the data into a form that corrects for the correlation and for which OLS provide estimates with lower error variance.

The Prais-Winsten Method for AR(1) Processes

There is one potential concern associated with the Cochrane-Orcutt method of correcting for autocorrelation. Because the procedure drops the first observation due to lagging the error term one period, the resulting estimates technically cannot be BLUE because they are missing that one small piece of information. While this is generally not considered to be that serious of a concern, the Prais-Winsten method solves the problem by incorporating estimates of the first period lagged error in every iteration, thereby guaranteeing that our estimates are indeed BLUE.

The Prais-Winsten method is computationally equivalent to the Cochrane-Orcutt procedure except that the Prais-Winsten takes the additional step of estimating the first observation in each iteration. With this in mind, the steps for performing the Prais-Winsten procedure are

1. Repeat the first four steps of the Cochrane-Orcutt procedure.
2. Use those estimates to calculate and $\tilde{y}_1 = \sqrt{(1 - \rho^2)} \cdot y_1$ and $\tilde{x}_1 = \sqrt{(1 - \rho^2)} \cdot x_1$, which are the estimated observations for the first time period. Notice that the observations for the remaining time periods are the same as those for the Cochrane-Orcutt method.

Table 11.11 presents the values that we calculate for our U.S. houses sold data.

TABLE 11.11 Calculating the Converted Data for the First Iteration of the Prais-Winsten Procedure for the First Five Observations for Our U.S. Houses Sold Data

Observation (t)	Houses Sold (y_t)	Real GDP (billions) (x_t)	Converted Houses Sold ($\tilde{y}_t = y_t - \hat{\rho}y_{t-1}$)	Converted Intercept ($\tilde{\beta}_0 = 1 - \hat{\rho}$)	Converted GDP ($\tilde{x}_t = x_t - \hat{\rho}x_{t-1}$)
1	2,374,000	4,061	1,432,078	0.20	$2,449.61
2	2,082,000	4,098	188,583	0.20	$ 859.51
3	2,160,000	4.117	499,472	0.20	$ 848.31
4	2,154,000	4,129	431,262	0.20	$ 845.02
5	2,023,000	4,149	305,047	0.20	$ 856.44

3. Estimate the population regression model

$$\tilde{y}_t = \beta_0 + \beta_1\tilde{x}_t + \varepsilon_t. \qquad 11.3.5$$

which now contains all n observations rather than the $n - 1$ observations in the Cochrane-Orcutt method.

Doing so for our U.S. houses sold data, we get Excel Regression Output 11.10.

Excel Regression Output 11.10: The First Iteration of the Prais-Winsten Method for Our U.S. Houses Sold Data

SUMMARY OUTPUT

Regression Statistics	
Multiple R	0.967692823
R Square	0.93642940
Adjusted R Square	0.922616795
Standard Error	142533.8626
Observations	79

Restores observation lost in Cochrane-Orcutt procedure

ANOVA

	df	SS	MS	F	Significance F
Regression	2	2.30433E+13	1.15217E+13	567.1258733	2.0972E-46
Residual	77	1.56432E+12	20315901985		
Total	79	2.46077E+13			

	Coefficients	Standard Error	*t* Stat	*p*-value	Lower 95%	Upper 95%
Intercept	0	#N/A	#N/A	#N/A	#N/A	#N/A
Converted Intercept	−1,318,884.872	484,670.433	−2.72119936	0.008039036	−2283986.986	−353782.757
Converted GDP	737.963	93.179	7.919819102	1.45114E-11	552.4192507	923.5064504

Note: Dependent variable is the number of houses sold in the U.S. in a given quarter. Highlighted variables are significant at the 5 percent level.

Notice that output for this first iteration is for all 79 quarters in our sample rather than for the 78 observations in the Cochrane-Orcutt procedure. This is due to restoring the first observation by estimating the value of the first period observation.

As with the Cochrane-Orcutt procedure, we repeat iterations of the Prais-Winsten until the estimated value of $\hat{\rho}$ converges to a stable value. We then use that estimated value to convert the dependent and independent variables, and we run OLS on the converted data to generate our BLUE estimates.

For our U.S. houses sold data, the procedure converges after 10 iterations. Table 11.12 presents our summary of the iterative process.

TABLE 11.12
Estimated Values of $\hat{\rho}$ from the Prais-Winsten Procedure for Our U.S. Houses Sold Data

	Estimated $\hat{\rho}$
Iteration 1	0.797564
Iteration 2	0.821284
Iteration 3	0.826091
⋮	⋮
Convergence	0.827600

Again, while these steps produce the desired results, it is much, much easier to perform the Prais-Winsten procedure in a more-advanced statistical package. After first setting the time period by typing "tsset time", using the Stata command

```
prais housessold realgdp
```

we get Empirical Results 11.2.

Empirical Results 11.2: The Prais-Winsten Correction for AR(1) for Our U.S. Houses Sold Data

Iterations:

Iteration 0: rho = 0.0000
Iteration 1: rho = 0.7976
Iteration 2: rho = 0.8213
Iteration 3: rho = 0.8261
Iteration 4: rho = 0.8272
Iteration 5: rho = 0.8275
Iteration 6: rho = 0.8276
Iteration 7: rho = 0.8276
Iteration 8: rho = 0.8276
Iteration 9: rho = 0.8276
Iteration 10: rho = 0.8276

Estimates:

	Coefficient	Standard Error
Intercept	−1,264,514.000	546,853.800
Real GDP	729.279	105.019
$\hat{\rho}$	0.7950685	
Significance F	0.0000	
R-Square	.5339	
Observations	79	

Durbin-Watson statistic (original) 0.296015
Durbin-Watson statistic (transformed) 2.329643

Note: Dependent variable is the number of houses sold in the U.S. in a given quarter. Highlighted variables are significant at the 5 percent level.

As discussed earlier, the primary benefit of the Prais-Winsten method is that it does not require us to drop an observation, and therefore, the resulting estimates are indeed BLUE so long as the time-series assumptions T1 through T5 are satisfied and the autoregressive process is correctly specified [i.e., we are estimating an AR(1) process and the error term actually follows an AR(1) process in the population].

Empirical Research Tool 11.4 summarizes the Prais-Winsten method.

EMPIRICAL RESEARCH TOOL 11.4: THE PRAIS-WINSTEN METHOD FOR AR(1) PROCESSES

How to Do It:

1. Repeat the first four steps of the Cochrane-Orcutt method.
2. Calculate the first observation $\tilde{y}_1 = \sqrt{(1 - \rho^2)} \cdot y_1$ and $\tilde{x}_1 = \sqrt{(1 - \rho^2)} \cdot x_1$.
3. Estimate the population regression model $\tilde{y}_t = \beta_0 + \beta_1 \tilde{x}_t + \varepsilon_t$ with all T observations included.

Why It Works:

This method works for the same reason as the Cochrane-Orcutt procedure, except that the resulting estimates are now BLUE because they do not drop the first observation as long as T1 through T5 hold.

Suppose that rather than AR(1), we suspect our data to be AR(2) or some other higher-ordered processes. These two GLS methods can be adjusted to such situations. For instance, if we know that the error term follows the AR(2) process, we would follow the exact same steps to perform the Cochrane-Orcutt and Prais-Winsten procedures, with the difference being that rather than estimating only one $\hat{\rho}$ in each iteration, we would now have to estimate the two value $\hat{\rho}_1$ and $\hat{\rho}_2$ in each iteration.

Newey-West Robust Standard Errors

As with White's heteroskedastic consistent standard errors, calculating Newey-West robust standard errors in a more-advanced statistical package is so simple and the costs of not controlling for potential autocorrelation so high, that most researchers simply use this command when working with time-series data without giving it any further thought. After first setting the time period by typing "tsset time" using the Stata command

```
newey housessold realgdp, lag(1)
```

we get Empirical Results 11.3.

Empirical Results 11.3: Newey-West Robust Standard Errors for Our U.S. Houses Sold Data

	Coefficient	Standard Error	*t* Stat	*p*-value	Lower 95%	Upper 95%
Intercept	−1,587,778.000	355,317.100	−4.47	0	−2295305	−880251.2
Real GDP	780.700	67.818	11.51	0	645.65730	915.74340
Significance F			0.0000			
Observations			79			

Note: Dependent variable is the number of houses sold in the U.S. in a given quarter. Standard errors are Newey-West robust standard errors. Highlighted variables are significant at the 5 percent level.

In addition to detecting and correcting for autocorrelation in our time-series data, there are other issues that we should consider.

11.4 UNDERSTAND UNIT ROOTS AND COINTEGRATION

Unit Roots

unit root
Occurs when the parameter on the AR(1) process is equal to 1.

In time-series analysis, a **unit root** occurs when the parameter on the AR(1) equation equals 1 (i.e., when $\rho = 1$). To understand the problems confronted by the presence of a unit root, start by considering that an alternative way to define an AR(1) process is to write the population regression model as

$$y_t = \rho y_{t-1} + u_t \qquad \textbf{11.4.1}$$

because the same process that governs the relationship between the error terms in the two periods also governs the relationship between the observed values of the dependent variables in the two periods. Accordingly, if a unit root exists in our data, then we can rewrite our population regression model as

$$\begin{aligned} y_t &= \rho y_{t-1} + u_t \\ &= (1) \cdot y_{t-1} + u_t \\ &= y_{t-1} + u_t \end{aligned} \qquad \textbf{11.4.2}$$

As should be evident from formula 11.4.2, if a unit root exists in our data, then our best prediction of the dependent variable in the current period, y_t, is the value of the dependent variable in the immediate prior period, y_{t-1}.

Notation:
- $I(0)$ A time series that is integrated of order 0.
- $I(1)$ A time series that is integrated of order 1.

By definition, dependent variables with a unit root are referred to as being integrated of order 1, or $I(1)$, and dependent variables that do not have a unit roots are referred to as being integrated of order 0, or $I(0)$.

In simplest terms, processes that are $I(0)$ cross their means frequently, while processes that are $I(1)$ wander off and cross their means infrequently. This becomes problematic for $I(1)$ processes because our OLS estimation is based on comparisons to the mean; thus, when the values no longer cross the mean with frequency, we are unable to generate reliable estimates. A common analogy for explaining this concept is that a unit root is like a drunk trying to find the way home from a bar. Owing to the intoxicated state, the drunk is likely to wander off from the normal path home. As a result, we are unable to accurately estimate the path that the drunk will take and the ultimate location of his or her journey.

Given the impact that a unit root can have on our estimation, we should be interested in identifying whether one exists in our data. To statistically test for the presence of a unit root, the appropriate null and alternative hypotheses are

$$\begin{aligned} H_0&: \rho = 1 \\ H_A&: \rho < 1 \end{aligned} \qquad \textbf{11.4.3}$$

explosive time series
Occurs when a random shock has an increasingly larger influence.

This alternative hypothesis is written as being one-sided for an important reason. If ρ is greater than 1, then y_t is an **explosive time series,** which is extremely difficult to model. If ρ is less than 1, on the other hand, then the time-series process is a stable AR(1), and we can use the methods introduced earlier in this chapter to deal with the problem. If ρ is exactly equal to 1, however, then the series is neither a stable AR(1) nor an explosive time series, and we need to use new tools to convert the data into a stable process before additional empirical analysis can be performed.

To perform the test for a unit root, we start by converting the initial data by subtracting y_{t-1} from both sides of the equation to get

$$y_t - y_{t-1} = \rho y_{t-1} - y_{t-1} + \varepsilon_t \qquad \textbf{11.4.4}$$

which we can re-write as

$$\Delta y_t = \theta y_{t-1} + \varepsilon_t \qquad \textbf{11.4.5}$$

where $\theta = (\rho - 1)$. When testing for a unit root in formula 11.4.5, the appropriate null and alternative hypotheses are

$$\begin{aligned} H_0&: \theta = 0 \\ H_A&: \theta < 0 \end{aligned} \qquad \textbf{11.4.6}$$

While it might seem at this point that we could perform the desired hypothesis test by regressing Δy_t on y_{t-1} and performing a one sided t-test of the estimated slope coefficient to determine if $\theta < 0$. We are actually unable to do so in this case. To see why, recall that when performing hypothesis tests of this type, we assume that the null hypothesis is true, and we attempt to find statistical evidence in our data to prove that the null hypothesis is unlikely to be correct. For this to work, we have to assume that $\theta = 0$. Unfortunately, if $\theta = 0$, then the distribution of the t-statistic $(\hat{\theta}/\text{se}(\hat{\theta}))$ is not even close to asymptotically normal, meaning that our usual estimated p-values are no longer correct. Due to this fact, rather than being able to perform a simple t-test, we need to perform a **Dickey-Fuller test** that is based on the asymptotically correct Dickey-Fuller distribution.

Dickey-Fuller test
A test for a unit root using the Dickey-Fuller distribution tables.

Using the Stata command (and prespecifying the number of lags included in the estimation to be 15, which is the optimal number determined by the statistical package)

```
dfuller housessold, lags(15)
```

we perform this test for our U.S. houses sold data and get Empirical Results 11.4.

Empirical Results 11.4: The Dickey-Fuller Test for a Unit Root for Our U.S. Houses Sold Data

Augmented Dickey-Fuller test for unit root Number of obs = 63

	-----Interpolated Dickey-Fuller-----			
	Test Statistic	1% Critical Value	5% Critical Value	10% Critical Value
Z(t)	0.977	−3.562	−2.92	−2.595

Note: MacKinnon approximate p-value for Z(t) = 0.9940

To interpret the results of this test, we need to compare the calculated test statistic to the appropriate critical value. In this case, assuming that we are testing at the 5 percent significance level, we would compare the test statistic of 0.977 to the 5 percent critical value of −2.92, and we would fail to reject the null hypothesis of $\rho = 1$, meaning that our data do have a unit root. Finally, note that due to prespecifying the number of lags to be 15 and due to including the lagged dependent variable in the specification (see formula 11.4.5), the number of observations included in the calculation of the test statistic is $79 - 15 - 1 = 63$.

What options do we have if the Dickey-Fuller test provides evidence consistent with the presence of a unit root? Many times, if y_t has a unit root, then the first-differenced values of y_t will not. Hence, if we fail to reject the null hypothesis of our Dickey-Fuller test, our first step might be to first-difference y_t and then run an additional Dickey-Fuller test to verify that the first-differenced model does not have a unit root.

Table 11.13 presents the first-differenced data for our U.S. houses sold data.

TABLE 11.13
Calculating the First-Differenced Data for Our U.S. Houses Sold Data

Time	Houses Sold (y_t)	First Differenced Houses Sold (x_t)	Real GDP (billions) (x_t)	First Differenced Real GDP (billions) ($x_t - x_{t-1}$)
1	2,374,000	—	4,061	—
2	2,082,000	−292,000	4,098	37
3	2,160,000	78,000	4,117	19
4	2,154,000	−6,000	4,129	12
5	2,023,000	131,000	4,149	21

We then perform a Dickey-Fuller test on the first-differenced data to see whether the first-differencing has removed the unit root. Doing so, we get Empirical Results 11.5.

Empirical Results 11.5: The Dickey-Fuller Test for a Unit Root for Our First-Differenced U.S. Houses Sold Data

Augmented Dickey-Fuller test for unit root Number of obs = 62

		-----Interpolated Dickey-Fuller-----		
	Test Statistic	**1% Critical Value**	**5% Critical Value**	**10% Critical Value**
Z(t)	−2.608	−3.563	−2.92	−2.595

Note: MacKinnon approximate *p*-value for Z(t) = 0.0913

Note that because we cannot first-difference data for the initial time period, we lose an additional observation. Further, note that while we do not reject the null hypothesis of a unit root at the 5 percent level we do reject it at the 10 percent level (because $-2.608 < -2.595$ and the approximate p-value $0.0913 < 0.10$).

Cointegration

There is another method for removing the potential negative effects of a unit root that is more technically sophisticated. Suppose that we are able to identify a different economic variable, w_t, that is also integrated of order 1, or $I(1)$, and is related to y_t in such a way that some linear combination of the two variables is $I(0)$. Because w_t and y_t are related in such a manner, we could theoretically remove the unit root by regressing y_t on w_t, leaving residuals that are $I(0)$. This alternative approach, proposed by Engle and Granger (1987), is referred to as **cointegration.**

cointegration
An alternative method of removing a unit root that does not require the use of first-differencing.

Continuing with our analogy, if a drunk trying to find the way home from a bar can be likened to a unit root, cointegration can be likened to the drunk leaving the bar at the same time that a stray dog wanders past. While the drunk and the dog are not going to follow the exact same path, it is possible that they wander in the same general direction. If so, then their movements are cointegrated, and by relating their movements we can remove the unit root from the drunk's path. If they do not move in the same general direction, then their movements are not cointegrated, and we cannot relate them in a way that removes the unit root.

The trick to successful cointegration is identifying the additional series for which (1) the series itself is $I(1)$ and (2) the linear regression of y_t on the series produces residuals that are $I(0)$. In practice, this is often not as easy as it might sound, and a great amount of literature has developed trying to identify macroeconomics time series that are cointegrated.

As an example that often works, consider the 3-month and 1-year bond rates on U.S. treasury bonds. In theory, these two series are likely to be cointegrated because if the relative yield on one of the bonds increases, rational investors should shift their investment portfolios away from the other bond toward the now-higher-yield bond. To demonstrate how we might use one of these series to remove the unit root from the other, we start by performing the Dickey-Fuller test for both series to confirm that they are indeed both $I(1)$. Doing so, we get Empirical Results 11.6.

Empirical Results 11.6: The Dickey-Fuller Test for a Unit Root of Our 3-Month and 1-Year Bond Rate Series

3-Month Bond Rate Series

Augmented Dickey-Fuller test for unit root Number of obs = 1582

-----Interpolated Dickey-Fuller-----

	Test Statistic	1% Critical Value	5% Critical Value	10% Critical Value
Z(t)	−2.424	−3.430	−2.86	−2.57

MacKinnon approximate *p*-value for Z(t) = 0.1350

1-Year Bond Rate Series

Augmented Dickey-Fuller test for unit root Number of obs = 1582

-----Interpolated Dickey-Fuller-----

	Test Statistic	1% Critical Value	5% Critical Value	10% Critical Value
Z(t)	−2.454	−3.430	−2.86	−2.57

Note: MacKinnon approximate *p*-value for Z(t) = 0.1272

Because both approximate p-values are greater than 0.10, we fail to reject the null hypothesis of a unit root for both series. To test whether we can use one of these $I(1)$ series to remove the unit root from the other $I(1)$ series, we need to regress one series on the other, determine the calculated residuals from that regression, and test whether the residuals possess a unit root.

Doing so for the population regression function

$$(3 - month\ yield)_t = \beta_0 + \beta_1(1 - year\ yield)_t + \varepsilon_t \qquad \textbf{11.4.7}$$

we get Empirical Results 11.7.

Empirical Results 11.7: The Dickey-Fuller Test for a Unit Root of Our Cointegrated Weekly Bond Rate Series

OLS Regression Results

	Coefficients	Standard Error	*t* Stat	*p*-value	Lower 95%	Upper 95%
Intercept	−0.1178064	0.0161243	−7.31	0	−0.1494333	−0.0861794
1-Year Bond Yield	0.9455079	0.0027109	348.78	0	0.9401906	0.9508253
R-squared			0.9870			
Prob > F			0.0000			
Observations			1598			

Notes: Dependent variables is 3-month bond yield. Highlighted variables are significant at the 5 percent level.

Calculated Residuals

Augmented Dickey-Fuller test for unit root Number of obs = 1582

-----Interpolated Dickey-Fuller-----

	Test Statistic	1% Critical Value	5% Critical Value	10% Critical Value
Z(t)	−5.281	−3.430	−2.86	−2.57

Note: MacKinnon approximate *p*-value for Z(t) = 0.0000

Because the approximate p-value of $0.0009 < 0.05$, we reject the null hypothesis of a unit root and conclude that our two bond yield series are indeed cointegrated.

ADDITIONS TO OUR EMPIRICAL RESEARCH TOOLKIT

In this chapter we have introduced a number of tools that will prove valuable when performing empirical research:

- Statistical tests for the presence of autocorrelation, including the Durbin-Watson test and the regression test for AR(1) and AR(2).
- Empirical methods for correcting the estimated standard errors in the presence of autocorrelation, including the Cochrane-Orcutt and Prais-Winsten methods and Newey-West robust standard errors.
- Empirical methods for testing for and dealing with unit roots.

OUR NEW EMPIRICAL TOOLS IN PRACTICE: USING WHAT WE HAVE LEARNED IN THIS CHAPTER

Understanding the potential consequences associated with not controlling for autocorrelation when it is present, our former student decided to perform a Durbin-Watson test for her data. Table 11.14 presents her calculations.

TABLE 11.14 Calculating the Durbin-Watson Statistic for Our Former Student's U.S. Deficit Data

Observation (t)	Predicted Real Surplus/ Deficit ($\hat{y}_t$)	Residuals (e_t)	Residuals Squared (e_t^2)	Lagged Residuals (e_{t-1})	Difference Squared ($(e_t - e_{t-1})^2$)
1	70.61505371	−106.9150537	11430.8287		
2	1.365476086	−60.46547609	3656.07380	−106.915054	2157.563261
3	−187.191580	−31.90841964	1018.14724	−60.4654761	815.5054731
4	−542.949011	11.24901058	126.540239	−31.9084196	1862.563783
5	−407.800500	−93.29950027	8704.79675	11.2490106	10930.39112
6	−564.213114	38.81311406	1506.45782	−93.2995003	17453.74286
7	−137.334383	−38.56561737	1487.30684	38.81311406	5987.468077
8	147.587171	−107.3871714	11532.0046	−38.5656174	4736.406301
9	169.400647	−57.90064703	3352.48493	−107.387171	2448.916096

$\sum_{t=2}^{T}(e_t - e_{t-1})^2 = 666{,}507.67$

$\sum_{t=1}^{T} e_t^2 = 678{,}922.88$

$d = 0.9817$

Given that the calculated Durbin-Watson statistic was positive and very close to 1, the student found the results to be inconclusive and performed a regression test for AR(1) that resulted in the sample regression function shown in Table 11.15.

TABLE 11.15 Regression Output for the Regression Test for AR(1) for Our Former Student's U.S. Deficit Data

SUMMARY OUTPUT	
Regression Statistics	
Multiple R	0.467905215
R Square	0.21893529
Adjusted R Square	0.204649576
Standard Error	86.3013398
Observations	71

ANOVA						
	df	SS	MS	F	Significance F	
Regression	1	146137.5667	146137.5667	19.62125562	3.46095E-05	
Residual	70	521354.4875	7447.92125			
Total	71	667492.0542				
	Coefficients	**Standard Error**	***t* Stat**	***p*-value**	**Lower 95%**	**Upper 95%**
Intercept	0	#N/A	#N/A	#N/A	#N/A	#N/A
Residuals Lagged One Period	0.500844848	0.113068027	4.429588651	3.40669E-05	0.275337782	0.726351914

Note: Dependent variables is the residual in a given period. Highlighted variables are significant at the 5 percent level.

Because the estimated slope coefficient for the residuals lagged one period was statistically significant at the 5 percent level, the student concluded that autocorrelation was present in her data. Accordingly, she estimated the sample regression function in Table 11.16 with Newey-West robust standard errors.

TABLE 11.16 **Regression Output with Newey-West Robust Standard Errors for Our Former Student's U.S. Deficit Data**

	Coefficient	Standard Error	*t*	*P* > |*t*|	Lower 95%	Upper 95%
Intercept	649.3974	249.8934	2.60	0.012	150.0253	1148.77
Real GDP (billions)	−0.1565502	0.0294235	−5.32	0	−0.2153484	−0.097752
Real Income Tax Receipts (millions)	0.0021728	0.0002426	8.96	0	0.001688	0.0026575
Real Defense Expenditures (millions)	−0.0009907	0.0001025	−9.67	0	−0.0011955	−0.0007859
Population (millions)	−0.0023981	0.0018269	−1.31	0.194	−0.0060489	0.0012527
Democratic President	−77.81235	33.65896	−2.31	0.024	−145.0744	−10.55028
Democratic Controlled Senate	37.46459	53.68219	0.70	0.488	−69.8107	144.7399
Democratic Controlled House	−50.9832	50.41317	−1.01	0.316	−151.7259	49.75949
Recession	−90.47031	32.75252	−2.76	0.008	−155.921	−25.01961
Significance F	0.0000					
Observations			72			

Note: Dependent variables is U.S. annual surplus (deficit). Standard errors are Newey-West robust standard errors. Highlighted variables are significant at the 5 percent level.

Based on this work, from data collection through economic theory, empirical analysis, and effective write-up, our former student was judged to have conducted a successful empirical research project.

LOOKING AHEAD TO CHAPTER 12

In addition to the possible violations of assumptions M6 and T6 for cross-section and time-series data, respectively, there are a number of other situations in which OLS is not the most preferred estimator. Chapter 12 starts our discussion of such situations by examining the case of binary and categorical dependent variables.

Problems

11.1 The following equation is estimated, where y_{t-1} is also an explanatory variable, and the following results are obtained:

$$y_t = 2.7 + 0.4x_t + 0.9y_{t-1}$$
$$(0.4) \quad (0.06)$$
$$N = 200,\ R^2 = 0.98, \text{ and } DW = 1.9$$

a. What does the DW (Durbin-Watson) statistic test? What assumptions are used to calculate the Durbin-Watson statistic? For a DW of 1.9, what does this imply about the regression equation? (You do not need the tables to answer the question.)

b. Irrespective of your answer in part (a), how would you correct for AR(1) in this model?

11.2 Consider the population regression model $y_t = \beta_0 + \beta_1 x_t + \varepsilon_t$, where the error term may be written as $\varepsilon_t = \rho\varepsilon_{t-1} + u_t$, with $E(\varepsilon_t) = E(u_t) = 0$, $Cov(x_t, \varepsilon_t) = Cov(u_t, \varepsilon_t) = 0$, $Var(\varepsilon_t) = \sigma_\varepsilon^2$, and $Var(u_t) = \sigma_u^2$ for all t.

a. Prove that this model suffers from autocorrelation.

b. What will be the consequence(s) of estimating the model with OLS?

c. Describe how you would test for the presence of autocorrelation, and explicitly state whatever assumptions you are making to ensure the validity of the test.

d. Describe in detail how you would correct for autocorrelation using the Cochrane-Orcutt procedure.

11.3 A researcher suggests the following model for average wages:

$$w_t = \gamma + \beta L_t + \varepsilon_t$$

where

w_t = Average wage in the economy at time t
γ = Constant long run wage
L_t = Labor force in the economy at time t

a. Suppose that the error term has the following structure:

$$\varepsilon_t = \rho\varepsilon_{t-1} + u_t$$

where ε_t is a random error term with

$$E(\varepsilon_t) = 0,\ Var(\varepsilon_t) = \sigma^2, \text{ and } E(\varepsilon_t, \varepsilon_{t-j}) = 0 \text{ for all } h \neq 0$$

Given the structure of the error term, will estimating the interest rate equation by OLS yield unbiased estimates? Will standard hypothesis tests be valid? Why or why not?

b. The accompanying graphs depict both average monthly wages and the civilian labor force in the U.S. economy from 1964 to 2006.

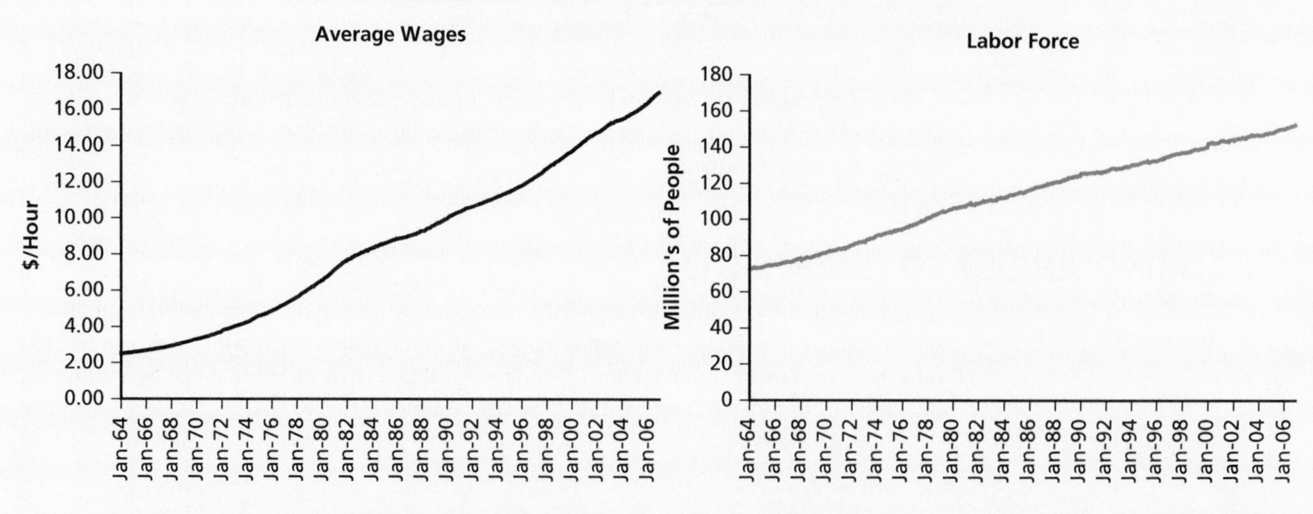

Estimating the model via OLS yields the following estimates (*t*-stats in parentheses):

$$\widehat{W}_t = -11.6 + 0.18L_t, R^2 = 0.98$$
$$(-90.8) \quad (161.9)$$

Do you really believe that the size of the labor force explains 98 percent of the variation in average wages? Why might your estimates be biased? Use the information in the graphs to support your answer. What would be a better model to estimate?

c. Describe how you would test for the presence of autocorrelation in this model with a Durbin-Watson test. Why does having a large sample size increase the chance that the DW test will yield a conclusive answer to the presence of serial correlation?

11.4 Consider the following AR(1) regression model:

$$y_t = \beta_0 + \beta_1 x_t + \varepsilon_t$$
$$\varepsilon_t = \rho\varepsilon_{t-1} + u_t \quad \text{(P.1)}$$

a. Discuss the consequences of estimating formula P.1 using OLS. Would your estimates be unbiased? Would your hypothesis tests be valid? Why or why not?

b. Describe in detail how you would properly estimate the preceding model (list the steps involved in your estimation procedure).

c. Now suppose the model was changed to

$$y_t = \beta_0 + \beta_1 x_t + \beta_2 y_{t-1} + \varepsilon_t$$
$$\varepsilon_t = \rho\varepsilon_{t-1} + u_t \quad \text{(P.2)}$$

Would OLS estimates of formula P.2 be unbiased? Efficient?

Exercises

E11.1 Use the data set **shipments.xls** for this problem. These data contain the number of shipments sent out for a shipping company each month and the number of calls they get each month.

a. Regress shipments on calls and save the residuals. Create a scatterplot with residuals on the *y*-axis and calls on the *x*-axis, and comment on the pattern.

b. Use the residuals to calculate the Durbin-Watson statistic. Use Durbin-Watson tables to test if these data follow an AR(1) process at the 5 percent level.

c. Use the regression test to test if these data follow an AR(1) process at a 5 percent significance level.

d. Do the tests from parts (b) and (c) agree? Which test do you prefer?

e. Use the regression test to test if these data follow an AR(3) process at a 5 percent significance level.

E11.2 Use the data set **dow jones.xls** for this problem.

a. Regress stock price on consumer confidence, and save the residuals. Create a scatterplot with residuals on the *y*-axis and calls on the *x*-axis and comment on the pattern.

b. Use the residuals to calculate the Durbin-Watson statistic. Use Durbin-Watson tables to test if these data follow an AR(1) process at the 5 percent level.

c. Use the regression test to test if these data follow an AR(1) process at a 5 percent significance level.

d. Do the tests from parts (b) and (c) agree? Which test do you prefer?

e. Use the regression test to test if these data follow an AR(3) process at a 5 percent significance level.

E11.3 Use the data set **shipments.xls** for this problem. These data contain the number of shipments sent out for a shipping company each month and the number of calls they get each month.

a. Use the Cochrane-Orcott method to correct for an AR(1) process in these data.

b. Use the Prais-Winston method to correct for an AR(1) process in these data.

c. Comment on the similarities and differences between your results in parts (a) and (b).

E11.4 Use the data set **shipments.xls** for this problem. These data contain the number of shipments sent out for a shipping company each month and the number of calls they get each month.

a. Use the Cochrane-Orcott method to correct for an AR(2) process in these data.

b. Use the Prais-Winston method to correct for an AR(2) process in these data.

c. Comment on the similarities and differences between your results in parts (a) and (b).

E11.5 Open file **dow jones.xls.**

a. Use the Dickey-Fuller test to see if stock price follows a unit root at a 5% percent significance level.

b. What are the implications if a time series follows a unit root?

c. First-difference the stock price, and use the Dickey-Fuller test to if the first-differenced stock price follows a unit root at a 5 percent significance level.

Chapter Twelve

Limited Dependent Variable Analysis

CHAPTER OBJECTIVES

After reading this chapter, you will be able to:

1. Estimate models with binary dependent variables.
2. Estimate models with categorical dependent variables.

A STUDENT'S PERSPECTIVE

Suppose that your boss at a travel agency has asked you to help develop a more effective marketing strategy using your data analysis skills. How might you do so?

This is exactly the situation encountered by one of our former students. In an effort to put his econometric skills to work, he turned to the Panel Study of Income Dynamics (PSID), which, according to the website http://psidonline.isr.umich.edu, "is the longest running longitudinal household survey in the world. The study began in 1968 with a nationally representative sample of over 18,000 individuals living in 5,000 families in the United States. Information on these individuals and their descendants has been collected continuously, including data covering employment, income, wealth, expenditures, health, marriage, childbearing, child development, philanthropy, education, and numerous other topics." After looking through the available data, the student realized that this source contained information on the vacationing decisions of families as well as a number of independent variables likely to affect such decisions. As a starting point for his analysis, the student calculated the summary statistics for families by their vacationing decisions in the past year in Table 12.1.

TABLE 12.1
Summary Statistics for Our Former Student's Vacation Data

	Took Vacation	Did Not Take Vacation
Age of Head of Family	42.393	45.233
	(12.719)	(16.780)
Head of Family Married	0.635	0.524
Number of Children	0.778	0.828
	(1.041)	(1.188)
Age of Youngest Child	2.904	2.874
	(4.888)	(4.777)
Head of Family Employed	0.941	0.685
Family Income	27,391.51	12,568.39
	(53,465.34)	(41,361.19)
Family Owns Home	0.650	0.531
Family Home's Value	173,852.50	117,840.90
	(323,502.00)	(194,875.00)
Observations	792	7,590

These entries suggested to our former student that families taking vacations had younger heads who were married, higher mean family incomes, and higher mean home values while families not taking vacations were likely to average more children and to have an unemployed head. Given his knowledge of econometrics, our former student knew that he needed to conduct a more advanced analysis to determine whether these differences in summary statistics pointed to true differences in estimated marginal effects. To get a better sense of the nature of his data, the student created the scatter diagram in Figure 12.1 of the dependent variable indicating whether the family took a vacation last year versus family income.

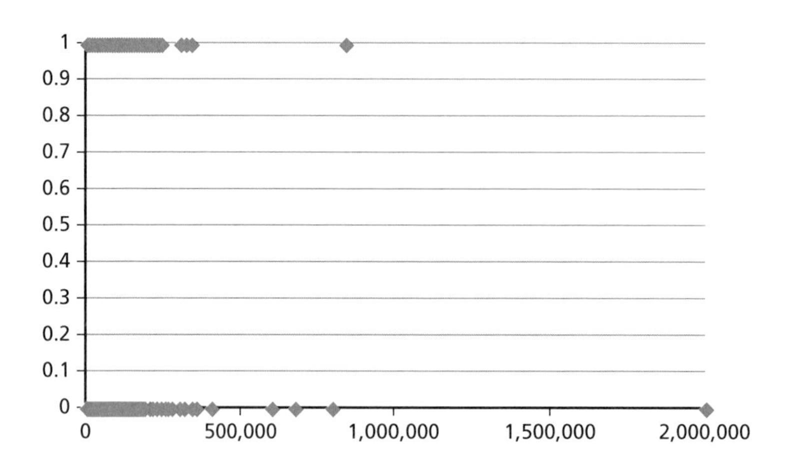

FIGURE 12.1
Scatter Diagram of Took Vacation versus Family Income for Our Former Student's Vacation Data

Looking at these data, our former student realized that the scatter diagram in Figure 12.1 looked much different than the scatter diagrams that he had previously encountered. In particular, the dependent variable was limited to only two possible outcomes, 1 and 0, depending on whether the family reported taking a vacation in the past year. This chapter introduces appropriate estimation techniques for models in which the dependent variable is limited by only having a fixed number of outcomes.

BIG PICTURE OVERVIEW

limited dependent variable
A dependent variable whose range of possible values is restricted in some way.

There are several situations in which OLS is not the best estimator to employ when dealing with cross-section data. In this chapter, we consider cases in which the dependent variable takes on a limited numbers of potential outcomes. As an example of such **limited dependent variables,** suppose we wish to examine the degree to which certain independent variables are correlated with the likelihood that an individual receives a college degree. As with the binary dummy variables in Chapter 7, because college graduate and noncollege graduate are qualities rather than quantities, we enter them in our regression analysis by defining a new variable, "College Graduate," that equals 1 if the individual received a degree and 0 if he or she did not.

Figure 12.2 depicts the empirical issue associated with a limited dependent variable such as the variable "College Graduate."

While we have so far discussed at length how to determine the best-fit line through the data on the left, it is not so obvious how we should determine the best-fit line through the data on the right (or whether a line would even be the appropriate estimator for those data). The remainder of this chapter introduces estimators to use when working with limited dependent variables. Figure 12.3 visually summarizes the empirical tools introduced in this chapter.

We start our discussion by considering the proper treatment of binary dependent variables. Before doing so, we need to introduce the data set that forms the baseline example for our discussion.

FIGURE 12.2
Visual Depiction of Continuous versus Binary Dependent Variables

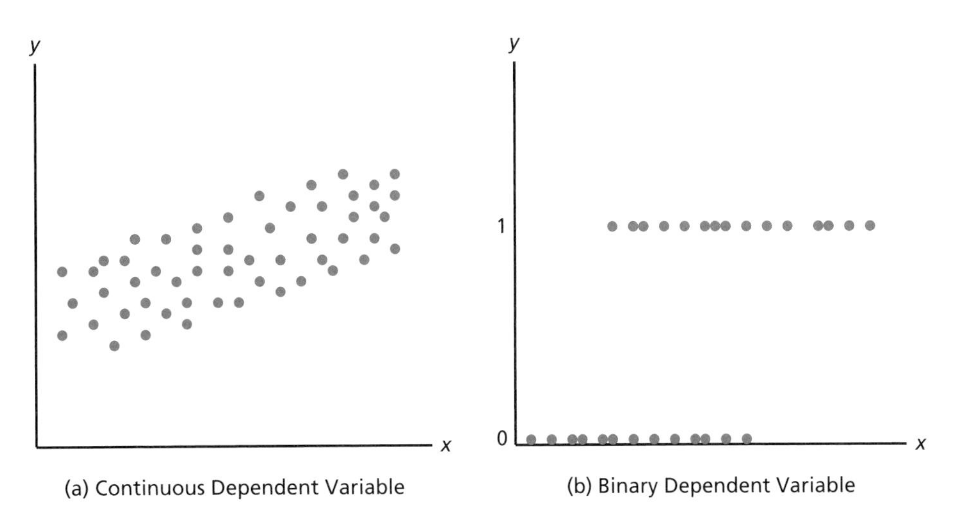

FIGURE 12.3
A Visual Depiction of the Empirical Tools Introduced in This Chapter

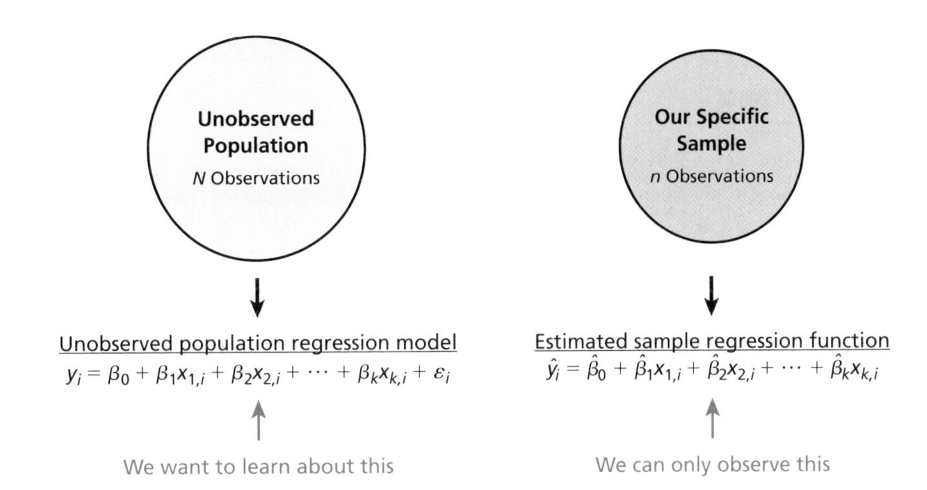

Question: What if the dependent variable has a discrete number of possible outcomes?

Answer: We can use non-linear estimators

If the dependent variable is binary } The Logit Model, The Probit Model

If the dependent variable is categorical } The Multinomial Logit, The Multinomial Probit, The Ordered Probit

DATA TO BE ANALYZED: OUR 2010 HOUSE ELECTION DATA

The U.S. House of Representatives, which along with the U.S. Senate composes the legislative branch of the U.S. government, is composed of 435 voting members who represent the 50 states in proportion to their population. Each House member is elected to serve a two-year term, meaning that all 435 representatives stand for election every two years. In 2010, a total of 28 House candidates ran unopposed, leaving 405 House seats that were determined in contested elections. These 405 elections are the focus of the following discussion.

A question of interest to economists (and other social scientists) is the degree to which certain independent factors are correlated with the observed outcome of congressional elections. As should be obvious, election outcomes are binary events: a candidate either wins or loses, making the outcome of an election qualitative rather than quantitative. For this reason, to enter the observed outcome of an election in our multiple linear regression analysis, we define a new variable, "Winner," that equals 1 if a given candidate won the election and 0 if he or she lost.

Economic theory suggests that several independent factors should affect the outcome of a House election. Given the two-party format of American politics, a candidate's party affiliation will clearly be important, as will the amount of campaign spending by both the candidate and his or her opponent. According to the website OpenSecrets.org, "Few things in life are more predictable than the chances of an incumbent member of the U.S. House of Representatives winning reelection" as evidenced by the fact incumbent reelection rates exceeded 90 percent in every election from 1994 to 2008. Finally, in the run-up to the elections, political pundits identified the rise of the "Tea Party" as a potentially deciding factor of many races (e.g., "Election Projections Fuel Tea Party Fervor," www.cnn.com/2010/POLITICS/11/03/tea.party/index.html).

Following the procedure in Appendix A, we collected data on these values for the 810 Democrats and Republicans running for the House in the 405 districts in which elections were contested in 2010. Table 12.2 presents simple summary statistics for these data.

TABLE 12.2
Simple Summary Statistics for Our 2010 House Election Data

	Winning Candidates	Losing Candidates
Democratic Incumbent	0.442	0.128
Republican Incumbent	0.323	0.005
Democrat in Open District	0.015	0.086
Republican in Open District	0.086	0.015
Tea Party Affiliated	0.101	0.212
Male	0.832	0.835
Opponent Male	0.835	0.832
Spending by Candidate	$1,473,642	$ 774,238
	($1,074,536)	($1,153,564)
Spending by Opponent	$ 774,238	$1,473,642
	($1,153,564)	($1,074,536)
Observations	405	405

Note: Standard deviations in parentheses.

A few things are notable about these data. First, because Democrats held a 256–178 edge in the House in the previous Congress, more Democratic than Republican incumbents were running for reelection in 2010. Second, 32 percent of the 405 contested races featured a Tea Party–affiliated candidate (all of whom were Republicans). Third, turning to the difference between winning and losing candidates, nearly 13 percent of Democratic incumbents lost to a Republican challenger, while less than 1 percent of Republican incumbents lost to a Democratic challenger. At the same time, 10 percent of Tea Party–affiliated candidates won election, while 21 percent lost. Finally, winning candidates outspent losing candidates by a nearly 2 to 1 margin, with winning candidates spending an average of nearly $1.5 million.

The scatter diagram of the dependent variable "Winner" versus the independent variable "Spending by Candidate" in Figure 12.4 highlights the empirical issue associated with binary dependent variables.

The next section introduces three different methods of estimation for answering this question: the linear probability, logit, and probit models. Before starting, we note two important things about the discussion of these alternative estimators. First, while the linear probability model directly provides estimated marginal effects, the logit and probit models do not. Accordingly, before interpreting our logit and probit results, we must first convert the estimated coefficients to estimated marginal effects. Second, because the estimated marginal effects for each of the three methods are broadly similar, we leave the full interpretation of the estimated marginal effects until the end of the section so as not to bore the reader by repeatedly offering similar interpretations.

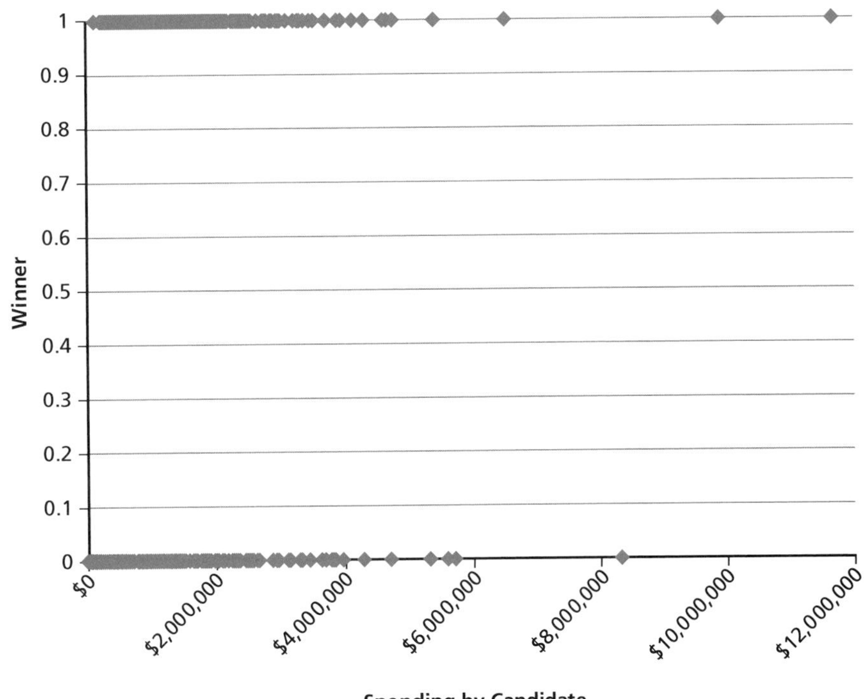

FIGURE 12.4
Scatter Diagram of the Binary Dependent Variable "Winner" versus "Spending by Candidate"

12.1 ESTIMATE MODELS WITH BINARY DEPENDENT VARIABLES

The Linear Probability Model

linear probability model An ordinary least square regression model with a binary dependent variable.

We start by noting that it is possible to estimate population regression models featuring binary dependent variables by OLS. Doing so is referred to as estimating a **linear probability model.** For our 2010 House election, if we estimate the population regression model

$$Winner = \beta_0 + \beta_1 Dem.\ incumbent_i + \beta_2 Rep.\ incumbent_i + \beta_3 Dem.\ open_i + \beta_4 Rep.\ open_i + \beta_5 Tea\ Party_i + \beta_6 Male_i + \beta_7 Opp.\ male_i + \beta_8 Spending\ for_i + \beta_9 Spending\ against_i + \varepsilon_i \quad (12.1.1)$$

by OLS, we get Excel Regression Output 12.1.

Excel Regression Output 12.1: Regression Output for the Linear Probability Model for Our 2010 House Election Data

SUMMARY OUTPUT	
Regression Statistics	
Multiple R	0.723909641
R Square	0.524045168
Adjusted R Square	0.518690676
Standard Error	0.347096625
Observations	810

ANOVA

	df	SS	MS	F	Significance F
Regression	9	106.1191465	11.79101628	97.87019606	1.2521E-122
Residual	800	96.38085347	0.120476067		
Total	809	202.5			

	Coefficients	Standard Error	*t* Stat	*p*-value	Lower 95%	Upper 95%
Intercept	0.125710561	0.048364437	2.599235505	0.009515301	0.030774379	0.220646744
Democratic Incumbent	0.618611434	0.039119489	15.81338228	3.23571E-49	0.541822471	0.695400397
Republican Incumbent	0.832026956	0.044309129	18.77777736	1.86227E-65	0.745051074	0.919002838
Democrat in Open District	0.018128587	0.059102398	0.30673184	0.759127307	−0.0978855	0.134142675
Republican in Open District	0.671121815	0.059242922	11.32830374	1.07544E-27	0.554831887	0.78741174
Tea Party Affiliated	0.130614883	0.037567253	3.476828101	0.000534745	0.056872855	0.20435691
Male	−0.020288906	0.032991341	−0.614976709	0.53874498	−0.08504872	0.044470908
Opponent Male	0.020730248	0.032965598	0.628844898	0.52963011	−0.043979035	0.085439531
Spending by Candidate	0.02583138	0.013508789	1.912190672	0.056208628	−0.000685477	0.052348238
Spending by Opponent	−0.020921013	0.013528948	−1.54638875	0.122406182	−0.047477441	0.005635415

Note: Dependent variable indicates whether individual won the election. Variables highlighted in blue are significant at the 5 percent level. Variables highlighted in gray are significant at the 10 percent level. Omitted group is nonincumbent candidates running in open districts against incumbent candidates.

While these results represent true estimated marginal effects, they are now interpreted as the effects that changes in the independent variables have on the probability of observing that the dependent variable takes on a value of 1 (i.e., the candidate won the election).

Can we improve on these estimates? To answer this question, consider that, as demonstrated in Figure 12.5, when estimating the relationship of interest by OLS, we are determining the *line* that best fits the observed data.

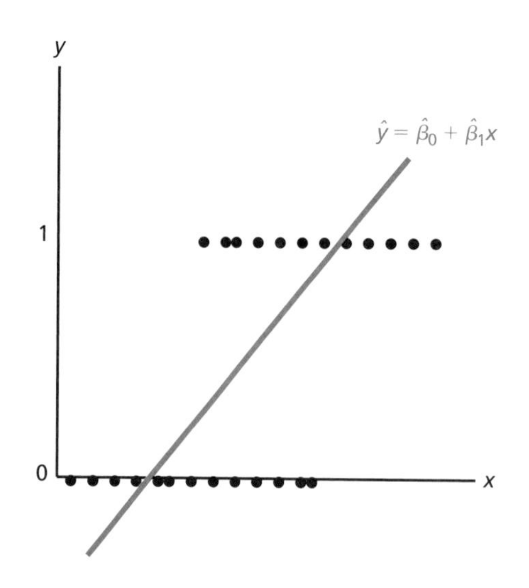

FIGURE 12.5
Estimating the Binary Relationship by OLS

Because the best-fit line in Figure 12.5 appears to more or less balance the 0s and 1s in the middle part of graph, we might expect OLS to describe the underlying relationship between the dependent and the independent variable reasonably well in the middle portion of the graph. To the more extreme left and right, however, the OLS estimates are not very accurate. To the left, the OLS best-fit line drastically underestimates the relationship by predicting negative values for the dependent variable, even though it is impossible to observe such values. To the right, the OLS best-fit line also drastically overestimates the relationship by predicting positive values for the dependent variable, even though it is impossible to observe such values.

Figure 12.6 depicts these facts.

FIGURE 12.6
A Visual Depiction of the Shortcomings of Estimating the Relationship between a Binary Dependent Variable and a Given Independent Variable with OLS

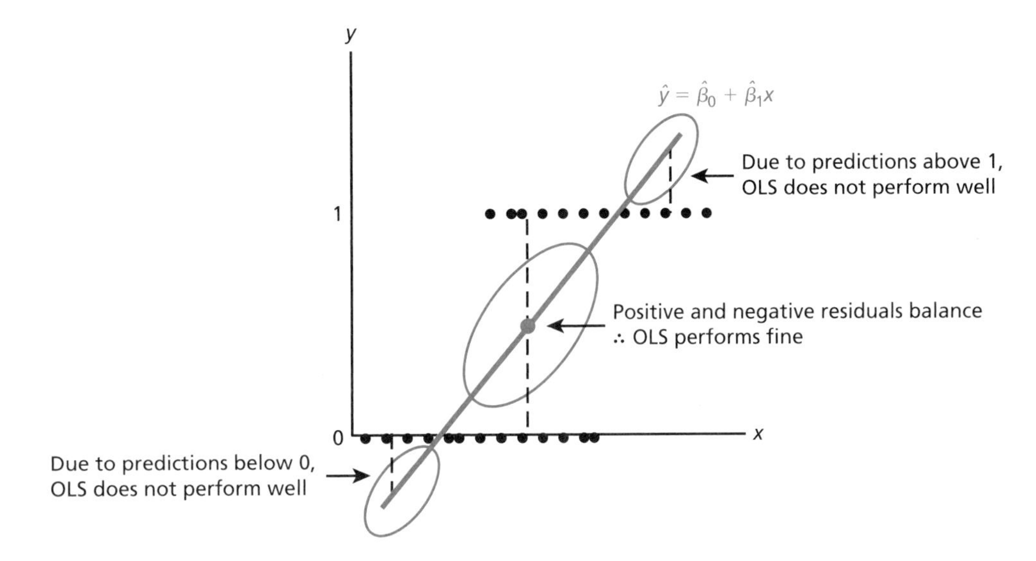

Given our expectation that OLS performs reasonably well in the middle of the data but poorly at the two extremes, we might clearly prefer an estimator more like the one in Figure 12.7.

FIGURE 12.7
Visual Depiction of What a More Preferred Estimator of the Relationship between a Binary Dependent Variable and a Given Independent Variable Might Look Like

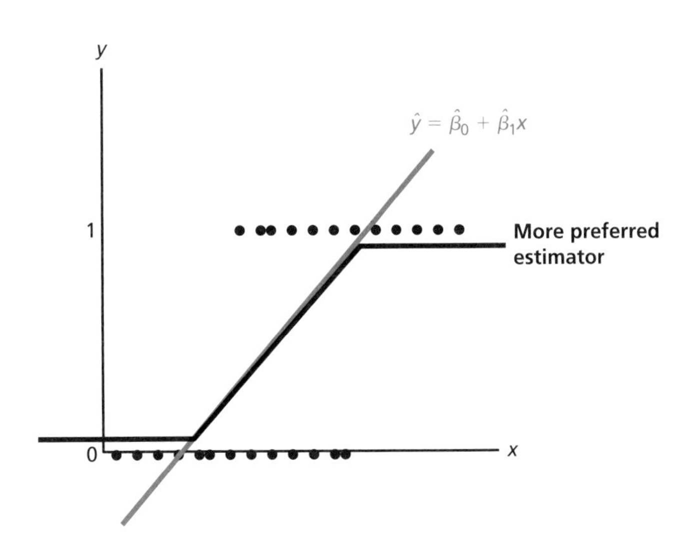

The Logit Model

logit model
A popular specification for estimating population regression models with binary dependent variables.

The **logit model** transforms the population regression model by plugging it into the logistic function

$$f(w) = \frac{e^w}{e^w + 1} = \frac{1}{1 + e^{-w}} \qquad 12.1.2$$

Predicted Value

where w is defined as the population regression model, meaning that

$$f(w) = \frac{1}{1 + e^{-(\beta_0 + \beta_1 x_{1,i} + \beta_2 x_{2,i} + \cdots + \beta_k x_{k,i} + \varepsilon_i)}} \quad \textbf{12.1.3}$$

This function improves on OLS because even though w can take on any values from $-\infty$ to ∞, $f(w)$ is constrained to fall between 0 and 1. Accordingly, applying the logistic function to our data solves the problem associated with OLS predicting values below 0 and above 1 for dependent variables that never actually take on such values.

Figure 12.8 provides a general approximation of the logistic function.

FIGURE 12.8
Visual Depiction of the Logistic Function

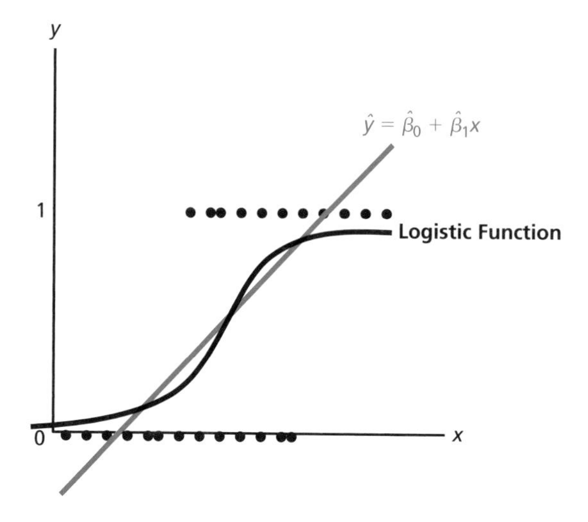

Notice that this approximation looks much more similar to the suggested estimator in Figure 12.7 than it does to the OLS estimator in Figure 12.5. Accordingly, applying the logistic function to our data should result in more desirable estimates of the underlying relationship between the binary dependent and the independent variables than does OLS.

While Excel does not estimate the logit model, more advanced statistical packages do. Using the Stata command

```
logit winner deminc repinc demopen repopen teaparty male oppmale
forspend againstspend
```

for our 2010 House election data, we get Empirical Results 12.1.

Empirical Results 12.1: Estimated *Coefficients* from the Logit Model for Our 2010 House Election Data

	Coefficients	Standard Error	t Stat	p-value	Lower 95%	Upper 95%
Intercept	−2.008893	0.4041252	−4.97	0.000	−2.800964	−1.216822
Democratic Incumbent	2.967275	0.3103075	9.56	0.000	2.359083	3.575466
Republican Incumbent	5.962943	0.7616428	7.83	0.000	4.470150	7.455735
Democrat in Open District	0.1836913	0.4932055	0.37	0.710	−0.782973	1.150356
Republican in Open District	3.401846	0.4907102	6.93	0.000	2.440072	4.363620
Tea Party Affiliated	0.9660699	0.2948818	3.28	0.001	0.388112	1.544028

	Coefficients	Standard Error	*t* Stat	*p*-value	Lower 95%	Upper 95%
Male	−0.1776630	0.2647990	−0.67	0.502	−0.6966594	0.3413334
Opponent Male	0.1977196	0.2817391	0.70	0.483	−0.3544789	0.7499182
Spending by Candidate	0.2287115	0.1156816	1.98	0.048	0.0019798	0.4554432
Spending by Opponent	−0.1770241	0.1128644	−1.57	0.117	−0.3982342	0.0441859
Log Likelihood			−312.206			
Prob > chi2			0.0000			
Observations			810			

Note: Dependent variable indicates whether individual won the election. Highlighted variables are significant at the 5 percent level. Omitted group is nonincumbent candidates running in open districts against incumbent candidates.

Notice that we have italicized the word *coefficients* in the box title for a very important reason. Rather than being true marginal effects, the estimated *coefficients* of the logit model are simply indications of the degree to which each independent variable adds to the likelihood that the dependent variable equals 1. For instance, the fact that the estimated coefficient for the "Democratic Incumbent" variable is 2.97 simply means that, all other independent variables constant, being a Democratic incumbent rather than a nonincumbent running against an incumbent (the omitted group) has a significantly statistic positive relationship to the likelihood of winning the election.

Technically, the estimated slope coefficient of 2.97 for the Democratic incumbent variable indicates that the log-odds ratio of winning the election is 2.97 times higher for a Democratic incumbent than for a nonincumbent running against an incumbent. What precisely does mean? It is hard to say because the log-odds ratio lacks a simple intuitive economic meaning. For this reason, it is very important to convert the estimated slope coefficients into estimated marginal effects before attempting interpretation.

Converting the estimated slope coefficients to estimated *marginal effects* by hand is possible, but doing so requires a series of calculations that are rather time-consuming and introduce the opportunity for user error. Instead, we can simply ask our chosen statistical package to perform the calculations for us. Using the postestimation Stata command

```
mfx
```

we get Empirical Results 12.2.

There are several things to note about the way that the preceding estimates are calculated and presented. First, in Stata (as in most other advanced statistical programs) the estimated marginal effect for a continuous independent variable is calculated by taking the derivative of the logistic function with respect to the variable (with all remaining variables being evaluated at the mean). This explains why the column containing the estimated marginal effects is given the heading $\partial y/\partial x$. Second, the estimated marginal effect for a binary dummy variable is calculated as the difference between the value of the logistic function when the variable takes on the value of 1 and the logistic function when the variable takes on the value of 0, with all other variables evaluated at the mean. Third, rather than calculating a traditional t-statistic, when converting the estimated coefficients to estimated marginal effects, we calculate an asymptotic t-statistic, which is labeled as z in the results due to the fact that the t-statistic becomes the z distribution as n becomes large. Finally, the estimated p-value is calculated as the probability of observing a value more extreme than the estimated marginal effect if the population parameter being estimated is truly equal to 0, which is calculated as $P(Z > |z|)$.

Empirical Results 12.2: Estimated *Marginal Effects* from the Logit Model for Our 2010 House Election Data

Estimated Marginal Effects ↓ (∂y/∂x); Asymptotic *t*-statistics ↓ (z); Estimated *p*-values ↓ (P > |z|)

	∂y/∂x	Standard Error	z	P > |z|	Lower 95%	Upper 95%
Democratic Incumbent	0.563235	0.04579	12.30	0.000	0.47348	0.65299
Republican Incumbent	0.674803	0.02651	25.45	0.000	0.62284	0.72677
Democrat in Open District	0.04483	0.11874	0.38	0.706	−0.18790	0.27756
Republican in Open District	0.456347	0.03838	11.89	0.000	0.38112	0.53157
Tea Party Affiliated	0.220444	0.06111	3.61	0.000	0.10067	0.34022
Male	−0.043509	0.06424	−0.68	0.498	−0.16941	0.08240
Opponent Male	0.049082	0.07019	0.70	0.484	−0.08849	0.18665
Spending by Candidate	0.056465	0.02857	1.98	0.048	0.00047	0.11246
Spending by Opponent	−0.043705	0.02788	−1.57	0.117	−0.09834	0.01093

Now that we have converted the estimated slope coefficients from the logit model into true estimated *marginal effects,* we can interpret the values in the manner to which we have become accustomed. Again, to avoid unnecessary repetition, we leave this discussion until the end of this section.

Empirical Research Tool 12.1 summarizes the logit model.

EMPIRICAL RESEARCH TOOL 12.1: THE LOGIT MODEL

How to Do It:

1. Estimate the population regression model in a more advanced statistical package.
2. Before interpreting the results, convert the estimated slope coefficients to estimated marginal effects.

Why It Works:

The problem associated with estimating models with binary dependent variables by OLS is that doing so predicts values of the dependent variable that are less than 0 and greater than 1, even though such values are factually impossible to observe. The logit model also allows the marginal effects to change as the values of the independent variable changes. The logit model solves this problem via the fact that while z can take on values from $-\infty$ to ∞, $f(z)$ is constrained to fall between 0 and 1. Accordingly, applying the logistic function to our data solves the problem associated with OLS predicting values below 0 and above 1 for dependent variables that never actually take on such values.

probit model
A popular specification for estimating population regression models with binary dependent variables.

The Probit Model

The **probit model** transforms the population regression model into the more desirable probit function. Assuming normality of the function that changes the linear function, w, into probabilities, the conditional probability that an individual chooses each possible outcome of the dependent variable is given by

$$Pr(y = 1|x_1, x_2, \ldots, x_k) = \Phi(w) \qquad \textbf{12.1.4}$$

where w is our population regression model $\beta_0 + \beta_1 x_1 + \beta_2 x_2 + \cdots + \beta_k x_k + \varepsilon_i$, and Φ is the *cumulative distribution function (CDF.)* of the standard normal distribution.

Like the logisitic function, the probit function is constrained to fall between 0 and 1, meaning that applying the probit model to our data solves the problem associated with OLS predicting the unrealistic outcomes less than 0 and greater than 1.

As might be expected, the probit model is not an option in Excel, and we instead need to estimate the model in a more advanced statistical package. Likewise, the estimated slope coefficients from the probit model will not represent true estimated marginal effects. Accordingly, we need to ask our chosen more advanced statistical package to convert the estimated slope coefficients to estimated marginal effects (see Appendix B). Using the Stata command

```
probit winner deminc repinc demopen repopen teaparty male oppmale
forspend againstspend
```

followed by

```
mfx
```

for our 2010 House election data, we get Empirical Results 12.3.

Empirical Results 12.3: Estimated *Coefficients* and *Marginal Effects* from the Probit Model for Our 2010 House Election Data

Estimated Coefficients:

	Coefficients	Standard Error	*t* Stat	*p*-value	Lower 95%	Upper 95%
Intercept	−1.191391	0.223871	−5.32	0.000	−1.630169	−0.752613
Democratic Incumbent	1.761182	0.172601	10.20	0.000	1.422891	2.099473
Republican Incumbent	3.224084	0.314902	10.24	0.000	2.606889	3.841280
Democrat in Open District	0.073330	0.271882	0.27	0.787	−0.459549	0.606209
Republican in Open District	2.009734	0.264883	7.59	0.000	1.490573	2.528895
Tea Party Affiliated	0.529923	0.161687	3.28	0.001	0.213022	0.846824
Male	−0.102762	0.149449	−0.69	0.492	−0.395676	0.190152
Opponent Male	0.115038	0.155863	0.74	0.460	−0.190448	0.420525
Spending by Candidate	0.139739	0.063810	2.19	0.029	0.014674	0.264803
Spending by Opponent	−0.099601	0.062121	−1.60	0.109	−0.221355	0.022154
Log Likelihood			−311.885			
Prob > chi2			0.0000			
Observations			810			

Note: Dependent variable indicates whether an individual won the election. Highlighted variables are significant at the 5 percent level. Omitted group is nonincumbent candidates running in open districts against incumbent candidates.

Estimated Marginal Effects:

	$\partial y/\partial x$	Standard Error	z	P > |z|	Lower 95%	Upper 95%
Democratic Incumbent	0.5724474	0.04158	13.77	0.000	0.490946	0.653948
Republican Incumbent	0.6692059	0.02395	27.94	0.000	0.622261	0.716151
Democrat in Open District	0.0290482	0.10724	0.27	0.786	−0.181148	0.239244
Republican in Open District	0.4838426	0.03032	15.96	0.000	0.424421	0.543265
Tea Party Affiliated	0.2018628	0.05777	3.49	0.000	0.088635	0.315091
Male	−0.0406921	0.05889	−0.69	0.490	−0.156111	0.074727
Opponent Male	0.0458203	0.06212	0.74	0.461	−0.075931	0.167572
Spending by Candidate	0.0555508	0.02538	2.19	0.029	0.005804	0.105297
Spending by Opponent	−0.0395946	0.02468	−1.60	0.109	−0.087975	0.008786

Because the last panel provides the desired marginal effects, we can now safely interpret our results. Once again, we leave this discussion until the end of this section.

Empirical Research Tool 12.2 summarizes the probit model.

EMPIRICAL RESEARCH TOOL 12.2: THE PROBIT MODEL

How to Do It:

1. Estimate the population regression model in a more-advanced statistical package.
2. Before interpreting the results, convert the estimated slope coefficients to estimated marginal effects.

Why It Works:

Similar to the logit model, the probit transforms the population regression model to values that are constrained to fall between 0 and 1 and allows the marginal effects to change as the values of the independent variables change.

Comparing the Three Estimators

Given that we have introduced three potential estimators, an obvious question might be, How do the three compare in their ability to explain the observed variation in the dependent variable? As a first pass at answering this question, Figure 12.9 presents line graphs of the predicted values of the dependent variable for each of the three estimators sorted from lowest to highest.

As should be clear from Figure 12.9, while the linear probability model predicts values for the dependent variable that are outside the bounds of 0 and 1, the logit and the probit both constrain the predicted values of the dependent variable to be between 0 and 1. Given that it is factually impossible for the dependent variable to be less than 0 or greater than 1, the latter two estimators clearly improve on the former estimator over this metric.

As a second pass, we might directly compare the estimated marginal effects resulting from each. To make this comparison easier, Table 12.3 consolidates the estimated marginal effects into a single table.

FIGURE 12.9 **Comparing Line Graphs of Predicted Values from the Linear Probability, Logit, and Probit Models**

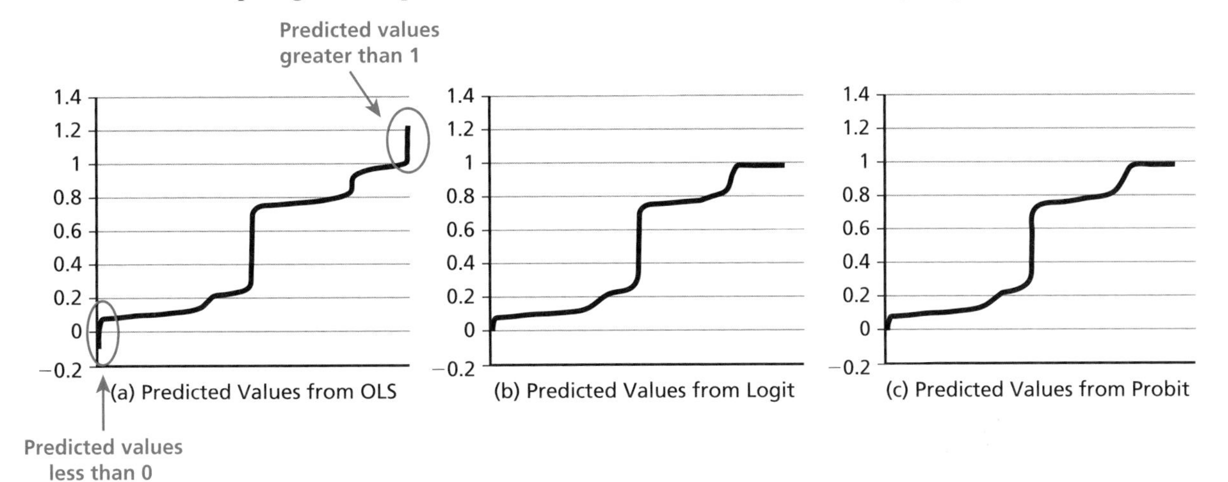

TABLE 12.3
A Comparison of the Estimated Coefficient from the Linear Probability, Logit, and Probit Models for Our 2010 House Election Data

	Method of Estimation		
	Linear Probability	Logit	Probit
Democratic Incumbent	0.6186 (0.0391)	0.5632 (0.0458)	0.5724 (0.0416)
Republican Incumbent	0.8320 (0.0443)	0.6748 (0.0265)	0.6692 (0.0240)
Democrat in Open District	0.0181 (0.0591)	0.0448 (0.1187)	0.0290 (0.1072)
Republican in Open District	0.6711 (0.0592)	0.4563 (0.0384)	0.4838 (0.0303)
Tea Party Affiliated	0.1306 (0.0376)	0.2204 (0.0611)	0.2019 (0.0578)
Male	−0.0203 (0.0330)	−0.0435 (0.0642)	−0.0407 (0.0589)
Opponent Male	0.0207 (0.0330)	0.0491 (0.0702)	0.0458 (0.0621)
Spending by Candidate / $1,000,000	0.0258 (0.0135)	0.0565 (0.0286)	0.0556 (0.0254)
Spending by Opponent / $1,000,000	−0.0209 (0.0135)	−0.0437 (0.0279)	−0.0396 (0.0247)
Log Likelihood		−312.21	−311.88
Observations	810	810	810

Note: Standard errors in parentheses. Values in blue are significant at the 5 percent level, values in light gray are significant at the 10 percent level.

Notice that all three estimators in Table 12.3 are consistent as to the independent variables they identify as achieving statistical significance. Beyond that, the estimated marginal effects from the probit and logit models are quite similar to each other at the mean value of the data but quite different from the linear probability model. Again, this highlights why we prefer the logit and probit models to the linear probability model.

Before interpreting the estimated marginal effects in Table 12.3, there are two important things to note about our independent variables. First, because we define dummy variables for all incumbents and for all candidates running for open seats, the omitted group to which these variables should be compared is the group of nonincumbent candidates running against incumbent candidates. Second, as the variable names suggest, the variables "Spending by Candidate/$1,000,000" and "Spending by Opponent/$1,000,000" represent the total amount of campaign spending in favor of the candidate and in opposition to the candidate opponent divided by $1,000,000.

With this in mind, looking at the estimated marginal effects from the logit and probit models (which are nearly the same for the statistically significant estimates), we can conclude that holding all other independent variables constant, Democratic incumbents, Republican incumbents, and Republicans running for open seats were roughly 57, 67, and 46 percent, respectively, more likely to have won their elections than otherwise similar nonincumbent candidates running against incumbent candidates. Likewise, candidates affiliated with the Tea Party were roughly 21 percent more likely to have won their election than non–Tea Party–affiliated, nonincumbent candidates. Finally, holding party affiliation and incumbency status constant, an additional $1,000,000 of campaign spending by a candidate increased the likelihood of that candidate's victory by roughly

5.6 percent.

Given how similar the logit and probit estimates appear to be, how do we choose which one to use? In a general sense, given that they provide similar results, the answer does not really matter. While true, we note that economists generally favor the probit models, while statisticians frequently estimate logit models.

While the preceding discussion has focused on binary dependent variables, a similar empirical issue exists when the dependent variable is categorical rather than binary in nature.

12.2 ESTIMATE MODELS WITH CATEGORICAL DEPENDENT VARIABLES

As an example of a categorical dependent variable, suppose that a restaurant is interested in determining the degree to which wait-staff visits to the table are related to the quality of service provided. To test this hypothesis, the restaurant owners might conduct a survey that asks customers to rate the quality of service as either excellent, good, fair, or poor. Because the responses to this survey are qualitative, they would need to enter them into a multiple linear regression by creating a new variable, "Quality of Service," that is equal to 0 if the response was "Poor," equal to 1 if the response was "Fair," equal to 2 if the response was "Good," and equal to 3 if the response was "Excellent." Figure 12.10 presents a scatter diagram of quality of this variable versus the dollar value of each customer's tip.

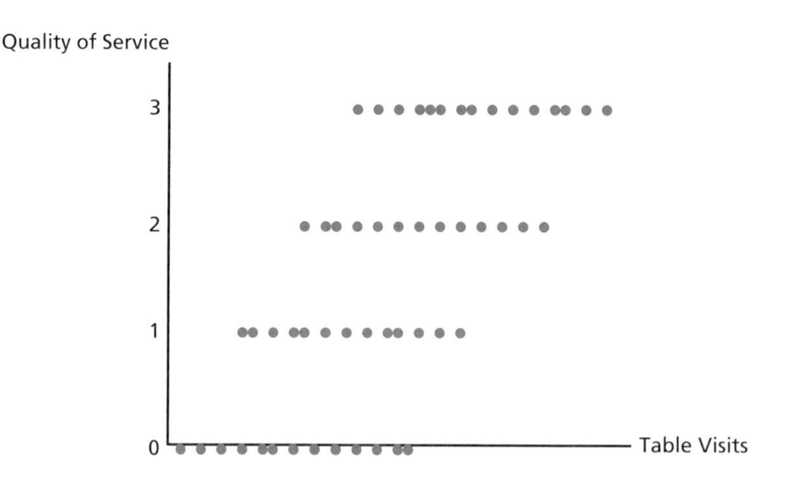

FIGURE 12.10
A Visual Depiction of a Scatter Diagram for Our Hypothetical Quality of Service Example

Before discussing how to most accurately estimate the underlying relationship between the nonlinear dependent variable and the independent variables, we first need to introduce a new data set that will form the baseline example for our discussion.

A New Data Set: Analyzing Educational Attainment Using Our SIPP Education Data

As mentioned at the beginning of the chapter, one of the classic examples involving limited dependent variables is educational attainment. While that initial example referred to the potential differences between college graduates and noncollege graduates, in reality there are many more categories of educational attainment that could be considered. To collect such data, we need to identify a source that provides detailed individual-level data on an individual's highest level of educational attainment. Following the procedure in Appendix A, we identified the *Survey of Income and Program Participation (SIPP)* as a source of such detailed individual-level data, and we collected a sample of 194,753 individuals living in the United States who were at least 30 years of age at the time of the most recent available survey (2008) and who provided information on the highest level of educational attainment. Based on these data, we constructed a new variable, "Highest Degree," that forms the dependent variable in our analysis. Table 12.4 presents summary statistics for this variable.

TABLE 12.4
Relative Frequency Distribution for Our SIPP Education Data

Highest Degree	Total	Percentage	Definition
0	21,785	0.112	Less than high school
1	50,906	0.261	High school
2	23,767	0.122	Some college
3	41,082	0.211	Associate's degree
4	35,281	0.181	Bachelor's degree
5	15,953	0.082	Master's degree
6	5,979	0.031	Professional degree/PhD
Total	194,753	1.000	

These data suggest that the modal level of educational attainment in our SIPP data is the high school diploma, which is the response of 26 percent of the sample. At the same time, nearly 63 percent of all individuals in the sample attended at least some college, with 18 percent receiving at most a bachelor's degree and 11 percent receiving a postgraduate degree.

Our question of interest is which independent factors affect the likelihood that individuals are observed in each of these educational attainment groups. According to economic theory, independent variables likely to affect education attainment fall under the broad groupings of (1) demographic factors, such as sex, race/ethnicity, marital status, and age; (2) socioeconomic status factors, such as income, home ownership, area of residence, and U.S. citizenship; and (3) scholastic aptitude factors, such as standardized test scores and high school GPA. Unfortunately, when collecting data, we often do not have access to all of the variables that we might desire, and in this case, the SIPP does not include any of the scholastic aptitude measures listed here. It does include many demographic and socioeconomic status factors, however, and Table 12.5 presents summary statistics for the independent variables in our analysis.

The scatter diagram of the dependent variable "Highest Degree" versus the independent variable "Household Income" in Figure 12.11 highlights the empirical issue associated with categorical dependent variables.

As with binary dependent variables, OLS estimates for categorical dependent variables would not be as desirable as those from other estimation techniques that take account of the nonlinear nature of the dependent variable. We introduce three methods for estimating models with categorical dependent variables.

TABLE 12.5 Summary Statistics for Our SIPP Education Data

		Highest Degree Earned						
	Overall	Less Than High School	High School	Some College	Associate's Degree	Bachelor's Degree	Master's Degree	Prof. Degree/ PhD
Demographic factors:								
Male	0.470	0.479	0.461	0.453	0.465	0.475	0.453	0.623
Black	0.105	0.135	0.116	0.110	0.126	0.071	0.067	0.061
Hispanic	0.096	0.310	0.097	0.069	0.078	0.042	0.030	0.028
Asian	0.042	0.044	0.028	0.020	0.030	0.070	0.069	0.086
Other Race	0.026	0.030	0.026	0.030	0.034	0.020	0.015	0.016
Current Age	53.48	57.48	55.30	52.25	52.53	50.72	52.82	53.04
	(14.65)	(16.31)	(15.05)	(14.54)	(13.77)	(13.77)	(13.64)	(13.79)
Currently Married	0.645	0.559	0.625	0.623	0.625	0.714	0.722	0.741
Socioeconomic status factors:								
Family Owns Home	0.772	0.634	0.748	0.762	0.777	0.840	0.864	0.857
Household Income	$6,261.24	$3,652.67	$4,876.39	$5,703.12	$5,765.65	$8,272.28	$9,397.50	$12,945.49
	($5,620.55)	($3,015.23)	($4,057.00)	($4,343.98)	($4,691.39)	($6,367.39)	($6,862.34)	($11,216.68)
Live in Metro Area	0.767	0.716	0.718	0.779	0.755	0.830	0.829	0.857
U.S. Citizen	0.935	0.790	0.941	0.975	0.958	0.957	0.951	0.932
Observations	194,753	21,785	50,906	23,767	41,082	35,281	15,953	5,979

Note: Standard deviations in parentheses.

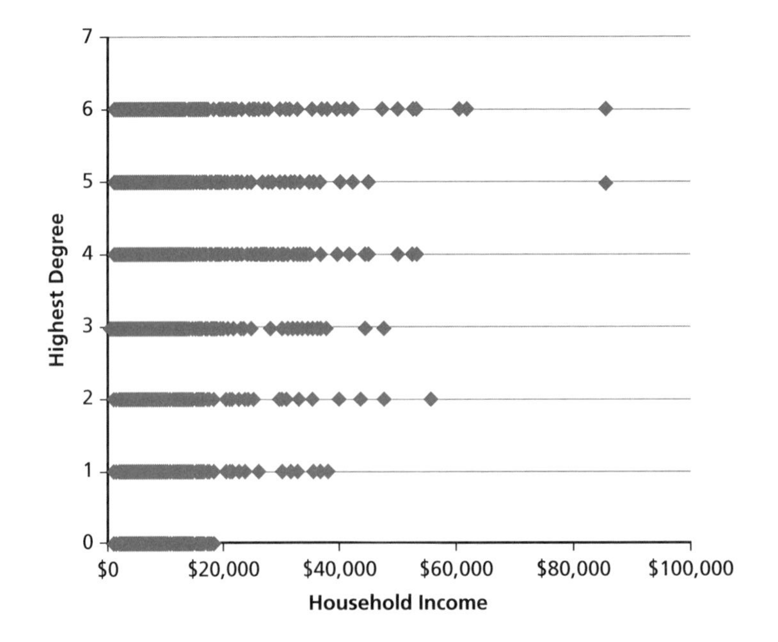

FIGURE 12.11 **Visual Depiction of Estimated Probit Relationship for the First 32,000 Observations in Our SIPP Education Data**

The Multinomial Logit

multinomial logit
A regression model that generalizes logistic regression to allow more than two discrete outcomes for the dependent variable.

The **multinomial logit** extends the logistic function to categorical dependent variables. For simplicity, assume that our categorical dependent variable y_i takes on three possible outcomes, 0, 1, and 2, with the chosen outcome being defined as

$$y_i \begin{array}{lll} = 2 & \text{if} & w_2 \geq max(w_1, w_0) \\ = 1 & \text{if} & w_1 \geq max(w_2, w_0) \\ = 0 & \text{if} & w_0 \geq max(w_2, w_1) \end{array} \quad \textbf{12.2.1}$$

where w_0, w_1, and w_2 are the multiple linear regression models for each of the three possible outcomes of the dependent variable. Note that to be consistent with utility maximization, most consumer choice models assume that w_0, w_1, and w_2 represent the utilities associated with each possible outcome (i.e., the individual chooses outcome w_2 if and only if outcome w_2 provides more utility than both outcomes w_0 and w_1, the individual chooses outcome w_1 if and only if outcome w_1 provides more utility than both outcomes w_0 and w_2, and so on).

The multinomial logit model transforms this specification into a likelihood function by making the following calculation

$$Pr(y_i = h) = \frac{exp(Z_h)}{1 + \sum_{j=0}^{J} exp(Z_j)} \quad \textbf{12.2.2}$$

where h indicates the specific outcome being considered (i.e., $y_i = 0$, or $y_i = 1$, or $y_i = 2$) and j is a counting term indicating each of the possible outcomes, with J being the highest possible outcome (i.e., in this case, j takes on three possible value, 0, 1, and 2, with J being 2).

Estimated slope coefficients are then calculated by maximizing the likelihood function, a complicated process that is fortunately pre-programmed in statistical packages such as Stata. Using the Stata command

```
mlogit highdegree male black hisp asian othrace age married ownhome income
metro uscit, base(0)
```

for our SIPP education data, we get Empirical Results 12.4.

Empirical Results 12.4: Estimated *Coefficients* from the Multinomial Logit Model for Our SIPP Education Data

Coefficient Estimates

	Coefficients	Standard Error	*t* Stat	*p*-value	Lower 95%	Upper 95%
Outcome 1:						
Intercept	0.965686	0.050058	19.29	0.000	0.867575	1.063797
Male	−0.153393	0.017226	−8.90	0.000	−0.187156	−0.119630
Black	−0.570631	0.026392	−21.62	0.000	−0.622359	−0.518903
Hispanic	−1.525498	0.025660	−59.45	0.000	−1.575791	−1.475206
Asian	−0.751345	0.046291	−16.23	0.000	−0.842074	−0.660616
Other Race	−0.575723	0.050243	−11.46	0.000	−0.674197	−0.477249
Current Age	−0.022869	0.000606	−37.75	0.000	−0.024056	−0.021681
Currently Married	0.089291	0.018364	4.86	0.000	0.053300	0.125283
Family Owns Home	0.219086	0.019853	11.04	0.000	0.180175	0.257997
Household Income/$1,000	0.115538	0.003501	33.00	0.000	0.108677	0.122400
Live in Metro Area	0.247506	0.019428	12.74	0.000	0.209428	0.285584
U.S. Citizen	0.898961	0.029587	30.38	0.000	0.840970	0.956953

	Coefficient Estimates					
	Coefficients	**Standard Error**	***t* Stat**	***p*-value**	**Lower 95%**	**Upper 95%**
Outcome 2:						
Intercept	−0.234576	0.0669483	−3.50	0.000	−0.365793	−0.103360
Male	−0.210114	0.0200727	−10.47	0.000	−0.249456	−0.170772
Black	−0.727586	0.0312207	−23.30	0.000	−0.788777	−0.666394
Hispanic	−1.902281	0.0337794	−56.31	0.000	−1.968488	−1.836075
Asian	−1.079328	0.0606528	−17.80	0.000	−1.198205	−0.960451
Other Race	−0.494593	0.0572962	−8.63	0.000	−0.606892	−0.382295
Current Age	−0.037821	0.0007138	−52.99	0.000	−0.039220	−0.036422
Currently Married	−0.032186	0.02153	−1.49	0.135	−0.074384	0.010012
Family Owns Home	0.265941	0.0237752	11.19	0.000	0.219343	0.312540
Household Income/$1,000	0.167726	0.0036992	45.34	0.000	0.160475	0.174976
Live in Metro Area	0.593495	0.0233588	25.41	0.000	0.547712	0.639277
U.S. Citizen	1.762638	0.0484022	36.42	0.000	1.667772	1.857505
} And so on through the maximum outcome (outcome 6 in this case)						
Log Likelihood			−324,995.48			
Prob > chi2			0.0000			
Observations			194,753			

Note: Dependent variable is individual's highest degree earned. Highlighted variables are significant at the 5 percent level.

Once again, it is important to note that these initial estimates represent estimated slope coefficients rather than estimated marginal effects. This means that they simply provide an indication of the degree to which a given independent variable is associated with the likelihood that an individual chooses a given outcome relative to the base outcome. For instance, the fact that the estimated slope coefficient for the variable "Male" has a statistically significant negative effect for "Outcome 1" suggests that, all other independent variables constant, males are less likely to choose Outcome 1 than the omitted outcome. Beyond knowing the direction of the estimated association between different independent variables and different possible outcomes of the dependent variable, we would like to estimate the exact degree to which marginal changes in the independent variables are associated with changes in the dependent variable. Accordingly, rather than focusing on the relatively uninformative coefficient estimates, we should convert the values to more meaningful estimated marginal effects. Fortunately, more advanced statistical programs make the desired conversions for us, although in a slightly more complicated way than for the binomial logit. Using the Stata command

```
mlogit highdegree male black hisp asian othrace age married ownhome income
metro uscit, base(0)
```

(which specifies that the base group for highedegree is 0), followed by the Stata commands

```
mfx, predict(p outcome(1))
mfx, predict(p outcome(2))
```

and so on for all possible outcomes of the dependent variable we get the estimated marginal effects that are consolidated in Table 12.6.

TABLE 12.6 Estimated Marginal Effects from Our Multinomial Logit Estimation of the Highest Degree Achieved for Our SIPP Education Sample

	Highest Degree Earned					
	High School Diploma	**Some College**	**AA Degree**	**BA Degree**	**MA Degree**	**Professional Degree/PhD**
Demographic Factors:						
Male	−0.0015 (0.0021)	−0.0083 (0.0016)	−0.0024 (0.0020)	−0.0036 (0.0018)	−0.0085 (0.0012)	0.0141 (0.0007)
Black	0.0198 (0.0036)	−0.0112 (0.0025)	0.0384 (0.0035)	−0.0660 (0.0026)	−0.0290 (0.0017)	−0.0092 (0.0009)
Hispanic	0.0241 (0.0041)	−0.0339 (0.0026)	−0.0291 (0.0037)	−0.1134 (0.0024)	−0.0593 (0.0014)	−0.0188 (0.0007)
Asian	−0.0688 (0.0053)	−0.0623 (0.0034)	−0.0432 (0.0052)	0.0889 (0.0053)	0.0316 (0.0035)	0.0136 (0.0019)
Other Race	−0.0117 (0.0064)	0.0052 (0.0049)	0.0577 (0.0067)	−0.0545 (0.0048)	−0.0352 (0.0029)	−0.0091 (0.0016)
Current Age	0.0022 (0.0001)	−0.0010 (0.0001)	−0.0012 (0.0001)	−0.0023 (0.0001)	0.0000 (0.0001)	0.0001 (0.0000)
Currently Married	0.0186 (0.0023)	−0.0073 (0.0018)	−0.0175 (0.0023)	0.0076 (0.0021)	0.0012 (0.0014)	−0.0011 (0.0008)
Socioeconomic Status Factors:						
Family Owns Home	−0.0352 (0.0028)	−0.0103 (0.0021)	0.0109 (0.0026)	0.0382 (0.0023)	0.0202 (0.0016)	0.0020 (0.0009)
Household Income/$1,000	−0.0152 (0.0003)	−0.0003 (0.0002)	0.0008 (0.0003)	0.0149 (0.0002)	0.0082 (0.0001)	0.0033 (0.0001)
Live in Metro Area	−0.0656 (0.0026)	0.0157 (0.0019)	−0.0133 (0.0025)	0.0632 (0.0020)	0.0259 (0.0013)	0.0108 (0.0007)
U.S. Citizen	−0.0350 (0.0052)	0.0730 (0.0029)	0.0539 (0.0044)	0.0371 (0.0040)	−0.0058 (0.0032)	−0.0103 (0.0019)
Log Likelihood			−324,995.48			
Observations			194,753			

Note: Dependent variable is individual's highest degree earned. Base group is individuals with less than a high school diploma. Standard errors in parentheses. Variables highlighted in blue are significant at the 5 percent level. Variables highlighted in gray are significant at the 10 percent level.

Looking at these results, one thing should stand out. As opposed to many previous applications, nearly all of the preceding estimated marginal effects achieve statistical significance at the 5 percent level. The reason? Our huge sample of nearly 195,000 individual observations drives down the estimated standard errors (which, as you should recall from previous chapters, depend on the number of observations) for all variables, thereby greatly increasing the chances that individual estimates achieve statistical significance. This is the one of the main reasons we love large sample sizes when performing empirical analysis.

For illustration purposes (and for the sake of brevity), rather than discussing all statistically significant estimates, we only discuss a few. From Table 12.6, we see that all other variables constant, relative to receiving less than a high school diploma (the omitted group), women in our sample are significantly more likely than men to attend some college, receive a bachelor's, or receive a master's degree, while men are significantly more likely than women to attain a professional degree or PhD. Similarly, all other variables constant, relative to individuals receiving less than a high school diploma, each additional \$1,000 of household income is negatively correlated with earning only a high school diploma and positively correlated with earning an associate's degree, a bachelor's degree, a master's degree, or a professional degree or PhD.

As a final point, we note that one important assumption about the underlying data must be satisfied in order for the multinomial logit to be the appropriate estimator to use. The **independence of irrelevant alternatives (IIA)** requires the data to possess the characteristic that if one of the possible outcomes of the dependent variable is eliminated, the relative probabilities of the remaining possible outcomes do not change. As an example, suppose that there are three possible outcomes, A, B, and C, and that the probability of each of these outcome occurring is 1/3. In this case, the relative probability that outcome B relative to outcome C is $1/3 \div 1/3 = 1$. For the IIA assumption to hold, it must be the case that when outcome A is eliminated, the relative probability that outcome B relative to outcome C remains 1. This can only happen if the individual probabilities of outcome B and outcome C occurring in the absence of outcome A both change to 1/2 (so that the relative probability that outcome B occurs instead of outcome C becomes $1/2 \div 1/2 = 1$). If this is not the case, then the IIA assumption is violated, and the multinomial logit is not the correct estimator to use.

independence of irrelevant alternatives (IIA)
A condition that is needed for multinomial logit to be theoretically valid.

The classic example of a violation of the IIA assumption is known as the "red bus/blue bus" paradox. Suppose that an individual initially has a choice between three modes of transportation, a red bus, a blue bus, and a bicycle, and that the individual probability of each outcome is 1/3. In such a case, the relative probability of choosing a blue bus rather than a bicycle is $1/3 \div 1/3 = 1$. Suppose now that the city decides to paint all of its red buses blue, thereby eliminating the option of riding a red bus. Does the individual care about this change (i.e., will the individual refuse to ride a bus if it is blue rather than red)? No, the individual only cares that a bus is a bus. Accordingly, after the change, the probability of riding a red bus should be added to the probability of riding a blue bus, meaning that the relative probability of riding a blue bus instead of a bicycle should become $2/3 \div 1/3 = 2$ instead of 1, thereby violating the IIA assumption. Note that we will return to this issue later.

Empirical Research Tool 12.3 summarizes the multinomial logit.

EMPIRICAL RESEARCH TOOL 12.3: THE MULTINOMIAL LOGIT

How to Do It:

1. Estimate the population regression model in a more-advanced statistical package.
2. Before interpreting the results, convert the estimated slope coefficients to estimated marginal effects.

Why It Works:

Similar to the logit and probit models, the multinomial logit model transforms the population regression model to values that are constrained to fall between 0 and the highest observed outcome of the dependent variable and allows the marginal effects to change as the values of the independent variables change.

The Multinomial Probit

As in the binary case, we can also estimate models for categorical dependent variables using the probit function rather than the logit function. Doing so is referred to estimating a **multinomial probit**. Unfortunately, due to the complexity of the calculations involved, actually estimating a multinomial probit is often quite difficult. Indeed, we attempted to estimate the model for our SIPP education sample, but after hours of waiting for the likelihood function to converge, we finally gave up! Accordingly, given that it is so much easier to estimate, we generally opt for the multinomial logit over the multinomial probit.

multinomial probit
A popular alternative to multinomial logit model; a generalization of the probit model by allowing more than two discrete, unordered outcomes.

The Ordered Probit

Suppose we know that the possible values of the categorical dependent variable follow a clear ordering, such that the highest possible outcome would be preferred to the second highest possible outcome, the second highest possible outcome would be preferred to the third highest possible outcome, and so on. Because this situation violates the IIA assumption, the multinomial logit will not be the correct estimator. To see why, consider that if we remove the highest possible outcome, the relative probabilities of the remaining outcomes do not remain constant because the probability of choosing the highest possible outcome shifts entirely to the second highest possible outcome, thereby changing the relative probabilities of choosing each of the remaining possible outcomes.

This situation is likely to apply to our education example. Given that, most individuals would agree that, all other independent variables constant, a PhD/professional degree is preferred to a master's degree, a master's degree is preferred to a bachelor's degree, and so on. Accordingly, if we were to remove the option of receiving a PhD/professional degree, almost all individuals preferring that option would switch to a master's degree instead of a high school diploma or less than a high school diploma, thereby changing the relative probabilities of the remaining options and violating the IIA assumption.

ordered probit
A regression model that generalizes the probit model to allow more than two discrete outcomes for the dependent variable.

Fortunately, estimating the **ordered probit** is a relatively straightforward way to deal with the ordered nature of the outcomes of the dependent variable. Again, for simplicity, assume that a dependent variable y_i has three potential ordered outcomes, 0, 1, and 2. We the define the categorical dependent variable as

$$\begin{aligned} &= 2 \quad \textit{if} \quad \alpha_2 < w < \infty \\ y_i &= 1 \quad \textit{if} \quad \alpha_1 < w < \alpha_2 \\ &= 0 \quad \textit{if} \quad -\infty < w < \alpha_1 \end{aligned} \qquad \textbf{12.2.3}$$

where w is our population regression model. Note that in this formulation, α_1 and α_2 partition the individual's choice of outcomes for the dependent variable, with α_2 being the minimum value at which the individual chooses outcome 2 and α_1 being the minimum value at which the individual chooses outcome 1.

Assuming normality of the function that changes the linear function, z, into probabilities, the conditional probability that an individual chooses each possible outcome of the dependent variable is given by

$$Pr(Y_i = 2|\textit{the x's}) = Pr(\alpha_2 < w < \infty|\textit{the x's}) = 1 - \Phi\left(\frac{\alpha_2 - (w)}{\sigma_i}\right) \qquad \textbf{12.2.4}$$

$$Pr(Y_i = 1|\textit{the x's}) = Pr(\alpha_1 < w < \alpha_2|\textit{the x's}) = \Phi\left(\frac{\alpha_2 - (w)}{\sigma_i}\right) - \Phi\left(\frac{\alpha_1 - (w)}{\sigma_i}\right) \qquad \textbf{12.2.5}$$

$$Pr(Y_i = 0|\textit{the x's}) = Pr(-\infty < w < \alpha_1|\textit{the x's}) = 1 - \Phi\left(\frac{\alpha_1 - (w)}{\sigma_i}\right) \qquad \textbf{12.2.6}$$

where w is as defined earlier and Φ is the cumulative distribution function (CDF) of the standard normal distribution.

While we could maximize this function by hand, more advanced statistical packages calculate the estimated coefficients quite easily. Using the Stata command

```
oprobit highdegree male black hisp asian othrace age married ownhome
income metro uscit
```

for our SIPP education data, we get Empirical Results 12.5.

Empirical Results 12.5: Estimated *Coefficients* from the Ordered Probit Model for Our SIPP Education Data

Coefficient Estimates

	Coefficients					
	Coefficients	Standard Error	*t* Stat	*p*-value	Lower 95%	Upper 95%
Male	0.0047304	0.0047346	1.00	0.318	−0.0045493	0.01401
Black	−0.2444167	0.0079472	−30.76	0.000	−0.259993	−0.2288405
Hispanic	−0.7690341	0.0090969	−84.54	0.000	−0.7868638	−0.7512045
Asian	0.1966657	0.0122147	16.10	0.000	0.1727253	0.2206061
Other Race	−0.1966015	0.014777	−13.30	0.000	−0.225564	−0.167639
Current Age	−0.0094343	0.0001691	−55.79	0.000	−0.0097658	−0.0091029
Currently Married	0.0061168	0.0052168	1.17	0.241	−0.004108	0.0163416
Family Owns Home	0.1837842	0.0060887	30.18	0.000	0.1718506	0.1957178
Household Income/$1,000	0.0581012	0.0004658	124.73	0.000	0.0571882	0.0590142
Live in Metro Area	0.2563663	0.0056772	45.16	0.000	0.2452391	0.2674935
U.S. Citizen	0.3825629	0.0108822	35.15	0.000	0.3612341	0.4038916
/cut 1	−0.8967788	0.0155429				
/cut 2	0.1102635	0.015366				
/cut 3	0.4529626	0.015366				
/cut 4	1.070267	0.0154452				
/cut 5	1.821578	0.0157319				
/cut 6	2.549235	0.0164972				
Log Likelihood			−330,197.81			
Prob > chi2			0.0000			
Observations			194,753			

Note: Dependent variable is individual's highest degree earned. Base group is individuals with less than a high school diploma. Highlighted variables are significant at the 5 percent level.

The entries in Empirical Results 12.5 are estimated coefficients rather than estimated marginal effects; thus, they inform us only of the estimated direction of change for each of the independent variables. We can, however, convert these estimates to marginal effects by plugging the estimated values back into formulas 12.2.4, 12.2.5, and 12.2.6 or by asking our preferred statistical package to provide them for us. Table 12.7 presents the results of doing the latter and condensing the results into one concise table.

Again, nearly all of these estimated marginal effects achieve statistical significance due to the extremely large number of observations. For illustration purposes, we only focus on interpreting the estimated marginal effects for a few variables. All other variables constant, relative to achieving less than a high school diploma (the omitted group), blacks are significantly more likely to earn a high school diploma or attend some college and significantly less likely to earn an associate's degree, a bachelor's degree, a master's degree, or a professional degree or PhD. Conversely, all other variables constant, relative to achieving less than a high school diploma, individuals living in metro areas are significantly less likely to earn a high school diploma or attend some college and significantly more likely to earn an associate's degree, a bachelor's degree, a master's degree, or a professional degree or PhD.

Empirical Research Tool 12.4 summarizes the ordered probit.

TABLE 12.7 Estimated Marginal Effects from Our Ordered Probit Estimation of the Highest Degree Achieved for Our SIPP Education Sample

	Highest Degree Earned					
	High School Diploma	**Some College**	**AA Degree**	**BA Degree**	**MA Degree**	**Professional Degree/PhD**
Demographic Factors:						
Male	−0.0010	−0.0001	0.0003	0.0008	0.0005	0.0002
	(0.0010)	(0.0001)	(0.0003)	(0.0008)	(0.0005)	(0.0002)
Black	0.0502	0.0028	−0.0208	−0.0421	−0.0249	−0.0091
	(0.0015)	(0.0001)	(0.0008)	(0.0014)	(0.0007)	(0.0003)
Hispanic	0.1222	−0.0122	−0.0861	−0.1211	−0.0602	−0.0195
	(0.0015)	(0.0001)	(0.0008)	(0.0014)	(0.0007)	(0.0003)
Asian	−0.0436	−0.0070	0.0093	0.0334	0.0244	0.0108
	(0.0027)	(0.0006)	(0.0004)	(0.0020)	(0.0017)	(0.0008)
Other Race	0.0406	0.0024	−0.0166	−0.0339	−0201	−0.0074
	(0.0029)	(0.0001)	(0.0015)	(0.0025)	(0.0014)	(0.0005)
Current Age	0.0020	0.0002	−0.0006	−0.0016	−0.0011	−0.0004
	(0.0000)	(0.0000)	(0.0000)	(0.0000)	(0.0000)	(0.0000)
Currently Married	−0.0013	−0.0001	0.0004	0.0011	0.0007	0.0003
	(0.0011)	(0.0001)	(0.0004)	(0.0009)	(0.0006)	(0.0002)
Socioeconomic Status Factors:						
Family Owns Home	−0.0389	−0.0033	0.0140	0.0318	0.0198	0.0076
	(0.0013)	(0.0001)	(0.0005)	(0.0011)	(0.0006)	(0.0003)
Household income/$1,000	−0.0126	−0.0014	0.0039	0.0101	0.0066	0.0026
	(0.0001)	(0.0000)	(0.0003)	(0.0001)	(0.0001)	(0.0000)
Live in Metro Area	−0.0535	−0.0039	0.0204	0.0442	0.0270	0.0102
	(0.0012)	(0.0001)	(0.0006)	(0.0010)	(0.0006)	(0.0002)
U.S. Citizen	−0.0742	−0.0009	0.0369	0.0648	0.0358	0.0124
	(0.0018)	(0.0003)	(0.0013)	(0.0018)	(0.0009)	(0.0003)
Log Likelihood			−330,197.81			
Observations			194,753			

Note: Dependent variable is individual's highest degree earned. Base group is individuals with less than a high school diploma. Standard errors in parentheses. Highlighted variables are significant at the 5 percent level.

EMPIRICAL RESEARCH TOOL 12.4: THE ORDERED PROBIT

How to Do It:

1. Estimate the population regression model in a more-advanced statistical package.
2. Before interpreting the results, convert the estimated slope coefficients to estimated marginal effects.

Why It Works:

Similar to the multinomial logit model, the ordered probit transforms the population regression model to values that are constrained to fall between 0 and the highest observed outcome of the dependent variable and allows the marginal effects to change as the values of the independent variables change. This specification should only be used if the values have some type of natural ordering.

ADDITIONS TO OUR EMPIRICAL RESEARCH TOOLKIT

In this chapter we have introduced a number of tools that will prove valuable when performing empirical research:

- Methods for dealing with binary dependent variables, including the linear probability, logit, and probit models.
- Methods for dealing with categorical dependent variables, including the multinomial logit and the ordered probit models.

OUR NEW EMPIRICAL TOOLS IN PRACTICE: USING WHAT WE HAVE LEARNED IN THIS CHAPTER

Based on the information in this chapter, our former student decided that he should estimate his population regression model as either a linear probability, a logit, or a probit model. Combining the results for all three produced the results in Table 12.8.

TABLE 12.8 Estimated Marginal Effects for Our Former Student's Vacation Data

	Method of Estimation		
	Linear Probability	Logit	Probit
Age of Head of Family	−0.0006 (0.0002)	−0.0006 (0.0002)	−0.0007 (0.0002)
Head of Family Married	0.0130 (0.0071)	0.0124 (0.0059)	0.0141 (0.0065)
Number of Children	−0.0093 (0.0032)	−0.0090 (0.0028)	−0.0106 (0.0031)
Age of Youngest Child	−0.0005 (0.0007)	−0.0002 (0.0006)	−0.0001 (0.0007)
Head of Family Employed	0.0881 (0.0078)	0.0946 (0.0057)	0.0941 (0.0056)
Family Income/100,000	0.0369 (0.0082)	0.0154 (0.0057)	0.0174 (0.0056)
Family Owns Home	0.0221 (0.0083)	0.0219 (0.0066)	0.0242 (0.0073)
Family Home's Value/100,000	0.0032 (0.0019)	0.0016 (0.0013)	0.0020 (0.0016)
Log Likelihood		−2,444.15	−2,442.42
Observations	8,382	8,382	8,382

Note: Dependent variables equals 1 if head of family reported that family took vacation. Standard errors in parentheses. Variables highlighted in blue and gray are significant at the 5 and 10 percent levels, respectively.

The student interpreted these data as follows. All other variables constant, the married heads of household who were employed, earning higher incomes, and owning their own homes were significantly more likely to have reported taking a vacation in the past year, while families with older heads and more children were significantly less likely to have done likewise. Given these results, our former student was able to suggest that his boss invest money advertising in areas that are more likely to be composed of younger, richer, married couples who own their own homes and have relatively fewer children.

On the basis of his work, from data to collection to empirical analysis and effective write-up, our former student was judged to have conducted a successful empirical research project.

LOOKING AHEAD TO CHAPTER 13

Rather than having access to strictly cross-section or strictly time-series data, we are sometimes lucky enough to have data on a cross-section that extends across a number of different time periods. We refer to such data as being panel data, and the fact that such data varies both across individuals and over time offers a number of empirical advantages. We discuss these in Chapter 13.

Problems

12.1 Draw a picture that explains why OLS is not the most appropriate estimator when the dependent variable only takes on two values. List four other reasons the Logit or Probit is preferred to OLS in this circumstance.

12.2 How are the multinomial logit and the ordered probit different? Why are the logit or probit not appropriate models in this circumstance?

12.3 A study tried to find the determinants of the increase in the number of households headed by a female. Using 1940 and 1960 historical census data, a logit model was estimated to predict whether a woman is the head of a household (living on her own) or whether she is living within another's household. The limited dependent variable takes on a value of 1 if the female lives on her own and is 0 if she shares housing. The results for 1960 using 6,051 observations on prime-age whites and 1,294 on nonwhites were as shown in the accompanying table:

Regression	(1) White	(2) Nonwhite
Regression Model	Logit	Logit
Constant	1.459	−2.874
	(0.685)	(1.423)
Age	−0.275	0.084
	(0.037)	(0.068)
Age Squared	0.00463	0.00021
	(0.00044)	(0.00081)
Education	−0.171	−0.127
	(0.026)	(0.038)
Farm Status	−0.687	−0.498
	(0.173)	(0.346)
South	0.376	−0.520
	(0.098)	(0.180)
Expected Family Earnings	0.0018	0.0011
	(0.00019)	(0.00024)
Family Composition	4.123	2.751
	(0.294)	(0.345)
Pseudo-R^2	0.266	0.189
Percent Correctly Predicted	82.0	83.4

where *Age* is measured in years, *Education* is years of schooling of the family head, *Farm status* is a binary variable taking the value of one if the family head lived on a farm, *South* is a binary variable for living in a certain region of the country, *Expected family earnings* was generated from a separate OLS regression to predict earnings from a set of regressors, and *Family composition* refers to the number of family members under the age of 18 divided by the total number in the family.

The mean values for the variables were as shown in the next table.

Variable	(1) White Mean	(2) Nonwhite Mean
Age	46.1	42.9
Age squared	2,263.5	1,965.6
Education	12.6	10.4
Farm status	0.03	0.02
South	0.3	0.5
Expected family earnings	2,336.4	1,507.3
Family composition	0.2	0.3

a. Interpret the results. Do the coefficients have the expected signs? Why do you think age was entered both in levels and in squares?

b. Calculate the difference in the predicted probability between whites and nonwhites and the sample mean values of the explanatory variables. Why do you think the study did not combine the observations and allow for a nonwhite binary variable to enter?

c. What would be the effect on the probability of a nonwhite woman living on her own, if *Education* and *Family composition* were changed from their current mean to the mean of whites, while all other variables were left unchanged at the nonwhite mean values?

d. How would you calculate marginal effects in a more advanced statistical package? Why are marginal effects more informative than the coefficient estimates printed in this problem?

e. What are the primary reasons probit or logit models are used instead of the linear probability model?

12.4 Suppose you were hired by the state of California to conduct a study of voter willingness to support a tax increase to fund new school spending. Define V_i such that:

$$V_i = 1 \text{ if voter } i \text{ supports the tax increase}$$

$$V_i = 0 \text{ if voter } i \text{ does not support the tax increase}$$

Thus, V_i is a binomial random variable with population mean, μ, and population variance, σ^2. You think that voter support of the tax increase is related to the income of each individual.

a. Suppose that you regress V_i on $Income_i$ using a linear probability model. What properties would this model have, assuming that income is the only factor that affects voting behavior? Is the estimate of the slope reliable?

b. How would your answer change in part (a) if you instead used a logit or probit model?

Exercises

E12.1 Use the file **Hunting Data.xls**, which is collected from the 2006 National Survey of Fishing, Hunting, and Wildlife Associated Recreation, for the following questions.

a. Use OLS to regress hunt on male married, divorced, somecol, hsonly, ba, somepost, postgrad, black, other, income, and south central. Comment on the results. Why is OLS not the appropriate estimation strategy in this circumstance?

b. Estimate the same model as in part (a) with a probit model. Comment on the results. Make sure to estimate the marginal effects.

c. Estimate the same model as in part (a) with a logit model. Comment on the results. Make sure to estimate the marginal effects

d. Which model do you think is the most appropriate to use and why?

E12.2 Using the file **Cigarette Data.xls**, which is collected from the 2003 National Health Interview Survey,

a. Using OLS, regress smoke on black, Hispanic, male, age, family size, married, and divorced. Comment on the results.

b. Estimate the same model as in part (a) with a probit model. Comment on the results. Make sure to estimate the marginal effects.

c. Estimate the same model as in part (a) with a logit model. Comment on the results. Make sure to estimate the marginal effects.

d. Which model do you think is the most appropriate to use and why?

E12.3 Using the file **Publication.xls**, estimate a multinomial logit to investigate the factors that lead a researcher to either not publish (publish = 0), be a moderate publisher (publish = 1), or be a prolific publisher (publish = 2). Make sure to obtain the marginal effects and comment on your results.

E12.4 Using the file **Publication.xls**, estimate an ordered probit to investigate the factors that lead a researcher to either not publish (publish = 0), be a moderate publisher (publish = 1), or be a prolific publisher (publish = 2). Make sure to obtain the marginal effects and comment on your results.

Chapter Thirteen

Panel Data

CHAPTER OBJECTIVES

After reading this chapter, you will be able to:

1. Understand the nature of panel data.
2. Employ pooled cross-section analysis.
3. Estimate panel data models.

A STUDENT'S PERSPECTIVE

Suppose that during a Summer Olympics year you get hooked on following the team medal count, and as a result, you become interested in determining the independent factors that are associated with nations winning more medals.

This is exactly the situation encountered by one of our former students. In an effort to bring her econometric skills to bear, the student collected data on the total medals won by all 102 countries in the 1996, 2000, 2004, and 2008 Olympics. Given that she had data on these 102 countries for four different time periods, the student had a total of 408 observations. Table 13.1 presents summary statistics for these data.

TABLE 13.1
Simple Summary Statistics for Our Former Student's Olympic Medal Count Data

	Total Medals	GDP Per Capita (thousands)	Population (millions)
Mean	8.60	12.37	51.74
Standard Deviation	16.81	16.22	166.91
Minimum	0	0.09	0.09
25th Percentile	0	1.33	4.18
Median	2	4.40	10.31
75th Percentile	8	19.64	38.28
Maximum	110	106.46	1,327.66
Observations	408	408	408

These data suggested to the student that there was a large variance not only in the number of medals won by countries sending athletes to the Olympic Games but also the GDP per capita and population of those countries. In particular, the total numbers of medals won by countries in these four Olympics ranged from 0 to 110, while the GDP per capita and population ranged from \$90.48 to \$106,460 and 85,000 to 1.33 million, respectively.

Having heard that host countries tend to earn more medals during the Olympics that they host (due to increased investment in training and perhaps due to increased national pride), the student added to these data a dummy variable equal to 1 if a given country was host during a given year (i.e., the United States in 1996, Australia in 2000, Greece in 2004, and China in 2008). To determine the degree to which these independent variables are correlated with the total medals won, our former student estimated the regression function in Table 13.2 by OLS.

TABLE 13.2 Regression Results for Our Former Student's Olympic Medal Count Data

SUMMARY OUTPUT	
Regression Statistics	
Multiple R	0.540904716
R Square	0.292577911
Adjusted R Square	0.287324777
Standard Error	14.19059846
Observations	408

ANOVA

	df	SS	MS	F	Significance F
Regression	3	33646.95032	11215.65011	55.69587481	3.77312E-30
Residual	404	81354.72615	201.3730845		
Total	407	115001.6765			

	Coefficients	Standard Error	*t* Stat	*p*-value	Lower 95%	Upper 95%
Intercept	3.10233584	0.92351270	3.35927795	0.000855731	1.28684545	4.91782623
GDP per Capita (thousands)	0.25806112	0.04360884	5.91763325	6.97481E-09	0.17233254	0.34378970
Population (millions)	0.03582928	0.00433408	8.26687093	2.00228E-15	0.02730912	0.04434945
Host Country	46.34122807	7.308093	6.34108352	6.11335E-10	31.97459006	60.70786607

Note: Dependent variable is total medals won. Highlighted variables are significant at the 5 percent level.

These results suggested to our former student that, all other variables constant, (1) each additional $1,000 in GDP per capita was associated with a country winning 0.26 more total medals, (2) each additional 1 million citizens was associated with a 0.036 increase in total medals, and (3) being a host country was associated with a 46.34 increase in total medals won in the year that the country hosted the games.

Our former student was concerned that having data on 102 different countries in four different time periods, she possessed neither pure cross-section data nor pure time-series data. Instead, she realized that she possessed data on a cross-section of countries over multiple periods of time. Given this fact, the student was not sure that OLS was the appropriate estimator for these data.

BIG PICTURE OVERVIEW

panel data
Data for a cross-section of individuals, firms, countries, etc., that are collected for multiple time-periods.

pooled cross-section
Occurs when more than one time period of cross-sectional data are estimated in the same model.

This chapter introduces another situation in which alternative estimators are preferred to OLS. **Panel data** refers to data for the same cross-section of observations that are collected over multiple time periods. For example, panel data sets might consist of a number of different countries for which data are collected over a number of different years, or the annual wages of a number of individual workers collected over a number of different time periods, or the crime rates of a number of U.S. cities collected over a number of different years.

As we have seen many times before, we can almost always estimate models by OLS. In the case of panel data, doing so is referred to as estimating a **pooled cross-section** because such a model simply pools the data from different time periods into one large cross-section for which no differentiation is made for the different time periods. While possible, estimating a pooled cross-section by OLS is not our best estimator because it fails to exploit the significant advantages offered by the panel nature of the data. Namely, because the data are observed for the same individuals over time, there are estimation strategies that control for this unique structure. In the following sections, we introduce three different methods for doing so.

Figure 13.1 depicts the empirical tools introduced in this chapter.

FIGURE 13.1
A Visual Depiction of the Empirical Tools Introduced in This Chapter

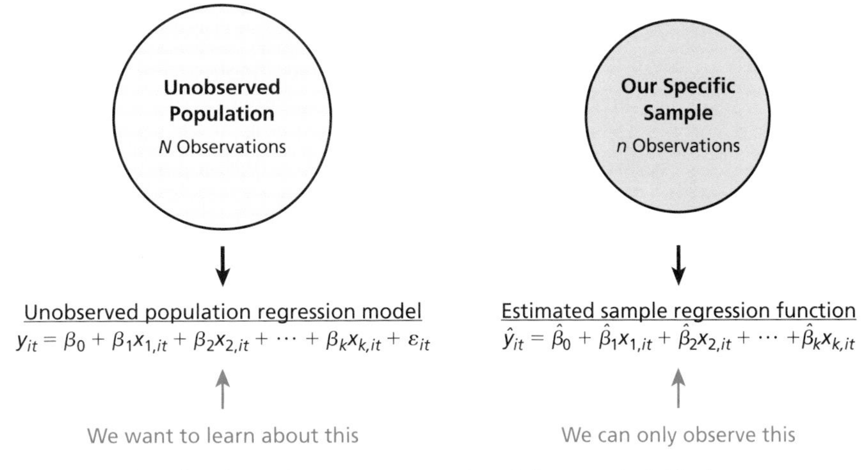

13.1 UNDERSTAND THE NATURE OF PANEL DATA

Given that panel data includes observations on a number of different individuals in a number of different time periods, we write the general population regression model as

$$y_{it} = \beta_0 + \beta_1 x_{1,it} + \beta_2 x_{2,it} + \cdots + \beta_k x_{k,it} + u_{it} \qquad \textbf{13.1.1}$$

where the i designation in the subscript refers to the individual (or firm, or country, etc.), the t designation in the subscript refers to the time period, and the combined it designation in the subscript reflects the fact that the observations vary across both individuals and time periods. As an example of how to read this notation, observation $y_{1,2}$ indicates that the given observation is for individual in time period 2, observation $y_{3,7}$ indicates that the given observation is for individual 3 in time period 7, $x_{2,4,6}$ is the second explanatory variable for individual 4 in time period 6, and so on. Note that whenever dealing with panel data, care should be taken to make sure that this appropriate designation for the subscript is used (we often find students using only one or the other designation but not both).

The distinguishing feature of panel data relates to assumptions that we make about the nature of the error term, u_{it}. As discussed in Chapter 4, the error term is believed to contain a great deal of different information, including factors affecting the dependent variable that are not included as independent variables, specification errors, and inherent randomness in human behavior. In the case of panel data, because the error terms are different in each period, an important concern is whether the composition of the error terms changes over time. To allow for the possibility that some components of the error term change over time while other components remain constant, our conventional assumption is that the error term for panel data is specified as

time-invariant component
The part of the error term that *does not* change over time.

time-variant component
The part of the error term that *does* change over time.

$$u_{it} = (\alpha_i + \varepsilon_{it}) \qquad \textbf{13.1.2}$$

where u_{it} is a composite error term that contains both a **time-invariant component,** α_i, which varies across individuals but not across time periods, and a **time-variant component,** ε_{it}, which varies across both individuals and time periods.

As an example of a composite error term, suppose that we are interested in explaining wage variation in a panel data set of individual workers. We might reasonably assume that an individual's innate work ethic, which is in the error term because it cannot be directly measured, is relatively constant over time for each individual (but varying across individuals), and we might reasonably assume that factors such as time-specific regional economic shocks vary across both individuals and time periods. If so, then the specification in formula 13.1.2 is appropriate.

There is another important assumption that we make about the nature of the time-invariant and the time-variant components of the error term. In addition to being constant over time, we assume that the time-invariant component of the error term is correlated with the independent variables in the population regression model. Conversely, while we assume that in addition to varying over time, the time-variant component of the error term is not correlated with the independent variables in any time period in the population regression model. While it might sound somewhat innocuous at this point, this assumption becomes very important when choosing the estimation technique that is most appropriate.

Before introducing the empirical methods for exploiting the advantages of panel data, we must introduce the data that are the focus of our analysis.

Data to Be Analyzed: Our NFL Team Value Panel

A natural situation in which panel data might be advantageous is firm-level data—such as firm profits, revenues, market values, etc.—that are collected over a number of time periods. Unfortunately, firm-level data are often difficult to come by due to the private nature of most firms. A clear exception to this general rule is NFL franchises, for whom *Forbes* releases widely publicized estimated team values every year (www.forbes.com/lists/2011/30/nfl-valuations-11_land.html). In addition to being publicly accessible firm-level data, the value of NFL teams to their home communities has gained widespread attention due to the contentious public policy question of whether taxpayers should subsidize the construction of new stadiums (McMaken, 2011, www.csmonitor.com/Business/The-Circle-Bastiat/2011/1009/Taxpayers-grumpy-about-funding-professional-sports-stadiums).

Economic theory suggests that a team's market value should depend on several different factors, including the number of fans that attend a team's home games; how much those fans pay for tickets, parking, concessions, and so on; as well as the team's success on the field. To test this theory, following the procedure outlined in Appendix A, we collected data on the estimated values of the 32 NFL teams in 2011, 2009, and 2007. Because these values are calculated at the beginning of the season, all of our independent variables are collected for the season immediately prior. The independent variables that we collect for the 2010, 2008, and 2006 seasons are (1) the total attendance for the eight regular-season home games for each team; (2) the fan cost index, which measures the average cost for a family of four to purchase tickets, pay for parking, and purchase food at each stadium; (3) the number of wins the team had during each season; and (4) whether the team qualified for the playoffs in each season. Figure 13.2 starts our summary analysis by presenting line graphs of the estimated values of the five highest- and lowest-valued teams in our sample.

By showing how the estimated values vary across both teams and time periods, these graphs clearly demonstrate the panel nature of our data. Notable perhaps is that the Dallas Cowboys and the New York Jets and Giants had steep increases in their estimated values between the 2009 and 2011 seasons—both of which coincide nicely with their opening new stadiums during between those time periods. Likewise, given that the St. Louis Rams, Oakland Raiders, Minnesota Vikings, and Jacksonville Jaguars are among the lowest-valued teams and all saw their market values decrease over the length of this panel, it is not surprising that they are all currently embroiled in controversies surrounding proposed new stadiums and are all mentioned as potential candidates to move to Los Angeles if and when a new stadium is built there (Wilson, 2011, http://footballpros.com/showthread.php/5692-NFP-News-AEG-discloses-five-candidates-for-Los-Angeles-relocation.html).

To get a better sense of our data, Table 13.3 presents further summary statistics.

FIGURE 13.2 **Line Graphs of Team Values for the Five Highest-Valued and Five Lowest-Valued NFL Teams in 2011**

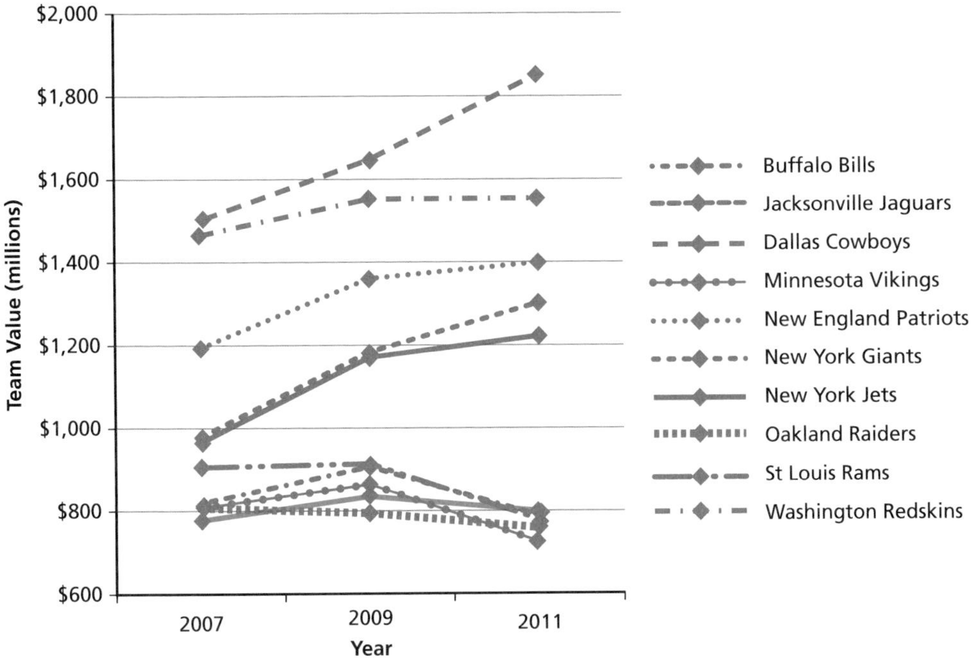

Team Value (millions)
$2,000
$1,800
$1,600
$1,400
$1,200
$1,000
$800
$600
2007
2009
2011
Year

Buffalo Bills
Jacksonville Jaguars
Dallas Cowboys
Minnesota Vikings
New England Patriots
New York Giants
New York Jets
Oakland Raiders
St Louis Rams
Washington Redskins

TABLE 13.3 **Simple Summary Statistics for Our NFL Team Value Data**

	Pooled Cross-Section	Yearly Data 2011	2009	2007
Value	1,012.13	1,036.31	1,042.66	957.41
	(200.60)	(237.50)	(188.49)	(163.48)
Attendance	540,114.40	531,474.10	541,696.10	547,172.90
	(61,592.46)	(71,943.81)	(54,267.46)	(58,083.54)
Fan Cost Index	394.51	420.51	396.36	366.66
	(69.25)	(81.21)	(62.37)	(52.06)
Wins	7.99	8.00	7.97	8.00
	(3.05)	(2.99)	(3.33)	(2.90)
Playoffs	0.375	0.375	0.375	0.375
Observations	96	32	32	32

The mean estimated value of the 32 NFL teams over this period was slightly more than $1 billion, while the mean attendance for the eight regular-season home games was roughly 540,000, or 67,500 per game, and the average cost for a family of four to attend a game and pay for parking, food, and drinks was nearly $400. Given that every team plays 16 games each season, in theory, the average number of wins should be 8.0 because exactly half the teams win should win each game and exactly half of the teams should lose each game. The mean in our sample is 7.99 due to a tie game having been played in the 2009 season. The percentage of teams making the playoffs is defined to be exactly 0.375 in each season because exactly 12 of the 32 teams make the playoffs each year. Note, however, that the identity of the 12 playoff teams changes from year to year. Finally, notice that while each individual year consists of 32 observations, or one for each individual team, our pooled cross-section consists of 96 observations, or three (2007, 2009, and 2011) for each individual team.

While not directly relevant to our analysis, the Mint.com website puts these estimated team values in perspective by comparing them to the GDP of small countries in the chart in Figure 13.3 (www.mint.com/blog/trends/is-your-nfl-team-worth-more-than-a-small-nation-092011/).

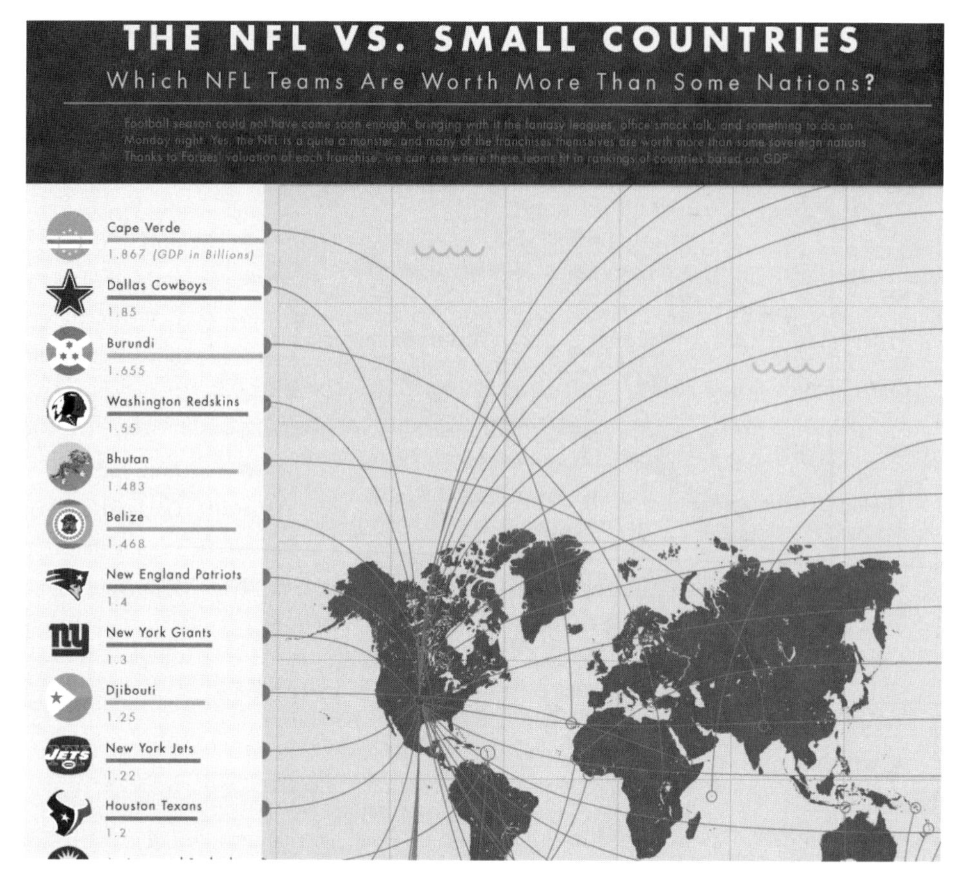

FIGURE 13.3
An Interesting Comparison between the Estimated Market Value of NFL Teams and the National GDP of Some Small Countries

Source: Reprinted with permission from Mint.com: www.mint.com/blog/trends/is-your-nfl-team-worth-more-than-a-small-nation-092011/.

13.2 EMPLOY POOLED CROSS-SECTION ANALYSIS

As a starting point to our analysis, we note that it is possible to treat panel data as regular cross-section data and to estimate OLS for the large pooled cross-section. In such a case, the population regression model that we would estimate can be written as

$$y_i = \beta_0 + \beta_1 x_{1i} + \beta_2 x_{2i} + \cdots + \beta_k x_{ki} + \varepsilon_i \qquad 13.2.1$$

owing to the fact that when estimating a pooled cross-section, we make no distinction between time periods and, therefore, do not need a time-period identifier in the specification of our model.

To estimate a pooled cross-section for our NFL team value data, we would estimate the population regression model

$$\begin{aligned} NFL\ team\ value_i = {} & \beta_0 + \beta_1 (Attendance/10{,}000)_i + \beta_2\,(Attendance/10{,}000_i)^2 \\ & + \beta_3 Fan\ cost\ index_i + \beta_4 (Fan\ cost\ index_i)^2 \\ & + \beta_5 Wins_i + \beta_6 Playoffs_i + \varepsilon_i \qquad 13.2.2 \end{aligned}$$

by OLS and get Excel Regression Output 13.1.

Excel Regression Output 13.1: Pooled Cross-Section for Our NFL Team Value Data

SUMMARY OUTPUT

Regression Statistics	
Multiple R	0.753430328
R Square	0.567657259
Adjusted R Square	0.538510557
Standard Error	136.2735251
Observations	96

ANOVA

	df	SS	MS	F	Significance F
Regression	6	2170056.346	361676.0577	19.47586609	2.19529E-14
Residual	89	1652772.154	18570.47363		
Total	95	3822828.5			

	Coefficients	Standard Error	*t* Stat	*p*-value	Lower 95%	Upper 95%
Intercept	925.5621248	770.2303216	1.20166929	0.23267954	−604.8690852	2455.993335
Attendance/ 10,000	−48.81804229	24.47665429	−1.99447366	0.049160364	−97.45263196	−0.18345262
Attendance/ 10,000 Squared	5.990679347	2.25652794	2.6548217	0.009400251	1.507006488	10.47435221
Fan Cost Index	3.359397701	1.69670767	1.97995079	0.05079838	−0.011924228	6.73071963
Fan Cost Index Squared	−0.002526798	0.00193411	−1.30643782	0.194769813	−0.006369838	0.00131624
Wins	6.463908645	6.94573101	0.93063043	0.354562257	−7.337110631	20.26492793
Playoffs	−49.38763293	42.73948266	−1.15555056	0.250957861	−134.3100728	35.53480694

Note: Dependent variable is a team's estimated market value in a given year. Highlighted variables are significant at the 10 percent level.

These results suggest that, all other independent variables equal, within our pooled cross-section, the most important determinants of a team's estimated market value are factors associated with the stadium in which the team plays. Namely, all other variables constant, beyond an annual home season attendance of 410,000, estimated team value is increasing with attendance at an increasing rate (to see this, recall from Chapter 8 the correct method for interpreting quadratic terms). At the same time, all other independent variables constant, for each dollar increase in the fan cost index, a team's estimated value is expected to increase by nearly $3.4 million. This latter fact likely explains why owners desire to build new stadiums that will allow them to charge higher prices for tickets, parking, and concessions—all of which increase the total cost of attending a home game for the fan but increase the value of the investment for the team's owner.

Pooled Cross-Section Analysis with Year Dummies

A basic first attempt at controlling, at least somewhat, for the cross-time variance in our data is to estimate the pooled cross-section data with dummy variables for $n - 1$ of the years covered in our panel (because we must omit one outcome when including a series of dummy variables). Table 13.4 demonstrates how we create binary dummy variables for the $n - 1$ years 2009 and 2011 (with 2007 as the omitted group) for our NFL team value data.

TABLE 13.4
Pooled Cross-Section Data with Year Dummies for the First Three Teams in Our NFL Team Value Data

Team ID	Team	Year	Value	2009	2011
1	Arizona Cardinals	2007	888	0	0
1	Arizona Cardinals	2009	935	1	0
1	Arizona Cardinals	2011	901	0	1
2	Atlanta Falcons	2007	796	0	0
2	Atlanta Falcons	2009	856	1	0
2	Atlanta Falcons	2011	814	0	1
3	Baltimore Ravens	2007	965	0	0
3	Baltimore Ravens	2009	1079	1	0
3	Baltimore Ravens	2011	1088	0	1

After calculating these variables, the population regression model that we wish to estimate can be written as

$$y_i = \beta_0 + \beta_1 x_{1i} + \beta_2 x_{2i} + \cdots + \beta_k x_{ki} + \beta_{k+1} t_{2i} + \cdots + \beta_{k+(T-1)} t_{Ti} + \varepsilon_i \qquad 13.2.3$$

where time period $t = 1$ (or t_{1i}) is the omitted time period and the subscripts on the independent variables include only the i term because we still are not controlling in any other way for the time element of our data.

For our NFL team value data, we would estimate the population regression model as

$$NFL\ team\ value_i = \beta_0 + \beta_1(Attendance/10{,}000)_i + \beta_2(Attendance/10{,}000_i)^2$$
$$+ \beta_3 Fan\ cost\ index_i + \beta_4(Fan\ cost\ index_i)^2$$
$$+ \beta_5 Wins_i + \beta_6 Playoffs_i + \beta_7 2009_i + \beta_8 2011_i + \varepsilon_i \qquad 13.2.4$$

by OLS and get Excel Regression Output 13.2.

Excel Regression Output 13.2: Pooled Cross-Section with Year Dummy Variables Output for Our NFL Team Value Data

SUMMARY OUTPUT

Regression Statistics	
Multiple R	0.763052548
R Square	0.582249191
Adjusted R Square	0.543835323
Standard Error	135.4850672
Observations	96

ANOVA

	df	SS	MS	F	Significance F
Regression	8	2225838.801	278229.8502	15.15726556	1.0521E-13
Residual	87	1596989.699	18356.20343		
Total	95	3822828.5			

	Coefficients	Standard Error	*t* Stat	*p*-value	Lower 95%	Upper 95%
Intercept	1092.278096	779.8786425	1.40057444	0.16489792	−457.8151209	2642.371312
Attendance/ 10,000	−53.4798999	24.86675656	−2.15065844	0.03427652	−102.9052702	−4.05452965
Attendance/ 10,000 Squared	6.46463105	2.29151073	2.82112188	0.00592768	1.91000545	11.01925665
Fan Cost Index	3.00326897	1.70003730	1.76659005	0.08080428	−0.375739177	6.382277126
Fan Cost Index Squared	−0.00223501	0.00193022	−1.15790835	0.25007034	−0.006071529	0.001601501
Wins	7.25997782	6.92275266	1.04871258	0.29721503	−6.499742419	21.01969805
Playoffs	−48.3899886	42.49716996	−1.13866379	0.25796916	−132.8577138	36.07773663
2009	61.74232114	35.44382892	1.74197662	0.08504669	−8.706125301	132.1907676
2011	35.09144796	36.42943486	0.96327182	0.33808096	−37.31599697	107.4988929

Note: Dependent variable is a team's estimated market value in a given year. Variables highlighted in blue are significant at the 10 percent level. Variables highlighted in gray are significant at the 5 percent level.

These estimates are fairly similar to those obtained in Excel Regression Output 13.1, but they now add the fact that, all other variables equal, the market value of NFL teams was estimated to be a statistically significant \$62 million higher in 2009 than 2007 but not significantly different in 2011 than 2007. This likely results from the decreases in attendance and total spending that accompanied the onset of the Great Recession in the United States. Note that in estimating this model, we are implicitly assuming that the estimated slope coefficients remain constant over time.

There is an important issue associated with employing pooled cross-section analysis for panel data. Recall that among the six assumptions required for OLS to provide estimates that are BLUE, assumption M5 is that the error term and the independent variables are uncorrelated, or $Cov(\varepsilon_i, x_i) = 0$. In the case of panel data, by assuming that the time-invariant component of the error term is correlated with the independent variables in the population regression model, we are implicitly assuming that assumption M5 is violated because if one component of the error term is correlated with the independent variables, then the composite error terms are also correlated with the independent variables (i.e., because $Cov(\alpha_i, x_i) \neq 0$, $Cov(\varepsilon_{it}, x_i) \neq 0$). In other words, given our assumption about the nature of the time-invariant component of the error term, estimating a pooled cross-section by OLS for panel data provides estimates that are biased.

The issue and consequences associated with pooled cross-section analysis for panel data are summarized in the following box.

The Issues and Consequences Associated with Employing Pooled Cross-Section Analysis for Panel Data

Problem:
Because we assume that the time-invariant component of the error-term, α_i, is correlated with the independent variables in the population regression model, assumption M5 that the error term is uncorrelated with the independent variables is violated.

Consequences:
Because assumption M5 is violated, our

1. Parameter estimates are biased.
2. Estimates are not BLUE.
3. Standard errors and statistical tests are incorrect.

Given that our estimates become biased due to the fact that the time-invariant component of the error term, α_i, is assumed to be correlated with the independent variables in the population regression model, a rather obvious solution for generating unbiased estimates might be to remove the time-invariant term from the population regression model. This is exactly the correction that we propose in the next section.

Before introducing those methods, there is a final point that we should consider concerning pooled cross-section analysis.

While not the focus of this chapter, there is a situation in which pooled cross-section analysis is appropriate for data containing observations on different individuals, firms, countries, and so on, in different time periods. Suppose that rather than possessing a true panel of data (observations on the same cross-section of individuals across different time-periods), we possess data on different cross-sections of individuals in different time periods. Perhaps the most well-known example of such data is the monthly Current Population Survey. According to www.census.gov/cps, "The Current Population Survey (CPS), sponsored jointly by the U.S. Census Bureau and the U.S. Bureau of Labor Statistics (BLS), is the primary source of labor force statistics for the population of the United States." The CPS collects data on a "probability selected sample" of about 60,000 occupied households from all 50 states and the District of Columbia that are in the survey for four consecutive months, out for eight, and then returned for another four months before leaving the sample permanently. Accordingly, the CPS data are not a true panel because the surveyed individuals move in and out of the sample, meaning that the monthly surveys are composed of different cross-sections of individuals. In such a case, it would be entirely appropriate to estimate a pooled cross-section with dummy variables for different time periods in order to increase the number of observations in addition to increase the variation in the independent variables.

13.3 ESTIMATE PANEL DATA MODELS

first-differenced data
Occurs when the previous observation of a variable is subtracted off the current period.

A first pass at controlling for time-period differences in panel data is to estimate a **first-differenced data** regression model. The process of first-differencing data consists of subtracting the values of both the dependent variable and the independent variables in the previous time period, $t - 1$, from the values of the dependent and independent variables in the current time period, t. The simplest way to demonstrate this process is in a two-period model.

First-Differenced Data in a Two-Period Model

After first-differencing the data in our two-period model, we have

$$\begin{aligned} \Delta y_{it} &= (y_{i2} - y_{i1}) \\ \Delta x_{1,it} &= (x_{1,i2} - x_{1,i1}) \\ \Delta x_{2,it} &= (x_{2,i2} - x_{2,i1}) \\ &\vdots \\ \Delta x_{k,it} &= (x_{k,i2} - x_{k,i1}) \end{aligned} \qquad \textbf{13.3.1}$$

and

$$\Delta u_{it} = u_{i2} - u_{i1} = (\alpha_i + \varepsilon_{i2}) - (\alpha_i + \varepsilon_{i1}) = \varepsilon_{i2} - \varepsilon_{i1} \qquad \textbf{13.3.2}$$

The population regression model that we then wish to estimate is then

$$\Delta y_{it} = \beta_0 + \beta_1 \Delta x_{1,it} + \beta_2 \Delta x_{2,it} + \cdots \beta_k \Delta x_{k,it} + \Delta u_{it} \qquad \textbf{13.3.3}$$

Formula 13.3.3 demonstrates the value of first-differencing our data. Namely, doing so theoretically solves the potential problem presented by the time-invariant component potentially being correlated with one or more of our independent variables by removing the time-invariant component from the error term (i.e., the error term in formula 13.3.2 now equals $\varepsilon_{i2} - \varepsilon_{i1}$, which no longer includes the time-invariant component α_i).

For illustration purposes, we create a two-period model by limiting our NFL team value data to the years 2007 and 2009. Table 13.5 demonstrates how we first-difference these data by subtracting the 2007 values from the 2009 values.

TABLE 13.5 Calculating the First-Differenced Data for the First Three Teams in Our 2007–2009 NFL Team Value Data

Team ID	Team (i)	Year (t)	Regular Data Value ($y_{i,t}$)	First-Differenced Data Value ($\Delta y_{it} = y_{i2} - y_{i1}$)	Regular Data Attendance/ 10,000 ($x_{i,t}$)	First-Differenced Data Attendance/10,000 ($\Delta x_{1,it} = x_{1,i2} - x_{1,i1}$)
1	Arizona Cardinals	2009	935	47	51.2775	0.3946
1	Arizona Cardinals	2007	888		50.8829	
2	Atlanta Falcons	2009	856	60	51.2527	−5.0935
2	Atlanta Falcons	2007	796		56.3462	
3	Baltimore Ravens	2009	1079	114	57.0152	0.3605
3	Baltimore Ravens	2007	965		56.6547	

Table 13.6 presents the results of completing the calculations for all 32 teams.

TABLE 13.6 The First-Differenced Data for the First Five Teams in Our 2007–2009 NFL Team Value Data

Team ID	Team	Value	Attendance/ 10,000	Attendance/ 10,000 Squared	Fan Cost Index	Fan Cost Index Squared	Wins	Playoffs
1	Arizona Cardinals	47	0.3946	4.031249384	14.46	10095.3936	4	1
2	Atlanta Falcons	60	−5.0935	−54.80549972	33.46	22724.0244	4	1
3	Baltimore Ravens	114	0.3605	4.097799895	14	11726.68	−2	0
4	Buffalo Bills	88	−4.1334	−43.02885934	24.13	13845.5527	0	0
5	Carolina Panthers	93	−0.2859	−3.357114993	31.51	19845.9433	4	1

We now estimate the first-differenced population regression model

$$\Delta NFL\ team\ value_i = \beta_0 + \beta_1\Delta(Attendance/10{,}000)_i + \beta_2\Delta(Attendance/10{,}000_i)^2 + \beta_3\Delta\ Fan\ cost\ index_i + \beta_4\Delta(Fan\ cost\ index_i)^2 + \beta_5\Delta Wins_i + \beta_6\Delta Playoffs_i + \Delta u_{it} \quad \textbf{13.3.4}$$

by OLS and get Excel Regression Output 13.3.

Excel Regression Output 13.3: OLS Regression for the First-Differenced Data for Our Two-Period NFL Team Value Data

SUMMARY OUTPUT

Regression Statistics	
Multiple R	0.787519788
R Square	0.620187417
Adjusted R Square	0.529032397
Standard Error	33.43993145
Observations	32

Total number of teams in the NFL in 2007 and 2009 combined

ANOVA

	df	SS	MS	F	Significance F
Regression	6	45648.27461	7608.045768	6.803656193	0.000228862
Residual	25	27955.72539	1118.229016		
Total	31	73604			

	Coefficients	Standard Error	*t* Stat	*p*-value	Lower 95%	Upper 95%
Intercept	84.50565489	11.74147626	7.197191649	1.52737E-07	60.32363206	108.6876777
Differenced Attendance/ 10,000	−54.72525073	18.30262704	−2.990021629	0.006184609	−92.42021643	−17.0302850
Differenced Attendance/ 10,000 Square	5.565247826	1.853717823	3.002208728	0.006006217	1.747444536	9.383051117
Differenced Fan Cost Index	−1.178124177	1.163788587	−1.012318036	0.321083945	−3.57499162	1.218743265
Differenced Fan Cost Index Squared	0.001743397	0.001185153	1.471031556	0.153758621	−0.000697471	0.004184266
Differenced Wins	7.571994673	2.465719286	3.070907024	0.005089077	2.493750786	12.65023856
Differenced Playoffs	−45.59396529	13.24268158	−3.442955645	0.002036479	−72.86777831	−18.32015227

Note: Dependent variable is a team's estimated market value in a given year. Highlighted variables are significant at the 10 percent level.

We interpret these results exactly the way that we would interpret any regular OLS estimates. Namely, all other independent variables equal, we estimate that a quadratic relationship exists between fan attendance and estimated team value, that each additional win during the season increases a team's estimated value by \$7.57 million, and that teams making the playoffs average estimated market values that are \$45.6 million lower than those for teams not making the playoffs.

Empirical Research Tool 13.1 summarizes the first-differenced method.

EMPIRICAL RESEARCH TOOL 13.1: FIRST-DIFFERENCED ESTIMATES FOR PANEL DATA

How to Do It:

1. Create new variables that equal the difference between the observed values in time period t and the observed values in time period $t - 1$ for the dependent variable and all of the independent variables (i.e., calculate $\Delta y_i = y_{i,t} - y_{i,t-1}$, $\Delta x_{1,i} = x_{1,i,t} - x_{1,i,t-1}$, and so on, through $\Delta x_{k,i}$).
2. Estimate the population regression model $\Delta y_i = \beta_0 + \beta_1 \Delta x_{1,i} + \beta_2 \Delta x_{2,i} + \cdots + \beta_k \Delta x_{k,i} + \Delta u_i$ by OLS.

Why It Works:

First-differencing the data removes the time-invariant component α_i from the error term because $\Delta u_i = u_{i2} - u_{i1} = (\alpha_i + \varepsilon_{i2}) - (\alpha_i + \varepsilon_{i1}) = \varepsilon_{i2} - \varepsilon_{i1}$. Doing so generates unbiased estimates because α_i, which is correlated with the independent variables, is removed through the differencing.

Notes:

In first-differenced models, it is impossible to estimate marginal effects for two types of independent variables:

1. Those that are constant across time periods, such as gender, years of education, marital status, and race, because all of the first-differenced values equal 0.
2. Those that increase by a fixed amount over time, such as years of age, work experience, and so on, because all of the first-differenced values will equal the same fixed value.

For the sake of simplicity, our discussion of first-differencing has focused on a two-period model. It should be noted that we can apply the technique to models with more than two time periods. As an example, for a four-period model, our first-differenced dependent variable would be

$$\begin{aligned} \Delta y_{4t} &= (y_{i4} - y_{i3}) \\ \Delta y_{3t} &= (y_{i3} - y_{i2}) \\ \Delta y_{2t} &= (y_{i2} - y_{i1}) \end{aligned} \qquad \textbf{13.3.5}$$

and so on while our first-differenced independent variables would be calculated in a similar fashion. We would then estimate the four-period first-differenced population regression model by OLS in the same way that we estimated the two-period first-differenced population regression model.

There are two alternative methods controlling for the time-invariant component of the error term that are more popular in empirical applications.

Fixed-Effects Panel Data Models

fixed-effects model
A method of removing the time-invariant component of the error term in panel data.

An alternative to first-differencing that can be used to remove the time-invariant component of the error term is referred to as a **fixed-effects model.** There are two possible methods of estimating such models. The first is to estimate a constant-free model that includes individual dummy variables for every single observation in the sample.

As an example, suppose that our sample consists of three individuals (or firms, or countries, etc.) *A*, *B*, and *C*. To implement this method for controlling for fixed effects, we would estimate the population regression model

$$y_i = \beta_1 x_{1i} + \beta_2 x_{2i} + \cdots + \beta_k x_{ki} + \beta_{k+1} A + \beta_{k+2} B + \beta_{k+3} C + \varepsilon_i \qquad \textbf{13.3.6}$$

where *A*, *B*, and *C* are binary dummy variables that are equal to 1 if the observation is for individual *A*, individual *B*, or individual *C*, respectively, and 0 otherwise.

The intuition behind this estimation method is that the estimated coefficients for the individual dummy variables provide estimates of α_i for each individual, thereby providing a simple way of removing the individual-specific component from the error term and putting it directly into the regression model. While this is the most straightforward approach to solving the problem, adding dummy variables for every individual is potentially time-consuming and consumes large numbers of degrees of freedom.

The second, more sophisticated method for estimating a fixed-effects model is to remove the individual effect α_i by "demeaning" the data (which is often referred to as applying a within-transformation to the data) and then estimating the quasi-differenced regression by OLS. The method for demeaning the data is to subtract the mean value for each individual from the individual observations for each individual:

$$\begin{aligned}
\tilde{y}_{it} &= (y_{it} - \bar{y}_i) \\
\tilde{x}_{1,it} &= (x_{1,it} - \bar{x}_{1,i}) \\
\tilde{x}_{2,it} &= (x_{2,it} - \bar{x}_{2,i}) \\
&\vdots \\
\tilde{x}_{k,it} &= (x_{k,it} - \bar{x}_{k,i})
\end{aligned} \qquad \textbf{13.3.7}$$

where

$$\begin{aligned}
\bar{y}_i &= \sum_{t=1}^{T} y_{it}/T \\
\bar{x}_{1,i} &= \sum_{t=1}^{T} x_{1,it}/T \\
\bar{x}_{2,i} &= \sum_{t=1}^{T} x_{2,it}/T \\
&\vdots \\
\bar{x}_{k,i} &= \sum_{t=1}^{T} x_{k,it}/T
\end{aligned}$$

and

$$\tilde{u}_{it} = u_{it} - \bar{u}_i = (\alpha_i + \varepsilon_{it}) - (\bar{\alpha}_i + \bar{\varepsilon}_i) = \varepsilon_{it} - \bar{\varepsilon}_i = \tilde{\varepsilon}_{it} \qquad \textbf{13.3.8}$$

where

$$\begin{aligned}
\bar{u}_i &= \sum_{t=1}^{T} u_{it}/T \\
\bar{\alpha}_i &= \sum_{t=1}^{T} \alpha_i/T = \alpha_i
\end{aligned}$$

The population regression model that we wish to estimate can then be written as

$$\tilde{y}_{it} = \beta_0 + \beta_1 \tilde{x}_{1,it} + \beta_2 \tilde{x}_{2,it} + \cdots \beta_k \tilde{x}_{k,it} + \tilde{\varepsilon}_{it} \qquad \textbf{13.3.9}$$

Formula 13.3.8 highlights the potential value of differencing the data in this manner because the quasi-differenced error term in formula 13.3.8 no longer includes the time-invariant component α_i.

After first declaring the data to be panel data (by typing "**xtset id time**"), using the Stata command

```
xtreg value attendance attendancesquared fancostindex
fancostindexsquared wins playoffs, fe
```

for our NFL team value data, we get Empirical Results 13.1.

Empirical Results 13.1: Estimating a Fixed-Effects Model for Our NFL Team Value Data

	Coefficient	Standard Error	t	P > |t|	Lower 95%	Upper 95%
Intercept	−232.73230	475.0128	−0.49	0.626	−1183.574	718.1092
Attendance/ 10,000	15.42717	15.71766	0.98	0.330	−16.03515	46.88948
Attendance/ 10,000 Squared	−1.22295	1.51063	−0.81	0.422	−4.24681	1.80092
Fan Cost Index	2.3211	1.15787	2.00	0.050	0.00337	4.63883
Fan Cost Index Squared	−0.00106	0.00126	−0.84	0.403	−0.00358	0.0014586
Wins	5.28042	3.46289	1.52	0.133	−1.65130	12.21214
Playoffs	−39.26036	19.7567	−1.99	0.052	−78.80768	0.28696

sigma u	158.09977
sigma e	50.489242
rho	0.90745358 (fraction of variance due to u_i)
Prob > F	0.0000
R-Squared:	
Within	0.5735
Between	0.3450
Overall	0.3631
Observations	96
Groups	32

Total number of teams in NFL in 2007, 2009, 2011 combined (→ Observations)

Number of NFL teams each year (→ Groups)

Note: Dependent variable is a team's estimated market value in a given year. Variables highlighted in blue are significant at the 10 percent level. Variables highlighted in gray are significant at the 5 percent level.

These results can be interpreted as follows. All other independent variables equal, after controlling for the team fixed effect, we estimate that each additional \$1 in a team's fan cost index is associated with a statistically significant increase of \$2.32 million in the team's estimated market value. Likewise, during the 2006, 2008, and 2010 seasons, the estimated market values of NFL teams making the playoffs averaged \$39.26 million less than the estimated market values of teams missing the playoffs, holding all other variables constant.

Empirical Research Tool 13.2 summarizes the fixed-effects model.

EMPIRICAL RESEARCH TOOL 13.2: FIXED-EFFECTS PANEL DATA MODEL

How to Do It:

1. Create new demeaned variables that equal the difference between the observed values and the average value for the individual over time for the dependent variable and all of the independent variables (i.e., calculate $\tilde{y}_{it} = (y_{it} - \bar{y}_i)$, $\tilde{x}_{1,it} = (x_{1,it} - \bar{x}_{1,i})$, and so on).
2. Estimate the population regression model $\tilde{y}_{it} = \beta_0 + \beta_1\tilde{x}_{1,it} + \beta_2\tilde{x}_{2,it} + \cdots \beta_k\tilde{x}_{k,it} + \tilde{\varepsilon}_{it}$ by OLS.

Why It Works:

Differencing the data removes the time-invariant component α_i from the error term because $\tilde{u}_{it} = u_{it} - \bar{u}_i = (\alpha_i + \varepsilon_{it}) - (\bar{\alpha}_i + \bar{\alpha}_i) = \varepsilon_{it} - \bar{\varepsilon}_i = \tilde{\varepsilon}_{it}$. Doing so increases the efficiency of our estimates by exploiting the panel nature of our data to control for an unobserved component of the error term that does not change over time.

Notes:
In fixed-effects models, it is impossible to estimate marginal effects for two types of independent variables.
1. Those that are constant across time periods, such as gender, years of education, marital status, and race, because all of the first-differenced values equal 0.
2. Those that increase by a fixed amount over time, such as years of age, work experience, and so on, because all of the first-differenced values will equal the same fixed value.

Note that this approach assumes that α_i is related to the independent variables. Suppose that this is not the case and that α_i is unrelated to the independent variables. In such a case, we do not need to remove α_i from our model (because it is not correlated with the independent variables), and therefore, its presence does not bias our estimates as it would if it were related to the independent variables. This does not mean that we should not take steps to account for the presence of α_i, however, because its presence will cause OLS to provide estimates that, while unbiased, will not be the most efficient estimates.

Random-Effects Panel Data Models

random-effects model
A method of removing the time-invariant component of the error term in panel data.

The **random-effects model** is similar to the fixed-effects model, but it allows us to control for that time-invariant component of the error term without completely removing the term itself. In doing so, it increases the efficiency of our estimates because it retains the information that is lost if we completely remove the time-invariant term.

To estimate the random-effects model, we start by quasi-differencing the data in a manner that accounts for potential differences across time-periods by calculating

$$\begin{aligned}\tilde{y}_{it} &= (y_{it} - \lambda\bar{y}_i)\\ \tilde{x}_{1,it} &= (x_{1,it} - \lambda\bar{x}_{1,i})\\ \tilde{x}_{2,it} &= (x_{2,it} - \lambda\bar{x}_{2,i})\\ &\vdots\\ \tilde{x}_{k,it} &= (x_{k,it} - \lambda\bar{x}_{k,i})\end{aligned} \tag{13.3.10}$$

and

$$\tilde{u}_{it} = u_{it} - \lambda\bar{u}_i \tag{13.3.11}$$

where λ is a weight between 0 and 1 that accounts for the fact that there is an individual component to the variance of the composite error term.

The population regression model that we wish to estimate can then be written as

$$\tilde{y}_{it} = \beta_0 + \beta_1\tilde{x}_{1,it} + \beta_2\tilde{x}_{2,it} + \cdots \beta_k\tilde{x}_{k,it} + \tilde{u}_{it} \tag{13.3.12}$$

The random-effects procedure estimates formula 13.2.12 by OLS after first estimating λ with our data. Note that the estimated value of λ provides valuable information about the correct specification of the model. If $\lambda = 0$, then the random-effects model is equivalent to the pooled OLS model presented earlier. If $\lambda = 1$, then the random-effects model is equivalent to the fixed-effects model.

After first declaring the data to be panel data (by typing "xtset id time"), using the Stata command

```
xtreg value attendance attendancesquared fancostindex
fancostindexsquared wins playoffs, re
```

for our NFL team value data, we get Empirical Results 13.2.

Empirical Results 13.2: Estimating a Random-Effects Model for Our NFL Team Value Data

	Coefficient	Standard Error	*t*	P > |*t*|	Lower 95%	Upper 95%
Intercept	−108.182	471.1432	−0.23	0.818	−1031.606	815.2418
Attendance	1.11487	15.56764	0.07	0.943	−29.39714	31.62688
Attendance Squared	0.450142	1.482184	0.30	0.761	−2.45489	3.35517
Fan Cost Index	3.074871	1.108368	2.77	0.006	0.90251	5.24723
Fan Cost Index Squared	−0.001986	0.001215	−1.63	0.102	−0.00437	0.000395
Wins	5.997044	3.499039	1.71	0.087	−0.86095	12.85503
Playoffs	−41.0834	20.39557	−2.01	0.044	−81.05799	−1.10881
sigma u			129.73777			
sigma e			50.489242			
rho			0.86847136 (fraction of variance due to u_i)			
Prob > F			0.0000			
R-Squared:						
Within			0.5535			
Between			0.4659			
Overall			0.4672			
Observations			96	← Total number of teams in NFL in 2007, 2009, 2011 combined		
Groups			32	← Number of NFL teams each year		

Note: Dependent variable is a team's estimated market value in a given year. Variables highlighted in blue are significant at the 10 percent level. Variables highlighted in gray are significant at the 5 percent level.

Notice that these results for the random-effects model are quite different than the results for the fixed-effects model in Empirical Results 13.1. In the random-effects model, all other variables constant, we estimate that each additional $1 a team in the fan cost index is associated with a statistically significant increase of $3.07 million in a team's estimated market value. Likewise, during the 2006, 2008, and 2010 seasons, the estimated market values of NFL teams making the playoffs averaged $41.08 million less than the estimated market values of teams missing the playoffs, holding all other variables constant. These two estimates are both somewhat larger than the estimates for the fixed-effects model. More significant differences are that we now estimate each additional game a team wins during these three seasons to increase a team's value by a marginally significant $6 million, all other variables equal, and we estimate the quadratic term for the fan cost index to achieve marginal significance. The reason for these differences is that random effects simply controls for the time-invariant component of the error rather than removing it completely.

Empirical Research Tool 13.3 summarizes the random-effects model.

Now that we have introduced the random-effects model, we note that it will generally be considered inappropriate for economic applications because, in nearly all of the

EMPIRICAL RESEARCH TOOL 13.3: RANDOM-EFFECTS PANEL DATA MODEL

How to Do It:

1. Create new variables that equal the difference between the observed values and the average value for the individual over time multiplied by λ for the dependent variable and all of the independent variables (i.e., calculate $\tilde{y}_{it} = (y_{it} - \lambda\bar{y}_i)$, $\tilde{x}_{1,it} = (x_{1,it} - \lambda\bar{x}_{1,i})$, and so on).
2. Estimate the population regression model $\tilde{y}_{it} = \beta_0 + \beta_1\tilde{x}_{1,it} + \beta_2\tilde{x}_{2,it} + \cdots \beta_k\tilde{x}_{k,it} + \tilde{\varepsilon}_{it}$ by OLS.

Why It Works:

Quasi-differencing the data in this case does not remove the time-invariant component α_i from the error term because it does not cause bias because the α_i are not correlated with the error term. This process does, however, increase efficiency because it accounts for the fact that the individual values are related to each other over time.

economic cases that we encounter, the time-invariant component of the error term, α_i, will be correlated with one or more the independent variables, rendering the fixed-effects model more appropriate.

ADDITIONS TO OUR EMPIRICAL RESEARCH TOOLKIT

In this chapter, we have introduced a number of tools that will prove valuable when performing empirical research:

- Methods for employing pooled cross-section analysis.
- Methods for estimating panel data models, including first-differencing, fixed effects, and panel effects.

OUR NEW EMPIRICAL TOOLS IN PRACTICE: USING WHAT WE HAVE LEARNED IN THIS CHAPTER

On the basis of her training, our former student decided to estimate a fixed-effects model for her Olympic medal count data, obtaining the results shown in Table 13.7.

TABLE 13.7 **Estimated Marginal Effects for the Fixed-Effects Estimation for Our Former Student's Olympics Medal Count Data**

	Coefficient	Standard Error	t	P > |t|	Lower 95%	Upper 95%
Intercept	6.416939	0.8109548	7.91	0.000	4.82112	8.01276
GDP per Capita (thousands)	0.0019489	0.0228597	0.09	0.932	−0.04304	0.04694
Population (millions)	0.038982	0.0144143	2.70	0.007	0.01062	0.06735
Host Country	14.79442	2.045549	7.23	0.000	10.76914	18.8197
sigma u			14.836322			
sigma e			3.5272125			
rho			0.9465026 (fraction of variance due to u_i)			
Prob > F			0.0000			
R-Squared:						
Within			0.1717			
Between			0.1957			
Overall			0.1947			
Observations			408			
Groups			102			

Note: Dependent variables is a team's estimated market value in a given year. Highlighted variables are significant at the 5 percent level.

The student interpreted these results as suggesting that, all other variables constant, every 1 million additional citizens is associated with a 0.039 increase in the total number of medals won, while being a host country is associated with an additional 14.79 medals won in the country that hosted the games. More importantly, the student focused on the fact that GDP per capita became statistically insignificant and the estimated marginal effect of being a host country shrank by roughly two-thirds when estimating the fixed-effects model rather than the pooled cross-section model. Considering these changes in more detail, the student decided that they were not that surprising given that the countries winning the most medals in the four Olympic Games included in the sample were the United States, Russia, and China and that of those countries, the United States (1996) and China (2008) both hosted the Olympics during the time periods covered by her panel.

Based on this work, from the initial idea through data collection, empirical analysis, interpretation of results, and effective write-up, our former student was judged to have conducted a successful empirical research project.

LOOKING AHEAD TO CHAPTER 14

We occasionally encounter situations in which, due to certain aspects of the data we collect, we are unable to uniquely identify the marginal effect that we wish to estimate. For instance, we have difficulty estimating the marginal effect of obesity on health because obese people are not only obese but they are also more likely to have high blood pressure, less likely to exercise regularly, etc. Accordingly, if we simply regress overall health on an indicator of obesity, we confound the effects that obesity, high blood pressure, lack of exercise, and so on, have on health, thereby rendering our estimated marginal effect of obesity on health biased. Fortunately, there are empirical tools that we can use to help us better identify the estimated marginal effects in such cases. We discuss these tools in Chapter 14.

Problems

13.1 You have a data set that has two years of individual data on wages, experience, education level, and score on a job proficiency test. Call the two time periods time period 1 and time period 2.

  a. Write out the model assuming you organize the data set as a pooled cross-section.
  b. Write out a new model that allows the intercept to change between the two years.
  c. Write out another model that allows both the slope and the intercept to change between the two years.
  d. Describe in detail how you would test if the slopes differ between the two time periods.

13.2 As in problem 13.1, you have a data set that has two years of individual data on wages, experience, education level, and score on a job proficiency test. Now you are going to exploit the time nature of these data.

  a. Describe how you would estimate this model through first-differencing.
  b. Describe how you would estimate this model through fixed effects by demeaning the observations.
  c. Describe how you would estimate this model through fixed effects using dummy variables.
  d. Will you get different results if you use first-differencing or fixed effects?
  e. Why would you use panel data techniques over pooled cross-section?
  f. What will happen to the education variable when you use either first-differencing or fixed effects?

13.3 Explain why you can't use an independent cross-section to use panel data techniques such as first-differencing and fixed effects.

Exercises

E13.1 Use the file **Life Expectancy.xls**.

a. Regress Life Expectancy on Population, GDP, and Health Expenditure as a pooled cross-section.

b. Regress Life Expectancy on Population, GDP, and Health Expenditure as a pooled cross-section controlling for the number of years.

c. Now regress Life Expectancy on GDP per Capita and Health Expenditure as a pooled cross-section, controlling for the number of years, and compare your results to what you found in parts (a) and (b). Which specification do you feel is a better fit?

E13.2 Use the file **Life Expectancy.xls**.

a. Use first differencing to estimate the regression of Life Expectancy on Population, GDP, and Health Expenditure.

b. Now use first-differencing to estimate the regression of Life Expectancy on GDP per Capita and Health Expenditure.

c. Compare your results to what you found in problem C13.1.

E13.3 Estimate a fixed-effects model using the NFL data with only using years 2007 and 2009. Comment on the results, and compare your estimates to the first-differenced estimates in Excel Regression Output 13.3.

E13.4 Estimate a random-effects model using the Olympics data. Comment on the results. Do you think that this is the best method to estimate this model? Explain.

E13.5 Use the file **Life Expectancy.xls**.

a. Estimate the model Life Expectancy on Population, GDP, and Health Expenditure using the dummy variable method of fixed effects.

b. Estimate the model Life Expectancy on Population, GDP, and Health Expenditure using the differencing method of fixed effects. Make sure your results match in parts (a) and (b).

c. Estimate the model Life Expectancy on Population, GDP, and Health Expenditure using random effects.

d. Comment on the differences.

Chapter **Fourteen**

Instrumental Variables for Simultaneous Equations, Endogenous Independent Variables, and Measurement Error

CHAPTER OBJECTIVES

After reading this chapter, you will be able to:

1. Use two-stage least squares to identify simultaneous demand and supply equations.
2. Use two-stage least squares to correct for endogeneity of an independent variable.
3. Use two-stage least squares to correct for measurement error.

A STUDENT'S PERSPECTIVE

Suppose that having been raised in a dairy farming family, you are interested in determining the relationship between milk output prices and milk input prices.

This is exactly the situation encountered by a former student of ours. In an effort to bring his econometric skills to bear, the student collected data on milk production and milk prices. Figure 14.1 presents line graphs for these data.

FIGURE 14.1 **Line Graphs for the Dependent and Independent Variables for Our Former Student's Milk Supply Data**

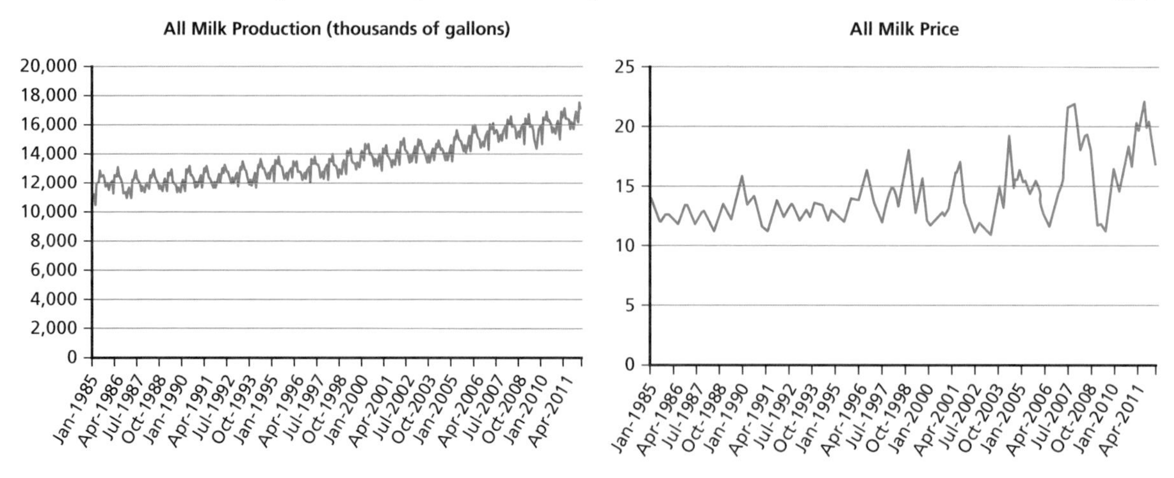

Looking at these line graphs, our former student concluded that milk production and milk prices tended to move upward in a somewhat similar fashion. To determine the exact degree to which the two were linearly related, he estimated the sample regression function in Table 14.1.

TABLE 14.1 **Estimated OLS Sample Regression Function for Our Former Student's Milk Supply Data**

SUMMARY OUTPUT	
Regression Statistics	
Multiple R	0.707400091
R Square	0.500414889
Adjusted R Square	0.497340519
Standard Error	1086.748495
Observations	328

ANOVA

	df	SS	MS	F	Significance F
Regression	2	384469764.6	192234882.3	162.7699016	1.05692E-49
Residual	325	383832244.9	1181022.292		
Total	327	768302009.5			

	Coefficients	Standard Error	*t* Stat	*p*-value	Lower 95%	Upper 9 5%
Intercept	12965.87754	466.4849849	27.79484433	6.81137E-88	12048.16629	13883.58879
All Milk Price	300.7062994	24.32584198	12.36159882	4.92761E-29	252.8503135	348.5622853
Milk Feed Price Ratio	−1298.252491	104.7035551	−12.39931624	3.58053E-29	−1504.23479	−1092.270233

Note: Dependent variable is all milk production (millions of gallons). Highlighted variables are significant at the 5 percent level.

These results suggested to the student that, as predicted by the law of supply, milk production was positively related to the output price of milk, holding all other variables constant. While consistent with theory, our former student was concerned about his ability to uniquely estimate milk supply because he realized that milk prices were not only a determinant of milk supply, but also of milk demand. Accordingly, he was unsure whether he had truly identified the effect of milk prices on milk production, holding all other variables constant.

BIG PICTURE OVERVIEW

instrumental variables
Variables that are correlated with the endogenous variable but not correlated with the error term.

Chapter 14 introduces three different situations in which we use **instrumental variables** (IVs) to calculate correct estimated marginal effects through a process known as **two-stage least squares.** Figure 14.2 depicts the empirical tools introduced in this chapter.

FIGURE 14.2
A Visual Depiction of the Empirical Tools Introduced in This Chapter

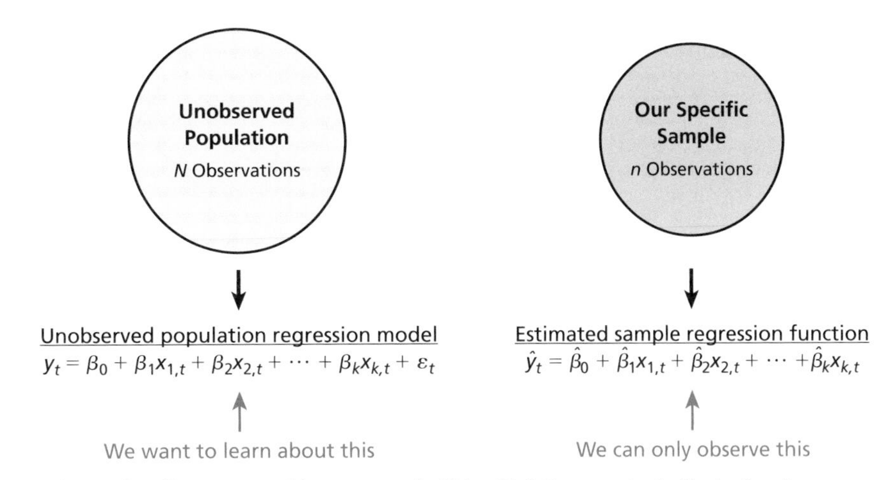

two-stage least squares
An instrumental variables estimation technique that involves estimating a first-stage identification function and using those results to correct the second-stage OLS regression to provide consistent estimates in a number of empirical situations.

There are three prominent situations in which we might wish to employ instrumental variables.

14.1 USE TWO-STAGE LEAST SQUARES TO IDENTIFY SIMULTANEOUS DEMAND AND SUPPLY EQUATIONS

simultaneous equation Occurs when two or more equations contain variables that are related to each other.

Simultaneous equations occur when our dependent variable and at least one of our independent variables are jointly determined. As a result of this joint determination, the OLS estimates are unable to distinguish between the exact degree to which each independent factor determines the observed variation in the dependent variable.

The classic example in which simultaneous equations occur is the case of quantity and price determination in markets. In such cases, the data points that a researcher observes are a series of price–quantity combinations, which might look like Figure 14.3.

FIGURE 14.3 **A Hypothetical Series of Price–Quantity Combinations in an Output Market**

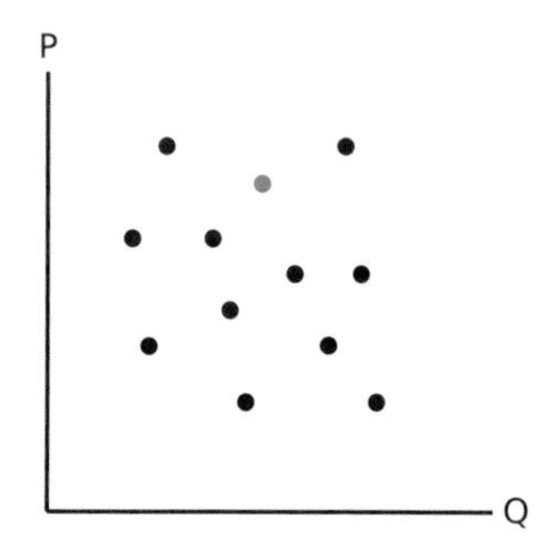

Unfortunately for the researcher, each of these individual price–quantity combinations is determined by the interaction between supply and demand. Accordingly, without further information it is not possible to determine the extent to which each of those factors is driving the observed variations in equilibrium prices and quantities. In other words, if we observe a specific price–quantity equilibrium (such as the blue dot in the Figure 14.3), we cannot say for certain whether that equilibrium price and quantity resulted from a change in supply or a change in demand from the prior equilibrium. Figure 14.4 depicts this potential confusion.

FIGURE 14.4 **A Visual Depiction of the Possible Causes of a Given Observed Price–Quantity Equilibrium**

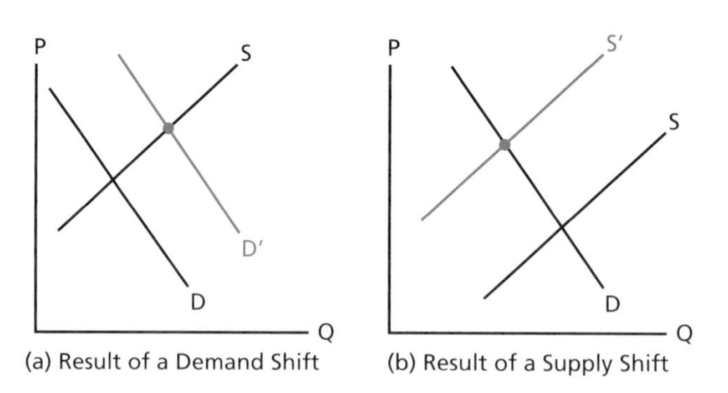

While the preceding scenarios are clearly different, OLS does not differentiate between them. As a result, OLS provides biased estimates of the marginal effect that the independent variable has on the dependent variable. To correctly identify the individual effects that supply and demand have on observed equilibrium prices and quantities, we need to develop a framework that allows us to distinguish between the two effects. Before introducing this framework, we need to introduce the data that will form the baseline example for our discussion.

DATA TO BE ANALYZED: OUR U.S. GASOLINE SALES DATA

For instrumental variables to be a viable solution in the case of simultaneous equations, we need (1) many, many observations and (2) at least one distinct independent variable that is likely to affect demand only and at least one distinct independent variable that is likely to affect supply only. To satisfy these two requirements, in this section we choose to focus on U.S. gasoline sales. The reason for this is that the U.S. average pump price for gasoline is released on a weekly basis; being a commodity that is an important part of an individual's budget, economic theory tells us that consumer income should affect the demand for gasoline; and being a major input in the production of gasoline, economic theory tells us that the price of crude oil should affect the supply of gasoline.

Following the process outlined in Appendix A, we collected monthly data on each of the preceding variables for the market for regular gasoline in the United States between August 1990 and March 2010. Figure 14.5 presents simple summary statistics for these variables.

FIGURE 14.5 Line Graphs of the Dependent and Independent Variables for Our U.S. Gasoline Sales Data

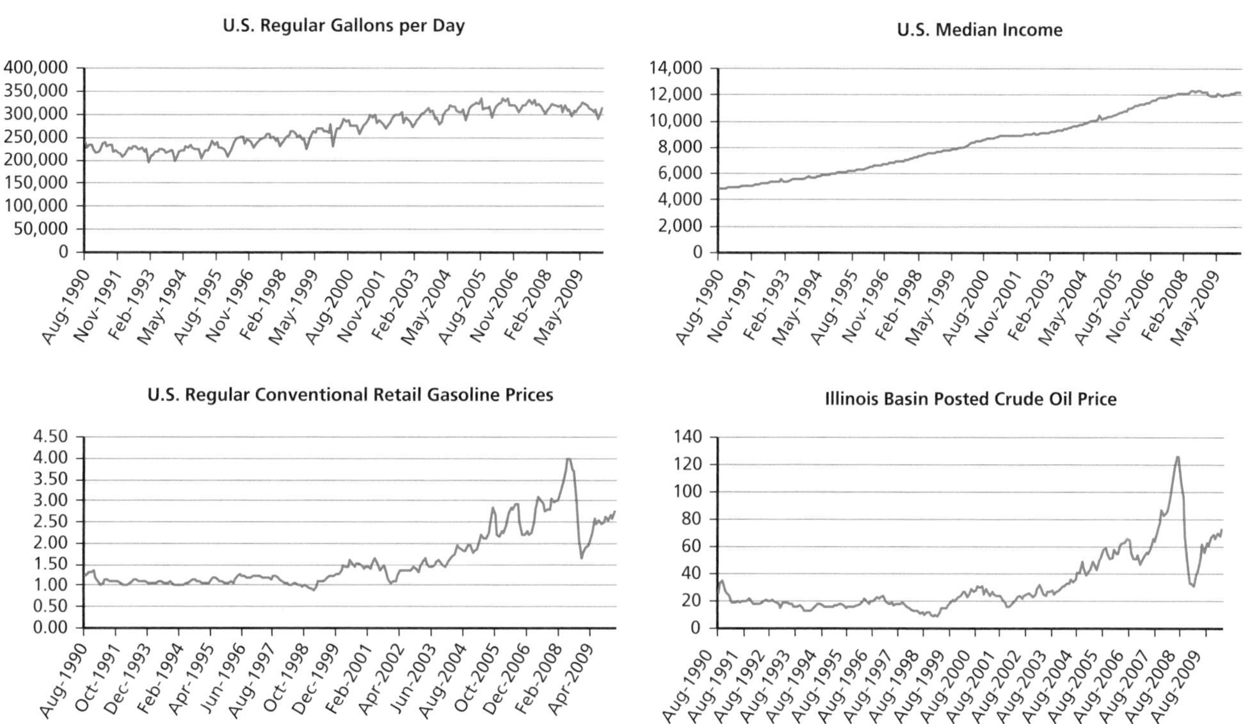

As discussed earlier, because each individual price–quantity observation results from the interaction of supply and demand, our first step is to identify the individual demand and supply equations. In general terms, these are

Demand Equation: $$Q_t^d = \beta_0 + \delta_1 P_t + \beta_1 x_{1t} + \cdots + \beta_k x_{kt} + \varepsilon_t \qquad \textbf{14.1.1}$$

where Q_t^d is the observed quantity demanded in each time period; P_t is the observed price in each time period; and $x_{1t}, x_{2t}, \ldots, x_{kt}$ are the observed values of independent factors that shift demand, such as income, the price of other goods, tastes and preferences, and the number of buyers, in each time period.

Supply Equation: $$Q_t^s = \gamma_0 + \mu_1 P_t + \gamma_1 w_{1t} + \cdots + \gamma_j w_{jt} + \varepsilon_t \qquad \textbf{14.1.2}$$

where Q_t^s is the observed quantity supplied in each time period; P_t is the observed price in each time period; and $w_{1t}, w_{2t}, \ldots, w_{jt}$ are independent factors that shift supply, such as input prices, technology, weather, the price of other goods, and the number of sellers, in each time period.

The obvious problem in this formulation is that the observed price in each time period is included as an independent variable in both the demand and supply equations. For this reason, OLS estimates cannot distinguish the exact degree to which price is correlated with each dependent variable.

We correct for this problem using a process known as two-stage least squares. To perform this two-stage process, we (1) estimate observed price as a function of the demand and supply shifters in the first-stage and use the results to calculate predicted prices for each observation in the data set and (2) include the predicted prices in place of the observed prices as independent variables in the second-stage demand and supply equations.

In general terms, we formulate this process as follows.

First Stage:

Estimate the population regression model

$$P_t = \varphi_0 + \varphi_1 x_{1t} + \cdots + \varphi_k x_{kt} + \varphi_{k+1} w_{1t} + \cdots + \varphi_{k+j} w_{jt} + \varepsilon_t \quad 14.1.3$$

and use the resulting estimates to calculate the predicted price

$$\hat{P}_t = \hat{\varphi}_0 + \hat{\varphi}_1 x_{1t} + \cdots + \hat{\varphi}_k x_{kt} + \hat{\varphi}_{k+1} w_{1t} + \cdots + \hat{\varphi}_{k+j} w_{jt} \quad 14.1.4$$

Second Stage:

Estimate the population regression models for the demand and supply equations

$$Q_t^d = \beta_0 + \delta_1 \hat{P}_t + \beta_1 x_{1t} + \cdots + \beta_k x_{kt} + \varepsilon_t \quad 14.1.5$$

$$Q_t^s = \gamma_0 + \mu_1 \hat{P}_t + \gamma_1 w_{1t} + \cdots + \gamma\beta_j w_{jt} + \varepsilon_t \quad 14.1.6$$

For comparison purposes, before estimating the two-stage least squares model for our U.S. gasoline data, we first estimate the demand and supply equations separately by OLS, and we get Excel Regression Output 14.1.

Excel Regression Output 14.1: Estimating the Demand and Supply Equations with Regular OLS for Our U.S. Gasoline Data

Demand Equation

SUMMARY OUTPUT

Regression Statistics	
Multiple R	0.940042395
R Square	0.883679705
Adjusted R Square	0.882681248
Standard Error	13306.27343
Observations	236

Number of months between August 1990 and March 2010 (→ Observations)

ANOVA

	df	SS	MS	F	Significance F
Regression	2	3.13407E+11	1.56703E+11	885.0449155	1.4089E-109
Residual	233	41254260664	177056912.7		
Total	235	3.54661E+11			

	Coefficients	Standard Error	*t* Stat	*p*-value	Lower 95%	Upper 95%
Intercept	141073.8145	3376.438732	41.78183753	3.2576E-110	134421.5632	147726.0658
Price per Gallon	−622.6915903	2378.576425	−0.26179171	0.793713312	−5308.957026	4063.573845
Income	15.43720063	0.69085326	22.34512236	7.25242E-60	14.07608323	16.79831803

Note: Dependent variable is total gallons of regular gasoline sold in the U.S. in a given month. Highlighted variables are significant at the 5 percent level.

Supply Equation

SUMMARY OUTPUT

Regression Statistics	
Multiple R	0.839647458
R Square	0.705007854
Adjusted R Square	0.702475733
Standard Error	21190.14472
Observations	236

Number of months between August 1990 and March 2010

ANOVA

	df	SS	MS	F	Significance F
Regression	2	2.50039E+11	1.25019E+11	278.4257687	1.70969E-62
Residual	233	1.04622E+11	449022233.4		
Total	235	3.54661E+11			

	Coefficients	Standard Error	*t* Stat	*p*-value	Lower 95%	Upper 95%
Intercept	159952.2622	6224.929237	25.69543462	6.18133E-70	147687.9219	172216.6026
Price per Gallon	110929.9575	9105.198754	12.18314509	9.5974E-27	92990.91724	128868.9977
Crude Price	−2097.1122	280.841344	−7.46724885	1.62903E12	−2650.425126	−1543.79927

Note: Dependent variable is total gallons of regular gasoline sold in the U.S. in a given month. Highlighted variables are significant at the 5 percent level.

These results can be interpreted as follows. Starting with the demand equation, we estimate that, all other independent variables constant, the price per gallon of regular gasoline is not statistically related to the quantity of regular gasoline demanded, which, if true, would suggest that the law of demand did not hold for regular gasoline. At the same time, we estimate that each additional dollar of consumer income is associated with an increase of 15.44 in the number of gallons sold; if true, this would suggest that regular gasoline is a normal good for American consumers. Turning to the supply equation, we estimate that each additional dollar per gallon in the price of regular gasoline is associated with a statistically significant increase of 110,930 (the quantity of regular gasoline sold in the United States), while we estimate that each additional dollar in the price of crude oil is associated with a statistically significant decrease of 2,097.1 (the quantity of regular gasoline sold), holding all other independent variables constant.

As discussed previously, a potential problem with these OLS estimates is that these separate regressions amalgamate the effects that variation in demand and supply have on observed quantities and prices and, therefore, result in biased estimates. We improve on these estimates by performing two-stage least squares. To do so, we first estimate the first-stage population regression model.

First Stage:

$$Gas\ price_t = \varphi_0 + \varphi_1\ U.S.median\ income_t + \varphi_2\ World\ crude\ price_t + \varepsilon_t \quad \textbf{14.1.7}$$

by OLS and get Excel Regression Output 14.2.

Note that we generally do not interpret these first-stage results. Instead, we look at the F-statistic for the overall significance of the sample regression function to make sure that we have identified sufficiently strong instruments. As a general rule, an F-statistic that exceeds 10 is considered sufficient evidence that we have strong instruments. In this case, the value of the F-statistic is 3,663.12, meaning that we can be satisfied with our chosen instruments.

Excel Regression Output 14.2: First-Stage Regression for Two-Stage Least Squares for Our U.S. Gasoline Data

SUMMARY OUTPUT

Regression Statistics	
Multiple R	0.984467759
R Square	0.969176769
Adjusted R Square	0.968912192
Standard Error	0.12236482
Observations	236

Number of months between August 1990 and March 2010

ANOVA

	df	SS	MS	F	Significance F
Regression	2	109.6967894	54.84839469	3663.116797	9.0013E-177
Residual	233	3.488743786	0.014973149		
Total	235	113.1855332			

	Coefficients	Standard Error	*t* Stat	*p*-value	Lower 95%	Upper 95%
Intercept	0.277283972	0.034057174	8.141719951	2.35224E-14	0.210184611	0.344383332
Income	6.17735E-05	5.44471E-06	11.34560511	4.84232E-24	5.10464E-05	7.25007E-05
Crude Price	0.024916924	0.000578199	43.0939964	5.507E-113	0.023777757	0.026056091

Note: Dependent variable is total gallons of regular gasoline sold in the U.S. in a given month. Highlighted variables are significant at the 5 percent level.

After estimating the first-stage sample regression function, we calculate the predicted prices (which are provided along with the estimated residuals when we check the "Residuals" box in the regression window), and we include those predicted values in the second-stage population regression models.

Second Stage:

Demand Equation: $Quantity_t^d = \beta_0 + \delta_1\, \widehat{Gas\ price}_t + \beta_1\, U.S.\ median\ income_t + \varepsilon_t$ **14.1.8**

Supply Equation: $Quantity_t^s = \gamma_0 + \mu_1\, \widehat{Gas\ price}_t + \gamma_1\, World\ crude\ price_t + \varepsilon_t$ **14.1.9**

by OLS, and we get Excel Regression Output 14.3.

Excel Regression Output 14.3: Second-Stage Regressions for the Demand and Supply Equations for Our U.S. Gasoline Price Data

Demand Equation

SUMMARY OUTPUT

Regression Statistics	
Multiple R	0.940784533
R Square	0.885075537
Adjusted R Square	0.884089061
Standard Error	13226.19551
Observations	236

Number of months between August 1990 and March 2010

ANOVA

	df	SS	MS	F	Significance F
Regression	2	3.13902E+11	1.56951E+11	897.2093252	3.4519E-110
Residual	233	40759213697	174932247.6		
Total	235	3.54661E+11			

	Coefficients	Standard Error	*t* Stat	*p*-value	Lower 95%	Upper 95%
Intercept	139351.1324	3379.337053	41.23623368	4.844E-109	132693.1708	146009.094
Predicted Price per Gallon	−4270.791529	2508.196686	−1.702733902	0.089951441	−9212.434484	670.8514259
Income	16.33847311	0.717185976	22.78136166	3.27889E-61	14.92547506	17.75147116

Note: Dependent variable is total gallons of regular gasoline sold in the U.S. in a given month. Variables highlighted in blue are significant at the 5 percent level. Variables highlighted in gray are significant at the 10 percent level.

Supply Equation

SUMMARY OUTPUT

Regression Statistics

Multiple R	0.940784533
R Square	0.885075537
Adjusted R Square	0.884089061
Standard Error	13226.19551
Observations	236

Number of months between August 1990 and March 2010

ANOVA

	df	SS	MS	F	Significance F
Regression	2	3.13902E+11	1.56951E+11	897.2093252	3.4519E-110
Residual	233	40759213697	174932247.6		
Total	235	3.54661E+11			

	Coefficients	Standard Error	*t* Stat	*p*-value	Lower 95%	Upper 95%
Intercept	66012.32831	6184.250904	10.67426425	6.50469E-22	53828.13236	78196.52427
Predicted Price per Gallon	260219.0872	9526.880049	27.31419792	1.392E-74	241449.2515	278988.9229
Crude Price	−6590.274218	289.2835957	−22.78136166	3.27889E-61	−7160.220048	−6020.328387

Note: Dependent variable is total gallons of regular gasoline sold in the U.S. in a given month. Highlighted variables are significant at the 5 percent level.

Notice that this approach to controlling for simultaneous equations has now cleared up the confusion surrounding whether the law of demand holds for our U.S. gasoline data, in particular in the second stage because, as in the demand equation, price per gallon is now estimated to have a statistically significant negative effect on the quantity demanded of gasoline. Aside from this important difference, the estimated signs and statistical significance are the same as those given earlier.

As we have seen for previous applications, such as White's heteroskedastic standard errors and Newey-West robust standard errors, once we understand what it is trying to accomplish it is much easier to perform two-stage least squares in a more-advanced statistical package. Using the Stata command

```
ivreg quantity income (pricepergallon = income crudeprice)
```

for our U.S. gasoline sales data, we get Empirical Results 14.1.

Empirical Results 14.1: Using Two-Stage Least Squares to Estimate the Demand and Supply Equations

Demand Equation

	Coefficients	Standard Error	t	P > |t|	Lower 95%	Upper 95%
Intercept	139,351.10	3,416.92	40.78	0.000	132,619.10	146,083.10
Price per Gallon	−4,270.79	2,536.09	−1.68	0.094	−9,267.39	725.80
Income	16.34	0.73	22.53	0.000	14.91	17.77
Prob > F			0.0000			
R-Squared			0.8825			
Observations			236			

Supply Equation

	Coefficients	Standard Error	t	P>|t|	Lower 95%	Upper 95%
Crude Price	66,012.33	14,540.73	4.54	0.000	37,364.21	94,660.45
Intercept	260,219.10	22,400.10	11.62	0.000	216,086.50	304,351.70
Price per Gallon	−6,590.27	680.18	−9.69	0.000	−7,930.36	−5,250.19
Prob > F			0.0000			
R-Squared			0.3647			
Observations			236			

Note: Dependent variable is total gallons of regular gasoline sold in the U.S. in a given month. Variables highlighted in blue are significant at the 5 percent level. Variables highlighted in gray are significant at the 10 percent level.

Notice that the coefficient estimates are exactly the same as those generated in Excel but that the estimated standard errors are different. The reason for this is that Stata is programmed to estimate standard errors that account for the two-stage least squares estimation process, while Excel makes no such modifications.

Empirical Research Tool 14.1 summarizes the use of the two-stage least squares model to identify simultaneous equations.

EMPIRICAL RESEARCH TOOL 14.1: USING TWO-STAGE LEAST SQUARES TO IDENTIFY SIMULTANEOUS EQUATIONS

How to Do It:

1. For each equation, identify an appropriate instrumental variable that shifts the dependent variable in the other equation but not in the given equation.

Perform two-stage least squares by:

2. Regressing the jointly determined independent variable on all remaining independent variables, including the instrumental variable.
3. Calculating the predicted value of the jointly determined independent variable.
4. Estimating the initial population regression model for one of the equations with the predicted values of the jointly determined independent variable substituted for the actual values.
5. Repeating step 4 for the remaining equation.

Why It Works:

For each of the simultaneous equations, two-stage least squares isolates the portion of the jointly determined variable that is not related to the error term, thereby yielding consistent estimates of the individual equations.

14.2 USE TWO-STAGE LEAST SQUARES TO CORRECT FOR ENDOGENEITY OF AN INDEPENDENT VARIABLE

endogenous independent variable
A variable that is correlated with the error term.

There is a second situation in which instrumental variables prove extremely valuable. Among the six assumptions required for OLS to produce estimates that are BLUE, one of the more likely to be violated is assumption M5, which states that *"the error term and the independent variables are uncorrelated."* We refer to independent variables that are correlated with the error term as being **endogenous independent variables.** Due to this correlation, we are unable to independently identify the marginal effect of the endogenous independent variable, because whenever that variable changes the error term also changes. As a result, in the presence of endogenous independent variables, OLS estimates are biased and inconsistent. Fortunately, instrumental variables solve this problem and allow us to estimate consistent marginal effects of the endogenous independent variables.

One of the most often cited situations in which we are likely to encounter endogenous independent variables is the case of the economic returns to educational attainment. A straightforward way to estimate the marginal effects of education on earnings is to estimate a population regression model of the general form

$$\ln Wage_i = \beta_0 + \beta_1 Education_i + \beta_2 Experience_i + \beta_3 Male_i + \cdots + \varepsilon_i \qquad \textbf{14.2.1}$$

where $Wage_i$ is the wage earned by individual i in a given time period; $Education_i$ is the highest level of education attained by i; $Experience_i$ is the number of years of work experience accumulated by i; $Male_i$ is a binary dummy variable indicating whether i is male; and the remaining independent variables—represented by the ". . ."—are other measurable values predicted by theory to be correlated with an individual's observed wage. In this formulation, because it measures the degree to which an individual's highest level of education is correlated with his or her observed wage, the coefficient estimate $\hat{\beta}_1$ provides an estimate of the economic return to educational attainment holding all other independent variables constant.

An important empirical issue associated with this approach is that an individual's educational attainment is likely dependent on his or her innate motivation/work ethic. Unfortunately, because many aspects of an individual's innate motivation/work ethic cannot be directly measured, they belong in the error term. Accordingly, the independent variable $Education_i$ is correlated with the error term ε_i, thereby violating assumption M5 and causing the OLS estimated coefficient $\hat{\beta}_1$ to be a biased and inconsistent estimate of the population parameter β_1 in which we are interested.

The issues and consequences associated with endogenous independent variables are summarized in the following box.

The Issues and Consequences Associated with Endogenous Independent Variables

Problem:
Endogenous independent variables violate assumption M5, which states that the error term and the independent variables are uncorrelated.

Consequences:
With endogenous independent variables,

1. Parameter estimates are biased.
2. Parameter estimates are inconsistent.
3. Standard errors are wrong.

The estimation method that we use in the presence of an endogenous independent variable relies on our ability to identify a different variable that is correlated with the endogenous variable but uncorrelated with the error term. If (and it's a big if) we are able

instrument
A variable that is correlated with the endogenous independent variable but not correlated with the error term.

to identify such an **instrument** for the endogenous independent variable, then we could use an instrumental variables approach to generate unbiased and consistent estimates. The steps for performing two-stage least squares in this case are: (1) regress the endogenous independent variable on both the instrument and the remaining independent variables; (2) use those estimates to calculate predicted values of the endogenous independent variable, and (3) estimate the original population regression model substituting the predicted values of the endogenous independent variable for the observed values of the endogenous independent variable.

Formally, suppose that we wish to estimate the population regression model

$$y_i = \beta_0 + \beta_1 x_{1,i} + \beta_2 x_{2,i} + \cdots + \beta_k x_{k,i} + \varepsilon_i \qquad 14.2.2$$

and we suspect that $x_{1,i}$ is correlated with ε_i (i.e. $E(x_{1,i}, \varepsilon_i) \neq 0$). Suppose further that we are able to identify the variable z_i that *is* correlated with $x_{1,i}$ but *is not* correlated with ε_i (i.e. $E(z_i, \varepsilon_i) = 0$). We can then estimate the first-stage population regression model

$$x_{1,i} = \gamma_0 + \gamma_1 z_i + \gamma_2 x_{2,i} + \cdots + \gamma_k x_{k,i} + \varepsilon_i \qquad 14.2.3$$

and use the resulting estimates to calculate the predicted values of $x_{1,i}$ as

$$\hat{\mathbf{x}}_{\mathbf{1},i} = \hat{\gamma}_0 + \hat{\gamma}_1 z_i + \hat{\gamma}_2 x_{2,i} + \cdots + \hat{\gamma}_k x_{k,i} \qquad 14.2.4$$

We then substitute the predicted values of the endogenous independent variable for the observed values and estimate the second-stage population regression model

$$y_i = \delta_0 + \delta_1 \hat{x}_{1,i} + \delta_2 x_{2,i} + \cdots + \delta_k x_{k,i} + u_i \qquad 14.2.5$$

The resulting coefficient estimate $\hat{\delta}_1$ should then provide a consistent estimate of the unobserved population parameter δ_1. The reason for this is that the first-stage regression in formula 14.2.3 isolates the part of the endogenous independent variable that is not correlated with the error term, meaning that the second-stage regression no longer suffers from the endogeneity.

Note that we have so far rather cavalierly assumed that a variable that is correlated with the endogenous independent variable but is *also* uncorrelated with the error term exists and is easy to identify. In reality, this is often far from the case: The entire issue associated with successfully employing instrumental variables relates to the ability to identify a plausible instrument. Unfortunately, doing so is often quite difficult. For instance, in the case of educational attainment, it is difficult to identify a plausible instrument because almost all factors that are correlated with educational attainment are also plausibly correlated with as motivation/work ethic. This is an issue, because this latter correlation is exactly the correlation that we wish to remove from our estimates. In summary, we stress that while IV approaches for dealing with endogenous independent variables are theoretically appealing, they are often difficult to implement in practice.

Before demonstrating how to use instrumental variables to correct for endogenous independent variables, we need to introduce the data that we use when doing so.

Our Empirical Example: The Effect of a Doctor's Advice to Reduce Drinking

An issue in which health economists might be interested is the degree to which patients actually follow their doctor's advice. For instance, we might question whether patients who are encouraged to cut back on alcohol consumption actually heed their doctor's advice. At first glance, it might seem that we could address this question by regressing the number of alcoholic drinks consumed on a dummy variable indicating whether a doctor had given the advice to reduce alcohol consumption, as well as other relevant independent variables. Unfortunately, receiving the advice to reduce alcohol consumption is likely correlated with unmeasurable personality traits that are included in the error term. If so, then receiving the advice to reduce alcohol consumption is endogenous and our OLS will be biased and inconsistent.

To control for this potential endogeneity, we need to identify variables that are correlated with receiving the advice to reduce alcohol consumption but are uncorrelated with the error term. We argue that potential candidates for such instruments are being advised by a doctor to lose weight and/or exercise more frequently. We make this argument for the following reasons. On the one hand, it is *plausible* that individuals who merit doctor interventions aimed at reducing their alcohol consumption are also overweight, nonexercisers who merit interventions aimed at decreasing their weight and/or increasing their exercise (i.e., individuals who drink too much might also be inclined to exercise too little and weigh too much). If so, then the endogenous independent variable would be correlated with the proposed instruments. On the other hand, it is *plausible* that individuals who merit doctor interventions aimed at decreasing weight and/or increasing exercise do not necessarily have the unobserved personality traits that lead to their also requiring doctor interventions aimed at reducing their alcohol consumption (i.e., many individuals who exercise too little and weigh too much do not drink to excess). If so, then the proposed instruments would not necessarily be correlated with the error term. Accordingly, it is *plausible* that being advised to lose weight and/or increase exercise are valid instruments for being advised to reduce alcohol consumption.

Note that we are careful to use the word *plausible* when discussing our chosen instrument for the very reason that identifying valid instruments is often quite difficult. Because of this fact, in the empirical work that follows, we are careful to statistically test for the validity of our proposed instruments.

Data to Be Analyzed: Our Doctor Advice Data

To carry out our proposed instrumental variables approach, we need to collect individual health data that contain information on alcohol consumption and doctor-recommended lifestyle modifications. Following the process outlined in Appendix A, we collected data for 14,589 individuals from the National Health Interview Survey that contained self-reported information on the number of days that an individual had five or more drinks during the previous year; whether the individual was advised by a doctor to reduce alcohol consumption, lose weight, and/or increase exercise; and other demographic data. Table 14.2 presents summary statistics for these data.

TABLE 14.2
Summary Statistics for Our Drinking Data

Days with 5+ drinks per year	12.098
	(45.230)
Advised to reduce drinking	0.048
Advised to lose weight	0.133
Advised to exercise	0.143
Male	0.490
Currently married	0.521
Black	0.117
Other race	0.032
Age 25–44	0.538
Age 45–64	0.376
Age 65–69	0.048
Age 70–74	0.037
Observations	14,589

Table 14.2 indicates that individuals in our sample had five or more drinks on an average of 12.1 days in the previous year. While true, there is a wide variance in individual responses (as evidenced by the standard deviation being nearly four times larger than the mean), with more than 10,200 of the nearly 14,600 individuals in our sample reporting 0 days of more than five drinks and 99 and 29, respectively, reporting 364 and 365 days. Turning to our doctor's advice variables, nearly 5 percent of our sample reported being advised to quit drinking, while 13 and 14 percent reported being advised to lose weight and to exercise more, respectively.

As a baseline for comparison, we estimate the population regression model

$$Days_i = \beta_0 + \beta_1 Quit_i + \beta_2 Male_i + \beta_3 Married_i + \beta_4 Black_i + \beta_5 Other_i + \beta_6(Age\ 25 - 44)_i + \beta_7(Age\ 55 - 64)_i + \beta_8(Age\ 65 - 69)_i + \varepsilon_i \qquad 14.2.6$$

by OLS and get Excel Regression Output 14.4.

Excel Regression Output 14.4: OLS Results for Number of Days with Five or More Drinks in the Past Year for Our Doctor's Advice Sample

SUMMARY OUTPUT

Regression Statistics	
Multiple R	0.214163908
R Square	0.045866179
Adjusted R Square	0.045342649
Standard Error	44.19306746
Observations	14,589

Number of individuals in our sample

ANOVA

	df	SS	MS	F	Significance F
Regression	8	1368828.674	171103.5842	87.60942151	1.4136E−142
Residual	14580	28475136.75	1953.027212		
Total	14588	29843965.42			

	Coefficients	Standard Error	*t* Stat	*p*-value	Lower 95%	Upper 95%
Intercept	2.17621478	1.970137522	1.10460044	0.26935099	−1.68550428	6.03793384
Advised to Reduce Drinking	21.23582547	1.733588889	12.24963174	2.48895E-34	17.83777169	24.63387925
Male	14.56154226	0.735868468	19.78824056	5.0424E-86	13.11914687	16.00393766
Currently Married	−7.19444955	0.744659958	−9.661389033	5.12034E-22	−8.65407738	−5.73482172
Black	−0.91143164	1.162764004	−0.783849208	0.43314133	−3.19059635	1.36773307
Other Race	−5.12066772	2.088322098	−2.452048814	0.01421618	−9.21404352	−1.02729193
Age 25–44	7.39307239	1.966779972	3.758972788	0.00017128	3.53793456	11.24821023
Age 45–64	4.74387695	1.989545386	2.384402477	0.01711959	0.84411602	8.64363788
Age 65–69	0.32345624	2.522993336	0.128203367	0.89798980	−4.62193023	5.26884271

Note: Dependent variable is number of days with 5+ drinks per year. Omitted age is 70–74. Highlighted variables are significant at the 5 percent level.

We can interpret these results as follows. Holding all other independent variables constant, individuals advised by their doctor to reduce alcohol consumption reported averaging 21.24 more days with five or more drinks in the previous year than otherwise similar individuals not advised by their doctor to quit drinking. Likewise, men reported having five or more drinks on an average of 14.56 more days than women, currently married individuals reported having five or more drinks on an average of 7.20 less days than otherwise similar unmarried individuals, other race individuals reported having five or more drinks on an average of 5.12 fewer days than whites, and individuals between ages 25 and 44 and ages 45 and 64 reported having five or more drinks on roughly 7 and 5 more days, respectively, than otherwise similar 18-to-24-year-olds.

Our two-stage least squares approach to controlling for the potential endogeneity of the doctor's advice to quit drinking starts with estimating the first-stage population regression model

$$\begin{aligned} Reduce_i = \beta_0 + \beta_1 Lose\ weight_i + \beta_2 Exercise\ more_i + \beta_3 Male_i \\ + \beta_4 Married_i + \beta_5 Black_i + \beta_6 Other_i + \beta_7 (Age\ 25 - 44)_i \\ + \beta_8 (Age\ 45 - 64)_i + \beta_9 (Age\ 65 - 69)_i + \varepsilon_i \end{aligned} \quad \textbf{14.2.6}$$

by OLS and using those results to calculate the predicted likelihood that an individual is advised by his or her doctor to reduce alcohol consumption as

$$\begin{aligned} \widehat{Reduce}_i = \hat{\beta}_0 + \hat{\beta}_1 Lose\ weight_i + \hat{\beta}_2 Exercise\ more_i + \hat{\beta}_3 Male_i \\ + \hat{\beta}_4 Married_i + \hat{\beta}_5 Black_i + \hat{\beta}_6 Other_i + \hat{\beta}_7 (Age\ 25 - 44)_i \\ + \hat{\beta}_8 (Age\ 45 - 64)_i + \hat{\beta}_9 (Age\ 65 - 69)_i \end{aligned} \quad \textbf{14.2.7}$$

We then substitute those predicted values for the observed values and estimate the second-stage population regression model

$$\begin{aligned} Days_i = \delta_0 + \beta_1 \widehat{Reduce}_i + \delta_2 Male_i + \delta_3 Married_i + \delta_4 Black_i + \delta_5 Other_i \\ + \delta_6 (Age\ 25 - 44)_i + \delta_7 (Age\ 45 - 64)_i + \delta_8 (Age\ 65 - 69)_i + \varphi_i \end{aligned} \quad \textbf{14.2.8}$$

While we could estimate this model step-by-step in Excel, it is much easier to learn the relatively simple commands required to estimate it in a more advanced statistical package. Using the Stata command

```
ivreg bingedays male married black othrace age2544 age4564 age6569
(quitdrink = losewgt exercise)
```

for our doctor's advice sample, we get Empirical Results 14.2.

Empirical Results 14.2: Using Two-Stage Least Squares to Control for the Potential Endogeneity of the Advice to Quit Drinking in Our Doctor's Advice Sample

First Stage

	Coefficient	Standard Error	t	P > |t|	Lower 95%	Upper 95%
Intercept	−0.0159122	0.0085537	−1.86	0.0630	−0.0326785	0.0008541
Advised to Lose Weight	0.1071945	0.0077260	13.87	0.0000	0.0920505	0.1223385
Advised to Exercise More	0.1893377	0.0075404	25.11	0.0000	0.1745575	0.2041178
Male	0.0277515	0.0031385	8.84	0.0000	0.0215997	0.0339033
Currently Married	−0.0123854	0.0031827	−3.89	0.0000	−0.0186240	−0.0061469
Black	0.0282409	0.0049764	5.67	0.0000	0.0184865	0.0379953
Other Race	0.0000313	0.0089306	0.00	0.9970	−0.0174739	0.0175365
Age 25–44	0.0107566	0.0085086	1.26	0.2060	−0.0059213	0.0274345
Age 45–64	0.0177250	0.0085388	2.08	0.0380	0.0009878	0.0344622
Age 65–69	−0.0045205	0.0107910	−0.42	0.6750	−0.0256722	0.0166312
Prob > F			0.0000			
R-squared			0.2220			
Obervations			14,589			

Note: Dependent variable equals 1 if individual was advised to reduce drinking. Omitted age is 70–74. Variables highlighted in blue are significant at the 5 percent level. Variables highlighted in light gray are significant at the 10 percent level.

Second Stage

	Coefficient	Standard Error	t	P > |t|	Lower 95%	Upper 95%
Intercept	3.747557	1.997955	1.88	0.0610	−0.168687	7.663801
Advised to Reduce Drinking	1.11814	3.905059	0.29	0.7750	−6.536269	8.772553
Male	15.28697	0.749926	20.38	0.0000	13.81702	16.75692
Currently Married	−7.45334	0.749442	−9.95	0.0000	−8.922342	−5.984339
Black	0.215959	1.184429	0.18	0.8550	−2.105672	2.537591
Other Race	−5.176274	2.097967	−2.47	0.0140	−9.288554	−1.063993
Age 25–44	5.958711	1.991495	2.99	0.0030	2.055128	9.862294
Age 45–64	4.303662	2.000175	2.15	0.0310	0.383066	8.224259
Age 65–69	0.007078	2.535214	0.00	0.9980	−4.962264	4.976419
Prob > F			0.0000			
R-squared			0.0371			
Observations			14,589			

Note: Dependent variable is number of days with 5+ drinks per year. Omitted age is 70–74. Variables highlighted in blue are significant at the 5 percent level. Variables highlighted in gray are significant at the 10 percent level.

Interpreting these results demonstrates the importance of controlling for the endogeneity of the "Advised to Reduce Drinking" variable. We start our interpretation by looking at the first-stage regression results for our chosen instruments. All other independent variables constant, individuals who are advised to lose weight and to exercise more are nearly 11 and 19 percent more likely to be advised to quit drinking.

We can statistically assess the potentially validity of our proposed instruments by performing an F-test of the joint significance of the instruments in the first-stage regression (or a t-test if there is only one instrument). In this case, because there is only one instrumental variable, we can rely on a t-test on the "Advised to Lose Weight" variable, which has a p-value of 0.0000, suggesting that we have chosen potentially valid instruments.

weak instrument
An instrumental variable that is not highly correlated to the endogenous independent variable.

We pause here to note that a large volume of recent empirical work has underscored the importance of statistically testing to ensure that we have not chosen a **weak instrument.** The reason for this is that if a chosen instrument is not strongly correlated with the endogenous independent variable, then IV does not yield less-biased estimates than OLS, and the hypothesis tests and estimated confidence intervals are incorrect. In reference to this fact, in their seminal work on the subject Bound, Jaeger, and Baker (1993) write that for instrumental variable approaches using weak instruments, "the cure can be worse than the disease." As a general rule, to avoid having weak instruments, we look for a calculated F-statistic greater than 10 for our F-test of the joint significance of the instruments in the first-stage regression. Because with only one variable the F-statistic is the t-statistic squared, in our example, the F-statistic is 192.38, or 13.87 squared.

Looking at the second-stage results, we see that the advised to quit drinking variable is no longer estimated to be statistically significant, suggesting that after controlling for the endogeneity of being advised to reduce alcohol consumption, individuals receiving such advice do not average statistically more days with five or more drinks than otherwise similar individuals not advised to reduce their drinking. The fact that the nonsignificance of this result stands in marked contrast to the estimated significance in the OLS estimates in Excel Regression Output 14.4 highlights the importance of controlling for the potential endogeneity of an independent variable.

Empirical Research Tool 14.2 summarizes the use of two-stage least squares to control for the endogeneity of an independent variable.

EMPIRICAL RESEARCH TOOL 14.2: USING TWO-STAGE LEAST SQUARES TO CONTROL FOR ENDOGENEITY OF AN INDEPENDENT VARIABLE

How to Do It:

1. Identify appropriate instrumental variable(s) that are related to the endogenous independent variable but not related to the error term. This step is not trivial.

Perform two-stage least squares by:

2. Regressing the endogenous independent variable on all remaining independent variables, including the instrumental variable(s), and calculating the predicted value.
3. Estimating the initial population regression model with the predicted values of the endogenous independent variable substituted for the actual variable.

Why It Works:
The first-stage regression isolates the part of the endogenous independent variable that is not correlated with the error term, meaning that the second-stage regression no longer suffers from the initial endogeneity.

There are two final practical issues associated with instrumental variables that should be mentioned. First, because instrumental variable analysis results in biased but consistent estimators, it should only be used with large samples. Second, in practice, it is quite often extremely difficult to find an instrument that is related to the endogenous independent variable but not related to the error term.

14.3 USE TWO-STAGE LEAST SQUARES TO CORRECT FOR MEASUREMENT ERROR

measurement error
Occurs when either the dependent variable or one or more independent variables are measured incorrectly.

A final situation in which instrumental variables is a valuable tool is the case of **measurement error.** To see why, consider that sometimes when collecting data, the values we actually observe do not exactly match the true values that we are intending to measure. Sometimes this happens for innocent enough reasons. For instance, we sometimes attempt to collect data for certain factors that are difficult for the respondent to remember correctly. As an example, suppose that we asked a random sample of individuals to report the number of times that they had attended the gym in the previous year. In such a case, those individuals who attended the gym every day and those who did not attend the gym for a single day would likely respond with correct information. But what of individuals who attended the gym on occasion? Would we expect their response as to the number of days that they attended the gym in the prior year to be exactly correct? Probably not. Likewise, sometimes the individuals recording responses accidentally record incorrect information. As an example, suppose that an individual responded that he or she had attended the gym 32 days in the prior year while the questioner accidentally recorded 23 instead. Other times, measurement error results for the more nefarious reason that the respondent intentionally reported untrue information. As an example, suppose that we ask someone who cheated on his or her income taxes to report his or her true gross income. Would this individual be likely to report the true amount if it would reveal the crime? Probably not. In all of these cases, regardless of the root cause, because the reported value was inaccurate, our OLS estimates based on the data would be biased and inconsistent if the measurement error occurs in the independent variables.

This mistake is referred to as measurement error. Another situation in which we are likely to encounter measurement error is the unintentional mis-recording of observed data. Suppose, for example, that when entering data you simply type in the wrong number (or the reporting agency makes such a mistake). This would create measurement error in the variable for which the data was misentered.

The degree to which measurement error is a potential concern depends in large part on whether the suspected measurement error occurs in our dependent or our independent variables.

Measurement Error in the Dependent Variable

Suppose we suspect that measurement error is present in our dependent variable. What effect would we expect this to have on our OLS estimates? To answer this question, assume that the true value of our dependent variable y_i is measured with error such that

$$y_i = y_i^* + u_i \tag{14.3.1}$$

where y_i^* is the value that we actually observe for the dependent variable and u_i is the measurement error associated with each observed value.

In such a case, while the true regression model would be

$$y_i = \beta_0 + \beta_1 x_{1i} + \beta_2 x_{2i} + \varepsilon_i \tag{14.3.2}$$

the regression model that we would be able to estimate would be

$$y_i^* = \beta_0 + \beta_1 x_{1i} + \beta_2 x_{2i} + \varepsilon_i^* \tag{14.3.3}$$

where $\varepsilon_i^* = \varepsilon_i + u_i$.

To determine how measurement error might affect our OLS estimates, we start by noting the composite nature of the error term in formula 14.3.2, in which the first component represents traditional unobservable factors and the second component represents the error with which we measure the dependent variable. It turns out that the exact degree to which this affects our OLS estimates depends on the manner in which the measurement error term, $u_{i,}$ is related to the independent variable, x_i. If the measurement error term is not systematically related to any of the independent variables, then our OLS estimates will be unbiased. On the other hand, if the measurement error term is systematically related to any of the independent variables, then our OLS estimates will be biased.

There is an important additional concern associated with measurement error in the dependent variable. Because measurement error introduces an additional component into the error term, the error variance is higher than it would have been without any measurement error, meaning that the estimated standard errors will be higher than they would have been without the measurement error.

Measurement Error in an Independent Variable

Suppose that instead of having measurement error in our dependent variable, we have measurement error in one of our independent variables. Similar to the previous discussion, we would assume that the true value our dependent variable x_{1i} is measured with error such that

$$x_{1i} = x_{1i}^* + u_{1i} \tag{14.3.4}$$

where x_{1i}^* is the value that we actually observe for the independent variable and u_i is the measurement error associated with each observed value. The true regression model in this case would be

$$y_i = \beta_0 + \beta_1 x_{1i} + \beta_2 x_{2i} + \varepsilon_i \tag{14.3.5}$$

but the model that we would be able to estimate would be

$$y_i = \beta_0 + \beta_1 (x_{1i}^* + u_{1i}) + \beta_2 x_{2i} + \varepsilon_i \tag{14.3.6}$$

which can be rewritten as

$$y_i = \beta_0 + \beta_1 x_{1i} + \beta_2 x_{2i} + (\varepsilon_i \mp \beta_1 u_{1i}) \tag{14.3.7}$$

or

$$y_i = \beta_0 + \beta_1 x_{1i} + \beta_2 x_{2i} + \varepsilon_i^* \tag{14.3.8}$$

where $\varepsilon_i^* = (\varepsilon_i - \beta_1 u_{1i})$.

Because $\beta_1 u_{1i}$ is now a component of the error term, our OLS estimate of β_1 is biased. One alternative to correct for this problem is to collect data that do not suffer from measurement error and use those data in place of the variable that suffers from measurement error. Unfortunately, this solution is often difficult to implement. Instead, we could attempt an instrumental variable approach to solving the problem. To do so, we would need another potential measure of x_{1i}—say, x'_{1i}—which is also measured with error. If we were able to identify such a variable, we could then use it as an instrument in the first stage of a two-stage least squares approach. As an example, suppose that we have data on an individual's self-reported salary, which are likely to suffer from measurement error because individuals are often unable to quote their previous year's earning correctly to the penny off the tops of their heads. Suppose that, in addition, we have salary data that are reported by the individual's spouse or significant other. While this new measure is also likely to be measured with error, the errors in the two reported values should be uncorrelated because the spouse or significant other is likely to report an entirely different number. In such a case, we could perform two-stage least squares by regressing x^*_{1i} on x'_{1i} and the remaining independent variables in the first stage, using those estimates to calculate predicted values x^*_{1i} and then regressing y_i on the predicted value of x^*_{1i} and the remaining independent variables in the second stage. Using instrumental variables in this manner with a large sample will result in biased but consistent estimates.

Our Empirical Example: Using a Spouse's Responses to Control for Measurement Error in an Individual's Self-Reported Drinking

As an example, consider that patients often misreport their true behavior to their doctors. For instance, in the June 8, 2009, *Los Angeles Times* article, "Body of Lies: Patients Aren't 100% Honest with Doctors," Karen Ravn writes that

> Of 1,500 responders to a 2004 online survey by WebMD, 45% admitted they hadn't always told it exactly like it was—with 13% saying they had "lied," and 32% saying they had "stretched the truth." In the survey, 22% lied about smoking, 17% about sex, 16% about drinking and 12% about recreational drug use.

Suppose that, given such evidence, we are concerned that the data for the number of days in which an individual consumed five or more drinks in our doctor's advice sample is subject to measurement error. Suppose further that in addition to collecting data on the number of days in which each individual self-reported excessive drinking, a doctor was able to collect data on the number of days in which the individual's spouse reported his or her having engaged in that behavior. If the individual were indeed likely to misreport the number of days in which he or she consumed five or more drinks, then the spouse's reported number of days might serve as a valid instrument for correcting the measurement error.

To see how, as a baseline for comparison, we estimate the population regression model

$$Reduce_i = \beta_0 + \beta_1 Days_i + \beta_2 Male_i + \beta_3 Married_i + \beta_4 Black_i + \beta_5 Other_i + \beta_6(Age\ 25 - 44)_i + \beta_7(Age\ 45 - 64)_i + \beta_8(Age\ 65 - 69)_i + \varepsilon_i \quad \textbf{14.3.9}$$

and get Excel Regression Output 14.5.

If we possess data on the number of days in which an individual's spouse reports that he or she consumed five or more drinks in the past year, then we might control for the potential measurement error in the self-reported number of days of binge drinking by estimating the first-stage population regression model

$$Days_i = \beta_0 + \beta_1 Spouse\ days_i + \beta_2 Male_i + \beta_3 Married_i + \beta_4 Black_i + \beta_5 Other_i + \beta_6(Age\ 25 - 44)_i + \beta_7(Age\ 45 - 64)_i + \beta_8(Age\ 65 - 69)_i + \varepsilon_i \quad \textbf{14.3.10}$$

Excel Regression Output 14.5: OLS Estimates for Being Advised to Reduce Alcohol Intake for Our Doctor's Advice Sample

SUMMARY OUTPUT

Regression Statistics	
Multiple R	0.196704244
R Square	0.038692560
Adjusted R Square	0.038165093
Standard Error	0.210041867
Observations	14589

ANOVA

	df	SS	MS	F	Significance F
Regression	8	25.89014134	3.236267668	73.35550192	4.4047E-119
Residual	14580	643.2344045	0.044117586		
Total	14588	669.1245459			

	Coefficients	Standard Error	*t* Stat	*p*-value	Lower 95%	Upper 95%
Intercept	0.07626792	0.00934278	8.16329904	3.52505E-16	0.05795489	0.09458096
Self-Reported Days with 5+ Drinks per Year	0.00047970	3.91606E-05	12.24963174	2.48895E-34	0.00040294	0.00055646
Male	0.02870659	0.00353613	8.11809320	5.11209E-16	0.02177534	0.03563784
Married	−0.00928651	0.00354972	−2.61612908	0.00890246	−0.01624441	−0.00232862
Black	0.05590614	0.00550710	10.15164834	3.9193E-24	0.04511153	0.06670076
Other Race	−0.00027947	0.00992747	−0.02815158	0.97754164	−0.01973858	0.01917963
Age 25–44	−0.07411870	0.00933212	−7.94232064	2.12859E-15	−0.09241084	−0.05582656
Age 45–64	−0.02393471	0.00945573	−2.53124038	0.011376413	−0.04246913	−0.00540029
Age 65–69	−0.01572136	0.01199064	−1.31113581	0.189832532	−0.03922454	0.00778182

Note: Dependent variable is whether individual was advised by a doctor to reduce alcohol intake. Omitted age is 70–74. Highlighted variables are significant at the 5 percent level.

calculating the predicted number of days in which the individual consumed five or more drinks as

$$\widehat{Days}_i = \hat{\beta}_0 + \hat{\beta}_1 Spouse\ days_i + \hat{\beta}_2 Male_i + \hat{\beta}_3 Married_i + \hat{\beta}_4 Black_i + \hat{\beta}_5 Other_i + \hat{\beta}_6 (Age\ 25-44)_i + \hat{\beta}_7 (Age\ 45-64)_i + \hat{\beta}_8 (Age\ 65-69)_i \quad \textbf{14.3.11}$$

and estimating the second-stage population regression model

$$Reduce_i = \beta_0 + \beta_1 \widehat{Days}_i + \beta_2 Male_i + \beta_3 Married_i + \beta_4 Black_i + \beta_5 Other_i + \beta_6 (Age\ 25-44)_i + \beta_7 (Age\ 45-64)_i + \beta_8 (Age\ 65-69)_i + \varepsilon_i \quad \textbf{14.3.12}$$

Using the Stata commands

```
ivreg reduce male married black othrace age2544 age4564 age6569
                    (days = spousedays)
```

we get Empirical Results 14.3.

Empirical Results 14.3: Using Two-Stage Least Squares to Control for the Potential Measurement Error of the Self-Reported Number of Days with Five or More Drinks per Year in Our Doctor's Advice Sample

First Stage

	Coefficient	Standard Error	t	P > |t|	Lower 95%	Upper 95%
Intercept	−0.474116	0.062572	−0.76	0.4490	−1.700615	0.752382
Spouse-Reported Days with 5+ Drinks per Year	0.931933	0.002577	361.68	0.0000	0.926882	0.936983
Male	1.42727	0.236523	6.03	0.0000	0.963655	1.890885
Currently Married	−0.493104	0.237702	−2.07	0.0380	−0.959030	−0.027179
Black	0.334921	0.368813	0.91	0.3640	−0.387999	1.057841
Other Race	−1.282229	0.664797	−1.93	0.0540	−2.585316	0.020857
Age 25–44	0.496652	0.624965	0.79	0.4270	−0.728357	1.721662
Age 45–64	0.218098	0.633255	0.34	0.7310	−1.023162	1.459359
Age 65–69	−0.235709	0.803020	−0.29	0.7690	−1.80973	1.338313
Prob > F			0.0000			
R-squared			0.9033			
Observations			14,589			

Note: Dependent variable is self-reported number of days with 5+ drinks per year. Omitted age is 70–74. Highlighted variables are significant at the 5 percent level. Variables highlighted in gray are significant at the 10 percent level.

Second Stage

	Coefficient	Standard Error	t	P > |t|	Lower 95%	Upper 95%
Intercept	0.076370	0.009343	8.17	0.0000	0.058056	0.09468
Predicted Self-Reported Days with 5+ Drinks per Year	0.000453	0.000041	10.97	0.0000	0.000372	0.000534
Male	0.029116	0.003542	8.22	0.0000	0.022174	0.036059
Currently Married	−0.009486	0.003551	−2.67	0.0080	−0.016447	−0.002525
Black	0.055914	0.005507	10.15	0.0000	0.045119	0.066708
Other Race	−0.000418	0.009928	−0.04	0.9660	−0.019878	0.019042
Age 25–44	−0.073962	0.009333	−7.93	0.0000	−0.092255	−0.055669
Age 45–64	−0.023820	0.009456	−2.52	0.0120	−0.042355	−0.005285
Age 65–69	−0.015722	0.011991	−1.31	0.1900	−0.039225	0.007782
Prob > F			0.0000			
R-squared			0.0387			
Observations			14,589			

Note: Dependent varaible is whether individual was advised by a dcotor to reduce alcohol intake. Omitted age is 70–74. Highlighted variables are significant at the 5 percent level.

Comparing these estimates to the OLS estimates in Excel Regression Output 14.5, we see that the results do not change much at all. This might suggest that while measurement error might be in our data, its presence is not that significant of a problem.

Empirical Research Tool 14.3 summarizes the use of two-stage least squares to correct for measurement error.

EMPIRICAL RESEARCH TOOL 14.3: USING TWO-STAGE LEAST SQUARES TO CORRECT FOR MEASUREMENT ERROR

How to Do It:

1. Identify another independent variable that is also measured with error. Note that the measurement errors from the two variables should not be related to each other.

Perform two-stage least squares by:

2. Regressing the independent variable that is measured with error on all remaining independent variables, including the additional variable found in step 1, and calculating the predicted value.
3. Estimating the initial population regression model with the predicted values of the independent variable that is measured with error substituted for the actual variable.

Why It Works:

The first-stage regression isolates the part of the variable that is measured with error that is not correlated with the error term, meaning that the second-stage regression no longer suffers from inconsistency that arises from the independent variable being measured with error.

ADDITIONS TO OUR EMPIRICAL RESEARCH TOOLKIT

In this chapter, we have introduced a number of tools that will prove valuable when performing empirical research:

- Using two-stage least squares to identify simultaneous demand and supply equations.
- Using two-stage least squares to correct for endogeneity of an independent variable.
- Using two-stage least squares to correct for measurement error.

OUR NEW EMPIRICAL TOOLS IN PRACTICE: USING WHAT WE HAVE LEARNED IN THIS CHAPTER

While our former student had estimated an upward-sloping supply curve for milk production in the United States through regular OLS, he was concerned that he had not correctly identified the true marginal effect of milk prices on milk production because milk prices are determined by both milk supply and milk demand. To correctly identify the milk supply equation, our former student realized that he needed to collect data on a variable that affected milk demand but not milk supply. Knowing that consumer confidence is a determinant of demand but not supply, our former student collected data on the consumer confidence for the time period covered in his sample. Figure 14.6 presents the line graph that he produced for these data.

FIGURE 14.6
Line Graphs of Consumer Confidence for Our Former Student's Milk Supply Data

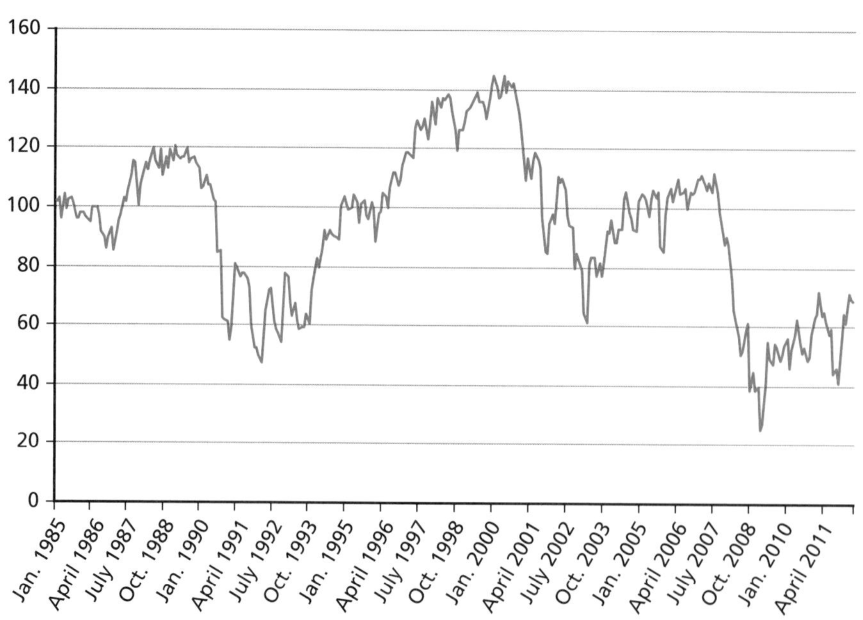

Using these data, our former student performed two-stage least squares and got the results in Table 14.3.

TABLE 14.3
Using Two-Stage Least Squares to Estimate Our Former's Students Milk Supply Equation

	Supply Equation					
	Coefficients	Standard Error	t	P > |t|	Lower 95%	Upper 95%
Intercept	12,057.69	1,909.19	6.32	0.000	8,301.77	15,813.61
All milk price	361.76	126.79	2.85	0.005	112.34	611.19
Milk feed price ratio	−1,282.92	110.23	−11.64	0.000	−1,499.78	– 1,066.07
Prob > F			0.0000			
R-squared			0.4907			
Observations			328			

Note: Dependent variable is all milk production (millions of gallons). Highlighted variables are significant at the 5 percent level.

These results suggested to him that the milk supply curve was indeed upward sloping but that the estimated marginal effect of milk prices on milk production using instrumental variables was lower than the marginal effect estimated through OLS while the estimated marginal effect of the milk–feed price ratio was similar to that estimated through OLS.

Based on this work, from the initial idea through data collection, empirical analysis, interpretation of results, and effective write-up, our former student was judged to have conducted a successful empirical research project.

LOOKING AHEAD TO CHAPTER 15

There are a number of other situations encountered by introductory econometrics students in which OLS is not the best possible estimator. For instance, we might sometimes wish to (1) learn about the estimated relationship between the dependent variable and the independent variables at points in the distribution other than the mean, (2) estimate models in which the dependent variable takes on non-negative count values, (3) control for sample-selection bias in our dependent variable, or (4) employ quasi-experimental techniques. We discuss the empirical tools required to address these situations in Chapter 15.

Problems

14.1 The following two equations describe property crime and police expenditures across U.S. cities:

$$Crime_i = \alpha_0 + \alpha_1 Police_i + \alpha_2 Income_i + u_{1,i}$$

$$Police_i = \beta_0 + \beta_1 Crime_i + \beta_2 Income_i + \beta_3 Liberal_i + u_{2,1}$$

$Crime_i$ = Number of crimes committed in city i last year
$Police_i$ = Total spending on the police force in city i last year
$Income_i$ = Average income in city i last year
$Liberal_i$ = Share of votes received by the liberal presidential candidate from city i in the last election

a. If you were to estimate these two equations with OLS, would you get consistent estimates? Why or why not?

b. Which of the two equations is fully identified? How do you know this?

c. Describe how you would estimate one or both of the equations using 2SLS. Describe the properties of the estimates in both equations.

d. Come up with another explanatory variable that you could add to one of these equations to make the system fully identified. Justify the inclusion of this variable.

e. Discuss practical and theoretical drawbacks of using 2SLS.

14.2 A public health researcher is trying to estimate the determinants of fertility rates in developing countries. She proposes the following model:

$$FR_i = \beta_0 + \beta_1 Age_i + \beta_2 Education_i + \beta_3 Urban_i + u_i$$

where FR_i is the fertility rate for individual i (measured as the number of children ever born), regressed on their age, their years of education, and whether or not they live in an urban area.

a. Another researcher argues that the Education variable suffers from a simultaneity bias with fertility rates. Identify the consequences of including an endogenous explanatory variable, and briefly outline the steps you would take to consistently estimate this model.

b. This study used two different methods to measure fertility rates: one for rural areas and one for urban areas. Each method generated some measurement error, though the rural methodology was quite a bit less accurate. Given this fact, what are the consequences of measurement error in this sample? What, if anything, can you do to remedy the potential problems associated with measurement error on the fertility variable? Be as specific as possible.

c. Consider your answer to part (b), and assume fertility rates no longer suffer from measurement error, but the education variable does suffer from measurement error. Also assume you have two different measures of education: one self-reported and the other obtained by asking the individual's closest relative. Given this fact, what are the consequences of measurement error in this sample? What, if anything, can you do to remedy the potential problems associated with measurement error on the education variable? Be as specific as possible.

14.3 The following two equations describe the interactions between fertility rates and average income of women in a cross-section of countries:

$$Fertility_i = \alpha_0 + \alpha_1 Income_i + \alpha_2 Education_i + \alpha_3 Rural_i + u_1$$

$$Income_i = \beta_0 + \beta_1 Fertility_i + \beta_2 Education_i + u_2$$

where the fertility rate (measured by average number of births per woman in country i) is a function of average female income in that country, the average years of female education, and the fraction of country i's population that lives in rural areas, and female income is a function of the fertility rate and female education.

a. If you were to estimate these two equations separately with OLS, would you get consistent parameter estimates? Explain why or why not.

b. Which of the two equations is fully identified? Explain why.

c. Describe how you would consistently estimate the identified equation.

d. Come up with another explanatory variable, Z_i, that you could add to this system so that both equations can be estimated. What two conditions must Z_i satisfy? Explain why the variable you selected meets these two criteria.

14.4 The following system of equations model the murder rate in a state and the total number of executions in that state:

$$M_i = \beta_0 + \beta_1 P_i + \beta_2 E_i + \beta_3 I_i + u_i$$

$$E_i = \gamma_0 + \gamma_1 M_i + \gamma_2 P_i + e_i$$

where M_i = Murder rate in state i

P_i = Total expenditures on the police force in state i

E_i = Total number of executions in state i

I_i = Average annual income in state i

a. Suppose you estimated each equation with OLS. Would you get consistent estimates? Why or why not?

b. Given what you know about needing both a demand and supply shifter, can both of these equations be estimated? If not, which one cannot be estimated?

c. Describe in detail how you would consistently estimate the equation that can be estimated using two-stage least squares.

14.5 Consider the following regression model:

$$y_i^* = \beta_0 + \beta_1 x_{1,i} + \beta_2 x_{2,i} + \varepsilon_i$$

where y_i^* is a dependent variable that is measured with error. Specifically, you never observe y_i^*, you actually observe $y_i = y_i^* + \eta$, where η is the measurement error in y_i^*.

a. Under what condition(s) will estimating $y_i = \beta_0 + \beta_1 x_{1,i} + \beta_2 x_{2,i} + \varepsilon_i$ yield inconsistent estimates?

b. Assuming that the condition(s) for consistency in part (a) are met, what will be the net effect of measurement error in y?

14.6 Consider a simple time-series model where the independent variable has classical measurement error

$$(1)\ y_t = \beta_0 + \beta_1 x_t^* + \varepsilon_t$$

and

$$(2)\ x_t = x_t^* + u_t$$

where ε_t has zero mean and is uncorrelated with x_t^* and u_t. We observe y_t and x_t only. Assume that u_t has zero mean and is uncorrelated with x_t^* and that x_t^* also has a zero mean (this last assumption is only to simplify the algebra).

a. Write $x_t^* = x_t - u_t$, and plug this into equation (1). Show that the error term in the new equation—say, v_t—is negatively correlated with x_t if $\beta_1 > 0$. What does this imply about the OLS estimator of β_1 from the regression of y_t on x_t?

b. In addition to the previous assumptions, assume that ε_t and u_t are uncorrelated with all past values of x_t^* and u_t—in particular, with x_{t-1}^* and u_{t-1}. Show that $E(x_{t-1}, v_t) = 0$, where v_t is the error term in the model from part (a).

c. Are x_t and x_{t-1} likely to be correlated? Explain.

d. What do parts (b) and (c) suggest as a useful strategy for consistently estimating β_0 and β_1?

Exercises

E14.1 Use the data in **Education.xls** to run an instrumental variable regression.

a. First estimate the model using OLS. Regress logwage on *Experience*, *Occupation* (equals 1 if blue collar occupation and 0 if white collar), Industry (equals 1 if manufacturing industry and 0 if not), *Married* (equals 1 if married and 0 if not), Union (equals 1 if in a union and 0 if not), *Education* (years of education), and *Black* (equals 1 if black and 0 if not).

b. Now use *South* (equals 1 if live in south and 0 if not) as an instrument for education. Run the first-stage regression by regressing *Education on South* and all other independent variables and get the predicted value for education. Run the second-stage regression by regressing logwage on the predicted value of *Education*, *Experience*, *Occupation*, *Industry*, *Married*, *Union*, and *Black*.

c. Comment on if you think that the dummy variable *South* is a valid instrument; that is, is *South* correlated with years of *Education* and uncorrelated with the error term in the regression in part (a)?

E14.2 Use the data in **Demand.xls** to run an instrumental variable regression.

a. First estimate the demand equation model using OLS. Regress *Quantity on Price and Consumer Confidence*.

b. Now use Milk feed price as an instrument for *Price*. Run the first- and second-stage regressions. Does your regression differ from what you found in part (a)?

c. Draw a picture that shows why it is important to use a supply shifter when estimating a demand equation.

E14.3 Use the data in **Measurement Error.xls** to correct for measurement error.

a. First estimate the model using OLS. Regress logwage on *Experience*, *Occupation* (equals 1 if blue collar occupation and 0 if white collar), *Industry* (equals 1 if manufacturing industry and 0 if not), *Married* (equals 1 if married and 0 if not), Union (equals 1 if in a union and 0 if not), *Education* (years of education), and *Black* (equals 1 if black and 0 if not).

b. Now use spouse experience as an instrument for experience to correct for the fact that experience may be measured with error. Run the first-stage regression by regressing *Education on Spouse Experience* and all other independent variables and get the predicted value for *Experience*. Run the second-stage regression by regressing logwage on the predicted value of *Experience*, *Education*, *Occupation*, *Industry*, *Married*, *Union*, and *Black*.

Chapter Fifteen

Quantile Regression, Count Data, Sample Selection Bias, and Quasi-Experimental Methods

CHAPTER OBJECTIVES

After reading this chapter, you will be able to:

1. Estimate quantile regression.
2. Estimate models with non-negative count data.
3. Control for sample selection bias.
4. Use quasi-experimental methods.

A STUDENT'S PERSPECTIVE

Suppose that as an economics student with an interest in public policy and health, you are interested in determining the relationship between changes in state cigarette taxes and future cigarette sales in the state.

This is exactly the situation encountered by one of our former students. In an effort to bring her econometric skills to bear, the student collected data on state cigarette tax rates (including the District of Columbia) in 2006 and 2007 as well as state cigarette sales per capita in the years immediately before and after (i.e., 2005 and 2008). Analyzing the data, the student noticed that 10 different states increased their tax rates between 2006 and 2007. This led her to question whether those 10 states observed a larger reduction in per capita cigarette sales than the 40 states (and the District of Columbia) that did not raise their tax rates.

Table 15.1 provides the summary statistics for these data.

As a baseline, our former student estimated the simple linear regression of 2008 per capita cigarette sales on a binary dummy variable indicating whether a state changed its cigarette tax rate between 2006 and 2007 that is presented in Table 15.2.

The student interpreted the results as suggesting that, all other independent variables constant, states that increased their cigarette tax rate between 2006 and 2007 averaged per capita cigarette sales in 2008 that were 11.6 percent lower than states that did not raise their cigarette tax rates. While potentially informative, our former student wondered whether OLS was indeed the most preferred estimator for answering her question of interest.

TABLE 15.1 Summary Statistics for Our Former Student's Change in Cigarette Tax Data

	Changed Cigarette Tax	2005 Sales per Capita	2008 Sales per Capita	Change	% Change
Alabama	0	79.967	79.585	−0.383	−0.005
Alaska	1	57.701	48.009	−9.692	−0.168
Arizona	1	37.337	33.768	−3.569	−0.096
Arkansas	0	79.079	78.876	−0.203	−0.003
California	0	32.299	30.848	−1.451	−0.045
Colorado	0	53.933	50.485	−3.448	−0.064
Connecticut	0	51.353	47.719	−3.634	−0.071
Delaware	0	169.971	137.504	−32.466	−0.191
D.C.	0	34.976	39.172	4.196	0.120
Florida	0	71.436	69.962	−1.474	−0.021
Georgia	0	64.610	64.680	0.070	0.001
Hawaii	1	46.111	44.683	−1.428	−0.031
Idaho	0	53.353	58.843	5.490	0.103
Illinois	0	51.405	48.496	−2.908	−0.057
Indiana	0	93.793	82.995	−10.798	−0.115
Iowa	1	82.463	58.304	−24.159	−0.293
Kansas	0	53.566	52.294	−1.273	−0.024
Kentucky	0	176.401	144.481	−31.921	−0.181
Louisiana	0	92.999	83.948	−9.051	−0.097
Maine	0	71.404	55.452	−15.952	−0.223
Maryland	0	48.122	43.583	−4.539	−0.094
Massachusetts	0	42.152	43.190	1.038	0.025
Michigan	0	58.490	52.312	−6.178	−0.106
Minnesota	1	64.114	51.872	−12.242	−0.191
Mississippi	0	87.626	94.231	6.604	0.075
Missouri	0	100.785	101.744	0.959	0.010
Montana	0	60.779	53.803	−6.976	−0.115
Nebraska	0	59.772	64.018	4.246	0.071
Nevada	0	62.573	66.121	3.548	0.057
New Hampshire	0	136.874	114.799	−22.075	−0.161
New Jersey	1	37.465	34.396	−3.069	−0.082
New Mexico	0	34.066	35.026	0.959	0.028
New York	0	32.036	31.433	−0.603	−0.019
North Carolina	1	86.854	77.127	−9.727	−0.112
North Dakota	0	65.473	74.462	8.989	0.137
Ohio	0	88.691	64.824	−23.867	−0.269
Oklahoma	0	94.938	88.893	−6.045	−0.064
Oregon	0	50.448	52.154	1.707	0.034
Pennsylvania	0	62.555	61.829	−0.726	−0.012
Rhode Island	0	50.819	43.309	−7.510	−0.148
South Carolina	0	88.040	92.460	4.421	0.050
South Dakota	1	65.904	50.557	−15.347	−0.233
Tennessee	0	91.989	71.533	−20.455	−0.222
Texas	1	51.165	46.026	−5.140	−0.100
Utah	0	29.747	33.103	3.356	0.113
Vermont	1	63.901	51.673	−12.229	−0.191
Virginia	0	79.417	75.198	−4.219	−0.053
Washington	0	35.363	33.032	−2.331	−0.066
West Virginia	0	102.344	113.303	10.958	0.107
Wisconsin	0	69.012	67.903	−1.110	−0.016
Wyoming	0	72.465	81.619	9.154	0.126

TABLE 15.2 OLS Regression Output for Our Former Student's Change in Cigarette Tax Data

SUMMARY OUTPUT	
Regression Statistics	
Multiple R	0.426873034
R Square	0.182220587
Adjusted R Square	0.165531211
Standard Error	0.099508158
Observations	51

ANOVA

	df	SS	MS	F	Significance F
Regression	1	0.108112205	0.108112205	10.91835845	0.001784866
Residual	49	0.485191806	0.009901874		
Total	50	0.593304012			

	Coefficients	Standard Error	*t* Stat	*p*-value	Lower 95%	Upper 95%
Intercept	−0.033739541	0.015540563	−2.171062885	0.034798441	−0.064969471	−0.002509610
Changed Cigarette Tax	−0.115965959	0.035095534	−3.304293941	0.001784866	−0.186493072	−0.045438845

Note: Dependent variable is percentage change in cigarette sales between 2004 and 2008. Highlighted variables are significant at the 5 percent level.

BIG PICTURE OVERVIEW

Chapter 15 finishes our discussion of more advanced topics that students sometimes encounter when conducting their own empirical research projects by introducing empirical tools for: (1) estimating linear relationships at points in the distribution other than the mean, (2) dealing with non-negative count data, (3) dealing with sample selection bias, and (4) performing quasi-experimental methods. Figure 15.1 summarizes the empirical tools used in this chapter.

FIGURE 15.1
A Visual Depiction of the Empirical Tools Introduced in This Chapter

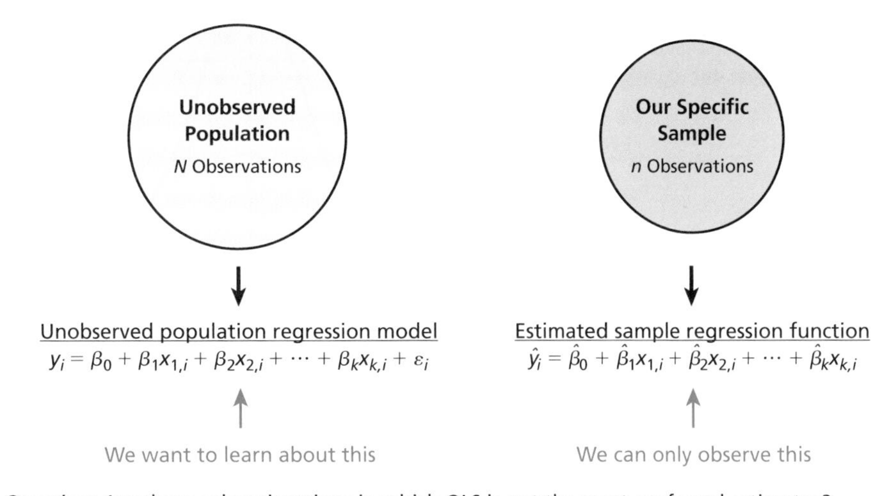

Question: Are there other situations in which OLS is not the most-preferred estimator?

Answer: Yes.

(1) When we want to estimate the linear relationship at points in the distribution other than the mean } Quantile Regression

(2) When our dependent variable is non-negative count data } Poisson, Negative Binomial

(3) When we think that our data suffers from sample-selection bias } Heckman Correction

(4) When we can use quasi-experimental methods } Difference-in-Difference

15.1 ESTIMATE QUANTILE REGRESSION

A potential concern associated with determining our OLS best-fit line by minimizing the sum of squared residuals is that, by definition, the estimated coefficients are based on comparisons to the mean values of each of the variables. Accordingly, the estimated linear relationships only truly apply for the mean values of those two distributions, and hence only provide estimates of the average marginal effect that an independent variable has on the dependent variable. While these estimates are of great potential value, they do not always provide all of the information in which we might be interested.

As an example of this concern, consider that in Chapter 6 we interpreted the estimated sample regression function

$$\begin{aligned} Salary_i = &-1{,}003{,}204.93 + 569{,}508.46 Experience_i + 212{,}460.86 Home\ runs_i \\ &(394{,}238.70) \quad (63{,}560.11) \qquad\qquad\qquad (23{,}578.03) \end{aligned}$$

as indicating that, holding home runs constant, each additional year of experience was estimated to be associated with a \$569,508.46 greater annual salary, *on average,* and that holding experience constant, each additional home run was estimated to be associated with a \$212,460.86 greater annual salary, *on average.* While these estimates answer the question "Are experience and home runs important determinants of player salaries?" they do not answer the question "Does the effect of experience on salary, holding home runs constant, differ for players with lower salaries than for players with higher salaries?" With modern computer power, there is a relatively simple method for answering the latter question.

For illustration purposes, suppose we are concerned that the estimated relationship between annual salary and experience, holding home runs constant, might be different for players at the 10th percentile of the salary distribution (or 75th percentile, or 90th percentile, etc.) than for players at the mean of the salary distribution. Figure 15.2 depicts this concern.

FIGURE 15.2
Distribution of the Dependent Variable, for example, Salaries

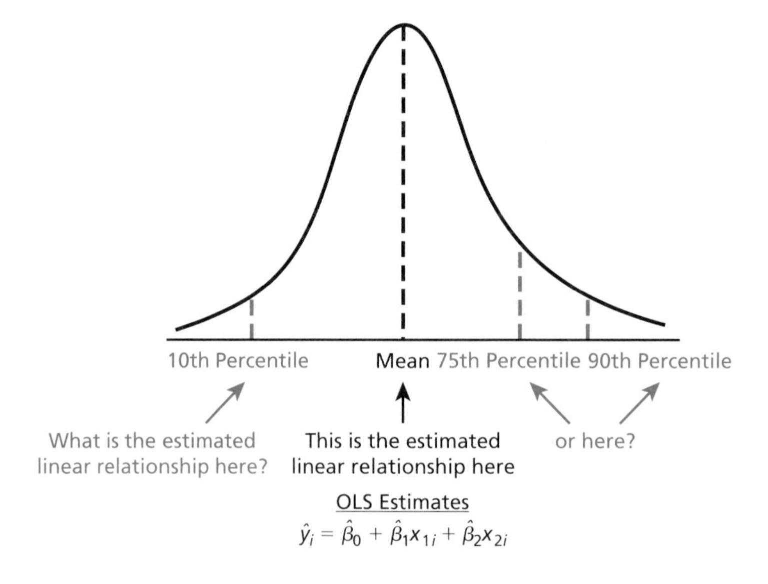

quantile regression
Results in estimates approximating either the median or other percentiles of the dependent variable.

Quantile regression estimates marginal effects at different points in the distribution of the dependent variable by minimizing a loss function rather than minimizing the sum of squared residuals. The solution to the quantile regression optimization problem does not provide a simple closed-form solution using differential calculus; instead, linear programming algorithms must be used to determine the estimated marginal effects at the different points in the distribution.

While quantile regression is not programmed in Excel, it is programmed in more-advanced statistical packages. Using the Stata commands,

```
qreg salary experience hr, quantile(.10)
qreg salary experience hr, quantile(.25)
qreg salary experience hr, quantile(.50)
qreg salary experience hr, quantile(.75)
qreg salary experience hr, quantile(.90)
```

and combining the estimated slope coefficients into one easy-to-read table, we get Empirical Results 15.1.

Empirical Results 15.1: Estimated Quantile Regression Slope Coefficients for Our MIB Position Player Sample

	OLS	Quantile Regression				
	Mean	10th Percentile	25th Percentile	Median	75th Percentile	90th Percentile
Intercept	−1,003,205.00	214,285.70	−167,692.30	−158,823.50	169,780.20	400,000.00
	(394,238.70)	(45,372.54)	(109,525.10)	(225,690.20)	(436,652.90)	(405,122.30)
Experience	569,508.50	89,285.71	257,307.70	429,411.80	703,736.30	1,171,129.00
	(63,560.11)	(10,728.26)	(23,377.08)	(36,078.75)	(57,729.61)	(51,331.69)
HR	212,460.90	12,142.86	78,076.92	111,764.70	230,219.80	230,971.10
	(23,578.03)	(3,424.94)	(7,487.22)	(13,425.58)	(23,544.63)	(17,874.61)
Observations	200	200	200	200	200	200

Note: Dependent variable is annual salary. Standard errors in parentheses. Highlighted values are significant at the 5 percent level.

These results can be interpreted as follows. All other independent variables constant, the estimated marginal effect of experience is statistically significant at all points in the distribution, with the estimated effect of an additional year of experience increasing monotonically (with each successive percentile) from a low of $89,285.71 for the 10th percentile of the MLB salary distribution to a high of $1,171,129.00 for the 90th percentile of the MLB salary distribution. These estimates are valuable because they paint a very different picture of the relationship between experience and salary than the one we found in the OLS regression.

As a final point, note that by calculating estimated marginal effects at different points in the distribution of the dependent variable, quantile regression is more robust than OLS for data sets containing significant outliers. For this reason, we encourage considering quantile regression rather than OLS for highly-skewed data sets. Quantile regression is also a valuable tool to use in policy analysis where there may be nonconstant effects over the distribution of the dependent variable.

Empirical Research Tool 15.1 summarizes quantile regression.

EMPIRICAL RESEARCH TOOL 15.1: QUANTILE REGRESSION

How to Do It:

Ask a more advanced statistical package to estimate quantile regressions at desired points in the distribution.

Why It Works:

Doing so estimates marginal effects based on the median and other percentile values of the dependent variable rather than the mean value of the dependent variable (which is how we estimate OLS).

15.2 ESTIMATE MODELS WITH NON-NEGATIVE COUNT DATA

non-negative count data
Occur when the data take on integers that are greater than or equal to 0 and the integers arise from counting rather than ranking.

Another situation in which a different estimator might be preferred to OLS is the case of dependent variables that take on specific, non-negative discrete values that are the result of counting rather than ranking. In such cases, which we refer to as **non-negative count data,** we prefer to use estimators based on distributions other than the normal distribution.

As an example of non-negative count data, suppose that we are interested in estimating the degree to which different independent factors are correlated with the number of children born to a given mother. In such a case, because the mother has exactly 0, exactly 1, exactly 2, and so on, children, the observed dependent variable is discrete and noncontinuous. Because such data are non-negative and noncontinuous, OLS is not the best-possible estimator. This is true for a number of reasons. First, as we saw with binary and categorical dependent variables, OLS can provide negative estimated values even though such values, by definition, can never occur. Second, because of the underlying nature of the data, OLS estimates are biased, inconsistent, and inefficient for count data models.

The issues and consequences associated with count data models are summarized in the following box.

The Issues and Consequences Associated with Estimating Non-Negative Count Models by OLS

Problem:

OLS does not account for the non-negative, noncontinuous nature of count data.

Consequences:

When estimating non-negative count data by OLS, the

1. Parameter estimates are biased.
2. Parameter estimates are inconsistent.
3. Parameter estimates are inefficient.

Given these issues, we need to develop an alternative estimator to OLS that accounts for the non-negative, noncontinuous nature of the dependent variable. Before discussing these methods, we need to introduce the empirical example that forms the basis of our discussion.

Our Empirical Example: Early-Career Publications by Economics PhDs

A well-known phrase related to academia is "publish or perish." This phrase derives from the fact that to achieve tenure within a given academic department, an individual faculty member must produce a record of academic publications commensurate with the standards of the department. Because PhD-granting academic departments invest heavily in producing students who go on to receive academic jobs at other institutions, an obvious concern is how successful their graduates are in terms of the number of academic articles that they produce. As such, PhD-granting departments might be very interested in determining which factors are associated with the future publishing success of their graduates. Because PhD recipients can only produce a non-negative, discrete number of articles, the dependent variable in such an analysis would be an example of non-negative count data.

Economic theory suggests that several independent factors should be associated with a student's future publishing success. Of particular concern, during graduate school an individual is surely influenced by his or her dissertation advisor as well as his or her classmates and whether he or she was able to produce publication-quality research. We focus on these specific measures in assembling our data set.

Data to Be Analyzed: Our Newly Minted Economics PhD Publication Data

Following the process outlined in Appendix A, combining information from the *Dissertation Abstracts* database and *Econlit,* which is the American Economic Association's database of worldwide economics journals, we assemble a data set of the total number of academic publications in the first 12 years after graduation for the cohort of 681 students receiving their PhD in economics in 1994 and reporting the identity of their dissertation advisor. Note that we choose this 12-year time period due to the fact that academic economists are generally granted tenure and promoted to associate professor after roughly 6 years and promoted to full professor after roughly 12 years at their initial institution. Note further that our measure of a PhD program's quality is provided by the National Research Council's (NRC) ranking of the top 106 PhD-granting economics programs in the United States in 1995, while our measure of a dissertation advisor's prominence is whether he or she was ranked among the top 250 worldwide economists (which we refer to as "star advisors") or among the worldwide economists ranked 251 − 1,000 (which we refer to as "ranked advisors") according to Coupe (2003).

Table 15.3 presents summary statistics for these data.

TABLE 15.3
Summary Statistic for Our New Economics PhD Publication Data

Total publications	4.379
	(7.003)
PhD program NRC rank	32.106
	(27.975)
Work with star advisor	0.151
Work with ranked advisor	0.192
Publish while PhD student	0.245
Ever coauthor with advisor	0.172
Male student	0.824
International student	0.529
Observations	681

Note: Standard deviations in parentheses.

According to Table 15.3, the 681 students in our sample averaged roughly 4.4 total publications, or roughly 0.3 published articles per year by 2006, and graduated from a program with an average NRC ranking of 32.1. Roughly 15 percent of these students worked with advisors ranked among the top 250 worldwide economists, while roughly 19 percent worked with advisors ranked between 251 and 100 worldwide, roughly 25 percent published an academic article while being a graduate student, and roughly 17 percent coauthored with their advisor. Finally, roughly 82 percent of our sample of economics PhD recipients are male, while roughly 53 percent are international students.

Table 15.4 demonstrates the non-negative count data nature of our dependent variable by tabulating the number of academic articles published in the first 12 years after PhD receipt.

Table 15.4 suggests that academic publishing is not as easy as some might think. More than half of the economics PhDs in our sample publish either 0 or 1 academic article in their first 12 years after graduation, and only 12 percent average 1 or more publications per year. At the same time, there are a large number of stars in this cohort of 1994 graduates: 15 individuals average more than 2 publications per year and 3 publish more than 40 articles in the 12-year period.

Based on the preceding discussion, we desire to estimate the population regression model

$$\begin{aligned} Articles_i &= \beta_0 + \beta_1 Rank_i + \beta_2 Star_i + \beta_3 Ranked_i + \beta_4 Publish\ as\ student_i \\ &\quad + \beta_5 Coauthor\ with\ Advisor_i + \beta_6 Male_i + \beta_7 International_i + \varepsilon_i \end{aligned} \qquad 15.2.1$$

TABLE 15.4 Total Number of Publications in the First 12 Years after PhD Receipt

Total Articles	Frequency	Percent	Cumulative Frequency	Total Articles	Frequency	Percent	Cumulative Frequency
0	265	38.91	38.91	18	4	0.59	95.30
1	81	11.89	50.81	19	3	0.44	95.74
2	58	8.52	59.32	20	7	1.03	96.77
3	39	5.73	65.05	21	1	0.15	96.92
4	30	4.41	69.46	22	4	0.59	97.50
5	34	4.99	74.45	23	2	0.29	97.80
6	16	2.35	76.80	24	1	0.15	97.94
7	15	2.20	79.00	25	3	0.44	98.38
8	19	2.79	81.79	26	1	0.15	98.53
9	10	1.47	83.26	28	1	0.15	98.68
10	12	1.76	85.02	29	1	0.15	98.83
11	16	2.35	87.37	33	1	0.15	98.97
12	8	1.17	88.55	34	1	0.15	99.12
13	15	2.20	90.75	37	3	0.44	99.56
14	13	1.91	92.66	42	1	0.15	99.71
15	3	0.44	93.10	51	1	0.15	99.85
16	6	0.88	93.98	63	1	0.15	100.00
17	5	0.73	94.71				
				Total	681	100	

As a baseline for comparison, we estimate the population regression model in formula 15.2.1 by OLS and get Excel Regression Output 15.1.

These results can be interpreted as follows. All other independent variables constant, students who graduate from PhD programs that are 10 places higher in the rankings average nearly 0.4 more articles in their first 12 years (0.039×10), while students working with a star advisor, students publishing while in graduate school, and students who coauthor with their advisor average 2.5, 5.7, and 3.7 more articles in their first 12 years, respectively.

Excel Regression Output 15.1: OLS Results for Total Number of Publications in First 12 Years after PhD Receipt

SUMMARY OUTPUT

Regression Statistics	
Multiple R	0.538822504
R Square	0.290329691
Adjusted R Square	0.282948276
Standard Error	5.930391852
Observations	681

Number of individuals in our sample

ANOVA

	df	SS	MS	F	Significance F
Regression	7	9683.150026	1383.307147	39.33252613	2.22423E-46
Residual	673	23669.10548	35.16954752		
Total	680	33352.25551			

	Coefficients	Standard Error	*t* Stat	*p*-value	Lower 95%	Upper 95%
Intercept	2.916802531	0.690251369	4.225710607	2.71047E-05	1.561497347	4.272107715
PhD Program NRC Rank	−0.038916222	0.009214737	−4.223259058	2.73936E-05	−0.057009313	−0.020823131
Work with Star Advisor	2.534971415	0.715771592	3.541592659	0.000425167	1.129557398	3.940385431
Work with Ranked Advisor	0.695305926	0.62460138	1.113199472	0.266020209	−0.531095825	1.921707678
Publish While PhD Student	5.686150788	0.566903079	10.03019916	3.6887E-22	4.573039368	6.799262209
Ever Coauthor with Advisor	3.681967474	0.642489167	5.730785298	1.50875E-08	2.420443139	4.943491809
Male Student	0.246242396	0.616593639	0.399359287	0.689755186	−0.964436195	1.456920987
International Student	−0.067179851	0.477357731	−0.140732718	0.888123208	−1.004469419	0.870109718

Note: Dependent variable is the number of publications in the first 12 years after PhD receipt. Variables highlighted in blue are significant at the 5 percent level.

A potential issue with these OLS estimates is that they do not account for the non-negative count nature of the dependent variable. There are, however, two well-known models that do account for the underlying nature of the data.

The Poisson Model

Poisson distribution
Appropriate for counting the number of times that a random event occurs in a given amount of time.

The **Poisson distribution** is a discrete probability distribution that expresses the probability of a given number of events occurring in a fixed interval of time and/or space. According to the Poisson distribution, the probability of exactly k events occurring in a given interval is

$$f(k, \lambda) = \frac{\lambda^k e^{-\lambda}}{k!} \qquad 15.2.2$$

Notation:
For the Poisson distribution:
- λ Expected number of occurrences
- k Non-negative integer

where λ is the expected number of occurrences in a given interval and k is a non-negative integer, such that $k = 0, 1, 2, \ldots, K$.

The log-likelihood function for this distribution is

$$L(\lambda) = \ln \prod_{i=1}^{n} f(k_i|\lambda) = \sum_{i=1}^{n} \ln\left(\frac{e^{-\lambda}\lambda^{ki}}{k_i!}\right)$$

$$= -n\lambda + \left(\sum_{i=1}^{n} k_i\right)\ln(\lambda) - \sum_{i=1}^{n}\ln(k_i!) \qquad 15.2.3$$

where $k_i! = k_i\,(k_i - 1)\,(k_i - 2) \times \cdots \times 2 \times 1$. This functional form constrains the estimates to be non-negative integers.

As always, we could estimate this model by hand. However, it is much easier to ask a more advanced statistical program to make the conversion for us (for detailed Stata and SAS commands, see Appendix B). Before presenting the results, it is important to note that, as with other nonlinear estimators such as the logit and probit, the estimated coefficients from the Poisson are not true estimated marginal effects. Accordingly, we need to ask our chosen program to make the desired conversion for us. Using the Stata command

```
poisson total nrcrank star ranked pubbyphd cowadv male intlstu
```

followed by

```
mfx
```

we get Empirical Results 15.2.

Empirical Results 15.2: Poisson Results for Total Number of Publications in First 12 Years after PhD Receipt for Our Newly Minted Economics PhD Publishing Data

Coefficient Estimates

	Coefficients	Standard Error	z	P > |z|	Lower 95%	Upper 95%
Intercept	1.179465	0.0606389	19.45	0.000	1.060615	1.298315
PhD Program NRC Rank	−0.013692	0.0009657	−14.18	0.000	−0.015585	−0.011799
Work with Star Advisor	0.294332	0.0491217	5.99	0.000	0.198055	0.390609
Work with Ranked Advisor	0.158275	0.0498576	3.17	0.002	0.060556	0.255994
Publish While PhD Student	1.037896	0.0398704	26.03	0.000	0.959751	1.11604
Ever Coauthor with Advisor	0.628039	0.0413019	15.21	0.000	0.547089	0.708989
Male Student	0.013599	0.0522141	0.26	0.795	−0.088739	0.115937
International Student	−0.042324	0.0381075	−1.11	0.267	−0.117013	0.032365
Prob > chi2			0.0000			
Log likelihood			−2,540.951			
Observations			681			

Marginal Effects

	Coefficients	Standard Error	z	P > |z|	Lower 95%	Upper 95%
PhD Program NRC Rank	−0.043943	0.00295	−14.91	0.000	−0.04972	−0.03817
Work with Star Advisor	1.050542	0.19569	5.37	0.000	0.66699	1.43409
Work with Ranked Advisor	0.533878	0.17661	3.02	0.003	0.18772	0.88003
Publish While PhD Student	4.536737	0.22179	20.45	0.000	4.10203	4.97144
Ever Coauthor with Advisor	2.517947	0.20244	12.44	0.000	2.12117	2.91472
Male Student	0.043455	0.16612	0.26	0.794	−0.28214	0.36905
International Student	−0.136011	0.12258	−1.11	0.267	−0.37627	0.10424

Note: Dependent variable is the number of publications in the first 12 years after PhD receipt. Highlighted variables are significant at the 5 percent level.

These results can be interpreted as follows. All other independent variables constant, students who graduate from PhD programs that are 10 places higher in the rankings average nearly 0.44 more articles in their first 12 years (0.044×10), while students working with a star advisor, students working with a ranked advisor, students publishing while in graduate school, and students who coauthor with their advisor average 1.0, 0.5, 4.5, and 2.5 more articles in their first 12 years, respectively. Notice that these results are quite different from the OLS results we found in Excel Regression Results 15.1.

One drawback of the Poisson model is that the mean needs to equal the variance in this distribution. This restriction is called equi-dispersion. If the mean is not equal to the variance then the Poisson model is not the appropriate count data model.

Empirical Research Tool 15.2 summarizes the Poisson model for non-negative count data.

EMPIRICAL RESEARCH TOOL 15.2: THE POISSON MODEL FOR NON-NEGATIVE COUNT DATA

How to Do It:

1. Estimate the Poisson model in a more advanced statistical package.
2. Convert the results to estimated marginal effects.

Why It Works:

The Poisson model accounts for the non-negative count nature of our data by modeling the empirical process using the Poisson distribution, which corrects for the discrete nature of the observed outcomes of the dependent variable.

Note:

The Poisson distribution is overly restrictive because it constrains the mean of the distribution to equal the variance, a condition we refer to as equi-dispersion. If this condition is not met, then the Poisson is inappropriate.

The Negative Binomial Model

negative binomial distribution
A distribution appropriate for counting the number of times that a random event occurs before a specified number of failures.

The **negative binomial distribution** is a discrete probability distribution of the number of successes in a sequence of Bernoulli trials (i.e., trials that result in either a success or a failure) before a specified number of failures (denoted as r) occur.

The log-likelihood function for the probability that there are exactly k occurrences of a given event for this distribution is equal to

$$L(r,p) = \sum_{i=1}^{N} \ln(\Gamma(k_i + r)) - \sum_{i=1}^{N} \ln(k_i!) - N\ln(\Gamma(r)) + Nr\ln(1-p) + \sum_{i=1}^{N} k_i \ln(p) \quad \textbf{15.2.4}$$

We estimate this model by maximizing the log-likelihood function in formula 15.2.4. Again, when asking a more advanced statistical package to estimate the model for us, we must ask that it convert the estimated coefficient into estimated marginal effects before attempting to interpret the results. Using the Stata command

```
nbreg total nrcrank star ranked pubbyphd cowadv male intlstu
```

followed by

```
mfx
```

we get Empirical Results 15.3.

Empirical Results 15.3: Negative Binomial Results for Total Number of Publications in First 12 Years after PhD Receipt

Coefficient Estimates

	Coefficients	Standard Error	z	P > |z|	Lower 95%	Upper 95%
Intercept	1.082933	0.165430	6.55	0.000	0.7586962	1.407169
PhD Program NRC Rank	−0.018146	0.002302	−7.88	0.000	−0.0226576	−0.013635
Work with Star Advisor	0.415895	0.162383	2.56	0.010	0.0976314	0.734160
Work with Ranked Advisor	0.253602	0.145951	1.74	0.082	−0.0324566	0.539660
Publish While PhD Student	1.246756	0.124018	10.05	0.000	1.003684	1.489827
Ever Coauthor with Advisor	0.910335	0.141722	6.42	0.000	0.6325659	1.188104
Male Student	0.012370	0.147579	0.08	0.933	−0.2768793	0.301620
International Student	−0.013488	0.113861	−0.12	0.906	−0.2366512	0.209676
alpha	1.549614	0.121550				
Prob > chi2			0.0000			
Log likelihood			−1,536.237			
Observations			681			

Marginal Effects

	Coefficients	Standard Error	z	P > |z|	Lower 95%	Upper 95%
PhD Program NEC Rank	−0.053286	0.00704	−7.57	0.000	−0.06708	−0.03949
Work with Star Advisor	1.422117	0.64775	2.20	0.028	0.15255	2.69169
Work with Ranked Advisor	0.807294	0.50461	1.60	0.110	−0.18172	1.7963
Publish While PhD Student	5.362114	0.80003	6.70	0.000	3.79409	6.93014
Ever Coauthor with Advisor	3.729763	0.8076	4.62	0.000	2.14689	5.31263
Male Student	0.036180	0.42992	0.08	0.933	−0.80644	0.87880
International Student	−0.039623	0.33462	−0.12	0.906	−0.69546	0.61621

Note: Dependent variable is the number of publications in the first 12 years after PhD receipt. Highlighted variables are significant at the 5 percent level.

We can interpret these results as follows. Holding all other independent variables constant, each one unit increase in the rank of a student's PhD program is associated with a decrease of 0.05 article in the first 12 years post-PhD receipt. Accordingly, all other independent variables constant, a student graduating from the 61st ranked program would be expected to publish 3.0 fewer articles in the first 12 years post-PhD than a student graduating from the 1st ranked program (60×0.05). Likewise, all other independent variables constant, a student working with an advisor ranked among the top 250 worldwide economists is estimated to publish 1.42 more articles in the first 12 years than an individual working with an unranked advisor, while a student publishing an article as a graduate student is estimated to publish 5.36 more total articles and a student publishing an article coauthored with the dissertation advisor is estimated to publish 3.73 more articles than a student not doing likewise.

Empirical Research Tool 15.3 summarizes the negative binomial model for non-negative count data.

EMPIRICAL RESEARCH TOOL 15.3: THE NEGATIVE BINOMIAL MODEL FOR NON-NEGATIVE COUNT DATA

How to Do It:

1. Estimate the negative binomial model in a more advanced statistical package.
2. Convert the results to estimated marginal effects.

Why It Works:

The negative binomial model accounts for the non-negative count nature of our data by modeling the empirical process using the negative binomial distribution, which corrects for the discrete nature of the observed outcomes of the dependent variable.

Note:

The negative binomial distribution does not require equi-dispersion of the data. Therefore, it can be used in many situations in which the Poisson may not.

Choosing between the Poisson and the Negative Binomial Models

Comparing Empirical Results 15.2 and Empirical Results 15.3, we notice that the estimated standard errors are much smaller for the Poisson model than for the negative binomial model. As a result, our estimated p-values are smaller for the Negative Binomial model and we estimate working with a star advisor to be statistically significant in that model while we estimate doing so to be insignificant in the negative binomial model.

Given the potentially significant difference between the estimates provided by the two models, we might be interested in determining which model is more appropriate for a given data set. There is a statistical test that helps us make this determination. A test of **over-dispersion** tests whether the conditional mean and the conditional variance of the data are equal, which must be the case if the Poisson is the appropriate model. Without getting too technical, the intuition behind the test is that the negative binomial model essentially adds the parameter, α, which can be thought of as the dispersion parameter. In practice, this term acts as an added random component that pulls the conditional variance away from the conditional mean if it is non-zero. Accordingly, the only way that the data can exhibit equi-dispersion is if $\alpha = 0$, meaning that the null hypothesis for testing for equi-dispersion is

over-dispersion
Occurs when the mean and the variance of the data are not equal.

$$H_0: \alpha = 0$$
$$H_A: \alpha \neq 0 \qquad \textbf{15.2.5}$$

Fortunately, more advanced statistical packages generally provide results of this test when estimating the negative binomial model. For instance, in Stata, the output for this test is included immediately below the negative binomial estimates. For our PhD recipient publication data, the reported test results are given below.

Likelihood-ratio test of alpha = 0: chibar2(01) = 2009.43 Prob> = chibar2 = 0.000

According to the estimated p-value of 0.000 given above, we reject the null hypothesis of equi-dispersion, and we conclude that the negative binomial is the more appropriate estimator for these data. In our experience, we find that we almost always reject the null hypothesis of equi-disperion, meaning that we almost always end up estimating negative binomial models for applications with non-negative count data. Nonetheless, given the ease of performing this test, we suggest always doing so when considering the Poisson and the negative binomial models for non-negative count data.

15.3 CONTROL FOR SAMPLE-SELECTION BIAS

sample-selection bias
Occurs when individuals nonrandomly select themselves into a given outcome of the dependent variable.

Another empirical issue in which OLS is not the preferred estimator occurs when individuals nonrandomly select themselves into different observed outcomes of the dependent variable. The problem with this so-called **sample-selection bias** is that the nonrandomness of the individual's decision biases the estimated coefficients and makes it difficult to distinguish causation from correlation.

As an example, consider the widely publicized correlation between exposure to classical music as an infant and improved performance on standardized tests (believers in causal effect of this relationship include Georgia Governor Zell Miller, who in 1998 proposed that all babies born in the state be given a classical music CD when leaving the hospital). While the correlation between these variables may indeed exist, the more important question is: Does its mere existence imply that we should force every mother to play Mozart around-the-clock in the hopes that her children will grow up smarter? Not necessarily.

The issue here is that without advance knowledge of this statistic, parents who self-select to play classical music for their babies are likely different from those who self-select to not play classical music for their babies. In particular, it is likely that individuals who regularly listen to classical music possess higher socioeconomic status and have higher education levels and higher innate educational ability and motivation than individuals who do not listen to classical music. Accordingly, given that many of these traits likely have genetic components that can be passed down to their children, it is likely that children of parents who listen to classical music are predisposed toward better standardized test performance than those children whose parents do not listen to classical music. As a consequence, the relationship between early exposure to classical music and future performance on standardized tests might be no more than simple correlation (or "statistical noise") rather than causation that should be acted upon.

In technical terms, sample-selection bias is problematic because it violates both assumption M2 that "the data are collected through independent, random sampling" (because individuals nonrandomly select into one of the outcomes of the dependent variable) and M5 that "the independent variables and the error term are uncorrelated." In violating these assumptions, sample-selection bias results in coefficient estimates that are biased and inconsistent.

The issue and consequences associated with sample-selection bias are summarized in the following box.

The Issues and Consequences Associated with Sample-Selection Bias

Problem:
Sample-selection bias violates assumption M2, which states that the data are collected through independent, random sampling, and assumption M5, which states that the independent variables and the error terms are uncorrelated.

Consequences:
In the presence of sample-selection bias,

1. Parameter estimates are biased.
2. Parameter estimates are inconsistent.

One of the most well-known examples of sample-selection bias occurs when estimating log salary regressions because some individuals choose not to work and therefore have no observed salary. Unfortunately, because individuals nonrandomly self-select into working or not working, simply estimating a log salary regression for the subsample of individuals choosing to work provides biased estimated marginal effects because it does not account for the nonrandom decisions of individuals choosing not to work and not being included in the sample.

Heckman selection correction
A two-stage procedure for controlling for sample-selection bias.

Nobel laureate James Heckman proposes a two-stage procedure for controlling for this type of sample-selection bias. The procedure, known as the **Heckman selection correction,** consists of: (1) estimating the individual's self-selection decision and using those estimates to calculate values known as the inverse Mills ratio and (2) including those calculated values in the second-stage regression to control for the potential sample-selection bias.

In general terms, suppose that we are interested in estimating the population regression model

$$y_i = \beta_0 + \beta_1 x_{1,i} + \beta_2 x_{2,i} + \cdots + \beta_k x_{k,i} + \varepsilon_i \qquad \textbf{15.3.1}$$

but that y_i is only observed if an individual nonrandomly self-selects outcome $w_i = 1$ and is not observed if the individual nonrandomly self-selects outcome $w_0 = 0$, meaning that we have to possible outcomes for each individual: either

$$y_i = \beta_0 + \beta_1 x_{1,i} + \beta_2 x_{2,i} + \cdots + \beta_k x_{k,i} + \varepsilon_i \quad \text{if } w_i = 1$$

or

$$y_i = 0 \quad \text{if } w_i = 0$$

In such a case, we would correct for sample-selection bias using the two-stage Heckman selection correction as follows. In the first stage, we would estimate the self-selection decision w as a function of independent variables likely to affect that decision. There is an issue here in terms of the independent variables that should be included in the first-stage population regression model. Generally, the independent variables included in the first stage are the same independent variables as in formula 15.3.1. However, for our estimates to be unbiased and consistent, we must make sure that our model is identified, To identify the model, we need to include a separate independent variable, v, that is correlated with the self-selection decision, w_i, but uncorrelated with the dependent variable, y_i. After determining an appropriate identification variable, we estimate the first-stage population regression Probit model

$$w_i = \gamma_0 + \gamma_1 x_{1,i} + \gamma_2 x_{2,i} + \cdots + \gamma_k x_{k,i} + \gamma_{k+1} v_i + \varphi_i \qquad \textbf{15.3.2}$$

and use the results to calculate the inverse Mills ratio for each individual:

$$\hat{\lambda}_i(\hat{w}_i) = \lambda_i \frac{\phi(\hat{w}_i)}{\Phi(\hat{w}_i)} \qquad \textbf{15.3.3}$$

where ϕ is the standard normal density function, Φ is the standard normal cumulative distribution function, and $\hat{w}_i$. is the predicted value of w_i.

To complete the model, we would estimate the second-stage population regression model:

$$y_i = \beta_0 + \beta_1 x_{1,i} + \beta_2 x_{2,i} + \cdots + \beta_k x_{k,i} + \theta\hat{\lambda}_i + \varepsilon_i \qquad \textbf{15.3.4}$$

The intuition behind this approach is that the inverse Mills ratio reflects the degree to which observable factors are related to the nonrandom self-selection decision, and therefore, including those measures in the second-stage regression controls for the potential effect that sample-selection bias has on the outcome of interest. In essence, the inverse Mills ratio "returns" randomness to the model by providing a measure of how an individual who is not self-selected into a given outcome (i.e., an individual who is chosen at random) would perform relative to an individual who is self-selected into the given outcome.

Data to Be Analyzed: Our CPS Salary Data

To estimate the preceding model, we need to collect data for a large sample of individuals, some of whom work and some of whom do not. Following the procedure outlined in Appendix A, we collected a very large sample of 100,731 individuals from the March 2011 supplement of the Consumer Population Survey (CPS). In addition to a typical set of independent variables that economic theory predicts to be correlated with salary, we need to determine an appropriate variable for identifying the Heckman selection correction model. Our choice in this instance is the number of children that an individual currently has that are under age 6 because it seems *plausible* that having young children at home is correlated with the decision of whether to work but uncorrelated with the salary that one earns when working.

Table 15.5 presents summary statistics for our CPS salary sample.

TABLE 15.5
Summary Statistics for Our CPS Salary Sample

	Workers	Nonworkers
Salary	48,213.64	—
	(55,014.15)	—
Current age	43.694	45.401
	(11.267)	(11.940)
Highest education	14.102	13.238
	(2.398)	(2.243)
Number of children under 6	0.255	0.273
	(0.579)	(0.625)
Male	0.508	0.387
White	0.797	0.749
Black	0.110	0.145
Asian	0.059	0.062
Other race	0.092	0.106
Currently married	0.637	0.574
Observations	77,602	23,129

These data suggest that, on average, nonworkers in the sample are a little older and a little less educated than workers. At the same time, nonworkers average more children under the age of 6 and are quite a bit more likely to be female than are workers, suggesting that women with young children might disproportionately be making the nonrandom decision to not work and that our chosen identification variable seems to be at the very least plausible.

As a baseline for comparison, we first estimate the population regression model

$$\ln Salary_i = \beta_0 + \beta_1 Male_i + \beta_2 Age_i + \beta_3 Age_i^2 + \beta_4 Married_i + \beta_5 Education_i + \beta_6 Black_i + \beta_7 Asian_i + \beta_8 Other\ race_i + \varepsilon_i \quad \textbf{15.3.5}$$

by OLS and get Excel Regression Output 15.2.

Excel Regression Output 15.2: OLS Results for CPS Salary Sample

SUMMARY OUTPUT

Regression Statistics	
Multiple R	0.433630622
R Square	0.188035517
Adjusted R Square	0.187951801
Standard Error	0.923237242
Observations	77.602

Number of individuals in our sample

ANOVA

	df	SS	MS	F	Significance F
Regression	8	15316.23524	1914.529405	2246.132704	0
Residual	77593	66137.713	0.852367005		
Total	77601	81453.94824			

	Coefficients	Standard Error	t Stat	p-value	Lower 95%	Upper 95%
Intercept	5.930950095	0.053389885	111.0875238	0	5.826306214	6.035593976
Male	0.449088447	0.006666962	67.36028539	0	0.436021238	0.462155655
Current Age	0.100171353	0.002319232	43.19159969	0	0.095625671	0.104717036
Current Age Squared	−0.001067231	2.56299E-05	−41.6400605	0	−0.001117465	−0.001016996
Currently Married	0.133612169	0.007206349	18.54089652	1.41513E-76	0.119487765	0.147736573
Highest Education	0.137696942	0.001401252	98.26705195	0	0.134950495	0.140443389
Black	−0.085328081	0.010819147	−7.88676629	3.1413E-15	−0.106533549	−0.064122613
Asian	0.056059273	0.022803116	2.45840410	0.013957772	0.011365292	0.100753254
Other Race	−0.094529049	0.018538405	−5.09909278	3.42086E-07	−0.130864222	−0.058193876

Note: Dependent variable is log annual salary. White is the omitted race. Highlighted variables are significant at the 5 percent level.

These results can be interpreted as follows. All other independent variables constant, male workers in our sample are estimated to earn roughly 45 percent higher salaries than otherwise similar female workers; age is estimated to have a quadratic effect on salary, with the inflection point occurring at roughly 47 years of age; currently married workers are estimated to earn 13 percent more than nonmarried workers; each additional year of education beyond the ninth grade (which is the minimum in our sample) is estimated to increase salary by nearly 14 percent; black and other race workers are estimated to earn roughly 9 percent less than otherwise similar white workers; and, finally, Asian workers are estimated to earn roughly 6 percent more than otherwise-similar white workers. Notice that because we are blessed with such a large sample size, all of these estimated slope coefficients achieve statistical significance and that all but one have calculated p-values of 0 or very close to 0.

Unfortunately, these OLS estimates do not account for the nonrandom decision of the 23,219 nonworkers in our sample that self-select into not working. As a result, the estimates are likely to suffer from sample-selection bias. To control for this potential bias using the two-stage Heckman selection correction, we estimate the first-stage population regression model

$$Work_i = \gamma_0 + \gamma_1 Children\ under\ 6_i + \gamma_2 Male_i + \gamma_3 Age_i + \gamma_4 Age_i^2 + \gamma_5 Married_i + \gamma_6 Education_i + \gamma_7 Black_i + \gamma_8 Asian_i + \gamma_9 Other\ race_i + \varepsilon_i \quad \textbf{15.3.6}$$

by Probit, and we use the resulting estimates to calculate the inverse Mills ratio $\hat{\lambda}_i$.

We then estimate the second-stage population regression model

$$\ln Salary_i = \beta_0 + \beta_1 Male_i + \beta_2 Age_i + \beta_3 Age_i^2 + \beta_4 Married_i + \beta_5 Education_i + \beta_6 Black_i + \beta_7 Asian_i + \beta_8 Other\ race_i + \theta\hat{\lambda}_i + \varepsilon_i \quad \textbf{15.3.7}$$

Again, while we could theoretically perform all of these calculations in Excel, doing so would be needlessly time-consuming and would introduce many opportunities for operator error. Instead, using the Stata command

```
heckman lsalary male age age2 married educ black asian othrace,
select(childrenu6 male age age2 married educ black asian othrace)
```

we get Empirical Results 15.4.

Empirical Results 15.4: Heckman Selection Correction Results for Our CPS Salary Data

ln(Salary) Equation

	Coefficients	Standard Error	z	P > |z|	Lower 95%	Upper 95%
Intercept	7.235784	0.0603703	119.86	0	7.11746	7.354107
Male	0.3043176	0.0075768	40.16	0	0.2894674	0.3191678
Current Age	0.0830065	0.0026124	31.77	0	0.0778863	0.0881267
Current Age Squared	−0.0008213	0.0000288	−28.52	0	−0.0008777	−0.0007648
Currently Married	0.0852341	0.0081503	10.46	0	0.0692598	0.1012085
Highest Education	0.0964123	0.0016026	60.16	0	0.0932713	0.0995533
Black	−0.0371814	0.0121271	−3.07	0.002	−0.06095	−0.0134127
Asian	0.0657361	0.0255719	2.57	0.01	0.015616	0.1158561
Other Race	−0.0274396	0.0206981	−1.33	0.185	−0.0680072	0.0131279

Selection Equation

	Coefficients	Standard Error	z	P > |z|	Lower 95%	Upper 95%
Intercept	−0.3331657	0.0657207	−5.07	0	−0.4619759	−0.2043556
Children Under 6	−0.0735301	0.0060047	−12.25	0	−0.0852992	−0.0617611
Male	0.2201362	0.0083119	26.48	0	0.2038452	0.2364271
Current Age	−0.0027502	0.0028262	−0.97	0.33	−0.0082894	0.002789
Current Age Squared	−0.000363	0.0000308	−1.18	0.239	−0.0000966	0.0000241
Currently Married	0.0639605	0.0089447	7.15	0	0.0464292	0.0814918
Highest Education	0.08055	0.0018215	44.22	0	0.0769799	0.0841201
Black	−0.0974382	0.0127112	−7.67	0	−0.1223517	−0.0725247
Asian	−0.0411779	0.0268741	−1.53	0.125	−0.0938501	0.0114944
Other Race	−0.0970935	0.0214981	−4.52	0	−0.139229	−0.054958
lambda	−0.9288846	0.0012971			−0.9313836	−0.9262981
Prob > chi2			0.000			
Log Likelihood			−151,080.80			
Observations			100,731			
Censored Observations			23,129			
Uncensored Observations			77,602			

LR test of indep. eqns. (rho = 0): chi2(1) = 9432.72 Prob > chi2 = 0.0000

Note: Dependent variable is log annual salary. White is the omitted race. Highlighted variables are significant at the 5 percent level.

These results can be interpreted as follows. Starting with the selection equation, holding all other independent variables constant, each additional child under the age of 6 reduces the likelihood that an individual works by nearly 7.5 percent. Among other independent variables, all other independent variables constant, men in the sample are 22 percent more likely to work than women, individuals who are currently married are 6.4 percent more likely to work than nonmarried individuals, each additional year of education increases the likelihood of working by 8 percent, and blacks and other race individuals are 9.7 percent less likely to work than otherwise-similar whites.

Turning to the log salary equation, after controlling for potential sample-selection bias, all other independent variables constant, males are estimated to earn percent more than otherwise-similar females; there is an estimated quadratic effect of age, with the inflection point occurring at 51 years of age; individuals who are currently married are estimated to earn 8.5 percent more than individuals who 30.4 are not currently married; each additional year of education is estimated to increase earnings by 9.6 percent; blacks are estimated to earn 3.7 percent less than otherwise-similar whites; and Asians are estimated to earn 6.6 percent more than otherwise-similar whites. Empirical Research Tool 15.4 summarizes the Heckman correlation for sample-selection bias.

EMPIRICAL RESEARCH TOOL 15.4: THE HECKMAN CORRECTION FOR SAMPLE-SELECTION BIAS

How to Do It:

1. Estimate the self-selection decision $w_i = \gamma_0 + \gamma_1 x_{1,i} + \gamma_2 x_{2,i} + \cdots + \gamma_k x_{k,i} + \gamma_{k+1} v_i + \varphi_i$ using a Probit model.
2. Use those results to calculate the inverse Mills ratio, $\hat{\lambda}_i$.
3. Estimate the population regression model $y_i = \beta_0 + \beta_1 x_{1,i} + \beta_2 x_{2,i} + \cdots + \beta_k x_{k,i} + \theta\hat{\lambda}_i + \varepsilon_i$.

Why It Works:

The inverse Mills ratio reflects the degree to which observable factors are related to the nonrandom self-selection decision, including those measures in the second-stage regression controls for the potential effect that sample-selection bias has on the outcome of interest. In essence, the inverse Mills ratio "returns" randomness to the model by providing a measure of how an individual who is not self-selected into a given outcome (i.e., an individual who is chosen at random) would perform relative to an individual who is self-selected into the given outcome.

15.4 USE QUASI-EXPERIMENTAL METHODS

quasi-experimental methods
Methods designed to look like randomized clinical trials, although they lack the randomized assignment.

randomized clinical trials
Experiments in controlled environments where participants are assigned by chance alone to different treatments.

treatment group
The randomized group that receives the intervention.

control group
The randomized base group that does not receive the intervention.

The discussion of sample-selection bias touches on an important issue concerning data that economists often encounter. Namely, while many statistical methods, such as OLS, are based on the assumption that data are collected randomly, the data confronted in many economic situations are not the result of purely random data-generating processes. This fact often forces economists to either gloss over the nonrandomness of the data collection process or to do whatever they can to minimize the potential damage resulting from it. Economists have recently employed advance methods for dealing with the nonrandomness of the data-collection process that are referred to as **quasi-experimental methods.**

The gold standard for data-generating processes that are purely random are the **randomized clinical trials** employed most often by medical researchers. As an example, suppose that a drug company wishes to test the efficacy of a new cholesterol-lowering drug. To do so, they would (1) recruit a (hopefully) large number of trial participants, (2) randomly assign each participant to either a **treatment group** that actually receives the drug or to a **control group** that receives a placebo rather than the actual drug, and (3) track and compare the health outcomes of the two groups. The beauty of such a process is that being a purely random trial, there would be no systematic reason for one group to observe different health outcomes than the other, and thus, any observed difference between the two groups would have to be due to the effect of the drug itself.

If economists have long tried to conduct randomized clinical trials to study outcomes of economic interest (the currently popular field of behavioral economics uses experimental design to collect data instead of relying on the outcomes of real-world decision making). Unfortunately, many of the outcomes in which we are interested cannot be generated by such trials. For instance, suppose that we wish to determine the effect that starting at a community college rather than a university has on a student's educational and economic future. While the ideal experiment would be to randomly assign college freshmen to community colleges and universities and compare their future outcomes, there is no way that we could practically conduct such an experiment because individuals would revolt against being forced into an attendance path other than the one they would have chosen on their own. In such cases, because we cannot perform the desired randomized clinical trial, we must employ methods that fit the results of nonrandom data-generating processes into empirical situations that mimic random trails. We refer to such approaches as *quasi-experimental methods,* and we discuss one of the most popular (and most straightforward to estimate) next.

difference-in-differences estimators
Estimators that attempt to replicate randomized clinical trials by comparing treatment and control groups before and after a treatment is imposed to estimate the impact of a given policy intervention.

Difference-in-differences estimators attempt to apply the structure of randomized clinical trials to data that result from nonrandom data-generating processes by using a given policy intervention (the "treatment") to divide the observations into control and treatment groups for which data are compared before and after the policy intervention to estimate the effect of the given treatment. A very well-known example of this procedure is the 1994 *American Economic Review* paper by David Card and Alan Kruger that exploits a change to the minimum wage law in New Jersey but not in neighboring Pennsylvania to estimate that, contrary to economic theory, an increase in the minimum wage may actually increase rather than decrease fast-food employment. In this section, we focus on a different policy intervention for which a difference-in-differences estimator might be appropriate.

Our Empirical Example: Changes in State Speed Limits

A governmental policy intervention that is well known to most citizens is the increase in a state's maximum allowable highway speed limit. In a 1999 study, the Insurance Institute for Highway Safety famously argued that 1996 motor vehicle deaths were 15 percent higher in 24 states that raised their maximum allowable speed limits than in 7 states that did not (www.iihs.org/news/1999/iihs_news_011499.pdf). An important question associated with this finding is whether the higher observed fatality rate in states that increased their speed limit was truly caused by the policy change or whether individuals in those states were more likely to die in traffic accidents for some other reason (such as drivers in those state being more reckless regardless of the change in the speed limit). In this section, we demonstrate how difference-in-differences estimators can be used to answer these questions.

Data to Be Analyzed: Our State Traffic Fatality Data

In order to answer these questions, we need to collect before and after data on the number of traffic fatalities in both states that did and did not increase their speed limits in a given time period. To demonstrate how, following the procedure described in Appendix A, we collect data on the number of traffic fatalities in 1994 and 1998 for the 31 states listed in Table 15.6: 24 of which increased their maximum speed limit in 1996 and 7 of which did not (as indicated by the variable "Changed Speed Limits"). Table 15.6 presents summary statistics for these 31 states.

Looking at Table 15.6, we see that overall, there was a 0.7 percent decrease in traffic fatalities between these two years. While true, there is a large variation across states, with Vermont seeing a 28.07 percent increase in traffic fatalities and California seeing a 16.76 percent decrease in traffic fatalities. Comparing states that did increase their speed limits to those that did not is not that revealing, because some states in both categories observed increases in traffic fatalities while others observed decreases.

To apply a difference-in-differences estimator to these data, we start by considering the 24 states that raised their maximum speed limit in 1996 to be the "treatment" group and the

TABLE 15.6 Summary 1994 and 1998 State Traffic Fatality Data

	Changed Speed Limits	1994 Traffic Deaths	1998 Traffic Deaths	Change	% Change
Alabama	1	1,080	1,038	−42	−3.89%
Arizona	1	911	964	53	5.82%
Arkansas	1	612	609	−3	−0.49%
California	1	4,374	3,641	−733	−16.76%
Colorado	1	615	656	41	6.67%
Connecticut	0	292	304	12	4.11%
Georgia	1	1,406	1,552	146	10.38%
Idaho	1	256	286	30	11.72%
Kansas	1	446	504	58	13.00%
Kentucky	0	708	759	51	7.20%
Maine	0	189	176	−13	−6.88%
Michigan	1	1,362	1,393	31	2.28%
Mississippi	1	800	900	100	12.50%
Missouri	1	1,097	1,172	75	6.84%
Montana	1	205	238	33	16.10%
Nebraska	1	261	320	59	22.61%
Nevada	1	324	404	80	24.69%
New Jersey	0	671	673	2	0.30%
New Mexico	1	452	431	−21	−4.65%
North Carolina	1	1,405	1,589	184	13.10%
North Dakota	1	86	102	16	18.60%
Oklahoma	1	706	752	46	6.52%
Oregon	0	515	548	33	6.41%
Rhode Island	1	62	74	12	19.35%
South Dakota	1	155	167	12	7.74%
Texas	1	3,280	3,711	431	13.14%
Utah	1	367	388	21	5.72%
Vermont	0	57	73	16	28.07%
Virginia	0	838	844	6	0.72%
Washington	1	665	688	23	3.46%
Wyoming	1	139	147	8	5.76%
Totals	22.58%	14,614	14,512	−102	−0.70%

7 states that did not change their speed limit in 1996 to be the "control" group. Likewise, we consider the number of traffic deaths in 1994 to be the "before" data for both groups, and the number of traffic deaths in 1998 to be the "after" data for both groups.

The difference-in-differences estimator is calculated by comparing the before and after data for the control and treatment groups. There are actually two different ways to calculate the desired difference-in-differences estimator. The first is a simple calculation that consists of computing the difference between the mean number of traffic deaths for the treatment group before and after the policy intervention and comparing that value to the difference between the mean number of traffic deaths for the control group before and after the policy intervention. Doing so, we obtain the data shown in Table 15.7.

TABLE 15.7 Calculations for the Difference-in-Differences Estimator for Our State Traffic Fatality Data

	Mean of 1998 Traffic Deaths	Mean of 1994 Traffic Deaths	Change	% Change
Did change speed limits (treatment group)	905.2500	877.7500	27.5000	3.13%
Did not change speed limits (control group)	482.4286	467.1429	15.2857	3.27%
Treatment group difference	27.5000			
Control group difference	15.2857			
Difference-in-differences estimator	12.2143			

As we can see by looking at these data, between 1994 and 1998 the mean number of traffic deaths in states that raised their speed limit increased by 27.5, while the mean number of traffic deaths in states that did not raise their speed limit increased by 15.2857. The resulting difference-in-differences estimator is the difference between these values, or 27.5 − 15.2857 = 12.2143. Assuming that all else is held constant between the states, we can interpret this estimate as saying that states that did increase their speed limits in 1996 experienced 12.2143 more traffic deaths, on average, than they would have had they not increased the speed limit.

Figure 15.3 depicts these differences.

FIGURE 15.3
The Difference-in-Differences Estimator

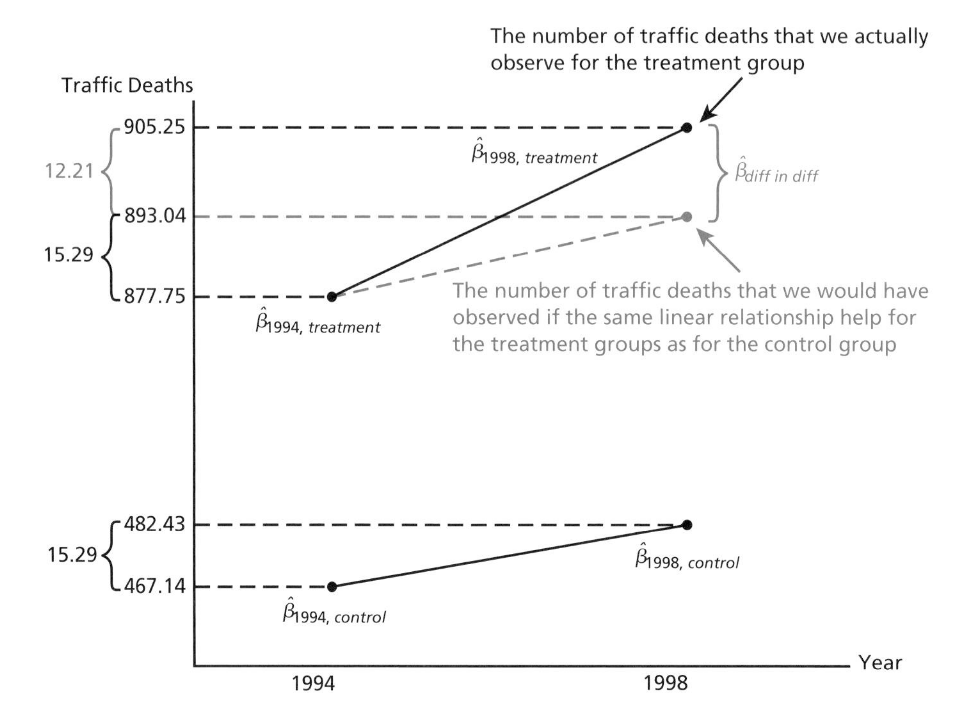

The second possible method for calculating the difference-in-differences estimator is performing OLS on a pooled cross-section of the before and after data. To do so, our population regression model would need to include (1) a binary dummy variable indicating the after data, (2) a binary dummy variable indicating the states receiving the treatment, and (3) an interaction term for the product between those two variables. Accordingly, for our traffic fatality application, we would calculate a difference-in-differences estimator by estimating the population regression model

$$Deaths_i = \beta_0 + \beta_1 1998_i + \beta_2 Treatment_i + \beta_3 (1998Treatment)_i + \varepsilon_i \quad \textbf{15.4.1}$$

where 1998_i is a dummy variable equal to 1 if the data is collected for 1998, $Treatment_i$ is a dummy variable equal to 1 if the state increased its speed limit in 1996, and $(1998\ Treatment)_i$ is the interaction between those two variables. In this model, the estimated coefficient on the interaction term (i.e., β_3) is the desired difference-in-differences estimator.

Estimating formula 15.4.1 by OLS for our traffic fatality data provides the results shown in Excel Regression Output 15.3.

These results can be interpreted as follows. All other independent variables constant, the 7 states in our sample that did not observe the treatment of increased maximum speed limits saw an average of 467.14 traffic deaths in 1994 and an average of 15.29 more traffic deaths in 1998 than 1994. At the same time, the 24 states that did receive the treatment of increased speed limits saw an average of 410.61 more traffic deaths in 1994 than states that did not receive the treatment. Finally, and most importantly for this analysis, while the states not receiving the treatment did see traffic deaths increase, on average, between 1994 and 1998, the average increase in the number of traffic deaths between those two years

Excel Regression Output 15.3: Difference-in-Differences Estimates for Our 1994 and 1998 State Traffic Death Data

SUMMARY OUTPUT

Regression Statistics	
Multiple R	0.19877503
R Square	0.039511513
Adjusted R Square	−0.010168926
Standard Error	890.5038439
Observations	62

Total a umber of states between the two years in our sample (i.e. 31·2)

ANOVA

	df	SS	MS	F	Significance F
Regression	3	1892043.348	630681.116	0.795313273	0.501478973
Residual	58	45993831.57	792997.0961		
Total	61	47885874.92			

	Coefficients	Standard Error	*t* Stat	*p*-value	Lower 95%	Upper 95%
Intercept	467.1428571	336.5788161	1.387915207	0.17047169	−206.5928384	1140.878553
1998	15.28571429	475.9943265	0.032113228	0.97449201	−937.5204438	968.0918723
Treatment	410.6071429	382.5269208	1.073407179	0.287534181	−355.1036764	1176.317962
1998 × Treatment	12.21428571	540.9747593	0.022578291	0.982064159	−1070.66434	1095.092911

Note: Dependent variable is the number of traffic fatalities.

was 12.21 more in states receiving the treatment. Note that this value is the difference-in-differences estimator and is exactly the same as the value we estimated in Table 15.7.

While we can see that it is possible for both methods to produce the same results, the OLS method is preferable to the algebraic method for two reasons. First, it allows us to calculate estimated standard errors for the difference-in-differences estimator—a fact that allows us to perform tests of statistical significance. Note that the p-value on the difference-in-differences estimator is a large 0.9821, implying that the change in the speed limit did not result in a statistically significant increase in the number of traffic fatalities. This fact is actually not that surprising given that our sample consists of only 51 observations, which necessarily leads to large estimated standard errors. Second, it allows us to control for additional factors that might change across time by including additional independent variables in the estimated sample regression function.

Empirical Research Tool 15.5 summarizes the difference-in-differences estimator.

EMPIRICAL RESEARCH TOOL 15.5: DIFFERENCE-IN-DIFFERENCES ESTIMATORS

How to Do It:

1. Identify a policy intervention that affected a specific "treatment" group but not a specific "control" group.
2. Gather data before and after the policy intervention for the two groups. Estimate the population regression model $y_i = \beta_0 + \beta_1 After_i + \beta_2\ Treatment_i + \beta_3(After \cdot Treatment)_i + \varepsilon_i$ by OLS.
3. Interpret $\hat{\beta}_3$ as the desired difference-in-differences estimator.

Why It Works:

Difference-in-differences estimation applies the structure of a randomized trial to a nonrandom data-generating process by comparing "before" and "after" data for two groups that are similar, except for the fact that one group received a given treatment and the other group did not.

ADDITIONS TO OUR EMPIRICAL RESEARCH TOOLKIT

In this chapter we have introduced a number of tools that will prove valuable when performing empirical research. They include:

- Quantile regression.
- Models for dealing with non-negative count data, including the Poisson and the negative binomial.
- Methods to control for sample selection bias, including the Heckman correction for sample-selection bias.
- Quasi-experimental methods, including difference-in-differences estimation.

OUR NEW EMPIRICAL TOOLS IN PRACTICE: USING WHAT WE HAVE LEARNED IN THIS CHAPTER

Based on her training, our former student realized that because she observed a specific policy intervention (i.e., some states raising their cigarette tax and other states not raising their cigarette tax), she might be able to employ a difference-in-differences estimator to more accurately estimate the marginal effect that increases in cigarette taxes have on smoking rates. Table 15.8 presents her estimated sample regression function.

TABLE 15.8 **Difference-in-Differences Estimation for Our Former Student's Cigarette Tax Change Data**

SUMMARY OUTPUT	
Regression Statistics	
Multiple R	0.234110868
R Square	0.054807898
Adjusted R Square	0.025873446
Standard Error	28.09473845
Observations	102

ANOVA					
	df	**SS**	**MS**	**F**	**Significance F**
Regression	3	4485.378823	1495.126274	1.894208961	0.135566774
Residual	98	77352.80421	789.3143286		
Total	101	81838.18303			

	Coefficients	**Standard Error**	***t* Stat**	***p*-value**	**Lower 95%**	**Upper 95%**
Intercept	71.5883703	4.387660993	16.31583899	1.08576E-29	62.88120008	80.29554052
Changed	−12.28666258	9.908733615	−1.239983136	0.217942492	−31.95022146	7.376896293
2008	−3.802439354	6.205089684	−0.612793617	0.541432261	−16.11623757	8.511358862
2008 × Changed	−5.857817886	14.01306546	−0.418025442	0.676843068	−33.66628953	21.95065376

These results indicated to our former student that states that increased cigarette taxes between 2006 and 2007 saw their cigarette sales per capita decrease by 5.86, all other independent variables constant, relative to states that did not increase their cigarette taxes. As a result, our former student concluded that increases in cigarette taxes are likely successful in reducing cigarette consumption, although in this circumstance, the coefficient on the difference-in-differences estimator is statistically insignificant.

Based on this work, from the initial idea through data collection, empirical analysis, interpretation of results, and effective write-up, our former student was judged to have conducted a successful empirical research project.

LOOKING AHEAD TO CHAPTER 16

At this point, we have filled our empirical toolkit with an extensive number of tools that apply to a wide variety of situations. Beyond being able to correctly estimate marginal effects, being able to coherently present the chosen estimation methods and empirical results is a skill for which the benefit cannot be underestimated. With this fact in mind, Chapter 16 provides tips for performing and writing up an empirical research project.

Problems

15.1 How do quantile regression estimates differ from OLS estimates?

15.2 Explain how the following situations suffer from sample selection bias.

a. Data on the salaries of people in the labor force.

b. Telephone survey respondents.

c. Number of years of education.

d. Drug trials for a lethal disease.

15.3 Compare and contrast difference-in-differences estimation to panel data techniques.

15.4 Given how difficult it is to estimate true marginal effects in economics, why aren't quasi-experimental techniques used more often?

Exercises

E15.1 Use the file **California Data.xls** for the following questions.

a. Regress Loan Amount on income, black, other race, and male. Comment on the results using OLS.

b. Estimate the same model using quantile regression at the 50th percentile. How do your results in parts (a) and (b) differ?

c. Estimate the model at the 10th, 25th, 75th, and 90th percentiles. Do these results differ from the results you found in parts (a) and (b)?

d. From a policy perspective, why do you think it is important to not just focus on average values but also consider the marginal values at different points in the distribution?

E15.2 Use the file **Hunting Data.xls**, which is collected from the 2006 National Survey of Fishing, Hunting, and Wildlife Associated Recreation, for the following questions.

a. Regress Hunt Days on male married, divorced, somecol, hsonly, ba, somepost, postgrad, black, other, income, and south central. Comment on the results. Why is OLS not the appropriate estimation strategy in this circumstance?

b. Estimate the same model as in part (a) with a Poisson model. Comment on the results.

c. Estimate the model with a negative binomial model. Test for over-dispersion. Do your results from parts (b) and (c) differ?

d. Which model do you think is the most appropriate to use, and why?

E15.3 Use the file **Cigarette Data.xls**, which is collected from the 2003 National Health Interview Survey, to answer the following questions.

a. Estimate a Heckman selection model in order to identify factors that affect the number of cigarettes smoked per day. The identification variable to be used in the first stage is dadattack (if the person's father had a heart attack) while the dependent variable is cigperday (number of cigarettes smoked per day), and the explanatory variables are black, Hispanic, male, age, family size, married, and divorced. Comment on the results.

b. Estimate the same model with OLS and compare and contrast the results with those you found in part (a).

E15.4 Using the file **Suicide Data.xls**, which is collected from the National Center for Health Statistic's 1998 mortality data, estimate a difference-in-differences model to estimate the effects of a policy change in the assisted suicide law in Oregon in 1997 in two ways.

a. First, estimate the sample mean of the number of suicides in Oregon in 1996 and the number of suicides in Washington in 1996, and then subtract the Washington mean from the Oregon mean. Second, estimate the sample mean of the number of suicides in Oregon in 1998 and the number of suicides in Washington in 1998, and then subtract the Washington mean from the Oregon mean. Finally, subtract the value from the first step from the value in the second step. This is the difference-in-differences estimator. Comment on the results.

b. Estimate the difference-in-differences estimator using a regression. Regress the number of suicides in Oregon, the year 1998 and Oregon × 1998. Verify that the difference-in-differences estimator is the same as what you found in part (a). Comment on the results.

c. From a policy perspective, why is the method employed in part (b) preferable to the method employed in part (a)?

d. Explain how this method does a better job of estimating the true effects of the policy change in Oregon than if only the 1998 data had been used.

Chapter Sixteen

How to Conduct and Write Up an Empirical Research Project

CHAPTER OBJECTIVES

After reading this chapter, you will be able to:

1. List the general steps and understand the approach to conducting a research project.
2. Understand the general approach to writing an empirical research project.
3. Identify the elements included in the write-up of our movie box office project.

A STUDENT'S PERSPECTIVE

Suppose that after having determined a question of sufficient interest, developed the appropriate economic theory, collected appropriate data, implemented the correct empirical approach, and drawn the correct conclusions, you are faced with the challenge effectively communicating the quality of your work to your future readers. This is exactly the situation encountered by all of our former students. In this chapter, we provide advice for effectively writing up an empirical research project.

BIG PICTURE OVERVIEW

The previous chapters introduce tools required to conduct empirical research projects using multiple linear regression analysis. What factors affect the ultimate quality of such projects? While the appropriateness and quality of the empirical analysis is certainly important, one should never underestimate the importance of effectively communicating the underlying motivation for the project and the significance of the results. Rigorous empirical projects often fail to reach their full potential due to an author's inability to effectively communicate the quality of the work, while less rigorous studies often generate more "buzz" than might have been expected due to the skill with which the author communicates to his or her audience. In other words, when conducting an empirical research project, the effective communication of the goals, process, and results are of great importance. Unfortunately, because the effective communication of these facets of an empirical research project are more art than a science, there are no clear-cut rules as to the best approach. Nonetheless, we present general guidelines below that you may wish to follow as you start to develop your own preferred approach.

As a tool for demonstrating many of the issues that must be considered when conducting a successful empirical research project, we develop a new application—empirically explaining movie box office receipts—that we work through from start to finish, culminating in an example write-up that we might actually produce were we to conduct this as a

An Important Caveat about Our Goals for This Chapter

The following discussion aims to relay some of the hints that we think budding researchers might find useful in developing their own approach to conducting and writing up empirical research projects. Successfully conducting and presenting empirical research is a highly personal endeavor. We certainly do not wish to suggest that these are the only skills required to become a successful researcher or that other researchers do not have additional, potentially more valuable insights to impart. Instead, these hints are only intended as a starting point for students who might be lacking experience in conducting and writing up such projects. We encourage all readers, even those with prior experience, to consult all potential sources of information while developing their own approach to conducting and writing up empirical research projects.

term project for an undergraduate course. We hope that you will use this as a guideline as to how to write up an empirical project of your own.

The above box presents an important caveat about the goals of this chapter.

16.1 GENERAL APPROACH TO CONDUCTING AN EMPIRICAL RESEARCH PROJECT

Before being able to write up an empirical research project, a researcher must

1. Decide on the question to be addressed.
2. Collect and summarize data that are appropriate for addressing the question.
3. Determine and implement an appropriate empirical technique, and correctly interpret the results.
4. Draw appropriate conclusions based on the estimates.

In our experience, it is best to complete all of these steps before starting the write-up because the decisions we make here will have great influence over the decisions we make when writing up our empirical results. Taking this advice to the extreme, note that when preparing our own papers for submission to academic journals, we never write even one word of text until we have constructed all of the tables that are to be presented and discussed.

Before starting into the details, we wish to mention one insight that guides our own approach to empirical work: One of our first graduate microeconomics professors continually repeated the mantra that "Economics is about telling stories." With this in mind, we approach every research project as a chance to tell our readers an economic story, and every decision we make in both the empirical work and the write-up is aimed at making that story as compelling as possible.

Step 1: Determine a Question of Interest

We initially discussed several points related to this important decision in Chapter 2. One of the points that we stressed is that we always strive to ensure that the chosen question will be of interest to the reader (if it is not, the reader will likely be inclined to not care much about the quality of the work and/or the results). With this in mind, continuing with our movie buff example, we start by asking whether analyzing the factors associated with box-office success sounds like it would be interesting to potential readers. While the answer to this question is certainly subjective, given that box-office numbers are widely publicized throughout the year and that the motion picture industry is a multi-billion dollar business, we might well expect the answer to be yes. Accordingly, we should be comfortable moving on to step 2.

One important point to note is that the ability to answer your chosen question is intimately related to the data that you are able to collect—just because a question is interesting does not mean that you will be able to empirically address the answer. Regardless of the brilliance of your question, if you are unable to collect appropriate data, you will not be able to complete the project. For instance, suppose that being a huge fan of the National Football League (NFL) and being concerned about the NFL's ongoing collective bargaining disputes, you decide to investigate the degree to which player on-field performance is correlated with a team's operating profit. While certainly an interesting question, there is absolutely no way that you will be able to collect the necessary data for such an empirical project because other than the Green Bay Packers, who are publicly owned, NFL owners do not open their accounting books for anyone (which is always a sticking point in their negotiations with the NFL Players Association). As a result, after reaching the data collection part of your project (step 3) you would be forced to reconsider your chosen question. Given this reality, an alternative approach to identifying a sufficiently appropriate question is to first identify interesting data that you know you are able to collect and then work backward to identifying an interesting question that can be asked *and answered* utilizing those data. As an example, recall that we arrived at the MLB position player salary example on which we focused Chapters 6 through 9 not because we had an overriding love of the game or an obvious question in mind, but rather because (1) the labor economic theory governing salary determination in professional labor markets is quite clear and (2) the salary and productivity data needed to test such theories are relatively easy to collect.

Step 2: Formulate the Appropriate Theory

Recall from Chapter 8 that for OLS to be the best linear unbiased estimator, the population multiple linear regression model must be *correctly specified.* This begs the obvious question of how to determine the *correct* specification. One of the things that distinguishes economists from other users of applied statistics is our belief that the correct specification should be guided by economic theory. To an economist, this means that the chosen empirical model should include all factors predicted by economic theory to affect the dependent variable, regardless of whether the individual coefficient estimates achieve statistical significance (i.e., we do not believe in either step-wise procedures that search across potential independent variables to determine the subset that are statistically significant or in dropping variables from our theory-driven model because they fail to achieve statistical significance).

There are two good starting points for determining the appropriate economic theory to guide our analysis: (1) our personal economic intuition and (2) the existing literature, which demonstrates the intuition and empirical evidence of other researchers.

For our movie box-office example, we might start by noting that our intuition tells us that a movie's box-office revenue is directly related to the number of consumers choosing to purchase tickets, and therefore, to increase a movie's box office, the producers must increase the demand for tickets. Further, our intuition tells us that the best way to do so is by increasing the "buzz" surrounding the movie by producing either (1) a blockbuster or (2) a film that is loved by the critics. Given these insights, we would expect a movie's box-office performance to depend on the independent variables listed in Table 16.1 that serve as measures of the degree to which a given movie meets these criteria.

TABLE 16.1
Independent Variables Suggested by Our Intuition

Production budget	Critical reviews
Sequel	Oscar buzz
Bankable star	Movie run time
MPAA rating	Theater run
Total theaters	

The intuition behind these variables should be clear. Besides having bigger production budgets, big-budget blockbusters are often sequels that feature bankable stars and have PG-13 ratings. Critical darlings, on the other hand, are often movies that have better critical reviews, nominations for major awards, such as the best picture Oscar, and longer run times owing to their more serious topics. In addition, we might expect a movie's performance to be directly related to the length of its theater run because the longer a movie is in theaters, the greater the opportunity it has to sell tickets.

After exhausting our personal intuition, we should consult the existing literature to double-check our thinking and to get additional ideas as to how we should approach our empirical work. We usually start our literature review by identifying a closely related article and then working back through the references listed in that paper to develop a somewhat exhaustive list of the important work in the field. In this case, because we are interested in learning how previous researchers have empirically modeled movie box-office receipts, we start with an Internet search of "empirical movie box office," and we identify the article in Figure 16.1 that appeared in the *Southwestern Economic Review* in 2005.

FIGURE 16.1
A Valuable Source Revealed by Our Literature Review

Source: N. Terry, M. Butler, and D. De'Armond, "The Determinants of Domestic Box Office Performance in the Motion Picture Industry," *Southwestern Economic Review* 32, no. 1 (2005), pp. 137–148.

THE DETERMINANTS OF DOMESTIC BOX OFFICE PERFORMANCE IN THE MOTION PICTURE INDUSTRY

Neil Terry, West Texas A&M University
Michael Butler, West Texas A&M University
De'Arno De'Armond, West Texas A&M University

ABSTRACT

This paper examines the determinants of box office revenue in the motion picture industry. The sample consists of 505 films released during 2001-2003. Regression results indicate the primary determinants of box office earnings are critic reviews, award nominations, sequels, Motion Picture Association of America rating, budget, and release exposure. Specific results include the observation that a ten percent increase in critical approval garners an extra seven million dollars at the box office, an academy award nomination is worth six million dollars, the built in audience from sequels are worth eighteen million dollars, and R-rated movies are penalized twelve million dollars.

Looking at the paper's abstract suggests that our personal intuition identified the key independent variables that these authors found to significantly influence a movie's box-office gross. Reading further through the article, we see that the authors include a "survey of the literature" in their paper, which happens to be a valuable resource for conducting our own literature review. By going to these papers and learning about the sources that informed their work (which are referenced in their papers), we are able to quickly stitch together a fairly exhaustive view of the existing literature and we are able to include many of these references in our write-up.

Through this process, we uncover several additional independent variables that we think should be included in our empirical analysis. Table 16.2 lists these additional independent variables.

TABLE 16.2
Additional Variables Suggested by Our Literature Review

Movie genre	Holiday release
Major studio	Advertising Budget

At this point, to help us prepare for step 3, it is useful to write out a general version of an empirical model that lists the independent variables that we have identified as likely being correlated with our dependent variable. For our movie box-office example, we have

$$\begin{aligned} \textit{Box office} = f(&\textit{Production budget, Sequel, Bankable star, MPAA rating,} \\ &\textit{Total theaters, Critical reviews, Oscar buzz,} \\ &\textit{Movie run time, Theater run, Movie genre, Studio,} \\ &\textit{Holiday release, Advertising budget}) \end{aligned} \quad \textbf{16.1.1}$$

While not required, this step is potentially useful because it clearly indicates the variables for which we will need to find appropriate data in the next step. It also helps us prepare for presenting our chosen empirical model when writing up our work.

Before moving on to step 3, we need to mention a potentially important limitation associated with Excel's regression analysis capabilities: Excel will not perform multiple linear regression analysis for specifications containing more than 16 independent variables. This introduces the following potential concern: Suppose that we are working on an application for which we wish to estimate a multiple linear regression with more than 16 independent variables. We have two basic options if we wish to perform our empirical analysis in Excel. We can choose to (1) limit our analysis to the 16 independent variables that seem most appropriate according to economic theory or (2) use a different statistical package. While this might sound like a major limitation to Excel's usefulness, we note that for many applications, economic theory specifies far fewer independent variables that should be included in the empirical analysis. Given that we have already identified 13 potentially important independent variables, however, and given that several of those (MPAA rating, Movie genre, and Major studio) are categorical, ours may be one of those cases in which the 16-independent-variable limit becomes a real concern.

Step 3: Gather Appropriate Data

Once we have identified the dependent variable and the important independent variables that form the basis of our empirical analysis, we need to collect usable data. In practice, this step is likely as important as any other in determining the ultimate success of our project. Every applied microeconomist likely has multiple war stories concerning brilliant ideas that he or she was unable to study because the necessary data were lacking. Oftentimes, this unfortunate result occurs because the researcher is unable to locate appropriate data, as with our earlier hypothetical NFL profit analysis. Other times, the problem reveals itself only after collecting and beginning to analyze the data, at which point we realize that the collected data are inadequate for addressing the question of interest. (This is particularly true when working with advanced econometric techniques, such as two-stage least squares, for which it is difficult to determine appropriate instruments and for which we often find that our chosen instruments are either weak or invalid.) What are we to do in such a case? We must either reformulate the question of interest into one that we can answer with the collected data or scrap the question altogether and begin working on an alternative question that leads to data that can be collected and analyzed.

Collecting Data for the Dependent Variables

Returning to our movie box-office example, does the fact that we were able to specify a question of sufficient interest guarantee that we will be able to find data appropriate for addressing its answer? Of course not. We can, however, quickly learn whether we will be able to do so by starting the data collection process. Because we will most certainly be dead in the water if we cannot find an appropriate measure of our dependent variable, we suggest this as a natural starting point. Because we are interested in explaining total box-office grosses, we start with an Internet search for "2009 yearly movie box office" (which is the most recent year for which the data are available). Clicking on the first entry takes us to the page titled "2009 Domestic Grosses" on the Box Office Mojo website shown in Figure 16.2.

Notice that this page contains data on the 100 highest-grossing films opening (but not necessarily closing) during the 2009 calendar year. Given that these represent the vast majority of films in wide release during the year, we might reasonably decide to limit our data set to only these movies. We then can follow the procedure detailed in Chapter 2 to import these data into Excel from the Web.

Is this one year's worth of data enough? Or should we repeat the data collection process for additional years? This is an important question for a number of reasons. First, if we only focus on one year, we open ourselves up to potential biases that can be caused by individual year aberrations in the data. For instance, because *Avatar* was by far the highest grossing film of all time (at least in nominal terms), if we only focus on the year in

FIGURE 16.2 **2009 Domestic Grosses According to boxofficemojo.com**

2009 DOMESTIC GROSSES

Top 10 Total Grosses of all Movies Released in 2009

Rank	Movie Title (click to view)	Studio	**Total Gross** / Theaters		Opening / Theaters		Open	Close
1	**Avatar**	Fox	**$749,766,139**	3,461	$77,025,481	3,452	12/18	8/12
2	**Transformers: Revenge of the Fallen**	P/DW	**$402,111,870**	4,293	$108,966,307	4,234	6/24	10/15
3	**Harry Potter and the Half-Blood Prince**	WB	**$301,959,197**	4,455	$77,835,727	4,325	7/15	12/17
4	**The Twilight Saga: New Moon**	Sum.	**$296,623,634**	4,124	$142,839,137	4,024	11/20	4/1
5	**Up**	BV	**$293,004,164**	3,886	$68,108,790	3,766	5/29	11/5
6	**The Hangover**	WB	**$277,322,503**	3,545	$44,979,319	3,269	6/5	12/17
7	**Star Trek**	Par.	**$257,730,019**	4,053	$75,204,289	3,849	5/8	10/1
8	**The Blind Side**	WB	**$255,959,475**	3,407	$34,119,372	3,110	11/20	6/3
9	**Alvin and the Chipmunks: The Squeakquel**	Fox	**$219,614,612**	3,747	$48,875,415	3,700	12/23	5/20
10	**Sherlock Holmes**	WB	**$209,028,679**	3,626	$62,304,277	3,626	12/25	4/29

Source: Adapted from Box Office Mojo, www.boxofficemojo.com.

which it was released, we might draw incorrect conclusions as the relationship between the various blockbuster measures and a movie's domestic gross. Second, as we learned in previous chapters, increasing the number of observations decreases the estimated standard errors, thereby increasing the precision of the regression estimates. While true, there is most definitely a cost associated with collecting additional data, particularly in terms of the time required for data entry. As such, when determining the ideal number of observations for a given research project, the researcher is faced with an important trade-off between the precision of the estimates and the time-cost of collecting data. So how many observations are enough? This, again, is a decision for the researcher conducting the project. When asked by students in our undergraduate courses for the correct solution to this trade-off, our short answer is they need to collect "enough" data. In this context, the precise definition of "enough" is left to the researcher: While it is true that, in general, more observations are always better, we would accept a much looser definition of "enough" from undergraduates in one-semester courses than from graduate students writing a master's thesis or from professors attempting to publish in academic journals. In the case of our movie box-office example, we choose to define "enough" as five consecutive years, which gives us a potential sample of 500 different movies (the top 100 of each calendar year for five consecutive years). To add data for the additional years to our data for 2009, we click the "Previous Year" tab and import data on the top 100 grossing films in 2008, 2007, 2006, and 2005. We then save the file as **Movie Data Master.xlsx**, and beyond creating the new variable discussed in the next paragraph and adding additional independent variables, we never perform any calculations or data transformations in this file (so that we can quickly and easily return to our initial data should we reach the point that we need to scrap our calculations and start over).

The fact that we are collecting data for multiple years brings up another important concern. As every student learns in their principles of economics class, to avoid the problem of "money illusion" when comparing dollar-denominated data over time it is important to compare real values rather than nominal values. Because the annual box-office data on the boxofficemojo.com website are presented in nominal rather than real dollars, therefore, we need to make the conversion to real values ourselves using CPI data from the Bureau of Labor Statistics website (http://data.bls.gov/timeseries/CUUR0000SA0?output_view=pct_1mth). Choosing the appropriate boxes from that website, we find the desired price indices for each year to be as shown in Table 16.3.

TABLE 16.3
Annual CPI Data to Be Used When Converting to Real Values

2005	195.3
2006	201.6
2007	207.342
2008	215.303
2009	214.537

We can easily use these values to convert the nominal domestic box office grosses to real domestic gross (in 2009 dollars) by creating a new column in which we multiply the 2005 box-office grosses by 214.537/195.3, the 2006 box-office grosses by 214.537/201.6, and so on. While it might not make much difference when comparing across five consecutive years, the following box highlights the importance of comparing real rather than nominal values across longer time periods. We note that students in our classes often fail to make such conversions, which always results in their losing a few points on their projects.

Real versus Nominal Box-Office Grosses

The importance of controlling for inflation when comparing movie box office across different years can easily be demonstrated by the following example. On February 3, 2010, the *Hollywood Reporter* heralded *Avatar* for passing *Titanic* as the highest grossing domestic film of all time (www.hollywoodreporter.com/news/avatar-tops-titanic-record-us-20231). As the following chart makes clear, however, this fact is only true in nominal but not real terms. When adjusted for inflation, the picture becomes quite different.

Rank	Title	Studio	Year	Unadjusted Gross	Adjusted Gross
1	Gone with the Wind	MGM	1939	$198,676,459	$1,606,254,800
2	Star Wars	Fox	1977	$460,998,007	$1,416,050,800
3	The Sound of Music	Fox	1965	$158,671,368	$1,132,202,200
4	E.T.: The Extra-Terrestrial	Uni.	1982	$435,110,554	$1,127,742,000
5	The Ten Commandments	Par.	1956	$ 65,500,000	$1,041,450,000
6	Titanic	Par.	1997	$600,788,188	$1,020,349,800
7	Jaws	Uni.	1975	$260,000,000	$1,018,226,600
8	Doctor Zhivago	MGM	1965	$111,721,910	$ 986,876,900
9	The Exorcist	WB	1973	$232,671,011	$ 879,020,900
10	Snow White and the Seven Dwarfs	Dis.	1937	$184,925,486	$ 866,550,000
11	101 Dalmatians	Dis.	1961	$144,880,014	$ 794,342,100
12	The Empire Strikes Back	Fox	1980	$290,475,067	$ 780,536,100
13	Ben-Hur	MGM	1959	$ 74,000,000	$ 779,100,000
14	Avatar	Fox	2009	$760,507,625	$ 773,179,400
15	Return of the Jedi	Fox	1983	$309,306,177	$ 747,772,300

Notice that after controlling for inflation, *Avatar* barely cracks the top 15 and that its adjusted gross is less than half that of *Gone With the Wind,* which was released in 1939. Notice further that only 1 of the 14 films remaining top-15 highest grossing films of all time—*Titanic*—was released after 1990. What does this tell you?

Collecting Data for the Independent Variables

Now that we have collected data on our dependent variable, we need to collect data on as many of our desired independent variables as possible. Recall from the previous section that based on our economic intuition and our literature review, we hypothesize a movie's real box-office gross to depend on the independent variables listed in Table 16.4.

TABLE 16.4
Independent Variables for Which We Wish to Collect Data

Production budget	Critical reviews	Sequel
Oscar buzz	Bankable star	Movie run time
MPAA rating	Theater run	Total theaters
Movie genre	Holiday release	Major studio
Advertising budget		

Where do we collect these data for each of the films in our sample? In addition to domestic box-office gross, notice that the data collected from the Box Office Mojo website also includes the studio releasing the film; the "Total Theaters" in which the film played; and the movies' domestic open and close dates, which can be used to calculate the movie's domestic "Theater Run" by subtracting the movie's open date from its close date. This last calculation introduces an issue that we might not have been expecting. Because the dates on the source webpage do not have the calendar year attached (i.e., the opening date for *Avatar* is listed as 12/8 as opposed to 12/8/2009), Excel's import wizard automatically assigns the current calendar year as the calendar year associated with the listed open and close dates. While this is not a concern for movies for that open and close in the same year, it is an issue for movies that open relatively late in one year and close relatively earlier in the following year. For instance, if we are importing the data at some point in 2011, Excel will automatically enter *Avatar*'s open date as 12/8/2011 and close date as 8/12/2011 (even though the film opened in December, 2008 and ran through August 2009); in doing so, Excel calculates a theatre run of −128 days for the film (12/8/2011−8/12/2011 = −128 days), which is obviously incorrect. While not 100 percent correct, the easiest way to calculate the correct theater run in this case is to change Avatar's open date to 12/18/2010, which will force Excel to calculate *Avatar*'s theater run as the correct 237 days. It is possible to make this change for all affected movies at one time by (1) sorting the entire data set on the "Theater Run" column, (2) identifying the movies with negative Theater Run values, and (3) using Excel's find and replace feature (CTRL+F) to switch all open dates from the current year to the previous year, which would be 2011 to 2010 in this example. (In the interest of exactness, we could, of course, change the open date to 12/18/2008 and the closing date to 8/12/2009, but that would require additional entries and it would result in the same outcome.)

Notice that because the entries result from mathematical calculations, in the formula bar in Excel, they will be entered as the calculations themselves (H2-G2) rather than as the results of the calculations. To keep this fact from causing problems in the future, we use the "copy" and "paste special—values" option (refer back to Chapter 2 for detailed instructions) to convert the entries in the "Theater Run" column from the calculations to the results of the calculations.

After completing this task, we can also turn the qualitative values for "Studio" into the binary dummy variable "Major Studio," which is equal to 1 if the movie is released by a major studio (BV, Fox, P/DW, Par., SonR, Sony, Uni., and WB) and equal to 0 otherwise. We can also construct the dummy variable "Sequel," which is equal to 1 if the movie is a sequel and equal to 0 if it is not, by scrolling through the movies in our data set and making note of those that are indeed sequels. Finally, we can sort all movies by their open dates and create the variable "Holiday Release" by entering a 1 in each cell if the movie is released around a major U.S. holiday (Memorial Day, Independence Day, Thanksgiving, Christmas, and New Year's) and 0 otherwise.

These steps provide data for several of our desired independent variables. Where do we turn to find data for the remaining variables? If we click on a movie's title on the

Box Office Mojo webpage shown in Figure 16.2, we are taken to another page that contains many of the remaining desired independent variables. For *Avatar,* this new page looks like Figure 16.3.

FIGURE 16.3
Webpage for *Avatar* on boxofficemojo.com

Source: Adapted from Box Office Mojo, www.boxofficemojo.com.

Avatar

Domestic Total Gross: **$749,766,139**
Domestic Lifetime Gross: $760,507,625

Distributor: **Fox**
Release Date: **December 18, 2009**
Genre: **Sci-Fi Adventure**
Runtime: **2 hrs. 40 min.**
MPAA Rating: **PG-13**
Production Budget: **N/A**

Summary Daily Weekend Weekly Releases Foreign

Total Lifetime Grosses
Domestic: **$760,507,625 27.3%**
+ Foreign $2,020,624,407 72.7%
= **Worldwide $2,781,132,032**
Domestic Summary
Opening Weekend: $77,025,481
(#1 Rank, 3,452 theaters, 22,313 average)
% of Total Gross: 10.3%
> View All 34 Weekends
Widest Release: 3,461 theaters
Close Date: August 12, 2010
In Release: 238 days / 34 weeks

The Players
Director: James Cameron
Writer: James Cameron
Actors: Sam Worthington
Zoe Saldana
Sigourney Weaver
Michelle Rodriguez
Giovanni Ribisi
Producers: James Cameron
Jon Landau
Composer: James Horner

Notice that these data are not in tabular form, meaning that if we import them directly into Excel they will fit nicely into the existing tables. As such, using Excel's import wizard is of little help because once in Excel we will need to physically move the data into tabular form, which promises to be a major hassle. Instead, we suggest creating a few new columns in the existing Excel file and entering the desired data for each film ourselves. In this case, we create the columns "Genre," "Rating," "Run Time," and "Budget (Millions)," and enter those data by hand. For *Avatar,* this looks like Table 16.2.

TABLE 16.5
Data That We Enter for *Avatar* in Our Excel File

Movie Title	Genre	Rating	Run Time	Budget (Millions)
Avatar	Sci-Fi Adventure	PG-13	160	237

Notice that two of these—"Genre" and "Rating"—are qualitative variables, meaning that we need to convert them to a series of dummy variables before we can include them in our multiple linear regression analysis. What particular dummy variables should we create for these qualitative variables? According to our literature review, previous researchers have found that, all other independent variables equal, adventure and science-fiction movies earn significantly different box-office grosses than movies in other genres. Accordingly, while there are many different potential genres, we create dummy variables equal to 1 if a given movie was listed as Adventure or Sci-Fi and 0 otherwise. In our empirical analysis all genres other than adventure and science fiction are our omitted group. Likewise, because there are only four different MPAA ratings, we create the three dummy variables PG, PG-13, and R, which are equal to 1 if a movie had one of those specific ratings and 0 otherwise, meaning that in our empirical analysis G-rated movies are our omitted group.

While boxofficemojo.com has been kind enough to provide us with much of our desired data, it has not provided data for all of our desired independent variables. In addition to the variables that we have so far collected, we also need data measuring "Critic Reviews," "Bankable Stars," "Oscar Buzz," and "Advertising Budget." While there are many potential sources of critic reviews, based on its current popularity we measure a movie's critical acclaim as the Rotten Tomatoes "tomatometer" percentage of critics recommending the movie. We found that the easiest way to determine this value for each movie was to conduct a search for the movie's title using the search engine provided on the Rotten Tomatoes homepage to pull up the movie's individual webpage and then to enter the value under the new column "RT Rating." To define bankable stars, we follow Joshi and Hanssen (2009) and consider an actor/actress as bankable if *Forbes* reported that he or she earned more than $10 million per movie in 2009 (www.forbes.com/2009/06/09/movies-sandler-depp-business-media-hollywood.html and www.forbes.com/2009/06/30/top-earning-actresses-business-entertainment-hollywood.html). For each movie starring one of those actors or actresses, we enter a 1 in the new column "Star Actor," and for all other we enter a 0 in that column. Finally, we define a film as garnering Oscar buzz with two new variables: If the movie was nominated for the Best Picture Oscar, we enter a 1 in the "Best Picture Nominee" column, and if the movie won the Best Picture Oscar, we enter a 1 in the "Best Picture Winner" column. For all other movies, we enter a 0 in those columns.

This leaves one last desired independent variable for which we have not yet collected data: a movie's advertising budget. From our literature review, we learned that a few previous researchers have included this measure in their empirical analysis. Reading their work, we learn that the source for these data is the Ad$pender data set compiled by the private firm TNS Media Intelligence. An Internet search reveals that gaining access to this data set requires one to either purchase a subscription from the firm or find a source that provides access to the data. While a few university libraries apparently subscribe to the service and allow on-campus access, our university library does not. What are we to do in this situation? If we were conducting a project that we hoped to one day submit to an academic journal, we would take the hit and pay the price required to subscribe to the service. If we were preparing an undergraduate paper, on the other hand, we would make note of the issue in our write-up (so that it was clear that we had considered the issue), and we would expect our professor to be reasonable enough to not expect us to pay the subscription cost out of our own pocket. For this reason, we are comfortable not including advertising budgets in our empirical analysis, although we do make note of the issue later in the conclusion of our sample write-up.

There is an additional issue that should be discussed at this point—missing data. Sometimes, our initial data source simply lacks data on certain variables. This is a potential concern because observations with missing values cannot be included in the estimation of the sample regression function. What should we do in such cases? The answer depends on the size and scope of the problem. If a very small percentage of observations are missing, and if those observations do not result from a systematic process, it likely makes little or no difference if we simply drop them from the sample. Likewise, if economic theory predicts that the independent variable for which observations are missing is of relatively little importance, it is likely acceptable to omit the variable from the analysis. If, however, the number of observations missing is large and/or the variable for which they are missing is vital to the analysis, then we likely should pursue a different tack.

As an example of how we might deal with missing data, after importing the data from boxofficemojo.com, we can see that the production budget is listed as N/A for what seems like an inordinate number of movies (81 our original 500 observations, or roughly 16 percent of our sample). We actually found this somewhat surprising because we expected the production budget for most recent movies to be readily available. Given the likely importance of a movie's production budget to its domestic box-office gross, we were neither comfortable dropping the observations with N/A values nor excluding the variable itself from our analysis. Instead, we conducted Internet searches for the movies with N/A budgets, finding reliable values for enough movies to increase our usable sample size from 419 to 471, an improvement of roughly 11 percent that seems well worth the time invested.

The preceding description might seem like a lot of work to devote to an empirical research project, but how long exactly did it take? In total, we were able to complete data construction in less than 20 hours, which, when completed over a number of days, does not strike us as too excessive a price to pay for the chance to receive a top grade and the lifetime reward that goes with it!

We now have exactly 16 independent variables that we hypothesize to be significant determinants of a movie's domestic box-office gross and that we, therefore, expect to form the core of our empirical analysis. These variables are saved in the file **moviedata.xlsx** and are listed in Table 16.6.

TABLE 16.6 **The Variables for Which We Have Collected Data**

Dependent variable:	Real Domestic Gross
Independent variables:	Total Theaters, Theater Run, Major Studio, Sequel, Holiday Release, Run Time, Budget (millions), Adventure, Sci-Fi, PG, PG-13, R, RT Rating, Star Actor, Best Picture Nominee, Best Picture Winner

Note that if desired, we can use these variables to construct additional variables that we can include in our empirical analysis. As an example, we could create a new variable that equals the square of run time and include that variable to test whether run time has a quadratic relationship with real box-office gross. Likewise, we could create a new variable that is the product of Sci-Fi and holiday release and include it as an independent variable to test whether there is a significant interaction effect between those two variables in determining a movie's real box-office gross.

Step 4: Conduct Empirical Analysis

After collecting data that are appropriate for addressing our chosen question, performing an appropriate empirical analysis is the real crux of an empirical paper. Once they are satisfied with the motivation and theory, experienced readers are likely to focus on the chosen empirical specification and the offered interpretation of the results. As such, the ability to adequately execute this section is of utmost importance in determining how the reader responds to your work. Having read many, many empirical papers (both by students and by professional colleagues), we can promise that nothing loses a reader more quickly than an improper empirical specification and/or an incorrect interpretation of the empirical results. For this reason, we strongly recommend making every effort to execute this stage to the best of our ability.

How do you make sure that our empirical specification is correct? This is an extremely complicated question without a definitive answer. Determining the appropriate empirical specification requires the researcher to make a number of decisions for which the correct option is rarely obvious. In a paper in the leading economics journal, Edward Leamer amusingly summarized this idea as follows.

> *"There are two things you are better off not watching in the making: sausages and econometric estimates".*
>
> *—Edward Leamer, "Let's Take the Con Out of Econometrics,"* American Economic Review *(1983)*

What does this mean? In most cases, determining the correct econometric specification is more of an art than a science, meaning that if we asked two equally talented researchers to investigate the same question of interest they might well make totally different decisions that result in different empirical specifications, with it being entirely possible that no obvious reason exists for preferring one to the other.

How might we determine the most correct empirical specification for our chosen empirical project? While we have already stressed the importance of letting economic theory be our primary guide, we ultimately have to make decisions between specifications that often seem equally supported by theory. In such cases, we determine our most preferred specification through trial and error. For instance, the theory underlying our movie box-office example is sufficiently general to allow for the possibility that the correlation between box-office gross and movie genre differs for holiday releases and nonholiday releases (i.e., it could be that sci-fi movies are less well-received during the Christmas season than during the rest of the year). How might we determine whether this is a realistic possibility? As we learned in Chapter 9, we could allow the effect of the science-fiction genre to differ with holiday release by including the interaction term "Sci−Fi · Holiday Release" in our population regression model. If we find this interaction term to be statistically significant, we would conclude that it should be included in our most preferred specification. If not, we could reasonably conclude that it should not be included (note that this decision would not be the same as simply dropping an independent variable because it lacks statistical significance—in this case, we would still be including Sci-Fi and Holiday Release in our model; we would just being leaving out the interaction term between those variables).

Continuing with our movie box-office example, now that we have our data, we need to decide what to do with it to produce the best possible empirical research project. This is where the art of empirical analysis really comes into play. As discussed in Chapter 3, we have always found a valuable starting point to be rolling up our sleeves and creating summary statistics and graphs to get a sense of what the data look like. To do so for our movie box office sample, we might begin by calculating the summary statistics for the dependent variable and for key independent variables. Table 16.7 presents these values.

TABLE 16.7 Summary Statistics Calculated in Excel

	Real Domestic Gross	Budget (Millions)	RT Rating	Run Time	Total Theaters	Theater Run
Mean	$ 90,604,967.89	$ 60.73	50.04	108.60	2,949.30	99.64
Standard deviation	$ 79,944,612.33	$ 51.06	26.39	18.71	701.31	40.74
Minimum	$ 24,457,504.61	$ 0.02	2	74	687	30
25th percentile	$ 40,456,756.06	$ 25.00	26	95	2,570	69
Median	$ 63,485,350.70	$ 45.00	50	106	3,026	97
75th percentile	$108,561,877.50	$ 80.00	73	119	3,453	125
Maximum	$749,766,139.00	$300.00	98	191	4,455	335
	Sequel	**Major Studio**	**Star Actor**	**Picture Nom**	**Picture Win**	**PG**
Mean	0.123	0.709	0.227	0.053	0.008	0.187
	PG-13	**R**	**Action**	**Sci-Fi**	**Holiday**	
Mean	0.486	0.291	0.130	0.040	0.193	

We learn several things from this exercise. First, both real domestic gross and production budget are sharply skewed to the right, as evidenced by the fact that the 25th percentiles of both distributions are much closer to the medians than are the 75th percentiles of both distributions. This should not be surprising given that there are relatively few blockbusters each year and that blockbusters tend to have larger budgets. Quickly scanning the data from highest to lowest gross suggests that this is indeed so. If the intuition behind the observed skewness were not so clear, we would recommend looking at the data much more closely because skewness can indicate that data have been entered incorrectly for some observations (i.e., if we had mistakenly added a 0 to the real box-office gross for *Avatar,* making it $7,497,661,390 rather than $749,766,139, the data would have been much further skewed to the right). Second, the remaining continuous variables, "RT Rating," "Runtime," "Total Theaters," and "Theater Run" are nearly symmetric in their distributions, with roughly one in eight movies being sequels; roughly 5 percent being nominated for the Best Picture Oscar, with less than 1 percent winning the award; nearly half of all movies being rated PG-13; roughly 13 percent and 4 percent being action and science-fiction movies, respectively; and nearly one in five being released around a major U.S. holiday.

One thing that might stand out in Table 16.7 is that there are a lot of numbers in each of the entries in the "Real Domestic Gross" column, making it somewhat difficult to digest all of the information. Given that all of the movie grosses in our sample are in the millions of dollars, we might decide to rescale our dependent variable as "Real Domestic Gross/1,000,000" so that the entries have fewer numbers to digest (i.e., the mean would be $90.605 million rather than $90,604,967.89). While not necessary, such a conversion likely makes our results easier to interpret.

Is this all of the information that we wish to know about the data? No, these summary statistics only provide a sense of the units of measurement and the central tendencies of the dependent and independent variables. Because we are actually more interested in determining the relationship between our dependent variable and each of our independent variables, we might next construct scatterplots between box-office gross and key independent variables. Figure 16.4 presents these figures for five important independent variables.

FIGURE 16.4 **Scatterplots of the Relationship between Real Domestic Gross and Several Key Independent Variables**

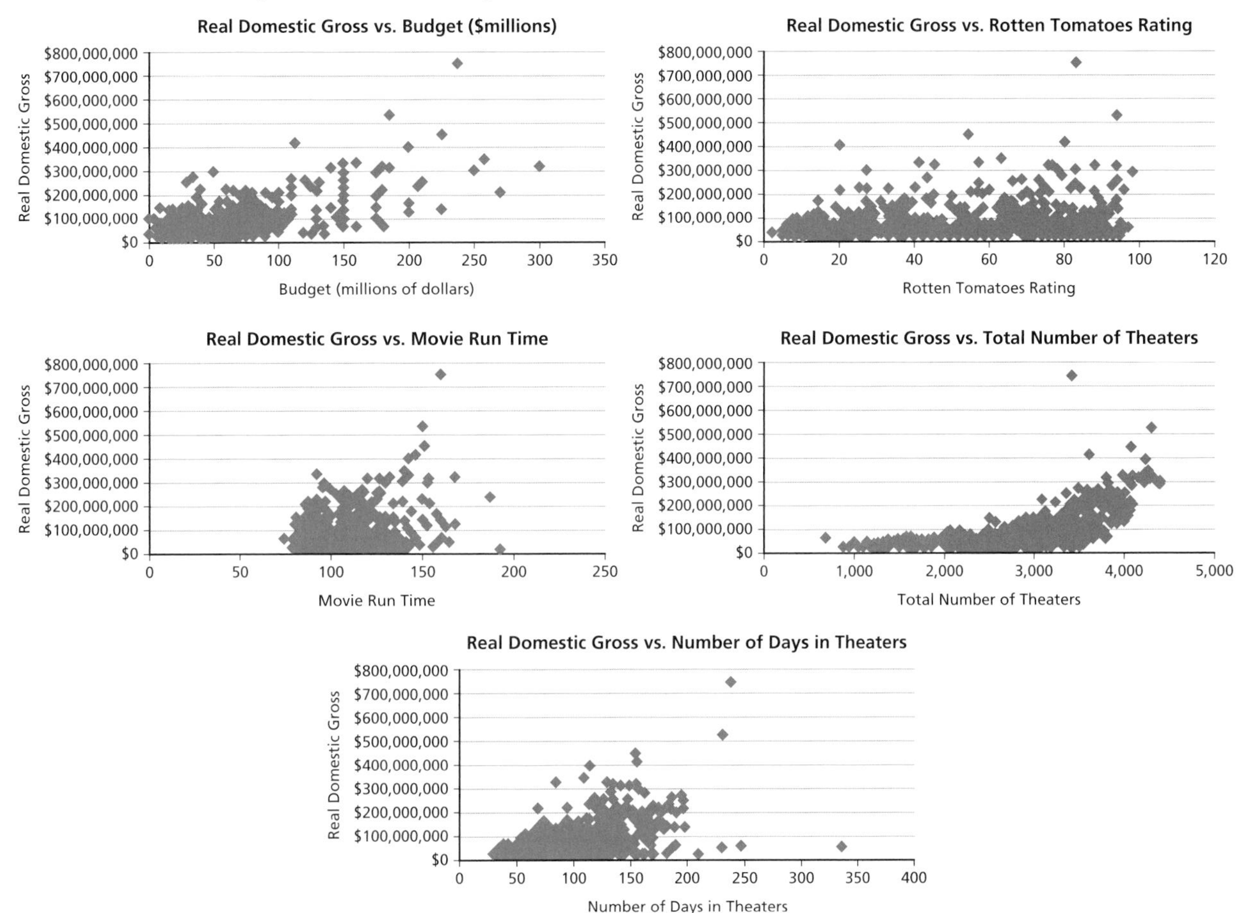

While not representing true marginal effects, these scatterplots provide general evidence as to the likely nature of the relationships between the dependent variable and each of these independent variables. In each case, it appears that a positive relationship likely exists and that there is no obvious reason to suspect the relationships to be quadratic in nature. In other words, this relatively simple analysis has established that real domestic gross is likely related in a linear fashion to all of these independent variables.

While informative, the preceding exercises do not specifically determine the most desirable empirical specification for our project. To narrow our search, we start with our best guess and see where it leads us. For our movie box-office sample, we might start by estimating a baseline regression controlling for the 16 independent variables outlined earlier. Table 16.8 presents the estimated sample regression function, with variables that are statistically significant at the 5 percent level being highlighted in blue and variables that are statistically significant at the 10 percent level being highlighted in light gray.

These results suggest that several of our independent variables are estimated to have a statistically significant correlation with our dependent variable. Recall that we have rescaled our dependent variable to be in millions of dollars, which will affect the correct interpretation of the estimated coefficients. Specifically, the estimated coefficient for "Budget (millions)" suggests that, all other independent variables constant, each $1 million increase is a movie's production budget is associated with a $423,000 (0.423 million) increase in the movie's real domestic gross. Before spending too much additional time interpreting

TABLE 16.8 A First Pass at Estimating the Sample Regression Function

SUMMARY OUTPUT	
Regression Statistics	
Multiple R	0.832902922
R Square	0.693727278
Adjusted R Squard	0.682933525
Standard Error	45.01573679
Observations	471

ANOVA

	df	SS	MS	F	Significance F
Regression	16	2083843.172	130240.1982	64.27118732	1.2122E-105
Residual	454	919993.1177	2026.416559		
Total	470	3003836.289			

	Coefficients	Standard Error	*t* Stat	*p*-value	Lower 95%	Upper 95%
Intercept	−205.3579594	21.44985898	−9.57386058	6.70693E-20	−247.5112843	−163.204635
Budget (millions)	0.42267205	0.064748116	6.52794355	1.78713E-10	0.295428863	0.54991523
RT Rating	0.38235514	0.095059171	4.02228563	6.74977E-05	0.19554458	0.56916570
Run Time	0.25351368	0.141369797	1.79290885	0.073653042	−0.024362029	0.53138939
Total Theaters	0.04446834	0.004282476	10.3837923	8.32259E-23	0.036052406	0.05288427
Theater Run	0.67457521	0.063379465	10.64343502	9.08732E-24	0.550021707	0.79912872
Sequel	24.53019949	6.852102386	3.57995227	0.000380699	11.06442806	37.99597092
Star Actor	−0.35565538	6.448181906	−0.05515592	0.956038513	−13.02764111	12.31633035
Star Actress	−1.85739996	7.342954559	−0.25294995	0.800421384	−16.2877955	12.57299557
Picture Nominee	14.21735661	11.70961548	1.21416084	0.225317499	−8.794413589	37.22912681
Picture Winner	−56.43791188	25.13614884	−2.24528874	0.025230094	−105.8355443	−7.04027947
PG	3.22134155	12.09295441	0.26638168	0.79006621	−20.54376743	26.98645033
PG-13	27.73891149	12.13060981	2.28668731	0.022673615	3.899802008	51.57802098
R	18.87884253	12.67048245	1.48998608	0.136922272	−6.02122624	43.77891129
Action	−14.53511634	6.87271669	−2.11490114	0.034982635	−28.04139906	−1.02883362
Sci-Fi	37.95145267	11.08960256	3.42225544	0.000677268	16.15813365	59.74477168
Holiday	15.33915664	5.509662798	2.78404636	0.005592763	4.511551376	26.16676191

these results, we might want to consider alternative specifications. For instance, we could allow for a potential quadratic effect of the length of a movie's theater run by including both the "Theater Run" and the created "Theater Run Squared" variables in the regression. Or, we could allow for the possibility that science-fiction movies released around holidays gross less than those released at other times by including the interaction term "Sci-Fi · Holiday Release" (recall that due to the 16-variable limit, to include these new variables, we need to drop a different independent variable, such as "Major Studio," which is estimated to be nearly insignificant in the former regression, from the population regression model that we estimate). We would then determine whether these new variables should be included in our most preferred specification by performing *t*-tests for the individual significance of the estimated coefficients and in certain situations *F*-tests for the joint significance of a subset of variables. Note that we did perform such tests for the inclusion of additional independent variables and we rejected all alternative specifications. As a result, we might consider the estimates in Table 16.8 to be our most-preferred (at least given the 16 independent variable constraint in Excel). Accordingly, we might consider ourselves either extremely good (or extremely lucky) that the initial specification suggested by our personal economic intuition couple with our literature review ended up being our most-preferred specification.

While true, there is an additional specification issue that we should consider. Given that our movie box-office data represent a pooled cross-section (a cross-section of yearly movie releases over a number of different years), we should test for the possibility that the estimated sample regression functions differ across the years in our sample. We can do so by performing a basic Chow test in which we compare the pooled cross-section estimates to the five individual year estimates. In this case, the calculated test statistics is 1.49 and the critical value is 1.38, meaning that we reject the null hypothesis of equal estimated coefficients across the five years in the pooled sample, and we conclude that we should estimate the sample regression functions separately for each of the years. Table 16.9 combines these

TABLE 16.9 The Results of Estimating the Sample Regression Function Separately by Movie Opening Year

	Overall	2005	2006	2007	2008	2009
Intercept	−205.444	−201.826	−199.378	−171.886	−156.589	−257.864
	(21.560)	(48.114)	(49.079)	(60.991)	(43.488)	(57.126)
Budget (millions)	0.4299	0.6022	0.4036	0.3374	0.4259	0.4363
	(0.0648)	(0.1590)	(0.1494)	(0.1528)	(0.1320)	(0.1699)
Run Time	0.2595	0.0851	0.3494	0.3596	−0.1835	0.7195
	(0.1415)	(0.3407)	(0.3086)	(0.3075)	(0.3369)	(0.3769)
Total Theaters	0.0449	0.0351	0.0490	0.0449	0.0340	0.0357
	(0.0043)	(0.0093)	(0.0098)	(0.0108)	(0.0098)	(0.0122)
Theater Run	0.6746	0.7668	0.5452	0.5042	0.7904	1.0255
	(0.0632)	(0.1390)	(0.1431)	(0.1827)	(0.1449)	(0.1702)
Sequel	23.6824	43.9318	23.1868	38.5126	20.7073	8.9257
	(6.9462)	(17.3507)	(12.9554)	(16.7697)	(14.1002)	(19.9104)
Major Studio	−2.2325	−6.0545	−1.3688	8.8269	−9.2513	−2.5600
	(5.2798)	(11.1990)	(12.1892)	(11.3334)	(11.7551)	(14.8908)
Star Actor	−2.8798	−15.1777	12.9678	−2.8120	8.3683	−29.1680
	(5.4176)	(13.5523)	(10.5891)	(12.1565)	(12.1839)	(14.7319)
Action	−14.6946	−31.2580	−41.7028	−0.8430	6.1915	−17.9602
	(6.9108)	(16.4808)	(13.0350)	(15.9928)	(13.0054)	(21.5246)
Sci-Fi	37.5511	19.4483	−14.3207	61.1400	−27.9152	34.7982
	(11.1044)	(18.3372)	(43.4251)	(26.5212)	(43.1887)	(25.5300)
Holiday	15.7616	7.1309	27.1348	−2.0923	10.7912	40.7200
	(5.5253)	(14.2806)	(14.1894)	(12.5011)	(12.3088)	(14.4618)
RT Rating	0.3847	0.4640	0.2692	0.2816	0.6944	0.0997
	(0.0950)	(0.2253)	(0.1949)	(0.1935)	(0.2219)	(0.2610)
Picture Nominee	13.9213	−14.4187	−25.6731	7.2349	−35.0726	60.0342
	(11.7426)	(27.7143)	(31.0781)	(27.1325)	(29.5525)	(25.8396)
Picture Winner	−57.2659	−139.8372	1.0341	7.5698	4.7141	—
	(25.1187)	(57.0001)	(48.1274)	(47.0418)	(52.8782)	—
PG	3.0034	30.8272	−6.7051	−4.5140	−7.7982	2.1645
	(12.0881)	(28.3677)	(21.1442)	(45.7511)	(22.5028)	(33.7937)
PG-13	27.6671	51.9261	17.0546	11.5934	35.7423	41.9496
	(12.1708)	(29.5554)	(21.1813)	(46.0544)	(21.8328)	(33.6292)
R	18.4646	45.1499	13.7514	−13.2605	22.4682	34.6868
	(12.7728)	(30.8017)	(23.7762)	(47.7652)	(23.1354)	(34.3478)
R Square	0.6940	0.7014	0.7348	0.7833	0.7364	0.7764
Observations	471	95	95	88	97	95

Note: Standard errors in parentheses. Values in blue and gray denote significance at the 5 and 10 percent levels.

separate-year estimates into one table of estimated coefficients, with those that are significant at the 5 percent level being highlighted in blue and those that are significant at the 10 percent level being highlighted in light gray.

One final thing to note concerning the choice of most desirable specification is that, just as we did for the dependent variable, in certain situations it may be desirable to transform some of the independent variables into more easily interpretable values. For instance, because our "Theater Run" variable is denominated in days, the estimated coefficient should be interpreted as the marginal effect that a one-day increase in a movie's theater run is expected to have on its real box-office gross. Suppose we believe that when making decisions, studios decide whether to extend a movie's run a week at a time rather than a day at a time. In such a case, we might want to rescale the variable as "Theater Run/7" so that the correct interpretation of the estimated coefficient would be the marginal effect that a one-*week* increase in a movie's theater run is expected to have on its real box-office gross.

Step 5: Draw Conclusions

This section provides a chance to summarize the results of our empirical analysis. In the previous section, we determined that several independent variables are estimated to have statistically significant marginal effects on our dependent variable. Do we need to focus on every single one in our write-up? No. We only need mention those results that most directly relate to the story that we wish to tell. How do we determine which results do so? It might help to create a box that summarizes all of our results, thereby allowing us to quickly compare the results to determine which might be deemed "more important" than others. For our movie box office example, we would have something like Table 16.10.

TABLE 16.10
Summary of the Results of Our Empirical Analysis

Summary of Empirical Results

In the Pooled Cross-Section Regression

Positively Related to Real Box-Office Gross:
Budget, Run Time, Total Theaters, Theater Run, Sequel, Sci-Fi, Holiday Release, RT Rating, PG-13

Negatively Related to Real Box-Office Gross:
Action, Best Picture Winner

In the Individual Year Regressions

Positively Related to Real Box-Office Gross:
Budget, Total Theaters, Theater Run—all years
Run Time—2009
Sequel—2005, 2006, 2007
Sci-Fi—2007
Holiday Release—2006, 2009
RT Rating—2005, 2009
PG-13—2005, 2008

Negatively Related to Real Box-Office Gross:
Action—2005, 2006
Best Picture Winner—2005
Star Actor—2009

At this point, we need to decide on which of these results we wish to focus. Again, our advice is to start with those results that relate directly to the story that we wish to tell. Beyond that, we can choose to include any results that we believe that readers will find particularly interesting.

Once we reach this point, we have completed the empirical work required for your empirical research project. This leaves the write-up as the only remaining task (as mentioned in Chapter 2, however, this is no small step—depending on the difficulty of the data collection process, in our professional work we often devote nearly as much time to the write-up as to the other steps combined).

The following box summarizes the key points discussed in this section.

Key Points on How to Conduct an Empirical Research Project

- Think of an interesting question.
- Use economic theory to guide dependent and independent variable selection.
- Search diligently for the corresponding data.
- Realize that data collection will likely be the most time-consuming part of the project.
- Use statistical analysis, economic theory, and the literature to guide model selection.
- Correctly interpret results.
- Draw appropriate conclusions.

16.2 GENERAL APPROACH TO WRITING UP AN EMPIRICAL RESEARCH PROJECT

Now that we've completed all of our empirical work, how do we produce a write-up that best conveys to our readers the work that we have done and the results that we have found? Again, this is more of an art than a science. Probably the best way to hone this art is to read many, many empirical papers; to identify what we do and do not like about different approaches; and to use those insights to formulate our preferred approach. This is how most academics hone their skills. Short of that, we offer some general hints as starting points toward developing your own style.

Recall that we view the write-up as a chance to tell the story that we wish to tell the reader. With this in mind, we recommend first thinking about the goal of the work. We undertook the project with our mind toward telling a specific story. To be most effective, our write-up should be streamlined to focus on this goal without including extraneous information that detracts from it. While preparing the write-up, a number of decisions need to be made regarding what should be included and what should not. In general, when preparing the write-up, we encourage making decisions that focus the reader on the story that we are trying to tell and against those that do not.

There is an additional caveat that we wish to stress: While the previous chapters have introduced many tools that *can* be used, the write-up of your empirical project is not the time to prove how many of those tools we know how to use. Rather, the write-up should include only those tools that help address the question of interest. Unfortunately, we find that students in our courses often feel compelled to work through every single tool introduced in the class, even though many of them are not actually applicable to their chosen project. As an example, if there is no theoretical reason to suspect structural differences between specific subsets of the data, then there is no reason to conduct a Chow test. Likewise, if there is no theoretical reason to suspect an interaction effect between independent variables, then there is no reason to include one in the estimated sample regression function. Adding further to this point, the write-up does not have to explicitly walk the reader through every single thing that we did when determining our chosen empirical specification. Similarly, we do not have to discuss in detail every single estimated coefficient and every single step of each individual hypothesis test that we conducted. Doing so often only serves to drown the reader in numbers, variables, alternate specifications, and hypothesis tests, which is a surefire way to confuse the reader and remove the focus from the story that we wish to tell. Instead, we encourage focusing on those aspects that move the story forward and help the reader understand the key points that we wish to make.

In general, an effective write-up should have five distinct parts: (1) introduction, (2) description of the data, (3) empirical approach and results, (4) conclusion, and (5) references. Each of these parts serves a particular purposes, which we discuss in the following sections.

Section 1: Introduction (and Economic Theory/Literature Review)

The purpose of this section is to present our chosen question and indicate why it is important enough to be the subject of your empirical project. To effectively gain the reader's attention, we recommend introducing the question as quickly as possible so that the reader does not need to work through multiple sections of text trying to decipher what the remainder of the paper will be about. We also recommend focusing as much as possible on the relevance of the work in order to capture the reader's attention. In other words, when writing up the empirical project, we advise considering the reader and what is essential to furthering his or her understanding of the work.

We include economic theory/literature review in parentheses in the title of this section for a specific reason: This is where the decisions start in terms of our write-up. While it is vital to include a discussion of the economic theory guiding our empirical specification at some point in the write-up, it is a matter of personal taste as to whether we work the discussion into the introduction or present it as a separate stand-alone economic theory section. If the goal of the paper is to develop a more formal theory (which is unlikely for undergraduate students), then we might prefer to include a separate theory section. Otherwise, it is likely preferable to incorporate a general description of the underlying theory into the introductory section.

Likewise, if one of the main thrusts of the paper is providing a thorough literature review, then we might want to present it in a separate section, as did Terry, Butler, and De'Armond (2005) in the paper referenced in Figure 16.1. If, instead, we wish to summarize key findings of a few directly relevant papers, we might wish to incorporate them within the introduction (as we do in the example write-up that we include at the end of the chapter).

Finally, in academic journal articles, it is traditional to conclude the introduction with a one-paragraph summary of the data analyzed and the main empirical results. Generally speaking, there are two compelling reasons for doing so. The more cynical is that owing to their time constraints, when reading journal articles, many academics quickly scan the introduction to determine whether it is worth their time to work through the remainder of the paper. The more practical reason is that by providing an overview of what we think are the most important aspects of the work, we can provide the reader with a road map for interpreting the remainder of the paper.

Section 2: Discussion of the Data (including Summary Statistics)

This purpose of this section is to (1) indicate why the data we collected are appropriate for addressing your chosen question, (2) inform the reader as to the sources of our data, and (3) provide the reader with a general sense of what the data look like (the units of denomination, central tendencies, etc.). To do so, we start by discussing the type of data required to address our chosen question. We then detail all of the sources from which the required data were collected (this does not need to be nearly as detailed a description as we included in Chapter 2 or in the preceding section). We then provide general summary statistics and discuss what those values tell us about the data.

Note that several important decisions need to be made in this section, particularly regarding the presentation of summary statistics. Chapter 3 discussed several different summary statistics that could be appropriately used in different situations. In general, most empirical papers start their discussion of summary statistics by presenting a list of sample means and standard deviations for continuous variables and sample percentages for binary and categorical variables. Beyond that, it is up to us to determine which other statistics might be valuable additions to your summary analysis. Again, the key deciding factors should be to include those tools that will be most helpful in developing your story for the reader. Depending on the situation, we might choose to include pictures, such as histograms that demonstrate the overall distribution of key variables for which the mean is not that informative. Even if only presenting a table of means, if we believe that there are likely important differences across specific subgroups of the data, it is often useful to provide separate summary statistics for each subgroup to provide the reader with a sense of how important variables might differ across groups. As a hypothetical example, if we have sufficient reason to believe that box-office gross might differ across movie genres, then we might want to present summary statistics separately for each different movie genre.

An important issue that should not be overlooked, but often is (even in academic journals), is the choice of title for our tables and figures. As a general rule, an effective title is one that perfectly describes the included data without forcing the reader to work through the text to figure out exactly what is being reported in the table. Again, the reason for this is that many trained readers will skim the text and read the tables in detail in order to get the maximum from the paper with the minimum time commitment.

A related but equally important issue is the choice of variable names presented in the write-up. Again, the chosen variable names should clearly indicate the values represented. If the variable names are unclear, then the reader will either be forever confused as to the results or continually forced to refer back to the text to refresh his or her memory as to the true meaning of the variables. Both of these outcomes are undesirable because they are likely to quickly turn the reader against the work. The choice of variable names becomes an issue because many statistical packages limit the number of characters than can be assigned to variable names. For instance, the variable name "Real Domestic Box-Office Gross" is not one that we would be able to easily use in a program such as Stata. Instead, we might choose the variable name "RBOG," which would certainly make sense to us while conducting your empirical work. Think about the reader, however. Is the variable name "RBOG" likely to conjure up a clear definition in his or her mind when reading the write-up? No, meaning that the reader will be forced to continually flip back through the text to recall exactly what the variable "RBOG" represents. Doing so will quickly become an annoyance, which will likely sour the reader to our work. Instead, we suggest making efforts to provide variable names that make clear sense to the readers (notice that there is no rule requiring us to use the same name in our chosen statistical package as we use when presenting the results in our write-up). For instance, even if we use the name "RBOG" when working with our data, in our write-up it might be better to report the variable as "Real Domestic Gross" in the presented tables.

While on the subject of presenting tables containing our results, in academic articles authors often present notes below their tables that explain additional issues associated with the estimates presented in the tables. For instance, it is common to represent different levels of statistical significance with different numbers of stars (*, **, or ***) in the table and then note the associated level of significance in the accompanying note (as we do in Table 3 in our example write-up). We could also use the notes to remind our readers of the units of measurement of the dependent variable or any other data issue that we might deem important.

Turning to more general issues, how do we decide which aspects of the data to highlight in this section? This is one of the reasons we suggest completing our entire empirical analysis before working on the write-up. Once we determine the main results that we wish to highlight, we are free to construct our entire write-up in a way that maximizes the story for the reader.

Finally, note that while we present all tables and figures together at the end of our write-up (which is standard for academic papers), we could just as easily incorporate them into the text close to the sections in which we are discussing them. For instance, we could insert Table 1 between the fourth and fifth paragraphs of the data description section; we could insert Table 2 between the first and second paragraphs of the empirical results section; and so on.

Section 3: Discussion of the Empirical Analysis

The purpose of this section is to (1) write out our chosen empirical model so that the reader knows exactly what we are going to estimate, (2) indicate why our chosen model is appropriate, (3) present the results of estimating our chosen model, and (4) provide a correct interpretation of our results.

We generally start this section by explicitly writing out our empirical model so that the reader knows exactly what model we will be estimating. After doing so, it is likely useful to remind the reader of the signs that economic theory predicts for our key variables of interest. A simple way to do this is to include a table summarizing the predictions for each of the independent variables, as Joshi and Hanssens (2009) do in table Table 2a of their paper and as we do in Table 2 of our example write-up. As a final step in this section, we present and discuss our results.

When discussing the results, there is no law requiring that we discuss each individual estimated coefficient. In fact, doing so often loses the reader's interest because he or she begins to feel led on a forced march through the results. Instead, we recommend that primarily focusing on those results that form the core of our analysis (i.e., the ones that relate directly to the story that we wish to tell). With regard to the relative importance of our time investment, we would argue that it is far more important to correctly interpret our empirical results than it is to discuss each and every estimated coefficient. Based on our experience, nothing creates negative reactions in readers (particularly instructors) faster than reading incorrect interpretations of results. Once the reader has been lost to such a mistake, it is very unlikely that he or she will be won back—no matter how well we might construct our write-up.

Note that while we have generally considered and estimated several alternate specifications in the course of determining our most-preferred specification, we only need present our chosen empirical specification in the write-up. To demonstrate the thoroughness of our thought process and to head off potential questions that might occur to readers, we might want to briefly mention relevant considerations made while determining the most preferred specification. For instance, we might state that "We also considered interaction terms between science-fiction movies and holiday releases, but found them to be statistically insignificant." A useful tool for making such points is to include them in a footnote that makes clear to the reader that we did indeed consider such factors without sidetracking the narrative in the text.

Further note that it is perfectly acceptable to report having performed a certain statistical test without listing every single step in the process and presenting tables containing results. For instance, when performing a Chow test, we might simply state, "A Chow test rejects the equality of the estimated sample regression functions across years at the 5 percent level, indicating that the box-office gross functions should be estimated separately by year," instead of writing out each individual step of the hypothesis testing process.

Section 4: Conclusion

This is our last chance to convince the reader as to the value of our work. Does the write-up need to mention everything that we did in the course of completing the project? No. We only need highlight those results on which we want the reader to focus. This is where the results table constructed earlier comes in handy. Making such a list should help us focus on which results are more important and which are less important.

There are a number of additional purposes that can be served in this section. For instance, suppose that we are surprised by some of the results but think that a data issue may be causing the confusion, such as an imperfection in your data-collection process or the undue influence of an outlier (i.e., the *Avatar* effect we referenced in several earlier instances)? Similarly, suppose that we are unable to collect data for some independent variables that we think might be important explanatory factors, such as a movie's advertising budget? Now is the time to discuss these issues. From our experience, readers (particularly college instructors) are likely to be far more sympathetic to the work if we acknowledge such potential shortcomings at this point rather than simply burying our head and pretending that they do not exist.

Finally, suppose that there are either additional things that we would have added to our work if we had more time or resources or if there are extensions of our work that we would like to pursue in the future? Now is the time stake our ground. As an example, for our movie box-office gross example, we might take the opportunity to mention that in the future we would like to collect data on advertising budgets so that we could estimate a movie's domestic operating profit in addition to its box office gross.

Section 5: References

To avoid plagiarizing other authors, we must acknowledge all sources that we cite in our write-up. The exact style to follow when listing references in this section is somewhat open to debate. If an instructor specifies a given style, then by all means follow that. Otherwise, we should list the references according to an accepted format such as the *Chicago Manual of Style* or the APA Reference Style. As a default example, in their Style Guideline Instructions for authors of accepted articles, the American Economic Association includes the following: "Reference section must be double-spaced, beginning on a new page following the text, giving full information. Use full names of authors or editors. List all author/editors up to/including ten names. Authors of articles and books and material without specific authors or editors, such as government documents or bulletins, are to be listed alphabetically. Please refer to Sample References: www.aeaweb.org/sample_references.pdf."

The following box summarizes the key points to consider when preparing the write-up of an empirical research project.

Key points to Consider when Preparing a Write-up of an Empirical Research Project

- You should focus on telling the story of your project.
- It should not matter how long your write-up is, but rather how good it is.
- It is not necessary to include every single step you went through to decide on the appropriate model.
- Make sure to focus on the results that pertain to your story. It is not necessary to interpret every single estimate.
- The project does not have to be perfect, but you should mention the shortcomings in the conclusion (i.e., data you would have liked to collect or possible extensions).

Before presenting our example write-up, we note that combining the text, references, and tables and figures, our entire write-up is 10 regular double-spaced pages, which in our view is a very appropriate length for an undergraduate term empirical research project, although this decision is ultimately up to each instructor. We also stress again that this is not intended as a template to directly follow for every single empirical project that you have to produce. Rather, it is intended as a (hopefully helpful) starting point in developing your own style. As mentioned earlier, we encourage you to critically read existing papers and openly discuss the topic with your professors to further develop your own style.

16.3 AN EXAMPLE WRITE-UP OF OUR MOVIE BOX-OFFICE PROJECT

Lights, Camera, Ticket Sales: An Analysis of the Determinants of Domestic Box-Office Gross

1. Introduction

A general statement of the overall importance of the market being studied is a useful way to introduce the importance of your chosen topic.

Note that we formally state our chosen question in the third sentence of our write-up.

The motion picture industry is a major part of the U.S. economy. In 2009, 522 movies were released in the United States, with the total box office gross being $17.565 billion. Given this importance, the motion picture industry is the focus of significant media attention, with weekend box office grosses being widely publicized, as well as the annual *Forbes* list of the most influential individual celebrities in Hollywood. What exactly makes an individual influential in Hollywood? Producing, directing, or starring in a movie that ranks among the top-grossing films of the year. Given the obvious importance of being associated with a high-grossing movie, an obvious question might be: Which factors are associated with a movie's total box-office gross? We attempt to answer this question by estimating real domestic box-office grosses for the top 100 highest-grossing movies between 2005 and 2009.

Previous researchers have addressed this topic on multiple occasions. Litman (1983) and Terry, Butler, and De'Armond (2005) find that, all other independent variables equal,

Because it is not a major focus of our write-up, we include our literature review in the introduction.

a movie's production budget is positively associated with domestic box-office gross, while Litman (1983) and Anast (1967) find that science-fiction and action movies, respectively, are correlated with box-office gross. Litman (1983), Sochay (1994), Radas and Shugan (1998), and Einav (2001) find further evidence that films released around Christmas or the major summer holidays gross significantly more than movies released at other times of the year. Litman (1983), Reinstein and Snyder (2000), and Terry, Butler, and De'Armond (2005) find that the better a movie's critical reviews, the higher its box-office gross. Litman (1983) and Nelson et al. (2001) estimate that both being nominated for and winning an Oscar are positively associated with box-office gross. Finally, Saehney and Eliashberg (1996) and Ravid (1999) estimate that a movie's MPAA rating is significantly related to its box-office success, with the former finding a negative effect associated with R-rated movies and the latter finding a positive affect associated with G and PG movies.

We summarize our major empirical findings in the last paragraph of the introduction to provide readers with an idea as to where our write-up is headed.

In this paper, we estimate real domestic box-office gross for the top 100 highest-grossing movies between 2005 and 2009, controlling for many of the independent variables just discussed. For our sample as a whole, we find that, all other independent variables equal, a movie's real domestic box-office gross is positively related to its production budget, movie run time, total theaters, theater run, and Rotten Tomato rating, as well as its being a sequel, in the science-fiction genre, having a holiday release, and/or a PG-13 rating. It is negatively related to being an action movie and/or winning the Best Picture Oscar. Estimating the real box-office gross functions separately by year reveals that aside from the core factors of production budget, total theater, and theater run, which are estimated to have a positive relationship in every year, many of the full-sample results are not consistent over time and are, instead, driven by specific movies released in specific years. For instance, while we estimate movie run time and holiday release to be significant in the full-sample regression, the only year in which we estimate movie run time to have a significant effect is 2009, and the only years in which we estimate holiday release to have significant effects are 2006 and 2009. Moreover, while we do not estimate being a Best Picture Oscar nominee to have a significant effect in the full-sample regression, we do estimate it to have a significant effect in 2009. None of these results should be that surprising—*Avatar,* the highest-grossing movie in our sample (and of all-time), was released during the Christmas holiday in 2009, was nominated for but did not win the Best Picture Oscar, and had a runtime of 2 hours and 40 minutes, which was the seventh-longest running in our sample. The remaining cross-year differences can be explained in a similar fashion.

2. Data Description

We start this section with our discussion of economic theory as a means of motivating the data that we need to collect.

A movie's box-office gross is directly related to the number of consumers purchasing tickets to view the movie in theaters. Economic theory suggests that the number of ticket-purchasing consumers is a function of consumer demand for seeing a given movie. Several factors are likely to affect consumer demand through the amount of "buzz" that a movie generates, with movies that generate more "buzz" selling more tickets and achieving higher box-office grosses. The factors affecting a movie's "buzz" likely include the movie's production budget, number of theaters, run time, theater run, rating, and whether the movie was a sequel, released around a holiday, and/or featuring a "bankable" star.

We briefly describe the sources from which we collect data. Note that we highlight decisions that we made when collecting the data, such as collecting data only for the top 100 highest-grossing movies of each year in our sample.

Data representing these economic factors are collected from publicly available Internet sources. Data on a movie's total domestic gross, opening and closing dates (which are used to calculate its theater run), total number of theaters, production budget, run time, and Motion Picture Association of America (MPAA) ratings are collected from the boxofficemojo.com website (and are also available from other sources, including IMDB, The Numbers, etc.). To ensure that we include the majority of all movies achieving wide release, we collect data for the top 100 highest-grossing films in specific calendar years; to avoid any single year biases in the data (i.e., the "*Avatar* effect" in 2009), we collect data for the five consecutive years from 2005 to 2009. To enable comparisons over time, domestic grosses are converted to real domestic grosses ($2009) using CPI data from the U.S. Bureau of Labor Statistics.

Additional data are collected from other easily accessible Internet sources. We measure the reaction of movie critics to each individual film by Rotten Tomatoes' "tomatometer" percentage of critics recommending each movie. We indicate the degree of "Oscar buzz" surrounding a movie by binary dummy variables indicating whether the movie was nominated for a Best Picture Oscar and whether it won the award. Following Joshi and Hanssens (2009), we define a movie as featuring a "bankable" star if it features one of the actors or actresses reported to make at least $10 million per movie according to the *Forbes* list of the top-paid actors and actresses in 2009.

Eliminating observations for which we were not able to collect reliable values for all of these variables (whose definitions are summarized in Table 2) leaves us with a sample of 471 movies. According to the summary statistics in Table 1, the average real domestic gross of movies ranked among the 100 annual highest-grossing movies between 2005 and 2009 was $90.604 million, with the maximum being the $749.766 million of *Avatar* in 2009. While true, the median real domestic gross is $63.485 million, suggesting that the distribution of movie box-office receipts is highly skewed to the left, a fact that is not surprising given that only a few extremely high-grossing films are released each year and that the remaining films are more tightly distributed around at lower values.

Given the skewness of our dependent variable, we decide to present an additional analysis of our Real Domestic Gross data.

Figure 1 expands on this point by demonstrating that nearly 72 percent of all movies in our sample gross between $24 and $97 million domestically, nearly 16 percent gross between $97 and $169 million, and only 5 percent gross more than $242 million. In other words, it appears that the movie market between 2005 and 2009 was driven by relatively few true blockbusters. Indeed, while the 471 movies in our sample gross a total of $42.674 billion, the 45 movies grossing more than $200 million have a total gross of 12.854 billion, which represents a full 30 percent of the total gross of all movies in our sample. As such, we might expect our empirical results to be driven in large part by the relatively few high-grossing movies in our sample. We will return to this point later.

Looking at the remaining summary statistics in Table 1, the average production budget of movies in our sample is $60.73 million, while the average film length is 108.60 minutes, the average theater run is 99.64 days, and the average number of theaters in which movies play is 2,949.30. At the same time, roughly 12 percent of movies in our sample are sequels, roughly 23 percent feature a bankable star, roughly 5 percent are nominated for Best Picture, and roughly 1 percent win the Oscar. Finally, only 4 percent of our movies are rated as G, while 19 percent are rated as PG, 49 percent as PG-13, and 29 percent as R by the MPAA.

While not absolutely necessary, adding facts that are likely to catch the reader's interest likely adds to their enjoyment and overall impression of your write-up.

While not central to our empirical work, it is interesting to consider these statistics for individual movies in more detail. Doing so further illustrates the market dominance of "blockbuster" movies by revealing that among the highest-grossing movie in each of our five calendar years, only 2006's *Spider Man 3* fails to rank as one of the five highest-grossing movies in our pooled cross-section, although it does rank sixth overall, trailing 2009's second highest-grossing move, *Transformers: Revenge of the Fallen* which ranks fifth. At the opposite extreme, the three lowest-grossing movies in our sample, each with real domestic grosses of roughly $25 million, were released in 2007. Turning to Rotten Tomatoes ratings, the highest-rated movie in our sample, *Up,* receives a tomatometer rating of 98, while the lowest-rated movies, *Epic Movie* and *Meet the Spartans,* receive tomatometer ratings of 2. Perhaps of further interest, of the four movies in our sample receiving tomatometer ratings of 96 or higher—*Up, The Queen, WALL-E,* and *Ratatouille*—three are animated features. In our pooled sample, only *Grindhouse* (which was later divided into two movies for its DVD release) and *King Kong* have run times greater than 3 hours, while *Hannah Montana/Miley Cyrus: Best of Both Worlds Concert Tour* and Tim Burton's *Corpse Bride* both have run times below 1 hour and 15 minutes. Finally, *Crash* has the longest observed theater run in our sample at 335 days, while *Zathura, We Own the Night,* and *The Grudge 2* have the shortest theater runs at 30 days.

3. Empirical Results

We start this section by stating outright what we wish to accomplish with our empirical analysis.

Our goal is to estimate the degree to which the independent variables discussed earlier are correlated with the real box-office grosses of movies in our sample. To do so, we estimate a standard real box-office gross function of the form

We then write out our chosen empirical specification so that the reader knows exactly what we are going to estimate.

$$\begin{aligned}
&\textit{Real domestic gross}/\$1{,}000{,}000_i \\
&\quad = \beta_0 + \beta_1 \textit{Budget}/\$1{,}000{,}000_i + \beta_2 \textit{Run time}_i + \beta_3 \textit{Theaters}_i \\
&\qquad + \beta_4 \textit{Theater run}_i + \beta_5 \textit{Sequel}_i + \beta_6 \textit{ Major studio}_i \\
&\qquad + \beta_7 \textit{Star actress}_i + \beta_8 \textit{Action}_i + \beta_9 \textit{SciFi}_i + \beta_{10} \textit{Holiday}_i \\
&\qquad + \beta_{11} \textit{Critic rating}_i + \beta_{12} \textit{Picture nominee}_i + \beta_{13} \textit{Picture winner}_i \\
&\qquad + \beta_{14} \textit{PG}_i + \beta_{15} \textit{PG13}_i + \beta_{16} \textit{R}_i + \epsilon_i
\end{aligned}$$

where *Real domestic gross*/$1,000,000$_i$ and the independent variables are defined as listed in Table 2. According to this formulation, the parameters of interest, $\beta_1 - \beta_{16}$, represent the

We often find it useful to prompt the reader as to how to correctly interpret the estimated coefficients in our multiple linear regression analysis.

estimated change in a movie's real domestic gross (in millions of dollars) that is associated with unit changes in each of the independent variables. As such, the estimated coefficient $\hat{\beta}_1$ should be interpreted as the estimated marginal effect of a $1 million increase in a movie's production budget on its real domestic gross (in millions of dollars); the estimated coefficient $\hat{\beta}_2$ should be interpreted as the estimated marginal effect a 1-minute increase in a movie's run time on its real domestic gross (in millions of dollars); and so on.

We often find it useful to summarize our expected coefficient estimates so that when the readers see those results, they are already expecting them.

As demonstrated in Table 2, based on the economic theory discussed earlier, we are able to make a number of predictions concerning the expected signs of the estimated marginal effects for our independent variables. Namely, holding all else constant, we expect variables that are associated with movies generating significant general interest (i.e., significant "buzz") being associated with their generating higher real box-office grosses. This is why we expect positive signs for a movie's production budget, number of theaters, whether it is a sequel, starring a bankable actor or actress, opening around a holiday, and being rated PG-13 but not rated R—which are all generally true for big-budget blockbusters. At the same time, all other independent variables equal, the more positive a movie's critical reviews the more the consumer should be willing to buy tickets and the higher the resulting box office. Finally, given that the Oscars have generally been nominating popular films but only honoring smaller, independent films in recent years, we might expect Best Picture nominees to achieve higher box-office receipts and Best Picture winners to achieve lower box-office receipts, holding all factors constant.

We recommend summarizing only those results that seem most important to the story that you wish to tell.

It is important to note how our results compare to those of previous researchers to provide the reader with a sense of where your work fits in the existing literature.

We highlight our new results and how they differ from previous studies.

According to the pooled sample estimates presented in column 1 of Table 3, most of our estimated coefficients exhibit the predicted signs and statistical significance. All other independent variables equal, we estimate that each additional $1 million in production budget is associated with an increase in real box-office gross of nearly $430,000, meaning that a movie increasing its production budget from the median to the mean (an increase of $15.73 million) would be expected to increase its real domestic gross by $6.76 million. We further estimate that longer run times, additional theaters, and longer theater runs are all associated with statistically higher real domestic grosses, with the estimated marginal effects being nearly $260,000 for each additional minute of run time, nearly $45,000 for each additional theater, and nearly $675,000 for each additional day of its theater run. Only one of our measures of critical acclaim has a statistically significant, positive relationship to box-office performance, with each one-unit increase in a movie's tomatometer rating being estimated to increase real box-office gross by roughly $385,000. Among our binary measures, all other independent variables equal, science-fiction movies are associated with real domestic grosses that are $37.6 million greater than films of other genres, while PG-13 movies, sequels, and holiday releases are associated with real domestic grosses that are roughly $27.7 million, $23.7 million, and $15.8 million greater, respectively, than movies not possessing those characteristics. Finally, being in the action genre and winning the Best Picture Oscar are estimated to have statistically significant, negative marginal effects, with the former being associated with real domestic grosses that are $14.7 million less than movies in other genres and Best Picture Winners being associated with real domestic grosses that are $57.3 million less than movies not winning the award. These results are generally consistent with previous research by Terry, Butler, and De'Armond (2005), Nelson et al. (2001), Einav (2001), Reinstein and Snyder (2000), Ravid (1999), Radas and Shugan (1998), Saehney and Eliashberg (1996), Sochay (1994), and Litman (1983).

Given that our pooled sample aggregates data over five different years, it might be natural to question the degree to which pooled-sample results hold across the different years. We actually might expect our estimated coefficients to differ across years if individual blockbusters released in different years are driving our results. A Chow test for this possibility yields a test statistic of 1.49 and a table value of 1.28, meaning that we reject the equality of estimated coefficients across years in our sample at the 5 percent level. As a result, columns 2–6 of Table 3 present the results of estimating our real domestic box-office gross function separately by year. Comparing across years, we see that a movie's production budget, total number of theaters, and length of theater run are estimated to have statistically significant, positive marginal effects on real domestic gross in each year in our sample, with the estimated marginal effect of a $1 million increase in budget being between $337,000 and $602,000, the estimated marginal effect of running in one additional theater being between $34,000 and $49,000, and the estimated marginal effect of running for one additional day being between $504,000 and $1.03 million. That these three key independent variables are estimated to be statistically significant in all five years in our sample might suggest that they are consistent drivers of movie box-office performance. The remaining independent variables do not demonstrate such consistency across years, suggesting that single-year aberrations related to the types of movies that are successful in different years are likely driving the remaining results. In particular, we only estimate Movie Run Time and Best Picture Nominee to be statistically significant in 2009, and we only estimate Holiday Release to be statistically significant in 2006 and 2009. These results are really not that surprising given that *Avatar,* which is by far the highest-grossing film in our sample, has the ninth-longest runtime of all 471 movies in our sample, was nominated for the Best Picture Oscar, and was released during the Christmas holiday. Similarly, Sci-Fi Movie is only estimated to be statistically significant in 2007 and the Rotten Tomato rating is only estimated to gross statistically significant premiums in 2005 and 2008. Again, these results are likely driven by the mix of movies released in those years because two of the three science-fiction movies opening in 2007 were among the six highest-grossing films for the year (*Transformers* and *I Am Legend*), the three movies with the highest tomatometer ratings in 2008 were among the five highest-grossing movies of the year, and the movie with the fourth highest rating in 2005 recorded the third highest box office gross—all of which are patterns not observed in other years in our sample. Best Picture Winner is only estimated to be statistically significant in 2005, which likely results from that year's winning movie *Crash* being only the 49th highest-grossing movie of the year, with a real domestic gross of $59,956,446, which is well below the $141 million, $77 million, and $141 million grossed by *The Departed, No Country For Old Men,* and *Slumdog Millionaire,* respectively, which are the remaining Best Picture winners in our sample. Finally, PG-13 movies are only estimated to gross statistically significant premiums in 2005 and 2008, which is due to four of the five highest-grossing films in each of those years having the PG-13 rating.

Given the limitations of linear regression analysis, we try to avoid declarative statements when discussing our results, choosing phrases such as "might suggest" rather than "proves."

Because these results differ from previous work, we devote attention to attempting to explain why they might do so.

4. Conclusion

In this paper, we estimate real domestic box-office gross for 471 of the top 100 grossing films of the year between 2005 and 2009. Our pooled sample regression results are generally consistent with Terry, Butler, and De'Armond (2005), Nelson et al. (2001), Einav (2001), Reinstein and Snyder (2000), Ravid (1999), Radas and Shugan (1998), Saehney and Eliashberg (1996), Sochay (1994), and Litman (1983) in that we estimate statistically significant, positive marginal effects for a movie's production budget, run time, number of theaters, theater run, critical reviews, being a sequel, a science-fiction, and/or a PG-13 movie and statistically significant negative marginal effects for being an action movie and/or winning a Best Picture Oscar. Estimating real domestic gross functions separately by years, however, suggests that beyond production budget, total theaters, and theater run, which are statistically significant in all years, the remaining results are likely driven by specific high-grossing movies that are released in specific years. For instance, *Avatar,* by far the highest-grossing movie in our sample, has the ninth-longest runtime of all 471 movies, a holiday release, and a Best Picture nomination, which likely drives that fact that those factors are only estimated to be statistically significant in 2009 and not other years (except for holiday release also being significant in 2006, thanks in part to that year's clear box-office winner, *Pirates of the Caribbean: Dead Man's Chest,* also having a holiday release).

We start the conclusion by summarizing our results and comparing them with the existing literature.

One important factor that we are not able to address in this study is the movie's real domestic operating profit as opposed to its real domestic gross. To get an accurate estimate of operating profit, we would need to subtract both a movie's production budget and advertising budget from its gross, and due to the proprietary nature of such data, we were unable to collect movie-specific advertising data. This becomes an issue because a ranking based on operating profit might look very different than a ranking based on box-office gross. For instance, while *Superman Returns* had a respectable-looking real domestic gross of $212.92 million (40th in our sample), it had a production budget of $270 million (2nd in our sample), while *The Blindside* grossed $255.96 million (24th in our sample) on a production budget of only $29 million (325th in our sample). Of course, while having the fifth-largest budget in our sample, *Avatar* performed so well at the box office that it still had the highest gross over budget of all movies in our sample by nearly $170 million.

We conclude the section by mentioning things that we would have liked to do but were unable to in this study.

References

We list all papers that we cite in our write-up following the chosen style guidelines.

Anast, Philip (1967). "Differential Movie Appeals as Correlates of Attendance." *Journalism Quarterly* 44: 86–90.

Einav, Liran (2001). "Seasonality and Competition in Time: An Empirical Analysis of Release Date Decisions in the U.S. Motion Picture Industry." Working Paper, Harvard University.

Joshi, Amit M., and Dominique M. Hanssens (2009). "Movie Advertising and the Stock Market Valuation of Studios: A Case of "Great Expectations?" *Marketing Science* 28(2): 239–250.

Litman, Barry R. (1983). "Predicting Success of Theatrical Movies: An Empirical Study." *Journal of Popular Culture* 16 (Spring): 159–175.

Nelson, Randy A., Michael R. Donihue, Donald M. Waldman, and Calbraith Wheaton (2001). "What's an Oscar Worth?" *Economic Inquiry* 39(1): 1–16.

Radas, Sonja, and Steven M. Shugan (1998). "Seasonal Marketing and Timing Introductions." *Journal of Marketing Research* 35(3): 296–315.

Ravid, S. Abraham (1999). "Information, Blockbusters, and Stars: A Study of the Film Industry." *Journal of Business* 72(4): 463–492.

Reinstein, David A., and Christopher M. Snyder (2000). "The Influence of Expert Reviews on Consumer Demand for Experience Goods: A Case Study of Movie Critics." Working Paper, University of California-Berkeley and George Washington University.

Sawhney, Mohanbir S., and Jehosua Eliashberg (1996). "A Parsimonious Model for Forecasting Gross Box Office Revenues of Motion Pictures." *Marketing Science* 15(2): 113–131.

Sochay, Scott (1994). "Predicting the Performance of Motion Pictures." *Journal of Media Economics* 7(4): 1–20.

Terry, Neil, Michael Butler, and De'Arno De'Armond (2005). "The Determinants of Domestic Box Office Performance in the Motion Picture Industry." *Southwestern Economics Review* 32(1): 137–148.

TABLE 1
Summary Statistics for Our Dependent and Independent Variables

Summary statistics tables generally include at least the mean and the standard deviation. Here, we add the median to demonstrate the high degree of skewness of our dependent variable.

While not necessary, here we separate the independent variables into distinct groups, indicating the type of measure that they represent.

	Mean	Standard Deviation	Median
Real Domestic Gross	$90,604,967.89	$79,944.612.33	$63,485,350.70
Production Measures:			
Budget/1,000,000	$60.73	$51.06	$45.00
Movie Run Time	108.60	18.71	106.00
Total Theaters	2949.30	701.31	3026.00
Theater Run	99.64	40.74	97.00
Sequel	0.123	—	—
Major Studio	0.709	—	—
Star Actor	0.227	—	—
Action Movie	0.130	—	—
Sci-Fi Movie	0.040	—	—
Holiday Release	0.193	—	—
Critical Acclaim:			
Rotten Tomato Rating	50.04	26.39	50.00
Best Picture Nominee	0.053	—	—
Best Picture Winner	0.008	—	—
MPAA Rating:			
PG	0.187	—	—
PG-13	0.486	—	—
R	0.291	—	—

FIGURE 1
Histogram of Real Domestic Box Office Grosses (in millions)

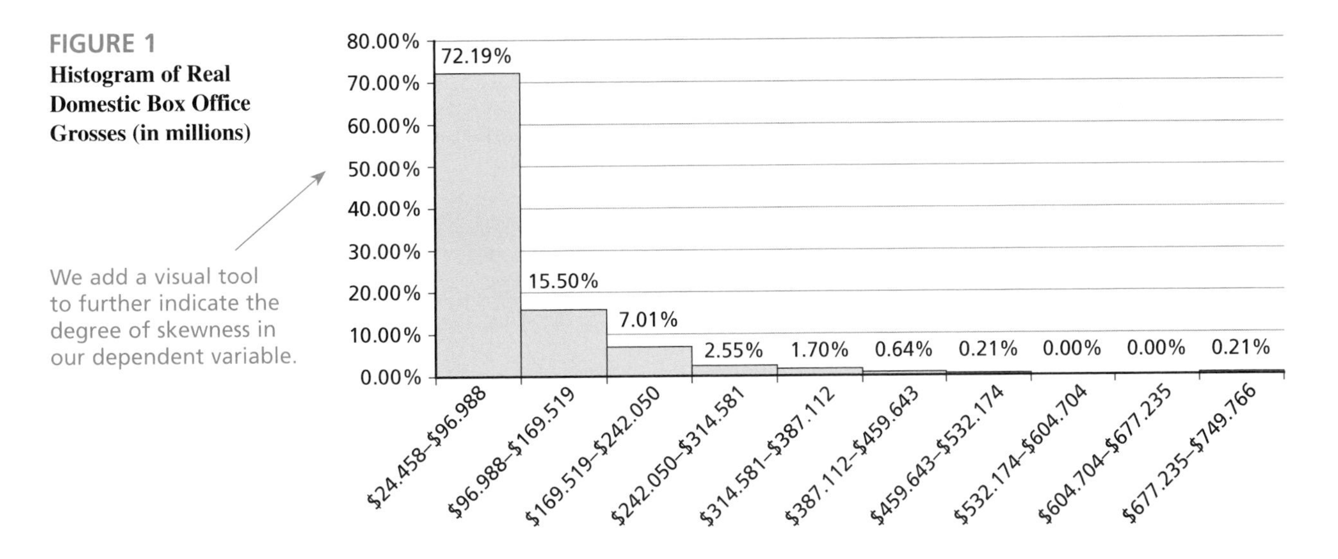

We add a visual tool to further indicate the degree of skewness in our dependent variable.

TABLE 2 Description and Predicted Signs for Independent Variables in Empirical Analysis

	Description	Predicted Sign
Production Measures:		
Budget/1,000,000	Movie's estimated production budget in millions of dollars	+
Movie Run Time	Length of movie in minutes	+/−
Total Theaters	Number of theaters in which movie is shown	+
Theater Run	Number of days that movie is shown in domestic theaters	+
Sequel	Dummy variable equal to 1 if movie is a sequel	+
Major Studio	Dummy variable equal to 1 if movie was released by a major studio	+
Star Actor	Dummy variable equal to 1 if movie stars actor/actress making $10 million per movie	+
Action Movie	Dummy variable equal to 1 if movie is in the action genre	−
Sci-Fi Movie	Dummy variable equal to 1 if movie is in the science-fiction genre	+
Holiday Release	Dummy variable equal to 1 if movie opens around a major U.S. holiday	+
Critical Acclaim:		
Rotten Tomato Rating	Rotten Tomatoes "tomatometer" percentage of critics recommending movie	+
Best Picture Nominee	Dummy variable equal to 1 if movie is nominated for Best Picture Oscar	+
Best Picture Winner	Dummy variable equal to 1 if movie wins Best Picture Oscar	−
MPAA Rating:		
PG	Dummy variable equal to 1 if movie is rated PG by the MPAA	+
PG-13	Dummy variable equal to 1 if movie is rated PG-13 by the MPAA	+
R	Dummy variable equal to 1 if movie is rated R by the MPAA	−

We add these columns so that the reader can refer to one spot for a quick reminder as to what each of the variables measures and to the predicted sign of the estimated coefficient rather than having to refer back to the text each time they arise.

TABLE 3 Real Gross Domestic Box Office (in millions) Regressions Overall and By Year Movie Opened

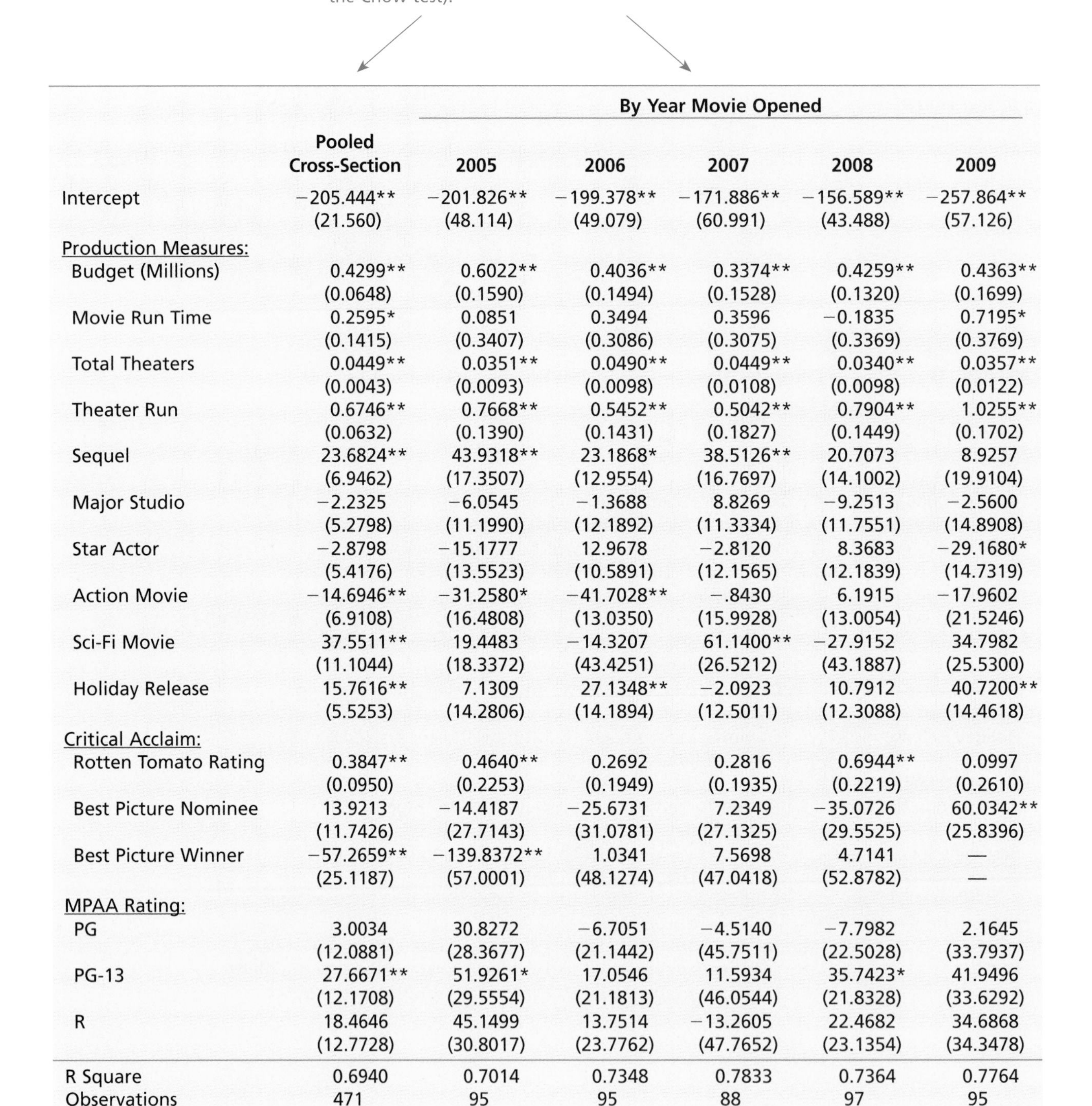

		By Year Movie Opened				
	Pooled Cross-Section	2005	2006	2007	2008	2009
Intercept	−205.444**	−201.826**	−199.378**	−171.886**	−156.589**	−257.864**
	(21.560)	(48.114)	(49.079)	(60.991)	(43.488)	(57.126)
Production Measures:						
Budget (Millions)	0.4299**	0.6022**	0.4036**	0.3374**	0.4259**	0.4363**
	(0.0648)	(0.1590)	(0.1494)	(0.1528)	(0.1320)	(0.1699)
Movie Run Time	0.2595*	0.0851	0.3494	0.3596	−0.1835	0.7195*
	(0.1415)	(0.3407)	(0.3086)	(0.3075)	(0.3369)	(0.3769)
Total Theaters	0.0449**	0.0351**	0.0490**	0.0449**	0.0340**	0.0357**
	(0.0043)	(0.0093)	(0.0098)	(0.0108)	(0.0098)	(0.0122)
Theater Run	0.6746**	0.7668**	0.5452**	0.5042**	0.7904**	1.0255**
	(0.0632)	(0.1390)	(0.1431)	(0.1827)	(0.1449)	(0.1702)
Sequel	23.6824**	43.9318**	23.1868*	38.5126**	20.7073	8.9257
	(6.9462)	(17.3507)	(12.9554)	(16.7697)	(14.1002)	(19.9104)
Major Studio	−2.2325	−6.0545	−1.3688	8.8269	−9.2513	−2.5600
	(5.2798)	(11.1990)	(12.1892)	(11.3334)	(11.7551)	(14.8908)
Star Actor	−2.8798	−15.1777	12.9678	−2.8120	8.3683	−29.1680*
	(5.4176)	(13.5523)	(10.5891)	(12.1565)	(12.1839)	(14.7319)
Action Movie	−14.6946**	−31.2580*	−41.7028**	−.8430	6.1915	−17.9602
	(6.9108)	(16.4808)	(13.0350)	(15.9928)	(13.0054)	(21.5246)
Sci-Fi Movie	37.5511**	19.4483	−14.3207	61.1400**	−27.9152	34.7982
	(11.1044)	(18.3372)	(43.4251)	(26.5212)	(43.1887)	(25.5300)
Holiday Release	15.7616**	7.1309	27.1348**	−2.0923	10.7912	40.7200**
	(5.5253)	(14.2806)	(14.1894)	(12.5011)	(12.3088)	(14.4618)
Critical Acclaim:						
Rotten Tomato Rating	0.3847**	0.4640**	0.2692	0.2816	0.6944**	0.0997
	(0.0950)	(0.2253)	(0.1949)	(0.1935)	(0.2219)	(0.2610)
Best Picture Nominee	13.9213	−14.4187	−25.6731	7.2349	−35.0726	60.0342**
	(11.7426)	(27.7143)	(31.0781)	(27.1325)	(29.5525)	(25.8396)
Best Picture Winner	−57.2659**	−139.8372**	1.0341	7.5698	4.7141	—
	(25.1187)	(57.0001)	(48.1274)	(47.0418)	(52.8782)	—
MPAA Rating:						
PG	3.0034	30.8272	−6.7051	−4.5140	−7.7982	2.1645
	(12.0881)	(28.3677)	(21.1442)	(45.7511)	(22.5028)	(33.7937)
PG-13	27.6671**	51.9261*	17.0546	11.5934	35.7423*	41.9496
	(12.1708)	(29.5554)	(21.1813)	(46.0544)	(21.8328)	(33.6292)
R	18.4646	45.1499	13.7514	−13.2605	22.4682	34.6868
	(12.7728)	(30.8017)	(23.7762)	(47.7652)	(23.1354)	(34.3478)
R Square	0.6940	0.7014	0.7348	0.7833	0.7364	0.7764
Observations	471	95	95	88	97	95

Note: Standard errors in parentheses. **, * denote significance at the 5 and 10 percent levels.

We include notes indicating important facts about the values presented in the table.

Appendix A: Data Collection

CHAPTERS 3, 4, AND 5

Our 200-Observation CEO Compensation Sample

Suppose that you are interested in investigating the relationship between compensation of company CEOs and company profits. How might you go about collecting data that are appropriate for testing the theory that CEO compensation is positively related to firm profit?

To collect compensation data for the CEOs of *Fortune* 500 firms, we first need to download the most recent list of *Fortune* 500 firms. We do so by performing the following Internet search.

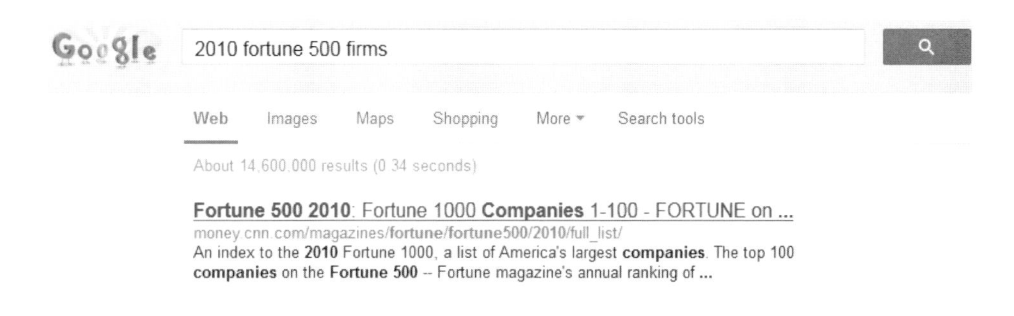

Clicking in the first entry takes us to the following website.

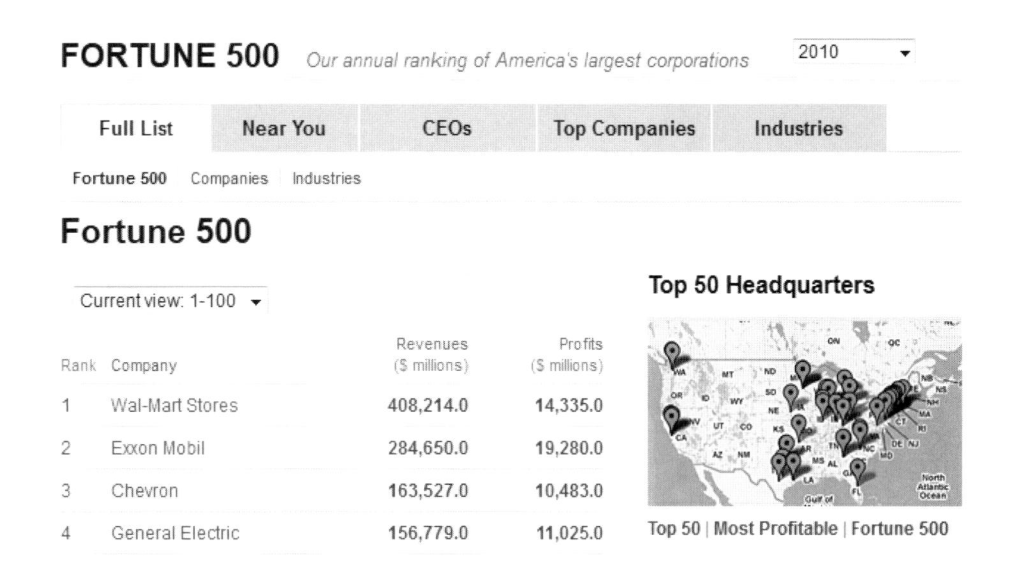

Rank	Company	Revenues ($ millions)	Profits ($ millions)
1	Wal-Mart Stores	408,214.0	14,335.0
2	Exxon Mobil	284,650.0	19,280.0
3	Chevron	163,527.0	10,483.0
4	General Electric	156,779.0	11,025.0

After downloading these data to Excel, we go back to the webpage and click the "Current View: 101–200" tab,

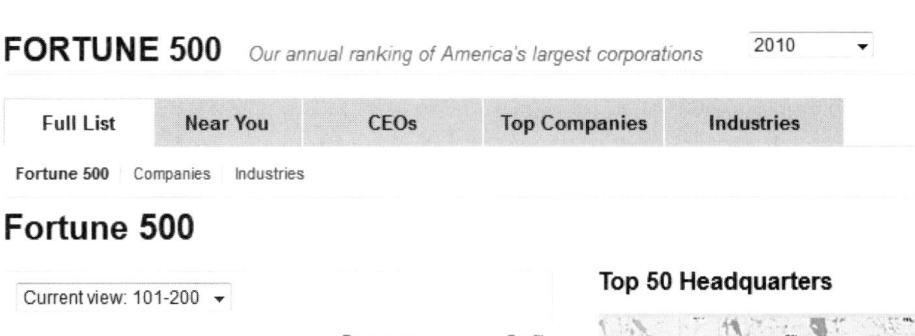

Rank	Company	Revenues ($ millions)	Profits ($ millions)
101	Staples	24,275.5	738.7
102	Google	23,650.6	6,520.4
103	Macy's	23,489.0	350.0
104	International Paper	23,366.0	663.0

Top 50 Headquarters

Top 50 | Most Profitable | Fortune 500

download, and add those data to our Excel master file. We then do the same for the remaining firms in the *Fortune* 500.

To add CEO compensation data for each of these *Fortune* 500 firms, we start with the following Internet search.

CEO Pay and the 99%
www.aflcio.org/Corporate-Watch/CEO-Pay-and-the-99/
Hyatt Hurts; Union Plus Ad; Labor Heritage Foundation; NLC Online; Union Sportsmen's Alliance Ad; The Union Boot Pro Ad; **Executive Paywatch**; Union ...

100 Highest-Paid CEOs
SEARCH CEO PAY DATABASE: OR LOOK UP CEO PAY BY ...

Trends in CEO Pay
CEO pay went up in 2011. Again. The average CEO pay of ...

Executive PayWatch Buttons
... provide a link back to the AFL-CIO Executive PayWatch site ...

CEO Pay by State
CEO pay is out of control. Take action now to rein it in. Take ...

CEO Pay by Industry
CEO Pay by Industry. Overall Average CEO Compensation ...

CEO Pay Data Sources
For a true picture of the vast inequities in the American ...

More results from aflcio.org »

Clicking on the link takes us to the following webpage.

To collect CEO compensation data, we enter each of the firms in our data set in the "Search CEO Pay Database" tab. For Walmart, we start by typing "wal" and once "Wal-Mart Stores Inc" became visible on the drop-down tab, we click on it.

Doing so takes us to the following webpage.

WAL-MART STORES INC

Michael T. Duke

President and CEO
WAL-MART STORES INC
Ticker: WMT
Headquarters: Bentonville, AR
Industry: General Merchandise Stores

In 2012, Michael T. Duke received $18,131,738 in total compensation. By comparison, the average worker made $34,053 in 2011. Michael T. Duke made 532 times the average worker's pay. See how other workers compared.

Tell a Friend Tweet 1,001
SHARE

How You Compare | How Others Compare | Mutual Fund Votes | CEO Pay Breakdown

CEO Pay Breakdown

2011	
Salary	$1,264,775
Bonus	$0
Value of Stock Awards	$13,066,877
Value of Option Awards	$0
Non-Equity Incentive Plan Compensation	$2,878,305
Change in Pension Value and Deferred Compensation Earnings	$544,523
All Other Compensation	$377,258
Total	$18,131,738

In our master Excel file, we enter 18,131,178 for Walmart's CEO compensation. We then move on to the next firm in our file and continue doing so until we had collected data on the 425 different *Fortune* 500 firms for which the data were available. As a final step, we save these data as the Excel file **CEO Compensation Data–Master.xlsx.**

To draw an independent, random sample from this "population," we copy and paste these data into a new worksheet many, many times (until we have a large number of observation, such as 30,000). We then use the random number generator in Excel (which is found in the Data Analysis Toolpak) to assign a unique, random number for each observation in the worksheet. Sorting the data on this unique number places the observation in random order. We then pick a random observation and select it along with the 199 following observations to create our 200-observation random sample.

CHAPTERS 6, 7, AND 8

Our MLB Position Player Sample

To collect our data, we start with the following simple Internet search.

Given that *USA Today* is a trusted source for these data, we start by clicking on the first entry. After doing so, we are taken to the baseball home page for the *USA Today* Salaries Database (which has salary data for a number of years for each of the four major professional sports in North America). Notice that for baseball salaries, there are drop-down tabs for "Team:" and for "Year:" The first step is to select the desired year (2009 season) from the "Year:" menu. The next step is to select the first team (Arizona Diamondbacks) from the "Team:" Doing so produces the following screen.

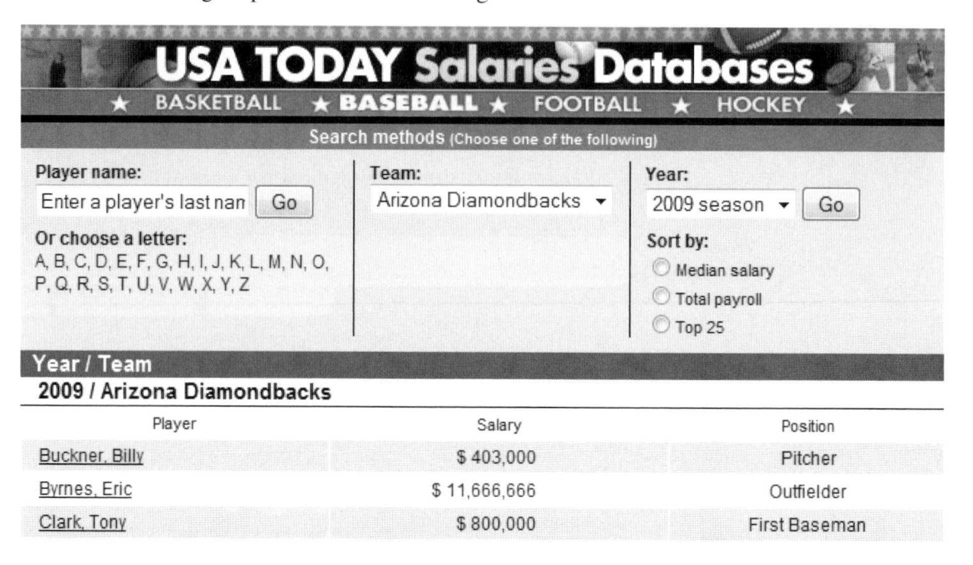

These are the salaries that we wish to collect for the players on the Arizona Diamondbacks' 2009 opening day roster (note that in addition to salary, this data source also provides each player's primary position). Following the Import wizard commands described in Chapter 2, we can import these data for the Arizona Diamondbacks as well as the remaining 29 MLB teams into Excel.

After completing these steps, we will have data on annual salary, position, and team for all players (both pitchers and position players) on the 2009 opening-day MLB rosters. To limit our data to only position players, we sort the data in Excel by the "Position" variable, and we delete all players for whom the listed position is pitcher.

While a matter of personal preference, at this point, we like to assign each individual a unique "id" number that can be used when sorting and merging the original data with additional data that we might wish to add later as we invariably decide to expand our project.

Next, we need to add data on each player's years of major league experience, which we can collect by clicking on each individual in the *USA Today* data set. To add data on an individual's offensive productivity in the 2008 season (because the individual's current salary should be based in large part on the individual's performance in the previous season), we start by conducting an Internet search for "2008 mlb player stats" (which we intentionally put in quotes to narrow the resulting website hits) and importing the resulting data into Excel following the usual procedure. Limiting the 2008 offensive statistics to only those players on 2009 opening-day rosters and merging those data with the existing salary results in the 411-observation population of MLB position players contained in the file **2009 Position Player Salary Data–Master.xlsx.**

We then follow the procedure outlined previously to create a 200-observation random sample from these data.

Our International GDP Sample

To make our Excel examples more meaningful, we wish to collect data of an entirely different nature. For international macroeconomists, an obvious concern is the degree to which different independent factors affect a country's observed gross domestic product (GDP). To collect data that allows us to address this concern, we start with the following simple Internet search.

world GDP 2009

About 40,700,000 results (0.20 seconds)

List of countries by GDP (nominal) - Wikipedia, the free encyclopedia
en.wikipedia.org/wiki/List_of_countries_by_GDP_(nominal)
- Block all en.wikipedia.org results
World map showing nominal **GDP** of countries for the year 2010 according to the IMF.
Legend: (in ..... 36, United Arab Emirates, 230252, **2009**. 37, Portugal ...

Clicking on this link takes us to data from reputable sources, such as the International Monetary Fund, which we can import into Excel. Searching for other variables that economic theory predicts are likely to affect GDP—such as population, labor force, unemployment life expectancy, capital investment, educational investment, etc.—and importing those values into Excel results in the 227-observation population contained in the file **GDP Population Data–Master.xlsx.**

We then follow the procedure outlined previously to create a 63-observation random sample from these data.

CHAPTER 9

Our California Home Mortgage Application Data

To identify and collect the appropriate housing expenditure data, we start with the following Internet search.

us home mortgage application data

About 3,710,000 results (0.20 seconds)

Citi **Mortgage Home** Loans - As low as 3.220% APR* Learn More*.
www.citi**mortgage**.com
Rates Have Dropped! Act Now.

Mortgage Bankers Association
www.mbaa.org/ - Cached
Housing Initiatives Promoted » · Banks in **U.S.** Overwhelmed by **Mortgage** Refinancing Boom After Reducing Jobs » · 26 Percent ... Weekly **Application** Survey ...

Home Mortgage Disclosure Act - Wikipedia, the free encyclopedia
en.wikipedia.org/wiki/**Home_Mortgage**_Disclosure_Act - Cached
The **United States Home Mortgage** Disclosure Act (or HMDA, pronounced ... It requires financial institutions to maintain and annually disclose **data** about **home** ... pre-approvals, **home** improvement, and refinance **applications** involving 1 to 4 ...

While Wikipedia may not be the preferred source of information, in this case, it does highlight an important potential data source: the Home Mortgage Disclosure Act (HMDA). Searching for "Home Mortgage Disclosure Act" takes us to the webpage www.ffiec.gov/hmda, which provides background on the act and the data collected. As that website makes clear, these data are critically linked with Census data, which we know is publicly available. Searching on "census data access tools" takes us to the page www.census.gov/main/www/access.html. Under the heading "Interactive Internet Tools" on this page, we see an entry for the DataFerrett tool. Clicking on the provided link takes us to http://dataferrett.census.gov. Clicking on the "Datasets Available" link takes us to a website containing the following,

Datasets Available

Description of Datasets Available using the DataFerrett:
This page contains brief overviews of the datasets that are available in the DataFerr
Survey/Sponsor's web site with further documentation for that dataset. You will be l
the DataFerrett site.

Click here for some of the Searchable Topics in the DataFerrett application.

American Community Survey (ACS)
American Housing Survey (AHS)
Behavioral Risk Factor Surveillance System (BRFSS)
Consumer Expenditure Survey (CES)
County Business Patterns (CBP)
Current Population Survey (CPS)
Decennial Census of Population and Housing (Census2000)
Decennial Census of Population and Housing (Census1990)
Home Mortgage Disclosure Act (HMDA) ← Desired Data
National Ambulatory Medical Care Survey (NAMCS)
National Center for Health Statistics Mortality-Underlying Cause-of-Death (MORT)
National Health and Nutrition Examination Survey (NHANES)
National Health Interview Survey (NHIS)
National Hospital Ambulatory Medical Care Survey (NHAMCS)
National Survey of Fishing, Hunting, and Wildlife-Associated Recreation (FHWAR)
New York City Housing and Vacancy Survey (NYCHVS)
Public Libraries Survey (PLS)
Small Area Health Insurance Estimates (SAHIE)
Small Area Income and Poverty Estimates (SAIPE)
Social Security Administration (SSA)
Survey of Income and Program Participation (SIPP)
Survey of Program Dynamics (SPD)

which indicates that the DataFerrett tool does indeed provide access to the HMDA dataset (a few of which we will use to collect data in future chapters).

To use the DataFerrett tool, we click on the "Get Data~Run:" link in the top right corner of the webpage:

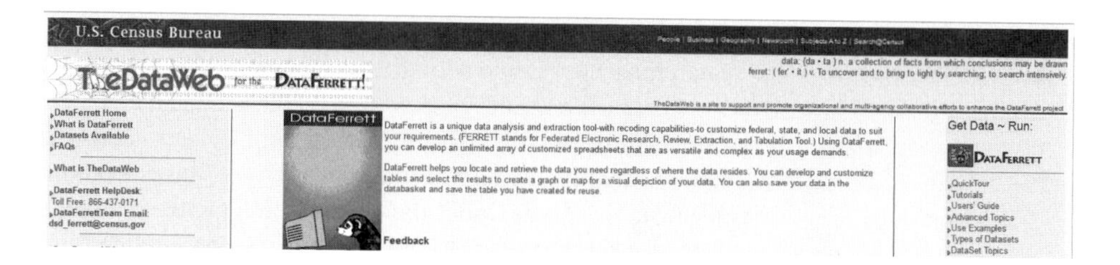

and click on the picture of the ferret in the next window.

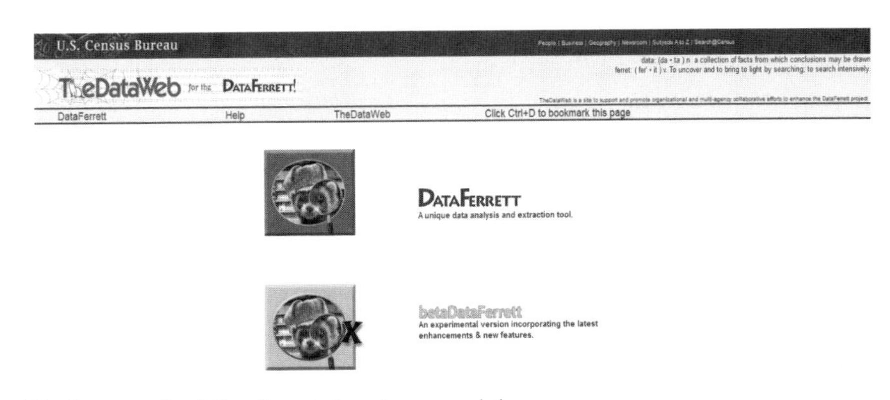

We then see the following picture in our web browser.

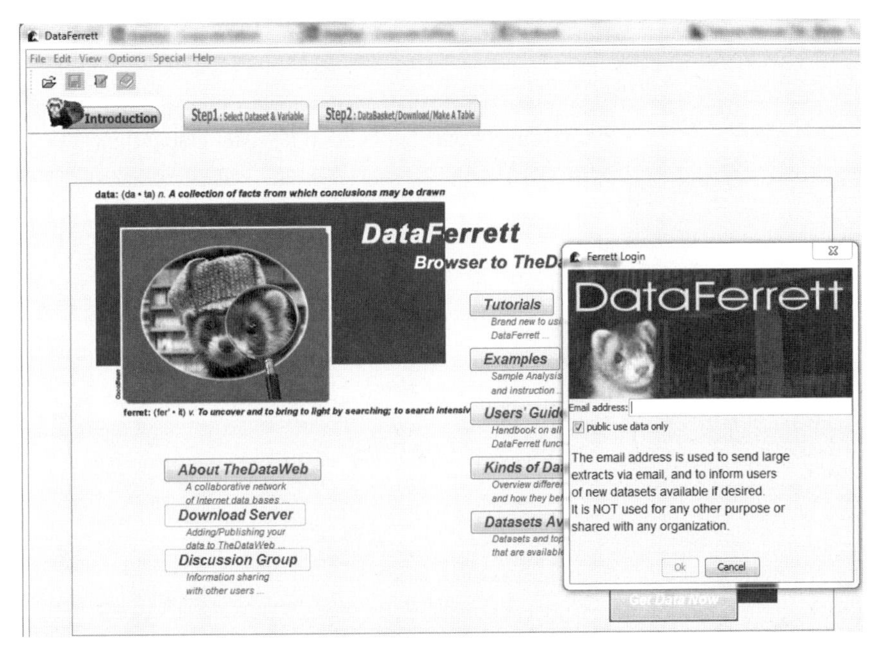

After entering our e-mail address in the window, we are given access to the following.

Clicking on the "Get Data Now" tab takes us to the following.

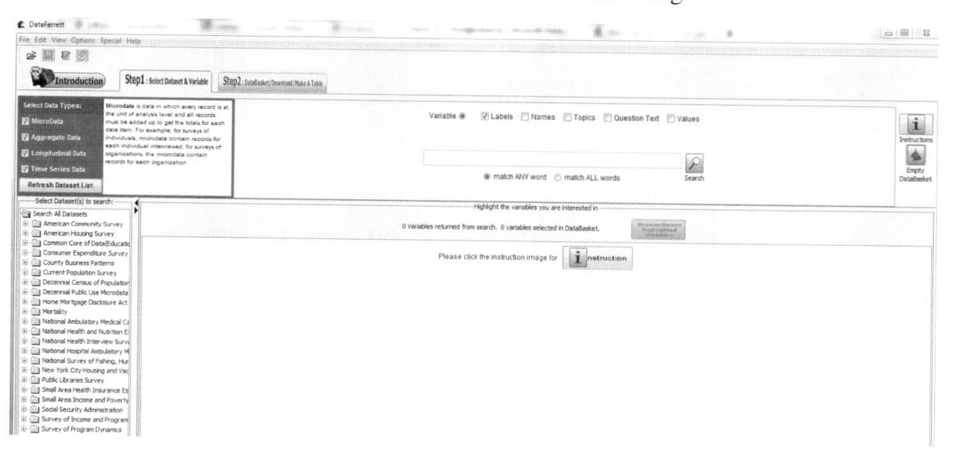

Under the "Select Database(s) to search" tab, we select "Home Mortgage Disclosure Act," then "Loan Application Register Data," then "2007," then "View Variables." Checking "Select All Topics" and clicking "Search Variables" provides access to the desired data set.

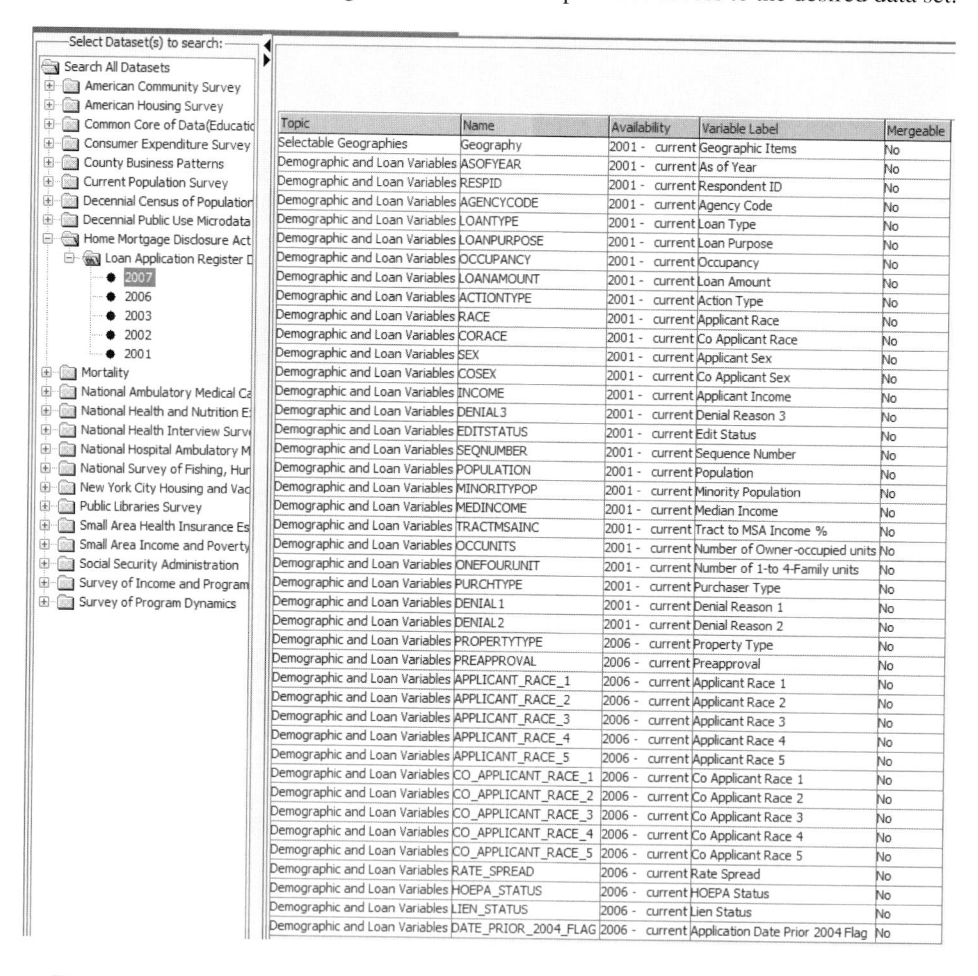

Topic	Name	Availability	Variable Label	Mergeable
Selectable Geographies	Geography	2001 - current	Geographic Items	No
Demographic and Loan Variables	ASOFYEAR	2001 - current	As of Year	No
Demographic and Loan Variables	RESPID	2001 - current	Respondent ID	No
Demographic and Loan Variables	AGENCYCODE	2001 - current	Agency Code	No
Demographic and Loan Variables	LOANTYPE	2001 - current	Loan Type	No
Demographic and Loan Variables	LOANPURPOSE	2001 - current	Loan Purpose	No
Demographic and Loan Variables	OCCUPANCY	2001 - current	Occupancy	No
Demographic and Loan Variables	LOANAMOUNT	2001 - current	Loan Amount	No
Demographic and Loan Variables	ACTIONTYPE	2001 - current	Action Type	No
Demographic and Loan Variables	RACE	2001 - current	Applicant Race	No
Demographic and Loan Variables	CORACE	2001 - current	Co Applicant Race	No
Demographic and Loan Variables	SEX	2001 - current	Applicant Sex	No
Demographic and Loan Variables	COSEX	2001 - current	Co Applicant Sex	No
Demographic and Loan Variables	INCOME	2001 - current	Applicant Income	No
Demographic and Loan Variables	DENIAL3	2001 - current	Denial Reason 3	No
Demographic and Loan Variables	EDITSTATUS	2001 - current	Edit Status	No
Demographic and Loan Variables	SEQNUMBER	2001 - current	Sequence Number	No
Demographic and Loan Variables	POPULATION	2001 - current	Population	No
Demographic and Loan Variables	MINORITYPOP	2001 - current	Minority Population	No
Demographic and Loan Variables	MEDINCOME	2001 - current	Median Income	No
Demographic and Loan Variables	TRACTMSAINC	2001 - current	Tract to MSA Income %	No
Demographic and Loan Variables	OCCUNITS	2001 - current	Number of Owner-occupied units	No
Demographic and Loan Variables	ONEFOURUNIT	2001 - current	Number of 1-to 4-Family units	No
Demographic and Loan Variables	PURCHTYPE	2001 - current	Purchaser Type	No
Demographic and Loan Variables	DENIAL1	2001 - current	Denial Reason 1	No
Demographic and Loan Variables	DENIAL2	2001 - current	Denial Reason 2	No
Demographic and Loan Variables	PROPERTYTYPE	2006 - current	Property Type	No
Demographic and Loan Variables	PREAPPROVAL	2006 - current	Preapproval	No
Demographic and Loan Variables	APPLICANT_RACE_1	2006 - current	Applicant Race 1	No
Demographic and Loan Variables	APPLICANT_RACE_2	2006 - current	Applicant Race 2	No
Demographic and Loan Variables	APPLICANT_RACE_3	2006 - current	Applicant Race 3	No
Demographic and Loan Variables	APPLICANT_RACE_4	2006 - current	Applicant Race 4	No
Demographic and Loan Variables	APPLICANT_RACE_5	2006 - current	Applicant Race 5	No
Demographic and Loan Variables	CO_APPLICANT_RACE_1	2006 - current	Co Applicant Race 1	No
Demographic and Loan Variables	CO_APPLICANT_RACE_2	2006 - current	Co Applicant Race 2	No
Demographic and Loan Variables	CO_APPLICANT_RACE_3	2006 - current	Co Applicant Race 3	No
Demographic and Loan Variables	CO_APPLICANT_RACE_4	2006 - current	Co Applicant Race 4	No
Demographic and Loan Variables	CO_APPLICANT_RACE_5	2006 - current	Co Applicant Race 5	No
Demographic and Loan Variables	RATE_SPREAD	2006 - current	Rate Spread	No
Demographic and Loan Variables	HOEPA_STATUS	2006 - current	HOEPA Status	No
Demographic and Loan Variables	LIEN_STATUS	2006 - current	Lien Status	No
Demographic and Loan Variables	DATE_PRIOR_2004_FLAG	2006 - current	Application Date Prior 2004 Flag	No

From here, we can click on each individual variable to learn about the information it contains. Highlighting the variables in which we are interested selects them for inclusion. We can then limit the reported values of those variables to only the outcomes in which we are interested. For our example, we are interested in collecting data on the loan amount for which the applicant applied and the applicant's income. Looking at the variable descriptions, we see that the HMDA data are collected for many different types of loans and many different types of housing. To make our data more easily interpretable, we limit our data to owner-occupied, single-family housing. Due to the large potentially sample size, we limited the state to California, and to eliminate unrealistic seeming data, we limited applicant income to a minimum of $1,000.

Downloading these data, we get the 73,046-observation sample in **California Home Mortgage Application Data–Master.xlsx** that we analyze in the chapter.

CHAPTERS 10 AND 11

Our U.S. Houses Sold Data

To identify and collect the appropriate data on houses sold in the United States, we start with the following Internet search (because we know that housing starts and sales are considered leading economic indicators and because we know that the U.S. Census Bureau collects and publishes such data).

us census bureau economic indicators

About 1,970,000 results (0.17 seconds)

Economic Indicators - U.S. Census Bureau
www.census.gov/cgi-bin/briefroom/BriefRm - Block all www.census.gov results
U.S. Census Bureau regular updates of U.S. **economic data** such as housing starts, retail merchant sales, international durable goods orders. Graphs of data.

After following the link, we search the webpage for the desired information, which we find in the following tab.

New Residential Sales CHART XML RSS Feed
Sales of new one-family houses in August 2011 were at a seasonally adjusted annual rate of 295,000. This is 2.3 percent below the revised July 2011 estimate of 302,000.

Current Press Release:	Archived Releases - 1995 - present	**Released:** September 26, 2011
PDF	Historic Time Series - 1963 - present	**Next release:** October 26, 2011
XLS	• Search Database	**Frequency:** Monthly
		Program Overview

Clicking on the "Historic Time Series – 1963-present" tab takes us to the following Excel data tables.

History Tables (below are in Excel)

- New Single-Family Houses Sold
- New Single-Family Houses For Sale and Months' Supply
- Median and Average Sales Price of New Houses Sold
- New Houses Sold and For Sale, by Stage of Const., Median Number of Months for Sale and Seasonal Factors
- New Houses Sold by Sales Price (1999-2005)
- New Houses Sold by Sales Price
- Median and Average Sales Price of New Houses Sold by Region
- New Houses Sold by Type of Financing
- Median and Average Sales Price of New Houses Sold by Type of Financing

Clicking on the very first link downloads the desired Excel data file, and clicking on the "Reg Sold" worksheet gives us the following.

Houses Sold by Region

(Components may not add to total because of rounding. Number of housing units in thousands.)

Period	Sold during period									
	Not seasonally adjusted					Seasonally adjusted annual rate				
	United States	North-east	Mid-West	South	West	United States	North-east	Mid-West	South	West
Jan 1963	42	(NA)	(NA)	(NA)	(NA)	591	(NA)	(NA)	(NA)	(NA)
Feb 1963	35	(NA)	(NA)	(NA)	(NA)	464	(NA)	(NA)	(NA)	(NA)
Mar 1963	44	(NA)	(NA)	(NA)	(NA)	461	(NA)	(NA)	(NA)	(NA)
Apr 1963	52	(NA)	(NA)	(NA)	(NA)	605	(NA)	(NA)	(NA)	(NA)
May 1963	58	(NA)	(NA)	(NA)	(NA)	586	(NA)	(NA)	(NA)	(NA)
Jun 1963	48	(NA)	(NA)	(NA)	(NA)	526	(NA)	(NA)	(NA)	(NA)

Notice that these data are collected on a monthly basis. Knowing that most other macroeconomic data are collected on a quarterly basis, we sum the individual monthly data into quarterly data to get the dependent variable for our analysis. Note that we also limit our data to starting in 1986Q2 because we know that several potentially important macroeconomic data series start with that time period.

The independent variable for our analysis in this chapter is the U.S. real GDP per quarter over the same time period. To calculate real GDP, we need two values: (1) U.S. nominal GDP by quarter and (2) the CPI per quarter.

To collect GDP data, we perform the following Internet search (because we know that the Bureau of Economic Analysis collects such data).

Bureau of Economic Analysis GDP

About 1,660,000 results (0.08 seconds)

News Release: **Gross Domestic ... - Bureau of Economic Analysis**
www.bea.gov/newsreleases/national/**gdp**/**gdp**newsrelease.htm
Sep 29, 2011 – Real **gross domestic product** -- the output of goods and services produced by labor and property located in the United States -- increased at an ...

Clicking on that link takes us to the Bureau of Economic Analysis (BEA) webpage. Clicking on the "Interactive Data" tab allows us to identify and download our desired GDP data as well as our desired price data, which we can use to convert the nominal GDP values to the desired real GDP values.

Downloading and combining these data, we get the 195-observation sample in **US Houses Sold Data–Master.xlsx** that we analyze in the chapter.

Our Three-Month and One-Year Bond Rate Series

To collect data on three-month and one-year bond rates, we start with the Internet search.

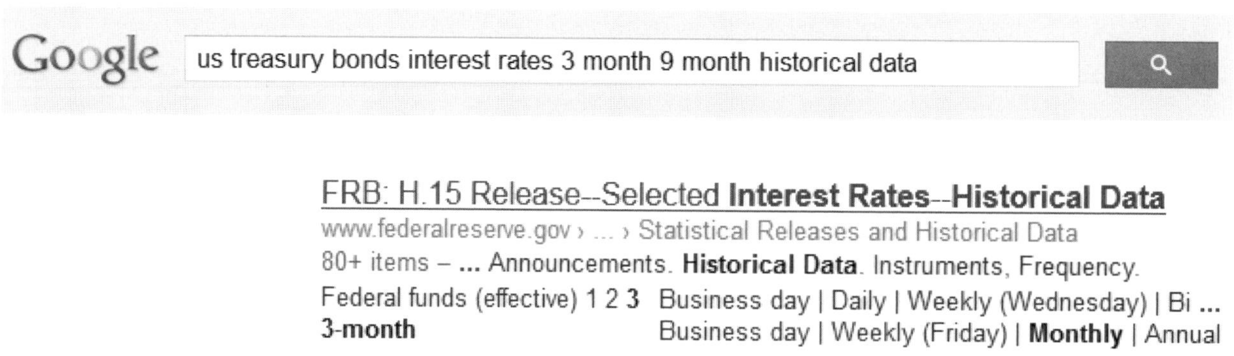

Google us treasury bonds interest rates 3 month 9 month historical data

FRB: H.15 Release--Selected **Interest Rates--Historical Data**
www.federalreserve.gov › ... › Statistical Releases and Historical Data
80+ items – **...** Announcements. **Historical Data**. Instruments, Frequency.
Federal funds (effective) 1 2 **3** Business day | Daily | Weekly (Wednesday) | Bi **...**
3-month Business day | Weekly (Friday) | **Monthly** | Annual

which takes us to the following webpage.

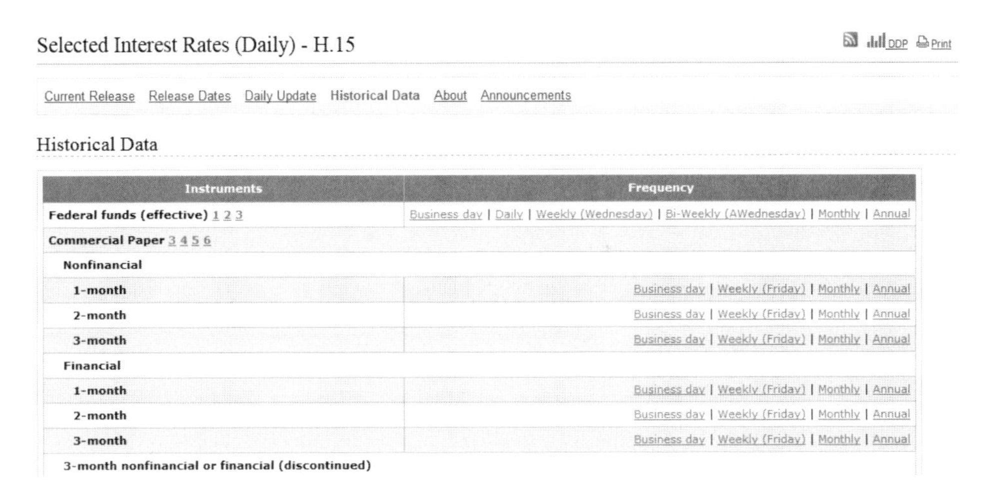
Selected Interest Rates (Daily) - H.15

DDP Print

Current Release Release Dates Daily Update Historical Data About Announcements

Historical Data

Instruments	Frequency
Federal funds (effective) 1 2 3	Business day | Daily | Weekly (Wednesday) | Bi-Weekly (AWednesday) | Monthly | Annual
Commercial Paper 3 4 5 6	
Nonfinancial	
1-month	Business day | Weekly (Friday) | Monthly | Annual
2-month	Business day | Weekly (Friday) | Monthly | Annual
3-month	Business day | Weekly (Friday) | Monthly | Annual
Financial	
1-month	Business day | Weekly (Friday) | Monthly | Annual
2-month	Business day | Weekly (Friday) | Monthly | Annual
3-month	Business day | Weekly (Friday) | Monthly | Annual
3-month nonfinancial or financial (discontinued)	

On this page, we scroll down to the section titled "U.S. government securities."

U.S. government securities	
Treasury bills (auction high) (discontinued) 3 4 24 25	
3-month (discontinued)	Business day | Weekly (Friday) | Monthly | Annual
6-month (discontinued)	Business day | Weekly (Friday) | Monthly | Annual
1-year (discontinued)	Business day | Weekly (Friday) | Monthly | Annual
Treasury bills (secondary market) 3 4	
4-week	Business day | Weekly (Friday) | Monthly | Annual
3-month	Business day | Weekly (Friday) | Monthly | Annual
6-month	Business day | Weekly (Friday) | Monthly | Annual
1-year	Business day | Weekly (Friday) | Monthly | Annual
Treasury constant maturities	
Nominal 11	
1-month	Business day | Weekly (Friday) | Monthly | Annual
3-month	Business day | Weekly (Friday) | Monthly | Annual
6-month	Business day | Weekly (Friday) | Monthly | Annual
1-year	Business day | Weekly (Friday) | Monthly | Annual
2-year	Business day | Weekly (Friday) | Monthly | Annual
3-year	Business day | Weekly (Friday) | Monthly | Annual
5-year	Business day | Weekly (Friday) | Monthly | Annual

From this section, we select the desired series, which in this case are the weekly three-month and one-year Treasury constant maturities series. Once we download the desired data to Excel, we combine the two series to produce the 1,598-observation sample in **T-bill Data–Master.xlsx** that we analyze in the chapter.

CHAPTER 12

Our 2010 U.S. House of Representative Election Results Data

The U.S. Congress is composed of two houses: the House of Representatives and the Senate. Each state receives representation in the House in proportion to its population (with each state being entitled to at least one representative and California having the current high of 53), while each state receives equal representation of two Senators, regardless of population. Members of the House are elected to serve two-year terms, meaning that all 435 representatives stand for election every two years. Senators are elected to serve six-year terms, with the terms staggered so that 33 (or 34) Senate seats are contested every two years.

Election results are available from all major news sources. We started to gather our U.S. House of Representative Election Results Data from http://elections.nytimes.com/2010/results/house/big-board, which appears as follows.

Democrats expected to win easily				Democrats expected to win narrowly				Tossup seats				Republicans expected to win narrowly				Republicans expected to win easily			
District	Dem.	Rep.	% Rpt.	District	Dem.	Rep.	% Rpt.	District	Dem.	Rep.	% Rpt.	District	Dem.	Rep.	% Rpt.	District	Dem.	Rep.	% Rpt.
Ala. 7	72%	28%	100%	Ark. 4	58%	40%	100%	Ala. 2	49%	51%	100%	Ark. 1	44%	52%	100%	Alaska 1	31%	69%	100%
Ariz. 4	67%	28%	100%	Calif. 18	58%	42%	100%	Ariz. 5	43%	52%	100%	Ariz. 1	44%	50%	100%	Ala. 1		83%	100%
Calif. 1	63%	31%	100%	Calif. 20	52%	48%	100%	Ariz. 7	50%	44%	100%	Ariz. 3	41%	52%	100%	Ala. 3	41%	59%	100%
Calif. 5	72%	25%	100%	Calif. 47	53%	39%	100%	Ariz. 8	49%	47%	100%	Calif. 3	43%	50%	100%	Ala. 4		Unc.	
Calif. 6	66%	30%	100%	Colo. 7	53%	42%	100%	Calif. 11	48%	47%	100%	Colo. 4	41%	52%	100%	Ala. 5	42%	58%	100%

Using the "Get External Data From Web" tool, we imported the election results from all 438 House races into Excel. By clicking on the link to each individual district, we obtained information on the candidates in each district. For instance, clicking on Ala. 7, we get the following.

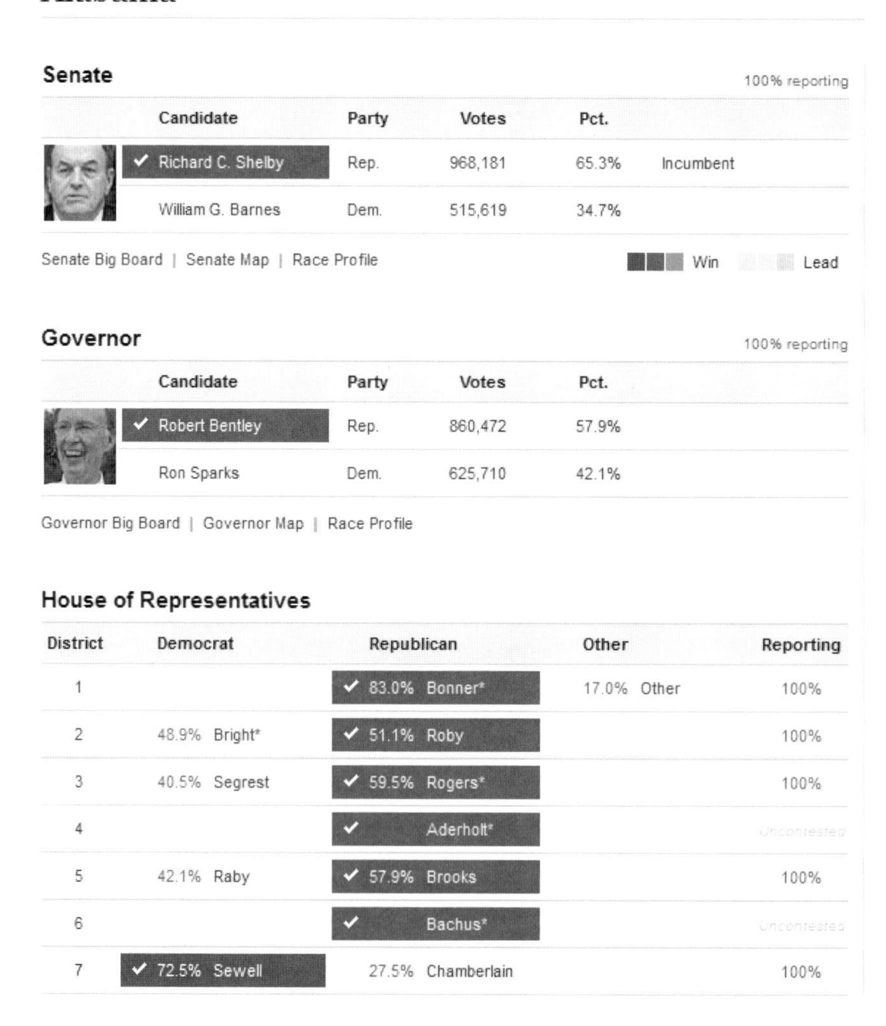

Alabama

Senate 100% reporting

Candidate	Party	Votes	Pct.	
✓ Richard C. Shelby	Rep.	968,181	65.3%	Incumbent
William G. Barnes	Dem.	515,619	34.7%	

Senate Big Board | Senate Map | Race Profile — Win, Lead

Governor 100% reporting

Candidate	Party	Votes	Pct.
✓ Robert Bentley	Rep.	860,472	57.9%
Ron Sparks	Dem.	625,710	42.1%

Governor Big Board | Governor Map | Race Profile

House of Representatives

District	Democrat	Republican	Other	Reporting
1		✓ 83.0% Bonner*	17.0% Other	100%
2	48.9% Bright*	✓ 51.1% Roby		100%
3	40.5% Segrest	✓ 59.5% Rogers*		100%
4		✓ Aderholt*		Uncontested
5	42.1% Raby	✓ 57.9% Brooks		100%
6		✓ Bachus*		Uncontested
7	✓ 72.5% Sewell	27.5% Chamberlain		100%

Looking at the election results for the House of Representatives, we determined which candidate won each race, whether that candidate was a Democrat or a Republican, and whether that candidate was an incumbent.

We found the amount of total spending on each candidate at www.washingtonpost.com/wp-srv/special/politics/election-results-2010/ by clicking on the "Campaign Finance" tab.

Finally, we obtained data on which candidates were affiliated with the Tea Party from www.nytimes.com/interactive/2010/10/15/us/politics/tea-party-graphic.html.

Combining these data, we get the 810-observation sample in **2010 House Election Data–Master.xlsx** that we analyze in the chapter.

Our SIPP Education Data

To collect educational attainment data, we return to DataFerrett by following the procedure outlined in the data collection section for Chapter 9. This time, we will be interested in the Survey of Income and Program Participation. Within this survey, we select the most recent survey, which is Wave 7 for the 2008 panel, which, when selected, looks as follows.

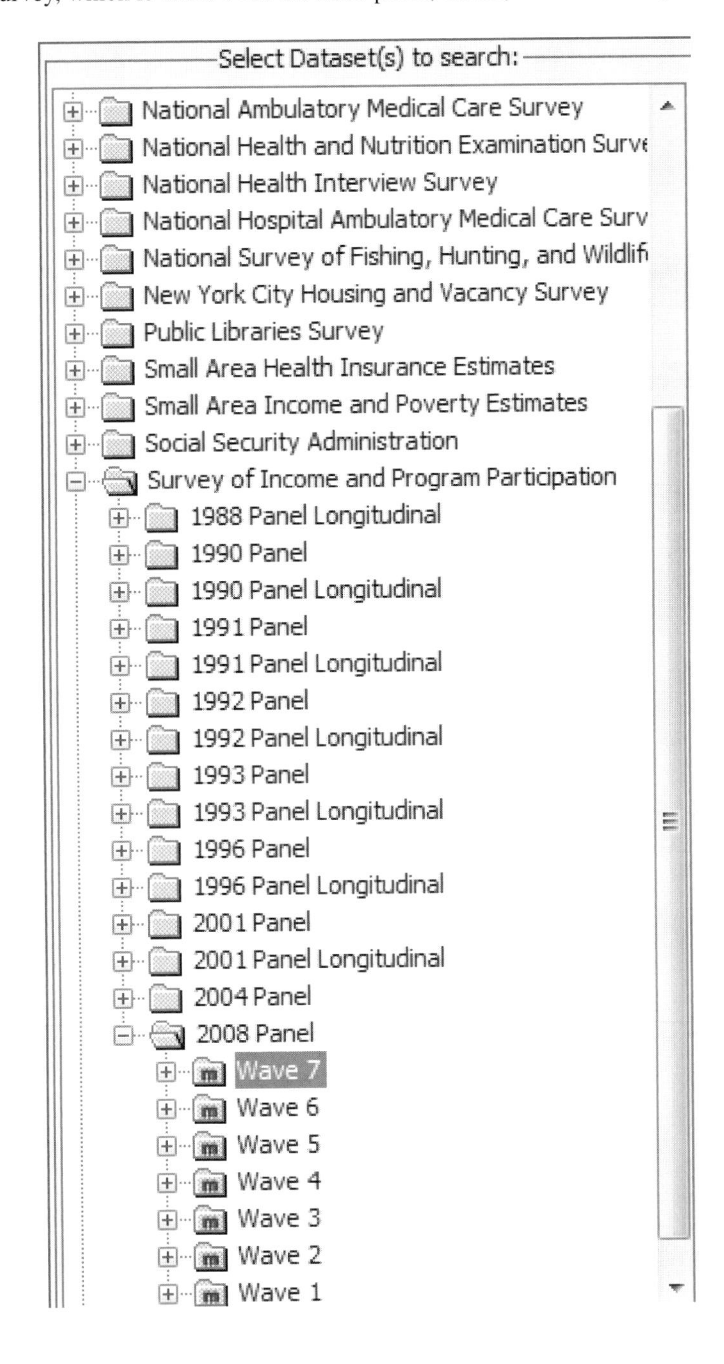

After clicking on this survey, and choosing the "View Variables" option, we start to select our desired dependent and independent variables by selecting the "View Variables" option. Knowing that we are interested in Education, Demographic, and Household data, we check each of those boxes, which looks as follows.

Select All Topics

- [ ] Person Variables
- [ ] Sample Unit Variables
- [ ] Armed Forces Variables
- [x] Education Variables
- [ ] Business Variables
- [ ] Assets Variables
- [x] Household Variables
- [x] Demographic Variables
- [ ] Family Variables
- [ ] Subfamily Variables
- [ ] Coverage Variables
- [ ] Job Variables
- [ ] General Income Variables
- [ ] Health Insurance Variables
- [ ] Labor Force Variables
- [ ] Weighting Variables

From resulting potential variables, we select EEDUCATE, which we limit to outcomes 31 through 47 and use to construct our dependent variable "Highest Degree"; ESEX, which we use to construct the independent variable "Male"; ERACE and EORIGIN, which we use to construct the independent variables "Black," "Hispanic," "Asian," and "Other Race"; TAGE, which we limit to ages 30 and above and use to construct the independent variable "Current Age"; EMS, which we use to construct the independent variable "Currently Married"; TMETRO, which we use to construct the independent variable "Live in Metro Area"; ETENURE, which we use to construct the independent variable "Family Owns Home"; THOTINC, which we limit to being greater than or equal to 1,000 and which we use to construct the independent variable "Household Income/$1,000"; and, finally, EORIGIN, which we use to construct the independent variable "U.S. Citizen."

Downloading these data, we get the 194,753-observation sample in **SIPP Education Data–Master.xlsx** that we analyze in the chapter.

CHAPTER 13

Our NFL Team Value Data

Given that *Forbes* publishes the estimated market values of each NFL team heading into each season, we obtain the dependent variable in our analysis by conducting a Internet search for each season. For instance, for the 2007 season, we start with the following search.

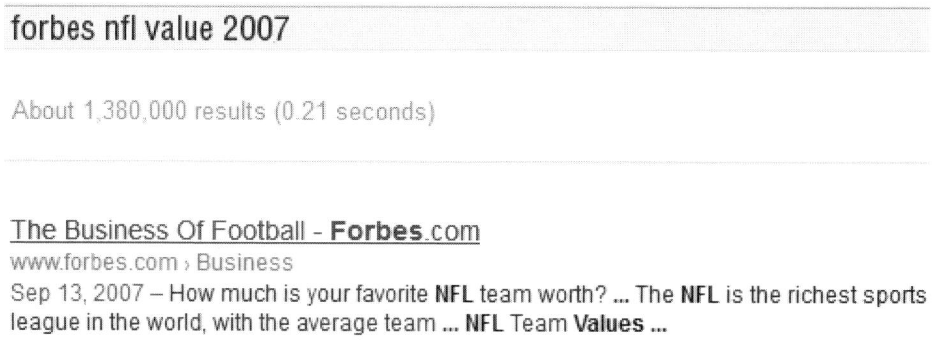

forbes nfl value 2007

About 1,380,000 results (0.21 seconds)

The Business Of Football - **Forbes**.com
www.forbes.com › Business
Sep 13, 2007 – How much is your favorite **NFL** team worth? ... The **NFL** is the richest sports league in the world, with the average team ... **NFL** Team **Values** ...

To these data, we add data on team performance, home attendance, and postseason performance by searching any of the popular sports websites, nfl.com, espn.com, and so on, to find team records for each desired season. The fan cost index for each season is found by conducting the following Internet search for each season:

nfl fan cost index 2009

About 128,000 results (0.09 seconds)

NFL average ticket prices rise; thank the Dallas Cowboys
content.usatoday.com/communities/.../post/2009/.../nfl...prices.../1
The average price of an **NFL** ticket rose 4% this season to $75. The increase ... Updated **2009**-09-10 2:06 AM. Going to ... The **Fan Cost Index** -- what it takes to bring a family of four to a game -- is $759 in Dallas, by far the highest in the league. ...

[PDF] **nfl** fci 2008.pmd
teammarketing.com.ismmedia.com/ISM3/.../nfl%20fci%20**2009**.pdf
File Format: PDF/Adobe Acrobat - Quick View
Steady as she goes: **NFL** prices facing tough times. Average ticket price increases 3.9 percent to $74.99; **Fan Cost Index** rises 4.1 percent to $412.64. Tickets to ...

with the second entry providing our desired data, which looks as follows.

8 **Team Marketing Report • Sept. 2009**

team marketing research

Team	Avg. Ticket	Pct. Change	Avg. Prem. Ticket	Beer	Soft Drink	Hot Dog	Parking	Program	Cap	FCI	Pct. Change
Dallas Cowboys^	$159.65	89.8%	$340.00	$7.00[12]	$5.00[16]	$5.00	$40.00	$6.00	$7.00	$758.58	74.2%
New England Patriots	117.84	0.0%	566.67	7.50[20]	4.00[20]	3.75	40.00	5.00	14.95	597.25	0.2%
Chicago Bears	88.33	0.0%	312.50	7.50[16]	4.50[20]	4.75	46.00	5.00	20.00	501.33	3.5%
New York Giants	88.63	0.6%	115.00	7.75[16]	4.25[20]	4.00	20.00	10.00	20.00	483.02	0.5%

Combining all of these data produces the 96-observation sample (32 teams over three different years) that we analyze in this chapter.

CHAPTER 14

Our U.S. Gasoline Sales Data

Given that we wish to collect data on U.S. gasoline sales, we start with the Internet search

us gasoline sales data

About 979,000,000 results (0.20 seconds)

U.S. Energy Information Administration (EIA)
www.eia.gov/
12 hours ago – **Sales**, revenue and prices, power plants, fuel **use**, stocks, ... Greenhouse **gas data**, voluntary **report**- ing, electric power plant emissions. ...
Petroleum & Other Liquids - Countries - International Energy Outlook - U.S. States

Clicking on this link takes us to a webpage that provides much of our desired data. Clicking on "Petroleum and Other Liquids" and then on the "Data" tab, "Consumption/Sales" tab, and the "Prime Supplier Sales Volume" tab takes us to the following webpage.

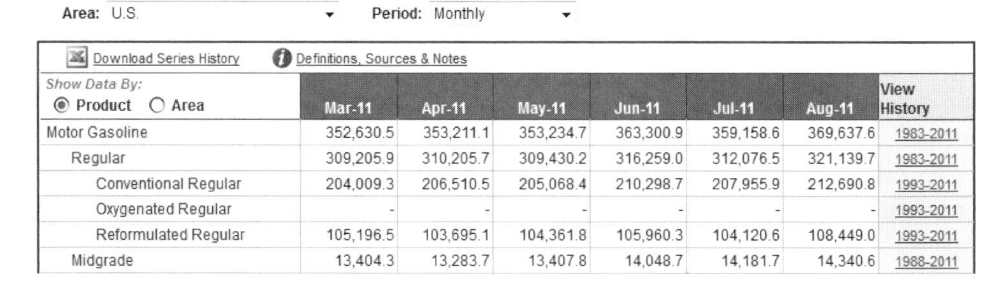

Prime Supplier Sales Volumes
(Thousand Gallons per Day)

Area: U.S. Period: Monthly

Download Series History | Definitions, Sources & Notes

Show Data By: ◉ Product ○ Area	Mar-11	Apr-11	May-11	Jun-11	Jul-11	Aug-11	View History
Motor Gasoline	352,630.5	353,211.1	353,234.7	363,300.9	359,158.6	369,637.6	1983-2011
Regular	309,205.9	310,205.7	309,430.2	316,259.0	312,076.5	321,139.7	1983-2011
Conventional Regular	204,009.3	206,510.5	205,068.4	210,298.7	207,955.9	212,690.8	1993-2011
Oxygenated Regular	-	-	-	-	-	-	1993-2011
Reformulated Regular	105,196.5	103,695.1	104,361.8	105,960.3	104,120.6	108,449.0	1993-2011
Midgrade	13,404.3	13,283.7	13,407.8	14,048.7	14,181.7	14,340.6	1988-2011

If we click the "View History" tab next to the "Regular" row, we get the observed monthly data for our dependent variable.

Next, from the "Petroleum and Other Liquids" and then on the "Data" tab, we select "Weekly Retail Gasoline and Diesel Prices," which provides the following.

Weekly Retail Gasoline and Diesel Prices
(Dollars per Gallon, Including Taxes)

Area: U.S. Period: Weekly

Download Series History | Definitions, Sources & Notes

Show Data By: ◉ Product ○ Area	09/19/11	09/26/11	10/03/11	10/10/11	10/17/11	10/24/11	View History
Gasoline - All Grades	3.657	3.568	3.492	3.476	3.533	3.520	1993-2011
All Grades - Conventional Areas	3.611	3.514	3.435	3.422	3.484	3.469	1994-2011
All Grades - Reformulated Areas	3.751	3.677	3.609	3.584	3.632	3.623	1994-2011
Regular	3.601	3.509	3.433	3.417	3.476	3.462	1990-2011

If we click the "View History" tab next to the "Regular" row, we get the observed monthly data for one of our important independent variables.

To collect data on personal income during this time series, we return to the BEA website and search for data on "Personal Income and Outlays." Doing so provides the following monthly data, which we can import to Excel and add to our data set.

```
Title:                 Personal Income
Series ID:             PI
Source:                U.S. Department of Commerce: Bureau of Economic Analysis
Release:               Personal Income and Outlays
Seasonal Adjustment:   Seasonally Adjusted Annual Rate
Frequency:             Monthly
Units:                 Billions of Dollars

Date Range:            1959-01-01 to 2010-03-01
Last Updated:          2010-05-03 10:17 AM CDT
Notes:                 A Guide to the National Income and Product Accounts of the Unitec
                       States (NIPA) - (http://www.bea.gov/national/pdf/nipaguid.pdf)

DATE          VALUE
1959-01-01    380.9
1959-02-01    383.1
1959-03-01    386.1
1959-04-01    389.4
1959-05-01    392.1
```

Finally, to collect data on crude oil prices, we perform the following Internet search.

crude oil prices history

About 7,640,000 results (0.14 seconds)

Crude Oil Price History
www.nyse.tv/crude-oil-price-history.htm
History of **Crude Oil Prices** at The New York Mercantile Exchange.

HISTORY OF **CRUDE OIL PRICES**
www.ioga.com/Special/crudeoil_Hist.htm
HISTORY OF ILLINOIS BASIN POSTED **CRUDE OIL PRICES**. **Crude Oil Price** ... **History** & Analysis of **Crude Oil Prices** from WTRG Economics. Year, Month ...

Clicking on the second link takes us to the following data, which we can import to Excel and add to our data set.

HISTORY OF ILLINOIS BASIN POSTED CRUDE OIL PRICES

Crude Oil Price
Chart from 1977 to 2003

Monthly Price Chart 1998-April 2009

History & Analysis of Crude Oil Prices from WTRG Economics

Year, Month, Monthly Average, and Yearly Average

2011

January	$84.47	July	$88.82
February	$81.32	August	$77.72
March	$94.72	September	$77.31
April	$102.15	October	
May	$92.92	November	
June	$87.92	December	
		2011 Average	$87.48

2010

January	$69.85	July	$67.91
February	$68.04	August	$68.34
March	$72.90	September	$67.18
April	$76.31	October	$73.63
May	$66.25	November	$76.00
June	$67.12	December	$81.01
		2010 Average	$71.21

Combining these data, we get the 236-observation sample in **US Gasoline Sales Data–Master.xlsx** that we analyze in the chapter.

Our Doctor Advice Data

Once again accessing DataFerret (http://dataferrett.census.gov/run.html), we identify the National Health Interview Survey as the dataset that we wish to access.

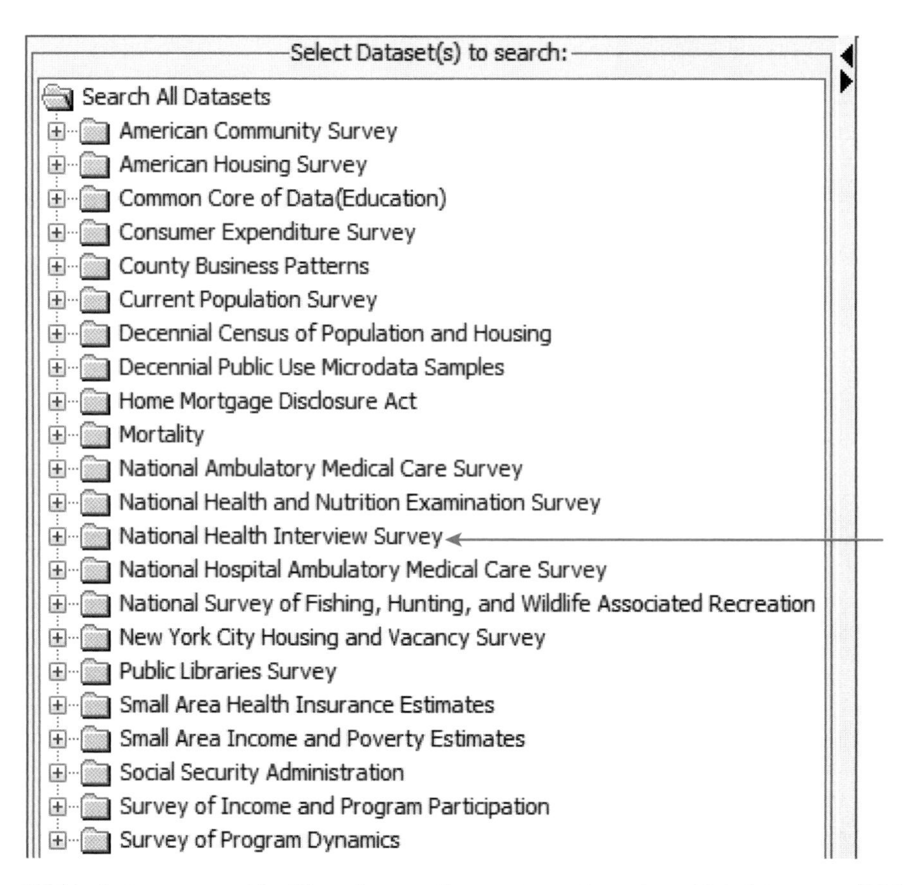

Within that survey, we identify and access the most recent year for which data are available.

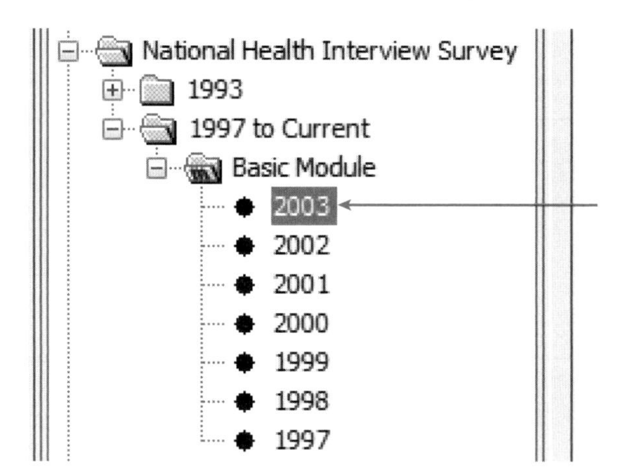

After selecting the view variables option, we search for the survey questions in which we are interested. Because we are interested in determining whether an individual has ever been advised to reduce alcohol consumption, lose weight, and/or exercise more, we perform the following search to identify the desired variables.

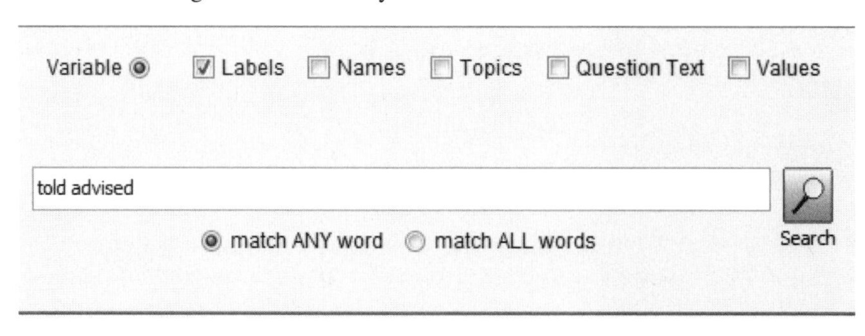

This search provides the following results.

Topic	Name	Availability	Variable Label	Mergeable
Sample Adult	MIEV	1997 - current	Ever been told you had a heart attack	No
Sample Child	CONDL9	1997 - current	Ever told - - had Congentl heart disease	No
Sample Child	AMR2	1997 - current	Ever told - - had mental retardation	No
Sample Child	CONDL10	1997 - current	Ever told - - had otr heart cond	No
Sample Child	CONDL8	1997 - current	Ever told - - had Arthritis	No
Sample Child	CASHMEV	1997 - current	Ever been told that - - had asthma	No
Sample Child	CONDL3	1997 - current	Ever told - - had Muscular Dystrophy	No
Sample Child	CONDL1	1997 - current	Ever told - - had Down's Syndrome	No
Sample Child	CONDL2	1997 - current	Ever told - - had Celebral Palsy	No
Sample Child	CONDL5	1997 - current	Ever told - - had Sickle Cell anemia	No
Sample Child	CONDL4	1997 - current	Ever told - - had Cystic Fibrosis	No
Sample Child	AODD1	1997 - current	Told - - had otr dev delay	No
Sample Child	AMR1	1997 - current	Told - - had mental retardation	No
Sample Child	CONDL7	1997 - current	Ever told - - had Diabetes	No
Sample Child	ADD2	1997 - current	Ever told - - had ADD	No
Sample Child	LEARND	1997 - current	Ever told - - had a learning disability	No
Sample Child	AODD2	1997 - current	Ever told - - had otr dev delay	No
Sample Child	CONDL6	1997 - current	Ever told - - had Autism	No
Sample Adult	ARTHPH	2002 - current	Ever told to exercise to help arthritis	No
Sample Adult	ARTH1	2002 - current	Ever told you had arthritis, gout, lupus	No
Sample Adult	ARTHWT	2002 - current	Ever told to lose weight to help arth	No
Sample Adult	AAPENVLN	2002 - current	Ever advised to change environment	No
Sample Child	CAPENVLN	2002 - current	Ever advised to change environment	No
Sample Adult	HYBPLEV	2003 - current	Told blood pressure was high/normal/low	No
Sample Adult	HYMDMED	2003 - current	Advised to stop taking medicine for HBP	No
Sample Adult	HBPALC	2003 - current	Ever told to reduce alcohol due to HBP	No
Sample Adult	CLHI	2003 - current	Told blood cholesterol level was high	No
Sample Adult	EXERC	2003 - current	Ever told to exercise due to HBP	No
Sample Adult	HLOSWGT	2003 - current	Ever advised to change diet to lower HBP	No

To obtain our key variables of interest, we select the three variables highlighted. We then need to identify our dependent variables, which we do by searching for "days drink," which provides the following. Note that the highlighted variable is the one that we choose as the dependent variable for our analysis.

Topic	Name	Availability	Variable Label	Mergeable
Sample Adult	ALCAMT	1997 - current	Average # drinks on days drank	No
Sample Adult	CIGDAMO	1997 - current	Number days smoked in past 30 days	No
Sample Adult	WKDAYR	1997 - current	Number of work loss days, past 12 months	No
Sample Adult	SAD	1997 - current	How often felt sad, past 30 days	No
Sample Adult	ALC12MWK	1997 - current	Freq drank alcohol: Days per week	No
Sample Adult	BEDDAYR	1997 - current	Number of bed days, past 12 months	No
Sample Adult	ALC5UPYR	1997 - current	Number of days had 5+ drinks past year	No
Sample Adult	HOPELESS	1997 - current	How often felt hopeless, past 30 days	No
Sample Adult	MHAMTMO	1997 - current	Feelings interfered w/life, past 30 days	No
Sample Adult	ALC5UPNO	1997 - current	Days had 5+ drinks, past year: # of days	No
Sample Adult	NERVOUS	1997 - current	How often felt nervous, past 30 days	No
Sample Adult	ALC5UPTP	1997 - current	Days had 5+ drinks past year: Time unit	No
Sample Adult	RESTLESS	1997 - current	How often restless/fidgety, past 30 days	No
Sample Adult	CIGQTYR	1997 - current	Tried quit smoking 1+ days, past 12 m	No
Sample Adult	WORTHLS	1997 - current	How often felt worthless, past 30 days	No
Sample Adult	ALC12MMO	1997 - current	Freq drank alcohol: Days per month	No
Sample Adult	ALC12MYR	1997 - current	Freq drank alcohol: Days in past year	No
Sample Child	SCHDAYR1	1997 - current	Days missed due to ill/inj, past 12 m	No
Sample Adult	AWZMSWK	2002 - current	# days missed due to asthma, past 12 mo.	No
Sample Adult	JNTPN	2002 - current	Rate your joint pain, past 30 days	No
Sample Child	CWZMSWK	2002 - current	# days school/work missed	No

Our final step is to search for other independent variables of interest and select those to include them in our data set. Note that because we wish to focus on adults, we limit our analysis to individuals who are 25 years of age or older. We also limit our analysis to only those individuals providing responses to the doctor advice and frequency of consuming five or more alcoholic drinks variables.

Combining these data, we get the 14,589-observation sample in **Drinking Data–Master.xlsx** that we analyze in the chapter.

CHAPTER 15

Our Newly Minted Economics PhD Publication Data

Collecting this entire data set is rather involved and time-consuming, but we include it because (in addition to be a good example of non-negative count data) it provides an example of how students can creatively use resources available to them to create their own data sets. We start by looking at the databases made available by our university library at http://library.sdsu.edu.

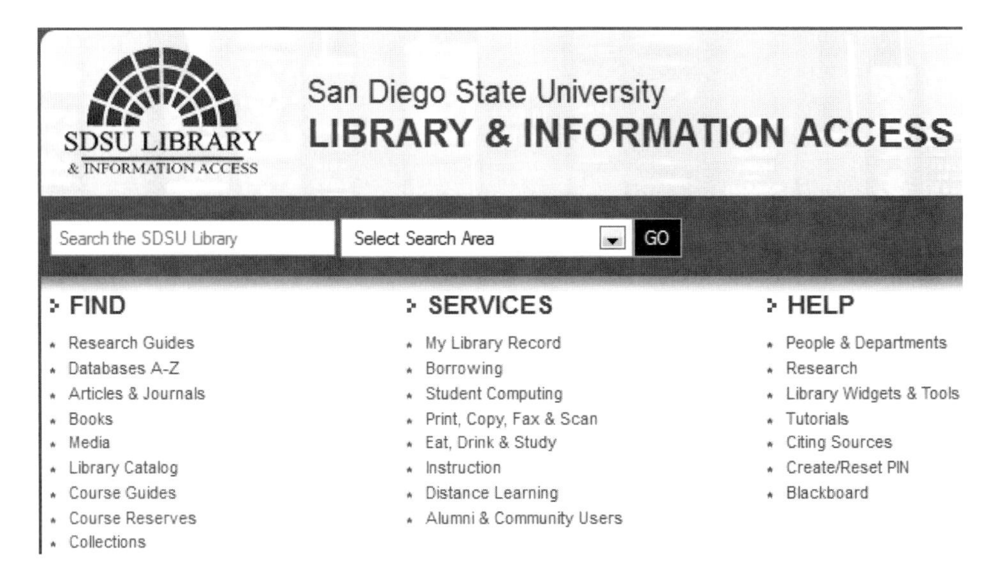

From the extensive list of available databases, we are interested in two: one containing information on students filing dissertations "Dissertations and Theses (ProQuest)" and the other containing information on the academic publications of economists "EconLit".

ARTICLE DATABASES: D – F

To view databases by subject area visit the ***Research Guides***

A B C D–F G–H I–L M–O P–R S–Z View All

- Defense Language Institute Ebook Collection [Details]
- Dictionary of Literary Biography Complete Online [SDSU] [Details]
- Directory of Open Access Journals [Details]
- Dissertations and Theses (ProQuest) [SDSU] ←
- Early American Imprints, Series I: Evans 1639-1800 [SDSU] [Details]
- Early English Books Online (EEBO) [SDSU] *1473-1700.* [Details]
- EBL Collection (eBooks) [Details]
- Ebrary (eBook Library) [SDSU]

Note: A personal account is required in order to download, or checkout, books from ebrary. In order to create an account, click on "sign in" the upper right-hand corner of the ebrary homepage, and then "create an account." Books may be viewed, but not downloaded, in their entirety online without creating an account by clicking on Table of Contents and then selecting a chapter/section.

- EcoAmericas [SDSU] *1999 to present.* [Details]
- EconLit [SDSU] *1969 to present.* [Details] ←

As discussed in the text, we wish to collect data for a cohort of economics PhD recipients for a year that allows significant time for individuals to establish an academic publication record. For our purposes, we limit our search in the "Dissertation Abstracts" database to individuals receiving their "Ph.D." in "Economics" in "1994."

ProQuest

Basic | Advanced | Browse | My Research 0 marked items

Databases selected: Dissertations & Theses

Advanced Search

Tools: Search Tips

Economics — Subject name/code — Look up subjects

AND Ph.D. — Degree

AND — Citation and abstract

Add a row | Remove a row — Search Clear

Database: Interdisciplinary - Dissertations & Theses — Select multiple databases

Date range: Within this year... 1994 About

Limit results to: Full text documents only

More Search Options

This search provides a series of individuals receiving the PhD in 1994 along with the title of the dissertation and the university awarding the degree. Clicking on the title of the dissertation takes us to a new page that contains information on many things, including the subject of the dissertation and the identity of the student's advisor. To start creating our data set, we enter all of this information into Excel. We determine whether the student's advisor is either a "star" (i.e., ranked 1–250) or "ranked" (i.e., ranked 251–1,000) by consulting Coupe's listing of the top 1,000 worldwide economists based on economics publications between 1969 and 2000 (http://student.ulb.ac.be/~tcoupe/update/nobelpub.html).

Once we have collected the information relating to the student's dissertation, we collect information on his or her early-career academic publishing record by moving to EconLit and performing a search for "Journal Articles" listing the individual as "Author."

We then count the total number of articles published and enter that as a new variable in our Excel file. We also count the number of articles published while in graduate school, which we define as actually being published by 1995 to allow for the often lengthy time-lag between acceptance and publication, and we count the number of articles ever coauthored with the advisor. This gives us the data set that we analyze in this chapter.

Combining these data, we get the 681-observation sample in **Publication Data–Master.xlsx** that we analyze in the chapter.

Our CPS Salary Data

We again return to DataFerrett (http://dataferrett.census.gov/run.html) and select the March 2011 supplement to the Current Population Survey (CPS).

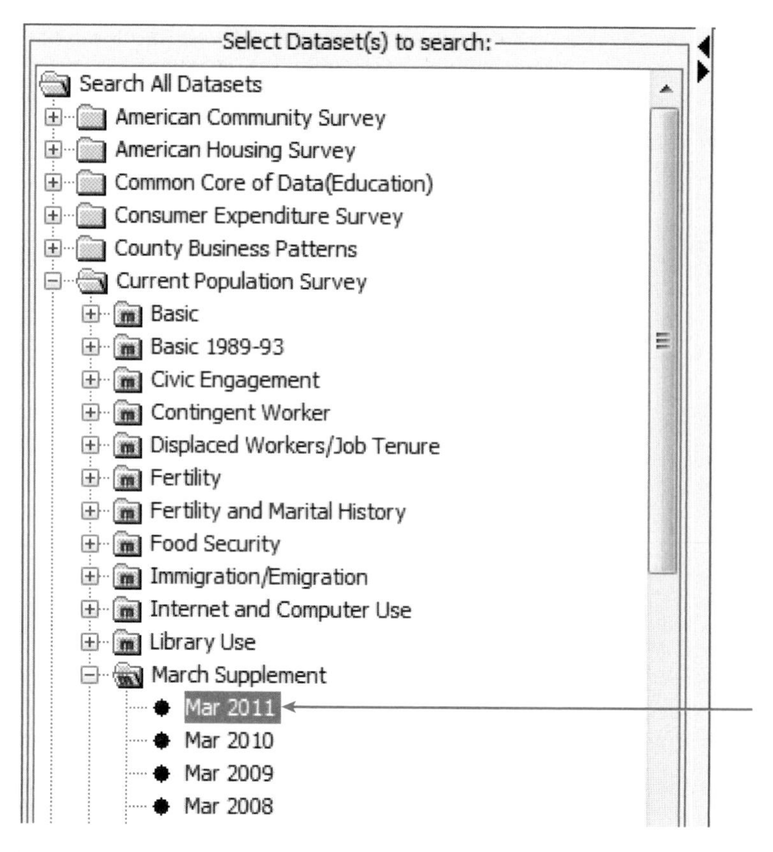

We then identify our dependent variable by conducting a search for "salary" and choosing the variable representing "total wage and salary earnings."

Topic	Name	Availability	Variable Label	Mergeable
Family Variables	FINC_WS	Mar 1992 - current	Wage and salary received Y/N - Family	No
Household Variables	HINC_WS	Mar 1992 - current	Wage and salary received Y/N - Household	No
Person Variables	TCWSVAL	Mar 1995 - current	Wage and salary earnings Top code flag- Person	No
Person Variables	WAGEOTR	Mar 1992 - current	Wage and salary earnings, other job Y/N	No
Person Variables	WSAL_VAL	Mar 1992 - current	Total wage and salary earnings amount - Person	No
Person Variables	WSAL_YN	Mar 1992 - current	Wage and salary earnings received Y/N - Person	No
Person Variables	WS_VAL	Mar 1992 - current	Wage and salary earnings, amount, other job - Person	No

We next find our selection correction identification variable by searching for "child" and choosing the variable representing the "number own child under 6."

Topic	Name	Availability	Variable Label	Mergeable
Person Variables	CH_HI	Mar 1992 - current	Health insurance - child covered Y/N	No
Person Variables	CH_MC	Mar 1992 - current	Health insurance - child covered by medicaid Y/N	No
Person Variables	CSP_VAL	Mar 1992 - current	Child support payments amounts - Person	No
Person Variables	CSP_YN	Mar 1992 - current	Child support payments received Y/N - Person	No
Family Variables	FCSPVAL	Mar 1992 - current	Child support amount - Family	No
Family Variables	FINC_CSP	Mar 1992 - current	Child support payments received Y/N - Family	No
Family Variables	FOWNU18	Mar 1992 - current	Family recode, number own child under 18	No
Family Variables	FOWNU6	Mar 1992 - current	Family Recode, number own child under 6	No
Household Variables	HCSPVAL	Mar 1992 - current	Child support amount - Household	No
Household Variables	HCSP_YN	Mar 1992 - current	Child support payments received Y/N - Household	No
Person Variables	TCSP_VAL	Mar 1999 - current	Topcode Flag,Child Support Payments Value	No
Person Variables	CTC_CRD	Mar 2005 - Mar 2011	Child tax credit	No
Person Variables	ACTC_CRD	Mar 2005 - Mar 2011	Child tax credit, additional	No
Household Variables	HRPAIDCC	Mar 2001 - current	Child care paid while working, anyone	No
Person Variables	PAIDCCYN	Mar 2001 - current	Child needed care while parent worked	No
Person Variables	PCHIP	Mar 2001 - current	Child covered by states CHIP	No
Person Variables	SSIKIDYN	Mar 2001 - current	Supplemental Security income, child recd	No
Person Variables	SSKIDYN	Mar 2001 - current	Social Security income, child recd	No
Household Variables	CARE_VAL	Mar 2011 - current	Annual amount paid for child care	No
Person Variables	CHSP_VAL	Mar 2011 - current	Annual amt paid for child support	No
Person Variables	CHSP_YN	Mar 2011 - current	Person required to pay child support	No
Person Variables	CHELSEW_YN	Mar 2011 - current	Child living outside the household	No

We complete the data set by searching for and adding the remaining economically relevant independent variables. Combining these data, we get the 100,731-observation sample in **CPS Salary Data–Master.xlsx** that we analyze in the chapter.

Our State Traffic Fatality Data

We return to DataFerrett (http://dataferrett.census.gov/run.html) and select the "Underlying Cause-of-Death" supplement to the "Mortality" survey. Note that to collect our before and after data, we repeat the following steps for both 1994 and 1998.

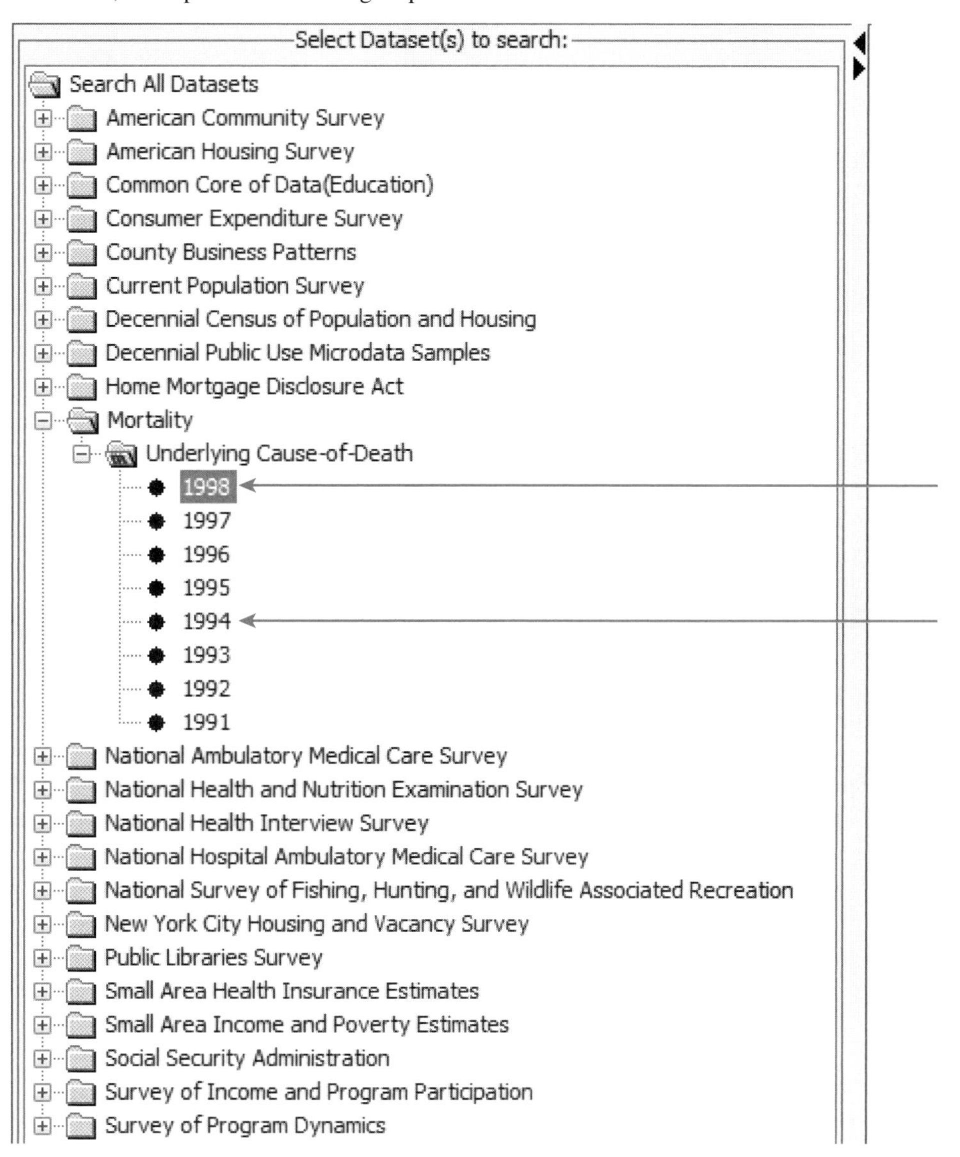

We ask the program to show us all of the "mortality variables," and choose the one representing the "34 Cause Recode."

Topic	Name	Availability	Variable Label	Mergeable
Mortality Variables	PLACDTH	1991 - current	Place of Death and Decedent's Status	No
Mortality Variables	HISPANR	1991 - current	Hispanic Origin Recode	No
Mortality Variables	MARSTAT	1991 - current	Marital Status	No
Mortality Variables	HISPANIC	1991 - current	Hispanic Origin	No
Mortality Variables	HSPANICR	1991 - current	Hispanic Origin/Race Recode	No
Mortality Variables	WEEKDAY	1991 - current	Day of Week of Death	No
Mortality Variables	INDUSTRY	1991 - current	Kind of Business or Industry	No
Mortality Variables	UCR52	1991 - current	52 Cause Recode	No
Mortality Variables	INJWORK	1993 - current	Injury at Work	No
Mortality Variables	RACEIMP	1992 - current	Race Imputation Flag	No
Mortality Variables	AGEFLAG	1991 - current	Age Substitution Flag	No
Mortality Variables	ACCIDENT	1991 - current	Place of Accident for Causes E850-E929	No
Mortality Variables	UCR282	1991 - current	282 Cause Recode	No
Mortality Variables	UCR72	1991 - current	72 Cause Recode	No
Mortality Variables	UCR61	1991 - current	61 Infant Cause Recode	No
Mortality Variables	UCR34	1991 - current	34 Cause Recode	No
Mortality Variables	DATAYEAR	1996 - current	Data Year - four digits	No
Mortality Variables	COUNTYOC	1997 - current	County of Occurrence	No
Mortality Variables	DIVSTOC	1997 - current	Division and State Subcode of Occurrence	No
Mortality Variables	COUNTYRS	1997 - current	County of Residence	No
Mortality Variables	STATERS	1997 - current	State of Residence	No
Mortality Variables	CITYRS	1997 - current	City of Residence	No
Mortality Variables	DIVSTRES	1997 - current	Division and State Subcode of Residence	No
Mortality Variables	EXSTARES	1997 - current	Expanded State of Residence Code	No
Mortality Variables	STATEBTH	1997 - current	State of Birth	No
Mortality Variables	OCCUP	1997 - current	Usual Occupation	No
Mortality Variables	FIPSCTYO	1997 - current	FIPS County of Occurrence	No
Mortality Variables	FIPSCTYR	1997 - current	FIPS County of Residence	No
Mortality Variables	FIPSPMSA	1997 - current	FIPS PMSA/MSA of Residence	No
Mortality Variables	UCOD	1997 - current	ICD Code (9th Revision)	No

We then limit the 34 possible cause-of-death codes to "Motor Vehicle Accidents."

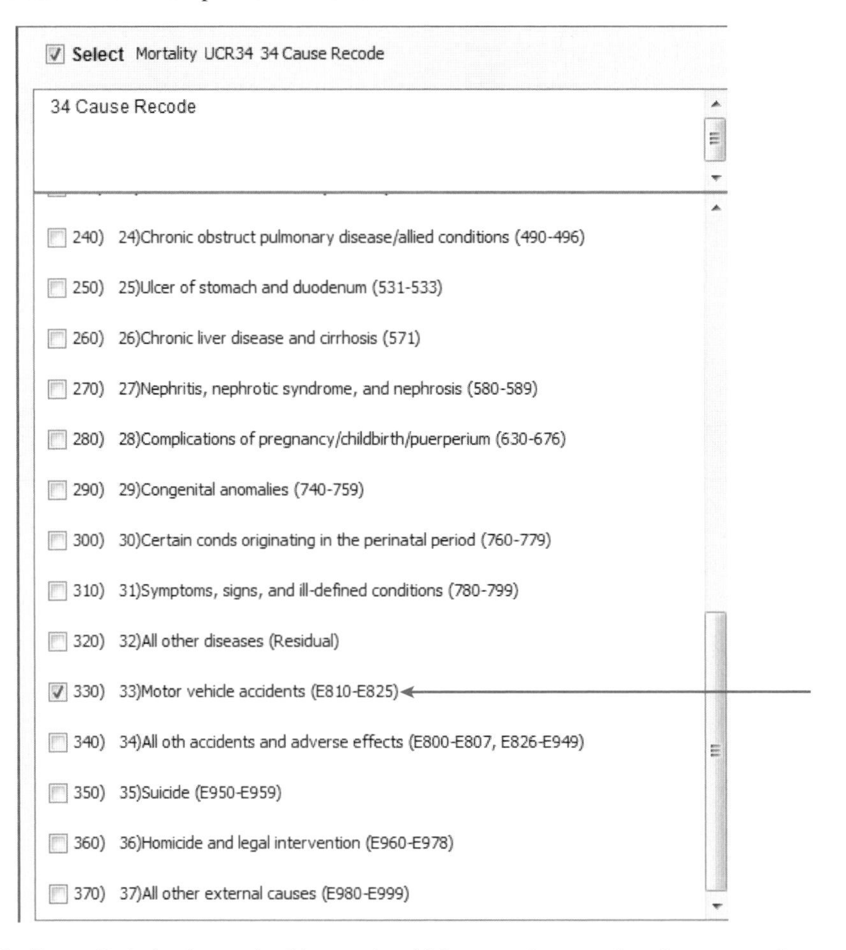

Finally, we limit the data to the 31 states in which we are interested, and we repeat the process for 1994 to assemble the sample in **Traffic Data–Master.xlsx** that we analyze in the chapter.

Appendix B: Stata Commands

SOME GENERAL COMMANDS THAT PROVE VALUABLE

While there are several different ways to move our data from Excel to Stata, our preferred method is to copy and paste the data directly into the Stata Data Editor. We do so as follows.

Importing the Data from Excel

1. Open Stata and click the Data Editor tab, which is shown here.

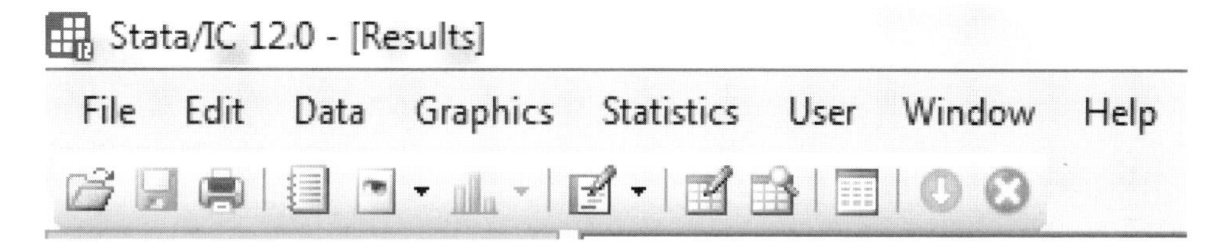

2. Highlight and copy the desired columns of data in Excel and paste those columns into the Data Editor.

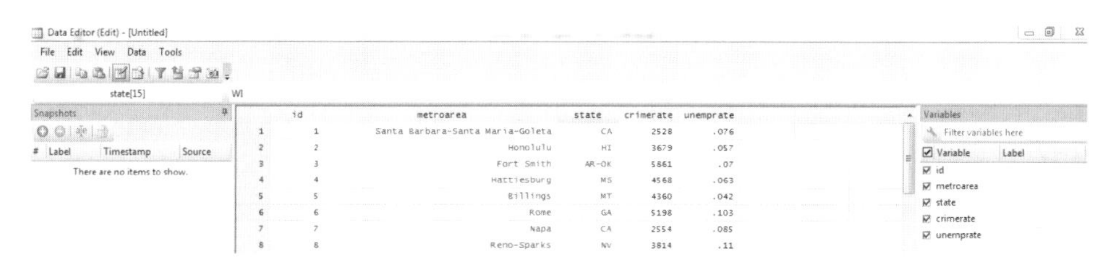

3. Create and save a new dataset in Stata format by typing

```
save crimesample
```

Note: As with Excel, when working with data in a different statistical package, when first importing data, we recommend saving two files: one a master file that contains our initial data and the other a working file in which we create new variables, make changes to existing variables, and estimate results.

Loading a Saved Dataset

Open Stata and access data by typing

```
use crimesample
```

Saving Changes to the Dataset

After making changes to the dataset, save those changes by typing

```
save crimesample, replace
```

Note: We try to remember to do this every time we create new variables or make changes to existing variables that we wish to be permanent, so that if we exit out of (or a thrown out of) Stata, we have access to those variables when returning to work with our data.

Visually Inspect the Data

Show the individual observations by typing

```
list
```

```
. list

     +------------------------------------------------------------------+
  1. | id                               metroarea |  state |  crimer~e |
     |  1   Santa Barbara-Santa Maria-Goleta      |     CA |      2528 |
     |------------------------------------------------------------------|
     |                          unempr~e                                |
     |                              .076                                |
     +------------------------------------------------------------------+

     +------------------------------------------------------------------+
  2. | id                               metroarea |  state |  crimer~e |
     |  2                                Honolulu |     HI |      3679 |
     |------------------------------------------------------------------|
     |                          unempr~e                                |
     |                              .057                                |
     +------------------------------------------------------------------+

     +------------------------------------------------------------------+
  3. | id                               metroarea |  state |  crimer~e |
     |  3                              Fort Smith |  AR-OK |      5861 |
     |------------------------------------------------------------------|
     |                          unempr~e                                |
     |                               .07                                |
     +------------------------------------------------------------------+
```

Create New Variables

Create a new variable (say, *crime rate*^{2}) by typing

```
gen x=crimerate^2
```

Note: When creating variables for which you want to specify different possible outcomes, you need to use the gen command for the first outcome and the replace command for subsequent outcomes.

For example, we could type

```
gen highcrime=1 if crimerate≥7000
```

To assign the value 0 for all remaining crime rates, we would then type

```
replace highcrime=0 if crimerate<7000
```

Tabulate the Outcomes of a Categorical Variable

Tabulate the variable by typing

```
tab highcrime
```

```
. tab highcrime
```

highcrime	Freq.	Percent	Cum.
0	142	94.67	94.67
1	8	5.33	100.00
Total	150	100.00	

Store the Commands and Results of a Given Session

Before performing all of the desired calculations, store a given session by typing

```
log using results.log
```

After entering all desired calculations, type

log close

CHAPTER 3

Constructing a Histogram

Ask Stata to construct a histogram with seven bins by typing

hist crimerate, bin(7)

```
. hist crimerate, bin(7)
(bin=7, start=1927, width=1111.1429)
```

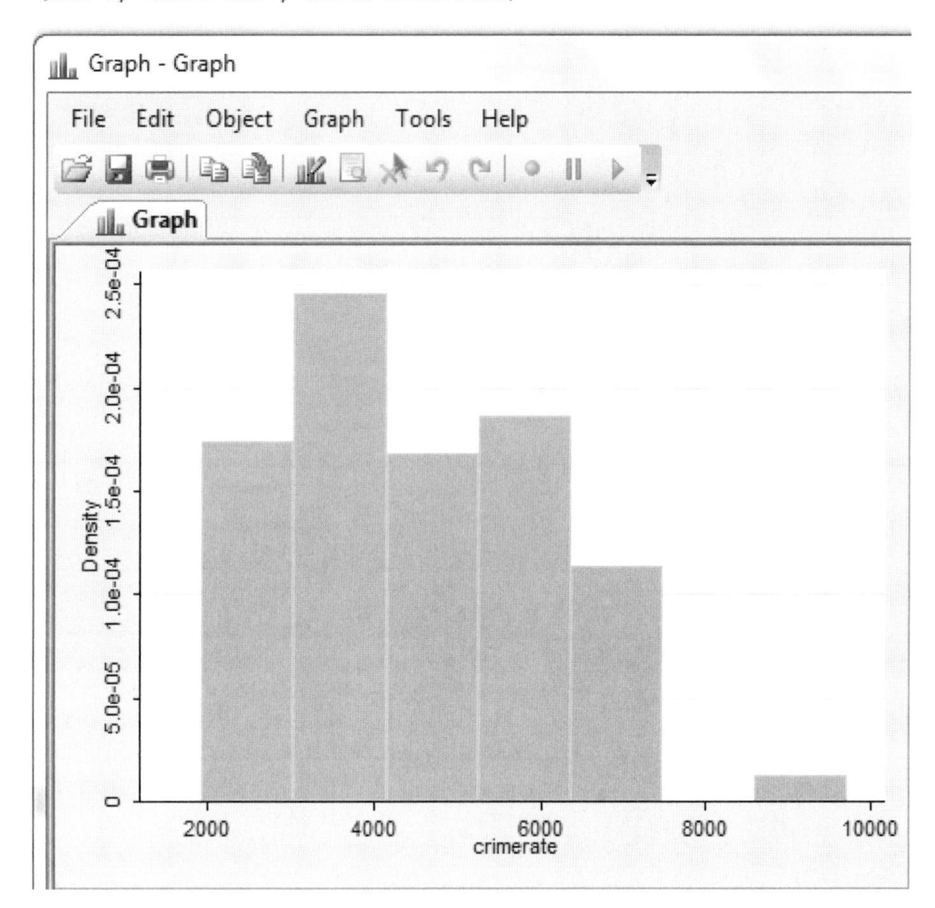

Calculating the Minimum, Maximum, Mean, and Standard Deviation

Summarize the data (which includes all four values) by typing

sum crimerate

```
. sum crimerate

    Variable |       Obs        Mean    Std. Dev.       Min        Max
-------------+--------------------------------------------------------
   crimerate |       150    4550.267    1500.039       1927       9705
```

Ordering the Data from Smallest to Largest

1. Order the data from smallest to largest by typing

sort crimerate

2. Visually inspect the ordered data by typing

list

```
. sort crimerate

. list
```

	id	metroarea	state	crimer~e	unempr~e
1.	111	Danbury	CT	1927	.069
2.	14	St. George	UT	2043	.066
3.	138	Madera-Chowchilla	CA	2160	.146
4.	97	Naples-Marco Island	FL	2378	.092
5.	59	Santa Rosa-Petaluma	CA	2423	.094
6.	88	Los Angeles-Long Beach-Santa Ana	CA	2444	.101
7.	96	Blacksburg-Christiansburg-Radford	VA	2481	.082
8.	87	Rochester-Dover	NH-ME	2486	.063
9.	47	Bend	OR	2528	.156
10.	17	Santa Barbara-Santa Maria-Goleta	CA	2528	.076

Calculating the Median and Other Percentiles

1. Calculate the median (the 50th percentile) by typing

centile crimerate, centile(50)

2. Calculate the 65th and 29th percentiles by typing

centile crimerate, centile(65)
centile crimerate, centile(29)

```
. centile crimerate, centile(50)
```

Variable	Obs	Percentile	Centile	— Binom. Interp. — [95% Conf.	Interval]
crimerate	150	50	4321.5	3958.336	4866.019

```
. centile crimerate, centile(65)
```

Variable	Obs	Percentile	Centile	— Binom. Interp. — [95% Conf.	Interval]
crimerate	150	65	5256.15	4830.778	5479.323

```
. centile crimerate, centile(29)
```

Variable	Obs	Percentile	Centile	— Binom. Interp. — [95% Conf.	Interval]
crimerate	150	29	3614.54	3194.163	3814

Constructing a Scatter Diagram

Ask Stata to construct the diagram by typing

dotplot crimerate, over(unemprate)

```
. dotplot crimerate, over(unemprate)
```

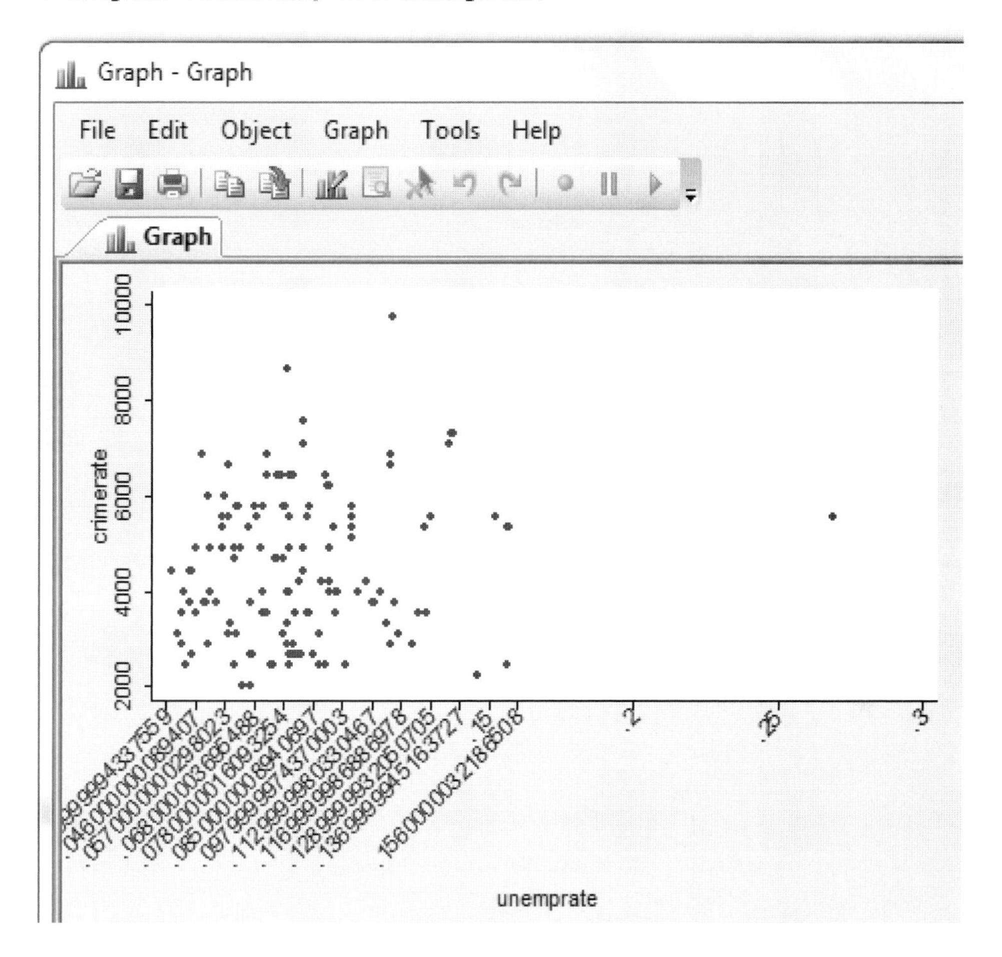

<u>**Calculating the Covariance and the Correlation Coefficient**</u>

1. Ask Stata to calculate the covariance by typing

   correlate crimerate unemprate, covariance

```
. correlate crimerate unemprate, covariance
(obs=150)

             |  crimer~e unempr~e
-------------+------------------
   crimerate |   2.3e+06
   unemprate |   7.38236  .000931
```

2. Ask Stata to calculate the correlation coefficient by typing

   correlate crimerate unemprate

```
. correlate crimerate unemprate
(obs=150)

             |  crimer~e unempr~e
-------------+------------------
   crimerate |    1.0000
   unemprate |    0.1613   1.0000
```

CHAPTER 4

Estimating the Sample Regression Function

Ask Stata to calculate the estimated sample regression function by typing

reg crimerate unemprate

```
. regress crimerate unemprate

      Source |       SS       df       MS              Number of obs =     150
-------------+------------------------------           F(  1,   148) =    3.95
       Model |  8723808.87     1  8723808.87           Prob > F      =  0.0486
    Residual |   326543462   148  2206374.75           R-squared     =  0.0260
-------------+------------------------------           Adj R-squared =  0.0194
       Total |   335267271   149  2250115.91           Root MSE      =  1485.4

------------------------------------------------------------------------------
   crimerate |      Coef.   Std. Err.      t    P>|t|     [95% Conf. Interval]
-------------+----------------------------------------------------------------
   unemprate |   7930.935   3988.513     1.99   0.049     49.14572    15812.72
       _cons |   3870.638   362.6691    10.67   0.000      3153.96    4587.317
------------------------------------------------------------------------------
```

CHAPTER 5

Constructing 95 Percent Confidence Intervals

Ask Stata to calculate a 95 percent confidence interval by typing

ci crimerate

```
. ci crimerate

    Variable |        Obs        Mean    Std. Err.       [95% Conf. Interval]
-------------+---------------------------------------------------------------
   crimerate |        150    4550.267    122.4776        4308.249    4792.284
```

CHAPTER 6

Estimating the Sample Regression Function

Ask Stata to calculate the estimated sample regression function by typing

reg salary experience hr

```
. reg salary experience hr

      Source |       SS       df       MS              Number of obs =     200
-------------+------------------------------           F(  2,   197) =  111.74
       Model |  2.5159e+15     2  1.2580e+15           Prob > F      =  0.0000
    Residual |  2.2177e+15   197  1.1258e+13           R-squared     =  0.5315
-------------+------------------------------           Adj R-squared =  0.5267
       Total |  4.7337e+15   199  2.3787e+13           Root MSE      =  3.4e+06

------------------------------------------------------------------------------
      salary |      Coef.   Std. Err.      t    P>|t|     [95% Conf. Interval]
-------------+----------------------------------------------------------------
  experience |   569508.5   63560.11     8.96   0.000     444162.9      694854
          hr |   212460.9   23578.03     9.01   0.000     165963.1    258958.6
       _cons |   -1003205   394238.7    -2.54   0.012     -1780675   -225735.1
------------------------------------------------------------------------------
```

Predicting Outcomes

Ask Stata to predict by typing

predict psalary

Note: This creates the new variable *psalary* in the variable window.

```
. predict psalary
(option xb assumed; fitted values)

. sum
```

Variable	Obs	Mean	Std. Dev.	Min	Max
id	200	100.5	57.87918	1	200
player	0				
salary	200	3699375	4877217	400000	2.39e+07
experience	200	4.245	3.894975	0	20
hr	200	10.755	10.49982	0	48
psalary	200	3699375	3555679	-1003205	1.54e+07

CHAPTER 7

Creating Binary Dummy Variable AL_i

Construct the binary dummy variable AL_i by typing

gen al=league=="American"

Note: This creates the new variable *al* in the variable window.

Creating the Categorical Variable $Position_i$

Construct the categorical variable $Position_i$ by typing

gen position=0 if positionname=="Catcher"
replace position=1 if positionname=="Infielder"
replace position=2 if positionname=="Outfielder"
replace position=3 if positionname=="Designated Hitter"

Note: This creates the new variable *position* in the variable window.

Creating the Dummy Variables $Infielder_i$, $Outfielder_i$ DH_i

Construct the dummy variables by typing

gen infielder=positionname=="Infielder"
gen outfielder=positionname=="Outfielder"
gen dh=positionname=="Designated Hitter"

Note: This creates the new variables *infielder, outfielder,* and *dh* in the variable window.

Creating the Interaction Term ($Experience_i \times AL_i$), $Outfielder_i$, DH_i

Construct the categorical variable ($Experience_i \times AL_i$) by typing

gen experienceal=experience×al

Note: This creates the new variable *experienceal* in the variable window.

Creating the Quadratic Experience Term

Construct the quadratic experience variable by typing

gen experience2=experience^2

Note: This creates the new variable *experience2* in the variable window.

Creating the Interaction between Two Quantitative Variables

Construct the quadratic experience variable by typing

```
gen experiencehr=experience×hr
```

Note: This creates the new variable *experiencehr* in the variable window.

Creating the Log-Linear Term

Construct the log salary variable by typing

```
gen logsalary=log(salary)
```

Note: This creates the new variable *logsalary* in the variable window.

CHAPTER 8

Perform the Reset Test

Regress logsalary on

```
reg logsalary experience experience2 hr experiencehr Japanese
    experience×Japanese infielder outfielder dh
```

Then perform the test by typing

```
estat ovtest
```

```
. reg  logsalary experience experiencesquared homeruns experiencehomeruns japanese experiencejapanese infi
> elder outfielder dh

      Source |       SS       df       MS              Number of obs =     200
-------------+------------------------------           F(  9,   190) =   91.18
       Model |  261.509071     9  29.0565634           Prob > F      =  0.0000
    Residual |  60.5475457   190  .318671293           R-squared     =  0.8120
-------------+------------------------------           Adj R-squared =  0.8031
       Total |  322.056617   199  1.61837496           Root MSE      =  .56451

------------------------------------------------------------------------------
   logsalary |      Coef.   Std. Err.      t    P>|t|     [95% Conf. Interval]
-------------+----------------------------------------------------------------
         experience |   .4466241   .0293268    15.23   0.000     .3887762    .5044721
  experiencesquared |  -.0208433   .0021118    -9.87   0.000    -.0250089   -.0166776
           homeruns |   .0391909   .0063903     6.13   0.000     .0265859     .051796
experiencehomeruns  |   .0013656   .0009222     1.48   0.140    -.0004535    .0031846
           japanese |   3.160626   .6919481     4.57   0.000     1.795739    4.525513
 experiencejapanese |  -.2970561   .1605917    -1.85   0.066    -.6138278    .0197156
          infielder |   .3753179   .1195052     3.14   0.002     .1395904    .6110454
         outfielder |   .3287464   .1228449     2.68   0.008     .0864314    .5710614
                 dh |   .5707603   .3540859     1.61   0.109    -.1276841    1.269205
              _cons |   12.31758   .1282572    96.04   0.000     12.06459    12.57057
------------------------------------------------------------------------------

. estat ovtest

Ramsey RESET test using powers of the fitted values of logsalary
       Ho:  model has no omitted variables
                F(3, 187) =      6.32
                 Prob > F =      0.0004
```

CHAPTER 9

Most of the Stata commands used in this chapter have either been introduced in previous chapters or are introduced within the text. There is one additional useful tool worth mentioning. Many outside researchers have written Stata code that was not originally canned in the program but can be accessed with a simple Internet search through Stata. The tool for doing so is the "findit" command, which can be used to access the command for performing weighted least squares.

Using findit Command to Get the Canned WLS Command

1. Use findit to locate the command.

findit wls

2. Go to the downloadable WLS command.

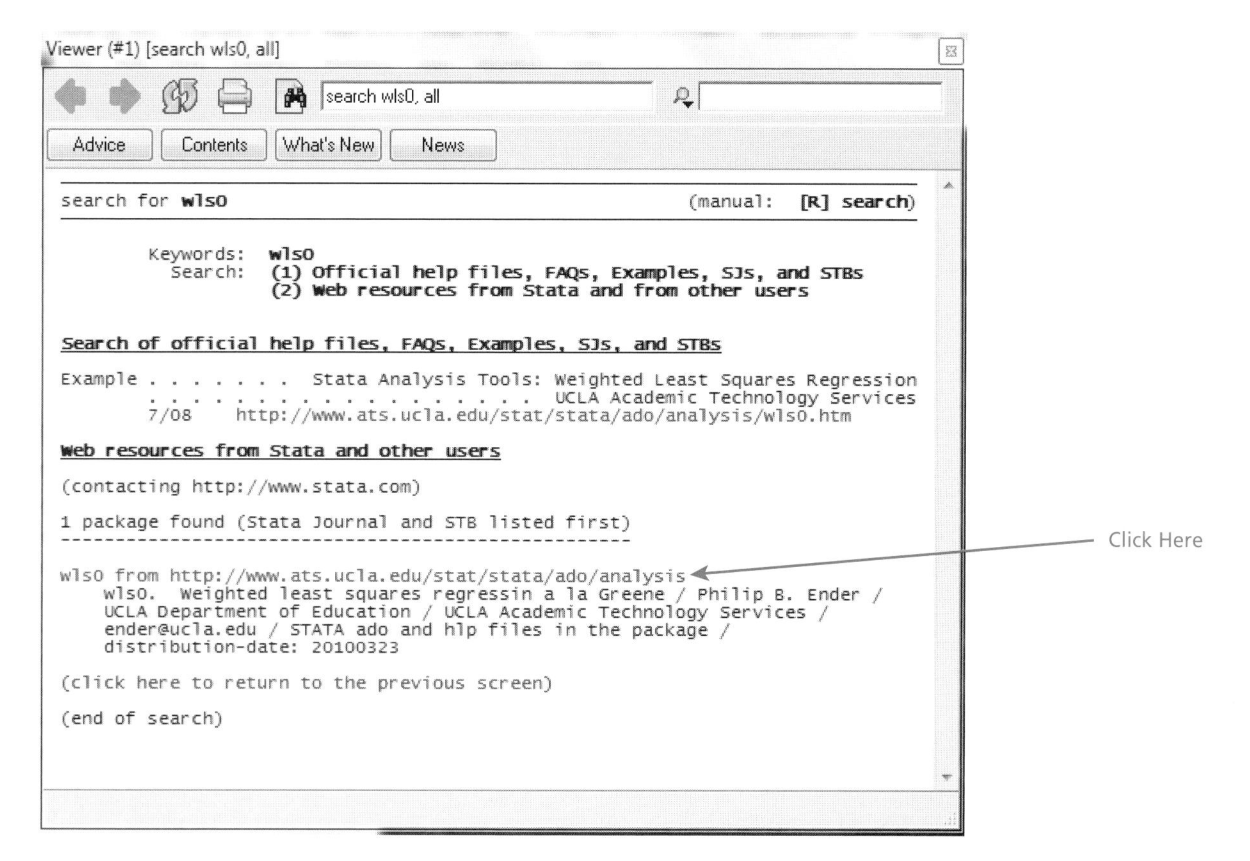

3. Install the command.

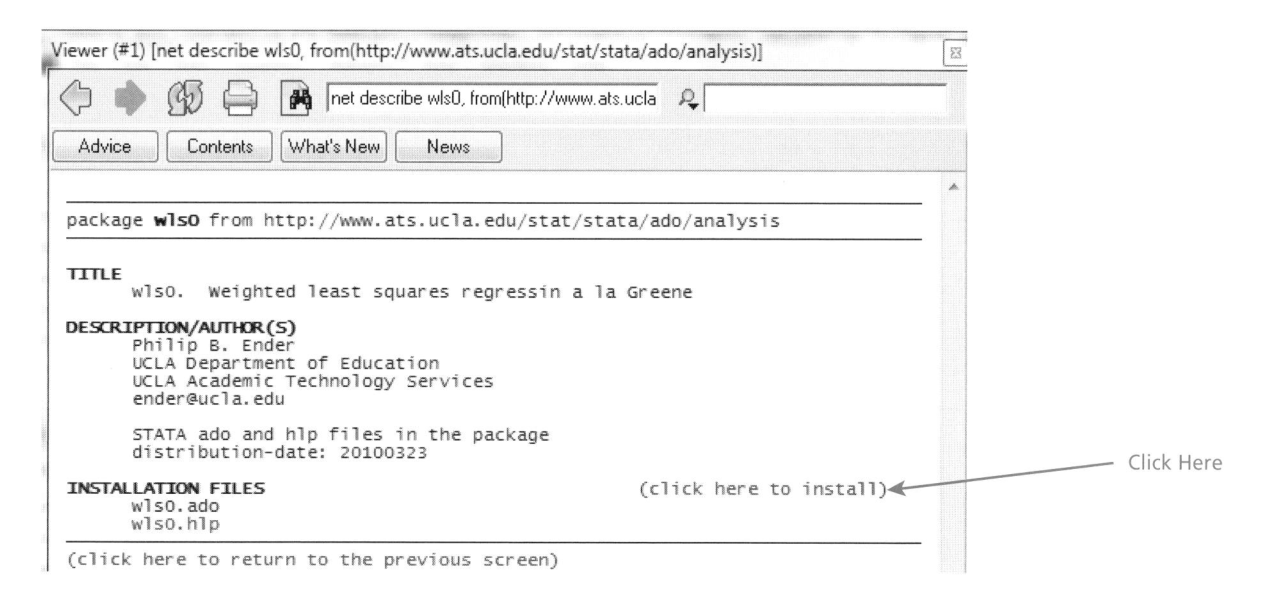

4. Run weighted least squares by typing

wls0 loanamount appincome, wvar(appincome) type(abse) noconst

```
. wls0 loanamount appincome, wvar(appincome) type(abse) noconst

WLS regression -  type: proportional to abs(e)

(sum of wgt is   1.8416e-05)

      Source |       SS       df       MS              Number of obs =   73046
-------------+------------------------------           F(  1, 73044) = 4811.51
       Model |  7.4829e+14     1  7.4829e+14           Prob > F      =  0.0000
    Residual |  1.1360e+16 73044  1.5552e+11           R-squared     =  0.0618
-------------+------------------------------           Adj R-squared =  0.0618
       Total |  1.2108e+16 73045  1.6576e+11           Root MSE      = 3.9e+05

------------------------------------------------------------------------------
  loanamount |      Coef.   Std. Err.      t    P>|t|     [95% Conf. Interval]
-------------+----------------------------------------------------------------
   appincome |  -1.812884   .0261354   -69.37   0.000     -1.86411   -1.761659
       _cons |   522950.2   1877.212   278.58   0.000     519270.9    526629.5
------------------------------------------------------------------------------
```

Estimating Our Model with White's Heteroskedastic Standard Errors

Run the desired regression while asking Stata to calculate White's heteroskedastic standard errors by typing

reg loanamount appincome, robust

```
. reg loanamount appincome, robust

Linear regression                                      Number of obs =   73046
                                                       F(  1, 73044) =  387.14
                                                       Prob > F      =  0.0000
                                                       R-squared     =  0.3933
                                                       Root MSE      = 3.0e+05

------------------------------------------------------------------------------
             |               Robust
  loanamount |      Coef.   Std. Err.      t    P>|t|     [95% Conf. Interval]
-------------+----------------------------------------------------------------
   appincome |   1.159802   .0589456    19.68   0.000     1.044269    1.275335
       _cons |   209474.6   9763.685    21.45   0.000     190337.8    228611.4
------------------------------------------------------------------------------
```

CHAPTER 11

Performing the Cochrane-Orcutt Procedure

1. Set the time variable by typing

tsset time

2. Ask Stata to run the Cochrane-Orcutt procedure by typing

prais housessold realgdp, corc

```
. tsset time
        time variable:  time, 1 to 79
                delta:  1 unit

. prais housessold realgdp, corc

Iteration 0:  rho = 0.0000
Iteration 1:  rho = 0.7976
Iteration 2:  rho = 0.7953
Iteration 3:  rho = 0.7951
Iteration 4:  rho = 0.7951
Iteration 5:  rho = 0.7951
Iteration 6:  rho = 0.7951

Cochrane-Orcutt AR(1) regression -- iterated estimates

      Source |       SS       df       MS              Number of obs =      78
-------------+------------------------------           F(  1,    76) =   89.16
       Model |  1.5467e+12     1  1.5467e+12           Prob > F      =  0.0000
    Residual |  1.3185e+12    76  1.7348e+10           R-squared     =  0.5398
-------------+------------------------------           Adj R-squared =  0.5338
       Total |  2.8652e+12    77  3.7210e+10           Root MSE      = 1.3e+05
```

```
------------------------------------------------------------------------------
  housessold |      Coef.   Std. Err.      t    P>|t|     [95% Conf. Interval]
-------------+----------------------------------------------------------------
     realgdp |   899.2937   95.24074     9.44   0.000     709.6053    1088.982
       _cons |   -2246219   506097.6    -4.44   0.000     -3254200    -1238239
-------------+----------------------------------------------------------------
         rho |   .7950685
------------------------------------------------------------------------------
Durbin-Watson statistic (original)    0.296015
Durbin-Watson statistic (transformed) 2.396826
```

Performing the Prais-Winsten Procedure

After setting the time variable, ask Stata to run the Prais-Winsten procedure by typing

prais housessold realgdp

```
. prais housessold realgdp

Iteration 0:  rho = 0.0000
Iteration 1:  rho = 0.7976
Iteration 2:  rho = 0.8213
Iteration 3:  rho = 0.8261
Iteration 4:  rho = 0.8272
Iteration 5:  rho = 0.8275
Iteration 6:  rho = 0.8276
Iteration 7:  rho = 0.8276
Iteration 8:  rho = 0.8276
Iteration 9:  rho = 0.8276
Iteration 10:  rho = 0.8276

Prais-Winsten AR(1) regression -- iterated estimates

      Source |       SS       df       MS              Number of obs =      79
-------------+------------------------------           F(  1,    77) =   88.20
       Model |  1.7611e+12     1  1.7611e+12           Prob > F      =  0.0000
    Residual |  1.5374e+12    77  1.9967e+10           R-squared     =  0.5339
-------------+------------------------------           Adj R-squared =  0.5279
       Total |  3.2986e+12    78  4.2289e+10           Root MSE      =  1.4e+05

------------------------------------------------------------------------------
  housessold |      Coef.   Std. Err.      t    P>|t|     [95% Conf. Interval]
-------------+----------------------------------------------------------------
     realgdp |   729.2792   105.0185     6.94   0.000     520.1605    938.3978
       _cons |   -1264514   546853.8    -2.31   0.023     -2353439     -175589
-------------+----------------------------------------------------------------
         rho |   .8276106
------------------------------------------------------------------------------
Durbin-Watson statistic (original)    0.296015
Durbin-Watson statistic (transformed) 2.329643
```

Estimating Our Model with Newey-West Robust Standard Errors

Ask Stata to calculate Newey-West robust standard errors for the desired regression by typing

newey housessold realgdp, lag(1)

```
. newey housessold realgdp, lag(1)

Regression with Newey-West standard errors          Number of obs  =        79
maximum lag: 1                                      F(  1,    77)  =    132.52
                                                    Prob > F       =    0.0000

------------------------------------------------------------------------------
             |             Newey-West
  housessold |      Coef.   Std. Err.      t    P>|t|     [95% Conf. Interval]
-------------+----------------------------------------------------------------
     realgdp |   780.7004   67.81807    11.51   0.000     645.6573    915.7434
       _cons |   -1587778   355317.1    -4.47   0.000     -2295305   -880251.2
------------------------------------------------------------------------------
```

Performing the Dickey-Fuller Test

Perform the Dickey-Fuller test by typing

dfgls housessold

```
. dfgls housessold

DF-GLS for housessold                                   Number of obs =    67
Maxlag = 11 chosen by Schwert criterion

               DF-GLS tau      1% Critical       5% Critical      10% Critical
  [lags]     Test Statistic        Value             Value             Value
------------------------------------------------------------------------------
    11           -1.005           -3.660            -2.731            -2.456
    10           -0.811           -3.660            -2.772            -2.496
    9            -0.956           -3.660            -2.813            -2.536
    8            -0.922           -3.660            -2.854            -2.576
    7            -1.173           -3.660            -2.894            -2.614
    6            -0.835           -3.660            -2.933            -2.651
    5            -0.859           -3.660            -2.971            -2.686
    4            -0.842           -3.660            -3.006            -2.718
    3            -0.863           -3.660            -3.038            -2.748
    2            -0.585           -3.660            -3.067            -2.774
    1            -0.601           -3.660            -3.093            -2.797

Opt Lag (Ng-Perron seq t) =  7 with RMSE    132022
Min SC   =  23.78632 at lag  1 with RMSE  137365.6
Min MAIC =  23.70235 at lag  1 with RMSE  137365.6
```

CHAPTER 12

Estimating a Logit Model

Estimate the logit model by typing

logit winner deminc repinc demopen repopen teaparty male oppmale forspend againstspend

```
. logit winner deminc repinc demopen repopen teaparty male oppmale forspend agai
> nstspend

Iteration 0:   log likelihood = -561.44922
Iteration 1:   log likelihood = -318.84967
Iteration 2:   log likelihood = -312.77374
Iteration 3:   log likelihood = -312.21519
Iteration 4:   log likelihood = -312.20605
Iteration 5:   log likelihood = -312.20604

Logistic regression                               Number of obs   =        810
                                                  LR chi2(9)      =     498.49
                                                  Prob > chi2     =     0.0000
Log likelihood = -312.20604                       Pseudo R2       =     0.4439

------------------------------------------------------------------------------
      winner |      Coef.   Std. Err.      z    P>|z|     [95% Conf. Interval]
-------------+----------------------------------------------------------------
      deminc |   2.967275   .3103075     9.56   0.000     2.359083    3.575466
      repinc |   5.962937    .761645     7.83   0.000      4.47014    7.455733
     demopen |   .1836913   .4932055     0.37   0.710    -.7829738    1.150356
     repopen |   3.401846   .4907102     6.93   0.000     2.440072     4.36362
    teaparty |   .9660699   .2948818     3.28   0.001     .3881122    1.544028
        male |   -.177663    .264799    -0.67   0.502    -.6966594    .3413335
     oppmale |   .1977196   .2817392     0.70   0.483     -.354479    .7499182
    forspend |   .2287115   .1156816     1.98   0.048     .0019798    .4554432
againstspend |  -.1770241   .1128644    -1.57   0.117    -.3982342    .0441859
       _cons |  -2.008893   .4041252    -4.97   0.000    -2.800964   -1.216822
------------------------------------------------------------------------------
```

Estimating the Marginal Effects

After estimating the logit model, ask Stata to calculate the desired marginal effects by typing

mfx

```
. mfx

Marginal effects after logit
      y  = Pr(winner) (predict)
         =  .55581565
```

variable	dy/dx	Std. Err.	z	P>|z|	[95% C.I.	]	X
deminc*	.563235	.04579	12.30	0.000	.47348	.65299	.285185
repinc*	.6748033	.02651	25.45	0.000	.622838	.726768	.164198
demopen*	.04483	.11874	0.38	0.706	-.187899	.277559	.050617
repopen*	.4563475	.03838	11.89	0.000	.381124	.531571	.050617
teaparty*	.2204441	.06111	3.61	0.000	.100668	.340221	.15679
male*	-.0435087	.06424	-0.68	0.498	-.169413	.082396	.833333
oppmale*	.0490823	.07019	0.70	0.484	-.088488	.186653	.833333
forspend	.0564653	.02857	1.98	0.048	.000468	.112462	1.12394
agains~d	-.0437045	.02788	-1.57	0.117	-.098342	.010933	1.12394

(*) dy/dx is for discrete change of dummy variable from 0 to 1

Estimating a Probit Model

Estimate the probit model by typing

probit winner deminc repinc demopen repopen teaparty male oppmale forspend againstspend

```
. probit winner deminc repinc demopen repopen teaparty male oppmale forspend aga
> instspend

Iteration 0:   log likelihood = -561.44922
Iteration 1:   log likelihood =  -318.3882
Iteration 2:   log likelihood = -312.03054
Iteration 3:   log likelihood =  -311.8847
Iteration 4:   log likelihood = -311.88457
Iteration 5:   log likelihood = -311.88457

Probit regression                                 Number of obs   =        810
                                                  LR chi2(9)      =     499.13
                                                  Prob > chi2     =     0.0000
Log likelihood = -311.88457                       Pseudo R2       =     0.4445
```

winner	Coef.	Std. Err.	z	P>|z|	[95% Conf.	Interval]
deminc	1.761182	.1726006	10.20	0.000	1.422891	2.099473
repinc	3.224084	.3149051	10.24	0.000	2.606882	3.841287
demopen	.07333	.2718819	0.27	0.787	-.4595488	.6062088
repopen	2.009734	.264883	7.59	0.000	1.490573	2.528895
teaparty	.5299228	.1616873	3.28	0.001	.2130215	.8468242
male	-.1027617	.1494487	-0.69	0.492	-.3956757	.1901524
oppmale	.1150382	.1558634	0.74	0.460	-.1904483	.4205248
forspend	.1397388	.0638097	2.19	0.029	.0146742	.2648034
againstspend	-.0996007	.0621208	-1.60	0.109	-.2213553	.0221539
_cons	-1.191391	.2238707	-5.32	0.000	-1.630169	-.7526123

After estimating the probit model, ask Stata to calculate the desired marginal effects by typing

mfx

```
. mfx

Marginal effects after probit
      y  = Pr(winner) (predict)
         =  .53352259
```

variable	dy/dx	Std. Err.	z	P>|z|	[95% C.I.	]	X
deminc*	.5724474	.04158	13.77	0.000	.490946	.653949	.285185
repinc*	.6692059	.02395	27.94	0.000	.622261	.716151	.164198
demopen*	.0290482	.10724	0.27	0.786	-.181148	.239244	.050617
repopen*	.4838426	.03032	15.96	0.000	.42442	.543265	.050617
teaparty*	.2018628	.05777	3.49	0.000	.088635	.315091	.15679
male*	-.0406921	.05889	-0.69	0.490	-.156111	.074727	.833333
oppmale*	.0458203	.06212	0.74	0.461	-.075931	.167572	.833333
forspend	.0555508	.02538	2.19	0.029	.005804	.105298	1.12394
agains~d	-.0395946	.02468	-1.60	0.109	-.087975	.008786	1.12394

(*) dy/dx is for discrete change of dummy variable from 0 to 1

Estimating a Multinomial Logit Model

Estimate the multinomial logit model by typing

mlogit highdegree male black hisp asian othrace age married ownhome income metro uscit, base(0)

Note: We must include the command ', base(0)' to have STATA treat less than high school as the base group. If we do not, Stata's default is to treat the modal group as the base group, which in this case would be high school diploma, which is outcome 1 in this case.

```
. mlogit highdegree male black hisp asian othrace age married ownhome income met
> ro uscit, base(0)

Iteration 0:   log likelihood = -350963.13
Iteration 1:   log likelihood = -333602.46
Iteration 2:   log likelihood = -325935.51
Iteration 3:   log likelihood = -325083.72
Iteration 4:   log likelihood = -324995.64
Iteration 5:   log likelihood = -324995.48
Iteration 6:   log likelihood = -324995.48

Multinomial logistic regression                   Number of obs   =     194753
                                                  LR chi2(66)     =   51935.30
                                                  Prob > chi2     =     0.0000
Log likelihood = -324995.48                       Pseudo R2       =     0.0740

------------------------------------------------------------------------------
  highdegree |      Coef.   Std. Err.      z    P>|z|     [95% Conf. Interval]
-------------+----------------------------------------------------------------
0            |  (base outcome)
-------------+----------------------------------------------------------------
1            |
        male |  -.1533926   .0172264    -8.90   0.000    -.1871557   -.1196295
       black |   -.570631   .0263921   -21.62   0.000    -.6223585   -.5189034
        hisp |  -1.525498   .0256597   -59.45   0.000    -1.575791   -1.475206
       asian |  -.7513452   .0462911   -16.23   0.000    -.8420741   -.6606164
     othrace |   -.575723   .0502426   -11.46   0.000    -.6741967   -.4772492
         age |  -.0228685   .0006058   -37.75   0.000    -.0240559   -.0216812
     married |   .0892914   .0183635     4.86   0.000     .0532995    .1252833
     ownhome |   .2190859   .0198527    11.04   0.000     .1801752    .2579965
      income |   .1155384    .003501    33.00   0.000     .1086766    .1224003
       metro |   .2475061   .0194277    12.74   0.000     .2094284    .2855837
       uscit |   .8989614   .0295879    30.38   0.000     .8409701    .9569527
       _cons |   .9656863   .0500575    19.29   0.000     .8675754    1.063797
-------------+----------------------------------------------------------------
2            |
        male |   -.210114   .0200727   -10.47   0.000    -.2494558   -.1707722
       black |  -.7275855   .0312207   -23.30   0.000     -.788777    -.666394
        hisp |  -1.902281   .0337794   -56.31   0.000    -1.968488   -1.836075
       asian |  -1.079328   .0606528   -17.80   0.000    -1.198205   -.9604505
     othrace |  -.4945934   .0572962    -8.63   0.000     -.606892   -.3822949
         age |  -.0378209   .0007138   -52.99   0.000    -.0392198   -.0364219
     married |  -.0321862     .02153    -1.49   0.135    -.0743841    .0100118
     ownhome |   .2659414   .0237752    11.19   0.000     .2193428    .3125401
      income |   .1677257   .0036992    45.34   0.000     .1604754    .1749761
       metro |   .5934945   .0233588    25.41   0.000      .547712    .6392769
       uscit |   1.762638   .0484022    36.42   0.000     1.667772    1.857505
       _cons |  -.2345761   .0669483    -3.50   0.000    -.3657925   -.1033598
-------------+----------------------------------------------------------------
3            |
        male |  -.1583278   .0180685    -8.76   0.000    -.1937415   -.1229142
       black |   -.487447   .0273998   -17.79   0.000    -.5411495   -.4337444
        hisp |  -1.743735   .0282849   -61.65   0.000    -1.799172   -1.688297
       asian |  -.6693378   .0484402   -13.82   0.000    -.7642788   -.5743967
     othrace |  -.3137187   .0507627    -6.18   0.000    -.4132117   -.2142256
         age |  -.0355082   .0006414   -55.36   0.000    -.0367653   -.0342511
     married |  -.0510816   .0192999    -2.65   0.008    -.0889087   -.0132546
     ownhome |   .3883777   .0212412    18.28   0.000     .3467456    .4300098
      income |   .1733844   .0035046    49.47   0.000     .1665154    .1802533
       metro |   .4152281   .0206466    20.11   0.000     .3747615    .4556947
       uscit |   1.273972   .0344121    37.02   0.000     1.206526    1.341419
       _cons |   .6063588   .0543474    11.16   0.000     .4998399    .7128777
------------------------------------------------------------------------------
```

To get STATA to calculate marginal effects, we again use the mfx command. In this case, however, the command is a little more complicated because there are more than two potential values for the dependent variable. Hence, the commands we need are as follows.

To get estimated marginal effects for outcome 1, type

```
mfx, predict(p outcome(1))
```

To get estimated marginal effects for outcome 2, type

```
mfx, predict(p outcome(2))
```

and so on through the maximum outcome (outcome 6 in this case).

```
. mfx, predict(p outcome(1))

Marginal effects after mlogit
      y  = Pr(highdegree==1) (predict, p outcome(1))
         =  .27770986
```

variable	dy/dx	Std. Err.	z	P>|z|	[95%	C.I.]	X
male*	-.0014822	.00214	-0.69	0.489	-.005677	.002712	.469831
black*	.0197922	.00356	5.55	0.000	.012807	.026777	.105477
hisp*	.0240947	.00406	5.94	0.000	.016145	.032044	.095716
asian*	-.0688026	.00529	-13.02	0.000	-.079163	-.058442	.041874
othrace*	-.011665	.00644	-1.81	0.070	-.024289	.000959	.026279
age	.0021565	.00008	28.25	0.000	.002007	.002306	53.4847
married*	.0185571	.00232	8.00	0.000	.014009	.023106	.645089
ownhome*	-.0351874	.00279	-12.63	0.000	-.040649	-.029726	.772455
income	-.0151813	.00032	-47.71	0.000	-.015805	-.014558	6.26124
metro*	-.0655641	.00261	-25.10	0.000	-.070684	-.060444	.766782
uscit*	-.0349601	.00522	-6.70	0.000	-.045186	-.024734	.935195

(*) dy/dx is for discrete change of dummy variable from 0 to 1

```
. mfx, predict(p outcome(2))

Marginal effects after mlogit
      y  = Pr(highdegree==2) (predict, p outcome(2))
         =  .13339476
```

variable	dy/dx	Std. Err.	z	P>|z|	[95%	C.I.]	X
male*	-.0082538	.00162	-5.10	0.000	-.011426	-.005081	.469831
black*	-.0112116	.0025	-4.48	0.000	-.01612	-.006303	.105477
hisp*	-.0338524	.00264	-12.83	0.000	-.039024	-.02868	.095716
asian*	-.0622957	.00342	-18.23	0.000	-.068992	-.055599	.041874
othrace*	.0051863	.00491	1.06	0.290	-.004428	.014801	.026279
age	-.0009587	.00006	-16.46	0.000	-.001073	-.000845	53.4847
married*	-.0072561	.0018	-4.03	0.000	-.010789	-.003723	.645089
ownhome*	-.0103147	.00212	-4.87	0.000	-.014467	-.006162	.772455
income	-.0003306	.00021	-1.54	0.124	-.000752	.00009	6.26124
metro*	.0157249	.00185	8.52	0.000	.012106	.019344	.766782
uscit*	.0730122	.00286	25.52	0.000	.067404	.07862	.935195

(*) dy/dx is for discrete change of dummy variable from 0 to 1

Estimating an Ordered Probit Model

Estimate the ordered probit model by typing

```
oprobit highdegree male black hisp asian othrace age married ownhome
income metro uscit
```

```
. oprobit highdegree male black hisp asian othrace age married ownhome income me
> tro uscit

Iteration 0:   log likelihood = -350963.13
Iteration 1:   log likelihood = -330228.84
Iteration 2:   log likelihood = -330197.81
Iteration 3:   log likelihood = -330197.81

Ordered probit regression                         Number of obs   =     194753
                                                  LR chi2(11)     =   41530.64
                                                  Prob > chi2     =     0.0000
Log likelihood = -330197.81                       Pseudo R2       =     0.0592

------------------------------------------------------------------------------
  highdegree |      Coef.   Std. Err.      z    P>|z|     [95% Conf. Interval]
-------------+----------------------------------------------------------------
        male |   .0047304   .0047346     1.00   0.318    -.0045493      .01401
       black |  -.2444167   .0079472   -30.76   0.000     -.259993   -.2288405
        hisp |  -.7690341   .0090969   -84.54   0.000    -.7868637   -.7512045
       asian |   .1966657   .0122147    16.10   0.000     .1727253    .2206061
     othrace |  -.1966015    .014777   -13.30   0.000     -.225564    -.167639
         age |  -.0094343   .0001691   -55.79   0.000    -.0097658   -.0091029
     married |   .0061168   .0052168     1.17   0.241     -.004108    .0163416
     ownhome |   .1837842   .0060887    30.18   0.000     .1718506    .1957178
      income |   .0581012   .0004658   124.73   0.000     .0571882    .0590142
       metro |   .2563663   .0056772    45.16   0.000     .2452391    .2674935
       uscit |   .3825629   .0108822    35.15   0.000     .3612341    .4038916
-------------+----------------------------------------------------------------
       /cut1 |  -.8967788   .0155429                     -.9272423   -.8663153
       /cut2 |   .1102635    .015366                      .0801468    .1403802
       /cut3 |   .4529626    .015366                      .4228458    .4830795
       /cut4 |   1.070267   .0154452                      1.039995    1.100539
       /cut5 |   1.821578   .0157319                      1.790744    1.852412
       /cut6 |   2.549235   .0164972                      2.516901    2.581568
------------------------------------------------------------------------------
```

To get estimated marginal effects for outcome 1, type

mfx, predict(p outcome(1))

To get estimated marginal effects for outcome 2, type

mfx, predict(p outcome(2))

and so on through the maximum outcome (outcome 6 in this case).

```
. mfx, predict(p outcome(1))

Marginal effects after oprobit
      y  = Pr(highdegree==1) (predict, p outcome(1))
         =  .27468311
------------------------------------------------------------------------------
variable |      dy/dx    Std. Err.     z    P>|z|  [    95% C.I.   ]      X
---------+--------------------------------------------------------------------
   male* |  -.0010256      .00103   -1.00   0.318  -.003038  .000986   .469831
  black* |   .0502471      .00154   32.66   0.000   .047231  .053263   .105477
   hisp* |   .1221851      .00101  120.98   0.000   .120206  .124165   .095716
  asian* |  -.0435831      .00274  -15.91   0.000  -.048951 -.038215   .041874
othrace* |   .0405793      .00286   14.18   0.000    .03497  .046189   .026279
     age |   .0020454      .00004   53.79   0.000   .001971   .00212   53.4847
married* |  -.0013257      .00113   -1.17   0.241  -.003541   .00089   .645089
ownhome* |  -.0388634      .00126  -30.80   0.000  -.041337  -.03639   .772455
  income |  -.0125964      .00011 -109.91   0.000  -.012821 -.012372   6.26124
  metro* |  -.0535385      .00116  -46.29   0.000  -.055805 -.051272   .766782
  uscit* |  -.0741832      .00181  -40.99   0.000  -.077731 -.070636   .935195
------------------------------------------------------------------------------
(*) dy/dx is for discrete change of dummy variable from 0 to 1

. mfx, predict(p outcome(2))

Marginal effects after oprobit
      y  = Pr(highdegree==2) (predict, p outcome(2))
         =  .13379581
------------------------------------------------------------------------------
variable |      dy/dx    Std. Err.     z    P>|z|  [    95% C.I.   ]      X
---------+--------------------------------------------------------------------
   male* |  -.0001152      .00012   -1.00   0.318  -.000342  .000111   .469831
  black* |   .0028432      .00009   30.65   0.000   .002661  .003025   .105477
   hisp* |  -.0121527      .00055  -22.23   0.000  -.013224 -.011081   .095716
  asian* |  -.0069585      .00057  -12.28   0.000  -.008069 -.005848   .041874
othrace* |   .0023788       .0007   31.88   0.000   .002233  .002525   .026279
     age |   .0002297      .00001   38.99   0.000   .000218  .000241   53.4847
married* |  -.0001482      .00013   -1.18   0.239  -.000395  .000098   .645089
ownhome* |  -.0032669       .0001  -33.47   0.000  -.003458 -.003076   .772455
  income |  -.0014144      .00003  -53.23   0.000  -.001466 -.001362   6.26124
  metro* |  -.0039258       .0001  -37.91   0.000  -.004129 -.003723   .766782
  uscit* |   -.000873      .00026   -3.34   0.001  -.001385 -.000361   .935195
------------------------------------------------------------------------------
(*) dy/dx is for discrete change of dummy variable from 0 to 1
```

CHAPTER 13

Estimating the Fixed-Effects Model

1. Declare the data to be panel data by typing

```
xtset teamid
```

2. Estimate the fixed-effects panel data model by typing

```
xtreg value attendance attendancesquared fancostindex
    fancostindexsquared wins playoffs, fe
```

Estimating the Random-Effects Model

After declaring the data to be panel data, estimate the random-effects panel data model by typing

```
xtreg value attendance attendancesquared fancostindex
    fancostindexsquared wins playoffs, re
```

CHAPTER 14

Estimating the Demand Equation by Two-Stage Least Squares

```
use gasdata
```

Estimate the desired two-stage least squares regression by typing

```
ivreg quantity income (pricepergallon=income crudeprice)
```

Dependent Variable **Demand Shifter** **Independent Variable** **Demand Shifter** **Supply Shifter**

```
. ivreg quantity income (pricepergallon= income crudeprice)

Instrumental variables (2SLS) regression

      Source |       SS       df       MS              Number of obs =     236
-------------+------------------------------           F(  2,   233) =  877.58
       Model |  3.1299e+11     2  1.5650e+11           Prob > F      =  0.0000
    Residual |  4.1671e+10   233   178844463           R-squared     =  0.8825
-------------+------------------------------           Adj R-squared =  0.8815
       Total |  3.5466e+11   235  1.5092e+09           Root MSE      =   13373

------------------------------------------------------------------------------
    quantity |      Coef.   Std. Err.      t    P>|t|     [95% Conf. Interval]
-------------+----------------------------------------------------------------
priceperga~n |  -4270.794   2536.089    -1.68   0.094     -9267.39    725.8012 *
      income |   16.33847   .7251613    22.53   0.000     14.90976    17.76718 **
       _cons |   139351.1   3416.916    40.78   0.000     132619.1    146083.1 **
------------------------------------------------------------------------------
Instrumented:  pricepergallon
Instruments:   income crudeprice
------------------------------------------------------------------------------
```

Estimating the Supply Equation by Two-Stage Least Squares

Estimate the desired two-stage least squares regression by typing

```
ivreg quantity crudeprice (pricepergallon=income crudeprice)
```

```
. ivreg quantity crudeprice (pricepergallon= income crudeprice)

Instrumental variables (2SLS) regression

      Source |       SS       df       MS              Number of obs =     236
-------------+------------------------------           F(  2,   233) =  162.29
       Model |  1.2933e+11     2  6.4664e+10           Prob > F      =  0.0000
    Residual |  2.2533e+11   233   967093402           R-squared     =  0.3647
-------------+------------------------------           Adj R-squared =  0.3592
       Total |  3.5466e+11   235  1.5092e+09           Root MSE      =   31098

------------------------------------------------------------------------------
    quantity |      Coef.   Std. Err.      t    P>|t|     [95% Conf. Interval]
-------------+----------------------------------------------------------------
priceperga~n |   260219.1    22400.1    11.62   0.000     216086.5    304351.7
  crudeprice |  -6590.274   680.1788    -9.69   0.000    -7930.361   -5250.188
       _cons |   66012.33   14540.73     4.54   0.000     37364.21    94660.45
------------------------------------------------------------------------------
Instrumented:  pricepergallon
Instruments:   crudeprice income
------------------------------------------------------------------------------
```

Estimating the Endogenous Independent Variable by Two-Stage Least Squares

Estimate the desired two-stage least squares regression by typing

ivreg quantity crudeprice (pricepergallon=income crudeprice)

```
. ivreg bingedays male married black othrace age2544 age4564 age6569 (quitdrink=
> losewgt exercise)

Instrumental variables (2SLS) regression

      Source |       SS       df       MS              Number of obs =   14589
-------------+------------------------------           F(  8, 14580) =   68.23
       Model |  1105818.83     8  138227.354           Prob > F      =  0.0000
    Residual |  28738146.6 14580   1971.0663           R-squared     =  0.0371
-------------+------------------------------           Adj R-squared =  0.0365
       Total |  29843965.4 14588  2045.78869           Root MSE      =  44.397

------------------------------------------------------------------------------
   bingedays |      Coef.   Std. Err.      t    P>|t|     [95% Conf. Interval]
-------------+----------------------------------------------------------------
   quitdrink |   1.118142   3.905059     0.29   0.775    -6.536269    8.772553
        male |   15.28697   .7499257    20.38   0.000     13.81702    16.75692
     married |   -7.45334    .749442    -9.95   0.000    -8.922342   -5.984339
       black |   .2159593   1.184429     0.18   0.855    -2.105672    2.537591
     othrace |  -5.176274   2.097967    -2.47   0.014    -9.288554   -1.063993
     age2544 |   5.958711   1.991495     2.99   0.003     2.055128    9.862294
     age4564 |   4.303662   2.000175     2.15   0.031     .3830655    8.224259
     age6569 |   .0070775   2.535214     0.00   0.998    -4.962264    4.976419
       _cons |   3.747557   1.997955     1.88   0.061    -.1686867    7.663801
------------------------------------------------------------------------------
Instrumented:  quitdrink
Instruments:   male married black othrace age2544 age4564 age6569 losewgt
               exercise
------------------------------------------------------------------------------
```

CHAPTER 15

Estimating Quantile Regressions

Ask Stata to run regressions for the 10th, 25th, 50th, 75th, and 90th, percentiles by typing

qreg gdpcapita edexp lifeexp unemprate, quantile(.10)
qreg gdpcapita edexp lifeexp unemprate, quantile(.25)
qreg gdpcapita edexp lifeexp unemprate, quantile(.50)
qreg gdpcapita edexp lifeexp unemprate, quantile(.75)
qreg gdpcapita edexp lifeexp unemprate, quantile(.90)

```
. qreg gdpcapita edexp lifeexp unemprate, quantile(.10)
Iteration  1:  WLS sum of weighted deviations =  1095795.5

Iteration  1: sum of abs. weighted deviations =  1115473.5
Iteration  2: sum of abs. weighted deviations =  1055078.2
Iteration  3: sum of abs. weighted deviations =  963662.07
Iteration  4: sum of abs. weighted deviations =  432519.27
Iteration  5: sum of abs. weighted deviations =  427182.13
Iteration  6: sum of abs. weighted deviations =  426137.83
Iteration  7: sum of abs. weighted deviations =  425664.81
Iteration  8: sum of abs. weighted deviations =  424951.28
Iteration  9: sum of abs. weighted deviations =  424129.45
Iteration 10: sum of abs. weighted deviations =  424003.13
Iteration 11: sum of abs. weighted deviations =   423995.9

.1 Quantile regression                          Number of obs =       155
  Raw sum of deviations 470821.8 (about 1928.3452)
  Min sum of deviations 423995.9                Pseudo R2     =    0.0995
```

gdpcapita	Coef.	Std. Err.	t	P>|t|	[95% Conf.	Interval]
edexp	44.04438	172.7389	0.25	0.799	-297.2529	385.3417
lifeexp	220.0777	30.06012	7.32	0.000	160.6849	279.4704 **
unemprate	-34.76091	24.88074	-1.40	0.164	-83.92024	14.39843
_cons	-11868.58	2872.485	-4.13	0.000	-17544.03	-6193.124 **

Estimating a Poisson Model

Estimate the Poisson model by typing

poisson total nrcrank star ranked pubbyphd cowadv male intlstu

```
. poisson total nrcrank star ranked pubbyphd cowadv male intlstu

Iteration 0:   log likelihood = -2542.5886
Iteration 1:   log likelihood = -2540.9512
Iteration 2:   log likelihood = -2540.9507
Iteration 3:   log likelihood = -2540.9507

Poisson regression                                Number of obs   =        681
                                                  LR chi2(7)      =    1929.56
                                                  Prob > chi2     =     0.0000
Log likelihood = -2540.9507                       Pseudo R2       =     0.2752
```

total	Coef.	Std. Err.	z	P>|z|	[95% Conf.	Interval]
nrcrank	-.0136917	.0009657	-14.18	0.000	-.0155845	-.0117989
star	.294332	.0491217	5.99	0.000	.1980552	.3906089
ranked	.1582752	.0498576	3.17	0.002	.0605562	.2559942
pubbyphd	1.037896	.0398704	26.03	0.000	.9597514	1.11604
cowadv	.6280391	.0413019	15.21	0.000	.5470889	.7089893
male	.0135992	.0522141	0.26	0.795	-.0887385	.115937
intlstu	-.042324	.0381075	-1.11	0.267	-.1170134	.0323654
_cons	1.179465	.0606389	19.45	0.000	1.060615	1.298315

To get estimated marginal effects, type

mfx

```
. mfx

Marginal effects after poisson
      y  = Predicted number of events (predict)
         =  3.2094416
```

variable	dy/dx	Std. Err.	z	P>|z|	[95% C.I.	]	X
nrcrank	-.0439428	.00295	-14.91	0.000	-.04972	-.038166	32.1057
star*	1.050542	.19569	5.37	0.000	.666992	1.43409	.151248
ranked*	.5338778	.17661	3.02	0.003	.187724	.880032	.192364
pubbyphd*	4.536737	.22179	20.45	0.000	4.10203	4.97144	.245228
cowadv*	2.517947	.20244	12.44	0.000	2.12117	2.91472	.171806
male*	.0434545	.16612	0.26	0.794	-.282143	.369052	.823789
intlstu*	-.1360111	.12258	-1.11	0.267	-.376265	.104242	.528634

(*) dy/dx is for discrete change of dummy variable from 0 to 1

Estimating a Negative Binomial Model

Estimate the negative binomial model by typing

nbreg total nrcrank star ranked pubbyphd cowadv male intlstu

```
. nbreg total nrcrank star ranked pubbyphd cowadv male intlstu

Fitting Poisson model:

Iteration 0:   log likelihood = -2542.5886
Iteration 1:   log likelihood = -2540.9512
Iteration 2:   log likelihood = -2540.9507
Iteration 3:   log likelihood = -2540.9507

Fitting constant-only model:

Iteration 0:   log likelihood = -1759.1282
Iteration 1:   log likelihood =  -1653.131
Iteration 2:   log likelihood = -1653.0696
Iteration 3:   log likelihood = -1653.0696

Fitting full model:

Iteration 0:   log likelihood = -1577.3708
Iteration 1:   log likelihood = -1537.4114
Iteration 2:   log likelihood = -1536.2369
Iteration 3:   log likelihood = -1536.2366
Iteration 4:   log likelihood = -1536.2366

Negative binomial regression                      Number of obs   =        681
                                                  LR chi2(7)      =     233.67
Dispersion     = mean                             Prob > chi2     =     0.0000
Log likelihood = -1536.2366                       Pseudo R2       =     0.0707
```

total	Coef.	Std. Err.	z	P>|z|	[95% Conf.	Interval]
nrcrank	-.0181461	.0023018	-7.88	0.000	-.0226576	-.0136346
star	.4158954	.1623826	2.56	0.010	.0976314	.7341595
ranked	.2536018	.1459509	1.74	0.082	-.0324566	.5396603
pubbyphd	1.246756	.1240184	10.05	0.000	1.003684	1.489827
cowadv	.9103349	.1417215	6.42	0.000	.6325659	1.188104
male	.0123702	.147579	0.08	0.933	-.2768793	.3016197
intlstu	-.0134877	.113861	-0.12	0.906	-.2366512	.2096758
_cons	1.082933	.1654298	6.55	0.000	.7586962	1.407169
/lnalpha	.4380058	.0784391			.2842679	.5917436
alpha	1.549614	.1215503			1.328789	1.807137

```
Likelihood-ratio test of alpha=0:  chibar2(01) = 2009.43 Prob>=chibar2 = 0.000
```

To get estimated marginal effects, type

mfx

```
. mfx

Marginal effects after nbreg
      y  = Predicted number of events (predict)
         =  2.936525
```

variable	dy/dx	Std. Err.	z	P>|z|	[95% C.I.	]	X
nrcrank	-.0532864	.00704	-7.57	0.000	-.067082	-.039491	32.1057
star*	1.422117	.64775	2.20	0.028	.152548	2.69169	.151248
ranked*	.8072938	.50461	1.60	0.110	-.181717	1.7963	.192364
pubbyphd*	5.362114	.80003	6.70	0.000	3.79409	6.93014	.245228
cowadv*	3.729763	.8076	4.62	0.000	2.14689	5.31263	.171806
male*	.0361804	.42992	0.08	0.933	-.806438	.878799	.823789
intlstu*	-.0396227	.33462	-0.12	0.906	-.69546	.616214	.528634

```
(*) dy/dx is for discrete change of dummy variable from 0 to 1
```

Estimating Heckman Two-Stage Regressions

Estimate the Heckman sample selection correction model by typing

heckman lsalary male age age2 married educ black asian othrace, select(childrenu6 male age age2 married educ black asian othrace)

```
. heckman lsalary male age age2 married educ black asian othrace, select(childre
> nu6 male age age2 married educ black asian othrace)

Iteration 0:   log likelihood = -155797.29  (not concave)
Iteration 1:   log likelihood = -155797.28  (not concave)
Iteration 2:   log likelihood = -155797.28  (not concave)
Iteration 3:   log likelihood = -155797.27  (not concave)
Iteration 4:   log likelihood = -155797.27  (not concave)
Iteration 5:   log likelihood = -155797.27  (not concave)
Iteration 6:   log likelihood = -155797.26  (not concave)
Iteration 7:   log likelihood = -155797.26  (not concave)
Iteration 8:   log likelihood = -155797.26  (not concave)
Iteration 9:   log likelihood = -155797.25  (not concave)
Iteration 10:  log likelihood = -155797.25  (not concave)
Iteration 11:  log likelihood = -155797.24  (not concave)
Iteration 12:  log likelihood = -155797.24  (not concave)
Iteration 13:  log likelihood = -155797.23  (not concave)
Iteration 14:  log likelihood =    -154544  (not concave)
Iteration 15:  log likelihood = -152244.59
Iteration 16:  log likelihood = -151172.06
Iteration 17:  log likelihood = -151081.26
Iteration 18:  log likelihood = -151080.85
Iteration 19:  log likelihood = -151080.85

Heckman selection model                         Number of obs      =    100731
(regression model with sample selection)        Censored obs       =     23129
                                                Uncensored obs     =     77602

                                                Wald chi2(8)       =   7580.56
Log likelihood = -151080.8                      Prob > chi2        =    0.0000

------------------------------------------------------------------------------
     lsalary |      Coef.   Std. Err.      z    P>|z|     [95% Conf. Interval]
-------------+----------------------------------------------------------------
lsalary      |
        male |   .3043176   .0075768    40.16   0.000     .2894674    .3191678
         age |   .0830065   .0026124    31.77   0.000     .0778863    .0881267
        age2 |  -.0008213   .0000288   -28.52   0.000    -.0008777   -.0007648
     married |   .0852341   .0081503    10.46   0.000     .0692598    .1012085
        educ |   .0964123   .0016026    60.16   0.000     .0932713    .0995533
       black |  -.0371814   .0121271    -3.07   0.002      -.06095   -.0134127
       asian |   .0657361   .0255719     2.57   0.010      .015616    .1158561
     othrace |  -.0274396   .0206981    -1.33   0.185    -.0680072    .0131279
       _cons |   7.235784   .0603703   119.86   0.000      7.11746    7.354107
-------------+----------------------------------------------------------------
select       |
  childrenu6 |  -.0735301   .0060047   -12.25   0.000    -.0852992   -.0617611
        male |   .2201362   .0083119    26.48   0.000     .2038452    .2364271
         age |  -.0027502   .0028262    -0.97   0.330    -.0082894     .002789
        age2 |  -.0000363   .0000308    -1.18   0.239    -.0000966    .0000241
     married |   .0639605   .0089447     7.15   0.000     .0464292    .0814918
        educ |     .08055   .0018215    44.22   0.000     .0769799    .0841201
       black |  -.0974382   .0127112    -7.67   0.000    -.1223517   -.0725247
       asian |  -.0411779   .0268741    -1.53   0.125    -.0938501    .0114944
     othrace |  -.0970935   .0214981    -4.52   0.000     -.139229    -.054958
       _cons |  -.3331657   .0657207    -5.07   0.000    -.4619759   -.2043556
-------------+----------------------------------------------------------------
     /athrho |  -1.650197    .009456  -174.51   0.000     -1.66873   -1.631663
    /lnsigma |   .1197583   .0029804    40.18   0.000     .1139168    .1255998
-------------+----------------------------------------------------------------
         rho |  -.9288846   .0012971                     -.9313836   -.9262981
       sigma |   1.127224   .0033596                      1.120659    1.133828
      lambda |  -1.047061    .004039                     -1.054978   -1.039145
------------------------------------------------------------------------------
LR test of indep. eqns. (rho = 0):   chi2(1) =  9432.72   Prob > chi2 = 0.0000
------------------------------------------------------------------------------
```

Appendix C: Statistical Tables

TABLE C.1
Standardized Normal Table (Z)

Example

Pr $(0 \leq Z \leq 1.96) = 0.4750$
Pr $(Z \geq 1.96) = 0.5 - 0.4750 = 0.025$

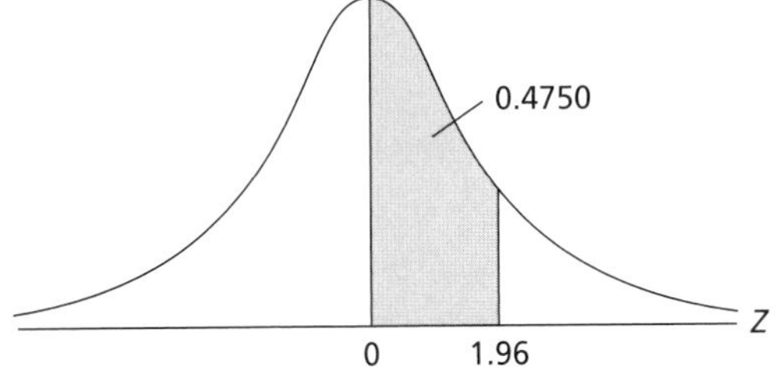

Z	.00	.01	.02	.03	.04	.05	.06	.07	.08	.09
0.0	.0000	.0040	.0080	.0120	.0160	.0199	.0239	.0279	.0319	.0359
0.1	.0398	.0438	.0478	.0517	.0557	.0596	.0636	.0675	.0714	.0753
0.2	.0793	.0832	.0871	.0910	.0948	.0987	.1026	.1064	.1103	.1141
0.3	.1179	.1217	.1255	.1293	.1331	.1368	.1406	.1443	.1480	.1517
0.4	.1554	.1591	.1628	.1664	.1700	.1736	.1772	.1808	.1844	.1879
0.5	.1915	.1950	.1985	.2019	.2054	.2088	.2123	.2157	.2190	.2224
0.6	.2257	.2291	.2324	.2357	.2389	.2422	.2454	.2486	.2517	.2549
0.7	.2580	.2611	.2642	.2673	.2704	.2734	.2764	.2794	.2823	.2852
0.8	.2881	.2910	.2939	.2967	.2995	.3023	.3051	.3078	.3106	.3133
0.9	.3159	.3186	.3212	.3238	.3264	.3289	.3315	.3340	.3365	.3389
1.0	.3413	.3438	.3461	.3485	.3508	.3531	.3554	.3577	.3599	.3621
1.1	.3643	.3665	.3686	.3708	.3729	.3749	.3770	.3790	.3810	.3830
1.2	.3849	.3869	.3888	.3907	.3925	.3944	.3962	.3980	.3997	.4015
1.3	.4032	.4049	.4066	.4082	.4099	.4115	.4131	.4147	.4162	.4177
1.4	.4192	.4207	.4222	.4236	.4251	.4265	.4279	.4292	.4306	.4319
1.5	.4332	.4345	.4357	.4370	.4382	.4394	.4406	.4418	.4429	.4441
1.6	.4452	.4463	.4474	.4484	.4495	.4505	.4515	.4525	.4535	.4545
1.7	.4454	.4564	.4573	.4582	.4591	.4599	.4608	.4616	.4625	.4633
1.8	.4641	.4649	.4656	.4664	.4671	.4678	.4686	.4693	.4699	.4706
1.9	.4713	.4719	.4726	.4732	.4738	.4744	.4750	.4756	.4761	.4767
2.0	.4772	.4778	.4783	.4788	.4793	.4798	.4803	.4808	.4812	.4817
2.1	.4821	.4826	.4830	.4834	.4838	.4842	.4846	.4850	.4854	.4857
2.2	.4861	.4864	.4868	.4871	.4875	.4878	.4881	.4884	.4887	.4890
2.3	.4893	.4896	.4898	.4901	.4904	.4906	.4909	.4911	.4913	.4916
2.4	.4918	.4920	.4922	.4925	.4927	.4929	.4931	.4932	.4934	.4936
2.5	.4938	.4940	.4941	.4943	.4945	.4946	.4948	.4949	.4951	.4952
2.6	.4953	.4955	.4956	.4957	.4959	.4960	.4961	.4962	.4963	.4964
2.7	.4965	.4966	.4967	.4968	.4969	.4970	.4971	.4972	.4973	.4974
2.8	.4974	.4975	.4976	.4977	.4977	.4978	.4979	.4979	.4980	.4981
2.9	.4981	.4982	.4982	.4983	.4984	.4984	.4985	.4985	.4986	.4986
3.0	.4987	.4987	.4987	.4988	.4988	.4989	.4989	.4989	.4990	.4990

Note: This table gives the area in the right-hand tail of the distribution (i.e., $Z \geq 0$). But since the normal distribution is symmetrical about $Z = 0$, the area in the left-hand tail is the same as the area in the corresponding right-hand tail. For example, $P(-1.96 \leq Z \leq 0) = 0.4750$. Therefore, $P(-1.96 \leq Z \leq 1.96) = 2(0.4750) = 0.95$.

TABLE C.2
Critical Values of the Student's *t* Distribution

	Significance level				
1-Tailed:	**0.10**	**0.05**	**0.025**	**0.01**	**0.005**
2-Tailed:	**0.20**	**0.10**	**0.05**	**0.02**	**0.01**
Degrees of Freedom					
1	3.08	6.31	12.71	31.82	63.66
2	1.89	2.92	4.30	6.97	9.93
3	1.64	2.35	3.18	4.54	5.84
4	1.53	2.13	2.78	3.75	4.60
5	1.48	2.02	2.57	3.37	4.03
6	1.44	1.94	2.45	3.14	3.71
7	1.42	1.90	2.36	3.00	3.50
8	1.40	1.86	2.31	2.90	3.36
9	1.38	1.83	2.26	2.82	3.25
10	1.37	1.81	2.23	2.76	3.17
11	1.36	1.80	2.20	2.72	3.11
12	1.36	1.78	2.18	2.68	3.06
13	1.35	1.77	2.16	2.65	3.01
14	1.35	1.76	2.15	2.62	2.98
15	1.34	1.75	2.13	2.60	2.95
16	1.34	1.75	2.12	2.58	2.92
17	1.33	1.74	2.11	2.57	2.90
18	1.33	1.73	2.10	2.55	2.88
19	1.33	1.73	2.09	2.54	2.86
20	1.33	1.73	2.09	2.53	2.85
21	1.32	1.72	2.08	2.52	2.83
22	1.32	1.72	2.07	2.51	2.82
23	1.32	1.71	2.07	2.50	2.81
24	1.32	1.71	2.06	2.49	2.80
25	1.32	1.71	2.06	2.49	2.79
26	1.31	1.71	2.06	2.48	2.78
27	1.31	1.70	2.05	2.47	2.77
28	1.31	1.70	2.05	2.47	2.76
29	1.31	1.70	2.05	2.46	2.76
30	1.31	1.70	2.04	2.46	2.75
40	1.30	1.68	2.02	2.42	2.70
60	1.30	1.67	2.00	2.39	2.66
90	1.29	1.66	1.99	2.37	2.63
120	1.29	1.66	1.98	2.36	2.62
infinity	1.28	1.65	1.96	2.33	2.58

Examples: The 2.5% critical value for a one-tailed test with 30 degrees of freedom is 2.04. The 5% critical value with large (>120) degrees of freedom is 1.96.

TABLE C.3 Critical Values for the *F* Distribution, Alpha = .05

Denominator DF	Numerator DF									
	1	2	3	4	5	6	7	8	9	10
1	161.448	199.500	215.707	224.583	230.162	233.986	236.768	238.883	240.543	241.882
2	18.513	19.000	19.164	19.247	19.296	19.330	19.353	19.371	19.385	19.396
3	10.128	9.552	9.277	9.117	9.013	8.941	8.887	8.845	8.812	8.786
4	7.709	6.944	6.591	6.388	6.256	6.163	6.094	6.041	5.999	5.964
5	6.608	5.786	5.409	5.192	5.050	4.950	4.876	4.818	4.772	4.735
6	5.987	5.143	4.757	4.534	4.387	4.284	4.207	4.147	4.099	4.060
7	5.591	4.737	4.347	4.120	3.972	3.866	3.787	3.726	3.677	3.637
8	5.318	4.459	4.066	3.838	3.687	3.581	3.500	3.438	3.388	3.347
9	5.117	4.256	3.863	3.633	3.482	3.374	3.293	3.230	3.179	3.137
10	4.965	4.103	3.708	3.478	3.326	3.217	3.135	3.072	3.020	2.978
11	4.844	3.982	3.587	3.357	3.204	3.095	3.012	2.948	2.896	2.854
12	4.747	3.885	3.490	3.259	3.106	2.996	2.913	2.849	2.796	2.753
13	4.667	3.806	3.411	3.179	3.025	2.915	2.832	2.767	2.714	2.671
14	4.600	3.739	3.344	3.112	2.958	2.848	2.764	2.699	2.646	2.602
15	4.543	3.682	3.287	3.056	2.901	2.790	2.707	2.641	2.588	2.544
16	4.494	3.634	3.239	3.007	2.852	2.741	2.657	2.591	2.538	2.494
17	4.451	3.592	3.197	2.965	2.810	2.699	2.614	2.548	2.494	2.450
18	4.414	3.555	3.160	2.928	2.773	2.661	2.577	2.510	2.456	2.412
19	4.381	3.522	3.127	2.895	2.740	2.628	2.544	2.477	2.423	2.378
20	4.351	3.493	3.098	2.866	2.711	2.599	2.514	2.447	2.393	2.348
21	4.325	3.467	3.072	2.840	2.685	2.573	2.488	2.420	2.366	2.321
22	4.301	3.443	3.049	2.817	2.661	2.549	2.464	2.397	2.342	2.297
23	4.279	3.422	3.028	2.796	2.640	2.528	2.442	2.375	2.320	2.275
24	4.260	3.403	3.009	2.776	2.621	2.508	2.423	2.355	2.300	2.255
25	4.242	3.385	2.991	2.759	2.603	2.490	2.405	2.337	2.282	2.236
26	4.225	3.369	2.975	2.743	2.587	2.474	2.388	2.321	2.265	2.220
27	4.210	3.354	2.960	2.728	2.572	2.459	2.373	2.305	2.250	2.204
28	4.196	3.340	2.947	2.714	2.558	2.445	2.359	2.291	2.236	2.190
29	4.183	3.328	2.934	2.701	2.545	2.432	2.346	2.278	2.223	2.177
30	4.171	3.316	2.922	2.690	2.534	2.421	2.334	2.266	2.211	2.165
31	4.160	3.305	2.911	2.679	2.523	2.409	2.323	2.255	2.199	2.153
32	4.149	3.295	2.901	2.668	2.512	2.399	2.313	2.244	2.189	2.142
33	4.139	3.285	2.892	2.659	2.503	2.389	2.303	2.235	2.179	2.133
34	4.130	3.276	2.883	2.650	2.494	2.380	2.294	2.225	2.170	2.123
35	4.121	3.267	2.874	2.641	2.485	2.372	2.285	2.217	2.161	2.114
36	4.113	3.259	2.866	2.634	2.477	2.364	2.277	2.209	2.153	2.106
37	4.105	3.252	2.859	2.626	2.470	2.356	2.270	2.201	2.145	2.098
38	4.098	3.245	2.852	2.619	2.463	2.349	2.262	2.194	2.138	2.091
39	4.091	3.238	2.845	2.612	2.456	2.342	2.255	2.187	2.131	2.084
40	4.085	3.232	2.839	2.606	2.449	2.336	2.249	2.180	2.124	2.077
41	4.079	3.226	2.833	2.600	2.443	2.330	2.243	2.174	2.118	2.071
42	4.073	3.220	2.827	2.594	2.438	2.324	2.237	2.168	2.112	2.065
43	4.067	3.214	2.822	2.589	2.432	2.318	2.232	2.163	2.106	2.059
44	4.062	3.209	2.816	2.584	2.427	2.313	2.226	2.157	2.101	2.054
45	4.057	3.204	2.812	2.579	2.422	2.308	2.221	2.152	2.096	2.049
46	4.052	3.200	2.807	2.574	2.417	2.304	2.216	2.147	2.091	2.044
47	4.047	3.195	2.802	2.570	2.413	2.299	2.212	2.143	2.086	2.039
48	4.043	3.191	2.798	2.565	2.409	2.295	2.207	2.138	2.082	2.035
49	4.038	3.187	2.794	2.561	2.404	2.290	2.203	2.134	2.077	2.030
50	4.034	3.183	2.790	2.557	2.400	2.286	2.199	2.130	2.073	2.026

Denominator DF	Numerator DF									
	1	2	3	4	5	6	7	8	9	10
51	4.030	3.179	2.786	2.553	2.397	2.283	2.195	2.126	2.069	2.022
52	4.027	3.175	2.783	2.550	2.393	2.279	2.192	2.122	2.066	2.018
53	4.023	3.172	2.779	2.546	2.389	2.275	2.188	2.119	2.062	2.015
54	4.020	3.168	2.776	2.543	2.386	2.272	2.185	2.115	2.059	2.011
55	4.016	3.165	2.773	2.540	2.383	2.269	2.181	2.112	2.055	2.008
56	4.013	3.162	2.769	2.537	2.380	2.266	2.178	2.109	2.052	2.005
57	4.010	3.159	2.766	2.534	2.377	2.263	2.175	2.106	2.049	2.001
58	4.007	3.156	2.764	2.531	2.374	2.260	2.172	2.103	2.046	1.998
59	4.004	3.153	2.761	2.528	2.371	2.257	2.169	2.100	2.043	1.995
60	4.001	3.150	2.758	2.525	2.368	2.254	2.167	2.097	2.040	1.993
61	3.998	3.148	2.755	2.523	2.366	2.251	2.164	2.094	2.037	1.990
62	3.996	3.145	2.753	2.520	2.363	2.249	2.161	2.092	2.035	1.987
63	3.993	3.143	2.751	2.518	2.361	2.246	2.159	2.089	2.032	1.985
64	3.991	3.140	2.748	2.515	2.358	2.244	2.156	2.087	2.030	1.982
65	3.989	3.138	2.746	2.513	2.356	2.242	2.154	2.084	2.027	1.980
66	3.986	3.136	2.744	2.511	2.354	2.239	2.152	2.082	2.025	1.977
67	3.984	3.134	2.742	2.509	2.352	2.237	2.150	2.080	2.023	1.975
68	3.982	3.132	2.740	2.507	2.350	2.235	2.148	2.078	2.021	1.973
69	3.980	3.130	2.737	2.505	2.348	2.233	2.145	2.076	2.019	1.971
70	3.978	3.128	2.736	2.503	2.346	2.231	2.143	2.074	2.017	1.969
71	3.976	3.126	2.734	2.501	2.344	2.229	2.142	2.072	2.015	1.967
72	3.974	3.124	2.732	2.499	2.342	2.227	2.140	2.070	2.013	1.965
73	3.972	3.122	2.730	2.497	2.340	2.226	2.138	2.068	2.011	1.963
74	3.970	3.120	2.728	2.495	2.338	2.224	2.136	2.066	2.009	1.961
75	3.968	3.119	2.727	2.494	2.337	2.222	2.134	2.064	2.007	1.959
76	3.967	3.117	2.725	2.492	2.335	2.220	2.133	2.063	2.006	1.958
77	3.965	3.115	2.723	2.490	2.333	2.219	2.131	2.061	2.004	1.956
78	3.963	3.114	2.722	2.489	2.332	2.217	2.129	2.059	2.002	1.954
79	3.962	3.112	2.720	2.487	2.330	2.216	2.128	2.058	2.001	1.953
80	3.960	3.111	2.719	2.486	2.329	2.214	2.126	2.056	1.999	1.951
81	3.959	3.109	2.717	2.484	2.327	2.213	2.125	2.055	1.998	1.950
82	3.957	3.108	2.716	2.483	2.326	2.211	2.123	2.053	1.996	1.948
83	3.956	3.107	2.715	2.482	2.324	2.210	2.122	2.052	1.995	1.947
84	3.955	3.105	2.713	2.480	2.323	2.209	2.121	2.051	1.993	1.945
85	3.953	3.104	2.712	2.479	2.322	2.207	2.119	2.049	1.992	1.944
86	3.952	3.103	2.711	2.478	2.321	2.206	2.118	2.048	1.991	1.943
87	3.951	3.101	2.709	2.476	2.319	2.205	2.117	2.047	1.989	1.941
88	3.949	3.100	2.708	2.475	2.318	2.203	2.115	2.045	1.988	1.940
89	3.948	3.099	2.707	2.474	2.317	2.202	2.114	2.044	1.987	1.939
90	3.947	3.098	2.706	2.473	2.316	2.201	2.113	2.043	1.986	1.938
91	3.946	3.097	2.705	2.472	2.315	2.200	2.112	2.042	1.984	1.936
92	3.945	3.095	2.704	2.471	2.313	2.199	2.111	2.041	1.983	1.935
93	3.943	3.094	2.703	2.470	2.312	2.198	2.110	2.040	1.982	1.934
94	3.942	3.093	2.701	2.469	2.311	2.197	2.109	2.038	1.981	1.933
95	3.941	3.092	2.700	2.467	2.310	2.196	2.108	2.037	1.980	1.932
96	3.940	3.091	2.699	2.466	2.309	2.195	2.106	2.036	1.979	1.931
97	3.939	3.090	2.698	2.465	2.308	2.194	2.105	2.035	1.978	1.930
98	3.938	3.089	2.697	2.465	2.307	2.193	2.104	2.034	1.977	1.929
99	3.937	3.088	2.696	2.464	2.306	2.192	2.103	2.033	1.976	1.928
100	3.936	3.087	2.696	2.463	2.305	2.191	2.103	2.032	1.975	1.927

Source: http://sph.bu.edu/otlt/MPH-Modules/BS/ BS704_HypothesisTesting-ANOVA/ftable.pdf.

Index